Beginning Java EE 7

Antonio Goncalves

Apress

Beginning Java EE 7

ISBN-13 (pbk): 978-1-4302-4626-8

ISBN-13 (electronic): 978-1-4302-4627-5

President and Publisher: Paul Manning
Lead Editor: Steve Anglin
Developmental Editor: James Markham
Technical Reviewer: Massimo Nardone
Editorial Board: Steve Anglin, Mark Beckner, Ewan Buckingham, Gary Cornell, Louise Corrigan, Morgan Ertel, Jonathan Gennick, Jonathan Hassell, Robert Hutchinson, Michelle Lowman, James Markham, Matthew Moodie, Jeff Olson, Jeffrey Pepper, Douglas Pundick, Ben Renow-Clarke, Dominic Shakeshaft, Gwenan Spearing, Matt Wade, Tom Welsh
Coordinating Editor: Katie Sullivan
Copy Editor: Lori Jacobs
Compositor: SPi Global
Indexer: SPi Global
Artist: SPi Global
Cover Designer: Anna Ishchenko

Distributed to the book trade worldwide by Springer Science+Business Media New York, 233 Spring Street, 6th Floor, New York, NY 10013. Phone 1-800-SPRINGER, fax (201) 348-4505, e-mail orders-ny@springer-sbm.com, or visit www.springeronline.com. Apress Media, LLC is a California LLC and the sole member (owner) is Springer Science + Business Media Finance Inc (SSBM Finance Inc). SSBM Finance Inc is a Delaware corporation. For information on translations, please e-mail rights@apress.com, or visit www.apress.com.

Apress and friends of ED books may be purchased in bulk for academic, corporate, or promotional use. eBook versions and licenses are also available for most titles. For more information, reference our Special Bulk Sales–eBook Licensing web page at www.apress.com/bulk-sales.

Any source code or other supplementary materials referenced by the author in this text is available to readers at www.apress.com. For detailed information about how to locate your book's source code, go to www.apress.com/source-code/.

Thanks daddy for playing and having fun with me while you were busy writing your book.

—Eloïse Goncalves

Contents at a Glance

Contents

Foreword

Java EE 7 builds upon the success of previous versions of the platform. It significantly improves developer productivity by providing a simplified Java Message Service API, a more cohesive integrated platform by leveraging Contexts and Dependency Injection (CDI) extensively, and cutting down boilerplate code. It also embraces technologies like WebSocket, JSON, Batch, and Concurrency, which are essential for modern web application development. This reduces the need for third-party frameworks, making your applications more lightweight.

Antonio played a very important role in shaping the Java EE 7 platform. His active role in the two key JSRs (Platform and Enterprise JavaBeans 3.2) demonstrates his technical depth and shapes the constantly evolving specifications. He highlighted several points in the specifications that made them easier to understand. He also participated in the transparency lists promoted by JCP and engaged with the community.

Antonio is the leader of Paris JUG (Java User Group) and a well-respected Java Champion; he uses Java EE in his consultant life to solve real-world problems. He is a passionate Java enthusiast who runs Devoxx France. In addition, a few years back he authored a book in French on Java EE 5, and then he wrote a highly rated book, *Beginning Java EE 6 Platform with GlassFish 3*. Altogether this makes him a great candidate for authoring this book.

The book has several practical code samples to get you started. It uses GlassFish for deploying the samples, but they would certainly run on any Java EE 7–compatible application server. All the code samples are also available on GitHub for you to get started. If you are looking for a pragmatic book written by one of the experts who understand the platform thoroughly, this is your source.

Arun Gupta
Java EE & GlassFish Guy

About the Author

Antonio Goncalves is a senior software architect living in Paris. Focused on Java development since the late 1990s, his career has taken him to different countries and companies where he works now as a Java EE consultant. As a former BEA consultant, he has great expertise in application servers such as WebLogic, JBoss, and, of course, GlassFish. He is particularly fond of open source and is a member of the OSSGTP (Open Source Solution Get Together Paris). He is also the cocreator and coleader of the Paris Java User Group and more recently Devoxx France.

Antonio wrote his first book on Java EE 5, in French, in 2007. He then joined the JCP to become an Expert Member of various JSRs (Java EE 6, JPA 2.0, and EJB 3.1) and wrote *Beginning Java EE 6* with Apress. Still involved in the JCP, Antonio joined the Java EE 7 and EJB 3.2 Expert Groups in 2010.

For the last few years, Antonio has given talks at international conferences mainly about Java EE, including JavaOne, Devoxx, GeeCon, The Server Side Symposium, Jazoon, and many Java User Groups. He has also written numerous technical papers and articles for IT web sites (DevX) and IT magazines (Programmez, Linux Magazine). Since 2009, he has been part of the French Java podcast called Les Cast Codeurs (influenced by the Java Posse). For all his work for the Java community, Antonio has been elected Java Champion.

Antonio is a graduate of the Conservatoire National des Arts et Métiers in Paris (with an engineering degree in IT), Brighton University (with an MSc in object-oriented design), and UFSCar University in Brazil (MPhil in Distributed Systems).

Follow Antonio on Tweeter (@agoncal) and on his blog (www.antoniogoncalves.org).

About the Technical Reviewer

 **Massimo Nardone** holds an MSc in computing science from the University of Salerno, Italy. He currently works as a PCI QSA and senior lead IT security/Cloud architect for IBM Finland, where his main responsibilities include Cloud, IT infrastructure, and security auditing/assessment. At IBM Finland Massimo is also the Finnish Invention Development Team Leader (FIDTL). His IT certifications include ITIL, Open Group Master Certified IT Architect, and Payment Card Industry (PCI) Qualified Security Assessor (QSA). He is a private, public, and desktop Cloud architecture expert.

With more than 19 years of experience in Cloud computing, IT infrastructure, mobile, security, and WWW technology areas for both national and international projects, Massimo has been a project manager, software engineer, research engineer, chief security architect, and software specialist. He was also a visiting lecturer and supervisor for exercises at the Networking Laboratory of the Helsinki University of Technology (Helsinki University of Technology TKK became a part of Aalto University).

Massimo is very familiar with security communication protocols testing tools and methodologies and has been developing Internet and mobile applications with evolving technologies and using many programming languages.

Massimo has been the technical reviewer for many book publishers in IT areas such as security, www-technology, database, and so on. Massimo holds four International Patents (PKI, SIP, SAML, and Proxy areas).

He dedicates this book to his beloved wife Pia and his children, Luna, Leo, and Neve.

Acknowledgments

In your hands you have my third book about the Java EE platform. And I tell you, to write a third book you need to be a bit crazy . . . and to be surrounded by people who help you in any possible way (so you don't get totally crazy). And this is the space to thank them.

First of all, I really want to thank Steve Anglin from Apress for giving me another opportunity to write for this great company. Throughout the writing process, I was constantly in contact with Jill Balzano, Kathleen Sullivan, and James Markham who reviewed the book and gave me precious advice. Thanks to Massimo Nardone who provided an in-depth technical review that improved the book.

A special thank you to my technical team who helped me throughout the 15 chapters and offered some insightful comments. Alexis Hassler lives in Beaujolais (France), but unlike his neighbors, he isn't a winemaker; he is a freelance software developer, a trainer, and a JUG leader in Lyon. Brice Leporini is an experienced engineer who has focused on Java for the last ten years and loves starting new projects, improving application performance, and coaching young geeks. Mathieu Ancelin is a developer who loves Java, the JVM, his Mac, and his guitar, and who is part of the CDI 1.1 expert group and works with CDI in OSGi. Antoine Sabot-Durand, senior software engineer at Red Hat, contributed to projects around CDI (like Seam 3 and Deltaspike) and is the tech lead on the Agorava framework (social media). I have to say that it was a real pleasure to work with such knowledgeable and cheerful senior developers.

I also need to thank Youness Teimoury, who coauthored Chapter 12 on XML and JSON.

It is a great honor to have Arun Gupta writing the foreword of this book. His devotion to Java EE is endless and his technical articles are priceless.

Thanks to my proofreader Tressan O'Donoghue, who added a Shakespearean touch to the book.

The diagrams in this book were made using the Visual Paradigm. I would like to thank both Visual Paradigm and JetBrains for providing me with a free license for their excellent products.

And a big kiss to my loving daughter, Eloïse. She is the best present life has given me.

I could not have written this book without the help and support of the Java community: blogs, articles, mailing lists, forums, Tweets . . . and particularly those involved in Java EE such as Bill Shannon, Linda DeMichiel, Reza Rahman, Adam Bien, Elias Dorneles, Emmanuel Bernard, Pete Muir, Marek Potociar, Çağatay Çivici, Arnaud Heritier, Nicolas de Loof, Jean-Michel Doudoux, and David Gageot.

More than anything I would like to thank a bunch of people who helped me in some way. Sometimes life can be difficult and a welcoming hand is comforting. Marianne, Gabriel, my first thank you goes to you. And in no special order I would like to thank José Paumard, Stephen Janssen, Nicolas Semczyk, Hugues Peron, Fred do Couto, Sebastien, Marion, Val, Karla, Stephane, Fabienne, Cricri, Chacha, La Fontaine, Le Café Livre, and the Navalhas, Eeckman, Soldado, and Martins families. A special thank you to Betty who brought me light during dark times and strength when I got weak.

Many thoughts go to my old friend Bruno Reau who got taken back too early.

Thank you all!

Introduction

In today's business world, applications need to access data, apply business logic, add presentation layers, be mobile, use geolocalization, and communicate with external systems and online services. That's what companies are trying to achieve while minimizing costs, using standard and robust technologies that can handle heavy loads. If that's your case, you have the right book in your hands.

Java Enterprise Edition appeared at the end of the 1990s and brought to the Java language a robust software platform for enterprise development. Challenged at each new version, badly understood or misused, overengineered, and competing with open source frameworks, J2EE was seen as a heavyweight technology. Java EE benefited from these criticisms to improve and today focuses on simplicity.

If you are part of the group of people who still think that "EJBs are bad, EJBs are evil," read this book, and you'll change your mind. EJBs (Enterprise Java Beans) are great, as is the entire Java EE 7 technology stack. If, on the contrary, you are a Java EE adopter, you will see in this book how the platform has found equilibrium through its ease of development and easy component model. If you are a beginner in Java EE, this is also the right book: it covers the most important specifications in a very understandable manner and is illustrated with a lot of code and diagrams to make it easier to follow.

Open standards are collectively one of the main strengths of Java EE. More than ever, an application written with JPA, CDI, Bean Validation, EJBs, JSF, JMS, SOAP web services, or RESTful web services is portable across application servers. Open source is another of Java EE's strengths. As you'll see in this book, most of the Java EE 7 Reference Implementations use open source licensing (GlassFish, EclipseLink, Weld, Hibernate Validator, Mojarra, OpenMQ, Metro, and Jersey).

This book explores the innovations of this new version, and examines the various specifications and how to assemble them to develop applications. Java EE 7 consists of nearly 30 specifications and is an important milestone for the enterprise layer (CDI 1.1, Bean Validation 1.1, EJB 3.2, JPA 2.1), for the web tier (Servlet 3.1, JSF 2.2, Expression Language 3.0), and for interoperability (JAX-WS 2.3 and JAX-RS 2.0). This book covers a broad part of the Java EE 7 specifications and uses the JDK 1.7 and some well-known design patterns, as well as the GlassFish application server, the Derby database, JUnit, and Maven. It is illustrated abundantly with UML diagrams, Java code, and screenshots.

How the Book Is Structured

This book concentrates on the most important Java EE 7 specifications and highlights the new features of this release. The structure of the book follows the architectural layering of an application.

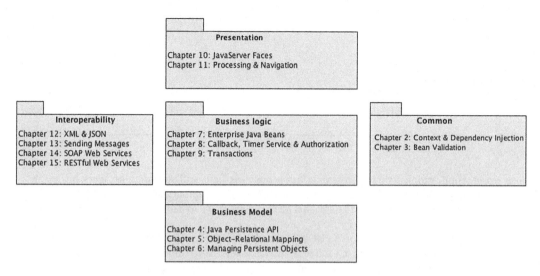

Chapter 1 briefly presents Java EE 7 essentials and Appendix A highlights the tools used throughout the book and how to install them (JDK, Maven, JUnit, Derby, and GlassFish).

In the first chapters, I explain the common concerns discussed throughout the book. Chapter 2 describes Context and Dependency Injection 1.1 and Chapter 3 looks at Bean Validation 1.1.

Chapters 4 through 6 describe the persistent tier and focus on JPA 2.1. After a general overview with some hands-on examples in Chapter 4, Chapter 5 dives into object-relational mapping (mapping attributes, relationships, and inheritance), while Chapter 6 shows you how to manage and query entities, their life cycle, callback methods, and listeners.

To develop a transaction business logic layer with Java EE 7, you can naturally use EJBs. Chapters 7 through 9 describe this process. After an overview of the specification and its history, Chapter 7 concentrates on session beans and their programming model. Chapter 8 focuses on the life cycle of EJBs, the timer service, and how to handle authorization. Chapter 9 explains transactions and how JTA 1.2 brings transactions to EJBs as well as CDI Beans.

In Chapters 10 and 11 you will learn how to develop a presentation layer with JSF 2.2. After an overview of the specification, Chapter 10 focuses on how to build a web page with JSF and Facelets components. Chapter 11 shows you how to interact with an EJB back end with CDI backing beans and navigate through pages.

Finally, the last chapters present different ways to interoperate with other systems. Chapter 12 explains how to process XML (using JAXB and JAXP) and JSON (JSON-P 1.0). Chapter 13 shows you how to exchange asynchronous messages with the new JMS 2.0 and Message-Driven Beans. Chapter 14 focuses on SOAP web services, while Chapter 15 covers RESTful web services with the new JAX-RS 2.0.

Downloading and Running the Code

The examples used in this book are designed to be compiled with the JDK 1.7, to be built with Maven 3, to be deployed on GlassFish v4 application server, and to store data in a Derby database. Appendix A shows you how to install all these software packages, and each chapter explains how to build, deploy, run, and test components depending on the technology used. The code has been tested on the Mac OS X platform (but should also work on Windows or Linux). The source code of the examples in the book is available from the Source Code page of the Apress web site at www.apress.com. You can also download the code straight from the public GitHub at https://github.com/agoncal/agoncal-book-javaee7.

Contacting the Author

If you have any questions about the content of this book, the code, or any other topic, please contact the author at antonio.goncalves@gmail.com. You can also visit his web site at www.antoniogoncalves.org and follow him on Twitter at @agoncal.

CHAPTER 1

■ ■ ■

Java EE 7 at a Glance

Enterprises today live in a globally competitive world. They need applications to fulfill their business needs, which are getting more and more complex. In this age of globalization, companies are distributed over continents, they do business 24/7 over the Internet and across different countries, have several datacenters, and internationalized systems which have to deal with different currencies and time zones—all that while reducing their costs, lowering the response times of their services, storing business data on reliable and safe storage, and offering several mobile and web interfaces to their customers, employees, and suppliers.

Most companies have to combine these complex challenges with their existing enterprise information systems (EIS) at the same time developing business-to-business applications to communicate with partners or business-to-customer systems using mobile and geolocalized applications. It is also not rare for a company to have to coordinate in-house data stored in different locations, processed by multiple programming languages, and routed through different protocols. And, of course, it has to do this without losing money, which means preventing system crashes and being highly available, scalable, and secure. Enterprise applications have to face change and complexity, and be robust. That's precisely why Java Enterprise Edition (Java EE) was created.

The first version of Java EE (originally known as J2EE) focused on the concerns that companies were facing back in 1999: distributed components. Since then, software applications have had to adapt to new technical solutions like SOAP or RESTful web services. The Java EE platform has evolved to respond to these technical needs by providing various ways of working through standard specifications. Throughout the years, Java EE has changed and became richer, simpler, easier to use, more portable, and more integrated.

In this chapter, I'll give you an overview of Java EE. After an introduction to its internal architecture, components, and services, I'll cover what's new in Java EE 7.

Understanding Java EE

When you want to handle collections of objects, you don't start by developing your own hashtable; you use the collection API (application programming interface). Similarly, if you need a simple Web application or a transactional, secure, interoperable, and distributed application, you don't want to develop all the low-level APIs: you use the Enterprise Edition of Java. Just as Java Standard Edition (Java SE) provides an API to handle collections, Java EE provides a standard way to handle transactions with Java Transaction API (JTA), messaging with Java Message Service (JMS), or persistence with Java Persistence API (JPA). Java EE is a set of specifications intended for enterprise applications. It can be seen as an extension of Java SE to facilitate the development of distributed, robust, powerful, and highly available applications.

Java EE 7 is an important milestone. Not only does it follow in the footsteps of Java EE 6 by focusing on an easier development model, but it also adds new specifications, as well as adding new functionalities to existing ones. Moreover, Context and Dependency Injection (CDI) is becoming the integration point between all these new specifications. The release of Java EE 7 coincides closely with the 13th anniversary of the enterprise platform. It combines the advantages of the Java language with experience gained over the last 13 years. Java EE profits from the dynamism of open source communities as well as the rigor of the JCP (Java Community Process) standardization process. Today Java EE is a well-documented platform with experienced developers, a large community, and many deployed applications running on companies' servers. Java EE is a suite of APIs that can be used to build standard component-based multitier applications. These components are deployed in different containers offering a series of services.

Architecture

Java EE is a set of specifications implemented by different containers. Containers are Java EE runtime environments that provide certain services to the components they host such as life-cycle management, dependency injection, concurrency, and so on. These components use well-defined contracts to communicate with the Java EE infrastructure and with the other components. They need to be packaged in a standard way (following a defined directory structure that can be compressed into archive files) before being deployed. Java EE is a superset of the Java SE platform, which means Java SE APIs can be used by any Java EE components.

Figure 1-1 shows the logical relationships between containers. The arrows represent the protocols used by one container to access another. For example, the web container hosts servlets, which can access EJBs through RMI-IIOP.

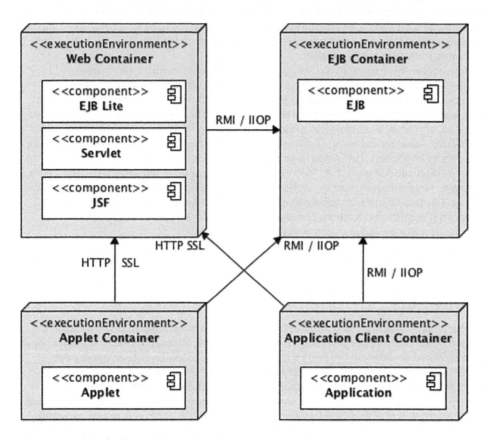

Figure 1-1. *Standard Java EE containers*

Components

The Java EE runtime environment defines four types of components that an implementation must support:

- *Applets* are GUI (graphic user interface) applications that are executed in a web browser. They use the rich Swing API to provide powerful user interfaces.

- *Applications* are programs that are executed on a client. They are typically GUIs or batch-processing programs that have access to all the facilities of the Java EE middle tier.

- *Web applications* (made of servlets, servlet filters, web event listeners, JSP and JSF pages) are executed in a web container and respond to HTTP requests from web clients. Servlets also support SOAP and RESTful web service endpoints. Web applications can also contain EJBs Lite (more on that in Chapter 7).

- *Enterprise applications* (made of Enterprise Java Beans, Java Message Service, Java Transaction API, asynchronous calls, timer service, RMI/IIOP) are executed in an EJB container. EJBs are container-managed components for processing transactional business logic. They can be accessed locally and remotely through RMI (or HTTP for SOAP and RESTful web services).

Containers

The Java EE infrastructure is partitioned into logical domains called containers (see Figure 1-1). Each container has a specific role, supports a set of APIs, and offers services to components (security, database access, transaction handling, naming directory, resource injection). Containers hide technical complexity and enhance portability. Depending on the kind of application you want to build, you will have to understand the capabilities and constraints of each container in order to use one or more. For example, if you need to develop a web application, you will develop a JSF tier with an EJB Lite tier and deploy them into a web container. But if you want a web application to invoke a business tier remotely and use messaging and asynchronous calls, you will need both the web and EJB containers. Java EE has four different containers:

- *Applet containers* are provided by most web browsers to execute applet components. When you develop applets, you can concentrate on the visual aspect of the application while the container gives you a secure environment. The applet container uses a sandbox security model where code executed in the "sandbox" is not allowed to "play outside the sandbox." This means that the container prevents any code downloaded to your local computer from accessing local system resources, such as processes or files.

- The *application client container* (ACC) includes a set of Java classes, libraries, and other files required to bring injection, security management, and naming service to Java SE applications (swing, batch processing, or just a class with a main() method). The ACC communicates with the EJB container using RMI-IIOP and the web container with HTTP (e.g., for web services).

- The *web container* provides the underlying services for managing and executing web components (servlets, EJBs Lite, JSPs, filters, listeners, JSF pages, and web services). It is responsible for instantiating, initializing, and invoking servlets and supporting the HTTP and HTTPS protocols. It is the container used to feed web pages to client browsers.

- The *EJB container* is responsible for managing the execution of the enterprise beans (session beans and message-driven beans) containing the business logic tier of your Java EE application. It creates new instances of EJBs, manages their life cycle, and provides services such as transaction, security, concurrency, distribution, naming service, or the possibility to be invoked asynchronously.

Services

Containers provide underlying services to their deployed components. As a developer, containers allow you to concentrate on implementing business logic rather than solving technical problems faced in enterprise applications. Figure 1-2 shows you the services provided by each container. For example, web and EJB containers provide connectors to access EIS, but not the applet container or the ACCs. Java EE offers the following services:

- *Java Transaction API*: This service offers a transaction demarcation API used by the container and the application. It also provides an interface between the transaction manager and a resource manager at the Service Provider Interface (SPI) level.

- *Java Persistence API*: Standard API for object-relational mapping (ORM). With its Java Persistence Query Language (JPQL), you can query objects stored in the underlying database.

- *Validation*: Bean Validation provides class and method level constraint declaration and validation facilities.

- *Java Message Service*: This allows components to communicate asynchronously through messages. It supports reliable point-to-point (P2P) messaging as well as the publish-subscribe (pub-sub) model.

- *Java Naming and Directory Interface*: This API, included in Java SE, is used to access naming and directory systems. Your application uses it to associate (bind) names to objects and then to find these objects (lookup) in a directory. You can look up data sources, JMS factories, EJBs, and other resources. Omnipresent in your code until J2EE 1.4, JNDI is used in a more transparent way through injection.

- *JavaMail*: Many applications require the ability to send e-mails, which can be implemented through use of the JavaMail API.

- *JavaBeans Activation Framework*: The JAF API, included in Java SE, provides a framework for handling data in different MIME types. It is used by JavaMail.

- *XML processing*: Most Java EE components can be deployed with optional XML deployment descriptors, and applications often have to manipulate XML documents. The Java API for XML Processing (JAXP) provides support for parsing documents with SAX and DOM APIs, as well as for XSLT. The Streaming API for XML (StAX) provides a pull-parsing API for XML.

- *JSON processing*: New in Java EE 7 the Java API for JSON Processing (JSON-P) allows applications to parse, generate, transform, and query JSON.

- *Java EE Connector Architecture*: Connectors allow you to access EIS from a Java EE component. These could be databases, mainframes, or enterprise resource planning (ERP) programs.

- *Security services*: Java Authentication and Authorization Service (JAAS) enables services to authenticate and enforce access controls upon users. The Java Authorization Service Provider Contract for Containers (JACC) defines a contract between a Java EE application server and an authorization service provider, allowing custom authorization service providers to be plugged into any Java EE product. Java Authentication Service Provider Interface for Containers (JASPIC) defines a standard interface by which authentication modules may be integrated with containers so that these modules may establish the authentication identities used by containers.

- *Web services*: Java EE provides support for SOAP and RESTful web services. The Java API for XML Web Services (JAX-WS), replacing the Java API for XML-based RPC (JAX-RPC), provides support for web services using the SOAP/HTTP protocol. The Java API for RESTful Web Services (JAX-RS) provides support for web services using the REST style.

- *Dependency Injection*: Since Java EE 5, some resources (data sources, JMS factories, persistence units, EJBs...) can be injected in managed components. Java EE 7 goes further by using CDI as well as the DI (Dependency Injection for Java) specifications.

- *Management*: Java EE defines APIs for managing containers and servers using a special management enterprise bean. The Java Management Extensions (JMX) API is also used to provide some management support.

- *Deployment*: The Java EE Deployment Specification defines a contract between deployment tools and Java EE products to standardize application deployment.

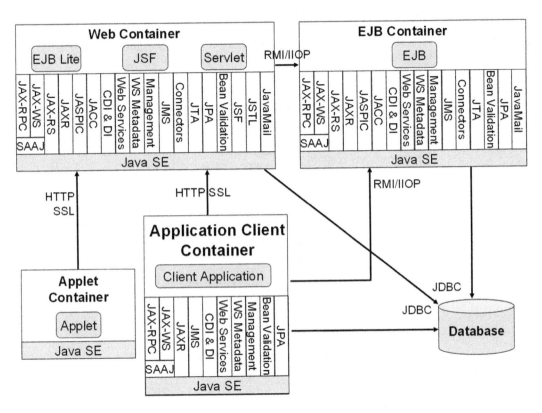

Figure 1-2. *Services provided by containers*

Network Protocols

As shown in Figure 1-2, components deployed in containers can be invoked through different protocols. For example, a servlet deployed in a web container can be called with HTTP as well as a web service with an EJB endpoint deployed in an EJB container. Here is the list of protocols supported by Java EE:

- *HTTP*: HTTP is the Web protocol and is ubiquitous in modern applications. The client-side API is defined by the java.net package in Java SE. The HTTP server-side API is defined by servlets, JSPs, and JSF interfaces, as well as SOAP and RESTful web services.

- *HTTPS* is a combination of HTTP and the Secure Sockets Layer (SSL) protocol.

- *RMI-IIOP*: Remote Method Invocation (RMI) allows you to invoke remote objects independently of the underlying protocol. The Java SE native RMI protocol is Java Remote Method Protocol (JRMP). RMI-IIOP is an extension of RMI used to integrate with CORBA. Java interface description language (IDL) allows Java EE application components to invoke external CORBA objects using the IIOP protocol. CORBA objects can be written in many languages (Ada, C, C++, Cobol, etc.) as well as Java.

Packaging

To be deployed in a container, components have first to be packaged in a standard formatted archive. Java SE defines Java Archive (jar) files, which are used to aggregate many files (Java classes, deployment descriptors, resources, or external libraries) into one compressed file (based on the ZIP format). As seen in Figure 1-3, Java EE defines different types of modules that have their own packaging format based on this common jar format.

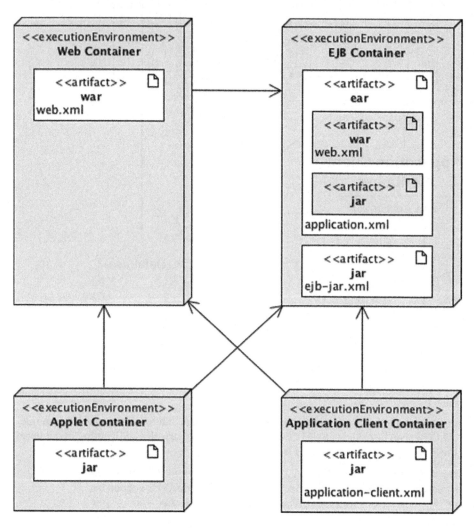

Figure 1-3. *Archives in containers*

- An application client module contains Java classes and other resource files packaged in a jar file. This jar file can be executed in a Java SE environment or in an application client container. Like any other archive format, the jar file contains an optional META-INF directory for meta information describing the archive. The META-INF/MANIFEST.MF file is used to define extension- and package-related data. If deployed in an ACC, the deployment descriptor can optionally be located at META-INF/application-client.xml.

- An EJB module contains one or more session and/or message-driven beans (MDBs) packaged in a jar file (often called an EJB jar file). It contains an optional META-INF/ejb-jar.xml deployment descriptor and can be deployed only in an EJB container.

- A web application module contains servlets, JSPs, JSF pages, and web services, as well as any other web-related files (HTML and XHTML pages, Cascading Style Sheets (CSS), Java-Scripts, images, videos, and so on). Since Java EE 6, a web application module can also contain EJB Lite beans (a subset of the EJB API described in Chapter 7). All these artifacts are packaged in a jar file with a .war extension (commonly referred to as a war file, or a Web Archive). The optional web deployment descriptor is defined in the WEB-INF/web.xml file. If the war contains EJB Lite beans, an optional deployment descriptor can be set at WEB-INF/ejb-jar.xml. Java.class files are placed under the WEB-INF/classes directory and dependent jar files in the WEB-INF/lib directory.

- An enterprise module can contain zero or more web application modules, zero or more EJB modules, and other common or external libraries. All this is packaged into an enterprise archive (a jar file with an .ear extension) so that the deployment of these various modules happens simultaneously and coherently. The optional enterprise module deployment descriptor is defined in the META-INF/application.xml file. The special lib directory is used to share common libraries between the modules.

Annotations and Deployment Descriptors

In programming paradigm, there are two approaches: imperative programming and declarative programming. Imperative programming specifies the algorithm to achieve a goal (*what has to be done*), whereas declarative programming specifies how to achieve this goal (*how it has to be done*). In Java EE, declarative programming is done by using metadata, that is, annotations or/and deployment descriptors.

As you've seen in Figure 1-2, components run in a container and this container gives the component a set of services. Metadata are used to declare and customize these services and associates additional information along with Java classes, interfaces, constructors, methods, fields or parameters.

Since Java EE 5, annotations have been proliferating in the enterprise platform. They decorate your code (Java classes, interfaces, fields, methods...) with metadata information. Listing 1-1 shows a POJO (Plain Old Java Object) that declares certain behavior using annotations on the class and on an attribute (more on EJBs, persistence context and annotations in the coming chapters).

Listing 1-1. An EJB with Annotations

```
@Stateless
@Remote(ItemRemote.class)
@Local(ItemLocal.class)
@LocalBean
public class ItemEJB implements ItemLocal, ItemRemote {

  @PersistenceContext(unitName = "chapter01PU")
  private EntityManager em;

  public Book findBookById(Long id) {
    return em.find(Book.class, id);
  }
}
```

The other manner of declaring metadata is by using deployment descriptors. A deployment descriptor (DD) refers to an XML configuration file that is deployed with the component in the container. Listing 1-2 shows an EJB deployment descriptor. Like most of the Java EE 7 deployment descriptors, it defines the http://xmlns.jcp.org/xml/ns/javaee namespace and contains a version attribute with the version of the specification.

Listing 1-2. An EJB Deployment Descriptor

```
<ejb-jar xmlns="http://xmlns.jcp.org/xml/ns/javaee" ↪
         xmlns:xsi="http://www.w3.org/2001/XMLSchema-instance" ↪
         xsi:schemaLocation="http://xmlns.jcp.org/xml/ns/javaee ↪
                             http://xmlns.jcp.org/xml/ns/javaee/ejb-jar_3_2.xsd" ↪
         version="3.2">

  <enterprise-beans>
    <session>
      <ejb-name>ItemEJB</ejb-name>
      <remote>org.agoncal.book.javaee7.ItemRemote</remote>
      <local>org.agoncal.book.javaee7.ItemLocal</local>
      <local-bean/>
      <ejb-class>org.agoncal.book.javaee7.ItemEJB</ejb-class>
      <session-type>Stateless</session-type>
      <transaction-type>Container</transaction-type>
    </session>
  </enterprise-beans>
</ejb-jar>
```

Deployment descriptors need to be packaged with the components in the special META-INF or WEB-INF directory to be taken in account. Table 1-1 shows the list of the Java EE deployment descriptors and the related specification (more on that in the coming chapters).

Table 1-1. *Deployment Descriptors in Java EE*

File	Specification	Paths
application.xml	Java EE	META-INF
application-client.xml	Java EE	META-INF
beans.xml	CDI	META-INF or WEB-INF
ra.xml	JCA	META-INF
ejb-jar.xml	EJB	META-INF or WEB-INF
faces-config.xml	JSF	WEB -INF
persistence.xml	JPA	META-INF
validation.xml	Bean Validation	META-INF or WEB-INF
web.xml	Servlet	WEB-INF
web-fragment.xml	Servlet	WEB-INF
webservices.xml	SOAP Web Services	META-INF or WEB-INF

Since Java EE 5 most deployment descriptors are optional and you can use annotations instead. But you can also use the best of both for your application. The biggest advantage of annotations is that they significantly reduce the amount of code a developer needs to write, and by using annotations you can avoid the need for deployment descriptors. On the other hand, deployment descriptors are external XML files that can be changed without requiring modifications to source code and recompilation. If you use both, then the metadata are overridden by the deployment descriptor (i.e., XML takes precedence over annotations) when the application or component is deployed.

■ **Note** In today's development annotations are preferred over deployment descriptors in Java EE. That is because there is a trend to replace a dual language programming (Java + XML) with only one (Java). This is also true because it's easy to analyze and prototype an application, when everything (data, methods, and metadata with annotations) is in one place.

Java EE uses the notion of Programming by Exception (a.k.a. Convention over Configuration) so that most of the common behavior doesn't need to be declared with metadata ("programming metadata is the exception, the container takes care of the defaults"). Which means that with only a small amount of annotations or XML the container can give you a default set of services with default behavior.

Standards

Java EE is based on standards. This means that Java EE goes through the standardizing process of the JCP and is described in a specification. In fact, Java EE is called an *umbrella specification* because it bundles together a number of other specifications (or Java Specification Requests). You might ask why standards are so important, as some of the most successful Java frameworks are not standardized (Struts, Spring, etc.). Throughout history, humans have created standards to ease communication and exchange. Some notable examples are language, currency, time, navigation, measurements, tools, railways, electricity, telegraphs, telephones, protocols, and programming languages.

In the early days of Java, if you were doing any kind of web or enterprise development, you were living in a proprietary world by creating your own frameworks or locking yourself to a proprietary commercial framework. Then came the days of open source frameworks, which are not always based on open standards. You can use open source and be locked to a single implementation, or use open source that implements standards and be portable. Java EE provides open standards that are implemented by several commercial (WebLogic, Websphere, MQSeries, etc.) or open source (GlassFish, JBoss, Hibernate, Open JPA, Jersey, etc.) frameworks for handling transactions, security, stateful components, object persistence, and so on. Today, more than ever in the history of Java EE, your application can be deployed to any compliant application server with very few changes.

JCP

The JCP is an open organization, created in 1998 by Sun Microsystems, that is involved in the definition of future versions and features of the Java platform. When the need for standardizing an existing component or API is identified, the initiator (a.k.a. specification lead) creates a JSR and forms a group of experts. This group, made of companies' representatives, organizations, universities, or private individuals, is responsible for the development of the JSR and has to deliver:

- One or more specifications that explain the details and define the fundamentals of the JSR (Java Specification Request),

- A *Reference Implementation* (RI), which is an actual implementation of the specification,

- *Compatibility Test Kit* (a.k.a. *Technology Compatibility Kit*, or TCK), which is a set of tests every implementation needs to pass before claiming to conform to the specification.

Once approved by the executive committee (EC), the specification is released to the community for implementation.

Portable

From its creation, the aim of Java EE was to enable the development of an application and its deployment to any application server without changing the code or the configuration files. This was never as easy as it seemed. Specifications don't cover all the details, and implementations end up providing nonportable solutions. That's what happened with JNDI names, for example. If you deployed an EJB to GlassFish, JBoss, or WebLogic, the JNDI name was different because it wasn't part of the specification, so you had to change your code depending on the application server you used. That particular problem, for example, was fixed in Java EE by specifying a syntax for JNDI names.

Today, the platform has introduced more portable configuration properties than ever, thus increasing portability. Despite having deprecated some APIs (pruning), Java EE applications keep their backward compatibility, letting you migrate your application to newer versions of an application server without too many problems.

Programming Model

Most of the Java EE 7 specifications use the same programming model. It's usually a POJO with some metadata (annotations or XML) deployed into a container. Most of the time the POJO doesn't even implement an interface or extend a superclass. Thanks to the metadata, the container knows which services to apply to this deployed component.

In Java EE 7, servlets, JSF backing beans, EJBs, entities, SOAP and REST web services are annotated classes with optional XML deployment descriptors. Listing 1-3 shows a JSF backing bean that turns out to be a Java class with a single CDI annotation.

Listing 1-3. A JSF Backing Bean

```
@Named
public class BookController {

  @Inject
  private BookEJB bookEJB;

  private Book book = new Book();
  private List<Book> bookList = new ArrayList<Book>();

  public String doCreateBook() {
    book = bookEJB.createBook(book);
    bookList = bookEJB.findBooks();
    return "listBooks.xhtml";
  }

  // Getters, setters
}
```

EJBs also follow the same model. As shown in Listing 1-4, if you need to access an EJB locally, a simple annotated class with no interface is enough. EJBs can also be deployed directly in a war file without being previously packaged in a jar file. This makes EJBs the simplest transactional component that can be used from simple web applications to complex enterprise ones.

Listing 1-4. A Stateless EJB

```
@Stateless
public class BookEJB {

  @Inject
  private EntityManager em;

  public Book findBookById(Long id) {
    return em.find(Book.class, id);
  }

  public Book createBook(Book book) {
    em.persist(book);
    return book;
  }
}
```

RESTful web services have been making their way into modern applications. Java EE 7 attends to the needs of enterprises by improving the JAX-RS specification. As shown in Listing 1-5, a RESTful web service is an annotated Java class that responds to HTTP actions (more in Chapter 15).

Listing 1-5. A RESTful Web Service

```
@Path("books")
public class BookResource {

  @Inject
  private EntityManager em;

  @GET
  @Produces({"application/xml", "application/json"})
  public List<Book> getAllBooks() {
    Query query = em.createNamedQuery("findAllBooks");
    List<Book> books = query.getResultList();
    return books;
  }
}
```

Throughout the chapters of this book you will come across this kind of code where components only contain business logic and where metadata are represented by annotations (or XML) to ensure that the container applies the right services.

Java Standard Edition 7

It's important to stress that Java EE is a superset of Java SE. This means that all the features of the Java language are available in Java EE as well as the APIs.

Java SE 7 was officially released on July 2011. It was developed under JSR 336 and brought many new features as well as continuing the ease of development introduced by Java SE 5 (autoboxing, annotations, generics, enumeration, etc.) and Java SE 6 (diagnosing, managing, and monitoring tools, JMX API, simplified execution of scripting languages in the Java Virtual Machine). Java SE 7 aggregates the JSR 334 (better known under the name of Project Coin), JSR 292 (InvokeDynamic, or support of dynamic languages in the JVM), JSR 203 (the new API I / O, commonly called NIO.2) and several updates of existing specifications (such as JDBC 4.1 (JSR 221). Even if this book does not explicitly cover Java SE 7, some of these enhancements will be used throughout the book samples so I just want to give you a quick overview of what the samples could look like.

String Case

Before Java SE 7 only numbers (byte, short, int, long, char) or enumerations could be used in switch cases. It is now possible to use a switch on a Strcompare alphanumerical values. This avoids long lists of if/then/else and makes the code more readable. Listing 1-6 shows you what you can now write in your applications.

Listing 1-6. A String Case

```
String action = "update";
switch (action) {
  case "create":
    create();
    break;
  case "read":
    read();
    break;
  case "udpate":
    udpate();
    break;
```

```
    case "delete":
      delete();
      break;
    default:
      noCrudAction(action);
  }
```

Diamond

Generics arrived with Java SE 5 with a rather verbose syntax. Java SE 7 brought a slightly lighter notation, called diamond, which does not repeat the declaration in the instantiation of an object. Listing 1-7 gives an example of declaring generics both with and without the diamond operator.

Listing 1-7. Declaring Generics with and Without Diamond

```
// Without diamond operator
List<String> list = new ArrayList<String>();
Map<Reference<Object>, Map<Integer, List<String>>> map =
    new HashMap<Reference<Object>, Map<Integer, List<String>>>();

// With diamond operator
List<String> list = new ArrayList<>();
Map<Reference<Object>, Map<Integer, List<String>>> map = new HashMap<>();
```

Try-with-Resources

In several Java APIs, closing resources have to be managed manually, usually by a call to a close method in a finally block. This is the case for resources managed by the operating system such as files, sockets, or JDBC connections. Listing 1-8 shows how it is necessary to put the closing code in a finally block with exception handling, which decreases the readability of the code.

Listing 1-8. Closing Input/Output Streams in Finally Blocks

```
try {
  InputStream input = new FileInputStream(in.txt);
  try {
    OutputStream output = new FileOutputStream(out.txt);
    try {
      byte[] buf = new byte[1024];
      int len;
      while ((len = input.read(buf)) >= 0)
        output.write(buf, 0, len);
    } finally {
      output.close();
    }
  } finally {
    input.close();
  }
} catch (IOException e) {
  e.printStrackTrace();
}
```

The try-with-resources overcomes this readability problem via a new simpler syntax. It allows the resources in the try to be automatically released at the end of the block. This notation described in Listing 1-9 can be used for any class that implements the new interface java.lang.AutoCloseable. This interface is now implemented by multiple classes (InputStream, OutputStream, JarFile, Reader, Writer, Socket, ZipFile...) and interfaces (java.sql.ResultSet).

Listing 1-9. Closing Input/Output Streams with Try-with-Resources

```
try (InputStream input = new FileInputStream(in.txt);
     OutputStream output = new FileOutputStream(out.txt)) {
  byte[] buf = new byte[1024];
  int len;
  while ((len = input.read(buf)) >= 0)
    output.write(buf, 0, len);
} catch (IOException e) {
  e.printStrackTrace();
}
```

Multicatch Exception

Until Java SE 6 the catch block could handle only one type of exception at a time. You therefore had to accumulate several catches to perform a specific action for each type of exception. And as shown in Listing 1-10 you often have to perform the same action for each exception.

Listing 1-10. Using Several Catch Exception Clauses

```
try {
  // Do something
} catch(SAXException e) {
  e.printStackTrace();
} catch(IOException e) {
  e.printStackTrace();
} catch(ParserConfigurationException e) {
  e.printStackTrace();
}
```

With Java SE 7 if the handling of each exception is identical, you can add as many exception types as you want, separated by a pipe character as shown in Listing 1-11.

Listing 1-11. Using Multicatch Exception

```
try {
  // Do something
} catch(SAXException | IOException | ParserConfigurationException e) {
  e.printStackTrace();
}
```

NIO.2

If like many Java developers you struggle each time you have to read or write a file, Java SE 7 came to your rescue by introducing a new IO package: `java.nio`. With a more expressive syntax, its goal is to replace the existing `java.io` package to allow:

- A cleaner exception handling.

- Full access to the file system with new features (support of specific operating system attributes, symbolic links, etc.).

- The addition of the notion of `FileSystem` and `FileStore` (e.g., a partition disk).

- Utility methods (move/copy files, read/write binary or text files, path, directories, etc.).

Listing 1-12 shows you the new `java.nio.file.Path` interface (used to locate a file or a directory in a file system) as well as the utility class `java.nio.file.Files` (used to get information about the file or to manipulate it). From Java SE 7 onward it is recommended to use the new NIO.2 even if the old `java.io` package has not been deprecated. The code in Listing 1-12 gets some information about the `source.txt` file, copies it to the `dest.txt` file, displays its content, and deletes it.

Listing 1-12. Using the New IO Package

```
Path path = Paths.get("source.txt");
boolean exists = Files.exists(path);
boolean isDirectory = Files.isDirectory(path);
boolean isExecutable = Files.isExecutable(path);
boolean isHidden = Files.isHidden(path);
boolean isReadable = Files.isReadable(path);
boolean isRegularFile = Files.isRegularFile(path);
boolean isWritable = Files.isWritable(path);
long size = Files.size(path);

// Copies a file
Files.copy(Paths.get("source.txt"), Paths.get("dest.txt"));
// Reads a text file
List<String> lines = Files.readAllLines(Paths.get("source.txt"), UTF_8);
for (String line : lines) {
  System.out.println(line);
}
// Deletes a file
Files.delete(path);
```

Java EE Specifications Overview

Java EE is an umbrella specification that bundles and integrates others. Today, an application server has to implement 31 specifications in order to be compliant with Java EE 7 and a developer has to know thousands of APIs to make the most of the container. Even if there are many specifications and APIs to know, Java EE 7 focuses on bringing simplicity to the platform by introducing a simple programming model based on POJO, a Web profile, and pruning some outdated technologies.

A Brief History of Java EE

Figure 1-4 summarizes 14 years of Java EE evolution. Java EE formerly called J2EE. J2EE 1.2, was first developed by Sun, and was released in 1999 as an umbrella specification containing ten JSRs. At that time people were talking about CORBA, so J2EE 1.2 was created with distributed systems in mind. Enterprise Java Beans (EJBs) were introduced with support for remote stateful and stateless service objects, and optional support for persistent objects (entity beans). They were built on a transactional and distributed component model using RMI-IIOP (Remote Method Invocation–Internet Inter-ORB Protocol) as the underlying protocol. The web tier had servlets and JavaServer Pages (JSPs), and JMS was used for sending messages.

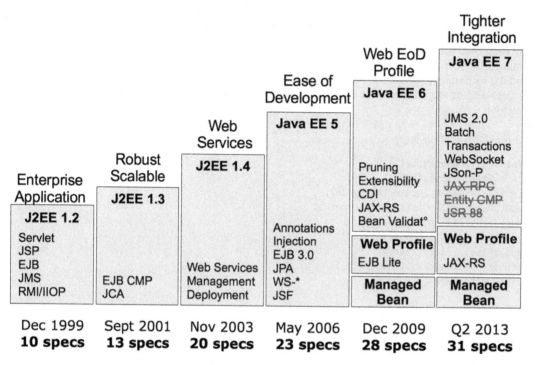

Figure 1-4. *History of J2EE/Java EE*

Starting with J2EE 1.3, the specification was developed by the Java Community Process (JCP) under the JSR 58. Support for entity beans was made mandatory, and EJBs introduced XML deployment descriptors to store metadata (which was serialized in a file in EJB 1.0). This version addressed the overhead of passing arguments by value with remote interfaces, by introducing local interfaces and passing arguments by reference. J2EE Connector Architecture (JCA) was introduced to connect Java EE to EIS.

■ **Note** CORBA originated about 1988 precisely because enterprise systems were beginning to be distributed (e.g., Tuxedo and CICS). EJBs and then J2EE followed on with the same assumptions, but ten years later. By the time J2EE was begun, CORBA was fully backed and at industrial strength, but companies found simpler, more decoupled ways to connect distributed systems, like SOAP or REST web services. So CORBA became redundant for most enterprise systems.

J2EE 1.4 (JSR 151) included 20 specifications in 2003 and added support for web services. EJB 2.1 allowed session beans to be invoked over SOAP/HTTP. A timer service was created to allow EJBs to be invoked at designated times or intervals. This version provided better support for application assembly and deployment. Although its supporters predicted a great future for it, not all of J2EE's promise materialized. The systems created with it were too complicated, and development time was frequently out of all proportion to the complexity of the user's requirements. J2EE was seen as a heavyweight component model: difficult to test, difficult to deploy, difficult to run. That's when frameworks such as Struts, Spring, or Hibernate emerged and showed a new way of developing an enterprise application.

Fortunately, in the second quarter of 2006, Java EE 5 (JSR 244) was released and turned out to be a remarkable improvement. It took some inspiration from open source frameworks by bringing back a POJO programming model. Metadata could be defined with annotations, and XML descriptors became optional. From a developer's point of view, EJB 3 and the new JPA were more of a quantum leap than an evolution of the platform .JavaServer Faces (JSF) was introduced as the standard presentation tier framework, and JAX-WS 2.0 replaced JAX-RPC as the SOAP web services API.

In 2009, Java EE 6 (JSR 316) followed the path of ease of development by embracing the concepts of annotations, POJO programming, and the configuration-by-exception mechanism throughout the platform, including the web tier. It came with a rich set of innovations such as the brand-new JAX-RS 1.1, Bean Validation 1.0, and CDI 1.0; it simplified mature APIs like EJB 3.1, and enriched others such as JPA 2.0 or the EJB timer service. But the major themes for Java EE 6 were portability (through standardizing global JNDI naming, for example), deprecation of some specifications (via pruning), and creating subsets of the platform through profiles.

Today Java EE 7 brings many new specifications (batch processing, websockets, JSON processing) as well as improving the others. Java EE 7 also improves integration between technologies by adopting CDI in most of the specifications. In this book, I want to show you these improvements and how much easier and richer Java Enterprise Edition has become.

Pruning

Java EE was first released in 1999, and ever since, new specifications have been added at each release (as shown previously in Figure 1-4). This became a problem in terms of size, implementation, and adoption. Some features were not well supported or not widely deployed because they were technologically outdated or other alternatives were made available in the meantime. So the expert group decided to propose the removal of some features through pruning. The pruning process (also known as marked for deletion) consists of proposing a list of features for possible removal in the following Java EE release. Note that none of the proposed removal items are actually removed from the current version but could be in the following one. Java EE 6 proposed the following specification and features to be pruned, and they indeed disappeared from Java EE 7:

- *EJB 2.x Entity Beans CMP (was part of JSR 318)*: The complex and heavyweight persistent component model of EJB 2.*x* entity beans has been replaced by JPA.

- *JAX-RPC (JSR 101)*: This was the first attempt to model SOAP web services as RPC calls. It has now been replaced by the much easier to use and robust JAX-WS.

- *JAXR (JSR 93)*: JAXR is the API dedicated to communicating with UDDI registries. Because UDDI is not widely used, JAXR has left Java EE and evolves as a separate JSR.

- *Java EE Application Deployment (JSR 88):* JSR 88 is a specification that tool developers can use for deployment across application servers. This API hasn't gained much vendor support, so it leaves Java EE 7 to evolve as a separate JSR.

Java EE 7 Specifications

The Java EE 7 specification is defined by the JSR 342 and contains 31 other specifications. An application server that aims to be Java EE 7 compliant has to implement all these specifications. Tables 1-2 to 1-6 list them all, grouped by technological domain, with their version and JSR numbers.

Table 1-2. *Java Enterprise Edition Specification*

Specification	Version	JSR	URL
Java EE	7.0	342	http://jcp.org/en/jsr/detail?id=342
Web Profile	7.0	342	http://jcp.org/en/jsr/detail?id=342
Managed Beans	1.0	316	http://jcp.org/en/jsr/detail?id=316

In the web service domain (Table 1-3) no improvement has been made to SOAP web service as no specification has been updated (see Chapter 14). REST web services have been heavily utilized lately in major web applications. JAX-RS 2.0 has followed a major update with the introduction of the client API for example (see Chapter 15). The new JSON-P (JSON Processing) specification is the equivalent of JAXP (Java API for XML Processing) but for JSON instead of XML (Chapter 12).

Table 1-3. *Web Services Specifications*

Specification	Version	JSR	URL
JAX-WS	2.2a	224	http://jcp.org/en/jsr/detail?id=224
JAXB	2.2	222	http://jcp.org/en/jsr/detail?id=222
Web Services	1.3	109	http://jcp.org/en/jsr/detail?id=109
Web Services Metadata	2.1	181	http://jcp.org/en/jsr/detail?id=181
JAX-RS	2.0	339	http://jcp.org/en/jsr/detail?id=339
JSON-P	1.0	353	http://jcp.org/en/jsr/detail?id=353

In the Web specifications (Table 1-4) no change has been made to JSPs or JSTL as these specifications have not been updated. Expression Language has been extracted from JSP and now evolves in its own JSR (341). Servlet and JSF (Chapters 10 and 11) have both been updated and the brand new WebSocket 1.0 has been introduced in Java EE 7.

Table 1-4. *Web Specifications*

Specification	Version	JSR	URL
JSF	2.2	344	http://jcp.org/en/jsr/detail?id=344
JSP	2.3	245	http://jcp.org/en/jsr/detail?id=245
Debugging Support for Other Languages	1.0	45	http://jcp.org/en/jsr/detail?id=45
JSTL (JavaServer Pages Standard Tag Library)	1.2	52	http://jcp.org/en/jsr/detail?id=52
Servlet	3.1	340	http://jcp.org/en/jsr/detail?id=340
WebSocket	1.0	356	http://jcp.org/en/jsr/detail?id=356
Expression Language	3.0	341	http://jcp.org/en/jsr/detail?id=341

In the enterprise domain (Table 1-5) there are two major updates: JMS 2.0 (Chapter 13) and JTA 1.2 (Chapter 9), which hadn't been updated for more than a decade. On the other hand EJBs (Chapters 7 and 8), JPA (Chapters 4, 5 and 6), and Interceptors (Chapter 2) specifications have evolved with minor updates.

Table 1-5. *Enterprise Specifications*

Specification	Version	JSR	URL
EJB	3.2	345	http://jcp.org/en/jsr/detail?id=345
Interceptors	1.2	318	http://jcp.org/en/jsr/detail?id=318
JavaMail	1.5	919	http://jcp.org/en/jsr/detail?id=919
JCA	1.7	322	http://jcp.org/en/jsr/detail?id=322
JMS	2.0	343	http://jcp.org/en/jsr/detail?id=343
JPA	2.1	338	http://jcp.org/en/jsr/detail?id=338
JTA	1.2	907	http://jcp.org/en/jsr/detail?id=907

Java EE 7 includes several other specifications (Table 1-6) such as the brand-new Batch processing (JSR 352) and Concurrency Utilities for Java EE (JSR 236). Some notable updates are Bean Validation 1.1 (Chapter 3), CDI 1.1 (Chapter 2), and JMS 2.0 (Chapter 13).

Table 1-6. *Management, Security, and Other Specifications*

Specification	Version	JSR	URL
JACC	1.4	115	http://jcp.org/en/jsr/detail?id=115
Bean Validation	1.1	349	http://jcp.org/en/jsr/detail?id=349
Contexts and Dependency Injection	1.1	346	http://jcp.org/en/jsr/detail?id=346
Dependency Injection for Java	1.0	330	http://jcp.org/en/jsr/detail?id=330
Batch	1.0	352	http://jcp.org/en/jsr/detail?id=352
Concurrency Utilities for Java EE	1.0	236	http://jcp.org/en/jsr/detail?id=236
Java EE Management	1.1	77	http://jcp.org/en/jsr/detail?id=77
Java Authentication Service Provider Interface for Containers	1.0	196	http://jcp.org/en/jsr/detail?id=196

Java EE 7 is not only composed of these 31 specifications as it heavily relies on Java SE 7. Table 1-7 shows some specifications that belong to Java SE but influence Java EE.

Table 1-7. *Related Enterprise Technologies in Java SE 7*

Specification	Version	JSR	URL
Common Annotations	1.2	250	http://jcp.org/en/jsr/detail?id=250
JDBC	4.1	221	http://jcp.org/en/jsr/detail?id=221
JNDI	1.2		
JAXP	1.3	206	http://jcp.org/en/jsr/detail?id=206
StAX	1.0	173	http://jcp.org/en/jsr/detail?id=173
JAAS	1.0		
JMX	1.2	3	http://jcp.org/en/jsr/detail?id=3
JAXB	2.2	222	http://jcp.org/en/jsr/detail?id=222
JAF	1.1	925	http://jcp.org/en/jsr/detail?id=925
SAAJ	1.3		http://java.net/projects/saaj

Web Profile 7 Specifications

Profiles were introduced in Java EE 6. Their main goal is to reduce the size of the platform to suit the developer's needs more efficiently. No matter the size or complexity of the Java EE 7 application you develop today, you will deploy it in an application server that offers you APIs and services for 31 specifications. A major criticism leveled against Java EE was that it was too large. Profiles are designed precisely to address this issue. As shown in Figure 1-5, profiles are subsets of the platform or supersets of it, and may overlap with the platform or with other profiles.

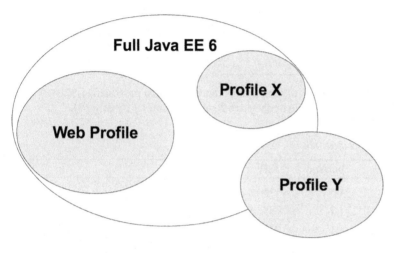

Figure 1-5. *Profiles in the Java EE platform*

Java EE 7 defines a single profile called the Web Profile. Its aim is to allow developers to create web applications with the appropriate set of technologies. Web Profile 7.0 is specified in a separate JSR and is, for now, the only profile of the Java EE 7 platform. Others might be created in the future (you could think of a minimal profile or a portal profile). Table 1-8 lists the specifications that are included in the Web Profile.

Table 1-8. *Web Profile 7.0 Specifications*

Specification	Version	JSR	URL
JSF	2.2	344	http://jcp.org/en/jsr/detail?id=344
JSP	2.3	245	http://jcp.org/en/jsr/detail?id=245
JSTL	1.2	52	http://jcp.org/en/jsr/detail?id=52
Servlet	3.1	340	http://jcp.org/en/jsr/detail?id=340
WebSocket	1.0	356	http://jcp.org/en/jsr/detail?id=356
Expression Language	3.0	341	http://jcp.org/en/jsr/detail?id=341
EJB Lite	3.2	345	http://jcp.org/en/jsr/detail?id=345
JPA	2.1	338	http://jcp.org/en/jsr/detail?id=338
JTA	1.2	907	http://jcp.org/en/jsr/detail?id=907
Bean Validation	1.1	349	http://jcp.org/en/jsr/detail?id=349

(continued)

Table 1-8. (*continued*)

Specification	Version	JSR	URL
Managed Beans	1.0	316	http://jcp.org/en/jsr/detail?id=316
Interceptors	1.2	318	http://jcp.org/en/jsr/detail?id=318
Contexts and Dependency Injection	1.1	346	http://jcp.org/en/jsr/detail?id=346
Dependency Injection for Java	1.0	330	http://jcp.org/en/jsr/detail?id=330
Debugging Support for Other Languages	1.0	45	http://jcp.org/en/jsr/detail?id=45
JAX-RS	2.0	339	http://jcp.org/en/jsr/detail?id=339
JSON-P	1.0	353	http://jcp.org/en/jsr/detail?id=353

The CD-BookStore Application

Throughout the book, you will see snippets of code dealing with entities, validation constraints, EJBs, JSF pages, JMS listeners, and SOAP or RESTful web services. They all belong to the CD-BookStore application. This application is an e-commerce web site that allows customers to browse a catalog of books and CDs on sale. Using a shopping cart, customers can add or remove items as they browse the catalog, and check out so they are able to pay and obtain a purchase order. The application has external interactions with a bank system to validate credit card numbers. The use case diagram in Figure 1-6 describes the system's actors and functionalities.

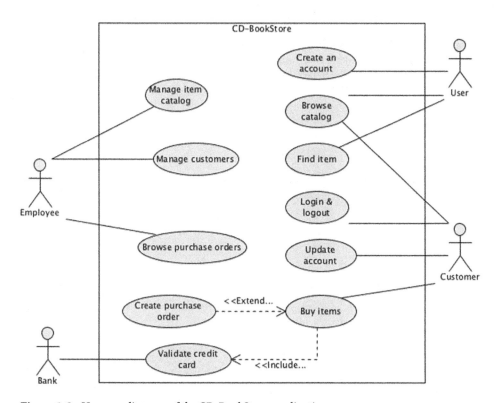

Figure 1-6. *Use case diagram of the CD-BookStore application*

The actors interacting with the system described in Figure 1-6 are

- *Employees* of the company who need to manage both the catalog of items and the customers' details. They can also browse the purchase orders.

- *Users* who are anonymous persons visiting the web site and consulting the catalog of books and CDs. If they want to buy an item, they need to create an account to become customers.

- *Customers* who can browse the catalog, update their account details, and buy items online.

- The *external bank* to which the system delegates credit card validations.

■ **Note**   You can download the code examples of this book from the Apress web site (`www.apress.com`) or straight from the Git repository at `https://github.com/agoncal/agoncal-book-javaee7`.

Summary

When a company develops a Java application and needs to add enterprise features such as transaction management, security, concurrency, or messaging, Java EE is an attractive choice. It is standard, components are deployed to different containers, which gives you many services, and it works with various protocols. Java EE 7 follows the path of its previous version by adding ease of use to the web tier. This version of the platform is lighter (thanks to pruning, profiles, and EJB Lite), easier to use (no need for interfaces on EJBs or annotations on the web tier), richer (it includes new specifications and new features), and more portable (it includes standardized deployment descriptor properties container and standard JNDI names).

In this chapter, I gave you a very quick overview of Java EE 7. The remaining chapters will be dedicated to a closer study of the Java EE 7 specifications. Each chapter has several snippets of code and a "Putting It All Together" section. You will need several tools and frameworks to compile, deploy, run, and test the code: JDK 1.7, Maven 3, JUnit 4, Derby 10.8, and GlassFish v4. Refer to Appendix A to set up your development environment.

CHAPTER 2

■ ■ ■

Context and Dependency Injection

The very first version of Java EE (J2EE at the time) introduced the concept of *inversion of control (IoC)*, meaning that the container would take control of your business code and provide technical services (such as transaction or security management). Taking control meant managing the life cycle of the components, bringing dependency injection and configuration to your components. These services were built in to the container and programmers had to wait until later versions of Java EE to have access to them. Component configuration was made possible in early versions with XML deployment descriptors, but we had to wait for Java EE 5 and Java EE 6 to have an easy and robust API to do life-cycle management and dependency injection.

Java EE 6 introduced Context and Dependency Injection to ease some of these concerns but mostly to become a central specification that ties all of these concepts together. Today CDI gives Managed Beans a first-class citizen programming model turning nearly all Java EE components into injectable, interceptable, and manageable beans. CDI is built on the concept of "loose coupling, strong typing," meaning that beans are loosely coupled but in a strongly typed way. Decoupling goes further by bringing interceptors, decorators, and events to the entire platform. And at the same time CDI brings the web tier and the back end together by homogenizing scopes. Thanks to its event bus CDI is also the standard way to extend Java EE and so becomes the extension platform for Java EE.

This chapter talks about dependency injection, scoping, and loose coupling, thereby covering most of the concepts behind CDI.

Understanding Beans

Java SE has JavaBeans, Java EE has Enterprise JavaBeans. But Java EE has other sorts of components such as Servlets, SOAP web services, RESTful web services, entities . . . and of course Managed Beans. But let's not forget our POJOs. POJOs are just Java classes that run inside the Java Virtual Machine (JVM). JavaBeans are just POJOs that follow certain patterns (e.g., a naming convention for accessors/mutators (getters/setters) for a property, a default constructor . . .) and are executed inside the JVM. All the other Java EE components also follow certain patterns (e.g., an Enterprise JavaBean must have metadata, a default constructor can't be final . . .) and are executed inside a container (e.g., the EJB container) that supplies some services (e.g., transaction, pooling, security . . .). This leaves us with Managed Beans and beans.

Managed Beans are container-managed objects that support only a small set of basic services: resource injection, life-cycle management, and interception. They were introduced in Java EE 6 to offer a lightweight component model aligned with the rest of the Java EE platform. They provide a common foundation for the different kinds of components that exist in the Java EE platform. For example, an Enterprise JavaBean can be seen as a Managed Bean with extra services. A Servlet can also be seen as a Managed Bean with extra services (different from an EJB), and so on.

Beans are CDI objects that are build on this basic Managed Bean model. Beans have an improved life cycle for stateful objects; are bound to well-defined contexts; bring a typesafe approach to dependency injection, interception, and decoration; are specialized with qualifier annotations; and can be used in expression language (EL). In fact, with very few exceptions, potentially every Java class that has a default constructor and runs inside a container is a bean. So JavaBeans and Enterprise JavaBeans can naturally take advantage of these CDI services.

Dependency Injection

Dependency Injection (DI) is a design pattern that decouples dependent components. It is part of inversion of control, where the concern being inverted is the process of obtaining the needed dependency. The term was first coined by Martin Fowler. One way to think about DI in a managed environment such as Java EE is to think of JNDI turned inside out. Instead of an object looking up other objects, the container injects those dependent objects for you. This is the so-called *Hollywood Principle*, "Don't call us?" (lookup objects), "we'll call you" (inject objects).

Java EE was created in the late 1990s and the first version already had EJBs, Servlets, and JMS. These components could use JNDI to look up container-managed resources such as JDBC DataSource, JMS factories or destinations. It allowed component dependencies and let the EJB container deal with the complexities of managing the life cycle of the resource (instantiating, initializing, sequencing, and supplying resource references to clients as required). But let's get back to talking about the resource injection performed by the container.

Java EE 5 introduced resource injection for developers. It allowed developers to inject container resources such as EJBs, entity managers, data sources, JMS factories, and destinations into a set of defined components (Servlets, JSF backing beans, and EJBs). For this purpose Java EE 5 introduced a new set of annotations (@Resource, @PersistenceContext, @PersistenceUnit, @EJB, and @WebServiceRef).

This first step taken in Java EE 5 wasn't enough, so Java EE 6 created two brand-new specifications to bring real DI to the platform: Dependency Injection (JSR 330) and Contexts and Dependency Injection (JSR 299). Today, in Java EE 7, DI goes even further to tie specifications together.

Life-Cycle Management

The life cycle of a POJO is pretty simple: as a Java developer you create an instance of a class using the new keyword and wait for the *Garbage Collector* to get rid of it and free some memory. But if you want to run a CDI Bean inside a container, you are not allowed to use the new keyword. Instead, you need to inject the bean and the container does the rest, meaning, the container is the one responsible for managing the life cycle of the bean: it creates the instance; it gets rid of it. So how do you initialize a bean if you can't call a constructor? Well, the container gives you a handle after constructing an instance and before destroying it.

Figure 2-1 shows the life cycle of a Managed Bean (and therefore, a CDI Bean). When you inject a bean, the container (EJB, Web, or CDI container) is the one responsible for creating the instance (using the new keyword). It then resolves the dependencies and invokes any method annotated with @PostConstruct before the first business method invocation on the bean. Then, the @PreDestroy callback notification signals that the instance is in the process of being removed by the container.

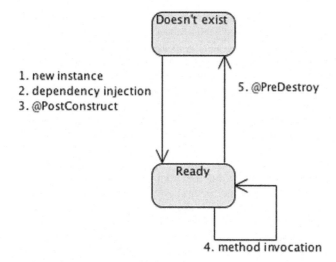

Figure 2-1. *Managed Bean life cycle*

As you'll see in the following chapters, most of the Java EE components follow the life cycle described in Figure 2-1.

Scopes and Context

CDI Beans may be stateful and are contextual, meaning that they live in a well-defined scope (CDI comes with predefined scopes: request, session, application, and conversation scopes). For example, a session context and its beans exist during the lifetime of an HTTP session. During this lifetime, the injected references to the beans are also aware of the context—that is, the entire chain of the bean dependencies is contextual. The container manages all beans inside the scope automatically for you and, at the end of the session, automatically destroys them.

Unlike stateless components (e.g., stateless session beans) or singletons (e.g., Servlets or singletons), different clients of a stateful bean see the bean in different states. When the bean is stateful (session, application and conversation scoped), it matters which bean instance the client has. Clients (e.g., other beans) executing in the same context will see the same instance of the bean. But clients in a different context may see a different instance (depending on the relationship between the contexts). In all cases, the client does not control the life cycle of the instance by explicitly creating and destroying it; the container does it according to the scope.

Interception

Interceptors are used to interpose on business method invocations. In this aspect, it is similar to aspect-oriented programming (AOP). AOP is a programming paradigm that separates cross-cutting concerns (concerns that cut across the application) from your business code. Most applications have common code that is repeated across components. These could be technical concerns (log the entry and exit from each method, log the duration of a method invocation, store statistics of method usage, etc.) or business concerns (perform additional checks if a customer buys more than $10,000 of items, send a refill order when the inventory level is too low, etc.). These concerns can be applied automatically through AOP to your entire application or to a subset of it.

Managed Beans support AOP-like functionality by providing the ability to intercept method invocation through interceptors. Interceptors are automatically triggered by the container when a Managed Bean method is invoked. As shown in Figure 2-2, interceptors can be chained and are called before and/or after the execution of a method.

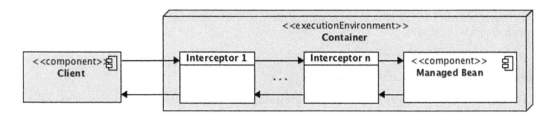

Figure 2-2. *A container intercepting a call and invoking interceptors*

Figure 2-2 shows you a number of interceptors that are called between the client and the Managed Bean. You could think of an EJB container as a chain of interceptors itself. When you develop a session bean, you just concentrate on your business code. But behind the scenes, when a client invokes a method on your EJB, the container intercepts the invocation and applies different services (life-cycle management, transaction, security, etc.). With interceptors, you add your own cross-cutting mechanisms and apply them transparently to your business code.

Loose Coupling and Strong Typing

Interceptors are a very powerful way to decouple technical concerns from business logic. Contextual life-cycle management also decouples beans from managing their own life cycles. With injection a bean is not aware of the concrete implementation of any bean it interacts with. But there is more to loose coupling in CDI. Beans can use event notifications to decouple event producers from event consumers or decorators to decouple business concerns. In other words, loose coupling is the DNA on which CDI has been built.

And all these facilities are delivered in a typesafe manner. CDI never relies on String-based identifiers to determine how objects fit together. Instead, CDI uses strongly typed annotations (e.g., qualifiers, stereotypes, and interceptor bindings) to wire beans together. Usage of XML descriptors is minimized to truly deployment-specific information.

Deployment Descriptor

Nearly every Java EE specification has an optional XML deployment descriptor. It usually describes how a component, module, or application (such as a web application or enterprise application) should be configured. With CDI, the deployment descriptor is called beans.xml and is mandatory. It can be used to configure certain functionalities (interceptors, decorators, alternatives, etc.), but it is essential to enable CDI. That's because CDI needs to identify the beans in your class path (this is called bean discovery).

It is during the bean discovery phase that the magic happens: that's when CDI turns POJOs into CDI Beans. At deployment time, CDI checks all of your application's jar and war files and each time it finds a beans.xml deployment descriptor it manages all the POJOs, which then become CDI Beans. Without a beans.xml file in the class path (under the META-INF or WEB-INF directory), CDI will not be able to use injection, interception, decoration, and so forth. Without this markup file CDI will not work. If your web application contains several jar files and you want to have CDI enabled across the entire application, each jar will need its own beans.xml to trigger CDI and bean discovery for each jar.

CDI Specifications Overview

Context and Dependency Injection is becoming a common ground for several specifications in Java EE. Some specifications heavily rely on it (Bean Validation, JAX-RS), others inspired it (EJB) and some work hand in hand with it (JSF). CDI 1.1 cuts across several specifications but would be nothing without others: Dependency Injection for Java 1.0 (JSR 330), Managed Bean 1.0 (JSR 342), Common Annotations 1.2 (JSR 250), Expression Language 3.0 (JSR 341), and Interceptors 1.2 (JSR 318).

A Brief History of CDI Specifications

In 2006, inspired from the Seam, Guice and Spring framework, Gavin King (the creator of Seam) became the specification lead of the JSR 299 which was then called Web Beans. Targeted for Java EE 6, Web Beans had to be renamed to Context and Dependency Injection 1.0 and was built on top of the new JSR 330: Dependency Injection for Java 1.0 (a.k.a. @Inject).

These two specifications were complementary and one could not be used without the other in Java EE. Dependency Injection for Java defined a set of annotations (@Inject, @Named, @Qualifier, @Scope, and @Singleton) mainly used for injection. CDI gave semantics to JSR 330 and added many more features such as context management, events, decorators, and enhanced interceptors (the JSR 318). Furthermore, CDI allowed the developer to extend the platform within standard, which was impossible until then. The aim of CDI was to fill all the gaps.

- Give more cohesion to the platform,

- Knit together the web tier and the transactional tier,

- Turn dependency injection into a first-class citizen, and

- Have the ability to add new extensions easily.

Today, with Java EE 7, CDI 1.1 is becoming the foundation of many JSRs and there have been some improvements.

What's New in CDI 1.1?

CDI 1.1 doesn't add any major features. Instead, this new version concentrates on integrating CDI with other specifications such as embracing interceptors, adding conversations in Servlet request, or having richer application life-cycle events in Java EE. The following new features can be found in CDI 1.1:

- The new CDI class provides programmatic access to CDI facilities from outside a Managed Bean;
- Interceptors, decorators, and alternatives can be prioritized (@Priority) and ordered for an entire application;
- Any type or package may be prevented from being considered a bean by CDI by adding the @Vetoed annotation on the type or package;
- The @New qualifier is deprecated in CDI 1.1 and applications are now encouraged to inject @Dependent scoped beans instead; and
- The new @WithAnnotations allows an extension to filter which types it sees.

Table 2-1 lists the main packages related to CDI. You will find the CDI annotations and classes in the javax.enterprise.inject and javax.decorator packages. Dependency Injection for Java APIs is in the javax.inject package and interceptors in javax.interceptor.

Table 2-1. *Main CDI-Related Packages*

Package	Description
javax.inject	Contains the core Dependency Injection for Java APIs (JSR 330)
javax.enterprise.inject	Core dependency injection APIs
javax.enterprise.context	CDI scopes and contextual APIs
javax.enterprise.event	CDI events and observers APIs
javax.enterprise.util	CDI utility package
javax.interceptor	Contains the Interceptor APIs (JSR 318)
javax.decorator	CDI decorator APIs

Reference Implementation

The reference implementation of CDI is Weld, an open source project from JBoss. Other implementations exist such as Apache OpenWebBeans or CanDi (from Caucho). It is also important to mention the Apache DeltaSpike project that references a set of CDI portable extensions.

Writing a CDI Bean

A CDI Bean can be any kind of class that contains business logic. It may be called directly from Java code via injection, or it may be invoked via EL from a JSF page. As you can see in Listing 2-1, a bean is a POJO that doesn't inherit or extend from anything, can inject references to other beans (@Inject), has its life cycle managed by the container (@PostConstruct), and can get its method invocation intercepted (here @Transactional is an interceptor binding—more on that later).

Listing 2-1. A BookService Bean Using Injection, Life-Cycle Management, and Interception

```
public class BookService {

    @Inject
    private NumberGenerator numberGenerator;
    @Inject
    private EntityManager em;

    private Date instanciationDate;

    @PostConstruct
    private void initDate() {
        instanciationDate = new Date();
    }

    @Transactional
    public Book createBook(String title, Float price, String description) {
        Book book = new Book(title, price, description);
        book.setIsbn(numberGenerator.generateNumber());
        book.setInstanciationDate(instanciationDate);
        em.persist(book);
        return book;
    }
}
```

Anatomy of a CDI Bean

According to the CDI 1.1 specification, the container treats any class that satisfies the following conditions as a CDI Bean:

- It is not a non-static inner class,

- It is a concrete class, or is annotated @Decorator, and

- It has a default constructor with no parameters, or it declares a constructor annotated @Inject.

Then a bean can have an optional scope, an optional EL name, a set of interceptor bindings, and an optional life-cycle management.

Dependency Injection

Java is an object-oriented programming language, meaning that the real world is represented using objects. A Book class represents a copy of "H2G2," a Customer represents you, and a PurchaseOrder represents you buying this book. These objects depend on each other: a book can be read by a customer and a purchase order refers to several books. This dependence is one value of object-oriented design.

For example, the process of creating a book (BookService) can be reduced to instantiating a Book object, generating a unique number using another service (NumberGenerator), and persisting the book to a database. The NumberGenerator service can generate an ISBN number made of 13 digits or an older format called ISSN with 8 digits. The BookService would then end up depending on either an IsbnGenerator or an IssnGenerator according to some condition or environment.

Figure 2-3 shows a class diagram of the NumberGenerator interface that has one method (String generateNumber()) and is implemented by IsbnGenerator and IssnGenerator. The BookService depends on the interface to generate a book number.

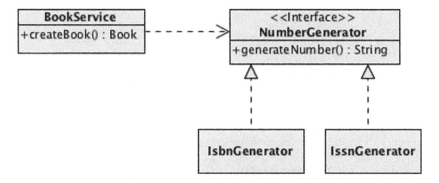

Figure 2-3. *Class diagram with the NumberGenerator interface and implementations*

How would you connect a BookService to the ISBN implementation of the NumberGenerator interface? One solution is to use the good old new keyword as shown in Listing 2-2.

Listing 2-2. A BookService POJO Creating Dependencies Using the New Keyword

```java
public class BookService {

  private NumberGenerator numberGenerator;

  public BookService() {
    this.numberGenerator = new IsbnGenerator();
  }

  public Book createBook(String title, Float price, String description) {
    Book book = new Book(title, price, description);
    book.setIsbn(numberGenerator.generateNumber());
    return book;
  }
}
```

The code in Listing 2-2 is pretty simple and does the job. In the constructor the BookService creates an instance of IsbnGenerator and affects it to the numberGenerator attribute. Invoking the numberGenerator.generateNumber() method would generate a 13-digit number.

But what if you want to choose between implementations and not just get wired to the IsbnGenerator? One solution is to pass the implementation to the constructor and leave an external class to choose which implementation it wants to use (see Listing 2-3).

Listing 2-3. A BookService POJO Choosing Dependencies Using the Constructor

```
public class BookService {

  private NumberGenerator numberGenerator;

  public BookService(NumberGenerator numberGenerator) {
    this.numberGenerator = numberGenerator;
  }

  public Book createBook(String title, Float price, String description) {
    Book book = new Book(title, price, description);
    book.setIsbn(numberGenerator.generateNumber());
    return book;
  }
}
```

So now an external class could use the BookService with the implementation it needs.

```
BookService bookService = new BookService(new IsbnGenerator())
BookService bookService = new BookService(new IssnGenerator())
```

This illustrates what inversion of control is: the control of creating the dependency between BookService and NumberGenerator is inverted because it's given to an external class, not the class itself. Since you end up connecting the dependencies yourself, this technique is referred to as construction by hand. In the preceding code we used the constructor to choose implementation (constructor injection), but another common way is to use setters (setter injection). However, instead of constructing dependencies by hand you can leave it for an injector (i.e., CDI) to do.

@Inject

As Java EE is a managed environment you don't need to construct dependencies by hand but can leave the container to inject a reference for you. In a nutshell, CDI dependency injection is the ability to inject beans into others in a typesafe way, which means no XML but annotations.

Injection already existed in Java EE 5 with the @Resource, @PersistentUnit or @EJB annotations, for example. But it was limited to certain resources (datasource, EJB . . .) and into certain components (Servlets, EJBs, JSF backing bean . . .). With CDI you can inject nearly anything anywhere thanks to the @Inject annotation. Note that in Java EE 7 you can still use the other injection mechanisms (@Resource . . .) but you should consider using @Inject whenever it is possible (see the "Producers" section later in this chapter).

Listing 2-4 shows how you would inject a reference of the NumberGenerator into the BookService using the CDI @Inject.

Listing 2-4. BookService Using @Inject to Get a Reference of NumberGenerator

```
public class BookService {

  @Inject
  private NumberGenerator numberGenerator;

  public Book createBook(String title, Float price, String description) {
    Book book = new Book(title, price, description);
    book.setIsbn(numberGenerator.generateNumber());
    return book;
  }
}
```

As you can see in Listing 2-4, a simple @Inject annotation on the property will inform the container that it has to inject a reference of a NumberGenerator implementation into the numberGenerator property. This is called the injection point (the place where the @Inject annotation is). Listing 2-5 shows the IsbnGenerator implementation. As you can see there are no special annotations and the class implements the NumberGenerator interface.

Listing 2-5. The IsbnGenerator Bean

```
public class IsbnGenerator implements NumberGenerator {

  public String generateNumber() {
    return "13-84356-" + Math.abs(new Random().nextInt());
  }
}
```

Injection Points

The @Inject annotation defines an injection point that is injected during bean instantiation. Injection can occur via three different mechanisms: property, setter, or constructor.

Until now, in all the previous code examples, you've seen the @Inject annotation on attributes (properties).

```
@Inject
private NumberGenerator numberGenerator;
```

Notice that it isn't necessary to create a getter and a setter method on an attribute to use injection. CDI can access an injected field directly (even if it's private), which sometimes helps eliminate some wasteful code. But instead of annotating the attributes, you can add the @Inject annotation on a constructor as follows:

```
@Inject
public BookService (NumberGenerator numberGenerator) {
  this.numberGenerator = numberGenerator;
}
```

But the rule is that you can only have one constructor injection point. The container is the one doing injection, not you (you can't invoke a constructor in a managed environment); therefore, there is only one bean constructor allowed so that the container can do its work and inject the right references.

The other choice is to use setter injection, which looks like constructor injection. You just need to annotate the setter with @Inject.

```
@Inject
public void setNumberGenerator(NumberGenerator numberGenerator) {
  this.numberGenerator = numberGenerator;
}
```

You may ask, "When should I use a field over a constructor or setter injection?" There is no real technical answer to that question; it's a matter of your own personal taste. In a managed environment, the container is the one doing all the injection's work; it just needs the right injection points.

Default Injection

Assume that NumberGenerator only has one implementation (IsbnGenerator). CDI will then be able to inject it simply by using @Inject on its own.

```
@Inject
private NumberGenerator numberGenerator;
```

This is termed *default injection*. Whenever a bean or injection point does not explicitly declare a qualifier, the container assumes the qualifier @javax.enterprise.inject.Default. In fact, the following code is identical to the previous one:

```
@Inject @Default
private NumberGenerator numberGenerator;
```

@Default is a built-in qualifier that informs CDI to inject the default bean implementation. If you define a bean with no qualifier, the bean automatically has the qualifier @Default. So code in Listing 2-6 is identical to the one in Listing 2-5.

Listing 2-6. The IsbnGenerator Bean with the @Default Qualifier

```
@Default
public class IsbnGenerator implements NumberGenerator {

  public String generateNumber() {
    return "13-84356-" + Math.abs(new Random().nextInt());
  }
}
```

If you only have one implementation of a bean to inject, the default behavior applies and a straightforward @Inject will inject the implementation. The class diagram in Figure 2-4 shows the @Default implementation (IsbnGenerator) as well as the default injection point (@Inject @Default). But sometimes you have to choose between several implementations. That's when you need to use qualifiers.

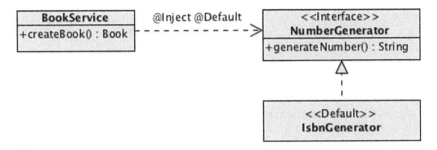

Figure 2-4. *Class diagram with @Default injection*

Qualifiers

At system initialization time, the container must validate that exactly one bean satisfying each injection point exists. Meaning that if no implementation of NumberGenerator is available, the container would inform you of an unsatisfied dependency and will not deploy the application. If there is only one implementation, injection will work using the @Default qualifier (see the diagram in Figure 2-4). If more than one default implementation were available, the container would inform you of an ambiguous dependency and will not deploy the application. That's because the typesafe resolution algorithm fails when the container is unable to identify exactly one bean to inject.

So how does a component choose which implementation (IsbnGenerator or IssnGenerator) is to get injected? Most frameworks heavily rely on external XML configuration to declare and inject beans. CDI uses qualifiers, which basically are Java annotations that bring typesafe injection and disambiguate a type without having to fall back on String-based names.

Let's say we have an application with a BookService that creates books with a 13-digit ISBN number and a LegacyBookService that creates books with an 8-digit ISSN number. As you can see in Figure 2-5, both services inject a reference of the same NumberGenerator interface. The services distinguish between the two implementations by using qualifiers.

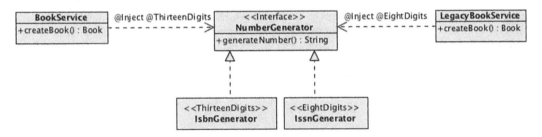

Figure 2-5. *Services using qualifiers for non-ambiguous injection*

A qualifier represents some semantics associated with a type that is satisfied by some implementation of that type. It is a user-defined annotation, itself annotated with @javax.inject.Qualifer. For example, we could introduce qualifiers to represent 13- and 8-digit number generators both shown in Listing 2-7 and Listing 2-8.

Listing 2-7. The ThirteenDigits Qualifier

```
@Qualifier
@Retention(RUNTIME)
@Target({FIELD, TYPE, METHOD})
public @interface ThirteenDigits { }
```

Listing 2-8. The EightDigits Qualifier

```
@Qualifier
@Retention(RUNTIME)
@Target({FIELD, TYPE, METHOD})
public @interface EightDigits { }
```

Once you have defined the needed qualifiers, they must be applied on the appropriate implementation. As you can see in both Listing 2-9 and Listing 2-10, the @ThirteenDigits qualifier is applied to the IsbnGenerator bean and @EightDigits to IssnGenerator.

Listing 2-9. The IsbnGenerator Bean with the @ThirteenDigits Qualifier

```
@ThirteenDigits
public class IsbnGenerator implements NumberGenerator {

  public String generateNumber() {
    return "13-84356-" + Math.abs(new Random().nextInt());
  }
}
```

Listing 2-10. The IssnGenerator Bean with the @EightDigits Qualifier

```
@EightDigits
public class IssnGenerator implements NumberGenerator {

  public String generateNumber() {
    return "8-" + Math.abs(new Random().nextInt());
  }
}
```

These qualifiers are then applied to injection points to distinguish which implementation is required by the client. In Listing 2-11 the BookService explicitly defines the 13-digit implementation by injecting a reference of the @ThirteenDigits number generator and in Listing 2-12 the LegacyBookService injects the 8-digit implementation.

Listing 2-11. BookService Using the @ThirteenDigits NumberGenerator Implementation

```
public class BookService {

  @Inject @ThirteenDigits
  private NumberGenerator numberGenerator;

  public Book createBook(String title, Float price, String description) {
    Book book = new Book(title, price, description);
    book.setIsbn(numberGenerator.generateNumber());
    return book;
  }
}
```

Listing 2-12. LegacyBookService Using the @EightDigits NumberGenerator Implementation

```java
public class LegacyBookService {

  @Inject @EightDigits
  private NumberGenerator numberGenerator;

  public Book createBook(String title, Float price, String description) {
    Book book = new Book(title, price, description);
    book.setIsbn(numberGenerator.generateNumber());
    return book;
  }
}
```

For this to work you don't need external configuration; that's why CDI is said to use strong typing. You can rename your implementations to whatever you want, rename your qualifier—the injection point will not change (that's loose coupling). As you can see, CDI is an elegant way to have typesafe injection. But if you start creating annotations each time you need to inject something, your application will end up being very verbose. That's when qualifiers with members can help you.

Qualifiers with Members

Each time you need to choose between implementations, you create a qualifier (i.e., an annotation). So if you need an extra two digits and a ten-digit number generator you will create extra annotations (e.g., @TwoDigits, @EightDigits, @TenDigits, @ThirteenDigits). Imagine that the generated numbers can either be odd or even, you would then end up with an large number of annotations: @TwoOddDigits, @TwoEvenDigits, @EightOddDigits, etc. One way to avoid the multiplication of annotations is to use members.

In our example we could replace all these qualifiers by using the single qualifier @NumberOfDigits with an enumeration as a value and a Boolean for the parity (see Listing 2-13).

Listing 2-13. The @NumberOfDigits with a Digits Enum and a Parity Boolean

```java
@Qualifier
@Retention(RUNTIME)
@Target({FIELD, TYPE, METHOD})
public @interface NumberOfDigits {

  Digits value();
  boolean odd();
}

public enum Digits {
  TWO,
  EIGHT,
  TEN,
  THIRTEEN
}
```

The manner in which you would use this qualifier with members doesn't change from what you've seen so far. The injection point will qualify the needed implementation by setting the annotation members as follows:

```
@Inject @NumberOfDigits(value = Digits.THIRTEEN, odd = false)
private NumberGenerator numberGenerator;
```

And the concerned implementation will do the same.

```
@NumberOfDigits(value = Digits.THIRTEEN, odd = false)
public class IsbnEvenGenerator implements NumberGenerator {...}
```

Multiple Qualifiers

Another way of qualifying a bean and an injection point is to specify multiple qualifiers. So instead of having multiple qualifiers for parity (@TwoOddDigits, @TwoEvenDigits ...) or having a qualifier with members (@NumberOfDigits), we could have used two different set of qualifiers: one set for the parity (@Odd and @Even) and another one for the number of digits. This is how you could qualify a generator of 13 even digits.

```
@ThirteenDigits @Even
public class IsbnEvenGenerator implements NumberGenerator {...}
```

The injection point would use the same syntax.

```
@Inject @ThirteenDigits @Even
private NumberGenerator numberGenerator;
```

Then only a bean that has both qualifier annotations would be eligible for injection. Qualifiers should be meaningful. Having the right names and granularity of qualifiers is important for an application.

Alternatives

Qualifiers let you choose between multiple implementations of an interface at development time. But sometimes you want to inject an implementation depending on a particular deployment scenario. For example, you may want to use a mock number generator in a testing environment.

Alternatives are beans annotated with the special qualifier javax.enterprise.inject.Alternative. By default alternatives are disabled and need to be enabled in the beans.xml descriptor to make them available for instantiation and injection. Listing 2-14 shows a mock number generator alternative.

Listing 2-14. A Default Mock Generator Alternative

```
@Alternative
public class MockGenerator implements NumberGenerator {

  public String generateNumber() {
    return "MOCK";
  }
}
```

As you can see in Listing 2-14, the MockGenerator implements the NumberGenerator interface as usual. It is annotated with @Alternative, meaning that CDI treats it as the default alternative of the NumberGenerator. As in Listing 2-6, this default alternative could have used the @Default built-in qualifier as follows:

```
@Alternative @Default
public class MockGenerator implements NumberGenerator {...}
```

Instead of a default alternative, you can specify the alternative by using qualifiers. For example, the following code tells CDI that the alternative of a 13-digit number generator is the mock:

```
@Alternative @ThirteenDigits
public class MockGenerator implements NumberGenerator {...}
```

By default, @Alternative beans are disabled and you need to explicitly enable them in the beans.xml descriptor as shown in Listing 2-15.

Listing 2-15. The beans.xml Deployment Descriptor Enabling an Alternative

```
<beans xmlns="http://xmlns.jcp.org/xml/ns/javaee"
       xmlns:xsi="http://www.w3.org/2001/XMLSchema-instance"
       xsi:schemaLocation="http://xmlns.jcp.org/xml/ns/javaee ⮕
                           http://xmlns.jcp.org/xml/ns/javaee/beans_1_1.xsd"
       version="1.1" bean-discovery-mode="all">

  <alternatives>
    <class>org.agoncal.book.javaee7.chapter02.MockGenerator</class>
  </alternatives>
</beans>
```

In terms of injection point, nothing changes. So your client code is not impacted. The code that follows injects the default implementation of a number generator. If the alternative is enabled, then the MockGenerator defined in Listing 2-14 will be injected.

```
@Inject
private NumberGenerator numberGenerator;
```

You can have several beans.xml files declaring several alternatives depending on your environment (development, production, test...).

Producers

I've shown you how to inject CDI Beans into other CDI Beans. But you can also inject primitives (e.g., int, long, float...), array types and any POJO that is not CDI enabled, thanks to producers. By CDI enabled I mean any class packaged into an archive containing a beans.xml file.

By default, you cannot inject classes such as a java.util.Date or java.lang.String. That's because all these classes are packaged in the rt.jar file (the Java runtime environment classes) and this archive does not contain a beans.xml deployment descriptor. If an archive does not have a beans.xml under the META-INF directory, CDI will not trigger bean discovery and POJOs will not be able to be treated as beans and, thus, be injectable. The only way to be able to inject POJOs is to use producer fields or producer methods as shown in Listing 2-16.

Listing 2-16. Producer Fields and Methods

```java
public class NumberProducer {

  @Produces @ThirteenDigits
  private String prefix13digits = "13-";

  @Produces @ThirteenDigits
  private int editorNumber = 84356;

  @Produces @Random
  public double random() {
    return Math.abs(new Random().nextInt());
  }
}
```

The NumberProducer class in Listing 2-16 has several attributes and methods all annotated with javax.enterprise.inject.Produces. This means that all the types and classes produced can now be injected with @Inject using a qualifier (@ThirteenDigits, @EightDigits or @Random).

The producer method (random() in Listing 2-16) is a method that acts as a factory of bean instances. It allows the return value to be injected. We can even specify a qualifier (e.g., @Random), a scope, and an EL name (as you will see later). A producer field (prefix13digits and editorNumber) is a simpler alternative to a producer method and it doesn't have any business code. It is just a property that becomes injectable.

In Listing 2-9 the IsbnGenerator generates an ISBN number with the formula "13-84356-" + Math.abs(new Random().nextInt()). Using the NumberProducer (Listing 2-16) we can use the produced types to change this formula. In Listing 2-17 the IsbnGenerator now injects both a String and an integer with @Inject @ThirteenDigits representing the prefix ("13-") and the editor identifier (84356) of an ISBN number. The random number is injected with @Inject @Random and returns a double.

Listing 2-17. IsbnGenerator Injecting Produced Types

```java
@ThirteenDigits
public class IsbnGenerator implements NumberGenerator {

  @Inject @ThirteenDigits
  private String prefix;

  @Inject @ThirteenDigits
  private int editorNumber;

  @Inject @Random
  private double postfix;

  public String generateNumber() {
    return prefix + editorNumber + postfix;
  }
}
```

In Listing 2-17 you can see strong typing in action. Using the same syntax (@Inject @ThirteenDigits), CDI knows that it needs to inject a String, an integer, or an implementation of a NumberGenerator. The advantage of using injected types (Listing 2-17) rather than a fixed formula (Listing 2-9) for generating numbers is that you can use all the CDI features such as alternatives (and have an alternative ISBN number generator algorithm if needed).

InjectionPoint API

In Listing 2-16 the attributes and return value produced by @Produces do not need any information about where they are injected. But there are certain cases where objects need to know something about the injection point into which they are injected. This can be a way of configuring or changing behavior depending on the injection point.

Let's take for example the creation of a logger. In the JDK, to create a java.util.logging.Logger you need to set the category of the class that owns it. For example, if you want a logger for the BookService you will write:

```
Logger log = Logger.getLogger(BookService.class.getName());
```

How would you produce a Logger that needs to know the class name of the injection point? CDI has an InjectionPoint API that provides access to metadata about an injection point (see Table 2-2). Thus you need to create a producer method that uses the InjectionPoint API to configure the right logger. Listing 2-18 shows how the createLogger method gets the injection point class name.

Table 2-2. *InjectionPoint API*

Method	Description
Type getType()	Gets the required type of injection point
Set<Annotation> getQualifiers()	Gets the required qualifiers of the injection point
Bean<?> getBean()	Gets the Bean object representing the bean that defines the injection point
Member getMember()	Gets the Field object in the case of field injection
Annotated getAnnotated()	Returns an AnnotatedField or AnnotatedParameter depending upon whether the injection point is an injected field or a constructor/method parameter
boolean isDelegate()	Determines if the injection point is a decorator delegate injection point
boolean isTransient()	Determines if the injection is a transient field

Listing 2-18. Logging Producer

```
public class LoggingProducer {

  @Produces
  private Logger createLogger(InjectionPoint injectionPoint) {
    return Logger.getLogger(injectionPoint.getMember().getDeclaringClass().getName());
  }
}
```

To use the produced logger in any bean you just inject it and use it. The logger's category class name will then be automatically set:

```
@Inject Logger log;
```

Disposers

In the previous examples (Listing 2-17 and Listing 2-18) we used producers to create datatypes or POJOs so they could be injected. We created them and didn't have to destroy or close them once used. But some producer methods return objects that require explicit destruction such as a Java Database Connectivity (JDBC) connection, JMS session, or entity manager. For creation, CDI uses producers, and for destruction, disposers. A disposer method allows the application to perform the customized cleanup of an object returned by a producer method.

Listing 2-19 shows a utility class that creates and closes a JDBC connection. The createConnection takes a Derby JDBC driver, creates a connection with a specific URL, deals with the exceptions, and returns an opened JDBC connection. This method is annotated with @Produces. On the other hand, the closeConnection method terminates the JDBC connection. It is annotated with @Disposes.

Listing 2-19. JDBC Connection Producer and Disposer

```java
public class JDBCConnectionProducer {

  @Produces
  private Connection createConnection() {
    Connection conn = null;
    try {
      Class.forName("org.apache.derby.jdbc.EmbeddedDriver").newInstance();
      conn = DriverManager.getConnection("jdbc:derby:memory:chapter02DB", "APP", "APP");

    } catch (InstantiationException | IllegalAccessException | ClassNotFoundException) {
      e.printStackTrace();
    }
    return conn;
  }

  private void closeConnection(@Disposes Connection conn) throws SQLException {
    conn.close();
  }
}
```

Destruction can be performed by a matching disposer method, defined by the same class as the producer method. Each disposer method, annotated with @Disposes, must have exactly one disposed parameter of the same type (here java.sql.Connection) and qualifiers (@Default) as the corresponding producer method return type (annotated @Produces). The disposer method (closeConnection()) is called automatically when the client context ends (in Listing 2-20 the context is @ApplicationScoped), and the parameter receives the object produced by the producer method.

Listing 2-20. JDBC Connection Producer and Disposer

```java
@ApplicationScoped
public class DerbyPingService {

  @Inject
  private Connection conn;

  public void ping() throws SQLException {
    conn.createStatement().executeQuery("SELECT 1 FROM SYSIBM.SYSDUMMY1");
  }
}
```

Listing 2-20 shows a bean injecting the created JDBC connection with `@Inject` and using it to ping a Derby database. As you can see, this client code doesn't deal with all the technical plumbing of creating and closing the JDBC connection or exception handling. Producers and disposers are a neat way of creating and closing resources.

Scopes

CDI is about Dependency Injection but also Context (the "C" in CDI). Every object managed by CDI has a well-defined scope and life cycle that is bound to a specific context. In Java, the scope of a POJO is pretty simple: you create an instance of a class using the new keyword and you rely on the garbage collection to get rid of it and free some memory. With CDI, a bean is bound to a context and it remains in that context until the bean is destroyed by the container. There is no way to manually remove a bean from a context.

While the web tier has well-defined scopes (application, session, request), there was no such thing for the service tier (see also Chapter 7 for stateless and stateful session beans). That's because when session beans or POJOs are used within web applications, they are not aware of the contexts of the web applications. CDI brought the web and service tiers together by binding them with meaningful scopes. CDI defines the following built-in scopes and even gives you extension points so you can create your own:

- *Application scope* (`@ApplicationScoped`): Spans for the entire duration of an application. The bean is created only once for the duration of the application and is discarded when the application is shut down. This scope is useful for utility or helper classes, or objects that store data shared by the entire application (but you should be careful about concurrency issues when the data have to be accessed by several threads).

- *Session scope* (`@SessionScoped`): Spans across several HTTP requests or several method invocations for a single user's session. The bean is created for the duration of an HTTP session and is discarded when the session ends. This scope is for objects that are needed throughout the session such as user preferences or login credentials.

- *Request scope* (`@RequestScoped`): Corresponds to a single HTTP request or a method invocation. The bean is created for the duration of the method invocation and is discarded when the method ends. It is used for service classes or JSF backing beans that are only needed for the duration of an HTTP request.

- *Conversation scope* (`@ConversationScoped`): Spans between multiple invocations within the session boundaries with starting and ending points determined by the application. Conversations are used across multiple pages as part of a multistep workflow.

- *Dependent pseudo-scope* (`@Dependent`): The life cycle is same as that the client. A dependent bean is created each time it is injected and the reference is removed when the injection target is removed. This is the default scope for CDI.

As you can see, all the scopes have an annotation you can use on your CDI Beans (all these annotations are in the `javax.enterprise.context` package). The first three scopes are well known. For example, if you have a session scoped shopping cart bean, the bean will be automatically created when the session begins (e.g., the first time a user logs in) and automatically destroyed when the session ends.

@SessionScoped

```
@SessionScoped
public class ShoppingCart implements Serializable {...}
```

An instance of the `ShoppingCart` bean is bound to a user session and is shared by all requests that execute in the context of that session. If you don't want the bean to sit in the session indefinitely, consider using another scope with a shorter life span, such as the request or conversation scope. Note that beans with scope `@SessionScoped` or `@ConversationScoped` must be serializable, since the container passivates them from time to time.

If a scope is not explicitly specified, then the bean belongs to the dependent pseudo-scope (@Dependent). Beans with this scope are never shared between different clients or different injection points. They are dependent on some other bean, which means their life cycle is bound to the life cycle of that bean. A dependent bean is instantiated when the object it belongs to is created, and destroyed when the object it belongs to is destroyed. The code that follows shows a dependent scoped ISBN generator with a qualifier:

```
@Dependent @ThirteenDigits
public class IsbnGenerator implements NumberGenerator {...}
```

Being the default scope, you can omit the @Dependent annotation and write the following:

```
@ThirteenDigits
public class IsbnGenerator implements NumberGenerator {...}
```

Scopes can be mixed. A @SessionScoped bean can be injected into a @RequestScoped or @ApplicationScoped bean and vice versa.

Conversation

The conversation scope is slightly different than the application, session, or request scope. It holds state associated with a user, spans multiple requests, and is demarcated programmatically by the application. A @ConversationScoped bean can be used for a long-running process where there is a definite beginning and end such as navigating through a wizard or buying items and checking out of an online store.

Request scoped objects have a very short life span that usually lasts for a single request (HTTP request or method invocation) while session scoped objects last for the entire duration of the user's session. But there are many cases that fall between these two extremes. There are some presentation tier objects that can be used across more than one page but not across the entire session. For that, CDI has a special conversation scope (@ConversationScoped). Unlike session scoped objects that are automatically timed out by the container, conversation scoped objects have a well-defined life cycle that explicitly starts and ends programmatically using the javax.enterprise.context.Conversation API.

As an example, think of a customer creation wizard web application. The wizard is composed of three steps. In the first step, the customer enters login information (e.g., username and password). In the second step, the customer enters account details such as the first name, last name, address, and e-mail address. The final step of the wizard confirms all the collected information and creates the account. Listing 2-21 shows the conversation scoped bean that implements the customer creator wizard.

Listing 2-21. A Wizard to Create a Customer Using a Conversation

```
@ConversationScoped
public class CustomerCreatorWizard implements Serializable {

  private Login login;
  private Account account;

  @Inject
  private CustomerService customerService;

  @Inject
  private Conversation conversation;
```

```
  public void saveLogin() {
    conversation.begin();

    login = new Login();
    // Sets login properties
  }

  public void saveAccount() {
    account = new Account();
    // Sets account properties
  }

  public void createCustomer() {
    Customer customer = new Customer();
    customer.setLogin(login);
    customer.setAccount(account);
    customerService.createCustomer(customer);

    conversation.end();
  }
}
```

The CustomerCreatorWizard in Listing 2-21 is annotated with @ConversationScoped. It then injects a CustomerService, to create the Customer, but more important, it injects a Conversation. This interface allows programmatic control over the life cycle of the conversation scope. Notice that when the saveLogin method is invoked, the conversation starts (conversation.begin()). The conversation is now started and is used for the duration of the wizard. Once the last step of the wizard is invoked, the createCustomer method is invoked and the conversation ends (conversation.end()). Table 2-3 gives you an overview of the Conversation API.

Table 2-3. *Conversation API*

Method	Description
void begin()	Marks the current transient conversation long-running
void begin(String id)	Marks the current transient conversation long-running, with a specified identifier
void end()	Marks the current long-running conversation transient
String getId()	Gets the identifier of the current long-running conversation
long getTimeout()	Gets the timeout of the current conversation
void setTimeout(long millis)	Sets the timeout of the current conversation
boolean isTransient()	Determines if the conversation is marked transient or long-running

Beans in Expression Language

One of the key features of CDI is that it knits together the transactional tier (see Chapter 9) and the web tier. But as you've seen so far, one of the primary characteristics of CDI is that DI is completely typesafe and does not depend on character-based names. While this is great in Java code, beans would not be resolvable without a character-based name outside Java such as EL in JSF pages for example.

By default, CDI Beans are not assigned any name and are not resolvable via EL binding. To assign a bean a name, it must be annotated with the @javax.inject.Named built-in qualifier as shown in Listing 2-22.

Listing 2-22. A BookService with a Character-Based Name

```
@Named
public class BookService {

  private String title, description;
  private Float price;
  private Book book;

  @Inject @ThirteenDigits
  private NumberGenerator numberGenerator;

  public String createBook() {
    book = new Book(title, price, description);
    book.setIsbn(numberGenerator.generateNumber());
    return "customer.xhtml";
  }
}
```

The @Named qualifier allows you to access the BookService bean through its name (which by default is the class name in camel case with the first letter in lowercase). The following code shows a JSF button invoking the createBook method:

```
<h:commandButton value="Send email" action="#{bookService.createBook}"/>
```

You can also override the name of the bean by adding a different name to the qualifier.

```
@Named("myService")
public class BookService {...}
```

Then you can use this new name on your JSF page.

```
<h:commandButton value="Send email" action="#{myService.createBook}"/>
```

Interceptors

Interceptors allow you to add cross-cutting concerns to your beans. As shown in Figure 2-2, when a client invokes a method on a Managed Bean (and therefore a CDI Bean, an EJB, a RESTful web service . . .), the container is able to intercept the call and process business logic before the bean's method is invoked. Interceptors fall into four types.

- *Constructor-level interceptors*: Interceptor associated with a constructor of the target class (@AroundConstruct),

- *Method-level interceptors*: Interceptor associated with a specific business method (@AroundInvoke),

- *Timeout method interceptors*: Interceptor that interposes on timeout methods with @AroundTimeout (only used with EJB timer service, see Chapter 8), and

- *Life-cycle callback interceptors*: Interceptor that interposes on the target instance life-cycle event callbacks (@PostConstruct and @PreDestroy).

■ **Note**   Since Java EE 6, interceptors have evolved into a separate specification (they used to be bundled with the EJB specification). They can be applied to Managed Bean, as you'll see in this section, but also to EJBs, SOAP, and RESTful web services.

Target Class Interceptors

There are several ways of defining interception. The simplest is to add interceptors (method-level, timeout, or life-cycle interceptors) to the bean itself as shown in Listing 2-23. CustomerService annotates logMethod() with @AroundInvoke. logMethod() is used to log a message when a method is entered and exited. Once this Managed Bean is deployed, any client invocation to createCustomer() or findCustomerById() will be intercepted, and the logMethod() will be applied. Note that the scope of this interceptor is limited to the bean itself (the target class).

Listing 2-23. A CustomerService Using Around-Invoke Interceptor

```
@Transactional
public class CustomerService {

  @Inject
  private EntityManager em;
  @Inject
  private Logger logger;

  public void createCustomer(Customer customer) {
    em.persist(customer);
  }

  public Customer findCustomerById(Long id) {
    return em.find(Customer.class, id);
  }

  @AroundInvoke
  private Object logMethod(InvocationContext ic) throws Exception {
    logger.entering(ic.getTarget().toString(), ic.getMethod().getName());
    try {
      return ic.proceed();
    } finally {
      logger.exiting(ic.getTarget().toString(), ic.getMethod().getName());
    }
  }
}
```

Despite being annotated with @AroundInvoke, logMethod() must have the following signature pattern:

```
@AroundInvoke
Object <METHOD>(InvocationContext ic) throws Exception;
```

The following rules apply to an around-invoke method (as well constructor, timeout, or life-cycle interceptors):

- The method can have public, private, protected, or package-level access but must not be static or final.
- The method must have a javax.interceptor.InvocationContext parameter and must return Object, which is the result of the invoked target method.
- The method can throw a checked exception.

The InvocationContext object allows interceptors to control the behavior of the invocation chain. If several interceptors are chained, the same InvocationContext instance is passed to each interceptor, which can add contextual data to be processed by other interceptors. Table 2-4 describes the InvocationContext API.

Table 2-4. *Definition of the InvocationContext Interface*

Method	Description
getContextData	Allows values to be passed between interceptor methods in the same InvocationContext instance using a Map.
getConstructor	Returns the constructor of the target class for which the interceptor was invoked.
getMethod	Returns the method of the bean class for which the interceptor was invoked.
getParameters	Returns the parameters that will be used to invoke the business method.
getTarget	Returns the bean instance that the intercepted method belongs to.
getTimer	Returns the timer associated with a @Timeout method.
proceed	Causes the invocation of the next interceptor method in the chain. It returns the result of the next method invoked. If a method is of type void, proceed returns null.
setParameters	Modifies the value of the parameters used for the target class method invocation. The types and the number of parameters must match the bean's method signature, or IllegalArgumentException is thrown.

To explain how the code works in Listing 2-23, let's take a look at the sequence diagram shown in Figure 2-6 to see what happens when a client invokes the createCustomer() method. First of all, the container intercepts the call and, instead of directly processing createCustomer(), first invokes the logMethod() method. logMethod() uses the InvocationContext interface to get the name of the invoked bean (ic.getTarget()) and invoked method (ic.getMethod()) to log an entry message (logger.entering()). Then, the proceed() method is called. Calling InvocationContext.proceed() is extremely important as it tells the container that it should proceed to the next interceptor or call the bean's business method. Not calling proceed() would stop the interceptors chain and would avoid calling the business method. The createCustomer() is finally invoked, and once it returns, the interceptor finishes its execution by logging an exit message (logger.exiting()). The same sequence would happen if a client invokes the findCustomerById() method.

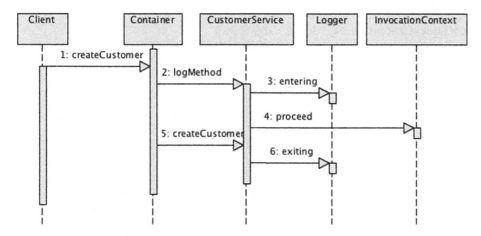

Figure 2-6. *A call to a business method being intercepted*

■ **Note**   Listing 2-23 uses the new `@javax.transaction.Transactional` annotation. It is used to control transaction boundaries on CDI Beans as well as Servlets, JAX-RS, and JAX-WS service endpoints. It provides the semantics of EJB transaction attributes in CDI. `@Transactional` is implemented via an interceptor. More on transactions in Chapter 9.

Class Interceptors

Listing 2-23 defines an interceptor that is only available for `CustomerService`. But most of the time you want to isolate cross-cutting concerns into a separate class and tell the container to intercept the calls on several beans. Logging is a typical example of a situation in which you want all the methods of all your beans to log entering and exiting messages. To specify a class interceptor, you need to develop a separate class and instruct the container to apply it on a specific bean or bean's method.

To share some code among multiple beans, let's take the `logMethod()` methods from Listing 2-23 and isolate it in a separate class as shown in Listing 2-24. Notice the `init()` method which is annotated with `@AroundConstruct` and will be invoked only when the constructor of the bean is called.

Listing 2-24. An Interceptor Class with Around-Invoke and Around-Construct

```
public class LoggingInterceptor {

  @Inject
  private Logger logger;

  @AroundConstruct
  private void init(InvocationContext ic) throws Exception {
    logger.fine("Entering constructor");
    try {
      ic.proceed();
    } finally {
      logger.fine("Exiting constructor");
    }
  }
}
```

```
@AroundInvoke
public Object logMethod(InvocationContext ic) throws Exception {
  logger.entering(ic.getTarget().toString(), ic.getMethod().getName());
  try {
    return ic.proceed();
  } finally {
    logger.exiting(ic.getTarget().toString(), ic.getMethod().getName());
  }
}
}
```

The LoggingInterceptor can now be wrapped transparently by any bean interested in this interceptor. To do this, the bean needs to inform the container with a@javax.interceptor.Interceptors annotation. In Listing 2-25, the annotation is set on the createCustomer() method. This means that any invocation of this method will be intercepted by the container, and the LoggingInterceptor class will be invoked (logging a message on entry and exit of the method).

Listing 2-25. CustomerService Uses an Interceptor on One Method

```
@Transactional
public class CustomerService {

  @Inject
  private EntityManager em;

  @Interceptors(LoggingInterceptor.class)
  public void createCustomer(Customer customer) {
    em.persist(customer);
  }

  public Customer findCustomerById(Long id) {
    return em.find(Customer.class, id);
  }
}
```

In Listing 2-25, @Interceptors is only attached to the createCustomer() method. This means that if a client invokes findCustomerById(), the container will not intercept the call. If you want the calls to both methods to be intercepted, you can add the @Interceptors annotation either on both methods or on the bean itself. When you do so, the interceptor is triggered if either method is invoked. And because the interceptor has an @AroundConstruct, the call to the constructor will be also intercepted.

```
@Transactional
@Interceptors(LoggingInterceptor.class)
public class CustomerService {
  public void createCustomer(Customer customer) {...}
  public Customer findCustomerById(Long id) {...}
}
```

If your bean has several methods, and you want to apply an interceptor to the entire bean except for a specific method, you can use the javax.interceptor.ExcludeClassInterceptors annotation to exclude a call from being intercepted. In the following code, the call to updateCustomer() will not be intercepted, but all others will:

```
@Transactional
@Interceptors(LoggingInterceptor.class)
public class CustomerService {
  public void createCustomer(Customer customer) {...}
  public Customer findCustomerById(Long id) {...}
  @ExcludeClassInterceptors
  public Customer updateCustomer(Customer customer) { ... }
}
```

Life-Cycle Interceptor

At the beginning of this chapter I explained the life cycle of a Managed Bean (Figure 2-2) and callback events. With a callback annotation, you can inform the container to invoke a method at a certain life-cycle phase (@PostConstruct and @PreDestroy). For example, if you want to log an entry each time a bean instance is created, you just need to add a @PostConstruct annotation on one method of your bean and add some logging mechanisms to it. But what if you need to capture life-cycle events across many types of beans? Life-cycle interceptors allow you to isolate some code into a class and invoke it when a life-cycle event is triggered.

Listing 2-26 shows the ProfileInterceptor class with two methods: logMethod(), used for postconstruction (@PostConstruct), and profile(), used for method interception (@AroundInvoke).

Listing 2-26. An Interceptor with Both Life-Cycle and Around-Invoke

```
public class ProfileInterceptor {

  @Inject
  private Logger logger;

  @PostConstruct
  public void logMethod(InvocationContext ic) throws Exception {
    logger.fine(ic.getTarget().toString());
      try {
      ic.proceed();
    } finally {
      logger.fine(ic.getTarget().toString());
    }
  }

  @AroundInvoke
  public Object profile(InvocationContext ic) throws Exception {
    long initTime = System.currentTimeMillis();
    try {
      return ic.proceed();
    } finally {
      long diffTime = System.currentTimeMillis() - initTime;
      logger.fine(ic.getMethod() + " took " + diffTime + " millis");
    }
  }
}
```

As you can see in Listing 2-26, life-cycle interceptors take an InvocationContext parameter and return void instead of Object. To apply the interceptor defined in Listing 2-26, the bean CustomerService (Listing 2-27) needs to use the @Interceptors annotation and define the ProfileInterceptor. When the bean is instantiated by the container, the logMethod() will be invoked prior to the init() method. Then, if a client calls createCustomer() or findCustomerById(), the profile() method will be invoked.

Listing 2-27. CustomerService Using an Interceptor and a Callback Annotation

```
@Transactional
@Interceptors(ProfileInterceptor.class)
public class CustomerService {

  @Inject
  private EntityManager em;

  @PostConstruct
  public void init() {
    // ...
  }

  public void createCustomer(Customer customer) {
    em.persist(customer);
  }

  public Customer findCustomerById(Long id) {
    return em.find(Customer.class, id);
  }
}
```

Chaining and Excluding Interceptors

You've seen how to intercept calls within a single bean (with @AroundInvoke) and across multiple beans (using @Interceptors). Interceptors 1.2 also lets you chain several interceptors.

In fact, the @Interceptors annotation is capable of attaching more than one interceptor, as it takes a comma-separated list of interceptors as a parameter. When multiple interceptors are defined, the order in which they are invoked is determined by the order in which they are specified in the @Interceptors annotation. For example, the code in Listing 2-28 uses @Interceptors at the bean and method level.

Listing 2-28. CustomerService Chaining Serveral Interceptors

```
@Stateless
@Interceptors({I1.class, I2.class})
public class CustomerService {
  public void createCustomer(Customer customer) {...}
  @Interceptors({I3.class, I4.class})
  public Customer findCustomerById(Long id) {...}
  public void removeCustomer(Customer customer) {...}
  @ExcludeClassInterceptors
  public Customer updateCustomer(Customer customer) {...}
}
```

When a client calls the updateCustomer() method, no interceptor is invoked because the method is annotated with @ExcludeClassInterceptors. When the createCustomer() method is called, interceptor I1 is executed followed by interceptor I2. When the findCustomerById() method is invoked, interceptors I1, I2, I3, and I4 get executed in this order.

Interceptor Binding

Interceptors are defined in their own specification (JSR 318) and can be used in any Managed Bean (EJBs, Servlets, RESTful web services . . .). But the CDI specification has extended it by adding interceptor binding, meaning that interceptor binding can only be used if CDI is enabled.

If you look at Listing 2-25 as an example, you can see the way interceptors work; you need to specify the implementation of the interceptor directly on the implementation of the bean (e.g., @Interceptors(LoggingInterceptor.class)). This is typesafe, but not loosely coupled. CDI provides interceptor binding that introduces a level of indirection and loose coupling. An interceptor binding type is a user-defined annotation that is itself annotated @InterceptorBinding which binds the interceptor class to the bean with no direct dependency between the two classes.

Listing 2-29 shows an interceptor binding called Loggable. As you can see, this code is very similar to a qualifier. An interceptor binding is an annotation itself annotated with @InterceptorBinding, which can be empty or have members (such as the ones seen in Listing 2-13).

Listing 2-29. Loggable Interceptor Binding

```
@InterceptorBinding
@Target({METHOD, TYPE})
@Retention(RUNTIME)
public @interface Loggable { }
```

Once you have an interceptor binding you need to attach it to the interceptor itself. This is done by annotating the interceptor with both @Interceptor and the interceptor binding (@Loggable in Listing 2-30).

Listing 2-30. Loggable Interceptor

```
@Interceptor
@Loggable
public class LoggingInterceptor {

  @Inject
  private Logger logger;

  @AroundInvoke
  public Object logMethod(InvocationContext ic) throws Exception {
    logger.entering(ic.getTarget().toString(), ic.getMethod().getName());
    try {
      return ic.proceed();
    } finally {
      logger.exiting(ic.getTarget().toString(), ic.getMethod().getName());
    }
  }
}
```

Now you can apply the interceptor to a bean by annotating the bean class with the same interceptor binding as shown in Listing 2-31. This gives you loose coupling (as the implementation class of the interceptor is not explicitly stated) and a nice level of indirection.

Listing 2-31. CustomerService using the Interceptor Binding

```
@Transactional
@Loggable
public class CustomerService {

  @Inject
  private EntityManager em;

  public void createCustomer(Customer customer) {
    em.persist(customer);
  }

  public Customer findCustomerById(Long id) {
    return em.find(Customer.class, id);
  }
}
```

In Listing 2-31 the interceptor binding is on the bean, meaning that every method will be intercepted and logged. But like interceptors, you can apply an interceptor binding to a method instead of an entire bean.

```
@Transactional
public class CustomerService {
  @Loggable
  public void createCustomer(Customer customer) {...}
  public Customer findCustomerById(Long id) {...}
}
```

Interceptors are deployment-specific and are disabled by default. Like alternatives, interceptors have to be enabled by using the CDI deployment descriptor beans.xml of the jar or Java EE module as shown in Listing 2-32.

Listing 2-32. The beans.xml Deployment Descriptor Enabling an Interceptor

```
<beans xmlns="http://xmlns.jcp.org/xml/ns/javaee"
       xmlns:xsi="http://www.w3.org/2001/XMLSchema-instance"
       xsi:schemaLocation="http://xmlns.jcp.org/xml/ns/javaee ➥
                           http://xmlns.jcp.org/xml/ns/javaee/beans_1_1.xsd"
       version="1.1" bean-discovery-mode="all">

  <interceptors>
    <class>org.agoncal.book.javaee7.chapter02.LoggingInterceptor</class>
  </interceptors>
</beans>
```

Prioritizing Interceptors Binding

Interceptor binding brings you a level of indirection, but you lose the possibility to order the interceptors as shown in Listing 2-28 (@Interceptors({I1.class, I2.class})). From CDI 1.1 you can prioritize them using the @javax.annotation.Priority annotation (or the XML equivalent in beans.xml) along with a priority value as shown in Listing 2-33.

Listing 2-33. Loggable Interceptor Binding

```
@Interceptor
@Loggable
@Priority(200)
public class LoggingInterceptor {

  @Inject
  private Logger logger;

  @AroundInvoke
  public Object logMethod(InvocationContext ic) throws Exception {
    logger.entering(ic.getTarget().toString(), ic.getMethod().getName());
    try {
      return ic.proceed();
    } finally {
      logger.exiting(ic.getTarget().toString(), ic.getMethod().getName());
    }
  }
}
```

@Priority takes an integer that can take any value. The rule is that interceptors with smaller priority values are called first. Java EE 7 defines platform-level priorities and you can then have your interceptors called before or after certain events. The javax.interceptor.Interceptor annotation defines the following set of constants:

- PLATFORM_BEFORE = 0: Start of range for early interceptors defined by the Java EE platform,

- LIBRARY_BEFORE = 1000: Start of range for early interceptors defined by extension libraries,

- APPLICATION = 2000: Start of range for interceptors defined by applications,

- LIBRARY_AFTER = 3000: Start of range for late interceptors defined by extension libraries, and

- PLATFORM_AFTER = 4000: Start of range for late interceptors defined by the Java EE platform.

So if you want your interceptor to be executed before any application interceptor, but after any early platform interceptor, you can write the following:

```
@Interceptor
@Loggable
@Priority(Interceptor.Priority.LIBRARY_BEFORE + 10)
public class LoggingInterceptor {...}
```

Decorators

Interceptors perform cross-cutting tasks and are perfect for solving technical concerns such as transaction management, security, or logging. By nature interceptors are unaware of the actual semantics of the actions they intercept and therefore are not appropriate for separating business-related concerns. The reverse is true for decorators.

Decorators are a common design pattern from the Gang of Four. The idea is to take a class and wrap another class around it (i.e., decorate it). This way, when you call a decorated class, you always pass through the surrounding decorator before you reach the target class. Decorators are meant to add additional logic to a business method. They are not able to solve technical concerns that cut across many disparate types. Interceptors and decorators, though similar in many ways, are complementary.

Let's take the example of an ISSN number generator. ISSN is an 8-digit number that has been replaced by ISBN (13-digit number). Instead of having two separate number generators (such as the one in Listing 2-9 and Listing 2-10) you can decorate the ISSN generator to add an extra algorithm that turns an 8-digit number into a 13-digit number. Listing 2-34 implements such an algorithm as a decorator. The FromEightToThirteenDigitsDecorator class is annotated with javax.decorator.Decorator, implements business interfaces (the NumberGenerator defined in Figure 2-3), and overrides the generateNumber method (a decorator can be declared as an abstract class so that it does not have to implement all the business methods of the interfaces if there are many). The generateNumber() method invokes the target bean to generate an ISSN, adds some business logic to transform such a number, and returns an ISBN number.

Listing 2-34. Decorator Transforming an 8-Digit Number to 13

```
@Decorator
public class FromEightToThirteenDigitsDecorator implements NumberGenerator {

    @Inject @Delegate
    private NumberGenerator numberGenerator;

    public String generateNumber() {
        String issn = numberGenerator.generateNumber();
        String isbn = "13-84356" + issn.substring(1);
        return isbn;
    }
}
```

Decorators must have a delegate injection point (annotated with @Delegate), with the same type as the beans they decorate (here the NumberGenerator interface). It allows the decorator to invoke the delegate object (i.e., the target bean IssnNumberGenerator) and therefore invoke any business method on it (such as numberGenerator.generateNumber() in Listing 2-34).

By default, all decorators are disabled like alternatives and interceptors. You need to enable decorators in the beans.xml as shown in Listing 2-35.

Listing 2-35. The beans.xml Deployment Descriptor Enabling a Decorator

```
<beans xmlns="http://xmlns.jcp.org/xml/ns/javaee"
       xmlns:xsi="http://www.w3.org/2001/XMLSchema-instance"
       xsi:schemaLocation="http://xmlns.jcp.org/xml/ns/javaee ➥
                           http://xmlns.jcp.org/xml/ns/javaee/beans_1_1.xsd"
       version="1.1" bean-discovery-mode="all">
```

```
<decorators>
  <class>org.agoncal.book.javaee7.chapter02.FromEightToThirteenDigitsDecorator</class>
</decorators>
</beans>
```

If an application has both interceptors and decorators, the interceptors are invoked first.

Events

DI, alternatives, interceptors, and decorators enable loose coupling by allowing additional behavior to vary, either at deployment time or at runtime. Events go one step further, allowing beans to interact with no compile time dependency at all. One bean can define an event, another bean can fire the event, and yet another bean can handle the event. The beans can be in separate packages and even in separate tiers of the application. This basic schema follows the observer/observable design pattern from the Gang of Four.

Event producers fire events using the javax.enterprise.event.Event interface. A producer raises events by calling the fire() method, passes the event object, and is not dependent on the observer. In Listing 2-36 the BookService fires an event (bookAddedEvent) each time a book is created. The code bookAddedEvent.fire(book) fires the event and notifies any observer methods observing this particular event. The content of this event is the Book object itself that will be carried from the producer to the consumer.

Listing 2-36. The BookService Fires an Event Each Time a Book Is Created

```
public class BookService {

  @Inject
  private NumberGenerator numberGenerator;

  @Inject
  private Event<Book> bookAddedEvent;

  public Book createBook(String title, Float price, String description) {
    Book book = new Book(title, price, description);
    book.setIsbn(numberGenerator.generateNumber());
    bookAddedEvent.fire(book);
    return book;
  }
}
```

Events are fired by the event producer and subscribed to by event observers. An observer is a bean with one or more observer methods. Each of these observer methods takes an event of a specific type as a parameter that is annotated with the @Observes annotation and optional qualifiers. The observer method is notified of an event if the event object matches the event type and all the qualifiers. Listing 2-37 shows the inventory service whose job is to keep the inventory of available books by increasing the book stock. It has an addBook method that observes any event typed with Book. The annotated parameter is called the event parameter. So once the event is fired from the BookService bean, the CDI container pauses the execution and passes the event to any registered observer. In our case the addBook method in Listing 2-37 will be invoked and the inventory updated, and the container will then continue the code execution where it paused in the BookService bean. This means that events in CDI are not treated asynchronously.

Listing 2-37. The InventoryService Observes the Book Event

```java
public class InventoryService {

  @Inject
  private Logger logger;
  List<Book> inventory = new ArrayList<>();

  public void addBook(@Observes Book book) {
    logger.info("Adding book " + book.getTitle() + " to inventory");
    inventory.add(book);
  }
}
```

Like most of CDI, event production and subscription are typesafe and allow qualifiers to determine which events observers will be observing. An event may be assigned one or more qualifiers (with or without members), which allows observers to distinguish it from other events of the same type. Listing 2-38 revisits the BookService bean by adding an extra event. When a book is created it fires a bookAddedEvent and when a book is removed it fires a bookRemovedEvent, both of type Book. To distinguish both events, each is qualified either by @Added or by @Removed. The code of these qualifiers is identical to the code in Listing 2-7: an annotation with no members and annotated with @Qualifier.

Listing 2-38. The BookService Firing Several Events

```java
public class BookService {

  @Inject
  private NumberGenerator numberGenerator;

  @Inject @Added
  private Event<Book> bookAddedEvent;

  @Inject @Removed
  private Event<Book> bookRemovedEvent;

  public Book createBook(String title, Float price, String description) {
    Book book = new Book(title, price, description);
    book.setIsbn(numberGenerator.generateNumber());
    bookAddedEvent.fire(book);
    return book;
  }

  public void deleteBook(Book book) {
    bookRemovedEvent.fire(book);
  }
}
```

The InventoryService in Listing 2-39 observes both events by declaring two separate methods observing either the book added event (@Observes @Added Book) or the book removed event (@Observes @Removed Book).

Listing 2-39. The InventoryService Observing Several Events

```java
public class InventoryService {

  @Inject
  private Logger logger;
  List<Book> inventory = new ArrayList<>();

  public void addBook(@Observes @Added Book book) {
    logger.warning("Adding book " + book.getTitle() + " to inventory");
    inventory.add(book);
  }

  public void removeBook(@Observes @Removed Book book) {
    logger.warning("Removing book " + book.getTitle() + " to inventory");
    inventory.remove(book);
  }
}
```

Because the event model uses qualifiers, you can benefit from having members on theses qualifiers or aggregating them. The code that follows observes all the added books which have a price greater than 100:

```java
void addBook(@Observes @Added @Price(greaterThan=100) Book book)
```

Putting It All Together

Now let's put some of these concepts together, write some beans, producers, use injection, qualifiers, alternatives, and interceptor binding. This example uses the Weld container to run a Main class in Java SE as well as an integration test to check if our injection is correct.

Figure 2-7 shows a class diagram with all the needed classes to run this sample and describes all the injection points.

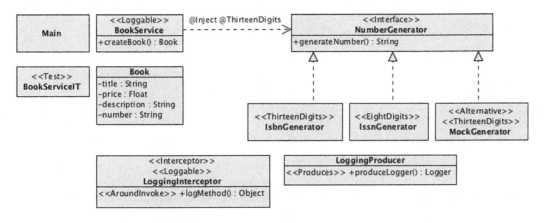

Figure 2-7. *Putting It All Together*

- The BookService bean has a method to create Book POJOs.

- The interface NumberGenerator has two implementations to generate ISBN and ISSN numbers (IsbnGenerator and IssnGenerator) and one alternative implementation for generating mock numbers for integration tests (MockGenerator).

- The NumberGenerator implementations use two qualifiers to avoid ambiguous dependency injection: @ThirteenDigits and @EightDigits.

- The LoggingProducer has a method-producer to allow Logger injection. The LoggingInterceptor coupled with the Loggable interceptor binding allows CDI Beans to log method entries.

- The Main class uses the BookService to create a Book and generate a number with the IsbnGenerator. The BookServiceIT integration test uses the MockGenerator alternative to generate a mock book number.

The classes described in Figure 2-7 follow the standard Maven directory structure.

- src/main/java: The directory for all the beans, qualifiers, interceptors, and Main class,

- src/main/resources: An empty beans.xml file so we can trigger CDI with no alternative nor interceptors,

- src/test/java: The directory for the integration tests BookServiceIT and the alternative MockGenerator,

- src/test/resources: A beans.xml enabling the MockGenerator alternative and the LoggingInterceptor interceptor, and

- pom.xml: The Maven Project Object Model (POM) describing the project and its dependencies.

Writing the Book and BookService Classes

The CD-BookStore application uses the BookService (Listing 2-41) to create books. The Book POJO (Listing 2-40) has a title, a description, and a price. The number of the book is generated by an external service and can be either an ISBN or an ISSN number.

Listing 2-40. The Book POJO

```
public class Book {

  private String title;
  private Float price;
  private String description;
  private String number;

  // Constructors, getters, setters
}
```

The BookService (Listing 2-41) has one method that takes a title, a price, and a description and returns a Book POJO. It uses injection (@Inject) and a qualifier (@ThirteenDigits) to invoke the generateNumber method of the IsbnGenerator to set the book's ISBN number.

Listing 2-41. The BookService Using Dependency Injection and Interception

```
@Loggable
public class BookService {

  @Inject  @ThirteenDigits
  private NumberGenerator numberGenerator;

  public Book createBook(String title, Float price, String description) {
    Book book = new Book(title, price, description);
    book.setNumber(numberGenerator.generateNumber());
    return book;
  }
}
```

The BookService in Listing 2-41 is annotated with the interceptor binding @Loggable (Listing 2-50) which logs the method entry and exit if enabled.

Writing the NumberGenerator Classes

The BookService in Listing 2-41 depends on the interface NumberGenerator (Listing 2-42). This interface has one method that generates and returns a book number. This interface is implemented by the IsbnGenerator, IssnGenerator, and MockGenerator classes.

Listing 2-42. The NumberGenerator Interface

```
public interface NumberGenerator {
    String generateNumber();
}
```

The IsbnGenerator (Listing 2-43) is qualified with @ThirteenDigits. This informs CDI that the number generated is made of 13 digits. Notice that the IsbnGenerator class also uses injection to get a java.util.logging.Logger (produced in Listing 2-48) and the interceptor binding @Loggable to log the method entry and exit

Listing 2-43. The IsbnGenerator Generates a 13-Digit Number

```
@ThirteenDigits
public class IsbnGenerator implements NumberGenerator {

  @Inject
  private Logger logger;

  @Loggable
  public String generateNumber() {
    String isbn = "13-84356-" + Math.abs(new Random().nextInt());
    logger.info("Generated ISBN : " + isbn);
    return isbn;
  }
}
```

The IssnGenerator in Listing 2-44 is the eight-digit implementation of the NumberGenerator.

Listing 2-44. The IssnGenerator Generates an Eight-Digit Number

```
@EightDigits
public class IssnGenerator implements NumberGenerator {

  @Inject
  private Logger logger;

  @Loggable
  public String generateNumber() {
    String issn = "8-" + Math.abs(new Random().nextInt());
    logger.info("Generated ISBN : " + issn);
    return issn;
  }
}
```

The MockGenerator in Listing 2-45 is an alternative (@Alternative) to the IsbnGenerator (because it is also qualified with @ThirteenDigits). The MockGenerator is only used for integration tests because it is only enabled in the beans.xml of the testing environment (see Listing 2-55).

Listing 2-45. Mock Number Generator as an Alternative to 13 Digits

```
@Alternative
@ThirteenDigits
public class MockGenerator implements NumberGenerator {

  @Inject
  private Logger logger;

  @Loggable
  public String generateNumber() {
    String mock = "MOCK-" + Math.abs(new Random().nextInt());
    logger.info("Generated Mock : " + mock);
    return mock;
  }
}
```

Writing the Qualifiers

Because there are several implementations of the NumberGenerator, CDI needs to qualify each bean and each injection point to avoid ambiguous injection. To do this, it uses the two qualifiers ThirteenDigits (Listing 2-46) and EightDigits (Listing 2-47) which are both annotated with javax.inject.Qualifier and have no members (just empty annotations). @ThirteenDigits is the one used in the IsbnGenerator bean (Listing 2-43) as well as the injection point in BookService (Listing 2-41).

Listing 2-46. The 13-Digits Qualifier

```
@Qualifier
@Retention(RUNTIME)
@Target({FIELD, TYPE, METHOD})
public @interface ThirteenDigits { }
```

Listing 2-47. The Eight-Digits Qualifier

```
@Qualifier
@Retention(RUNTIME)
@Target({FIELD, TYPE, METHOD})
public @interface EightDigits { }
```

Writing the Logger

The sample application uses logging in several ways. As you can see in Listings 2-43, 2-44, and 2-45, all the NumberGenerator implementations use injection to get a java.util.logging.Logger and write logs. Because Logger belongs to the JDK, it is not injectable by default (the rt.jar file does not have a beans.xml file) and you then need to produce it. The LoggingProducer class in Listing 2-48 has a producer method (produceLogger) annotated with @Produces that will create and return a Logger parameterized with the injection point class name.

Listing 2-48. Logging Producer

```
public class LoggingProducer {

  @Produces
  public Logger produceLogger(InjectionPoint injectionPoint) {
    return Logger.getLogger(injectionPoint.getMember().getDeclaringClass().getName());
  }
}
```

The LoggingInterceptor in Listing 2-49 uses the produced Logger to log the entering and exiting of methods. Because logging can be treated as a cross-cutting concern it is externalized as an interceptor (@AroundInvoke on logMethod). The LoggingInterceptor defines the @Loggable interceptor binding (Listing 2-50) and can then be used in any bean (e.g., BookService in Listing 2-41).

Listing 2-49. Interceptor Logging Methods on Entry and on Exit

```
@Interceptor
@Loggable
public class LoggingInterceptor {

  @Inject
  private Logger logger;

  @AroundInvoke
  public Object logMethod(InvocationContext ic) throws Exception {
    logger.entering(ic.getTarget().getClass().getName(), ic.getMethod().getName());
    try {
      return ic.proceed();
    } finally {
      logger.exiting(ic.getTarget().getClass().getName(), ic.getMethod().getName());
    }
  }
}
```

Listing 2-50. The Loggable Inteceptor Binding

```
@InterceptorBinding
@Target({METHOD, TYPE})
@Retention(RUNTIME)
public @interface Loggable { }
```

Writing the Main Class

To run the sample application we need a main class that triggers the CDI container and invokes the BookService.createBook method. CDI 1.1 does not have a standard API to bootstrap the container, so the code in Listing 2-51 is Weld specific. It first initializes the WeldContainer and returns a fully constructed and injected instance of the BookService.class. Invoking the createBook method will then use all the container services: the IsbnGenerator and the Logger will be injected into the BookService and a Book with an ISBN number will be created and displayed.

Listing 2-51. Main Class Using the CDI Container to Invoke the BookService

```
public class Main {

  public static void main(String[] args) {

    Weld weld = new Weld();
    WeldContainer container = weld.initialize();

    BookService bookService = container.instance().select(BookService.class).get();

    Book book = bookService.createBook("H2G2", 12.5f, "Geeky scifi Book");

    System.out.println(book);

    weld.shutdown();
  }
}
```

The code in Listing 2-51 is Weld specific and therefore not portable. It will not work in other CDI implementations such as OpenWebBeans (Apache) or CanDI (Caucho). One goal of a future CDI release will be to standardize a bootstrapping API.

Trigger CDI with beans.xml

To trigger CDI and allow this sample to work, we need a beans.xml file in the class path of the application. As you can see in Listing 2-52 the beans.xml file is completely empty, but without it CDI will not be triggered, bean discovery will not happen, and injection will not work.

Listing 2-52. Empty beans.xml File to Trigger CDI

```
<beans xmlns="http://xmlns.jcp.org/xml/ns/javaee"
       xmlns:xsi="http://www.w3.org/2001/XMLSchema-instance"
       xsi:schemaLocation="http://xmlns.jcp.org/xml/ns/javaee ↵
                           http://xmlns.jcp.org/xml/ns/javaee/beans_1_1.xsd"
       version="1.1" bean-discovery-mode="all">
</beans>
```

Compiling and Executing with Maven

All the classes need now to be compiled before running the Main class and the BookServiceIT integration test. The pom.xml in Listing 2-53 declares all the necessary dependencies to compile the code (org.jboss.weld.se:weld-se contains the CDI API and the Weld implementation) and run the test (junit:junit). Setting the version to 1.7 in the maven-compiler-plugin explicitly specifies that you want to use Java SE 7 (<source> 1.7 </source>). Notice that we use the exec-maven-plugin to be able to execute the Main class with Maven.

Listing 2-53. The pom.xml File to Compile, Run, and Test

```xml
<?xml version="1.0" encoding="UTF-8"?>
<project xmlns="http://maven.apache.org/POM/4.0.0" ➥
         xmlns:xsi="http://www.w3.org/2001/XMLSchema-instance" ➥
         xsi:schemaLocation="http://maven.apache.org/POM/4.0.0 ➥
         http://maven.apache.org/xsd/maven-4.0.0.xsd">
  <modelVersion>4.0.0</modelVersion>

  <parent>
    <groupId>org.agoncal.book.javaee7</groupId>
    <artifactId>chapter02</artifactId>
    <version>1.0</version>
  </parent>

  <groupId>org.agoncal.book.javaee7.chapter02</groupId>
  <artifactId>chapter02-putting-together</artifactId>
  <version>1.0</version>

  <dependencies>
    <dependency>
      <groupId>org.jboss.weld.se</groupId>
      <artifactId>weld-se</artifactId>
      <version>2.0.0</version>
    </dependency>
    <dependency>
      <groupId>junit</groupId>
      <artifactId>junit</artifactId>
      <version>4.11</version>
      <scope>test</scope>
    </dependency>
  </dependencies>

  <build>

    <plugins>
      <plugin>
        <groupId>org.apache.maven.plugins</groupId>
        <artifactId>maven-compiler-plugin</artifactId>
        <version>2.5.1</version>
        <configuration>
          <source>1.7</source>
          <target>1.7</target>
        </configuration>
      </plugin>
```

```
    <plugin>
      <groupId>org.codehaus.mojo</groupId>
      <artifactId>exec-maven-plugin</artifactId>
      <version>1.2.1</version>
      <executions>
        <execution>
          <goals>
            <goal>java</goal>
          </goals>
          <configuration>
            <mainClass>org.agoncal.book.javaee7.chapter02.Main</mainClass>
          </configuration>
        </execution>
      </executions>
    </plugin>

    <plugin>
      <groupId>org.apache.maven.plugins</groupId>
      <artifactId>maven-failsafe-plugin</artifactId>
      <version>2.12.4</version>
      <executions>
        <execution>
          <id>integration-test</id>
          <goals>
            <goal>integration-test</goal>
            <goal>verify</goal>
          </goals>
        </execution>
      </executions>
    </plugin>
  </plugins>
 </build>
</project>
```

To compile the classes, open a command line in the root directory containing the pom.xml file and enter the following Maven command:

```
$ mvn compile
```

Running the Main Class

Thanks to the exec-maven-plugin configured in the pom.xml in Listing 2-53, we can now very easily execute the Main class defined in Listing 2-51. Open a command line in the root directory containing the pom.xml file and enter the following Maven command:

```
$ mvn exec:java
```

This will execute the Main class that uses the BookService to create a Book. Thanks to injection the Logger will display the following output:

```
Info: Generated ISBN : 13-84356-1864341788
Book{title='H2G2', price=12.5, description='Geeky scifi Book', isbn='13-84356-1864341788'}
```

Writing the BookServiceIT Class

Listing 2-54 shows the BookServiceIT class testing the BookService bean. It uses the same Weld-specific API to bootstrap CDI as the Main class shown in Listing 2-51. Once the BookService.createBook is invoked, the integration test checks that the generated number starts with "MOCK". That's because the integration test uses the MockGenerator alternative (instead of the IsbnGenerator).

Listing 2-54. The BookServiceIT Integration Test

```java
public class BookServiceIT {

  @Test
  public void shouldCheckNumberIsMOCK () {

    Weld weld = new Weld();
    WeldContainer container = weld.initialize();

    BookService bookService = container.instance().select(BookService.class).get();

    Book book = bookService.createBook("H2G2", 12.5f, "Geeky scifi Book");

    assertTrue(book.getNumber().startsWith("MOCK"));

    weld.shutdown();
  }
}
```

Enabling Alternatives and Interceptors in beans.xml for Integration Testing

The BookServiceIT integration test in Listing 2-54 needs the MockGenerator to be enabled. This is done by having a different beans.xml file for testing (Listing 2-55) and enabling alternatives (with the <alternatives> tag). In a testing environment you might want to increase the logs. You can do so by enabling the LoggingInterceptor in the beans.xml.

Listing 2-55. Enabling Alternatives and Interceptors in beans.xml File

```xml
<beans xmlns="http://xmlns.jcp.org/xml/ns/javaee"
       xmlns:xsi="http://www.w3.org/2001/XMLSchema-instance"
       xsi:schemaLocation="http://xmlns.jcp.org/xml/ns/javaee ↩
       http://xmlns.jcp.org/xml/ns/javaee/beans_1_1.xsd"
       version="1.1" bean-discovery-mode="all">
  <alternatives>
    <class>org.agoncal.book.javaee7.chapter02.MockGenerator</class>
  </alternatives>
```

```
<interceptors>
  <class>org.agoncal.book.javaee7.chapter02.LoggingInterceptor</class>
</interceptors>
</beans>
```

Running the Integration Test

To execute the integration tests with the Maven Failsafe plugin (defined in the pom.xml in Listing 2-53) enter the following Maven command:

```
$ mvn integration-test
```

The BookServiceIT should run one successful integration test. You should also see several logs or methods entering and exiting.

Summary

In this chapter you have learned the difference between a POJO, a Managed Bean, and a CDI Bean and which services apply to which component model. Dependency Injection (JSR 330) and Contexts and Dependency Injection (JSR 299) both bring a standard, portable, and typesafe support for dependency injection to Java EE. CDI adds extra features such as scopes and contexts but also enhanced interceptors, decorators, and events. In fact, CDI natively implements several design patterns like the bridge (with alternatives), the observer/observable (with events), the decorator, the factory (with producers), and of course interception and injection.

Interceptors are the AOP-like mechanism of Java EE, allowing the container to invoke cross-cutting concerns on your application. Interceptors are easy to use, are powerful, and can be chained together or prioritized to apply several concerns to your beans.

CDI, being a vertical specification, is used in other Java EE specifications. In fact, the next chapters of this book will use some of these CDI services in some way.

CHAPTER 3

■ ■ ■

Bean Validation

The previous chapter talked about Context and Dependency Injection which has become a central and common specification across Java EE. It solves recurrent problems (injection, alternatives, stereotypes, producers . . .) that developers have in their day-to-day job. Validating data is also a common task that is spread across several, if not all, layers of today's applications (from presentation to database). Because processing, storing, and retrieving valid data are crucial for an application, each layer defines validation rules its own way. Often the same validation logic is implemented in each layer, proving to be time-consuming, harder to maintain, and error prone. To avoid duplication of these validations in each layer, developers often bundle validation logic directly into the domain model, cluttering domain classes with validation code that is, in fact, metadata about the class itself.

Bean Validation solves the problem of code duplication and cluttering domain classes by allowing developers to write a constraint once, use it, and validate it in any layer. Bean Validation implements a constraint in plain Java code and then defines it by an annotation (metadata). This annotation can then be used on your bean, properties, constructors, method parameters, and return value. In a very elegant yet powerful way, Bean Validation exposes a simple API so that developers can write and reuse business logic constraints.

This chapter demonstrates why validation is crucial to an application and why it needs to be duplicated across layers. You will learn how to write constraints: from aggregating existing ones to developing your own. You will see how to apply these constraints on your application, from the presentation layer right through to the business model layer. You will then learn how to validate these constraints (whether within a Java EE container or not).

Understanding Constraints and Validation

Application developers spend most of their time making sure the data they process and store are valid. They write data constraints, apply these constraints to their logic and model, and make sure the different layers validate these constraints in a consistent manner. This means applying these constraints in their client application (e.g., web browser if developing a web application), presentation layer, business logic layer, business model (a.k.a. domain model), database schema, and, to some degree, the interoperability layer (see Figure 3-1). And, of course, for consistency, they have to keep all these rules synchronized across layers and technologies.

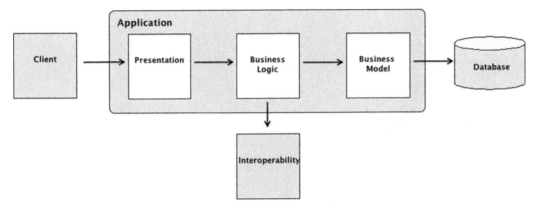

Figure 3-1. *Validation occurs in several layers*

In heterogeneous applications, developers have to deal with several technologies and languages. So even a simple validation rule, such as "this piece of data is mandatory and cannot be null," has to be expressed differently in Java, JavaScript, database schema, or XML schema.

Application

No matter if you develop a one tier or n-tier application; you still need to make sure the data you process are correct: for example, if the delivery address of the purchase order is empty you will never be able to ship the items to your customer. In Java you will commonly write code that checks if an entry is valid (if order.getDeliveryAddress() == null) and throws an exception or asks for feedback to correct it. Application-level validation is able to provide finer-grained control and allows more complex constraints (is this date a public holiday in France? is the customer's annual total bill amount greater than the average?).

Application-level validation may reside in multiple places to ensure that the data are correct.

- *Presentation layer*: In this layer you validate the data because the data could have been sent from several clients (a web browser, a command line tool such as cURL, which allows you to send HTTP commands, or a native application). You also want to give your users a quicker feedback.

- *Business logic layer*: This layer orchestrates the calls to your internal and external services, to your domain model . . . so the processed data have to be valid.

- *Business model layer*: This layer usually maps your domain model to the database, so you need to validate it before storing data.

In a complex application you will repeat the exact same constraint in several layers, resulting in a large amount of code duplication.

Database

At the end of the day, what you really want is to store valid data in your database so the data can be processed later. Constraints are enforced in relational databases because they use schemas. A *data definition language* (DDL, or data description language) uses a syntax for defining and constraining database structures. You can then make sure data in a column cannot be null (NOT NULL), have to be numerical (INTEGER), or have to have a maximum length (VARCHAR(20)). In this last example, trying to insert a 20-character-long string into a column will fail.

However, letting the database handle validation has several drawbacks: it has a performance cost and error messages are out of context. Invalid data must cross all application layers before being sent to the remote database server, which will then handle the validation before sending back an error. At the database level constraints are only aware of the data, not what the user is doing. So error messages are not aware of the context and cannot be very explicit. That's why we tend to validate the data earlier in the application or in the client.

Client

On the client side it is important to validate data so the user is quickly informed that she has entered wrong data. It reduces the number of roundtrips to the server and provides a better user experience through early error feedback. It is crucial when developing mobile applications that may use a low-bandwidth network connection.

In a typical web application, for example, JavaScript is executed in the browser for simple field-level validations and the server-side layer is used for more complex business rule validations. Native applications written in Java (Swing, Android mobile applications) can use the full power of the Java language to write and validate data.

Interoperability

Often enterprise applications need to exchange data with external partners and external systems. These business-to-business applications receive data in any kind of format, process them, store them, and send them back to their partner. Validating custom formats can be a complex and expensive task. Nowadays XML is the preferred language to exchange data between heterogeneous systems. Like databases that use DDL to define their structure, XML can use XSD (XML Schema Definition) to constrain XML documents. XSD expresses a set of rules to which an XML document must conform in order to be considered valid according to that schema. XML parsing and validation is a common task and easy to do with Java frameworks (more on XSD and XML validation in Chapter 16).

Bean Validation Specification Overview

As you can see validation is spread throughout layers (from client to database) and technologies (JavaScript, Java, DDL, XSD). This means that developers have to duplicate code in several layers and in different languages. This common practice is time-consuming, error prone, and harder to maintain with time. In addition, some of these constraints are so frequently used that they could be considered standards (check for a value, its size, its range . . .). It would good to be able to centralize these constraints in one place and share them across layers. That's when Bean Validation comes into play.

Bean Validation is targeted at Java even if some attempts have been made to integrate other languages such as DDL or XSD. It allows you to write a constraint once and use it in any application layer. Bean Validation is layer agnostic, meaning that the same constraint can be used from the presentation to the business model layer. Bean Validation is available for both server-side applications as well as rich Java client graphical interfaces (Swing, Android . . .). It is seen as an extension of the JavaBeans object model and, as such, can be used as a core component in other specifications (as you'll see in most of the chapters of this book).

Bean Validation allows you to apply already defined common constraints in your application, and also write your own and use them to validate beans, attributes, constructors, method returned types, and parameters. The API is very easy to use and flexible as it encourages you to define your constraints using annotations (XML is also possible).

A Brief History of Bean Validation

Developers have been constraining and validating their business model since Java was first developed. Homemade code and frameworks gave birth to practices that were implemented in early open source projects. For example, back in 2000, Struts, the famous Web MVC framework, already implemented a user input validation. But we had to wait some time for validation frameworks that were dedicated solely to Java (and not just web interaction). The best known are probably the Commons Validator from the Apache Commons and Hibernate Validator. Others are iScreen, OVal, and the ubiquitous Spring framework that comes with its own validation package.

Inspired by these validation frameworks, Bean Validation 1.0 (JSR 303) standardized data validation and was included in Java EE 6 in 2009.

What's New in Bean Validation 1.1?

Today Bean Validation 1.1 (JSR 349) is integrated into Java EE 7. This minor release brings many new features and improves existing ones. The major new features are as follows:

- Constraints can now be applied to method parameters and return value. Thus Bean Validation can be used to describe and validate the contract (pre- and postconditions) of a given method.

- Constraints can also be applied on constructors.

- There is a new API to obtain metadata information on constraints and constrained objects.

- Integration with Context and Dependency Injection has been increased (injection in validators is now possible).

Table 3-1 lists the main packages defined in Bean Validation 1.1 today.

Table 3-1. *Main Bean Validation Packages*

Package	Description
`javax.validation`	This package contains the core Bean Validation APIs
`javax.validation.bootstrap`	Classes used to bootstrap Bean Validation and to create a provider agnostic configuration
`javax.validation.constraints`	This package contains all the built-in constraints
`javax.validation.groups`	Default Bean Validation group
`javax.validation.metadata`	Metadata repository for all defined constraints and query API
`javax.validation.spi`	APIs defining the contract between the validation bootstrap mechanism and the provider engine

Reference Implementation

Hibernate Validator is the open source reference implementation of Bean Validation. The project was originally launched in Hibernate Annotations in 2005 by JBoss, became an independent project in 2007, and became the reference implementation in 2009 (with Hibernate Validator 4). Today, Hibernate Validator 5 implements Bean Validation 1.1 and adds specific features, which include a fail fast mode (return from the current validation as soon as the first constraint violation occurs), a programmatic constraint configuration API, and extra built-in constraints.

At the time of writing this book, Hibernate Validator is the only Bean Validation 1.1 compliant implementation. Apache BVal implemented Bean Validation 1.0 and is in the process of getting the 1.1 certification. Oval doesn't implement the full Bean Validation specification but knows how to process Bean Validation's constraints.

Writing Constraints

So far I've talked about constraints applied to several layers of your application, possibly written in different languages and technologies, but I also mentioned the duplication of validation code. So how difficult it is to apply a constraint to your Java classes with Bean Validation? Listing 3-1 shows how simple it is to add constraints to your business model.

Listing 3-1. A Book POJO with Constraint Annotations

```java
public class Book {

    @NotNull
    private String title;
    @NotNull @Min(2)
    private Float price;
    @Size(max = 2000)
    private String description;
    private String isbn;
    private Integer nbOfPage;

    // Constructors, getters, setters
}
```

Listing 3-1 shows the Book class with attributes, constructors, getters, setters, and annotations. Some of these attributes are annotated with built-in constraints such as @NotNull, @Min, and @Size. This indicates to the validation runtime that the title of the book cannot be null and that the description cannot be longer than 2000 characters. As you can see, an attribute can have several constraints attached to it (such as price that cannot be null and whose value cannot be lower than 2).

Anatomy of a Constraint

Constraints are defined by the combination of a constraint annotation and a list of constraint validation implementations. The constraint annotation is applied on types, methods, fields, or other constraint annotations in case of composition. In most of the Java EE specifications, developers use already defined annotations (e.g., @Entity, @Stateless, and @Path). But with CDI (which you saw in the previous chapter) and Bean Validation, developers need to write their own annotations. Because a constraint in Bean Validation is made of

- An annotation defining the constraint.
- A list of classes implementing the algorithm of the constraint on a given type (e.g., String, Integer, MyBean).

While the annotation expresses the constraint on the domain model, the validation implementation decides whether a given value passes the constraint or not.

Constraint Annotation

A constraint on a JavaBean is expressed through one or more annotations. An annotation is considered a constraint if its retention policy contains RUNTIME and if the annotation itself is annotated with javax.validation.Constraint (which refers to its list of constraint validation implementations). Listing 3-2 shows the NotNull constraint annotation. As you can see, @Constraint(validatedBy = {}) points to the implementation class NotNullValidator.

Listing 3-2. The NotNull Constraint Annotation

```
@Target({METHOD, FIELD, ANNOTATION_TYPE, CONSTRUCTOR, PARAMETER})
@Retention(RUNTIME)
@Documented
@Constraint(validatedBy = NotNullValidator.class)
public @interface NotNull {

  String message() default "{javax.validation.constraints.NotNull.message}";

  Class<?>[] groups() default {};

  Class<? extends Payload>[] payload() default {};
}
```

Constraint annotations are just regular annotations, so they must define some meta-annotations.

- `@Target({METHOD, FIELD, ...})`: Specifies the target to which the annotation can be used (more on that later).

- `@Retention(RUNTIME)`: Specifies how the annotation will be operated. It is mandatory to use at least RUNTIME to allow the provider to inspect your objects at runtime.

- `@Constraint(validatedBy = NotNullValidator.class)`: Specifies the class (zero, in case of constraint aggregation, or a list of classes) that encapsulates the validation algorithm.

- `@Documented`: This optional meta-annotation specifies that this annotation will be included in the Javadoc or not.

On top of these common meta-annotations, the Bean Validation specification requires each constraint annotation to define three extra attributes.

- `message`: This attribute (which generally is defaulted to a key) provides the ability for a constraint to return an internationalized error message if the constraint is not valid.

- `groups`: Groups are typically used to control the order in which constraints are evaluated, or to perform partial validation.

- `payload`: This attribute is used to associate metadata information with a constraint.

Once your constraint defines all the mandatory meta-annotations and elements, you can add any specific parameter you need. For example, a constraint that validates the length of a String can use an attribute named `length` to specify the maximum length.

Constraint Implementation

Constraints are defined by the combination of an annotation and zero or more implementation classes. The implementation classes are specified by the `validatedBy` element of `@Constraint` (as seen in Listing 3-2). Listing 3-3 shows the implementation class for the `@NotNull` annotation. As you can see, it implements the `ConstraintValidator` interface and uses generics to pass the name of the annotation (NotNull) and the type this annotation applies to (here it's Object).

Listing 3-3. The NotNull Constraint Implementation

```
public class NotNullValidator implements ConstraintValidator<NotNull, Object> {

  public void initialize(NotNull parameters) {
  }

  public boolean isValid(Object object, ConstraintValidatorContext context) {
    return object != null;
  }
}
```

The ConstraintValidator interface defines two methods that need to be implemented by the concrete classes.

- initialize: This method is called by the Bean Validation provider prior to any use of the constraint. This is where you usually initialize the constraint parameters if any.

- isValid: This is where the validation algorithm is implemented. This method is evaluated by the Bean Validation provider each time a given value is validated. It returns false if the value is not valid, true otherwise. The ConstraintValidatorContext object carries information and operations available in the context the constraint is validated to (as you'll see later).

A constraint implementation performs the validation of a given annotation for a given type. In Listing 3-3 the @NotNull constraint is typed to an Object (which means that this constraint can be used on any datatype). But you could have a constraint annotation that would have different validation algorithms depending on the datatype. For example, you could check the maximum characters for a String, but also the maximum number of digits for a BigDecimal, or the maximum number of elements in a Collection. In the code that follows notice that you have several implementations for the same annotation (@Size) but for different datatypes (String, BigDecimal, and Collection<?>):

```
public class SizeValidatorForString     implements<Size, String>      {...}
public class SizeValidatorForBigDecimal implements<Size, BigDecimal>   {...}
public class SizeValidatorForCollection implements<Size, Collection<?>> {...}
```

Applying a Constraint

Once you have an annotation and an implementation, you can apply the constraint on a given element type (attribute, getter, constructor, parameter, return value, bean, interface, or annotation). This is a design decision that developers have to make and implement using the @Target(ElementType.*) meta-annotation (see Listing 3-2).

- FIELD for constrained attributes,

- METHOD for constrained getters and constrained method return values,

- CONSTRUCTOR for constrained constructor return values,

- PARAMETER for constrained method and constructor parameters,

- TYPE for constrained beans, interfaces and superclasses, and

- ANNOTATION_TYPE for constraints composing other constraints.

As you can see, constraint annotations can be applied to most of the element types defined in Java. Only static fields and static methods cannot be validated by Bean Validation. Listing 3-4 shows an Order class that uses constraint annotations on the class itself, attributes, constructor, and a business method.

Listing 3-4. A POJO Using Constraints on Several Element Types

```
@ChronologicalDates
public class Order {

  @NotNull @Pattern(regexp = "[C,D,M][A-Z][0-9]*")
  private String orderId;
  private Date creationDate;
  @Min(1)
  private Double totalAmount;
  private Date paymentDate;
  private Date deliveryDate;
  private List<OrderLine> orderLines;

  public Order() {
  }

  public Order(@Past Date creationDate) {
    this.creationDate = creationDate;
  }

  public @NotNull Double calculateTotalAmount(@GreaterThanZero Double changeRate) {
    // ...
  }

  // Getters and setters
}
```

In Listing 3-4 @ChronologicalDates is a class-level constraint which is based on several properties of the Order class (in this case it makes sure that the creationDate, paymentDate, and deliveryDate are all chronological). The orderId attribute has two constraints as it cannot be null (@NotNull) and it has to follow a regular expression pattern (@Pattern). The Order constructor makes sure that the creationDate parameter has to be in the past. The calculateTotalAmount method (which calculates the total amount of the purchase order) checks that the changeRate is @GreaterThanZero and that the returned amount is not null.

■ **Note** So far the examples I've shown annotate attributes, but you could annotate getters instead. You just have to define constraints either on the attribute or on the getter but not on both at the same time. It is best to stay consistent and use annotations always on attributes or always on getters.

Built-In Constraints

Bean Validation is a specification that allows you to write your own constraints and validate them. But it also comes with some common built-in constraints. You've already seen a few in the previous examples but Table 3-2 gives you an exhaustive list of all the built-in constraints (i.e., all the constraints that you can use out of the box in your code without developing any annotation or implementation class). All of the built-in constraints are defined in the javax.validation.constraints package.

Table 3-2. *Exhaustive List of Built-In Constraint Annotations*

Constraint	Accepted Types	Description
AssertFalse AssertTrue	Boolean, boolean	The annotated element must be either false or true
DecimalMax DecimalMin	BigDecimal, BigInteger, CharSequence, byte, short, int, long, and respective wrappers	The element must be greater or lower than the specified value
Future Past	Calendar, Date	The annotated element must be a date in the future or in the past
Max Min	BigDecimal, BigInteger, byte, short, int, long, and their wrappers	The element must be greater or lower than the specified value
Null NotNull	Object	The annotated element must be null or not
Pattern	CharSequence	The element must match the specified regular expression
Digits	BigDecimal, BigInteger, CharSequence, byte, short, int, long, and respective wrappers	The annotated element must be a number within accepted range
Size	Object[], CharSequence, Collection<?>, Map<?, ?>	The element size must be between the specified boundaries

Defining Your Own Constraints

As you've just seen, the Bean Validation API provides standard built-in constraints, but they cannot meet all your application's needs. Therefore, the API allows you to develop and use your own business constraints. There are several ways to create your own constraints (from aggregating existing constraints to writing one from scratch) and also different styles (generic or class-level).

Constraint Composition

An easy way to create new constraints is by aggregating already existing ones without having an implementation class. This is pretty easy to do if the existing constraints have a @Target(ElementType.ANNOTATION_TYPE), which means that an annotation can be applied on another annotation. This is called constraints composition and allows you to create higher-level constraints.

Listing 3-5 shows how to create an Email constraint just by using built-in constraints from the Bean Validation API. This Email constraint makes sure that the e-mail address is not null (@NotNull), the minimum size is seven characters (@Size(min = 7)) and that it follows a complex regular expression (@Pattern). A composed constraint also has to define the message, groups, and payload attributes. Note that there is no implementation class (validatedBy = {}).

Listing 3-5. An E-mail Constraint Made of Other Constraints

```
@NotNull
@Size(min = 7)
@Pattern(regexp = "[a-z0-9!#$%&'*+/=?^_`{|}~-]+(?:\\.[a-z0-9!#$%&'*+/=?^_`{|}~-]+)*" ↩
        + "@(?:[a-z0-9](?:[a-z0-9-]*[a-z0-9])?\\.)+[a-z0-9](?:[a-z0-9-]*[a-z0-9])?")
@Constraint(validatedBy = {})
```

```
@Target({METHOD, FIELD, ANNOTATION_TYPE, CONSTRUCTOR, PARAMETER})
@Retention(RetentionPolicy.RUNTIME)
public @interface Email {

  String message() default "Email address doesn't look good";
  Class<?>[] groups() default {};
  Class<? extends Payload>[] payload() default {};
}
```

Each built-in constraint (@NotNull, @Size, and @Pattern) already has its own error message (the message() element). This means that if you have a null e-mail address, the constraint in Listing 3-5 will throw the @NotNull error message upon validation instead of the one defined ("E-mail address doesn't look good"). You may want to have a single error message for the Email constraints rather than having several ones. For that, you could add the @ReportAsSingleViolation annotation (as you'll see later in Listing 3-24). If you do, the evaluation of the composing constraints stops at the first failing constraint and the error report corresponding to the composed constraint (here, the @Email constraint) is generated and returned.

Constraint composition is useful because it avoids code duplication and facilitates the reuse of more primitive constraints. It is encouraged to create simple constraints rather than consolidate them to create more complex validation rules.

■ **Note**   When you create a new constraint, make sure you give it a meaningful name. A carefully chosen annotation name will make constraints more readable in the code.

Generic Constraint

Simple constraint composition is good practice but is usually not enough. Often you need to have complex validation algorithms; check a value in a database, delegate some validation to helper classes, and so on. That's when you need to add an implementation class to your constraint annotation.

Listing 3-6 shows a POJO that represents a network connection to the CD-BookStore items server. This POJO has several attributes of type String, all representing a URL. You want a URL to have a valid format, and even set a specific protocol (e.g., http, ftp . . .), host, and/or port number. The custom @URL constraint makes sure the different String attributes of the ItemServerConnection class respect the URL format. For example, the resourceURL attribute can be any kind of valid URL (e.g., file://www.cdbookstore.com/item/123). On the other hand, you want to constrain the itemURL attribute to have an http protocol and a host name starting with www.cdbookstore.com (e.g., http://www.cdbookstore.com/book/h2g2).

Listing 3-6. A URL Constraint Annotation Used on Several Attributes

```
public class ItemServerConnection {

  @URL
  private String resourceURL;
  @NotNull @URL(protocol = "http", host = "www.cdbookstore.com")
  private String itemURL;
  @URL(protocol = "ftp", port = 21)
  private String ftpServerURL;
  private Date lastConnectionDate;

  // Constructors, getters, setters
}
```

The first thing to do to create such a custom URL constraint is to define an annotation. Listing 3-7 shows the annotation that follows all the Bean Validation prerequisites (@Constraint meta-annotation, message, groups, and payload attributes) but also adds specific attributes: protocol, host, and port. These attributes are mapped to the annotation element names (e.g., @URL(protocol = "http")). A constraint may use any attribute of any datatype. Also note that these attributes have default values such as an empty String for the protocol and host or -1 for the port number.

Listing 3-7. The URL Constraint Annotation

```
@Constraint(validatedBy = {URLValidator.class})
@Target({METHOD, FIELD, ANNOTATION_TYPE, CONSTRUCTOR, PARAMETER})
@Retention(RUNTIME)
public @interface URL {

  String message() default "Malformed URL";
  Class<?>[] groups() default {};
  Class<? extends Payload>[] payload() default {};

  String protocol() default "";
  String host() default "";
  int port() default -1;
}
```

Listing 3-7 could have aggregated already existing constraints such as @NotNull. But the main difference between a constraint composition and a generic constraint is that it has an implementation class declared in the validatedBy attribute (here it refers to URLValidator.class).

Listing 3-8 shows the URLValidator implementation class. As you can see it implements the ConstraintValidator interface and therefore the initialize and isValid methods. The important thing to note is that URLValidator has the three attributes defined in the annotation (protocol, host, and port) and initializes them in the initialize(URL url) method. This method is invoked when the validator is instantiated. It receives as a parameter the constraint annotation (here URL) so it can extract the values to use for validation (e.g., the value for the itemURL protocol attribute in Listing 3-6 is the String "http").

Listing 3-8. The URL Constraint Implementation

```
public class URLValidator implements ConstraintValidator<URL, String> {

  private String protocol;
  private String host;
  private int port;

  public void initialize(URL url) {
    this.protocol = url.protocol();
    this.host = url.host();
    this.port = url.port();
  }

  public boolean isValid(String value, ConstraintValidatorContext context) {
    if (value == null || value.length() == 0) {
      return true;
    }
```

```
java.net.URL url;
try {
  // Transforms it to a java.net.URL to see if it has a valid format
  url = new java.net.URL(value);
} catch (MalformedURLException e) {
return false;
}

// Checks if the protocol attribute has a valid value
if (protocol != null && protocol.length() > 0 && !url.getProtocol().equals(protocol)) {
  return false;
}

if (host != null && host.length() > 0 && !url.getHost().startsWith(host)) {
  return false;
}

if (port != -1 && url.getPort() != port) {
  return false;
}

    return true;
  }
}
```

The isValid method implements the URL validation algorithm shown in Listing 3-8. The value parameter contains the value of the object to validate (e.g., file://www.cdbookstore.com/item/123). The context parameter encapsulates information about the context in which the validation is done (more on that later). The return value is a boolean indicating whether the validation was successful or not.

The main task of the validation algorithm in Listing 3-8 is to cast the passed value to a java.net.URL and see if the URL is malformed or not. Then, the method checks that the protocol, host, and port attributes are valid too. If one of these attributes is not valid then the method returns false. As you'll see later in the "Validating Constraints" section of this chapter, the Bean Validation provider will use this Boolean to create a list of ConstraintViolation.

Note that the isValid method considers null as a valid value (if (value == null ... return true)). The Bean Validation specification recommends as good practice to consider null as valid. This way you do not duplicate the code of the @NotNull constraint. You would have to use both @URL and @NotNull constraints to express that you want a value to represent a valid URL that is not null (such as the itemURL attribute in Listing 3-6).

The class signature defines the datatype to which the constraint is associated. In Listing 3-8 the URLValidator is implemented for a type String (ConstraintValidator<URL, String>). That means that if you apply the @URL constraint to a different type (e.g., to the lastConnectionDate attribute) you will get a javax.validation.UnexpectedTypeException at validation because no validator could be found for type java.util.Date. If you need a constraint to be applied to several datatypes, you either need to use superclasses when it is possible (e.g., we could have defined the URLValidator for a CharSequence instead of a String by writing ConstraintValidator<URL, CharSequence>) or need to have several implementation classes (one for String, CharBuffer, StringBuffer, StringBuilder . . .) if the validation algorithm is different.

■ **Note**   A constraint implementation is considered to be a Managed Bean. This means that you can use all the Managed Bean services such as injecting any helper class, an EJB, or even injecting an `EntityManager` (more on that in the following chapters). You can also intercept or decorate both `initialize` and `isValid` methods, or even use life-cycle management (`@PostConstruct` and `@PreDestroy`).

Multiple Constraints for the Same Target

Sometimes it is useful to apply the same constraint more than once on the same target with different properties or groups (as you'll see later). A common example is the `@Pattern` constraint, which validates that its target matches a specified regular expression. Listing 3-9 shows how to apply two regular expressions on the same attribute. Multiple constraints use the AND operator; this means that the `orderId` attribute needs to follow the two regular expressions to be valid.

Listing 3-9. A POJO Applying Multiple Pattern Constraints on the Same Attribute

```
public class Order {

    @Pattern.List({
            @Pattern(regexp = "[C,D,M][A-Z][0-9]*"),
            @Pattern(regexp = ".[A-Z].*?")
    })
    private String orderId;
    private Date creationDate;
    private Double totalAmount;
    private Date paymentDate;
    private Date deliveryDate;
    private List<OrderLine> orderLines;

    // Constructors, getters, setters
}
```

To be able to have the same constraint multiple times on the same target, the constraint annotation needs to define an array of itself. Bean Validation treats constraint arrays in a special way: each element of the array is processed as a regular constraint. Listing 3-10 shows the `@Pattern` constraint annotation that defines an inner interface (arbitrarily called `List`) with an element `Pattern[]`. The inner interface must have the retention RUNTIME and must use the same set of targets as the initial constraint (here METHOD, FIELD, ANNOTATION_TYPE, CONSTRUCTOR, PARAMETER).

Listing 3-10. The Pattern Constraint Defining a List of Patterns

```
@Target({METHOD, FIELD, ANNOTATION_TYPE, CONSTRUCTOR, PARAMETER})
@Retention(RUNTIME)
@Constraint(validatedBy = PatternValidator.class)
public @interface Pattern {

    String regexp();
    String message() default "{javax.validation.constraints.Pattern.message}";
    Class<?>[] groups() default {};
    Class<? extends Payload>[] payload() default {};
```

```
// Defines several @Pattern annotations on the same element
@Target({METHOD, FIELD, ANNOTATION_TYPE, CONSTRUCTOR, PARAMETER})
@Retention(RUNTIME)
@interface List {
    Pattern[] value();
  }
}
```

■ **Note** When you develop your own constraint annotation, you should add its corresponding multivalued annotation. The Bean Validation specification does not mandate it but strongly recommends the definition of an inner interface named List.

Class-Level Constraint

So far you've seen different ways of developing a constraint that is applied to an attribute (or a getter). But you can also create a constraint for an entire class. The idea is to express a constraint which is based on several properties of a given class.

Listing 3-11 shows a purchase order class. This purchase order follows a certain business life cycle: it is created into the system, paid by the customer, and then delivered to the customer. This class keeps track of all these events by having a corresponding creationDate, paymentDate, and deliveryDate. The class-level annotation @ChronologicalDates is there to check that these three dates are in chronological order.

Listing 3-11. A Class-Level Constraint Checking Chronological Dates

```
@ChronologicalDates
public class Order {

  private String orderId;
  private Double totalAmount;
  private Date creationDate;
  private Date paymentDate;
  private Date deliveryDate;
  private List<OrderLine> orderLines;
  // Constructors, getters, setters
}
```

Listing 3-12 shows the implementation of the @ChronologicalDates constraint. Like the constraints you've seen so far, it implements the ConstraintValidator interface whose generic type is Order. The isValid method checks that the three dates are in chronological order and returns true if they are.

Listing 3-12. The ChronologicalDates Class-Level Constraint Implementation

```
public class ChronologicalDatesValidator implements ConstraintValidator<ChronologicalDates, Order> {

  @Override
  public void initialize(ChronologicalDates constraintAnnotation) {
  }
```

```
@Override
public boolean isValid(Order order, ConstraintValidatorContext context) {
  return order.getCreationDate().getTime() < order.getPaymentDate().getTime() && ↪
         order.getPaymentDate().getTime()  < order.getDeliveryDate().getTime();
 }
}
```

Method-Level Constraint

Method-level constraints were introduced in Bean Validation 1.1. These are constraints declared on methods as well as constructors (getters are not considered constrained methods). These methods can be added to the method parameters (called parameter constraints) or to the method itself (called return value constraints). In this way Bean Validation can be used to describe and validate the contract applied to a given method or constructor. This enables the well-known *Programming by Contract* programming style.

- Preconditions must be met by the caller before a method or constructor is invoked.

- Postconditions are guaranteed to the caller after a method or constructor invocation returns.

Listing 3-13 shows how you can use method-level constraints in several ways. The CardValidator service validates a credit card following a specific validation algorithm. This algorithm is passed to the constructor and cannot be null. For that, the constructor uses the @NotNull constraint on the ValidationAlgorithm parameter. Then, the two validate methods return a Boolean (is the credit card valid or not?) with an @AssertTrue constraint on the returned type and a @NotNull and @Future constraint on the method parameters.

Listing 3-13. A Service with Constructor and Method-Level Constraints

```
public class CardValidator {

  private ValidationAlgorithm validationAlgorithm;

  public CardValidator(@NotNull ValidationAlgorithm validationAlgorithm) {
    this.validationAlgorithm = validationAlgorithm;
  }

  @AssertTrue
  public Boolean validate(@NotNull CreditCard creditCard) {

    return validationAlgorithm.validate(creditCard.getNumber(), creditCard.getCtrlNumber());
  }

  @AssertTrue
  public Boolean validate(@NotNull String number, @Future Date expiryDate, ↪
                          Integer controlNumber, String type) {

    return validationAlgorithm.validate(number, controlNumber);
  }
}
```

Constraint Inheritance

Often a business model has inheritance. And with Bean Validation you end up with constraints on your business model classes, superclasses, or interfaces. Constraint inheritance on properties works like normal inheritance in Java: it is cumulative. This means that when a bean inherits from another, its constraints are also inherited and will be validated.

Listing 3-15 shows the CD class that extends from Item (Listing 3-14). Both have attributes and constraints on these attributes. If an instance of CD is validated, not only its constraints are validated but also the constraint from the parent class.

Listing 3-14. An Item Superclass Using Constraints

```
public class Item {

  @NotNull
  protected Long id;
  @NotNull @Size(min = 4, max = 50)
  protected String title;
  protected Float price;
  protected String description;

  @NotNull
  public Float calculateVAT() {
    return price * 0.196f;
  }

  @NotNull
  public Float calculatePrice(@DecimalMin("1.2") Float rate) {
    return price * rate;
  }
}
```

Listing 3-15. A CD Class Extending Item

```
public class CD extends Item {

  @Pattern(regexp = "[A-Z][a-z]{1,}")
  private String musicCompany;
  @Max(value = 5)
  private Integer numberOfCDs;
  private Float totalDuration;
  @MusicGenre
  private String genre;

  // ConstraintDeclarationException : not allowed when method overriding
  public Float calculatePrice(@DecimalMin("1.4") Float rate) {
    return price * rate;
  }
}
```

The same inheritance mechanism applies to method-level constraints. The calculateVAT method declared in Item is inherited by CD. But in case of method overriding, special care must be taken when defining parameter constraints. Only the root method of an overridden method may be annotated with parameter constraints. The reason for this restriction is that the preconditions must not be strengthened in subtypes. Conversely, return value constraints may be added in subtypes without any restrictions (you can strengthen the postconditions).

So when you validate the calculatePrice of the CD class (see Listing 3-15), the Bean Validation runtime will throw a javax.validation.ConstraintDeclarationException saying that only the root method of an overridden method may use parameter constraints.

Messages

As seen earlier (Listing 3-2), a constraint annotation definition has several mandatory attributes: message, groups, and payload. Every constraint must define a default message of type String which is used to create the error message if there is a constraint violation when validating a bean.

The value of the default message can be hard coded, but it is recommended to use a resource bundle key to allow internationalization. By convention the resource bundle key should be the fully qualified class name of the constraint annotation concatenated to .message.

```
// Hard coded error message
String message() default "Email address doesn't look good";
// Resource bundle key
String message() default "{org.agoncal.book.javaee7.Email.message}";
```

By default the resource bundle file is named ValidationMessages.properties and must be in the class path of the application. The file follows the key/value pair format, so this is what you need to write to externalize and internationalize an error message.

```
org.agoncal.book.javaee7.Email.message=Email address doesn't look good
```

This default message defined in the constraint annotation can then be overridden on a per-usage basis at declaration time.

```
@Email(message = "Recovery email is not a valid email address")
private String recoveryEmail;
```

Thanks to message interpolation (javax.validation.MessageInterpolator interface), the error message can contain placeholders. The goal of interpolation is to determine the error message by resolving the message strings and the parameters between braces. The error message that follows is interpolated so the {min} and {max} placeholders are replaced by the value of the corresponding elements:

```
javax.validation.constraints.Size.message = size must be between {min} and {max}
```

Listing 3-16 shows a Customer class that uses error messages in several ways. The userId attribute is annotated with @Email, meaning that if the value is not a valid e-mail address, the default error message will be used. On the other hand the recoveryEmail overrides the default error message. Note that for the firstName and age attributes, the default error messages are overridden with messages using placeholders.

Listing 3-16. A Customer Class Declaring Several Error Messages

```
public class Customer {

  @Email
  private String userId;
  @NotNull @Size(min = 4, max = 50, message = "Firstname should be between {min} and {max}")
  private String firstName;
  private String lastName;
  @Email(message = "Recovery email is not a valid email address")
  private String recoveryEmail;
  private String phoneNumber;
  @Min(value = 18, message = "Customer is too young. Should be older that {value}")
  private Integer age;

  // Constructors, getters, setters
}
```

ConstraintValidator Context

So far you've seen that constraint implementation classes need to implement `ConstraintValidator` and, thus, to define their own `isValid` method. The `isValid` method signature takes the datatype to which the constraint is applied but also a `ConstraintValidationContext`. This interface encapsulates data related to the context in which the validation is executed by the Bean Validation provider. Table 3-3 lists the methods defined in the `javax.validation.ConstraintValidatorContext` interface.

Table 3-3. *Methods of the ConstraintValidationContext Interface*

Method	Description
disableDefaultConstraintViolation	Disable the default `ConstraintViolation` object generation
getDefaultConstraintMessageTemplate	Returns the current uninterpolated default message
buildConstraintViolationWithTemplate	Returns a `ConstraintViolationBuilder` to allow the building of a custom violation report

The `ConstraintValidatorContext` interface allows redefinition of the default constraint message. The `buildConstraintViolationWithTemplate` method returns a `ConstraintViolationBuilder`, based on the fluent API pattern, to allow building custom violation reports. The code that follows adds a new constraint violation to the report:

```
context.buildConstraintViolationWithTemplate("Invalid protocol")
      .addConstraintViolation();
```

This technique allows you to generate and create one or more custom report messages. If we take the example of the @URL constraint (Listing 3-7) we notice that there is only one error message for the entire constraint ("Malformed URL"). But this constraint has several attributes (`protocol`, `host`, and `port`) and we might want to have specific error messages for each attribute such as "Invalid protocol" or "Invalid host."

■ **Note** The ConstraintViolation interface describes a constraint violation. It exposes the constraint violation context as well as the message describing the violation. More on that later in the "Validating Constraints" section.

Listing 3-17 revisits the URL constraint class implementation and uses the ConstraintValidatorContext to change the error message. The code completely disables the default error message generation (disableDefaultConstraintViolation) and solely defines custom error messages for each attribute.

Listing 3-17. *The URL Constraint Using the ConstraintValidatorContext to Customize Error Messages*

```
public class URLValidator implements ConstraintValidator<URL, String> {

  private String protocol;
  private String host;
  private int port;

  public void initialize(URL url) {
    this.protocol = url.protocol();
    this.host = url.host();
    this.port = url.port();
  }

  public boolean isValid(String value, ConstraintValidatorContext context) {
    if (value == null || value.length() == 0) {
      return true;
    }

    java.net.URL url;
    try {
      url = new java.net.URL(value);
    } catch (MalformedURLException e) {
      return false;
    }

    if (protocol != null && protocol.length() > 0 && !url.getProtocol().equals(protocol)) {
      context.disableDefaultConstraintViolation();
      context.buildConstraintViolationWithTemplate("Invalid protocol").addConstraintViolation();
      return false;
    }

    if (host != null && host.length() > 0 && !url.getHost().startsWith(host)) {
      context.disableDefaultConstraintViolation();
      context.buildConstraintViolationWithTemplate("Invalid host").addConstraintViolation();
      return false;
    }

    if (port != -1 && url.getPort() != port) {
      context.disableDefaultConstraintViolation();
```

```
    context.buildConstraintViolationWithTemplate("Invalid port").addConstraintViolation();
      return false;
    }

    return true;
  }
}
```

Groups

When a bean is validated it means that all the constraints are validated once at the same time. But what if you need to partially validate your bean (a subset of constraints) or to control the order in which constraints are evaluated? That's when groups come into play. Groups allow you to restrict the set of constraints applied during validation.

In terms of code a group is just an empty interface.

```
public interface Payment {}
```

In terms of business logic a group has a meaning. For example, in a workflow "Payment" would suggest that attributes belonging to this group will be validated during the payment phase or the purchase order. To apply this group to a set of constraints you just need to use the groups attribute and pass it the interface.

```
@Past(groups = Payment.class)
private Date paymentDate;
```

You can have as many groups as your business logic needs and you can apply multiple groups to a constraint as the groups attribute allows an array of groups.

```
@Past(groups = {Payment.class, Delivery.class})
private Date deliveryDate;
```

Every constraint annotation must define a groups element. If no group is specified then the default javax.validation.groups.Default group is considered declared. So the following constraints are equivalent and are both part of the Default group:

```
@NotNull
private Long id;
@Past(groups = Default.class)
private Date creationDate;
```

Let's take the previous-use case seen with the @ChronologicalDates and apply groups to it. The Order class in Listing 3-18 has several dates to keep track of the purchase order workflow: creationDate, paymentDate, and deliveryDate. When you first create a purchase order the creationDate attribute is set but not the paymentDate and deliveryDate. You want to validate these two last dates later in a different workflow phase, but not at the same time as the creationDate. By applying groups you can validate the creationDate during the default group (since no group is specified for this annotation its default group is javax.validation.groups.Default), the paymentDate during the Payment phase, and deliveryDate and @ChronologicalDates during the Delivery phase.

Listing 3-18. A Class Using Several Groups

```java
@ChronologicalDates(groups = Delivery.class)
public class Order {

  @NotNull
  private Long id;
  @NotNull @Past
  private Date creationDate;
  private Double totalAmount;

  @NotNull(groups = Payment.class)  @Past(groups = Payment.class)
  private Date paymentDate;

  @NotNull(groups = Delivery.class) @Past(groups = Delivery.class)
  private Date deliveryDate;

  private List<OrderLine> orderLines;

  // Constructors, getters, setters
}
```

As you'll soon see, during the validation you just need to explicitly mention which group(s) you want to validate and the Bean Validation provider will do partial validation.

Deployment Descriptors

Like most Java EE 7 technologies, Bean Validation allows you to define metadata using annotations (what I've been doing so far in all the examples) as well as XML. Bean Validation can have several optional files under the META-INF directory. The first one, validation.xml, can be used by applications to refine some of the Bean Validation behavior (such as the default Bean Validation provider, the message interpolator, or specific properties). Then, you can have several files describing constraints declarations on your beans. Like all the deployment descriptors in Java EE 7, the XML overrides the annotations.

Listing 3-19 shows the validation.xml deployment descriptor that has a validation-config XML root element but, more important, defines one external constraint mapping file: constraints.xml (Listing 3-20).

Listing 3-19. A validation.xml File Declaring a Constraint Mapping File

```xml
<?xml version="1.0" encoding="UTF-8"?>
<validation-config
        xmlns="http://jboss.org/xml/ns/javax/validation/configuration"
        xmlns:xsi="http://www.w3.org/2001/XMLSchema-instance"
        xsi:schemaLocation="http://jboss.org/xml/ns/javax/validation/configuration ➥
                        validation-configuration-1.1.xsd"
        version="1.1">

  <constraint-mapping>META-INF/constraints.xml</constraint-mapping>

</validation-config>
```

Listing 3-20. A File Defining Constraints on a Bean

```xml
<?xml version="1.0" encoding="UTF-8"?>
<constraint-mappings
        xmlns="http://jboss.org/xml/ns/javax/validation/mapping"
        xmlns:xsi="http://www.w3.org/2001/XMLSchema-instance"
        xsi:schemaLocation="http://jboss.org/xml/ns/javax/validation/mapping ↪
                        validation-mapping-1.1.xsd"
        version="1.1">

  <bean class="org.agoncal.book.javaee7.chapter03.Book" ignore-annotations="false">
    <field name="title">
      <constraint annotation="javax.validation.constraints.NotNull">
        <message>Title should not be null</message>
      </constraint>
    </field>
    <field name="price">
      <constraint annotation="javax.validation.constraints.NotNull"/>
      <constraint annotation="javax.validation.constraints.Min">
        <element name="value">2</element>
      </constraint>
    </field>
    <field name="description">
      <constraint annotation="javax.validation.constraints.Size">
        <element name="max">2000</element>
      </constraint>
    </field>
  </bean>
</constraint-mappings>
```

The `constraints.xml` file in Listing 3-20 defines the XML metadata for declaring constraints on the Book class. It first applies a `@NotNull` constraint on the attribute `title` and redefines the default error message (`Title should not be null`). For the `price` attribute two distinct constraints are applied and the minimum value is set to 2. This resembles the code in Listing 3-1 where metadata was defined using annotations.

Validating Constraints

So far we've been dealing with constraints, defining them, aggregating them, implementing our own, customizing error messages, affecting groups—but without a validation runtime the constraints cannot be validated. Like most Java EE technologies the code needs to run inside a container or be managed by a provider.

Constraints can be applied to beans, attributes, getters, constructors, method parameters, and return values. So validation can occur on all these element types. You can validate beans, properties, values, methods, and groups but also a graph of objects with their own constraints. For all these constraints to be validated at runtime you need a validation API.

Validation APIs

The validation runtime uses a small set of APIs to be able to validate constraints. The main API is the `javax.validation.Validator` interface. It holds the contracts to validate objects and objects graphs independently of the layer in which it is implemented (presentation layer, business layer, or business model). Upon validation failure a set of `javax.validation.ConstraintViolation` interfaces is returned. This interface exposes the constraint violation context as well as the message describing the violation.

Validator

The main entry point for validation is the `Validator` interface. Its API is able to validate instances of beans using only a few methods described in Table 3-4. All these validation methods have the following routine for each constraint declaration:

- Determine the appropriate `ConstraintValidator` implementation to use for the constraint declaration (e.g., determine the `ConstraintValidator` for the `@Size` constraint on a `String`).

- Execute the `isValid` method.

- If `isValid` returns `true`, continue to the next constraint.

- If `isValid` returns `false`, the Bean Validation provider adds a `ConstraintViolation` to the list of constraint violations.

Table 3-4. *Methods of the Validator Interface*

Method	Description
`<T> Set<ConstraintViolation<T>> validate` `(T object, Class<?>... groups)`	Validates all constraints on an object
`<T> Set<ConstraintViolation<T>> validateProperty` `(T object, String propName, Class<?>... groups)`	Validates all constraints placed on a property
`<T> Set<ConstraintViolation<T>> validateValue` `(Class<T> beanType, String propName, Object value,` `Class<?>... groups)`	Validates all constraints placed on a property for a given value
`BeanDescriptor getConstraintsForClass(Class<?> clazz)`	Returns the descriptor object describing bean constraints
`ExecutableValidator forExecutables()`	Returns a delegate for validating parameters and return values on methods & constructors

If some unrecoverable failure happens during this validation routine, it raises a `ValidationException`. This exception can be specialized in some situations (invalid group definition, invalid constraint definition, invalid constraint declaration).

The methods `validate`, `validateProperty`, and `validateValue` are used, respectively, for validating an entire bean, a property, or a property for a given value. All methods take a varargs parameter that can be used to specify the groups to validate. The `forExecutables` provides access to a `ExecutableValidator` for validating methods and constructor parameters and return value. Table 3-5 describes the `ExecutableValidator` API.

Table 3-5. *Methods of the ExecutableValidator Interface*

Method	Description
`<T> Set<ConstraintViolation<T>> validateParameters` `(T object, Method` `method, Object[] params, Class<?>... groups)`	Validates all constraints placed on the parameters of a method
`<T> Set<ConstraintViolation<T>> validateReturnValue` `(T object, Method` `method, Object returnValue, Class<?>... groups)`	Validates all return value constraints of a method
`<T> Set<ConstraintViolation<T>> validateConstructorParameters` `(Constructor<T> constructor, Object[] params, Class<?>... groups)`	Validates all constraints placed on the parameters of a constructor
`<T> Set<ConstraintViolation<T>> validateConstructorReturnValue` `(Constructor<T> constructor, T createdObject, Class<?>... groups)`	Validates all return value constraints of a constructor

ConstraintViolation

All the validating methods listed in Tables 3-4 and 3-5 return a set of `ConstraintViolation` which can be iterated in order to see which validation errors occurred. If the set is empty then the validation succeeds. Otherwise a `ConstraintViolation` instance is added to the set for each violated constraint. The `ConstraintViolation` describes a single constraint failure and its API gives a lot of useful information about the cause of the failure. Table 3-6 gives an overview of this API.

Table 3-6. *Methods of the ConstraintViolation Interface*

Method	Description
`String getMessage()`	Returns the interpolated error message for this constraint violation
`String getMessageTemplate()`	Return the non-interpolated error message
`T getRootBean()`	Returns the root bean being validated
`Class<T> getRootBeanClass()`	Returns the class of the root bean being validated
`Object getLeafBean()`	Returns the leaf bean the constraint is applied on
`Path getPropertyPath()`	Returns the property path to the value from the root bean
`Object getInvalidValue()`	Returns the value failing to pass the constraint
`ConstraintDescriptor<?> getConstraintDescriptor()`	Returns the constraint metadata

Obtaining a Validator

The first step toward validating a bean is to get hold of a `Validator` instance. Like most of the Java EE specifications you can either get a `Validator` programmatically (if your code is executed outside a container) or get it injected (if your code is executed in an EJB or web container).

If you do it programmatically you need to start with the `Validation` class which bootstraps the Bean Validation provider. Its `buildDefaultValidatorFactory` method builds and returns a `ValidatorFactory` which in turn is used to build a `Validator`. The code looks like the following:

```
ValidatorFactory factory = Validation.buildDefaultValidatorFactory();
Validator validator = factory.getValidator();
```

You then need to manage the life cycle of the `ValidatorFactory` and programmatically close it.

```
factory.close();
```

If your application runs in a Java EE container, then the container must make the following instances available under JNDI:

- `ValidatorFactory` under `java:comp/ValidatorFactory`
- `Validator` under `java:comp/Validator`

Then you can look up these JNDI names and get an instance of `Validator`. But instead of looking the instances up via JNDI, you can request them to be injected via the `@Resource` annotation.

```
@Resource ValidatorFactory validatorFactory;
@Resource Validator validator;
```

If your container is using CDI (which by default it is in Java EE 7), the container must allow the injection via @Inject.

```
@Inject ValidatorFactory;
@Inject Validator;
```

Either way (with @Resource or @Inject) the container looks after the life cycle of the factory. So you do not need to manually create or close the ValidatorFactory.

Validating Beans

Once the Validator is obtained programmatically or by injection we can use its methods to validate either an entire bean or just a single property. Listing 3-21 shows a CD class with constraints set on properties and on method parameters and return value.

Listing 3-21. A Bean with Property and Method Constraints

```
public class CD {

  @NotNull @Size(min = 4, max = 50)
  private String title;
  @NotNull
  private Float price;
  @NotNull(groups = PrintingCatalog.class)
  @Size(min = 100, max = 5000, groups = PrintingCatalog.class)
  private String description;
  @Pattern(regexp = "[A-Z][a-z]{1,}")
  private String musicCompany;
  @Max(value = 5)
  private Integer numberOfCDs;
  private Float totalDuration;

  @NotNull @DecimalMin("5.8")
  public Float calculatePrice(@DecimalMin("1.4") Float rate) {
    return price * rate;
  }

  @DecimalMin("9.99")
  public Float calculateVAT() {
    return price * 0.196f;
  }
}
```

To validate the entire bean properties we just need to create an instance of CD and call the Validator.validate() method. If the instance is valid, then an empty set of ConstraintViolation is returned. The code that follows shows a valid CD instance (with a title and a price) that is validated. The code then checks that the set of constraints violations is empty.

```
CD cd = new CD("Kind of Blue", 12.5f);
Set<ConstraintViolation<CD>> violations = validator.validate(cd);
assertEquals(0, violations.size());
```

On the other hand the following code will return two ConstraintViolation objects—one for the title and another one for the price (both violating @NotNull):

```
CD cd = new CD();
Set<ConstraintViolation<CD>> violations = validator.validate(cd);
assertEquals(2, violations.size());
```

Validating Properties

The previous examples validate the entire bean properties. But with the help of the Validator.validateProperty() method, we can validate a single named property of a given object. This method is useful for partial object validation.

The code below creates a CD object with null title and price, meaning that the bean is not valid. But because we only validate the numberOfCDs property, the validation succeeds and the set of constraint violations is empty.

```
CD cd = new CD();
cd.setNumberOfCDs(2);
Set<ConstraintViolation<CD>> violations = validator.validateProperty(cd, "numberOfCDs");
assertEquals(0, violations.size());
```

On the contrary, the following code raises one constraint violation because the maximum number of CDs should be 5 and not 7. Notice that we use the ConstraintViolation API to check the number of violations, the interpolated message returned by the violation, the invalid value, and the message template.

```
CD cd = new CD();
cd.setNumberOfCDs(7);
Set<ConstraintViolation<CD>> violations = validator.validateProperty(cd, "numberOfCDs");
assertEquals(1, violations.size());
assertEquals("must be less than or equal to 5", violations.iterator().next().getMessage());
assertEquals(7, violations.iterator().next().getInvalidValue());
assertEquals("{javax.validation.constraints.Max.message}",
                violations.iterator().next().getMessageTemplate());
```

Validating Values

Using the Validator.validateValue() method, you can check whether a single property of a given class can be validated successfully, if the property had the specified value. This method is useful for ahead-of-time validation because you don't even have to create an instance of the bean or populate or update its values.

The code that follows doesn't create a CD object but just refers to the numberOfCDs attribute of the CD class. It passes a value and checks that the property is valid (number of CDs lower or equal than 5) or not:

```
Set<ConstraintViolation<CD>> constr = validator.validateValue(CD.class, "numberOfCDs", 2);
assertEquals(0, constr.size());
Set<ConstraintViolation<CD>> constr = validator.validateValue(CD.class, "numberOfCDs", 7);
assertEquals(1, constr.size());
```

Validating Methods

The methods for the validation of parameters and return values of methods and constructors can be found on the interface javax.validation.ExecutableValidator. The Validator.forExecutables() returns this ExecutableValidator on which you can invoke validateParameters, validateReturnValue, validateConstructorParameters, or validateConstructorReturnValue.

The code that follows calls the calculatePrice method passing the value 1.2. This will cause a constraint violation on the parameter as it violates @DecimalMin("1.4"). To do that, the code first needs to create a java.lang.reflect.Method object targeting the calculatePrice method with a parameter of type Float. Then it gets the ExecutableValidator object and invokes validateParameters passing the bean, the method to invoke, and the parameter value (here 1.2). It then checks that there are no constraints violated.

```
CD cd = new CD("Kind of Blue", 12.5f);
Method method = CD.class.getMethod("calculatePrice", Float.class);
ExecutableValidator methodValidator = validator. forExecutables();
Set<ConstraintViolation<CD>> violations = methodValidator.validateParameters(cd, method,
                                                       new Object[]{new Float(1.2)});
assertEquals(1, violations.size());
```

Validating Groups

A group defines a subset of constraints. Instead of validating all constraints for a given bean, only a subset is validated. Each constraint declaration defines the list of groups it belongs to. If no group is explicitly declared, a constraint belongs to the Default group. From a validation point of view all the validation methods have a varargs parameter which can be used to specify which validation groups shall be considered when performing the validation. If the parameter is not specified, the default validation group (javax.validation.groups.Default) will be used. If a group other than Default is specified, then Default is not validated.

In Listing 3-21 all the constraints belong to the Default group except for the description attribute. A description is needed (@NotNull @Size(min = 100, max = 5000)) only if it has to be printed on a catalog (the PrintingCatalog group). So if we create a CD with no title, no price, and a description and validate the Default group, then only the two @NotNull constraints on title and price will be violated.

```
CD cd = new CD();
cd.setDescription("Best Jazz CD ever");
Set<ConstraintViolation<CD>> violations = validator.validate(cd, Default.class);
assertEquals(2, violations.size());
```

Note that the previous code explicitly mentions the Default group during validation, but it can be omitted. So the following code is identical:

```
Set<ConstraintViolation<CD>> violations = validator.validate(cd);
```

On the other hand, if we decided to validate the CD for only the PrintingCatalog group, then the code that follows will only violate the constraint on description as its value is too short:

```
CD cd = new CD();
cd.setDescription("Too short");
Set<ConstraintViolation<CD>> violations = validator.validate(cd, PrintingCatalog.class);
assertEquals(1, violations.size());
```

If you want to validate your bean for both, the Default and the PrintingCatalog, you will end up with three constraints violated (@NotNull constraints on title and price and description too short):

```
CD cd = new CD();
cd.setDescription("Too short");
Set<ConstraintViolation<CD>> violations = validator.validate(cd, Default.class, PrintingCatalog.class);
assertEquals(3, violations.size());
```

Putting It All Together

Now let's put all these concepts together and write Java Beans where we can apply built-in constraint as well as developing our own. This example uses CDI and Bean Validation constraints running in Java SE (no need to deploy anything in GlassFish for now) and two integration tests to check if our constraints are correct.

Figure 3-2 shows a Customer class that has a delivery address (Address). Both beans have built-in constraints (@NotNull, @Size, and @Past) on their attributes. But they also use two constraints that we need to develop.

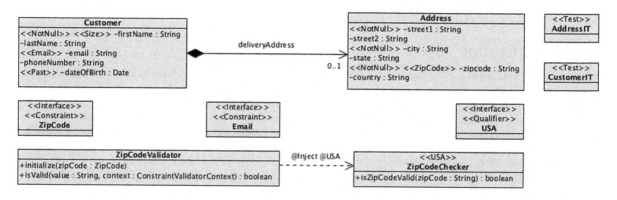

Figure 3-2. *Putting it all together*

- @Email, an aggregated constraint that checks that the e-mail address is valid.

- @ZipCode that checks if the zip code is valid for the United States. This constraint is made of an annotation as well as an implementation class (ZipCodeValidator). Note that ZipCodeValidator injects the helper class ZipCodeChecker with @Inject (and the CDI qualifier @USA).

The classes described in Figure 3-2 follow the Maven directory structure and have to be placed in the following directories:

- src/main/java: The directory for the Customer, Address beans and ZipCode, and Email constraints.

- src/main/resources: The beans.xml file so we can use CDI as well as the ValidationMessages.properties file for the constraints error messages.

- src/test/java: The directory for the integration tests AddressIT and CustomerIT.

- pom.xml: The Maven Project Object Model (POM) describing the project and its dependencies.

Writing the Customer Bean

In the CD-BookStore application a customer buys items online and these items are then delivered to his home address. To do so, the application needs valid information to ship the items such as the customers' name, e-mail address, and delivery address. The date of birth allows the application to send an annual birthday e-mail. Listing 3-22 shows the Customer bean with some built-in constraints on attributes (firstname cannot be null and the dateOfBirth has to be in the past), as well the @Email constraint that we will develop, and checks that a String is a valid e-mail address.

Listing 3-22. A Customer Bean with Built-In and E-mail Constraints

```java
public class Customer {

  @NotNull @Size(min = 2)
  private String firstName;
  private String lastName;
  @Email
  private String email;
  private String phoneNumber;
  @Past
  private Date dateOfBirth;
  private Address deliveryAddress;

  // Constructors, getters, setters
}
```

Writing the Address Bean

A Customer has zero or one delivery address. An Address is a bean that has all the needed information for an item to be shipped: street, city, state, zip code, and country. Listing 3-23 shows the Address bean with the @NotNull constraint applied on crucial attributes (street1, city, and zipcode) as well as the @ZipCode constraint that checks that a zip code is valid (developed later).

Listing 3-23. An Address Bean with Built-In and @ZipCode Constraints

```java
public class Address {

  @NotNull
  private String street1;
  private String street2;
  @NotNull
  private String city;
  private String state;
  @NotNull @ZipCode
  private String zipcode;
  private String country;

  // Constructors, getters, setters
}
```

Writing the @Email Constraint

The @Email constraint is not built in Bean Validation, so we need to develop it. There is no need to have an implementation class (@Constraint(validatedBy = {})) as a simple constraint annotation with the right regular expression (@Pattern) and size will work. Listing 3-24 shows the @Email constraint annotation.

Listing 3-24. *The E-mail Constraint Annotation with Built-In Constraints Aggregation*

```
@Size(min = 7)
@Pattern(regexp = "[a-z0-9!#$%&'*+/=?^_`{|}~-]+(?:\\."
        + "[a-z0-9!#$%&'*+/=?^_`{|}~-]+)*"
        + "@(?:[a-z0-9](?:[a-z0-9-]*[a-z0-9])?\\.)+[a-z0-9](?:[a-z0-9-]*[a-z0-9])?")
@ReportAsSingleViolation
@Constraint(validatedBy = {})
@Target({METHOD, FIELD, ANNOTATION_TYPE, CONSTRUCTOR, PARAMETER})
@Retention(RUNTIME)
public @interface Email {

  String message() default "{org.agoncal.book.javaee7.chapter03.Email.message}";
  Class<?>[] groups() default {};
  Class<? extends Payload>[] payload() default {};

  @Target({METHOD, FIELD, ANNOTATION_TYPE, CONSTRUCTOR, PARAMETER})
  @Retention(RUNTIME)
  @interface List {
    Email[] value();
  }
}
```

Notice that in Listing 3-24 the error message is a bundle key that is defined in the META-INF/ ValidationMessages.properties file.

```
org.agoncal.book.javaee7.chapter03.Email.message=invalid email address
```

Writing the @ZipCode Constraint

The @ZipCode constraint is more complex to write than @Email. A zip code has a certain format (e.g., five digits in the United States) and this can be easily checked with a regular expression. But to be sure that the zip code is not just syntactically correct but valid, we need to access an external service that will check if a certain zip code exists in a database or not. That's why the ZipCode constraint annotation in Listing 3-25 needs an implementation class (ZipCodeValidator).

Listing 3-25. *The @ZipCode Constraint Annotation*

```
@Constraint(validatedBy = ZipCodeValidator.class)
@Target({METHOD, FIELD, ANNOTATION_TYPE, CONSTRUCTOR, PARAMETER})
@Retention(RUNTIME)
public @interface ZipCode {

  String message() default "{org.agoncal.book.javaee7.chapter03.ZipCode.message}";
  Class<?>[] groups() default {};
  Class<? extends Payload>[] payload() default {};
```

```
@Target({METHOD, FIELD, ANNOTATION_TYPE, CONSTRUCTOR, PARAMETER})
@Retention(RUNTIME)
@interface List {
    ZipCode[] value();
  }
}
```

Listing 3-26 shows the ZipCode constraint implementation class: ZipCodeValidator implements the javax.validation.ConstraintValidator interface with the generic type String. The isValid method implements the validation algorithm that consists of matching a regular expression pattern and calling an external service: ZipCodeChecker. The code of the ZipCodeChecker is not shown here because it is not relevant. What's important is to note that it is injected (@Inject) with a CDI qualifier (@USA shown in Listing 3-27). So you can see both CDI and Bean Validation specifications working together.

Listing 3-26. The ZipCodeValidator Constraint Implementation

```
public class ZipCodeValidator implements ConstraintValidator<ZipCode, String> {

    @Inject @USA
    private ZipCodeChecker checker;
    private Pattern zipPattern = Pattern.compile("\\d{5}(-\\d{5})?");

    public void initialize(ZipCode zipCode) {
    }

    public boolean isValid(String value, ConstraintValidatorContext context) {
      if (value == null)
        return true;

      Matcher m = zipPattern.matcher(value);
      if (!m.matches())
        return false;

      return checker.isZipCodeValid(value);
    }
}
```

Listing 3-27. The USA CDI Qualifier

```
@Qualifier
@Retention(RUNTIME)
@Target({FIELD, TYPE, METHOD})
public @interface USA {
}
```

■ **Note**   In the next chapters, you will see how to integrate Bean Validation with other specifications such as JPA (you can add constraints to your entities) or JSF (you can constrain your backing beans).

Writing the CustomerIT and AddressIT Integration Tests

How can we now test our constraints on our beans? We can't really write unit tests for @Email, as it is a constraints aggregation annotation, or for @ZipCode because it needs injection to work (which is a container service). The easiest is to write an integration test; that is, use the ValidatorFactory to get a Validator and validate our beans.

Listing 3-28 shows the CustomerIT class that integration-tests the Customer bean. The init() method initializes the Validator (using the ValidatorFactory) and the close() method releases the factory. Then the class consists of two tests: one creating a valid Customer object and another one creating an object with an invalid e-mail address and checking whether the validation fails.

Listing 3-28. The CustomerIT Integration Test

```
public class CustomerIT {

  private static ValidatorFactory vf;
  private static Validator validator;

  @BeforeClass
  public static void init() {
    vf = Validation.buildDefaultValidatorFactory();
    validator = vf.getValidator();
  }

  @AfterClass
  public static void close() {
    vf.close();
  }

  @Test
  public void shouldRaiseNoConstraintViolation() {

    Customer customer = new Customer("John", "Smith", "jsmith@gmail.com");

    Set<ConstraintViolation<Customer>> violations = validator.validate(customer);
    assertEquals(0, violations.size());
  }

  @Test
  public void shouldRaiseConstraintViolationCauseInvalidEmail() {

    Customer customer = new Customer("John", "Smith", "DummyEmail");

    Set<ConstraintViolation<Customer>> violations = validator.validate(customer);
    assertEquals(1, violations.size());
    assertEquals("invalid email address", violations.iterator().next().getMessage());
    assertEquals("dummy", violations.iterator().next().getInvalidValue());
    assertEquals("{org.agoncal.book.javaee7.chapter03.Email.message}",
                            violations.iterator().next().getMessageTemplate());
  }
}
```

Listing 3-29 follows the same pattern (creating a Validator with a factory, validating a bean, and closing the factory) but for the Address bean.

Listing 3-29. The AddressIT Integration Test

```
public class AddressIT {

  @Test
  public void shouldRaiseConstraintViolationCauseInvalidZipCode() {

    ValidatorFactory vf = Validation.buildDefaultValidatorFactory();
    Validator validator = vf.getValidator();

    Address address = new Address("233 Spring Street", "New York", "NY", "DummyZip", "USA");

    Set<ConstraintViolation<Address>> violations = validator.validate(address);
    assertEquals(1, violations.size());

    vf.close();
  }
}
```

Compiling and Testing with Maven

All the classes need now to be compiled before they get tested. The pom.xml in Listing 3-30 declares all necessary dependencies to compile the code: Hibernate Validator (the reference implementation for Bean Validation) and Weld (for CDI). Notice that the pom.xml declares the Failsafe plug-in that is designed to run integration tests (used to run both CustomerIT and AddressIT integration test classes).

Listing 3-30. The pom.xml File to Compile and Test the Constraints

```
<?xml version="1.0" encoding="UTF-8"?>
<project xmlns="http://maven.apache.org/POM/4.0.0" ➥
         xmlns:xsi="http://www.w3.org/2001/XMLSchema-instance" ➥
         xsi:schemaLocation="http://maven.apache.org/POM/4.0.0 ➥
         http://maven.apache.org/xsd/maven-4.0.0.xsd">
  <modelVersion>4.0.0</modelVersion>

  <parent>
    <artifactId>chapter03</artifactId>
    <groupId>org.agoncal.book.javaee7</groupId>
    <version>1.0</version>
  </parent>

  <groupId>org.agoncal.book.javaee7.chapter03</groupId>
  <artifactId>chapter03-putting-together</artifactId>
  <version>1.0</version>
```

```xml
<dependencies>
  <dependency>
    <groupId>org.hibernate</groupId>
    <artifactId>hibernate-validator</artifactId>
    <version>5.0.0.Final</version>
  </dependency>
  <dependency>
    <groupId>org.jboss.weld.se</groupId>
    <artifactId>weld-se</artifactId>
    <version>2.0.0.Final</version>
  </dependency>

  <dependency>
    <groupId>junit</groupId>
    <artifactId>junit</artifactId>
    <version>4.11</version>
    <scope>test</scope>
  </dependency>
</dependencies>

<build>
  <plugins>
    <plugin>
      <artifactId>maven-compiler-plugin</artifactId>
      <version>2.5.1</version>
      <configuration>
        <source>1.7</source>
        <target>1.7</target>
      </configuration>
    </plugin>
    <plugin>
      <artifactId>maven-failsafe-plugin</artifactId>
      <version>2.12.4</version>
      <executions>
        <execution>
          <id>integration-test</id>
          <goals>
            <goal>integration-test</goal>
            <goal>verify</goal>
          </goals>
        </execution>
      </executions>
    </plugin>
  </plugins>
</build>
</project>
```

To compile the classes, open a command line in the root directory containing the pom.xml file and enter the following Maven command:

```
$ mvn compile
```

To execute the integration tests with the Maven Failsafe plug-in enter the following:

```
$ mvn integration-test
```

Summary

Bean Validation has a very comprehensive approach to validation problems and solves most of the use cases by validating properties or methods in any application layer. If you find that some cases have been ignored or forgotten, the API is flexible enough to be extended to properly fit your needs.

In this chapter you saw that a constraint is made of an annotation and a separate class implementing the validation logic. You can then aggregate these constraints to build new ones or reuse existing ones. Bean Validation comes with already built-in constraints, although it is regrettable that there are some missing (@Email, @URL, @CreditCard...).

In the first version of the specification, Bean Validation only allowed the validation of beans and attributes. This gave us better Domain-Driven Design, by putting the shallow domain validation in the POJO itself and in this way avoiding the anemic object anti-pattern. In Bean Validation 1.1, validating constructors and method parameters and return value were introduced. This now gives us pre- and postconditions validation, something close to design by contract.

In the following chapters you will see how Bean Validation is integrated in Java EE, particularly with JPA and JSF, and how it can be used in most of the specifications.

CHAPTER 4

■ ■ ■

Java Persistence API

Applications are made up of business logic, interaction with other systems, user interfaces . . . and data. Most of the data that our applications manipulate have to be stored in databases, retrieved, and analyzed. Databases are important: they store business data, act as a central point between applications, and process data through triggers or stored procedures. Persistent data are everywhere, and most of the time they use relational databases as the underlying persistence engine (as opposed to schemaless databases). Relational databases store data in tables made of rows and columns. Data are identified by primary keys, which are special columns with uniqueness constraints and, sometimes, indexes. The relationships between tables use foreign keys and join tables with integrity constraints.

All this vocabulary is completely unknown in an object-oriented language such as Java. In Java, we manipulate objects that are instances of classes. Objects inherit from others, have references to collections of other objects, and sometimes point to themselves in a recursive manner. We have concrete classes, abstract classes, interfaces, enumerations, annotations, methods, attributes, and so on. Objects encapsulate state and behavior in a nice way, but this state is only accessible when the Java Virtual Machine (JVM) is running: if the JVM stops or the garbage collector cleans its memory content, objects disappear, as well as their state. Some objects need to be persistent. By persistent data, I mean data that are deliberately stored in a permanent form on magnetic media, flash memory, and so forth. An object that can store its state to get reused later is said to be persistent.

The principle of object-relational mapping (ORM) is to bring the world of database and objects together. It involves delegating access to relational databases to external tools or frameworks, which in turn give an object-oriented view of relational data, and vice versa. Mapping tools have a bidirectional correspondence between the database and objects. Several frameworks achieve this, such as Hibernate, TopLink, and Java Data Objects (JDO), but Java Persistence API (JPA) is the preferred technology and is part of Java EE 7.

This chapter is an introduction to JPA, and in the two following chapters I concentrate on ORM and querying and managing persistent objects.

Understanding Entities

When talking about mapping objects to a relational database, persisting objects, or querying objects, the term "entity" should be used rather than "object." Objects are instances that just live in memory. Entities are objects that live shortly in memory and persistently in a database. They have the ability to be mapped to a database; they can be concrete or abstract; and they support inheritance, relationships, and so on. These entities, once mapped, can be managed by JPA. You can persist an entity in the database, remove it, and query it using a query language Java Persistence Query Language, or JPQL). ORM lets you manipulate entities, while under the covers the database is being accessed. And, as you will see, an entity follows a defined life cycle. With callback methods and listeners, JPA lets you hook some business code to life-cycle events.

As a first example, let's start with the simplest entity that we can possibly have. In the JPA persistence model, an entity is a Plain Old Java Object (POJO). This means an entity is declared, instantiated, and used just like any other Java class. An entity has attributes (its state) that can be manipulated via getters and setters. Listing 4-1 shows a simple entity.

Listing 4-1. *Simple Example of a Book Entity*

```
@Entity
public class Book {

    @Id @GeneratedValue
    private Long id;
    private String title;
    private Float price;
    private String description;
    private String isbn;
    private Integer nbOfPage;
    private Boolean illustrations;

    public Book() {
    }

    // Getters, setters
}
```

The example in Listing 4-1 represents a Book entity from which I've omitted the getters and the setters for clarity. As you can see, except for some annotations, this entity looks exactly like any Java class: it has several attributes (id, title, price, etc.) of different types (Long, String, Float, Integer, and Boolean), a default constructor, and getters and setters for each attribute. So how does this map to a table? The answer is thanks to annotations.

Anatomy of an Entity

For a class to be an entity it has be to annotated with @javax.persistence.Entity, which allows the persistence provider to recognize it as a persistent class and not just as a simple POJO. Then, the annotation @javax.persistence.Id defines the unique identifier of this object. Because JPA is about mapping objects to relational tables, objects need an ID that will be mapped to a primary key. The other attributes in Listing 4-1 (title, price, description, etc.) are not annotated, so they will be made persistent by applying a default mapping.

This example of code has only attributes, but, as you will later see, an entity can also have business methods. Note that this Book entity is a Java class that does not implement any interface or extend any class. In fact, to be an entity, a class must follow these rules.

- The entity class must be annotated with @javax.persistence.Entity (or denoted in the XML descriptor as an entity).

- The @javax.persistence.Id annotation must be used to denote a simple primary key.

- The entity class must have a no-arg constructor that has to be public or protected. The entity class may have other constructors as well.

- The entity class must be a top-level class. An enum or interface cannot be designated as an entity.

- The entity class must not be final. No methods or persistent instance variables of the entity class may be final.

- If an entity instance has to be passed by value as a detached object (e.g., through a remote interface), the entity class must implement the Serializable interface.

■ **Note**   In previous versions of Java EE, the persistent component model was called Entity Bean, or to be more precise, Entity Bean CMP (Container-Managed Persistence), and was associated with Enterprise JavaBeans. This model of persistence lasted from J2EE 1.3 until 1.4, but was heavyweight and finally replaced by JPA since Java EE 5. JPA uses the term "Entity" instead of "Entity Bean."

Object-Relational Mapping

The principle of ORM is to delegate to external tools or frameworks (in our case, JPA) the task of creating a correspondence between objects and tables. The world of classes, objects, and attributes can then be mapped to relational databases made of tables containing rows and columns. Mapping gives an object-oriented view to developers who can transparently use entities instead of tables. And how does JPA map objects to a database? Through *metadata*.

Associated with every entity are metadata that describe the mapping. The metadata enable the persistence provider to recognize an entity and to interpret the mapping. The metadata can be written in two different formats.

- *Annotations*: The code of the entity is directly annotated with all sorts of annotations that are described in the javax.persistence package.

- *XML descriptors*: Instead of (or in addition to) annotations, you can use XML descriptors. The mapping is defined in an external XML file that will be deployed with the entities. This can be very useful when database configuration changes depending on the environment, for example.

The Book entity (shown in Listing 4-1) uses JPA annotations so the persistence provider can synchronize the data between the attributes of the Book entity and the columns of the BOOK table. Therefore, if the attribute isbn is modified by the application, the ISBN column will be synchronized (if the entity is managed, if the transaction context is set, etc.).

As Figure 4-1 shows, the Book entity is mapped in a BOOK table, and each column is named after the attribute of the class (e.g., the isbn attribute of type String is mapped to a column named ISBN of type VARCHAR). These default mapping rules are an important part of the principle known as *configuration by exception*.

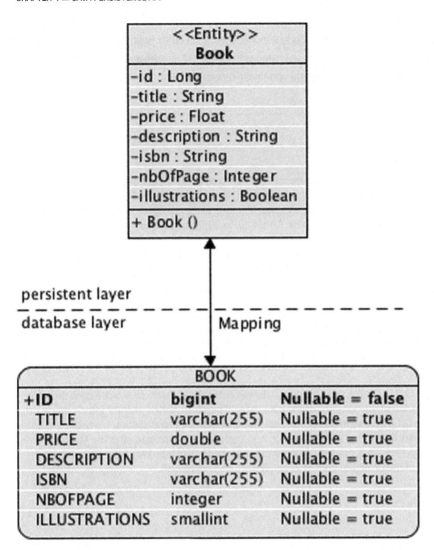

Figure 4-1. *Data synchronization between the entity and the table*

Java EE 5 introduced the idea of configuration by exception (sometimes referred to as *programming by exception* or *convention over configuration*) and is still heavily used today in Java EE 7. This means, unless specified differently, the container or provider should apply the default rules. In other words, having to supply a configuration is the exception to the rule. This allows you to write the minimum amount of code to get your application running, relying on the container and provider defaults. If you don't want the provider to apply the default rules, you can customize the mapping to your own needs using metadata. In other words, having to supply a configuration is the exception to the rule.

Without any annotation, the Book entity in Listing 4-1 would be treated just like a POJO and not be persisted. That is the rule: if no special configuration is given, the default should be applied, and the default for the persistence provider is that the Book class has no database representation. But because you need to change this default behavior, you annotate the class with @Entity. It is the same for the identifier. You need a way to tell the persistence provider that the id attribute has to be mapped to a primary key, so you annotate it with @Id, and the value of this identifier is automatically generated by the persistence provider, using the optional @GeneratedValue annotation. This type of decision characterizes the configuration-by-exception approach, in which annotations are not required for the more common cases and are only used when an override is needed. This means that, for all the other attributes, the following default mapping rules will apply:

- The entity name is mapped to a relational table name (e.g., the Book entity is mapped to a BOOK table). If you want to map it to another table, you will need to use the @Table annotation, as you'll see later in the "Elementary Mapping" section of the next chapter.

- Attribute names are mapped to a column name (e.g., the id attribute, or the getId() method, is mapped to an ID column). If you want to change this default mapping, you will need to use the @Column annotation.

- JDBC rules apply for mapping Java primitives to relational data types. A String will be mapped to VARCHAR, a Long to a BIGINT, a Boolean to a SMALLINT, and so on. The default size of a column mapped from a String is 255 (a String is mapped to a VARCHAR(255)). But keep in mind that the default mapping rules are different from one database to another. For example, a String is mapped to a VARCHAR in Derby and a VARCHAR2 in Oracle. An Integer is mapped to an INTEGER in Derby and a NUMBER in Oracle. The information of the underlying database is provided in the persistence.xml file, which you'll see later.

Following these rules, the Book entity will be mapped to a Derby table that has the structure described in Listing 4-2.

Listing 4-2. Script Creating the BOOK Table Structure

```
CREATE TABLE BOOK (
  ID BIGINT NOT NULL,
  TITLE VARCHAR(255),
  PRICE FLOAT,
  DESCRIPTION VARCHAR(255),
  ISBN VARCHAR(255),
  NBOFPAGE INTEGER,
  ILLUSTRATIONS SMALLINT DEFAULT 0,
  PRIMARY KEY (ID)
)
```

JPA 2.1 has an API and a standard mechanism to generate the database automatically from the entities and generate scripts such as Listing 4-2. This feature is very convenient when you are in development mode. However, most of the time you need to connect to a legacy database that already exists.

Listing 4-1 shows an example of a very simple mapping. As you will see in the next chapter, the mapping can be much richer, allowing you to map all kinds of things from objects to relationships. The world of object-oriented programming abounds with classes and associations between classes (and collections of classes). Databases also model relationships, only differently: using foreign keys or join tables. JPA has a set of metadata to manage the mapping of relationships. Even inheritance can be mapped. Inheritance is commonly used by developers to reuse code, but this concept is natively unknown in relational databases (as they have to emulate inheritance using foreign keys and constraints). Even if inheritance mapping throws in several twists, JPA supports it and gives you three different strategies to choose from.

> ■ **Note** JPA is aimed at relational databases. The mapping metadata (annotations or XML) are designed to map entities to structured tables and attributes to columns. The new era of NoSQL (Not Only SQL) databases (or schemaless) has emerged with different storage structures: key-values, column, document, or graph. At the moment JPA is not able to map entities to these structures. Hibernate OGM is an open source framework that attempts to address this issue. EclipseLink also has some extensions to map NoSQL structures. Hibernate OGM or EclipseLink extensions are beyond the scope of this book, but you should have a look at them if you plan to use NoSQL databases.

Querying Entities

JPA allows you to map entities to databases and also to query them using different criteria. JPA's power is that it offers the ability to query entities and their relationships in an object-oriented way without having to use the underlying database foreign keys or columns. The central piece of the API responsible for orchestrating entities is the `javax.persistence.EntityManager`. Its role is to manage entities, read from and write to a given database, and allow simple CRUD (create, read, update, and delete) operations on entities as well as complex queries using JPQL. In a technical sense, the entity manager is just an interface whose implementation is done by the persistence provider (e.g., EclipseLink). The following snippet of code shows you how to obtain an entity manager and persist a Book entity:

```
EntityManagerFactory emf = Persistence.createEntityManagerFactory("chapter04PU");
EntityManager em = emf.createEntityManager();
em.persist(book);
```

In Figure 4-2, you can see how the `EntityManager` interface can be used by a class (here `Main`) to manipulate entities (in this case, `Book`). With methods such as `persist()` and `find()`, the entity manager hides the JDBC calls to the database and the INSERT or SELECT SQL (Structured Query Language) statement.

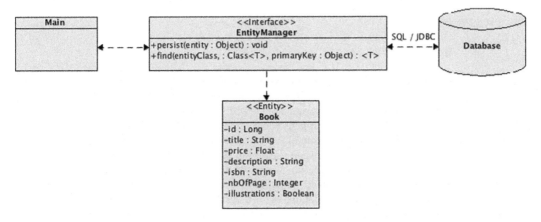

Figure 4-2. *The entity manager interacts with the entity and the underlying database*

The entity manager also allows you to query entities. A *query* in this case is similar to a database query, except that, instead of using SQL, JPA queries over entities using JPQL. Its syntax uses the familiar object dot (`.`) notation. To retrieve all the books that have the title *H2G2*, you can write the following:

```
SELECT b FROM Book b WHERE b.title = 'H2G2'
```

Notice that `title` is the name of the Book attribute, not the name of a column in a table. JPQL statements manipulate objects and attributes, not tables and columns. A JPQL statement can be executed with dynamic queries (created dynamically at runtime) or static queries (defined statically at compile time). You can also execute native SQL statement and even stored procedures. Static queries, also known as named queries, are defined using either annotations (@NamedQuery) or XML metadata. The previous JPQL statement can, for example, be defined as a named query on the Book entity. Listing 4-3 shows a Book entity defining the `findBookH2G2` named query using the @NamedQuery annotation (more on queries in Chapter 6).

Listing 4-3. Book Entity with a `findBookH2G2` Named Query

```
@Entity
@NamedQuery(name = "findBookH2G2", ↪
            query = "SELECT b FROM Book b WHERE b.title ='H2G2'")
public class Book {

  @Id @GeneratedValue
  private Long id;
  private String title;
  private Float price;
  private String description;
  private String isbn;
  private Integer nbOfPage;
  private Boolean illustrations;

  // Constructors, getters, setters
}
```

The `EntityManager` can be obtained in a standard Java class using a factory. Listing 4-4 shows such a class creating an instance of the Book entity, persisting it into a table, and calling a named query. It follows steps 1 through 5.

1. *Creates an instance of the Book entity*: Entities are annotated POJOs, managed by the persistence provider. From a Java viewpoint, an instance of a class needs to be created through the new keyword as with any POJO. It is important to emphasize that, up to this point in the code, the persistence provider is not aware of the Book object.

2. *Obtains an entity manager and a transaction*: This is the important part of the code, as an entity manager is needed to manipulate entities. First, an entity manager factory is created for the "chapter04PU" persistence unit. This factory is then employed to obtain an entity manager (the em variable), used throughout the code to get a transaction (tx variable), and persist and retrieve a Book.

3. *Persists the book to the database*: The code starts a transaction (`tx.begin()`) and uses the `EntityManager.persist()` method to insert a Book instance. When the transaction is committed (`tx.commit()`), the data is flushed to the database.

4. *Executes the named query*: Again, the entity manager is used to retrieve the book using the `findBookH2G2` named query.

5. *Closes the entity manager and the entity manager factory.*

Listing 4-4. *A Main Class Persisting and Retrieving a Book Entity*

```java
public class Main {

  public static void main(String[] args) {

    // 1-Creates an instance of book
    Book book = new Book("H2G2", "The Hitchhiker's Guide to the Galaxy", 12.5F, ↪
                         "1-84023-742-2", 354, false);

    // 2-Obtains an entity manager and a transaction
    EntityManagerFactory emf = Persistence.createEntityManagerFactory("chapter04PU");
    EntityManager em = emf.createEntityManager();

    // 3-Persists the book to the database
    EntityTransaction tx = em.getTransaction();
    tx.begin();
    em.persist(book);
    tx.commit();

    // 4-Executes the named query
    book = em.createNamedQuery("findBookH2G2", Book.class).getSingleResult();

    // 5-Closes the entity manager and the factory
    em.close();
    emf.close();
  }
}
```

Notice in Listing 4-4 the absence of SQL queries or JDBC calls. As shown in Figure 4-2 the Main class interacts with the underlying database through the EntityManager interface, which provides a set of standard methods that allow you to perform operations on the Book entity. Behind the scenes, the EntityManager relies on the persistence provider to interact with the databases. When you invoke the EntityManager method, the persistence provider generates and executes a SQL statement through the corresponding JDBC driver.

Persistence Unit

Which JDBC driver should you use? How should you connect to the database? What's the database name? This information is missing from our previous code. When the Main class (Listing 4-4) creates an EntityManagerFactory, it passes the name of a persistence unit as a parameter; in this case, it's called chapter04PU. The persistence unit indicates to the entity manager the type of database to use and the connection parameters, which are defined in the persistence.xml file, shown in Listing 4-5, that have to be accessible in the class path.

Listing 4-5. The persistence.xml File Defining the Persistence Unit

```xml
<?xml version="1.0" encoding="UTF-8"?>
<persistence xmlns="http://xmlns.jcp.org/xml/ns/persistence"
             xmlns:xsi="http://www.w3.org/2001/XMLSchema-instance"
             xsi:schemaLocation="http://xmlns.jcp.org/xml/ns/persistence ↪
             http://xmlns.jcp.org/xml/ns/persistence/persistence_2_1.xsd"
             version="2.1">

  <persistence-unit name="chapter04PU" transaction-type="RESOURCE_LOCAL">
    <provider>org.eclipse.persistence.jpa.PersistenceProvider</provider>
    <class>org.agoncal.book.javaee7.chapter04.Book</class>
    <properties>
      <property name="javax.persistence.schema-generation-action" value="drop-and-create"/>
      <property name="javax.persistence.schema-generation-target" value="database"/>
      <property name="javax.persistence.jdbc.driver" ↪
                value="org.apache.derby.jdbc.ClientDriver"/>
      <property name="javax.persistence.jdbc.url" ↪
                value="jdbc:derby://localhost:1527/chapter04DB;create=true"/>
      <property name="javax.persistence.jdbc.user" value="APP"/>
      <property name="javax.persistence.jdbc.password" value="APP"/>
    </properties>
  </persistence-unit>
</persistence>
```

The chapter04PU persistence unit defines a JDBC connection for the chapter04DB Derby database running on localhost and port 1527. It connects with a user (APP) and a password (APP) at a given URL. The <class> tag tells the persistence provider to manage the Book class (there are other tags to implicitly or explicitly denote managed persistence classes such as <mapping-file>, <jar-file>, or <exclude-unlisted-classes>). Without a persistent unit, entities can be manipulated as POJOs without having persistent repercussions.

Entity Life Cycle and Callbacks

Entities are just POJOs. When the entity manager manages the POJOs, they have a persistence identity (a key that uniquely identifies an instance equivalent to a primary key), and the database synchronizes their state. When they are not managed (i.e., they are detached from the entity manager), they can be used like any other Java class. This means that entities have a life cycle, as shown in Figure 4-3. When you create an instance of the Book entity with the new operator, the object exists in memory, and JPA knows nothing about it (it can even end up being garbage collected). When it becomes managed by the entity manager, the BOOK table maps and synchronizes its state. Calling the EntityManager.remove() method deletes the data from the database, but the Java object continues living in memory until it gets garbage collected.

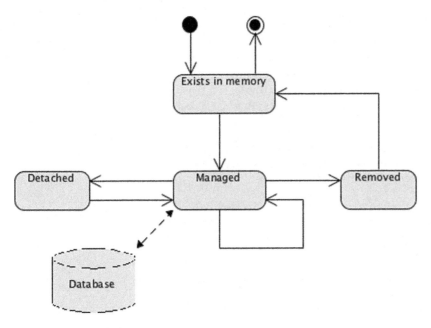

Figure 4-3. *The life cyle of an entity*

The operations made to entities fall into four categories—persisting, updating, removing, and loading—which correspond to the database operations of inserting, updating, deleting, and selecting, respectively. Each operation has a "pre" and "post" event (except for loading, which only has a "post" event) that can be intercepted by the entity manager to invoke a business method. As you will see in Chapter 6, you will have @PrePersist and @PostPersist annotations, and so on. JPA allows you to hook business logic to the entity when these events occur. These annotations can be set on entity methods (a.k.a. callback methods) or in external classes (a.k.a. listeners). You can think of callback methods and listeners as analogous triggers in a relational database.

Integration with Bean Validation

Bean Validation, which was explained in the previous chapter, has several hooks into Java EE. One of them is its integration with JPA and the entity life cycle. Entities may include Bean Validation constraints and be automatically validated. In fact, automatic validation is achieved because JPA delegates validation to the Bean Validation implementation upon the pre-persist, pre-update, and pre-remove entity life-cycle events. Of course, validation can still be achieved manually, by calling the validate method of a Validator on an entity if needed.

Listing 4-6 shows a Book entity with two Bean Validation constraints (@NotNull and @Size). If the title attribute is null and you want to persist this entity (by invoking EntityManager.persist()), the JPA runtime will throw a ConstraintViolation exception and the data will not be inserted in the database.

Listing 4-6. An Entity with Bean Validation Annotations

```
@Entity
public class Book {

  @Id @GeneratedValue
  private Long id;
  @NotNull
  private String title;
```

```
    private Float price;
    @Size(min = 10, max = 2000)
    private String description;
    private String isbn;
    private Integer nbOfPage;
    private Boolean illustrations;

    // Constructors, getters, setters
}
```

JPA Specification Overview

JPA 1.0 was created with Java EE 5 to solve the problem of data persistence. It brought the object-oriented and relational models together. In Java EE 7, JPA 2.1 follows the same path of simplicity and robustness and adds new functionalities. You can use this API to access and manipulate relational data from EJBs, web components, and Java SE applications.

JPA is an abstraction above JDBC that makes it possible to be independent of SQL. All classes and annotations of this API are in the javax.persistence package. The main components of JPA are

- ORM, which is the mechanism to map objects to data stored in a relational database.

- An entity manager API to perform database-related operations, such as CRUD.

- The JPQL, which allows you to retrieve data with an object-oriented query language.

- Transactions and locking mechanisms which Java Transaction API (JTA) provides when accessing data concurrently. JPA also supports resource-local (non-JTA) transactions.

- Callbacks and listeners to hook business logic into the life cycle of a persistent object.

A Brief History of JPA

ORM solutions have been around for a long time, even before Java. Products such as TopLink originally started with Smalltalk in 1994 before switching to Java. Commercial ORM products like TopLink have been available since the earliest days of the Java language. They were successful but were never standardized for the Java platform. A similar approach to ORM was standardized in the form of JDO, which failed to gain any significant market penetration.

In 1998, EJB 1.0 was created and later shipped with J2EE 1.2. It was a heavyweight, distributed component used for transactional business logic. Entity Bean CMP was introduced as optional in EJB 1.0, became mandatory in EJB 1.1, and was enhanced through versions up to EJB 2.1 (J2EE 1.4). Persistence could only be done inside the container through a complex mechanism of instantiation using home, local, or remote interfaces. The ORM capabilities were also very limited, as inheritance was difficult to map.

Parallel to the J2EE world was a popular open source solution that led to some surprising changes in the direction of persistence: Hibernate, which brought back a lightweight, object-oriented persistent model.

After years of complaints about Entity CMP 2.x components and in acknowledgment of the success and simplicity of open source frameworks such as Hibernate, the persistence model of the Enterprise Edition was completely rearchitected in Java EE 5. JPA 1.0 was born with a very lightweight approach that adopted many Hibernate design principles. The JPA 1.0 specification was bundled with EJB 3.0 (JSR 220). In 2009 JPA 2.0 (JSR 317) shipped with Java EE 6 and brought new APIs, extended JPQL, and added new functionalities such as second-level cache, pessimistic locking, or the criteria API.

Today, with Java EE 7, JPA 2.1 follows the path of ease of development and brings new features. It has evolved in the JSR 338.

What's New in JPA 2.1?

If JPA 1.0 was a revolution from its Entity CMP 2.*x* ancestor because a completely new persistence model, JPA 2.0, was a continuation of JPA 1.0, and today JPA 2.1 follows the same steps and brings many new features and improvements.

- *Schema generation*: JPA 2.1 has standardized database schema generation by bringing a new API and a set of properties (defined in the `persistence.xml`).

- *Converters*: These are new classes that convert between database and attributes representations.

- *CDI support*: Injection is now possible into event listeners.

- *Support for stored procedures*: JPA 2.1 allows now dynamically specified and named stored procedure queries.

- *Bulk update and delete criteria queries*: Criteria API only had select queries; now update and delete queries are also specified.

- *Downcasting*: The new `TREAT` operator allows access to subclass-specific state in queries.

Table 4-1 lists the main packages defined in JPA 2.1 today.

Table 4-1. *Main JPA Packages*

Package	Description
`javax.persistence`	API for the management of persistence and object/relational mapping
`javax.persistence.criteria`	Java Persistence Criteria API
`javax.persistence.metamodel`	Java Persistence Metamodel API
`javax.persistence.spi`	SPI for Java Persistence providers

Reference Implementation

EclipseLink 2.5 is the open source reference implementation of JPA 2.1. It provides a powerful and flexible framework for storing Java objects in a relational database. EclipseLink is a JPA implementation, but it also supports XML persistence through Java XML Binding (JAXB) and other means such as Service Data Objects (SDO). It provides support not only for ORM but also for object XML mapping (OXM), object persistence to enterprise information systems (EIS) using Java EE Connector Architecture (JCA), and database web services.

EclipseLink's origins stem from the Oracle TopLink product given to the Eclipse Foundation in 2006. EclipseLink is the JPA reference implementation and is the persistence framework used in this book. It is also referred to as the *persistence provider*, or simply the *provider*.

At the time of writing this book EclipseLink is the only JPA 2.1 implementation. But Hibernate and OpenJPA will soon follow and you will have several implementations to choose from.

Putting It all Together

Now that you know a little bit about JPA, EclipseLink, entities, the entity manager, and JPQL, let's put them all together and write a small application that persists an entity to a database. The idea is to write a simple `Book` entity with Bean Validation constraints and a `Main` class that persists a book. You'll then compile it with Maven and run it with EclipseLink and a Derby client database. To show how easy it is to integration-test an entity, I will show you how to write a test class (`BookIT`) with JUnit 4 and use the embedded mode of Derby for persisting data using an in-memory database.

This example follows the Maven directory structure, so classes and files described in Figure 4-4 have to be placed in the following directories:

- `src/main/java`: For the Book entity and the `Main` class;

- `src/main/resources`: For the `persistence.xml` file used by the `Main` and `BookIT` classes as well as the `insert.sql` database loading script;

- `src/test/java`: For the `BookIT` class, which is used for integration testing; and

- `pom.xml`: For the Maven POM, which describes the project and its dependencies on other external modules and components.

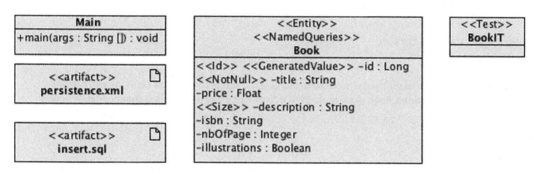

Figure 4-4. *Putting it all together*

Writing the Book Entity

The Book entity, shown in Listing 4-7, needs to be developed under the `src/main/java` directory. It has several attributes (a title, a price, etc.) of different data types (`String`, `Float`, `Integer`, and `Boolean`), some Bean Validation annotations (`@NotNull` and `@Size`), as well as some JPA annotations.

- `@Entity` informs the persistence provider that this class is an entity and that it should manage it.

- The `@NamedQueries` and `@NamedQuery` annotations define two named-queries that use JPQL to retrieve books from the database.

- `@Id` defines the id attribute as being the primary key.

- The `@GeneratedValue` annotation informs the persistence provider to autogenerate the primary key using the underlying database id utility.

Listing 4-7. A Book Entity with a Named Query

```
package org.agoncal.book.javaee7.chapter04;
@Entity
@NamedQueries({
  @NamedQuery(name = "findAllBooks", query = "SELECT b FROM Book b"),
  @NamedQuery(name = "findBookH2G2", query = "SELECT b FROM Book b WHERE b.title ='H2G2'")
})
```

```
public class Book {

    @Id @GeneratedValue
    private Long id;
    @NotNull
    private String title;
    private Float price;
    @Size(min = 10, max = 2000)
    private String description;
    private String isbn;
    private Integer nbOfPage;
    private Boolean illustrations;

    // Constructors, getters, setters
}
```

Note that for better readability I've omitted the constructor, getters, and setters of this class. As you can see in this code, except for a few annotations, Book is a simple POJO. Now let's write a Main class that persists a book to the database.

Writing the Main Class

The Main class, shown in Listing 4-8, is under the same package as the Book entity. It commences by creating a new instance of Book (using the Java keyword new) and sets some values to its attributes. There is nothing special here, just pure Java code. It then uses the Persistence class to get an instance of an EntityManagerFactory that refers to a persistence unit called chapter04PU, which I'll describe later in the section "Writing the Persistence Unit." This factory creates an instance of an EntityManager (em variable). As mentioned previously, the entity manager is the central piece of JPA in that it is able to create a transaction, persist the book object using the EntityManager.persist() method, and then commit the transaction. At the end of the main() method, both the EntityManager and EntityManagerFactory are closed to release the provider's resources

Listing 4-8. A Main Class Persisting the Book Entity

```
package org.agoncal.book.javaee7.chapter04;
public class Main {

    public static void main(String[] args) {

        // Creates an instance of book
        Book book = new Book("H2G2", "The Hitchhiker's Guide to the Galaxy", 12.5F, ↵
                             "1-84023-742-2", 354, false);

        // Obtains an entity manager and a transaction
        EntityManagerFactory emf = Persistence.createEntityManagerFactory("chapter04PU");
        EntityManager em = emf.createEntityManager();

        // Persists the book to the database
        EntityTransaction tx = em.getTransaction();
        tx.begin();
        em.persist(book);
        tx.commit();
```

```
    // Closes the entity manager and the factory
    em.close();
    emf.close();
  }
}
```

Again, for readability I've omitted exception handling. If a persistence exception occurs, you would have to roll back the transaction, log a message, and close the `EntityManager` in the finally block.

Writing the BookIT Integration Test

One complaint made about the previous versions of Entity CMP 2.x was the difficulty of integration testing persistent components. One of the major selling points of JPA is that you can easily test entities without requiring a running application server or live database. But what can you test? Entities themselves usually don't need to be tested in isolation. Most methods on entities are simple getters or setters with only a few business methods. Verifying that a setter assigns a value to an attribute and that the corresponding getter retrieves the same value does not give any extra value (unless a side effect is detected in the getters or the setters). So unit testing an entity has limited interest.

What about testing the database queries? Making sure that the `findBookH2G2` query is correct? Or injecting data into the database and testing complex queries bringing multiple values? These integration tests would need a real database with real data, or you would unit test in isolation with mocks to simulate a query. Using an in-memory database and JPA transactions is a good compromise. CRUD operations and JPQL queries can be tested with a very lightweight database that doesn't need to run in a separate process (just by adding a jar file to the class path). This is how you will run our `BookIT` class, by using the embedded mode of Derby.

Maven uses two different directories, one to store the main application code and another for the test classes. The `BookIT` class, shown in Listing 4-9, goes under the `src/test/java` directory and tests that the entity manager can persist a book and retrieve it from the database and checks that Bean Validation constraints are raised.

Listing 4-9. Test Class That Creates and Retrieves Books from the Database

```
public class BookIT {

  private static EntityManagerFactory emf =  ⤶
                 Persistence.createEntityManagerFactory("chapter04TestPU");
  private EntityManager em;
  private EntityTransaction tx;

  @Before
  public void initEntityManager() throws Exception {
    em = emf.createEntityManager();
    tx = em.getTransaction();
  }

  @After
  public void closeEntityManager() throws Exception {
    if (em != null) em.close();
  }
```

```java
@Test
public void shouldFindJavaEE7Book() throws Exception {
  Book book = em.find(Book.class, 1001L);
  assertEquals("Beginning Java EE 7", book.getTitle());
}

@Test
public void shouldCreateH2G2Book() throws Exception {

  // Creates an instance of book
  Book book = new Book("H2G2", "The Hitchhiker's Guide to the Galaxy", 12.5F, ⮑
                    "1-84023-742-2", 354, false);

  // Persists the book to the database
  tx.begin();
  em.persist(book);
  tx.commit();
  assertNotNull("ID should not be null", book.getId());

  // Retrieves all the books from the database
  book = em.createNamedQuery("findBookH2G2", Book.class).getSingleResult();
  assertEquals("The Hitchhiker's Guide to the Galaxy", book.getDescription());
}

@Test(expected = ConstraintViolationException.class)
public void shouldRaiseConstraintViolationCauseNullTitle() {

  Book book = new Book(null, "Null title, should fail", 12.5F, ⮑
                    "1-84023-742-2", 354, false);
  em.persist(book);
}
}
```

Like the Main class, BookIT in Listing 4-9 needs to create an EntityManager instance using an EntityManagerFactory. To initialize these components, you can use the JUnit 4 fixtures. The @Before and @After annotations allow executions of some code before and after a test is executed. That's the perfect place to create and close an EntityManager instance and get a transaction.

The shouldFindJavaEE7Book() test case relies on data already being present in the database (more on insert.sql script later) as it finds the book with id 1001 and checks that the title is "Beginning Java EE 7". The shouldCreateH2G2Book() method persists a book (using the EntityManager.persist() method) and checks whether the id has been automatically generated by EclipseLink (with assertNotNull). If so, the findBookH2G2 named query is executed and checks whether the returned book has "The Hitchhiker's Guide to the Galaxy" as its description. The last test case creates a Book with a null title, persists it, and checks that a ConstraintViolationException has been thrown.

Writing the Persistence Unit

As you can see in the Main class (Listing 4-8), the EntityManagerFactory needs a persistence unit called chapter04PU. And the integration test BookIT (Listing 4-9) uses a different persistent unit (chapter04TestPU). These two persistence units have to be defined in the persistence.xml file under the src/main/resources/META-INF directory (see Listing 4-10). This file, required by the JPA specification, is important as it links the JPA provider (EclipseLink in our case) to the database (Derby). It contains all the necessary information to connect to the database (URL, JDBC driver, user, and password) and informs the provider of the database schema-generation mode (drop-and-create means that tables will be dropped and then created). The <provider> element defines the persistence provider, in our case, EclipseLink. The persistence units list all the entities that should be managed by the entity manager. Here, the <class> tag refers to the Book entity.

The two persistent units differ in the sense that chapter04PU uses a running Derby database and chapter04TestPU an in memory one. Notice that both use the load script insert.sql to insert data into the database at runtime.

Listing 4-10. persistence.xml File

```xml
<?xml version="1.0" encoding="UTF-8"?>
<persistence xmlns="http://xmlns.jcp.org/xml/ns/persistence"
             xmlns:xsi="http://www.w3.org/2001/XMLSchema-instance"
             xsi:schemaLocation="http://xmlns.jcp.org/xml/ns/persistence ↪
             http://xmlns.jcp.org/xml/ns/persistence/persistence_2_1.xsd"
             version="2.1">

  <persistence-unit name="chapter04PU" transaction-type="RESOURCE_LOCAL">
    <provider>org.eclipse.persistence.jpa.PersistenceProvider</provider>
    <class>org.agoncal.book.javaee7.chapter04.Book</class>
    <properties>
      <property name="javax.persistence.schema-generation-action" value="drop-and-create"/>
      <property name="javax.persistence.schema-generation-target" ↪
                value="database-and-scripts"/>
      <property name="javax.persistence.jdbc.driver" ↪
                value="org.apache.derby.jdbc.ClientDriver"/>
      <property name="javax.persistence.jdbc.url" ↪
                value="jdbc:derby://localhost:1527/chapter04DB;create=true"/>
      <property name="javax.persistence.jdbc.user" value="APP"/>
      <property name="javax.persistence.jdbc.password" value="APP"/>
      <property name="javax.persistence.sql-load-script-source" value="insert.sql"/>
    </properties>
  </persistence-unit>

  <persistence-unit name="chapter04TestPU" transaction-type="RESOURCE_LOCAL">
    <provider>org.eclipse.persistence.jpa.PersistenceProvider</provider>
    <class>org.agoncal.book.javaee7.chapter04.Book</class>
    <properties>
      <property name="javax.persistence.schema-generation-action" value="drop-and-create"/>
      <property name="javax.persistence.schema-generation-target" value="database"/>
      <property name="javax.persistence.jdbc.driver" ↪
                value="org.apache.derby.jdbc.EmbeddedDriver"/>
      <property name="javax.persistence.jdbc.url" ↪
                value="jdbc:derby:memory:chapter04DB;create=true"/>
      <property name="javax.persistence.sql-load-script-source" value="insert.sql"/>
    </properties>
  </persistence-unit>
</persistence>
```

Writing an SQL Script to Load Data

Both persistence units defined in Listing 4-10 load the insert.sql script (using the javax.persistence.sql-load-script-source property). This means that the script in Listing 4-11 is executed for database initialization and inserts three books.

Listing 4-11. insert.sql File

```
INSERT INTO BOOK(ID, TITLE, DESCRIPTION, ILLUSTRATIONS, ISBN, NBOFPAGE, PRICE) values ⮑
        (1000, 'Beginning Java EE 6', 'Best Java EE book ever', 1, '1234-5678', 450, 49)
INSERT INTO BOOK(ID, TITLE, DESCRIPTION, ILLUSTRATIONS, ISBN, NBOFPAGE, PRICE) values ⮑
        (1001, 'Beginning Java EE 7', 'No, this is the best ', 1, '5678-9012', 550, 53)
INSERT INTO BOOK(ID, TITLE, DESCRIPTION, ILLUSTRATIONS, ISBN, NBOFPAGE, PRICE) values ⮑
        (1010, 'The Lord of the Rings', 'One ring to rule them all', 0, '9012-3456', 222, 23)
```

If you look carefully at the BookIT integration test (method shouldFindJavaEE7Book) you'll see that the test expects the book id 1001 to be in the database. Thanks to the database initialization, this is done before the tests are run.

Compiling and Testing with Maven

We have all the ingredients to compile and test the entity before running the Main application: the Book entity, the BookIT integration test, and the persistence units binding the entity to the Derby database. To compile this code, instead of using the javac compiler command directly, you will use Maven. You must first create a pom.xml file that describes the project and its dependencies such as the JPA and Bean Validation API. You also need to inform Maven that you are using Java SE 7 by configuring the maven-compiler-plugin as shown in Listing 4-12.

Listing 4-12. Maven pom.xml File to Compile, Test, and Execute the Application

```xml
<?xml version="1.0" encoding="UTF-8"?>
<project xmlns="http://maven.apache.org/POM/4.0.0" ⮑
        xmlns:xsi="http://www.w3.org/2001/XMLSchema-instance" ⮑
        xsi:schemaLocation="http://maven.apache.org/POM/4.0.0 ⮑
        http://maven.apache.org/xsd/maven-4.0.0.xsd">
  <modelVersion>4.0.0</modelVersion>

  <parent>
    <artifactId>parent</artifactId>
    <groupId>org.agoncal.book.javaee7</groupId>
    <version>1.0</version>
  </parent>

  <groupId>org.agoncal.book.javaee7</groupId>
  <artifactId>chapter04</artifactId>
  <version>1.0</version>

  <dependencies>
    <dependency>
      <groupId>org.eclipse.persistence</groupId>
      <artifactId>org.eclipse.persistence.jpa</artifactId>
      <version>2.5.0</version>
    </dependency>
```

```xml
  <dependency>
    <groupId>org.hibernate</groupId>
    <artifactId>hibernate-validator</artifactId>
    <version>5.0.0</version>
  </dependency>
  <dependency>
    <groupId>org.apache.derby</groupId>
    <artifactId>derbyclient</artifactId>
    <version>10.9.1.0</version>
  </dependency>

  <dependency>
    <groupId>org.apache.derby</groupId>
    <artifactId>derby</artifactId>
    <version>10.9.1.0</version>
    <scope>test</scope>
  </dependency>
  <dependency>
    <groupId>junit</groupId>
    <artifactId>junit</artifactId>
    <version>4.11</version>
    <scope>test</scope>
  </dependency>
</dependencies>

<build>
  <plugins>
    <plugin>
      <groupId>org.apache.maven.plugins</groupId>
      <artifactId>maven-compiler-plugin</artifactId>
      <version>2.5.1</version>
      <configuration>
        <source>1.7</source>
        <target>1.7</target>
      </configuration>
    </plugin>
    <plugin>
      <groupId>org.apache.maven.plugins</groupId>
      <artifactId>maven-failsafe-plugin</artifactId>
      <version>2.12.4</version>
      <executions>
        <execution>
          <id>integration-test</id>
          <goals>
            <goal>integration-test</goal>
            <goal>verify</goal>
          </goals>
        </execution>
      </executions>
    </plugin>
```

```
        <plugin>
          <groupId>org.codehaus.mojo</groupId>
          <artifactId>exec-maven-plugin</artifactId>
          <version>1.2.1</version>
          <executions>
            <execution>
              <goals>
                <goal>java</goal>
              </goals>
            </execution>
          </executions>
          <configuration>
            <mainClass>org.agoncal.book.javaee7.chapter04.Main</mainClass>
          </configuration>
        </plugin>
      </plugins>
    </build>
</project>
```

First, to be able to compile the code, you need the JPA API that defines all the annotations and classes that are in the javax.persistence package. You will get these and the EclipseLink runtime (i.e., the persistence provider) through the org.eclipse.persistence.jpa artifact ID. As seen in the previous chapter, the Bean Validation API is in the hibernate-validator artifact. You then need the JDBC drivers to connect to Derby. The derbyclient artifact ID refers to the jar that contains the JDBC driver to connect to Derby running in server mode (the database runs in a separate process and listens to a port) and the derby artifact ID contains the classes to use Derby as an embedded database. Note that this artifact ID is scoped for testing (<scope>test</scope>) and as well as the artifact for JUnit 4.

To compile the classes, open a command-line interpreter in the root directory that contains the pom.xml file and enter the following Maven command:

```
$ mvn compile
```

You should see the BUILD SUCCESS message informing you that the compilation was successful. Maven creates a target subdirectory with all the class files as well as the persistence.xml file. To run the integration tests you also rely on Maven by entering the following command:

```
$ mvn integration-test
```

You should see some logs about Derby creating a database and tables in memory. The BookIT class is then executed, and a Maven report should inform you that the three test cases are successful:

```
Results :
Tests run: 3, Failures: 0, Errors: 0, Skipped: 0

[INFO] ------------------------------------------------------------------------
[INFO] BUILD SUCCESS
[INFO] ------------------------------------------------------------------------
[INFO] Total time: 5.192s
[INFO] Finished
[INFO] Final Memory: 18M/221M
[INFO] ------------------------------------------------------------------------
```

Running the Main Class with Derby

Before executing the Main class, you need to start Derby. The easiest way to do this is to go to the $DERBY_HOME/bin directory and execute the startNetworkServer script. Derby starts and displays the following messages in the console:

```
Security manager installed using the Basic server security policy.
Apache Derby Network Server - 10.9.1.0 - (802917) started and ready to accept
connections on port 1527
```

The Derby process is listening on port 1527 and waiting for the JDBC driver to send any SQL statement. To execute the Main class, you can use the java interpreter command or use the exec-maven-plugin as follows:

```
$ mvn exec:java
```

When you run the Main class, several things occur. First, Derby will automatically create the chapter04DB database once the Book entity is initialized. That is because in the persistence.xml file you've added the create=true property to the JDBC URL.

```
<property name="javax.persistence.jdbc.url" ↪
        value="jdbc:derby://localhost:1527/chapter04DB;create=true"/>
```

This shortcut is very useful when you are in development mode, as you do not need any SQL script to create the database. Then, the javax.persistence.schema-generation-action property informs EclipseLink to automatically drop and create the BOOK table. Finally, the book is inserted into the table (with an automatically generated ID).

Let's use Derby commands to display the table structure: enter the ij command in a console (as explained in Appendix A, the $DERBY_HOME/bin directory has to be in your PATH variable). This runs the Derby interpreter, and you can execute commands to connect to the database, show the tables of the chapter04DB database (show tables), check the structure of the BOOK table (describe book), and even show its content by entering SQL statements such as SELECT * FROM BOOK.

```
$ ij
version 10.9.1.0

ij> connect 'jdbc:derby://localhost:1527/chapter04DB';

ij> show tables;
TABLE_SCHEM     |TABLE_NAME      |REMARKS
------------------------------------------------------------------------
APP             |BOOK            |
APP             |SEQUENCE        |

ij> describe book;
COLUMN_NAME    |TYPE_NAME|DEC&|NUM&|COLUM&|COLUMN_DEF|CHAR_OCTE&|IS_NULL&
------------------------------------------------------------------------
ID             |BIGINT   |0    |10  |19    |NULL      |NULL      |NO
TITLE          |VARCHAR  |NULL |NULL|255   |NULL      |510       |YES
PRICE          |DOUBLE   |NULL |2   |52    |NULL      |NULL      |YES
ILLUSTRATIONS  |SMALLINT |0    |10  |5     |0         |NULL      |YES
DESCRIPTION    |VARCHAR  |NULL |NULL|255   |NULL      |510       |YES
ISBN           |VARCHAR  |NULL |NULL|255   |NULL      |510       |YES
NBOFPAGE       |INTEGER  |0    |10  |10    |NULL      |NULL      |YES
```

Coming back to the code of the Book entity (Listing 4-7), because you've used the @GeneratedValue annotation (to automatically generate an ID), EclipseLink has created a sequence table to store the numbering (the SEQUENCE table). For the BOOK table structure, JPA has followed certain default conventions to name the table and the columns after the entity name and attributes (e.g., Strings are mapped to VARCHAR(255)).

Checking the Generated Schema

In the persistence.xml file described in Listing 4-10 we have informed EclipseLink to generate the schema database as well as creating the drop and create scripts, thanks to the following property:

```
<property name="javax.persistence.schema-generation.database.action" ↪
        value="drop-and-create"/>
<property name="javax.persistence.schema-generation.scripts.action" ↪
        value="drop-and-create"/>
```

By default the provider will generate two SQL scripts: createDDL.jdbc (Listing 4-13) with all the SQL statements to create the entire database and the dropDDL.jdbc (Listing 4-14) to drop all the tables. This is useful when you need to execute scripts to create a database in your continuous integration process.

Listing 4-13. The createDDL.jdbc Script

```
CREATE TABLE BOOK (ID BIGINT NOT NULL, DESCRIPTION VARCHAR(255), ↪
                ILLUSTRATIONS SMALLINT DEFAULT 0, ISBN VARCHAR(255), NBOFPAGE INTEGER, ↪
                PRICE FLOAT, TITLE VARCHAR(255), PRIMARY KEY (ID))
CREATE TABLE SEQUENCE (SEQ_NAME VARCHAR(50) NOT NULL, SEQ_COUNT DECIMAL(15), ↪
                PRIMARY KEY (SEQ_NAME))
INSERT INTO SEQUENCE (SEQ_NAME, SEQ_COUNT) values ('SEQ_GEN', 0)
```

Listing 4-14. The dropDDL.jdbc Script

```
DROP TABLE BOOK
DELETE FROM SEQUENCE WHERE SEQ_NAME = 'SEQ_GEN'
```

Summary

This chapter contained a quick overview of JPA 2.1. Like most of the other Java EE 7 specifications, JPA focuses on a simple object architecture, leaving its ancestor, a heavyweight component model (a.k.a. EJB CMP 2.*x*), behind. The chapter also covered entities, which are persistent objects that map metadata through annotations or XML.

Thanks to the "Putting It All Together" section, you have seen how to run a JPA application with EclipseLink and Derby. Integration testing is an important topic in projects, and, with JPA and in memory databases such as Derby, it is now very easy to test persistence.

In the following chapters, you will learn more about the main JPA components. Chapter 5 will show you how to map entities, relationships, and inheritance to a database. Chapter 6 will focus on the entity manager API, the JPQL syntax, and how to use queries and locking mechanisms as well as explaining the life cycle of entities and how to hook business logic in callback methods in entities and listeners.

CHAPTER 5

■ ■ ■

Object-Relational Mapping

In the previous chapter I went through the basics of object-relational mapping (ORM), which is basically mapping entities to tables and attributes to columns. I also introduced configuration by exception which allows the JPA provider to map an entity to a database table using all the defaults. But defaults are not always suitable, especially if you map your domain model to an existing database. JPA comes with a rich set of metadata so you can customize the mapping.

In this chapter I cover elementary mapping, but I also concentrate on more complex mappings such as relationships, composition, and inheritance. A domain model is made of objects interacting with each other. Objects and databases have different ways to store relationship information (references in objects and foreign keys in databases). Inheritance is not a feature that relational databases naturally have, and therefore the mapping is not as obvious. In this chapter I go into some detail and show examples that demonstrate how to map attributes, relationships, and inheritance from a domain model to a database.

Elementary Mapping

There are significant differences in the way Java data handles data compared to the way a relational database handles data. In Java, we use classes to describe both attributes for holding data and methods to access and manipulate that data. Once we define a class, we can create as many instances as we need with the new keyword. In a relational database, data are stored in non-object structures (columns and rows), and dynamic behavior is stored functionally as table triggers and stored procedures that are not bound tightly to the data structures, as they are with objects. Sometimes mapping Java objects to the underlying database can be easy, and the default rules can be applied. At other times, these rules do not meet your needs, and you must customize the mapping. Elementary mapping annotations focus on customizing the table, the primary key, and the columns, and they let you modify certain naming conventions or typing (not-null column, length, etc.).

Tables

Rules for configuration-by-exception mapping state that the entity and the table name are the same (a Book entity is mapped to a BOOK table, an AncientBook entity is mapped to an ANCIENTBOOK table, etc.). This might suit you in most cases, but you may want to map your data to a different table, or even map a single entity to several tables.

@Table

The @javax.persistence.Table annotation makes it possible to change the default values related to the table. For example, you can specify the name of the table in which the data will be stored, the catalog, and the database schema. You can also define unique constraints to the table using the @UniqueConstraint annotation in conjunction with @Table. If the @Table annotation is omitted, the name of the table will be the name of the entity. If you want to change the name to T_BOOK instead of BOOK, you would do as shown in Listing 5-1.

Listing 5-1. *The Book Entity Being Mapped to a T_BOOK Table*

```
@Entity
@Table(name = "t_book")
public class Book {

@Id
  private Long id;
  private String title;
  private Float price;
  private String description;
  private String isbn;
  private Integer nbOfPage;
  private Boolean illustrations;

  // Constructors, getters, setters
}
```

▧ **Note**   In the @Table annotation, I include a lowercase table name (t_book). By default, most databases will map the entity to an uppercase table name (and that's the case with Derby) except if you configure them to honor case.

@SecondaryTable

Up to now, I have assumed that an entity gets mapped to a single table, also known as a *primary table*. But sometimes when you have an existing data model, you need to spread the data across multiple tables, or *secondary tables*. To do this, you need to use the annotation @SecondaryTable to associate a secondary table to an entity or @SecondaryTables (with an "s") for several secondary tables. You can distribute the data of an entity across columns in both the primary table and the secondary tables simply by defining the secondary tables with annotations and then specifying for each attribute which table it belongs to (with the @Column annotation, which I describe in the "Attributes" section in more detail). Listing 5-2 shows an Address entity mapping its attributes to one primary table and two secondary tables.

Listing 5-2. *Attributes of the Address Entity Mapped in Three Different Tables*

```
@Entity
@SecondaryTables({
  @SecondaryTable(name = "city"),
 @SecondaryTable(name = "country")
})
public class Address {

  @Id
  private Long id;
  private String street1;
  private String street2;
  @Column(table = "city")
  private String city;
  @Column(table = "city")
  private String state;
  @Column(table = "city")
  private String zipcode;
```

```
@Column(table = "country")
private String country;

  // Constructors, getters, setters
}
```

By default, the attributes of the Address entity are mapped to the primary table (which has the default name of the entity, so the table is called ADDRESS). The annotation @SecondaryTables informs you that there are two secondary tables: CITY and COUNTRY. You then need to specify which attribute is stored in which secondary table (using the annotation @Column(table="city") or @Column(table="country")). Figure 5-1 shows the tables structure to which the Address entity will be mapped. Each table contains different attributes, but they all have the same primary key (to join the tables together). Again, remember that Derby translates lowercase table names (city) into uppercase (CITY).

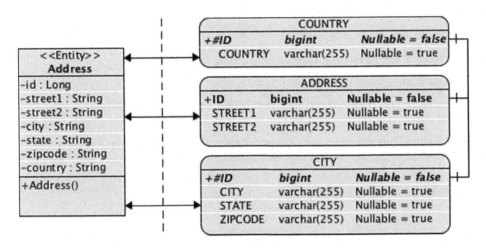

Figure 5-1. *The Address entity is mapped to three tables*

As you probably understand by now, you can have several annotations in the same entity. If you want to rename the primary table, you can add the @Table annotation as demonstrated in Listing 5-2.

Listing 5-2. The Primary Table Is Renamed to T_ADDRESS

```
@Entity
@Table(name = "t_address")
@SecondaryTables({
  @SecondaryTable(name = "t_city"),
  @SecondaryTable(name = "t_country")
})
public class Address {

  // Attributes, constructor, getters, setters
}
```

■ **Note** When you use secondary tables, you must consider the issue of performance. Every time you access an entity, the persistence provider accesses several tables and has to join them. On the other hand, secondary tables can be a good thing when you have expensive attributes such as binary large objects (BLOBs) that you want to isolate in a different table.

Primary Keys

In relational databases, a primary key uniquely identifies each row in a table. It comprises either a single column or set of columns. Primary keys must be unique, as they identify a single row (a null value is not allowed). Examples of primary keys are a customer identifier, a telephone number, an order reference, and an ISBN. JPA requires entities to have an identifier mapped to a primary key, which will follow the same rule: uniquely identify an entity by either a single attribute or a set of attributes (composite key). This entity's primary key value cannot be updated once it has been assigned.

@Id and @GeneratedValue

A simple (i.e., noncomposite) primary key must correspond to a single attribute of the entity class. The @Id annotation that you've seen before is used to denote a simple primary key. @javax.persistence.Id annotates an attribute as being a unique identifier. It can be one of the following types:

- *Primitive Java types*: byte, int, short, long, char
- *Wrapper classes of primitive Java types*: Byte, Integer, Short, Long, Character
- *Arrays of primitive or wrapper types*: int[], Integer[], etc.
- *Strings, numbers, and dates*: java.lang.String, java.math.BigInteger, java.util.Date, java.sql.Date

When creating an entity, the value of this identifier can be generated either manually by the application or automatically by the persistence provider using the @GeneratedValue annotation. This annotation can have four possible values.

- SEQUENCE and IDENTITY specify use of a database SQL sequence or identity column, respectively.
- TABLE instructs the persistence provider to store the sequence name and its current value in a table, increasing the value each time a new instance of the entity is persisted. As an example, EclipseLink creates a SEQUENCE table with two columns: the sequence name (which is an arbitrary name) and the sequence value (an integer automatically incremented by Derby).
- The generation of a key is done automatically (AUTO) by the underlying persistence provider, which will pick an appropriate strategy for a particular database (EclipseLink will use the TABLE strategy). AUTO is the default value of the @GeneratedValue annotation.

If the @GeneratedValue annotation is not defined, the application has to create its own identifier by applying any algorithm that will return a unique value. The code in Listing 5-3 shows how to have an automatically generated identifier. GenerationType.AUTO being the default value, I could have omitted the strategy element. Note that the attribute id is annotated twice, once with @Id and once with @GeneratedValue.

Listing 5-3. The Book Entity with an Automatically Generated Identifier

```
@Entity
public class Book {

    @Id
    @GeneratedValue(strategy = GenerationType.AUTO)
    private Long id;
    private String title;
    private Float price;
    private String description;
```

```
  private String isbn;
  private Integer nbOfPage;
  private Boolean illustrations;

  // Constructors, getters, setters
}
```

Composite Primary Keys

When mapping entities, it is good practice to designate a single dedicated column as the primary key. However, there are cases where a composite primary key is required (such as having to map to a legacy database or when the primary keys have to follow certain business rules–e.g., a date and a value or a country code and a time stamp need to be included). To do this, a primary key class must be defined to represent the composite key. Then, we have two available annotations for defining this class, depending on how we want to structure the entity: @EmbeddedId and @IdClass. As you'll see, the final result is the same, and you will end up having the same database schema, but the way to query the entity is slightly different.

For example, the CD-BookStore application needs to post news frequently on the main page where you can see daily news about books, music, or artists. The news has content, a title, and, because it can be written in several languages, a language code (EN for English, PT for Portuguese, etc.). The primary key of the news could then be the title and the language code because an article can be translated into multiple languages but keep its original title. So the primary key class NewsId is composed of two attributes of type String: title and language. Primary key classes must include method definitions for equals() and hashCode() in order to manage queries and internal collections (equality for these methods must be consistent with the database equality), and their attributes must be in the set of valid types listed previously. They must also be public, implement Serializable if they need to cross architectural layers (e.g., they will be managed in the persistent layer and used in the presentation layer), and have a no-arg constructor.

@EmbeddedId

As you will see later in this chapter, JPA uses different sorts of embedded objects. To summarize, an embedded object doesn't have any identity (no primary key of its own), and its attributes will end up as columns in the table of the entity that contains it.

Listing 5-4 shows the NewsId class as an embeddable class. It is just an embedded object (annotated with @Embeddable) that happens to be composed of two attributes (title and language). This class must have no-arg constructor, getter, setter, equals(), and hashCode() implementations; that is, it needs to use the JavaBean conventions. The class itself doesn't have an identity of its own (no @Id annotation). That's a characteristic of an embeddable.

Listing 5-4. The Primary Key Class Is Annotated with @Embeddable

```
@Embeddable
public class NewsId {

  private String title;
  private String language;

  // Constructors, getters, setters, equals, and hashcode
}
```

The News entity, shown in Listing 5-5, then has to embed the primary key class NewsId with the @EmbeddedId annotation. With this approach, there is no need to use @Id. Every @EmbeddedId must refer to an embeddable class marked with @Embeddable.

Listing 5-5. *The Entity Embeds the Primary Key Class with @EmbeddedId*

```
@Entity
public class News {

    @EmbeddedId
    private NewsId id;
    private String content;

    // Constructors, getters, setters
}
```

In the next chapter I describe how to find entities using their primary key. Just as a first glimpse, here is how it works: the primary key is a class with a constructor. You have to instantiate this class with the values that form your unique key, and pass this object to the entity manager (the em attribute) as shown in the code that follows:

```
NewsId pk = new NewsId("Richard Wright has died on September 2008", "EN")
News news = em.find(News.class, pk);
```

@IdClass

The other method of declaring a composite key is through the @IdClass annotation. It's a different approach whereby each attribute on the primary key class also needs to be declared on the entity class and annotated with @Id.

The composite primary key in the example NewsId in Listing 5-6 is just a POJO that does not require any annotation (in the previous example of Listing 5-5, the primary key class needs to be annotated with @EmbeddedId).

Listing 5-6. *The Primary Key Class Has No Annotation*

```
public class NewsId {

private String title;
  private String language;

  // Constructors, getters, setters, equals, and hashcode
}
```

Then, the entity News, shown in Listing 5-7, has to define the primary key using the @IdClass annotation and annotate each key with @Id. To persist the News entity, you will have to set a value to the title and the language attributes.

Listing 5-7. *The Entity Defines Its Primary Class with the @IdClass Annotation*

```
@Entity
@IdClass(NewsId.class)
public class News {

@Id private String title;
@Id private String language;
private String content;

  // Constructors, getters, setters
}
```

Both approaches, @EmbeddedId and @IdClass, will be mapped to the same table structure. This structure is defined in Listing 5-8 using the data definition language (DDL). The attributes of the entity and the primary key will end up in the same table, and the primary key will be formed with the attributes of the composite class (title and language).

Listing 5-8. DDL of the NEWS Table with a Composite Primary Key

```
create table NEWS (
    CONTENT VARCHAR(255),
    TITLE VARCHAR(255) not null,
    LANGUAGE VARCHAR(255) not null,
    primary key (TITLE, LANGUAGE)
);
```

The @IdClass approach is more prone to error, as you need to define each primary key attribute in both the @IdClass and the entity, taking care to use the same name and Java type. The advantage is that you don't need to change the code of the primary key class (no annotation is needed). For example, you could use a legacy class that, for legal reasons, you are not allowed to change but that you can reuse.

One visible difference is in the way you reference the entity in JPQL. In the case of @IdClass, you would do something like the following:

```
select n.title from News n
```

With @EmbeddedId, you would have something like the following:

```
select n.newsId.title from News n
```

Attributes

An entity must have a primary key (simple or compound) to be able to have an identity in a relational database. It also has all sorts of different attributes, making up its state, that have to be mapped to the table. This state can include almost every Java type that you could want to map.

- Java primitive types (int, double, float, etc.) and the wrapper classes (Integer, Double, Float, etc.);

- Arrays of bytes and characters (byte[ ], Byte[ ], char[ ], Character[ ]);

- String, large numeric, and temporal types (java.lang.String, java.math.BigInteger, java.math.BigDecimal, java.util.Date, java.util.Calendar, java.sql.Date, java.sql.Time, java.sql.Timestamp);

- Enumerated types and user-defined types that implement the Serializable interface; and

- Collections of basic and embeddable types.

Of course, an entity can also have entity attributes, collections of entities, or embeddable classes. This requires introducing relationships between entities (which will be covered in the "Relationship Mapping" section).

As you've seen, with configuration by exception, attributes are mapped using default mapping rules. However, sometimes you need to customize parts of this mapping. That's where JPA annotations (or their XML equivalent) come into play.

@Basic

The optional @javax.persistence.Basic annotation (see Listing 5-9) is the simplest type of mapping to a database column, as it overrides basic persistence.

Listing 5-9. *@Basic Annotation Elements*

```
@Target({METHOD, FIELD}) @Retention(RUNTIME)
public @interface Basic {
  FetchType fetch() default EAGER;
  boolean optional() default true;
}
```

This annotation has two parameters: optional and fetch. The optional element gives a hint as to whether the value of the attribute may be null. It is disregarded for primitive types. The fetch element can take two values: LAZY or EAGER. It gives a hint to the persistence provider runtime that data should be fetched lazily (only when the application asks for the property) or eagerly (when the entity is initially loaded by the provider).

For example, take the Track entity shown in Listing 5-10. A CD album is made up of several tracks, and each track has a title, a description, and a WAV file of a certain duration that you can listen to. The WAV file is a BLOB that can be a few megabytes long. When you access the Track entity, you don't want to eagerly load the WAV file; you can annotate the attribute with @Basic(fetch = FetchType.LAZY) so the data will be retrieved from the database lazily (only when you access the wav attribute using its getter, for example).

Listing 5-10. *The Track Entity with Lazy Loading on the WAV Attribute*

```
@Entity
public class Track {

  @Id @GeneratedValue(strategy = GenerationType.AUTO)
  private Long id;
  private String title;
  private Float duration;
  @Basic(fetch = FetchType.LAZY)
  @Lob
  private byte[] wav;
  private String description;

  // Constructors, getters, setters
}
```

Note that the wav attribute of type byte[ ] is also annotated with @Lob to store the value as a large object (LOB). Database columns that can store these types of large objects require special JDBC calls to be accessed from Java. To inform the provider, an additional @Lob annotation must be added to the basic mapping.

@Column

The @javax.persistence.Column annotation, shown in Listing 5-11, defines the properties of a column. You can change the column name (which by default is mapped to an attribute of the same name); specify the size; and authorize (or not) the column to have a null value, to be unique, or to allow its value to be updatable or insertable. Listing 5-11 shows the @Column annotation API with the elements and their default values.

Listing 5-11. @Column Annotation Elements

```
@Target({METHOD, FIELD}) @Retention(RUNTIME)
public @interface Column {
  String name() default "";
  boolean unique() default false;
  boolean nullable() default true;
  boolean insertable() default true;
  boolean updatable() default true;
  String columnDefinition() default "";
  String table() default "";
  int length() default 255;
  int precision() default 0; // decimal precision
  int scale() default 0;     // decimal scale
}
```

To redefine the default mapping of the original Book entity (Listing 5-1), you can use the @Column annotation in various ways (see Listing 5-12). For example, you can change the name of the title and nbOfPage column or the length of the description, and not allow null values. Note that not all the combinations of attributes on datatypes are valid (e.g., length only applies to string-valued column, scale and precision only to decimal column).

Listing 5-12. Customizing Mapping for the Book Entity

```
@Entity
public class Book {

  @Id @GeneratedValue(strategy = GenerationType.AUTO)
  private Long id;
  @Column(name = "book_title", nullable = false, updatable = false)
  private String title;
  private Float price;
  @Column(length = 2000)
  private String description;
  private String isbn;
  @Column(name = "nb_of_page", nullable = false)
  private Integer nbOfPage;
  private Boolean illustrations;

  // Constructors, getters, setters
}
```

The Book entity in Listing 5-12 will get mapped to the table definition in Listing 5-13.

Listing 5-13. BOOK Table Definition

```
create table BOOK (
  ID BIGINT not null,
  BOOK_TITLE VARCHAR(255) not null,
  PRICE DOUBLE(52, 0),
  DESCRIPTION VARCHAR(2000),
  ISBN VARCHAR(255),
```

```
NB_OF_PAGE INTEGER not null,
ILLUSTRATIONS SMALLINT,
 primary key (ID)
);
```

Most of the elements of the @Column annotation have an influence on the mapping. If you change the length of the description attribute to 2000, the destination column length will also be set at 2000. The updatable and insertable settings default to true, which means that any attribute can be inserted or updated in the database, and have an influence during runtime. You can set them to false when you want the persistence provider to ensure that it will not insert or update the data to the table in response to changes in the entity. Note that this does not imply that the entity attribute will not change in memory. You can still change the value in memory, but it will not be synchronized with the database. That's because the generated SQL statement (INSERT or UPDATE) will not include the columns. In other words, these elements do not affect the relational mapping; they affect the dynamic behavior of the entity manager when accessing the relational data.

■ **Note**   As seen in Chapter 3, Bean Validation defines constraints only within the Java space. So @NotNull reads as a piece of Java code that checks that an attribute's value is not null. On the other hand, the JPA @Column(nullable = false) is used in the database space to generate the database schema. Both JPA and Bean Validation annotations can coexist on an attribute.

@Temporal

In Java, you can use java.util.Date and java.util.Calendar to store data and then have several representations of it, such as a date, an hour, or milliseconds. To specify this in ORM, you can use the @javax.persistence.Temporal annotation. This has three possible values: DATE, TIME, or TIMESTAMP precision (i.e., the actual date, only the time, or both). Listing 5-14 defines a Customer entity that has a date of birth and a technical attribute that stores the exact time it was created in the system (this uses the TIMESTAMP value).

Listing 5-14. The Customer Entity with Two @Temporal Attributes

```
@Entity
public class Customer {

  @Id @GeneratedValue
  private Long id;
  private String firstName;
  private String lastName;
  private String email;
  private String phoneNumber;
  @Temporal(TemporalType.DATE)
  private Date dateOfBirth;
  @Temporal(TemporalType.TIMESTAMP)
  private Date creationDate;

  // Constructors, getters, setters
}
```

The Customer entity in Listing 5-14 will get mapped to the table defined in Listing 5-15. The dateOfBirth attribute is mapped to a column of type DATE and the creationDate attribute to a column of type TIMESTAMP.

Listing 5-15. CUSTOMER Table Definition

```
create table CUSTOMER (
  ID BIGINT not null,
  FIRSTNAME VARCHAR(255),
  LASTNAME VARCHAR(255),
  EMAIL VARCHAR(255),
  PHONENUMBER VARCHAR(255),
  DATEOFBIRTH DATE,
  CREATIONDATE TIMESTAMP,
  primary key (ID)
);
```

@Transient

With JPA, as soon as a class is annotated with @Entity, all its attributes are automatically mapped to a table. If you do not need to map an attribute, you can use the @javax.persistence.Transient annotation or the java transient keyword. For example, let's take the same Customer entity and add an age attribute (see Listing 5-16). Because age can be automatically calculated from the date of birth, the age attribute does not need to be mapped and therefore can be transient.

Listing 5-16. The Customer Entity with a Transient Age

```
@Entity
public class Customer {

  @Id @GeneratedValue
  private Long id;
  private String firstName;
  private String lastName;
  private String email;
  private String phoneNumber;
  @Temporal(TemporalType.DATE)
  private Date dateOfBirth;
  @Transient
  private Integer age;
  @Temporal(TemporalType.TIMESTAMP)
  private Date creationDate;

  // Constructors, getters, setters
}
```

As a result, the age attribute doesn't need any AGE column to be mapped to.

@Enumerated

Java SE 5 introduced enumeration types, which are now so frequently used that they are commonly part of the developer's life. The values of an enum are constants and have an implicit ordinal assignment that is determined by the order in which they are declared. This ordinal cannot be modified at runtime but can be used to store the value of the enumerated type in the database. Listing 5-17 shows a credit card–type enumeration.

Listing 5-17. Credit Card–Type Enumeration

```
public enum CreditCardType {
  VISA,
  MASTER_CARD,
  AMERICAN_EXPRESS
}
```

The ordinals assigned to the values of this enumerated type at compile time are 0 for VISA, 1 for MASTER_CARD, and 2 for AMERICAN_EXPRESS. By default, the persistence providers will map this enumerated type to the database assuming that the column is of type Integer. Looking at the code in Listing 5-18, you see a CreditCard entity that uses the previous enumeration with the default mapping.

Listing 5-18. Mapping an Enumerated Type with Ordinals

```
@Entity
@Table(name = "credit_card")
public class CreditCard {

  @Id
  private String number;
  private String expiryDate;
  private Integer controlNumber;
  private CreditCardType creditCardType;

  // Constructors, getters, setters
}
```

Because the defaults are applied, the enumeration will get mapped to an integer column, and it will work fine. But imagine introducing a new constant to the top of the enumeration. Because ordinal assignment is determined by the order in which values are declared, the values already stored in the database will no longer match the enumeration. A better solution would be to store the name of the value as a String instead of storing the ordinal. You can do this by adding an @Enumerated annotation to the attribute and specifying a value of STRING (ORDINAL is the default value), as shown in Listing 5-19.

Listing 5-19. Mapping an Enumerated Type with String

```
@Entity
@Table(name = "credit_card")
public class CreditCard {

  @Id
  private String number;
  private String expiryDate;
  private Integer controlNumber;
  @Enumerated(EnumType.STRING)
  private CreditCardType creditCardType;

  // Constructors, getters, setters
}
```

Now the CreditCardType database column will be of type VARCHAR and a Visa card will be stored with the String "VISA."

Access Type

Until now I have shown you annotated classes (@Entity or @Table) and attributes (@Basic, @Column, @Temporal, etc.), but the annotations applied on an attribute (or field access) can also be set on the corresponding getter method (or property access). For example, the annotation @Id can be set on the id attribute or on the getId() method. As this is largely a matter of personal preference, I tend to use property access (annotate the getters), as I find the code more readable. This allows me to quickly read the attributes of an entity without drowning in annotations. In this book, for easy readability, I've decided to annotate the attributes. But in some cases (e.g., with inheritance), it is not simply a matter of personal taste, as it can have an impact upon your mapping.

■ **Note** Java defines a field as an instance attribute. A property is any field with accessor (getter and setter) methods that follow the Java bean pattern (starts with getXXX, setXXX, or isXXX for a Boolean).

When choosing between field access (attributes) or property access (getters), you are specifying *access type*. By default, a single access type applies to an entity: it is either field access or property access, but not both (i.e., the persistence provider accesses persistent state either via attributes or via the getter methods). The specification states that the behavior of an application that mixes the placement of annotations on fields and properties, without explicitly specifying the access type, is undefined. When you use field-based access (see Listing 5-20), the persistence provider maps the attributes.

Listing 5-20. The Customer Entity with Annotated Fields

```
@Entity
public class Customer {

    @Id @GeneratedValue
    private Long id;
    @Column(name = "first_name", nullable = false, length = 50)
    private String firstName;
    @Column(name = "last_name", nullable = false, length = 50)
    private String lastName;
    private String email;
    @Column(name = "phone_number", length = 15)
    private String phoneNumber;

    // Constructors, getters, setters
}
```

When you use property-based access, as shown in Listing 5-21, the mapping is based on the getters rather than the attributes. All getters not annotated with the @Transient annotation are persistent.

Listing 5-21. The Customer Entity with Annotated Properties

```
@Entity
public class Customer {

    private Long id;
    private String firstName;
    private String lastName;
```

```java
  private String email;
  private String phoneNumber;

  // Constructors

  @Id @GeneratedValue
  public Long getId() {
    return id;
  }
  public void setId(Long id) {
    this.id = id;
  }

  @Column(name = "first_name", nullable = false, length = 50)
  public String getFirstName() {
    return firstName;
  }
  public void setFirstName(String firstName) {
    this.firstName = firstName;
  }

  @Column(name = "last_name", nullable = false, length = 50)
  public String getLastName() {
    return lastName;
  }
  public void setLastName(String lastName) {
    this.lastName = lastName;
  }

  public String getEmail() {
    return email;
  }
  public void setEmail(String email) {
    this.email = email;
  }

  @Column(name = "phone_number", length = 15)
  public String getPhoneNumber() {
    return phoneNumber;
  }
  public void setPhoneNumber(String phoneNumber) {
    this.phoneNumber = phoneNumber;
  }
}
```

In terms of mapping, the two entities in Listings 5-20 and 5-21 are completely identical because the attribute names happen to be the same as the getter names. But instead of using the default access type, you can explicitly specify the type by means of the @javax.persistence.Access annotation.

This annotation takes two possible values, FIELD or PROPERTY, and can be used on the entity itself and/or on each attribute or getter. For example, when an @Access(AccessType.FIELD) is applied to the entity, only mapping annotations placed on the attributes will be taken into account by the persistence provider. It is then possible to selectively designate individual getters for property access with @Access(AccessType.PROPERTY).

Explicit access types can be very useful (e.g., with embeddables and inheritance), but mixing them often results in errors. Listing 5-22 shows an example of what might happen when you mix access types.

Listing 5-22. The Customer Entity That Explicitly Mixes Access Types

```
@Entity
@Access(AccessType.FIELD)
public class Customer {

  @Id @GeneratedValue
  private Long id;
  @Column(name = "first_name", nullable = false, length = 50)
  private String firstName;
  @Column(name = "last_name", nullable = false, length = 50)
  private String lastName;
  private String email;
  @Column(name = "phone_number", length = 15)
  private String phoneNumber;

  // Constructors, getters, setters

  @Access(AccessType.PROPERTY)
  @Column(name = "phone_number", length = 555)
  public String getPhoneNumber() {
    return phoneNumber;
  }
  public void setPhoneNumber(String phoneNumber) {
    this.phoneNumber = phoneNumber;
  }
}
```

The example in Listing 5-22 explicitly defines the access type as being FIELD at the entity level. This indicates to the persistence manager that it should only process annotations on attributes. The phoneNumber attribute is annotated with @Column, which restricts its length to 15. Reading this code, you expect to end up with a VARCHAR(15) in the database, but this is not what happens. The getter method shows the access type for the getPhoneNumber() method has been explicitly changed, and so has the length of the phone number (to 555). In this case, the entity AccessType.FIELD is overwritten by AccessType.PROPERTY. You will then get a VARCHAR(555) in the database.

Collection of Basic Types

Collections of things are extremely common in Java. In the upcoming sections, you will learn about relationships between entities (which can be collections of entities). Basically, this means that one entity has a collection of other entities or embeddables. In terms of mapping, each entity is mapped to its own table, and references between primary and foreign keys are created. As you know, an entity is a Java class with an identity and many other attributes. But what if you only need to store a collection of Java types such as Strings or Integers? Since JPA 2.0, you can easily do this without having to go through the trouble of creating a separate class by using the @ElementCollection and @CollectionTable annotations.

We use the @ElementCollection annotation to indicate that an attribute of type java.util.Collection contains a collection of instances of basic types (i.e., nonentities) or embeddables (more on that in the "Embeddables" section). In fact, this attribute can be of the following types:

- java.util.Collection: Generic root interface in the collection hierarchy.

- java.util.Set: Collection that prevents the insertion of duplicate elements.

- java.util.List: Collection used when the elements need to be retrieved in some user-defined order.

In addition, the @CollectionTable annotation allows you to customize details of the collection table (i.e., the table that will join the entity table with the basic types table) such as its name. If this annotation is missing, the table name will be the concatenation of the name of the containing entity and the name of the collection attribute, separated by an underscore.

Once again, using the example Book entity, let's see how to add an attribute to store tags. Today, tags and tag clouds are everywhere; these tend to be very useful for sorting data, so imagine for this example you want to add as many tags as you can to a book to describe it and to find it quickly. A tag is just a String, so the Book entity could have a collection of Strings to store this information, as shown in Listing 5-23.

Listing 5-23. The Book Entity with a Collection of Strings

```
@Entity
public class Book {

  @Id @GeneratedValue
  private Long id;
  private String title;
  private Float price;
  private String description;
  private String isbn;
  private Integer nbOfPage;
  private Boolean illustrations;
  @ElementCollection(fetch = FetchType.LAZY)
  @CollectionTable(name = "Tag")
  @Column(name = "Value")
  private List<String> tags = new ArrayList<>();

  // Constructors, getters, setters
}
```

The @ElementCollection annotation in Listing 5-23 is used to inform the persistence provider that the tags attribute is a list of Strings and should be fetched lazily. If @CollectionTable is missing, the table name defaults to BOOK_TAGS (a concatenation of the name of the containing entity and the name of the collection attribute, separated by an underscore) instead of TAG as specified in the name element (name = "Tag"). Notice that I've added a complementary @Column annotation to rename the column to VALUE (if not, the column would be named like the attribute, TAGS). Figure 5-2 shows the result.

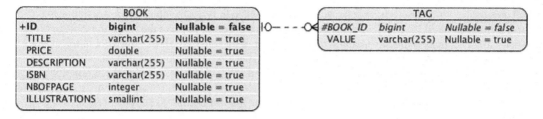

Figure 5-2. *Relationship between the BOOK and the TAG tables*

■ **Note**   In JPA 1.0, these annotations didn't exist. However, you were still able to store a list of primitive types as a BLOB in the database. Why? Because `java.util.ArrayList` implements `Serializable`, and JPA can map `Serializable` objects to BLOBs automatically. However, if you used `java.util.List` instead, you would have an exception as it doesn't extend `Serializable`. The `@ElementCollection` is a more elegant and useful way of storing lists of basic types. Storing lists in an inaccessible binary format makes it opaque to queries and not portable to other languages (since only Java runtimes can make use of the underlying serialized object—not Ruby, PHP . . .).

Map of Basic Types

Like collections, maps are very useful to store data. In JPA 1.0, keys could only be a basic datatype and values only entities. Now, maps can contain any combination of basic types, embeddable objects, and entities as keys or values, which brings significant flexibility to the mapping. But let's focus on maps of basic types.

When the map employs basic types, the `@ElementCollection` and `@CollectionTable` annotations can be used in the same way you saw previously with collections. A collection table is then used to store the data of the map.

Let's take an example with a CD album that contains tracks (see Listing 5-24). A track can be seen as a title and a position (the first track of the album, the second track of the album, etc.). You could then have a map of tracks with an integer for the position (the key of the map) and a String for the title (the value of the map).

Listing 5-24. A CD Album with a Map of Tracks

```
@Entity
public class CD {

  @Id @GeneratedValue
  private Long id;
  private String title;
  private Float price;
  private String description;
  @Lob
  private byte[] cover;
  @ElementCollection
  @CollectionTable(name="track")
  @MapKeyColumn (name = "position")
  @Column(name = "title")
  private Map<Integer, String> tracks = new HashMap<>();

  // Constructors, getters, setters
}
```

As discussed previously, the @ElementCollection annotation is used to indicate the objects in the map that are stored in a collection table. The @CollectionTable annotation changes the default name of the collection table to TRACK.

The difference with collections is the introduction of a new annotation: @MapKeyColumn. This annotation is used to specify the mapping for the key column of the map. If it is not specified, the column is named with the concatenation of the name of the referencing relationship attribute and _KEY. Listing 5-24 shows the annotation renamed to POSITION from the default (TRACK_KEY) to be clearer.

The @Column annotation indicates that the column containing the map value should be renamed TITLE. Figure 5-3 shows the result.

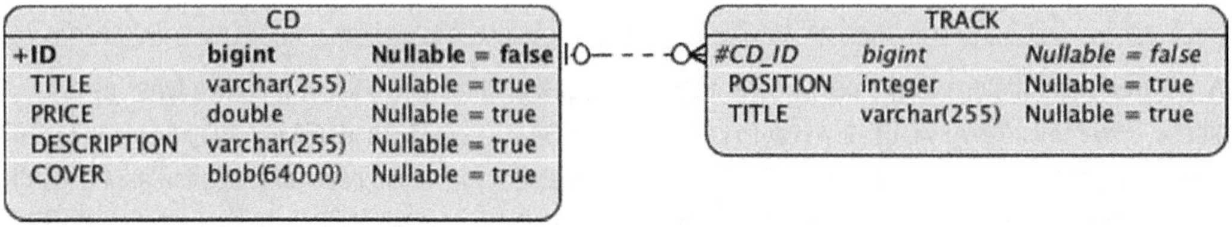

Figure 5-3. *Relationship between the CD and the TRACK tables*

Mapping with XML

Now that you are more familiar with elementary mapping using annotations, let's take a look at XML mapping. If you have used an object-relational framework such as the early versions of Hibernate, you will be familiar with how to map your entities in a separate XML deployment descriptors file. Since the beginning of this chapter, you haven't seen a single line of XML, just annotations. JPA also offers, as an option, an XML syntax to map entities. I will not go into too much detail about the XML mapping, as I've decided to focus on annotations (because they are easier to use in a book and most developers choose them over XML mapping). Keep in mind that every single annotation you see in this chapter has an XML equivalent, and this section would be huge if I covered them all. I encourage you to check Chapter 12 (XML Object/Relational Mapping Descriptor) of the JPA 2.1 specification, which covers all the XML tags in more detail.

XML deployment descriptors are an alternative to using annotations. However, although each annotation has an equivalent XML tag and vice versa, there is a difference in that the XML overrides annotations. If you annotate an attribute or an entity with a certain value, and at the same time you deploy an XML descriptor with a different value, the XML will take precedence.

The question is, when should you use annotations over XML and why? First of all, it's a matter of taste, as the behavior of both is exactly the same. When the metadata are really coupled to the code (e.g., a primary key), it does make sense to use annotations, since the metadata are just another aspect of the program. Other kinds of metadata, such as the column length or other schema details, can be changed depending on the deployment environment (e.g., the database schema is different in the development, test, or production environment). A similar situation arises when a JPA-based product needs to support several different database vendors. Certain id generation, column options, and so on may need to be adjusted depending on the database type in use. This may be better expressed in external XML deployment descriptors (one per environment) so the code doesn't have to be modified.

Let's again turn to the Book entity example. This time imagine you have two environments, and you want to map the Book entity to the BOOK table in the development environment and to the BOOK_XML_MAPPING table in the test environment. The class will only be annotated with @Entity (see Listing 5-25) and not include information about the table it should be mapped to (i.e., it will have no @Table annotation). The @Id annotation defines the primary key as being autogenerated, and a @Column annotation sets the size of the description to 500 characters long.

Listing 5-25. The Book Entity with Only a Few Annotations

```
@Entity
public class Book {
  @Id @GeneratedValue
  private Long id;
  private String title;
  private Float price;
  @Column(length = 500)
  private String description;
  private String isbn;
  private Integer nbOfPage;
  private Boolean illustrations;
  // Constructors, getters, setters
}
```

In a separate book_mapping.xml file (see Listing 5-26), following a specified XML schema, you can change the mapping for any data of the entity. The <table> tag allows you to change the name of the table to which the entity will be mapped (BOOK_XML_MAPPING instead of the default BOOK). Inside the <attributes> tag, you can customize the attributes, specifying not only their name and length but also their relationships with other entities. For example, you can change the mapping for the title column and the number of pages (nbOfPage).

Listing 5-26. Mapping the File META-INF/book_mapping.xml

```
<?xml version="1.0" encoding="UTF-8"?>
<entity-mappings xmlns="http://java.sun.com/xml/ns/persistence/orm"
                 xmlns:xsi="http://www.w3.org/2001/XMLSchema-instance"
                 xsi:schemaLocation="http://java.sun.com/xml/ns/persistence/orm ↪
                 http://java.sun.com/xml/ns/persistence/orm_2_1.xsd"
                 version="2.1">

  <entity class="org.agoncal.book.javaee7.chapter05.Book">
    <table name="book_xml_mapping"/>
    <attributes>
      <basic name="title">
        <column name="book_title" nullable="false" updatable="false"/>
      </basic>
      <basic name="description">
        <column length="2000"/>
      </basic>

      <basic name="nbOfPage">
        <column name="nb_of_page" nullable="false"/>
      </basic>
    </attributes>
  </entity>

</entity-mappings>
```

An important notion to always have in mind is that the XML takes precedence over annotations. Even if the `description` attribute is annotated by `@Column(length = 500)`, the length of the column used is the one in the `book_mapping.xml` file (Listing 5-26), which is 2000. This can be confusing as you look at the code and see 500 and then check the DDL and see 2000; always remember to check the XML deployment descriptor.

A result of merging the XML metadata and the annotations metadata is that the Book entity will get mapped to the `BOOK_XML_MAPPING` table structure defined in Listing 5-27. If you want to completely ignore the annotations and define your mapping with XML only, you can add the`<xml-mapping-metadata-complete>` tag to the `book_mapping.xml` file (in this case, all the annotations will be ignored even if the XML does not contain an override).

Listing 5-27. BOOK_XML_MAPPING Table Structure

```
create table BOOK_XML_MAPPING (
  ID BIGINT not null,
  BOOK_TITLE VARCHAR(255) not null,
  DESCRIPTION VARCHAR(2000),
  NB_OF_PAGE INTEGER not null,
  PRICE DOUBLE(52, 0),
  ISBN VARCHAR(255),
  ILLUSTRATIONS SMALLINT,
  primary key (ID)
);
```

There is only one piece of information missing to make this work. In your `persistence.xml` file, you need to reference the `book_mapping.xml` file, and for this you have to use the`<mapping-file>` tag. The `persistence.xml` defines the entity persistence context and the database it should be mapped to. It is the central piece of information that the persistence provider needs to reference external XML mapping. Deploy the Book entity with both XML files in the `META-INF` directory and you are done (see Listing 5-28).

Listing 5-28. A persistence.xml File Referring to an External Mapping File

```
<?xml version="1.0" encoding="UTF-8"?>
<persistence xmlns="http://java.sun.com/xml/ns/persistence"
             xmlns:xsi="http://www.w3.org/2001/XMLSchema-instance"
             xsi:schemaLocation="http://java.sun.com/xml/ns/persistence ↪
             http://java.sun.com/xml/ns/persistence/persistence_2_1.xsd"
             version="2.1">

  <persistence-unit name="chapter05PU" transaction-type="RESOURCE_LOCAL">
    <provider>org.eclipse.persistence.jpa.PersistenceProvider</provider>
    <class>org.agoncal.book.javaee7.chapter05.Book</class>
    <mapping-file>META-INF/book_mapping.xml</mapping-file>
    <properties>
      <!--Persistence provider properties-->
    </properties>
  </persistence-unit>
</persistence>
```

Embeddables

In the "Composite Primary Keys" section earlier in the chapter, you saw how a class could be embedded and used as a primary key with the @EmbeddedId annotation. Embeddables are objects that don't have a persistent identity on their own; they can only be embedded within owning entities. The owning entity can have collections of embeddables as well as a single embeddable attribute. They are stored as an intrinsic part of an owning entity and share the identity of this entity. This means each attribute of the embedded object is mapped to the table of the entity. It is a strict ownership relationship (a.k.a. composition), so that if the entity is removed, the embedded object is also removed.

This composition between two classes uses annotations. The included class uses the @Embeddable annotation, whereas the entity that includes the class uses @Embedded. Let's take the example of a customer that has an identifier, a name, an e-mail address, and an address. All these attributes could be in a Customer entity (see Listing 5-30), but, for object-modeling reasons, they are split into two classes: Customer and Address. Because Address has no identity of its own but is merely part of the Customer state, it is a good candidate to become an embeddable object instead of an entity (see Listing 5-29).

Listing 5-29. The Address Class Is an Embeddable

```
@Embeddable
public class Address {

  private String street1;
  private String street2;
  private String city;
  private String state;
  private String zipcode;
  private String country;

  // Constructors, getters, setters
}
```

As you can see in Listing 5-29, the Address class is not annotated as being an entity but as an embeddable. The @Embeddable annotation specifies that Address can be embedded in another entity class (or another embeddable). On the other side of the composition, the Customer entity has to use the @Embedded annotation to specify that Address is a persistent attribute that will be stored as an intrinsic part and share its identity (see Listing 5-30).

Listing 5-30. The Customer Entity Embedding an Address

```
@Entity
public class Customer {

  @Id @GeneratedValue
  private Long id;
  private String firstName;
  private String lastName;
  private String email;
  private String phoneNumber;
  @Embedded
  private Address address;

  // Constructors, getters, setters
}
```

Each attribute of Address is mapped to the table of the owning entity Customer. There will only be one table with the structure defined in Listing 5-31. As you'll see later in the section "Overriding Attributes," entities can override the attributes of embeddables (using the @AttributeOverrides annotation).

Listing 5-31. Structure of the CUSTOMER Table with All the Address Attributes

```
create table CUSTOMER (
  ID BIGINT not null,
  LASTNAME VARCHAR(255),
  PHONENUMBER VARCHAR(255),
  EMAIL VARCHAR(255),
  FIRSTNAME VARCHAR(255),
  STREET2 VARCHAR(255),
  STREET1 VARCHAR(255),
  ZIPCODE VARCHAR(255),
  STATE VARCHAR(255),
  COUNTRY VARCHAR(255),
  CITY VARCHAR(255),
  primary key (ID)
);
```

■ **Note** In the previous sections I showed you how to map collections and maps of basic datatypes. In JPA 2.1, the same is possible with embeddables. You can map collections of embeddables as well as maps of embeddables (the embeddable can be either the key or the value of the map).

Access Type of an Embeddable Class

The access type of an embeddable class is determined by the access type of the entity class in which it exists. If the entity explicitly uses a property access type, an embeddable object will implicitly use property access as well. A different access type for an embeddable class can be specified by means of the @Access annotation.

The Customer entity (see Listing 5-32) and Address entity (see Listing 5-33) use different access types.

Listing 5-32. The Customer Entity with Field Access Type

```
@Entity
@Access(AccessType.FIELD)
public class Customer {

  @Id @GeneratedValue
  private Long id;
  @Column(name = "first_name", nullable = false, length = 50)
  private String firstName;
  @Column(name = "last_name", nullable = false, length = 50)
  private String lastName;
  private String email;
  @Column(name = "phone_number", length = 15)
  private String phoneNumber;
```

```
@Embedded
private Address address;

// Constructors, getters, setters
}
```

Listing 5-33. The Embeddable Object with Property Access Type

```
@Embeddable
@Access(AccessType.PROPERTY)
public class Address {

  private String street1;
  private String street2;
  private String city;
  private String state;
  private String zipcode;
  private String country;

  // Constructors

  @Column(nullable = false)
  public String getStreet1() {
    return street1;
  }
  public void setStreet1(String street1) {
    this.street1 = street1;
  }

  public String getStreet2() {
    return street2;
  }
  public void setStreet2(String street2) {
    this.street2 = street2;
  }

  @Column(nullable = false, length = 50)
  public String getCity() {
    return city;
  }
  public void setCity(String city) {
    this.city = city;
  }

  @Column(length = 3)
  public String getState() {
    return state;
  }
  public void setState(String state) {
    this.state = state;
  }
```

```
@Column(name = "zip_code", length = 10)
public String getZipcode() {
  return zipcode;
}
public void setZipcode(String zipcode) {
  this.zipcode = zipcode;
}

public String getCountry() {
  return country;
}
public void setCountry(String country) {
  this.country = country;
}
}
```

Explicitly setting the access type on embeddables is strongly recommended to avoid mapping errors when an embeddable is embedded by multiple entities. For example, let's extend our model by adding an Order entity as shown in Figure 5-4. Address is now embedded by Customer (the home address of the customer) and Order (the delivery address).

Figure 5-4. *Address is embedded by Customer and Order*

Each entity defines a different access type: Customer uses field access, whereas Order uses property access. As an embeddable object's access type is determined by the access type of the entity class in which it is declared, Address will be mapped in two different ways, which can cause mapping problems. To avoid this, the Address access type should be set explicitly.

■ **Note**   Explicit access types are also very helpful in inheritance. By default, the leaf entities inherit the access type of their root entity. In a hierarchy of entities, each can be accessed differently from the other classes in the hierarchy. Including an @Access annotation will cause the default access mode in effect for the hierarchy to be locally overridden.

Relationship Mapping

The world of object-oriented programming abounds with classes and associations between classes. These associations are structural in that they link objects of one kind to objects of another, allowing one object to cause another to perform an action on its behalf. Several types of associations can exist between classes.

First of all, an association has a direction. It can be *unidirectional* (i.e., one object can navigate toward another) or *bidirectional* (i.e., one object can navigate toward another and vice versa). In Java, you use the dot (.) syntax to navigate through objects. For example, when you write customer.getAddress().getCountry(), you navigate from the object Customer to Address and then to Country.

In Unified Modeling Language (UML), to represent a unidirectional association between two classes, you use an arrow to indicate the orientation. In Figure 5-5, Class1 (the source) can navigate to Class2 (the target), but not the inverse.

Figure 5-5. *A unidirectional association between two classes*

To indicate a bidirectional association, no arrows are used. As demonstrated in Figure 5-6, Class1 can navigate to Class2 and vice versa. In Java, this is represented as Class1 having an attribute of type Class2 and Class2 having an attribute of type Class1.

Figure 5-6. *A bidirectional association between two classes*

An association also has a *multiplicity* (or *cardinality*). Each end of an association can specify how many referring objects are involved in the association. The UML diagram in Figure 5-7 shows that one Class1 refers to zero or more instances of Class2.

Figure 5-7. *Multiplicity on class associations*

In UML, a cardinality is a range between a minimum and a maximum number. So 0..1 means that you will have at minimum zero objects and at maximum one object. 1 means that you have one and only one instance. 1..* means that you can have one or many instances, and 3..6 means that you have a range of between three and six objects. In Java, an association that represents more than one object uses collections of type java.util.Collection, java.util.Set, java.util.List, or even java.util.Map.

A relationship has an ownership (i.e., the owner of the relationship). In a unidirectional relationship, ownership is implied: in Figure 5-5, there is no doubt that the owner is Class1, but in a bidirectional relationship, as depicted in Figure 5-6, the owner has to be specified explicitly. You then show the owner, which specifies the physical mapping, and the inverse side (the non-owning side).

In the next sections, you'll see how to map collections of objects with JPA annotations.

Relationships in Relational Databases

In the relational world, things are different because, strictly speaking, a relational database is a collection of *relations* (also called *tables*), which means anything you model is a table. To model an association, you don't have lists, sets, or maps; you have tables. In JPA when you have an association between one class and another, in the database you will get a table reference. This reference can be modeled in two different ways: by using a *foreign key* (a *join column*) or by using a *join table*. In database terms, a column that refers to a key of another table is a *foreign key column*.

As an example, consider that a customer has one address. In Listing 5-32 and Listing 5-33 we modeled this relation as an embeddable, but let's now turn it into a *one-to-one relationship*. In Java, you would have a Customer class with an Address attribute. In a relational world, you could have a CUSTOMER table pointing to an ADDRESS through a foreign key column (or join column), as described in Figure 5-8.

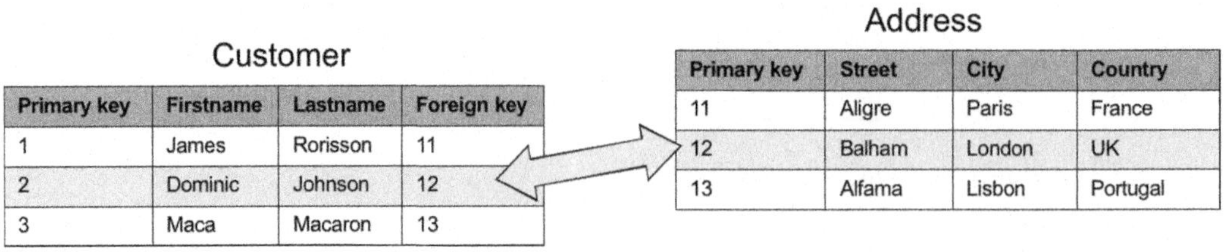

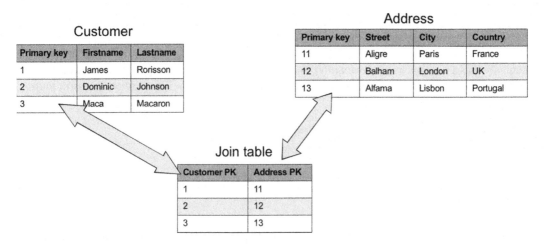

Figure 5-8. *A relationship using a join column*

There is a second way of modeling—using a join table. The CUSTOMER table in Figure 5-9 doesn't store the foreign key of the ADDRESS anymore. An intermediate table is created to hold the relationship information by storing the foreign keys of both tables.

Figure 5-9. *A relationship using a join table*

You wouldn't use a join table to represent a one-to-one relationship, as this could have performance issues (you always need to access a third table to get the address of a customer). Join tables are generally used when you have one-to-many or many-to-many cardinalities. As you will see in the following section, JPA uses these two modes to map object associations.

Entity Relationships

Now back to JPA. Most entities need to be able to reference, or have relationships with, other entities. This is what produces the domain model graphs that are common in business applications. JPA makes it possible to map associations so that an entity can be linked to another in a relational model. Like the elementary mapping annotations that you saw previously, JPA uses configuration by exception for associations. It has a default way of storing a relationship, but, if this doesn't suit your database model, you have several annotations you can use to customize the mapping.

The cardinality between two entities may be one-to-one, one-to-many, many-to-one, or many-to-many. Each respective mapping is named after the cardinality of the source and target:@OneToOne, @OneToMany, @ManyToOne, or @ManyToMany annotations. Each annotation can be used in a unidirectional or bidirectional way. Table 5-1 shows all the possible combinations between cardinalities and directions.

Table 5-1. *All Possible Cardinality-Direction Combinations*

Cardinality	Direction
One-to-one	Unidirectional
One-to-one	Bidirectional
One-to-many	Unidirectional
Many-to-one/one-to-many	Bidirectional
Many-to-one	Unidirectional
Many-to-many	Unidirectional
Many-to-many	Bidirectional

You will see that unidirectional and bidirectional are repetitive concepts that apply in the same way to all cardinalities. Next, you will see the difference between unidirectional and bidirectional relationships and then implement some of these combinations. I will not go through the complete catalog of the combinations but just focus on a subset. Explaining all the combinations would get repetitive. The important point is that you understand how to map cardinality and direction in relationships.

Unidirectional and Bidirectional

From an object-modeling point of view, direction between classes is natural. In a unidirectional association, object A points only to object B; in a bidirectional association, both objects refer to each other. However, some work is necessary when mapping a bidirectional relationship to a relational database, as illustrated by the following example involving a customer who has a home address.

In a unidirectional relationship, a Customer entity has an attribute of type Address (see Figure 5-10). The relationship is one-way, navigating from one side to the other. Customer is said to be the owner of the relationship. In terms of the database, this means the CUSTOMER table will have a foreign key (join column) pointing to ADDRESS, and, when you own a relationship, you are able to customize the mapping of this relationship. For example, if you need to change the name of the foreign key, the mapping will be done in the Customer entity (i.e., the owner).

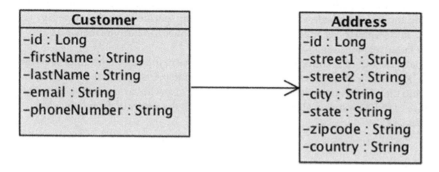

Figure 5-10. *A unidirectional association between* Customer *and* Address

As mentioned previously, relationships can also be bidirectional. To be able to navigate between Address and Customer, you need to transform a unidirectional relationship into a bidirectional one by adding a Customer attribute to the Address entity (see Figure 5-11). Note that UML class diagrams do not show attributes representing a relationship.

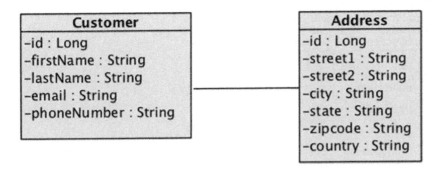

Figure 5-11. *A bidirectional association between* Customer *and* Address

In terms of Java code and annotations, it is similar to having two separate one-to-one mappings, one in each direction. You can think of a bidirectional relationship as a pair of unidirectional relationships, going both ways (see Figure 5-12).

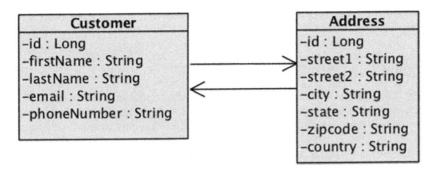

Figure 5-12. *A bidirectional association represented with two arrows*

How do you map a pair of unidirectional relationships? Who is the owner of this bidirectional relationship? Who owns the mapping information of the join column or the join table? If unidirectional relationships have an owning side, bidirectional ones have both an owning and an inverse side, which have to be explicitly specified with the mappedBy element of the @OneToOne, @OneToMany, and @ManyToMany annotations. mappedBy identifies the attribute that owns the relationship and is required for bidirectional relationships.

By way of explanation, let's compare the Java code (on one side) and the database mapping (on the other). As you can see on the left side of Figure 5-13, both entities point to each other through attributes: Customer has an address attribute annotated with @OneToOne, and the Address entity has a customer attribute also with an annotation. On the right side, the database mapping shows a CUSTOMER and an ADDRESS table. CUSTOMER is the owner of the relationship because it contains the ADDRESS foreign key.

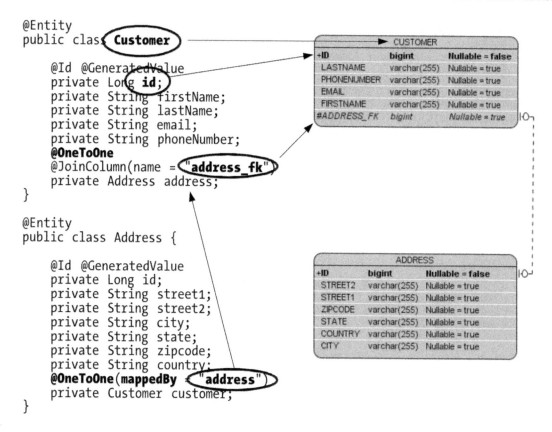

Figure 5-13. *Customer and Address code with database mapping*

In Figure 5-13 the Address entity uses the mappedBy element on its @OneToOne annotation. Address is called the inverse owner of the relationship because it has a mappedBy element. The mappedBy element indicates that the join column (address) is specified at the other end osf the relationship. In fact, at the other end, the Customer entity defines the join column by using the @JoinColumn annotation and renames the foreign key to address_fk. Customer is the owning side of the relationship, and, as the owner, it is the one to define the join column mapping. Address is the inverse side where the table of the owning entity contains the foreign key (the CUSTOMER table is the one with the ADDRESS_FK column).

There is a mappedBy element on the @OneToOne, @OneToMany, and @ManyToMany annotations, but not on the @ManyToOne annotation. You cannot have a mappedBy attribute on both sides of a bidirectional association. It would also be incorrect to not have it on either side as the provider would treat it as two independent unidirectional relationships. This would imply that each side is the owner and can define a join column.

■ **Note** If you are familiar with earlier versions of Hibernate, you might think of the JPA mappedBy as the equivalent of the Hibernate inverse attribute.

@OneToOne Unidirectional

A one-to-one unidirectional relationship between entities has a reference of cardinality 1, which can be reached in only one direction. Referring to the example of a customer and her address, assume the customer has only one address (cardinality 1). It is important to navigate from the customer (the source) toward the address (the target) to know where the customer lives. However, for some reason, in our model shown in Figure 5-14, you don't need to be able to navigate in the opposite direction (e.g., you don't need to know which customer lives at a given address).

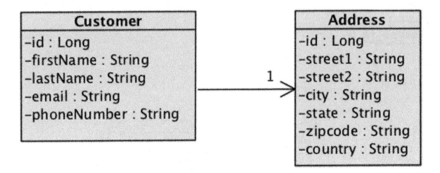

Figure 5-14. *One customer has one address*

In Java, a unidirectional relationship means that the Customer will have an Address attribute (Listing 5-34) but Address will not have a Customer attribute (Listing 5-35).

Listing 5-34. A Customer with One Address

```
@Entity
public class Customer {

    @Id @GeneratedValue
    private Long id;
    private String firstName;
    private String lastName;
    private String email;
    private String phoneNumber;
    private Address address;

    // Constructors, getters, setters
}
```

Listing 5-35. An Address Entity

```
@Entity
public class Address {

    @Id @GeneratedValue
    private Long id;
    private String street1;
    private String street2;
    private String city;
    private String state;
```

```
  private String zipcode;
  private String country;

  // Constructors, getters, setters
}
```

As you can see in Listings 5-34 and 5-35, these two entities have the minimum required annotations: @Entity plus @Id and @GeneratedValue for the primary key, that's all. With configuration by exception, the persistence provider will map these two entities to two tables and a foreign key for the relationship (from the customer pointing to the address). A one-to-one mapping is triggered by the fact that Address is declared an entity and includes the Customer entity as an attribute. We automatically imply a relationship by using an entity as a property on another entity so we don't need a @OneToOne annotation, as it relies on the defaults (see Listings 5-36 and 5-37).

Listing 5-36. The CUSTOMER Table with a Foreign Key to Address

```
create table CUSTOMER (
  ID BIGINT not null,
  FIRSTNAME VARCHAR(255),
  LASTNAME VARCHAR(255),
  EMAIL VARCHAR(255),
  PHONENUMBER VARCHAR(255),
  ADDRESS_ID BIGINT,
  primary key (ID),
  foreign key (ADDRESS_ID) references ADDRESS(ID)
);
```

Listing 5-37. The ADDRESS Table

```
create table ADDRESS (
  ID BIGINT not null,
  STREET1 VARCHAR(255),
  STREET2 VARCHAR(255),
  CITY VARCHAR(255),
  STATE VARCHAR(255),
  ZIPCODE VARCHAR(255),
  COUNTRY VARCHAR(255),
  primary key (ID)
);
```

As you now know, with JPA, if you do not annotate an attribute, the default mapping rules are applied. So, by default, the name of the foreign key column is ADDRESS_ID (see Listing 5-36), which is the concatenation of the name of the relationship attribute (here address), the symbol _, and the name of the primary key column of the destination table (here it will be the column ID of the ADDRESS table). Also notice that, in the DDL, the ADDRESS_ID column is nullable by default, meaning that, by default, a one-to-one association is mapped to a zero (null value) or one.

To customize the mapping, you can use two annotations. The first one is @OneToOne (that's because the cardinality of the relation is one), and it can modify some attributes of the association itself such as the way it has to be fetched. Listing 5-38 defines the API of the @OneToOne annotation.

Listing 5-38. @OneToOne Annotation API

```
@Target({METHOD, FIELD}) @Retention(RUNTIME)
public @interface OneToOne {
  Class targetEntity() default void.class;
  CascadeType[] cascade() default {};
  FetchType fetch() default EAGER;
  boolean optional() default true;
  String mappedBy() default "";
  boolean orphanRemoval() default false;
}
```

The other is @JoinColumn (its API is very similar to @Column shown in Listing 5-11). It is used to customize the join column, meaning the foreign key, of the owning side. Listing 5-39 shows how you would use these two annotations.

Listing 5-39. The Customer Entity with Customized Relationship Mapping

```
@Entity
public class Customer {

  @Id @GeneratedValue
  private Long id;
  private String firstName;
  private String lastName;
  private String email;
  private String phoneNumber;
  @OneToOne (fetch = FetchType.LAZY)
  @JoinColumn(name = "add_fk", nullable = false)
  private Address address;

  // Constructors, getters, setters
}
```

In JPA, a foreign key column is called a join column. The @JoinColumn annotation allows you to customize the mapping of a foreign key. It Listing 5-39 uses it to rename the foreign key column to ADD_FK and make the relationship obligatory by refusing the null value (nullable=false). The @OneToOne annotation gives the persistence provider a hint to fetch the relationship lazily (more on that later).

@OneToMany Unidirectional

A one-to-many relationship is when one source object refers to an ensemble of target objects. For example, a purchase order is composed of several order lines (see Figure 5-15). The order line could refer to the purchase order with a corresponding @ManyToOne annotation, but it's not the case as the relationship is unidirectional. Order is the "one" side and the source of the relationship, and OrderLine is the "many" side and the target.

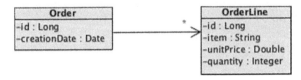

Figure 5-15. One order has several lines

The cardinality is multiple, and the navigation is done only from Order toward OrderLine. In Java, this multiplicity is described by the Collection, List, and Set interfaces of the java.util package. Listing 5-40 shows the code of the Order entity with a one-way, one-to-many relationship toward OrderLine (see Listing 5-41).

Listing 5-40. An Order Contains OrderLines

```
@Entity
public class Order {

  @Id @GeneratedValue
  private Long id;
  @Temporal(TemporalType.TIMESTAMP)
  private Date creationDate;
  private List<OrderLine> orderLines;

  // Constructors, getters, setters
}
```

Listing 5-41. An OrderLine

```
@Entity
@Table(name = "order_line")
public class OrderLine {

  @Id @GeneratedValue
  private Long id;
  private String item;
  private Double unitPrice;
  private Integer quantity;

  // Constructors, getters, setters
}
```

The Order in Listing 5-40 doesn't have any special annotation and relies on the configuration-by-exception paradigm. The fact that a collection of an entity type is being used as an attribute on this entity triggers a OneToMany relationship mapping by default. By default, one-to-many unidirectional relationships use a join table to keep the relationship information, with two foreign key columns. One foreign key column refers to the table ORDER and has the same type as its primary key, and the other refers to ORDER_LINE. The name of this joined table is the name of both entities, separated by the _ symbol. The join table is named ORDER_ORDER_LINE and will result in the schema structure illustrated in Figure 5-16.

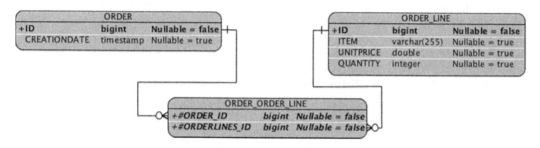

Figure 5-16. *Join table between ORDER and ORDER_LINE*

If you don't like the join table and foreign key names, or if you are mapping to an existing table, you can use JPA annotations to redefine these default values. The default value for a join column is the concatenation of the name of the entity, the symbol _, and the name of the referenced primary key. As the @JoinColumn annotation can be used to change the foreign key columns, the @JoinTable annotation (see Listing 5-42) can do the same for the join table mapping. You can also use the @OneToMany annotation (see Listing 5-43), which like @OneToOne customizes the relationship itself (using fetch mode, etc.).

Listing 5-42. @JoinTable Annotation API

```java
@Target({METHOD, FIELD}) @Retention(RUNTIME)
public @interface JoinTable {
  String name() default "";
  String catalog() default "";
  String schema() default "";
  JoinColumn[] joinColumns() default {};
  JoinColumn[] inverseJoinColumns() default {};
  UniqueConstraint[] uniqueConstraints() default {};
  Index[] indexes() default {};
}
```

Listing 5-43. The Order Entity with Annotated One-to-Many Relationship

```java
@Entity
public class Order {

  @Id @GeneratedValue
  private Long id;
  @Temporal(TemporalType.TIMESTAMP)
  private Date creationDate;
  @OneToMany
  @JoinTable(name = "jnd_ord_line",
    joinColumns = @JoinColumn(name = "order_fk"),
    inverseJoinColumns = @JoinColumn(name = "order_line_fk") )
  private List<OrderLine> orderLines;

  // Constructors, getters, setters
}
```

On the API of the @JoinTable annotation in Listing 5-42, you can see two attributes that are of type @JoinColumn: joinColumns and inverseJoinColumns. These two attributes are distinguished by means of the owning side and the inverse side. The joinColumns element describes the owning side (the owner of the relationship) and, in our example, refers to the ORDER table. The inverseJoinColumns element specifies the inverse side, the target of the relationship, and refers to ORDER_LINE.

Using the Order entity (see Listing 5-43), you can add the @OneToMany and @JoinTable annotations on the orderLines attribute by renaming the join table to JND_ORD_LINE (instead of ORDER_ORDER_LINE), as well as the two foreign key columns.

The Order entity in Listing 5-43 will be mapped to the join table described in Listing 5-44.

Listing 5-44. Structure of the Join Table Between Order and Order_Line

```
create table JND_ORD_LINE (
  ORDER_FK BIGINT not null,
  ORDER_LINE_FK BIGINT not null,
  primary key (ORDER_FK, ORDER_LINE_FK),
  foreign key (ORDER_LINE_FK) references ORDER_LINE(ID),
  foreign key (ORDER_FK) references ORDER(ID)
);
```

The default rule for a one-to-many unidirectional relationship is to use a join table, but it is very easy (and useful for legacy databases) to change to using foreign keys. The Order entity has to provide a @JoinColumn annotation instead of a @JoinTable, allowing the code to be changed as shown inListing 5-45.

Listing 5-45. The Order Entity with a Join Column

```
@Entity
public class Order {

  @Id @GeneratedValue
  private Long id;
  @Temporal(TemporalType.TIMESTAMP)
  private Date creationDate;
  @OneToMany(fetch = FetchType.EAGER)
  @JoinColumn(name = "order_fk")
  private List<OrderLine> orderLines;

  // Constructors, getters, setters
}
```

The code of the OrderLine entity (shown previously in Listing 5-41) doesn't change. Notice that in Listing 5-45 the @OneToMany annotation is overriding the default fetch mode (turning it to EAGER instead of LAZY). By using @JoinColumn, the foreign key strategy then maps the unidirectional association. The foreign key is renamed to ORDER_FK by the annotation and exists in the target table (ORDER_LINE). The result is the database structure shown in Figure 5-17. There is no join table, and the reference between both tables is through the foreign key ORDER_FK.

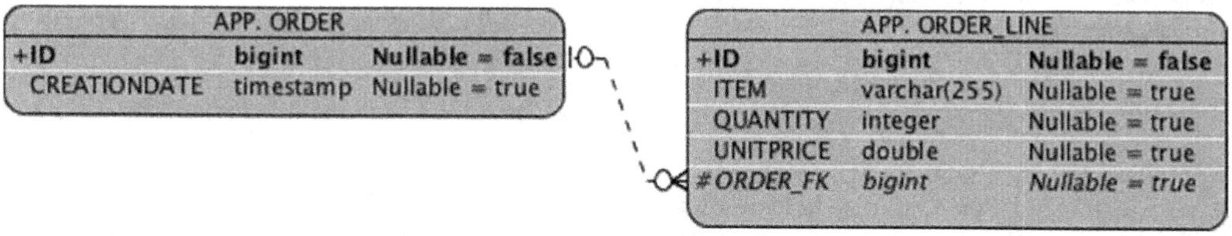

APP. ORDER		
+ID	bigint	Nullable = false
CREATIONDATE	timestamp	Nullable = true

APP. ORDER_LINE		
+ID	bigint	Nullable = false
ITEM	varchar(255)	Nullable = true
QUANTITY	integer	Nullable = true
UNITPRICE	double	Nullable = true
# ORDER_FK	bigint	Nullable = true

Figure 5-17. *Join column between Order and Order_Line*

@ManyToMany Bidirectional

A many-to-many bidirectional relationship exists when one source object refers to many targets, and when a target refers to many sources. For example, a CD album is created by several artists, and an artist appears on several albums. In the Java world, each entity will have a collection of target entities. In the relational world, the only way to map a many-to-many relationship is to use a join table (a join column does not work), and, as you've seen previously, in a bidirectional relationship you need to explicitly define the owner (with the mappedBy element).

Assuming the Artist entity is the owner of the relationship means that the CD is the reverse owner (see Listing 5-46) and needs to use the mappedBy element on its @ManyToMany annotation. mappedBy tells the persistence provider that appearsOnCDs is the name of the corresponding attribute of the owning entity.

Listing 5-46. Several Artists Appear in One CD

```
@Entity
public class CD {

  @Id @GeneratedValue
  private Long id;
  private String title;
  private Float price;
  private String description;
  @ManyToMany(mappedBy = "appearsOnCDs")
  private List<Artist> createdByArtists;

  // Constructors, getters, setters
}
```

So, if the Artist is the owner of the relationship, as shown in Listing 5-47, it is the one to customize the mapping of the join table via the @JoinTable and @JoinColumn annotations.

Listing 5-47. One Artist Appears on Several CD Albums

```
@Entity
public class Artist {

  @Id @GeneratedValue
  private Long id;
  private String firstName;
  private String lastName;
  @ManyToMany
  @JoinTable(name = "jnd_art_cd", ↵
    joinColumns = @JoinColumn(name = "artist_fk"), ↵
    inverseJoinColumns = @JoinColumn(name = "cd_fk"))
  private List<CD>appearsOnCDs;

  // Constructors, getters, setters
}
```

As you can see in Listing 5-47, the join table between Artist and CD is renamed to JND_ART_CD as well as each join column (thanks to the @JoinTable annotation). The joinColumns element refers to the owning side (the Artist) and the inverseJoinColumns refers to the inverse owning side (the CD). Figure 5-18 illustrates the database structure.

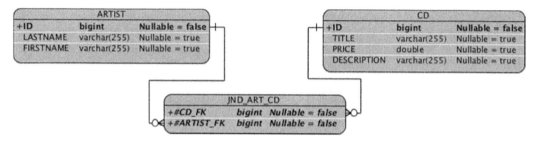

Figure 5-18. *Artist, CD, and the join table*

Note that on a many-to-many and one-to-one bidirectional relationship, either side may be designated as the owning side. No matter which side is designated as the owner, the other side should include the mappedBy element. If not, the provider will think that both sides are the owner and will treat it as two separate one-to-many unidirectional relationships. That could result in four tables: ARTIST and CD, plus two joining tables, ARTIST_CD and CD_ARTIST. Nor would it be legal to have a mappedBy on both sides.

Fetching Relationships

All the annotations that you have seen (@OneToOne, @OneToMany, @ManyToOne, and @ManyToMany) define a fetching attribute, specifying the associated objects to be loaded immediately (eagerly) or deferred (lazily), with a resulting impact on performance. Depending on your application, certain relationships are accessed more often than others. In these situations, you can optimize performance by loading data from the database when the entity is initially read (eagerly) or when it is accessed (lazily). As an example, let's look at some extreme cases.

Imagine four entities all linked to each other with different cardinalities (one-to-one, one-to-many). In the first case (see Figure 5-19), they all have eager relationships. This means that, as soon as you load Class1 (by a find by ID or a query), all the dependent objects are automatically loaded in memory. This can have an impact on the performance of your system.

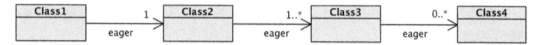

Figure 5-19. *Four entities with eager relationships*

Looking at the opposite scenario, all the relationships use a lazy fetch mode (see Figure 5-20). When you load Class1, nothing else is loaded (except the direct attributes of Class1, of course). You need to explicitly access Class2 (e.g., by using the getter method) to tell the persistence provider to load the data from the database, and so on. If you want to manipulate the entire object graph, you need to explicitly call each entity.

```
class1.getClass2().getClass3().getClass4()
```

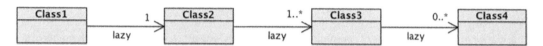

Figure 5-20. *Four entities with lazy relationships*

But don't think that EAGER is evil and LAZY is good. EAGER will bring all the data into memory using a small amount of database access (the persistence provider will probably use join queries to join the tables together and extract the data). With LAZY, you don't take the risk of filling up your memory because you control which object is loaded. But you have to access the database every time.

The fetch parameter is very important because if it is misused, it can cause performance problems. Each annotation has a default fetch value that you have to be aware of and, if not appropriate, change (see Table 5-2).

Table 5-2. *Default Fetching Strategies*

Annotation	Default Fetching Strategy
@OneToOne	EAGER
@ManyToOne	EAGER
@OneToMany	LAZY
@ManyToMany	LAZY

If, when you load a purchase order in your application, you always need to access its order lines, then it may be efficient to change the default fetch mode of the @OneToMany annotation to EAGER (see Listing 5-48).

Listing 5-48. An Order with an Eager Relationship to OrderLine

```
@Entity
public class Order {

  @Id @GeneratedValue
  private Long id;
  @Temporal(TemporalType.TIMESTAMP)
  private Date creationDate;
  @OneToMany(fetch = FetchType.EAGER)
  private List<OrderLine> orderLines;

  // Constructors, getters, setters
}
```

Ordering Relationships

With one-to-many or many-to-many relationships, your entities deal with collections of objects. On the Java side, these collections are usually unordered. Neither do relational databases preserve any order in their tables. Therefore, if you want an ordered list, it is necessary to either sort your collection programmatically or use a JPQL query with an Order By clause. JPA has easier mechanisms, based on annotations that can help in ordering relationships.

@OrderBy

Dynamic ordering can be done with the @OrderBy annotation. "Dynamically" means that you order the elements of a collection when you retrieve the association.

The example of the CD-BookStore application allows a user to write news about music and books. This news is displayed on the web site and once published, people are allowed to add comments (see Listing 5-49). On the web site you want to display the comments chronologically, so ordering comes into account.

Listing 5-49. A Comment Entity with a Posted Date

```
@Entity
public class Comment {

  @Id @GeneratedValue
  private Long id;
  private String nickname;
  private String content;
  private Integer note;
  @Column(name = "posted_date")
  @Temporal(TemporalType.TIMESTAMP)
  private Date postedDate;

  // Constructors, getters, setters
}
```

The comments are modeled using the Comment entity, shown in Listing 5-49. It has content, is posted by a user (identified by a nickname) who leaves a note on the news, and has a posted date of type TIMESTAMP which the system automatically creates. In the News entity, shown in Listing 5-50, you want to be able to arrange the list of comments ordered by posted date in descending order. To achieve this, you use the @OrderBy annotation in conjunction with the @OneToMany annotation.

Listing 5-50. The Comments of a News Entity Are Ordered by Descending Posted Date

```
@Entity
public class News {

  @Id @GeneratedValue
  private Long id;
  @Column(nullable = false)
  private String content;
  @OneToMany(fetch = FetchType.EAGER)
  @OrderBy("postedDate DESC")
  private List<Comment> comments;

  // Constructors, getters, setters
}
```

The @OrderBy annotation takes the names of the attributes on which the sorting has to be made (the postedDate attribute), as well as the method (ascending or descending). The String ASC or DESC can be used for sorting in either an ascending or descending manner, respectively. You can have several columns used in the @OrderBy annotation. If you need to order by posted date and note, you can use OrderBy("postedDate DESC, note ASC").

The @OrderBy annotation doesn't have any impact on the database mapping. The persistence provider is simply informed to use an order by clause when the collection is retrieved at runtime.

@OrderColumn

JPA 1.0 supported dynamic ordering using the @OrderBy annotation but did not include support for maintaining a persistent ordering. Since JPA 2.0 this is possible by adding the annotation @OrderColumn (its API is similar to @Column on Listing 5-11). This annotation informs the persistence provider that it is required to maintain the ordered list using a separate column where the index is stored. The @OrderColumn defines this separate column.

Let's use the news and comments example and change it slightly. This time the Comment entity, shown in Listing 5-51, has no postedDate attribute, and therefore there is no way to chronologically sort the comments.

Listing 5-51. A Comment Entity with No Posted Date

```
@Entity
public class Comment {

  @Id @GeneratedValue
  private Long id;
  private String nickname;
  private String content;
  private Integer note;

  // Constructors, getters, setters
}
```

To keep an ordering without posted date, the News entity (shown in Listing 5-52) can annotate the relationship with @OrderColumn. The persistence provider will then map the News entity to a table with an additional column to store the ordering.

Listing 5-52. The Ordering of Comments Is Persisted

```
@Entity
public class News {

  @Id @GeneratedValue
  private Long id;
  @Column(nullable = false)
  private String content;
  @OneToMany(fetch = FetchType.EAGER)
  @OrderColumn(name = "posted_index")
  private List<Comment> comments;

  // Constructors, getters, setters
}
```

In Listing 5-52, the @OrderColumn renames the additional column to POSTED_INDEX. If the name is not overridden, by default the column name is the concatenation of the name of the entity attribute and the _ORDER string (COMMENTS_ORDER in our example). The type of this column must be a numerical type. This ordered relationship will map to a separate join table as shown in the following:

```
create table NEWS_COMMENT (
    NEWS_ID BIGINT not null,
    COMMENTS_ID BIGINT not null,
    POSTED_INDEX INTEGER
);
```

There are performance impacts to be aware of; as with the @OrderColumn annotation, the persistence provider must also track changes to the index. It is responsible for maintaining the order upon insertion, deletion, or reordering. If data are inserted in the middle of an existing, sorted list of information, the persistence provider will have to reorder the entire index.

Portable applications should not expect a list to be ordered by the database, under the pretext that some database engines automatically optimize their indexes so that the data table appears as sorted. Instead, it should use either the @OrderColumn or @OrderBy construct. Note that you can't use both annotations at the same time.

Inheritance Mapping

Since their creation, object-oriented languages have used the inheritance paradigm. C++ allows multiple inheritance, and Java supports single-class inheritance. In object-oriented languages, developers commonly reuse code by inheriting attributes and behavior of root classes.

You have just studied relationships, and relationships between entities have a very straightforward mapping to a relational database. This is not the case with inheritance. Inheritance is a completely unknown concept and not natively implemented in a relational world. The concept of inheritance throws in several twists when saving objects into a relational database.

How do you organize a hierarchical model into a flat relational one? JPA has three different strategies you can choose from.

- *A single-table-per-class hierarchy strategy*: The sum of the attributes of the entire entity hierarchy is flattened down to a single table (this is the default strategy).

- *A joined-subclass strategy*: In this approach, each entity in the hierarchy, concrete or abstract, is mapped to its own dedicated table.

- *A table-per-concrete-class strategy*: This strategy maps each concrete entity hierarchy to its own separate table.

■ **Note** Support for the table-per-concrete-class inheritance mapping strategy is still optional in JPA 2.1. Portable applications should avoid using it until officially mandated.

Leveraging the easy use of annotations, JPA 2.1 delivers declarative support for defining and mapping inheritance hierarchies, including entities, abstract entities, mapped classes, and transient classes. The @Inheritance annotation is used on the root entity to dictate the mapping strategy to itself and to the leaf classes. JPA also transposes the object notion of overriding to the mapping, which allows root class attributes to be overridden by child classes. In the upcoming section, you will also see how the access type can be used with inheritance to mix field access and property access.

Inheritance Strategies

When it comes to mapping inheritance, JPA supports three different strategies. When an entity hierarchy exists, it always has an entity as its root. The root entity class can define the inheritance strategy by using the strategy element of @Inheritance to one of the options defined in the javax.persistence.InheritanceType enumerated type. If it doesn't, the default single-table-per-class hierarchy strategy will be applied. To explore each strategy, I discuss how to map a CD and a Book entity, both inheriting from the Item entity (see Figure 5-21).

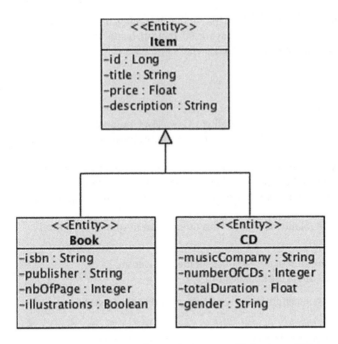

Figure 5-21. *Inheritance hierarchy between CD, Book, and* Item

The Item entity is the root entity and has an identifier, a title, a description, and a price. Both the CD and Book entities inherit from Item. Each of these leaf classes adds extra attributes such as an ISBN for the Book entity or a total time duration for the CD entity.

Single-Table-per-Class Hierarchy Strategy

The default inheritance mapping strategy is the single-table-per-class strategy, in which all the entities in the hierarchy are mapped to a single table. As it is the default, you can completely omit the @Inheritance annotation on the root entity (thanks to configuration by exception), and that's what the Item entity does (see Listing 5-53).

Listing 5-53. The Item Entity Uses the Default Single-Table-per-Class Strategy

```
@Entity
public class Item {

  @Id @GeneratedValue
  protected Long id;
  protected String title;
  protected Float price;
  protected String description;

  // Constructors, getters, setters
}
```

Item (Listing 5-53) is the root class for the Book entity (see Listing 5-54) and CD entity (see Listing 5-55). These entities inherit the attributes from Item as well as the default inheritance strategy and therefore don't have to use the @Inheritance annotation.

Listing 5-54. Book Extends Item

```
@Entity
public class Book extends Item {

  private String isbn;
  private String publisher;
  private Integer nbOfPage;
  private Boolean illustrations;

  // Constructors, getters, setters
}
```

Listing 5-55. CD Extends Item

```
@Entity
public class CD extends Item {

  private String musicCompany;
  private Integer numberOfCDs;
  private Float totalDuration;
  private String genre;

  // Constructors, getters, setters
}
```

With what you have seen so far, without inheritance, these three entities would be mapped into their own, separate tables, but with inheritance it's different. With the single-table-per-class strategy (the default one), they all end up in the same database table, which defaults to the name of the root class: ITEM. Figure 5-22 shows the ITEM table structure.

ITEM		
+ID	bigint	Nullable = false
DTYPE	varchar(31)	Nullable = true
TITLE	varchar(255)	Nullable = false
PRICE	double	Nullable = false
DESCRIPTION	varchar(255)	Nullable = true
ILLUSTRATIONS	smallint	Nullable = true
ISBN	varchar(255)	Nullable = true
NBOFPAGE	integer	Nullable = true
PUBLISHER	varchar(255)	Nullable = true
MUSICCOMPANY	varchar(255)	Nullable = true
NUMBEROFCDS	integer	Nullable = true
TOTALDURATION	double	Nullable = true
GENRE	varchar(255)	Nullable = true

Figure 5-22. *ITEM table structure*

As you can see in Figure 5-22, the ITEM table sums all the attributes of the Item, Book, and CD entities. But there's an additional column that doesn't relate to any of the entities' attributes: it's the discriminator column, DTYPE.

The ITEM table will be filled with items, books, and CD albums. When accessing the data, the persistence provider needs to know which row belongs to which entity. This way, the provider will instantiate the appropriate object type (Item, Book, or CD) when reading the ITEM table. That's why a discriminator column is used to explicitly type each row.

Figure 5-23 shows a fragment of the ITEM table with some data. As you can see, the single-table-per-class strategy has some holes; not every column is useful for each entity. The first row is the data stored for an Item entity (the DTYPE column contains the name of the entity). Items only have a title, a price, and a description (see Listing 5-53 earlier); they don't have a music company, an ISBN, and so on. So these columns will always remain empty.

ID	DTYPE	TITLE	PRICE	DESCRIPTION	MUSIC COMPANY	ISBN	...
1	Item	Pen	2.10	Beautiful black pen			...
2	CD	Soul Trane	23.50	Fantastic jazz album	Prestige		...
3	CD	Zoot Allures	18	One of the best of Zappa	Warner		...
4	Book	The robots of dawn	22.30	Robots everywhere		0-554-456	...
5	Book	H2G2	17.50	Funny IT book ;o)		1-278-983	...

Figure 5-23. Fragment of the ITEM table filled with data

The discriminator column is called DTYPE by default, is of type String (mapped to a VARCHAR), and contains the name of the entity. If the defaults don't suit, the @DiscriminatorColumn annotation allows you to change the name and the datatype. By default, the value of this column is the entity name to which it refers, although an entity may override this value using the @DiscriminatorValue annotation.

Listing 5-56 renames the discriminator column to DISC (instead of DTYPE) and changes its datatype to Char instead of String; each entity should then change its discriminator value to I for Item, B for Book (see Listing 5-57), and C for CD (see Listing 5-58).

Listing 5-56. Item Redefines the Discriminator Column

```
@Entity
@Inheritance(strategy = InheritanceType.SINGLE_TABLE)
@DiscriminatorColumn (name="disc", ↪
                      discriminatorType = DiscriminatorType.CHAR)
@DiscriminatorValue("I")
public class Item {

  @Id @GeneratedValue
  protected Long id;
  protected String title;
  protected Float price;
  protected String description;

  // Constructors, getters, setters
}
```

Listing 5-57. Book Redefines the Discriminator Value to B

```
@Entity
@DiscriminatorValue("B")
public class Book extends Item {

  private String isbn;
  private String publisher;
  private Integer nbOfPage;
  private Boolean illustrations;

  // Constructors, getters, setters
}
```

Listing 5-58. CD Redefines the Discriminator Value to C

```
@Entity
@DiscriminatorValue("C")
public class CD extends Item {

  private String musicCompany;
  private Integer numberOfCDs;
  private Float totalDuration;
  private String genre;

  // Constructors, getters, setters
}
```

The root entity Item defines the discriminator column once for the entire hierarchy with @DiscriminatorColumn. It then changes its own default value to I with the @DiscriminatorValue annotation. Child entities have to redefine their own discriminator value only.

Figure 5-24 shows the result. The discriminator column and its values are different from those shown earlier in Figure 5-23.

ID	DISC	TITLE	PRICE	DESCRIPTION	MUSIC COMPANY	ISBN	...
1	I	Pen	2.10	Beautiful black pen			...
2	C	Soul Trane	23.50	Fantastic jazz album	Prestige		...
3	C	Zoot Allures	18	One of the best of Zappa	Warner		...
4	B	The robots of dawn	22.30	Robots everywhere		0-554-456	...
5	B	H2G2	17.50	Funny IT book ;o)		1-278-983	...

Figure 5-24. *The ITEM table with a different discriminator name and values*

The single-table-per-class strategy is the default, is the easiest to understand, and works well when the hierarchy is relatively simple and stable. However, it has some drawbacks; adding new entities to the hierarchy, or adding attributes to existing entities, involves adding new columns to the table, migrating data, and changing indexes. This strategy also requires the columns of the child entities to be nullable. If the ISBN of the Book entity happens to be non-null, you cannot insert a CD anymore, because the CD entity doesn't have an ISBN.

Joined-Subclass Strategy

In the joined-subclass strategy, each entity in the hierarchy is mapped to its own table. The root entity maps to a table that defines the primary key to be used by all tables in the hierarchy, as well as the discriminator column. Each subclass is represented by a separate table that contains its own attributes (not inherited from the root class) and a primary key that refers to the root table's primary key. The nonroot tables do not hold a discriminator column.

You can implement a joined-subclass strategy by annotating the root entity with the @Inheritance annotation as shown in Listing 5-59 (the code of CD and Book is unchanged, the same as before).

Listing 5-59. The Item Entity with a Joined-Subclass Strategy

```
@Entity
@Inheritance(strategy = InheritanceType.JOINED)
public class Item {

    @Id @GeneratedValue
    protected Long id;
    protected String title;
    protected Float price;
    protected String description;

    // Constructors, getters, setters
}
```

From a developer's point of view, the joined-subclass strategy is natural, as each entity, abstract or concrete, will have its state mapped to a different table. Figure 5-25 shows how the Item, Book, and CD entities will be mapped.

BOOK		
+#ID	bigint	Nullable = false
ILLUSTRATIONS	smallint	Nullable = true
ISBN	varchar(255)	Nullable = true
NBOFPAGE	integer	Nullable = true
PUBLISHER	varchar(255)	Nullable = true

ITEM		
+ID	bigint	Nullable = false
DTYPE	varchar(31)	Nullable = true
TITLE	varchar(255)	Nullable = true
PRICE	double	Nullable = true
DESCRIPTION	varchar(255)	Nullable = true

CD		
+#ID	bigint	Nullable = false
MUSICCOMPANY	varchar(255)	Nullable = true
NUMBEROFCDS	integer	Nullable = true
TOTALDURATION	double	Nullable = true
GENRE	varchar(255)	Nullable = true

Figure 5-25. *Mapping inheritance with a joined-subclass strategy*

You can still use @DiscriminatorColumn and @DiscriminatorValue annotations in the root entity to customize the discriminator column and values (the DTYPE column is in the ITEM table).

The joined-subclass strategy is intuitive and is close to what you know from the object inheritance mechanism. But querying can have a performance impact. This strategy is called *joined* because, to reassemble an instance of a subclass, the subclass table has to be joined with the root class table. The deeper the hierarchy, the more joins needed to assemble a leaf entity. This strategy provides good support for polymorphic relationships but requires one or more join operations to be performed when instantiating entity subclasses. This may result in poor performance for extensive class hierarchies. Similarly, queries that cover the entire class hierarchy require join operations between the subclass tables, resulting in decreased performance.

Table-per-Concrete-Class Strategy

In the table-per-class (or table-per-concrete-class) strategy, each entity is mapped to its own dedicated table like the joined-subclass strategy. The difference is that all attributes of the root entity will also be mapped to columns of the child entity table. From a database point of view, this strategy denormalizes the model and causes all root entity attributes to be redefined in the tables of all leaf entities that inherit from it. With the table-per-concrete-class strategy, there is no shared table, no shared columns, and no discriminator column. The only requirement is that all tables must share a common primary key that matches across all tables in the hierarchy.

Mapping our example to this strategy is a matter of specifying a TABLE_PER_CLASS on the @Inheritance annotation (see Listing 5-60) of the root entity (Item).

Listing 5-60. *The Item Entity with a Table-per-Concrete-Class Strategy*

```
@Entity
@Inheritance(strategy = InheritanceType.TABLE_PER_CLASS)
public class Item {

  @Id @GeneratedValue
  protected Long id;
  protected String title;
  protected Float price;
  protected String description;

  // Constructors, getters, setters
}
```

Figure 5-26 shows the ITEM, BOOK, and CD tables. You can see that BOOK and CD duplicate the ID, TITLE, PRICE, and DESCRIPTION columns of the ITEM table. Note that the tables are not linked.

BOOK

+ID	bigint	Nullable = false
TITLE	varchar(255)	Nullable = true
PRICE	double	Nullable = true
ILLUSTRATIONS	smallint	Nullable = true
DESCRIPTION	varchar(255)	Nullable = true
ISBN	varchar(255)	Nullable = true
NBOFPAGE	integer	Nullable = true
PUBLISHER	varchar(255)	Nullable = true

ITEM

+ID	bigint	Nullable = false
TITLE	varchar(255)	Nullable = true
PRICE	double	Nullable = true
DESCRIPTION	varchar(255)	Nullable = true

CD

+ID	bigint	Nullable = false
MUSICCOMPANY	varchar(255)	Nullable = true
NUMBEROFCDS	integer	Nullable = true
TITLE	varchar(255)	Nullable = true
TOTALDURATION	double	Nullable = true
PRICE	double	Nullable = true
DESCRIPTION	varchar(255)	Nullable = true
GENRE	varchar(255)	Nullable = true

Figure 5-26. *BOOK and CD tables duplicating ITEM columns*

Of course, remember that each table can be redefined by annotating each entity with the @Table annotation.

The table-per-concrete-class strategy performs well when querying instances of one entity, as it is similar to using the single-table-per-class strategy: the query is confined to a single table. The downside is that it makes polymorphic queries across a class hierarchy more expensive than the other strategies (e.g., finding all the items, including CDs and books); it must query all subclass tables using a UNION operation, which is expensive when a large amount of data are involved. Support for this strategy is still optional in JPA 2.1.

Overriding Attributes

With the table-per-concrete-class strategy, the columns of the root class are duplicated on the leaf tables. They keep the same name. But what if a legacy database is being used and the columns have a different name? JPA uses the @AttributeOverride annotation to override the column mapping and @AttributeOverrides to override several.

To rename the ID, TITLE, and DESCRIPTION columns in the BOOK and CD tables, the code of the Item entity doesn't change, but the Book entity (see Listing 5-61) and CD entity (see Listing 5-62) have to use the @AttributeOverride annotation.

Listing 5-61. Book Overrides Some Item Columns

```
@Entity
@AttributeOverrides({
  @AttributeOverride(name = "id", ↪
                     column = @Column(name = "book_id")),
  @AttributeOverride(name = "title", ↪
                     column = @Column(name = "book_title")),
  @AttributeOverride(name = "description", ↪
                     column = @Column(name = "book_description"))
})
public class Book extends Item {

  private String isbn;
  private String publisher;
  private Integer nbOfPage;
  private Boolean illustrations;

  // Constructors, getters, setters
}
```

Listing 5-62. CD Overrides Some Item Columns

```
@Entity
@AttributeOverrides({
  @AttributeOverride(name = "id", ↪
                     column = @Column(name = "cd_id")),
  @AttributeOverride(name = "title", ↪
                     column = @Column(name = "cd_title")),
  @AttributeOverride(name = "description", ↪
                     column = @Column(name = "cd_description"))
})
public class CD extends Item {

  private String musicCompany;
  private Integer numberOfCDs;
  private Float totalDuration;
  private String genre;

  // Constructors, getters, setters
}
```

Because there is more than one attribute to override, you need to use @AttributeOverrides, which takes an array of @AttributeOverride annotations. Each annotation then points to an attribute of the Item entity and redefines the mapping of the column using the @Column annotation. So name = "title" refers to the title attribute of the Item entity, and @Column(name = "cd_title") informs the persistence provider that the title has to be mapped to a CD_TITLE column. Figure 5-27 shows the result.

BOOK		
+BOOK_ID	bigint	Nullable = false
BOOK_TITLE	varchar(255)	Nullable = true
BOOK_DESCRIPTION	varchar(255)	Nullable = true
PRICE	double	Nullable = true
ILLUSTRATIONS	smallint	Nullable = true
ISBN	varchar(255)	Nullable = true
NBOFPAGE	integer	Nullable = true
PUBLISHER	varchar(255)	Nullable = true

ITEM		
+ID	bigint	Nullable = false
TITLE	varchar(255)	Nullable = true
PRICE	double	Nullable = true
DESCRIPTION	varchar(255)	Nullable = true

CD		
+CD_ID	bigint	Nullable = false
CD_TITLE	varchar(255)	Nullable = true
CD_DESCRIPTION	varchar(255)	Nullable = true
PRICE	double	Nullable = true
MUSICCOMPANY	varchar(255)	Nullable = true
NUMBEROFCDS	integer	Nullable = true
TOTALDURATION	double	Nullable = true
GENRE	varchar(255)	Nullable = true

Figure 5-27. BOOK and CD tables overriding ITEM columns

■ **Note** In the "Embeddables" section earlier in the chapter, you saw that an embeddable object can be shared by several entities (Address was embedded by Customer and Order). Because embeddable objects are an intrinsic part of an owning entity, each entity's table also duplicates their columns. The @AttributeOverrides can then be used if you need to override the embeddable columns.

Type of Classes in the Inheritance Hierarchy

The previous examples used to explain the mapping strategies only use entities. Item is an entity as well as Book and CD. But entities don't always have to inherit from entities. A hierarchy of classes can mix all sorts of different classes: entities and also nonentities (or transient classes), abstract entities, and mapped superclasses. Inheriting from these different types of classes will have an impact on the mapping.

Abstract Entity

In the previous examples, the Item entity was a concrete class. It was annotated with @Entity and didn't have an abstract keyword, but an abstract class can also be specified as an entity. An abstract entity differs from a concrete entity only in that it cannot be directly instantiated with the new keyword. It provides a common data structure for its leaf entities (Book and CD) and follows the mapping strategies. For the persistence provider, an abstract entity is mapped as an entity. The only difference is in the Java space, not in the mapping.

Nonentity

Nonentities are also called *transient classes*, meaning they are POJOs. An entity may subclass a nonentity or may be extended by a nonentity. Why would you have nonentities in a hierarchy? Object modeling and inheritance are the means through which state and behavior are shared. Nonentities can be used to provide a common data structure to leaf entities. The state of a nonentity superclass is not persistent because it is not managed by the persistence provider (remember that the condition for a class to be managed by the persistence provider is the presence of an @Entity annotation).

For example, Book is an entity (Listing 5-64) and extends from an Item nonentity (Item doesn't have any annotation) as shown in Listing 5-63.

Listing 5-63. Item Is a Simple POJO with No @Entity

```java
public class Item {

  protected String title;
  protected Float price;
  protected String description;

  // Constructors, getters, setters
}
```

The Book entity (Listing 5-64) inherits from Item, so the Java code can access the title, price, and description attributes, plus any other method that is defined, in a normal, object-oriented way. Item can be concrete or abstract and does not have any impact on the final mapping.

Listing 5-64. The Book Entity Extends from a POJO

```java
@Entity
public class Book extends Item {

  @Id @GeneratedValue
  private Long id;
  private String isbn;
  private String publisher;
  private Integer nbOfPage;
  private Boolean illustrations;

  // Constructors, getters, setters
}
```

Book is an entity and extends Item. But only the attributes of Book would be mapped to a table. No attributes from Item appear in the table structure defined in Listing 5-65. To persist a Book, you need to create an instance of Book, set values to any attributes you want (title, price, isbn, publisher, etc.), but only the Book's attributes (id, isbn, etc.) will get persisted.

Listing 5-65. The BOOK Table Has No Attributes from Item

```sql
create table BOOK (
  ID BIGINT not null,
  ILLUSTRATIONS SMALLINT,
  ISBN VARCHAR(255),
  NBOFPAGE INTEGER,
  PUBLISHER VARCHAR(255),
  primary key (ID)
);
```

Mapped Superclass

JPA defines a special kind of class, called a *mapped superclass*, to share state and behavior, as well as mapping information entities inherit from. However, mapped superclasses are not entities. They are not managed by the persistence provider, do not have any table to be mapped to, and cannot be queried or be part of a relationship, but they may provide persistent properties to any entities that extend it. They are similar to embeddable classes except they can be used with inheritance. A class is indicated as being a mapped superclass by annotating it with the @MappedSuperclass annotation.

Using the root class, Item is annotated with @MappedSuperclass, not @Entity, as Listing 5-66 illustrates. It defines an inheritance strategy (JOINED) and annotates some of its attributes with @Column, but because mapped superclasses are not mapped to tables, the @Table annotation is not permitted.

Listing 5-66. Item Is a Mapped Superclass

```java
@MappedSuperclass
@Inheritance(strategy = InheritanceType.JOINED)
public class Item {

  @Id @GeneratedValue
  protected Long id;
  @Column(length = 50, nullable = false)
  protected String title;
  protected Float price;
  @Column(length = 2000)
  protected String description;

  // Constructors, getters, setters
}
```

As you can see in Listing 5-66, the title and description attributes are annotated with @Column. Listing 5-67 shows the Book entity extending Item.

Listing 5-67. Book Extends from a Mapped Superclass

```java
@Entity
public class Book extends Item {

  private String isbn;
  private String publisher;
  private Integer nbOfPage;
  private Boolean illustrations;

  // Constructors, getters, setters
}
```

This hierarchy will be mapped into only one table. Item is not an entity and does not have any table. Attributes of Item and Book would be mapped to columns of the BOOK table, but mapped superclasses also share their mapping information. The @Column annotations of Item will be inherited. But, as mapped superclasses are not managed entities, you would not be able to persist or query them, for example. Listing 5-68 shows the BOOK table structure with customized TITLE and DESCRIPTION columns.

Listing 5-68. The BOOK Table Has All the Attributes from Item

```sql
create table BOOK (
  ID BIGINT not null,
  TITLE VARCHAR(50) not null,
  PRICE DOUBLE(52, 0),
  DESCRIPTION VARCHAR(2000),
  ILLUSTRATIONS SMALLINT,
```

```
    ISBN VARCHAR(255),
    NBOFPAGE INTEGER,
    PUBLISHER VARCHAR(255),
    primary key (ID)
);
```

Summary

Thanks to configuration by exception, not much is required to map entities to tables; inform the persistence provider that a class is actually an entity (using @Entity) and an attribute is its identifier (using @Id), and JPA does the rest. This chapter could have been much shorter if it stuck to the defaults. JPA has a very rich set of annotations to customize every little detail of ORM (as well as the equivalent XML mapping).

Elementary annotations can be used on attributes (@Basic, @Temporal, etc.) or classes to customize the mapping. You can change the table's name or the primary key type, or even avoid mapping with the @Transient annotation. With JPA you can map collections of basic types or embeddables. Depending on your business model, you can map relationships (@OneToOne, @ManyToMany, etc.) of different directions and multiplicity. The same thing applies to inheritance (@Inheritance, @MappedSuperclass, etc.) where you can use different strategies to map a hierarchy of entities and nonentities mixed together.

This chapter focused on the static part of JPA, or how to map entities to tables. The next chapter deals with the dynamic aspects: how to manage and query these entities.

CHAPTER 6

■ ■ ■

Managing Persistent Objects

Java Persistence API has two sides. The first is the ability to map objects to a relational database. Configuration by exception allows persistence providers to do most of the work without much code, but the richness of JPA also allows customized mapping from objects to tables using either annotation or XML descriptors. From simple mapping (changing the name of a column) to more complex mapping (inheritance), JPA offers a wide spectrum of customizations. As a result, you can map almost any object model to a legacy database.

The other aspect of JPA is the ability to query these mapped objects. In JPA, the centralized service to manipulate instances of entities is the entity manager. It provides an API to create, find, remove, and synchronize objects with the database. It also allows the execution of different sorts of JPQL queries, such as dynamic, static, or native queries, against entities. Locking mechanisms are also possible with the entity manager.

The database world relies on Structured Query Language. This programming language is designed for managing relational data (retrieval, insertion, updating, and deletion), and its syntax is table oriented. You can select columns from tables made of rows, join tables together, combine the results of two SQL queries through unions, and so on. There are no objects here, only rows, columns, and tables. In the Java world, where we manipulate objects, a language made for tables (SQL) has to be twisted to suit a language made of objects (Java). This is where Java Persistence Query Language comes into play.

JPQL is the language defined in JPA to query entities stored in a relational database. JPQL syntax resembles SQL but operates against entity objects rather than directly with database tables. JPQL does not see the underlying database structure or deal with tables or columns but rather objects and attributes. And, for that, it uses the dot (.) notation that Java developers are familiar with.

In this chapter, you will learn how to manage persistent objects. This means you will learn how to do create, read, update, and delete (CRUD) operations with the entity manager as well as complex queries using JPQL. This chapter also talks about how JPA handles concurrency as well as second-level cache. The chapter ends by explaining the life cycle of an entity and how JPA allows you to hook in your own business logic when certain events occur on the entity.

Entity Manager

The entity manager is a central piece of JPA. It manages the state and life cycle of entities as well as querying entities within a persistence context. The entity manager is responsible for creating and removing persistent entity instances and finding entities by their primary key. It can lock entities for protecting against concurrent access by using optimistic or pessimistic locking and can use JPQL queries to retrieve entities following certain criteria.

When an entity manager obtains a reference to an entity, it is said to be "managed." Until that point, the entity is seen as a regular POJO (i.e., detached). The strength of JPA is that entities can be used as regular objects by different layers of an application and become managed by the entity manager when you need to load or insert data into the database. When an entity is managed, you can carry out persistence operations, and the entity manager will automatically synchronize the state of the entity with the database. When the entity is detached (i.e., not managed), it returns to a simple POJO and can then be used by other layers (e.g., a JavaServer Faces, or JSF, presentation layer) without synchronizing its state with the database.

With regard to persistence, the real work begins with the entity manager. EntityManager is an interface implemented by a persistence provider that will generate and execute SQL statements. The javax.persistence.EntityManager interface provides the API to manipulate entities (subset shown in Listing 6-1).

Listing 6-1. Subset of the EntityManager API

```java
public interface EntityManager {

    // Factory to create an entity manager, close it and check if it's open
    EntityManagerFactory getEntityManagerFactory();
    void close();
    boolean isOpen();

    // Returns an entity transaction
    EntityTransaction getTransaction();

    // Persists, merges and removes and entity to/from the database
    void persist(Object entity);
    <T> T merge(T entity);
    void remove(Object entity);

    // Finds an entity based on its primary key (with different lock mecanisms)
    <T> T find(Class<T> entityClass, Object primaryKey);
    <T> T find(Class<T> entityClass, Object primaryKey, LockModeType lockMode);
    <T> T getReference(Class<T> entityClass, Object primaryKey);

    // Locks an entity with the specified lock mode type (optimistic, pessimistic...)
    void lock(Object entity, LockModeType lockMode);

    // Synchronizes the persistence context to the underlying database
    void flush();
    void setFlushMode(FlushModeType flushMode);
    FlushModeType getFlushMode();

    // Refreshes the state of the entity from the database, overwriting any changes made
    void refresh(Object entity);
    void refresh(Object entity, LockModeType lockMode);

    // Clears the persistence context and checks if it contains an entity
    void clear();
    void detach(Object entity);
    boolean contains(Object entity);

    // Sets and gets an entity manager property or hint
    void setProperty(String propertyName, Object value);
    Map<String, Object> getProperties();

    // Creates an instance of Query or TypedQuery for executing a JPQL statement
    Query createQuery(String qlString);
    <T> TypedQuery<T> createQuery(CriteriaQuery<T> criteriaQuery);
    <T> TypedQuery<T> createQuery(String qlString, Class<T> resultClass);
```

```
// Creates an instance of Query or TypedQuery for executing a named query
Query createNamedQuery(String name);
<T> TypedQuery<T> createNamedQuery(String name, Class<T> resultClass);

// Creates an instance of Query for executing a native SQL query
Query createNativeQuery(String sqlString);
Query createNativeQuery(String sqlString, Class resultClass);
Query createNativeQuery(String sqlString, String resultSetMapping);

// Creates a StoredProcedureQuery for executing a stored procedure in the database
StoredProcedureQuery createStoredProcedureQuery(String procedureName);
StoredProcedureQuery createNamedStoredProcedureQuery(String name);

// Metamodel and criteria builder for criteria queries (select, update and delete)
CriteriaBuilder getCriteriaBuilder();
Metamodel getMetamodel();
Query createQuery(CriteriaUpdate updateQuery);
Query createQuery(CriteriaDelete deleteQuery);

// Indicates that a JTA transaction is active and joins the persistence context to it
void joinTransaction();
boolean isJoinedToTransaction();

// Return the underlying provider object for the EntityManager
<T> T unwrap(Class<T> cls);
Object getDelegate();

// Returns an entity graph
<T> EntityGraph<T> createEntityGraph(Class<T> rootType);
EntityGraph<?> createEntityGraph(String graphName);
<T> EntityGraph<T> getEntityGraph(String graphName);
<T> List<EntityGraph<? super T>> getEntityGraphs(Class<T> entityClass);
}
```

Don't get scared by the API in Listing 6-1, as this chapter covers most of the methods. In the next section, I explain how to get an instance of an EntityManager.

Obtaining an Entity Manager

The entity manager is the central interface used to interact with entities, but it first has to be obtained by an application. Depending on whether it is a container-managed environment (like you'll see in Chapter 7 with EJBs) or an application-managed environment, the code can be quite different. For example, in a container-managed environment, the transactions are managed by the container. That means you don't need to explicitly write the commit or rollback, which you have to do in an application-managed environment.

The term "application managed" means an application is responsible for explicitly obtaining an instance of EntityManager and managing its life cycle (it closes the entity manager when finished, for example). The code in Listing 6-2 demonstrates how a class running in a Java SE environment gets an instance of an entity manager. It uses the Persistence class to bootstrap an EntityManagerFactory associated with a persistence unit (chapter06PU), which is then used to create an entity manager. Notice that in an application-managed environment the developer is responsible for creating and closing the entity manager (i.e., managing its life cycle).

Listing 6-2. A Main Class Creating an EntityManager with an EntityManagerFactory

```
public class Main {

  public static void main(String[] args) {

    // Creates an instance of book
    Book book = new Book("H2G2", "The Hitchhiker's Guide to the Galaxy", 12.5F, ↪
                          "1-84023-742-2", 354, false);

    // Obtains an entity manager and a transaction
    EntityManagerFactory emf = Persistence.createEntityManagerFactory("chapter06PU");
    EntityManager em = emf.createEntityManager();

    // Persists the book to the database
    EntityTransaction tx = em.getTransaction();
    tx.begin();
    em.persist(book);
    tx.commit();

    // Closes the entity manager and the factory
    em.close();
    emf.close();
  }
}
```

Creating an application-managed entity manager is simple enough using a factory, but what differentiates application managed from container managed is how the factory is acquired. A container-managed environment is when the application evolves in a Servlet or an EJB container. In a Java EE environment, the most common way to acquire an entity manager is by the @PersistenceContext annotation, or by JNDI lookup. The component running in a container (Servlet, EJB, web service, etc.) doesn't need to create or close the entity manager, as its life cycle is managed by the container. Listing 6-3 shows the code of a stateless session bean into which we inject a reference of the chapter06PU persistence unit.

Listing 6-3. A Stateless EJB Injected with a Reference of an Entity Manager

```
@Stateless
public class BookEJB {

  @PersistenceContext(unitName = "chapter06PU")
  private EntityManager em;

  public void createBook() {

    // Creates an instance of book
    Book book = new Book("H2G2", "The Hitchhiker's Guide to the Galaxy", 12.5F, ↪
                          "1-84023-742-2", 354, false);

    // Persists the book to the database
    em.persist(book);
  }
}
```

Compared with Listing 6-2, the code in Listing 6-3 is much simpler. First, there is no `Persistence` or `EntityManagerFactory` as the container injects the entity manager instance. The application is not responsible for managing the life cycle of the `EntityManager` (creating and closing the `EntityManager`). Second, because stateless beans manage the transactions, there is no explicit commit or rollback. Chapter 7 demonstrates this style of entity manager.

■ **Note**　If you refer to the "Producers" section of Chapter 2 (Context and Dependency Injection) you will understand that you can also @Inject an EntityManager if you produce it (using the @Produces annotation).

Persistence Context

Before exploring the `EntityManager` API in detail, you need to understand a crucial concept: the *persistence context*. A persistence context is a set of managed entity instances at a given time for a given user's transaction: only one entity instance with the same persistent identity can exist in a persistence context. For example, if a Book instance with an ID of 12 exists in the persistence context, no other book with this ID can exist within that same persistence context. Only entities that are contained in the persistence context are managed by the entity manager, meaning that changes will be reflected in the database.

The entity manager updates or consults the persistence context whenever a method of the `javax.persistence.EntityManager` interface is called. For example, when a `persist()` method is called, the entity passed as an argument will be added to the persistence context if it doesn't already exist. Similarly, when an entity is found by its primary key, the entity manager first checks whether the requested entity is already present in the persistence context. The persistence context can be seen as a first-level cache. It's a short, live space where the entity manager stores entities before flushing the content to the database. By default, objects just live in the persistent context for the duration of the transaction.

To summarize, let's look at Figure 6-1 where two users need to access entities whose data are stored in the database. Each user has his own persistence context that lasts for the duration of his own transaction. User 1 gets the Book entities with IDs equal to 12 and 56 from the database, so both get stored in his persistence context. User 2 gets the entities 12 and 34. As you can see, the entity with ID = 12 is stored in each user's persistence context. While the transaction runs, the persistence context acts like a first-level cache storing the entities that can be managed by the `EntityManager`. Once the transaction ends, the persistence context ends and the entities are cleared.

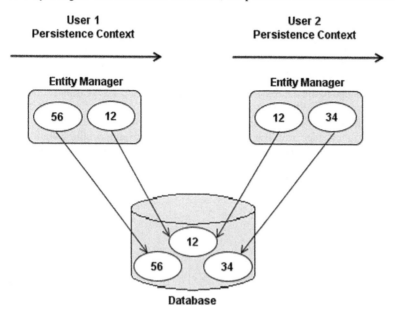

Figure 6-1. *Entities living in different users' persistence context*

The configuration for an entity manager is bound to the factory that created it. Whether application or container managed, the factory needs a persistence unit from which to create an entity manager. A persistence unit dictates the settings to connect to the database and the list of entities that can be managed in a persistence context. The persistence.xml file (see Listing 6-4) located in the META-INF directory defines the persistence unit. The persistence unit has a name (chapter06PU) and a set of attributes.

Listing 6-4. A Persistence Unit with a Set of Manageable Entities

```xml
<?xml version="1.0" encoding="UTF-8"?>
<persistence xmlns="http://xmlns.jcp.org/xml/ns/persistence"
             xmlns:xsi="http://www.w3.org/2001/XMLSchema-instance"
             xsi:schemaLocation="http://xmlns.jcp.org/xml/ns/persistence ↪
             http://xmlns.jcp.org/xml/ns/persistence/persistence_2_1.xsd"
             version="2.1">

  <persistence-unit name="chapter06PU" transaction-type="RESOURCE_LOCAL">
    <provider>org.eclipse.persistence.jpa.PersistenceProvider</provider>
    <class>org.agoncal.book.javaee7.chapter06.Book</class>
    <class>org.agoncal.book.javaee7.chapter06.Customer</class>
    <class>org.agoncal.book.javaee7.chapter06.Address</class>
    <properties>
      <property name="javax.persistence.schema-generation.database.action" ↪
                value="drop-and-create"/>
      <property name="javax.persistence.jdbc.driver" ↪
                value="org.apache.derby.jdbc.EmbeddedDriver"/>
      <property name="javax.persistence.jdbc.url" ↪
                value="jdbc:derby:memory:chapter06DB;create=true"/>
      <property name="eclipselink.logging.level" value="INFO"/>
    </properties>
  </persistence-unit>
</persistence>
```

The persistence unit is the bridge between the persistence context and the database. On one hand, the <class> tag lists all the entities that could be managed in the persistence context, and, on the other, it gives all the information to physically connect to the database (using properties). This is because you are in an application-managed environment (transaction-type="RESOURCE_LOCAL"). As you'll see in Chapter 7, in a container-managed environment, the persistence.xml would define a data source instead of the database connection properties and set the transaction type to JTA (transaction-type="JTA").

In JPA 2.1, some properties of the persistence.xml file have been standardized (see Table 6-1). They all start with javax.persistence such as javax.persistence.jdbc.url. JPA providers are required to support these standard properties, but they may provide custom properties of their own, such as the EclipseLink property in the example (e.g., eclipselink.logging.level).

Table 6-1. *Standard JPA Properties*

Property	Description
`javax.persistence.jdbc.driver`	Fully qualified name of the driver class
`javax.persistence.jdbc.url`	Driver-specific URL
`javax.persistence.jdbc.user`	Username used by database connection
`javax.persistence.jdbc.password`	Password used by database connection
`javax.persistence.database-product-name`	Name of the targeted database (e.g., Derby)
`javax.persistence.database-major-version`	Version number of the targeted database
`javax.persistence.database-minor-version`	Minor version number of the targeted database
`javax.persistence.ddl-create-script-source`	Name of the script creating the database
`javax.persistence.ddl-drop-script-source`	Name of the script dropping the database
`javax.persistence.sql-load-script-source`	Name of the script loading data into the database
`javax.persistence.schema-generation.database.action`	Specifies the action to be taken with regard to the database (none, `create`, `drop-and-create`, `drop`)
`javax.persistence.schema-generation.scripts.action`	Specifies the action to be taken with regard to DDL scripts (none, `create`, `drop-and-create`, `drop`)
`javax.persistence.lock.timeout`	Value in milliseconds for pessimistic lock timeout
`javax.persistence.query.timeout`	Value in milliseconds for query timeout
`javax.persistence.validation.group.pre-persist`	Groups targeted for validation upon pre-persist
`javax.persistence.validation.group.pre-update`	Groups targeted for validation upon pre-update
`javax.persistence.validation.group.pre-remove`	Groups targeted for validation upon pre-remove

Manipulating Entities

Being the central piece of JPA, we use the entity manager for both simple entity manipulation and complex JPQL query execution. When manipulating single entities, the `EntityManager` interface can be seen as a generic Data Access Object (DAO), which allows CRUD operations on any entity (see Table 6-2).

Table 6-2. *EntityManager Interface Methods to Manipulate Entities*

Method	Description
`void persist(Object entity)`	Makes an instance managed and persistent
`<T> T find(Class<T> entityClass, Object primaryKey)`	Searches for an entity of the specified class and primary key
`<T> T getReference(Class<T> entityClass, Object primaryKey)`	Gets an instance, whose state may be lazily fetched
`void remove(Object entity)`	Removes the entity instance from the persistence context and from the underlying database

(continued)

Table 6-2. (*continued*)

Method	Description
`<T> T merge(T entity)`	Merges the state of the given entity into the current persistence context
`void refresh(Object entity)`	Refreshes the state of the instance from the database, overwriting changes made to the entity, if any
`void flush()`	Synchronizes the persistence context to the underlying database
`void clear()`	Clears the persistence context, causing all managed entities to become detached
`void detach(Object entity)`	Removes the given entity from the persistence context, causing a managed entity to become detached
`boolean contains(Object entity)`	Checks whether the instance is a managed entity instance belonging to the current persistence context

To help you gain a better understanding of these methods, I use a simple example of a one-way, one-to-one relationship between a Customer and an Address. Both entities have automatically generated identifiers (thanks to the @GeneratedValue annotation), and Customer (see Listing 6-5) has a lazy fetch to Address (see Listing 6-6).

Listing 6-5. The Customer Entity with a One-Way, One-to-One Address

```
@Entity
public class Customer {

    @Id @GeneratedValue
    private Long id;
    private String firstName;
    private String lastName;
    private String email;
    @OneToOne (fetch = FetchType.LAZY)
    @JoinColumn(name = "address_fk")
    private Address address;

    // Constructors, getters, setters
}
```

Listing 6-6. The Address Entity

```
@Entity
public class Address {

    @Id @GeneratedValue
    private Long id;
    private String street1;
    private String city;
    private String zipcode;
    private String country;

    // Constructors, getters, setters
}
```

These two entities will get mapped into the database structure shown in Figure 6-2. Note the ADDRESS_FK column is the foreign key to ADDRESS.

CUSTOMER		
+ID	bigint	Nullable = false
LASTNAME	varchar(255)	Nullable = true
EMAIL	varchar(255)	Nullable = true
FIRSTNAME	varchar(255)	Nullable = true
# ADDRESS_FK	bigint	Nullable = true

ADDRESS		
+ID	bigint	Nullable = false
STREET1	varchar(255)	Nullable = true
ZIPCODE	varchar(255)	Nullable = true
COUNTRY	varchar(255)	Nullable = true
CITY	varchar(255)	Nullable = true

Figure 6-2. CUSTOMER and ADDRESS tables

For better readability, the fragments of code used in the upcoming section assume that the em attribute is of type EntityManager and tx of type EntityTransaction.

Persisting an Entity

Persisting an entity means inserting data into the database when the data don't already exist (otherwise an EntityExistsException is thrown). To do so, it's necessary to create a new entity instance using the new operator, set the values of the attributes, bind one entity to another when there are associations, and finally call the EntityManager.persist() method as shown in the JUnit test case in Listing 6-7.

Listing 6-7. Persisting a Customer with an Address

```
Customer customer = new Customer("Antony", "Balla", "tballa@mail.com");
Address address = new Address("Ritherdon Rd", "London", "8QE", "UK");
customer.setAddress(address);

tx.begin();
em.persist(customer);
em.persist(address);
tx.commit();

assertNotNull(customer.getId());
assertNotNull(address.getId());
```

In Listing 6-7, customer and address are just two objects that reside in the JVM memory. Both become managed entities when the entity manager (variable em) takes them into account by persisting them (em.persist(customer)). At this time, both objects become eligible to be inserted in the database. When the transaction is committed (tx.commit()), the data are flushed to the database, an address row is inserted into the ADDRESS table, and a customer row is inserted into the CUSTOMER table. As the Customer is the owner of the relationship, its table holds the foreign key to ADDRESS. The assertNotNull expressions check that both entities have received a generated identifier (thanks to the persistence provider and the @Id and @GeneratedValue annotations).

Note the ordering of the persist() methods: a customer is persisted and then an address. If it were the other way round, the result would be the same. Earlier, the entity manager was described as a first-level cache. Until the transaction is committed, the data stay in memory and there is no access to the database. The entity manager caches data and, when ready, flushes the data in the order that the underlying database is expecting (respecting integrity constraints). Because of the foreign key in the CUSTOMER table, the insert statement for ADDRESS will be executed first, followed by that for CUSTOMER.

■ **Note**   Most of the entities in this chapter do not implement the Serializable interface. That's because entities don't have to be in order to get persisted in the database. They are passed by reference from one method to the other, and, when they have to be persisted, the EntityManager.persist() method is invoked. But, if you need to pass entities by value (remote invocation, external EJB container, etc.), they must implement the java.io.Serializable marker (no method) interface. It indicates to the compiler that it must enforce all fields on the entity class to be serializable, so that any instance can be serialized to a byte stream and passed using Remote Method Invocation (RMI).

Finding by ID

To find an entity by its identifier, you can use two different methods. The first is the EntityManager.find() method, which has two parameters: the entity class and the unique identifier (see Listing 6-8). If the entity is found, it is returned; if it is not found, a null value is returned.

Listing 6-8. Finding a Customer by ID

```
Customer customer = em.find(Customer.class, 1234L)
if (customer!= null) {
  // Process the object
}
```

The second method is getReference() (see Listing 6-9). It is very similar to the find operation, as it has the same parameters, but it retrieves a reference to an entity (via its primary key) but does not retrieve its data. Think of it as a proxy to an entity, not the entity itself. It is intended for situations where a managed entity instance is needed, but no data, other than potentially the entity's primary key, being accessed. With getReference(), the state data are fetched lazily, which means that if you don't access state before the entity is detached, the data might not be there. If the entity is not found, an EntityNotFoundException is thrown.

Listing 6-9. Finding a Customer by Reference

```
try {
  Customer customer = em.getReference(Customer.class, 1234L)
  // Process the object
} catch(EntityNotFoundException ex) {
  // Entity not found
}
```

Removing an Entity

An entity can be removed with the EntityManager.remove() method. Once removed, the entity is deleted from the database, is detached from the entity manager, and cannot be synchronized with the database anymore. In terms of Java objects, the entity is still accessible until it goes out of scope and the garbage collector cleans it up. The code in Listing 6-10 shows how to remove an object after it has been created.

Listing 6-10. Creating and Removing Customer and Address Entities

```
Customer customer = new Customer("Antony", "Balla", "tballa@mail.com");
Address address = new Address("Ritherdon Rd", "London", "8QE", "UK");
customer.setAddress(address);
```

```
tx.begin();
em.persist(customer);
em.persist(address);
tx.commit();

tx.begin();
em.remove(customer);
tx.commit();

// The data is removed from the database but the object is still accessible
assertNotNull(customer);
```

The code in Listing 6-10 creates an instance of Customer and Address, links them together (customer.setAddress(address)), and persists them. In the database, the customer row is linked to the address through a foreign key; later on in the code, only the Customer is deleted. Depending on how the cascading is configured (discussed later in this chapter), the Address could be left with no other entity referencing it and the address row becomes an orphan.

Orphan Removal

For data consistency, orphans are not desirable, as they result in having rows in a database that are not referenced by any other table, without means of access. With JPA, you can inform the persistence provider to automatically remove orphans or cascade a remove operation as you'll see later. If a target entity (Address) is privately owned by a source (Customer), meaning a target must never be owned by more than one source, and that source is deleted by the application, the provider should also delete the target.

Associations that are specified as one-to-one or one-to-many support the use of the orphan-removal option. To include this option in the example, let's look at how to add the orphanRemoval=true element to the @OneToOne annotation (see Listing 6-11).

Listing 6-11. The Customer Entity Dealing with Orphan Address Removal

```
@Entity
public class Customer {

  @Id @GeneratedValue
  private Long id;
  private String firstName;
  private String lastName;
  private String email;
  @OneToOne (fetch = FetchType.LAZY, orphanRemoval=true)
  private Address address;

  // Constructors, getters, setters
}
```

With this mapping, the code in Listing 6-10 will automatically remove the Address entity when the customer is removed, or when the relationship is broken (by setting the address attribute to null, or by removing the child entity from the collection in a one-to-many case). The remove operation is applied at the time of the flush operation (transaction committed).

Synchronizing with the Database

Until now, the synchronization with the database has been done at commit time. The entity manager is a first-level cache, waiting for the transaction to be committed to flush the data to the database, but what happens when a customer and an address need to be inserted?

```
tx.begin();
em.persist(customer);
em.persist(address);
tx.commit();
```

All pending changes require anSQL statement; here two insert statements are produced and made permanent only when the database transaction commits. For most applications, this automatic data synchronization is sufficient. Although it is not known at exactly which point in time the provider actually flushes the changes to the database, you can be sure it happens when the transaction is committed. The database is synchronized with the entities in the persistence context, but data can be explicitly flushed (flush) to the database, or entities refreshed with data from the database (refresh). If the data are flushed to the database at one point, and if later in the code the application calls the rollback() method, the flushed data will be taken out of the database.

Flushing an Entity

With the EntityManager.flush() method, the persistence provider can be explicitly forced to flush the data to the database but does not commit the transaction. This allows a developer to manually trigger the same process used by the entity manager internally to flush the persistence context.

```
tx.begin();
em.persist(customer);
em.flush();
em.persist(address);
tx.commit();
```

Two interesting things happen in the preceding code. The first is that em.flush() will not wait for the transaction to commit and will force the provider to flush the persistence context. An insert statement will be generated and executed at the flush. The second is that this code will not work because ofthe integrity constraint. Without an explicit flush, the entity manager caches all changes and orders and executes them in a coherent way for the database. With an explicit flush, the insert statement to CUSTOMER will be executed, but the integrity constraint on the address foreign key will be violated (the ADDRESS_FK column in CUSTOMER). That will lead the transaction to roll back. Data that have been flushed will also get rolled back Explicit flushes should be carefully used and only when needed.

Refreshing an Entity

The refresh() method is used for data synchronization in the opposite direction of the flush, meaning it overwrites the current state of a managed entity with data as they are present in the database. A typical case is when you use the EntityManager.refresh() method to undo changes that have been made to the entity in memory only. The test case snippet in Listing 6-12 finds a Customer by ID, changes its first name, and undoes this change using the refresh() method.

Listing 6-12. Refreshing the Customer Entity from the Database

```
Customer customer = em.find(Customer.class, 1234L)
assertEquals(customer.getFirstName(), "Antony");

customer.setFirstName("William");

em.refresh(customer);
assertEquals(customer.getFirstName(), "Antony");");
```

Content of the Persistence Context

The persistence context holds the managed entities. With the EntityManager interface, you can check whether an entity is being managed, detach it, or clear all entities from the persistence context.

Contains

Entities are either managed or not by the entity manager. The EntityManager.contains() method returns a Boolean and allows you to check whether or not a particular entity instance is currently managed by the entity manager within the current persistence context. In the test case in Listing 6-13, a Customer is persisted, and you can immediately check whether the entity is managed (em.contains(customer)). The answer is true. Afterward, the remove() method is called, and the entity is removed from the database and from the persistence context (em.contains(customer) returns false).

Listing 6-13. Test Case for Whether the Customer Entity Is in the Persistence Context

```
Customer customer = new Customer("Antony", "Balla", "tballa@mail.com");

tx.begin();
em.persist(customer);
tx.commit();

assertTrue(em.contains(customer));

tx.begin();
em.remove(customer);
tx.commit();

assertFalse(em.contains(customer));
```

Clear and Detach

The clear() method is straightforward: it empties the persistence context, causing all managed entities to become detached. The detach(Object entity) method removes the given entity from the persistence context. Changes made to the entity will not be synchronized to the database after such eviction has taken place. Listing 6-14 creates an entity, checks that it is managed, detaches it from the persistence context, and checks that it is detached.

Listing 6-14. Checking Whether the Customer Entity Is in the Persistence Context

```
Customer customer = new Customer("Antony", "Balla", "tballa@mail.com");

tx.begin();
em.persist(customer);
tx.commit();

assertTrue(em.contains(customer));

em.detach(customer);

assertFalse(em.contains(customer));
```

Merging an Entity

A detached entity is no longer associated with a persistence context. If you want to manage it, you need to reattach it (i.e., merge it). Let's take the example of an entity that needs to be displayed in a JSF page. The entity is first loaded from the database into the persistent layer (it is managed), it is returned from an invocation of a local EJB (it is detached because the transaction context ends), the presentation layer displays it (it is still detached), and then it returns to be updated to the database. However, at that moment, the entity is detached and needs to be attached again, or merged, to synchronize its state with the database.

Listing 6-15 simulates this case by clearing the persistence context (em.clear()), which detaches the entity.

Listing 6-15. Clearing the Persistence Context and Merging an Entity

```
Customer customer = new Customer("Antony", "Balla", "tballa@mail.com");

tx.begin();
em.persist(customer);
tx.commit();

em.clear();

// Sets a new value to a detached entity
customer.setFirstName("William");

tx.begin();
em.merge(customer);
tx.commit();
```

The code in Listing 6-15 creates and persists a customer. The call to em.clear() forces the detachment of the customer entity, but detached entities continue to live outside the persistence context in which they were, and their state is no longer guaranteed to be synchronized with the database state. That's what happens with customer.setFirstName("William"); this is executed on a detached entity, and the data are not updated in the database. To replicate this change to the database, you need to reattach the entity (i.e., merge it) with em.merge(customer) inside a transaction.

Updating an Entity

Updating an entity is simple, yet at the same time it can be confusing to understand. As you've just seen, you can use EntityManager.merge() to attach an entity and synchronize its state with the database. But, if an entity is currently managed, changes to it will be reflected in the database automatically. If not, you will need to explicitly call merge().

Listing 6-16 demonstrates persisting a customer with a first name set to Antony. When you call the em.persist() method, the entity is managed, so any changes made to the entity will be synchronized with the database. When you call the setFirstName() method, the entity changes its state. The entity manager caches any action starting at tx.begin() and synchronizes it when committed.

Listing 6-16. Updating the Customer's First Name

```
Customer customer = new Customer("Antony", "Balla", "tballa@mail.com");

tx.begin();
em.persist(customer);

customer.setFirstName("Williman");

tx.commit();
```

Cascading Events

By default, every entity manager operation applies only to the entity supplied as an argument to the operation. But sometimes, when an operation is carried out on an entity, you want to propagate it on its associations. This is known as *cascading an event*. The examples so far have relied on default cascade behavior and not customized behavior. In Listing 6-17, to create a customer, you instantiate a Customer and an Address entity, link them together (customer.setAddress(address)), and then persist the two.

Listing 6-17. Persisting a Customer with an Address

```
Customer customer = new Customer("Antony", "Balla", "tballa@mail.com");
Address address = new Address("Ritherdon Rd", "London", "8QE", "UK");
customer.setAddress(address);

tx.begin();
em.persist(customer);
em.persist(address);
tx.commit();
```

Because there's a relationship between Customer and Address, you could cascade the persist action from the customer to the address. That would mean that a call to em.persist(customer) would cascade the persist event to the Address entity if it allows this type of event to be propagated. You could then shrink the code and do away with the em.persist(address) as shown in Listing 6-18.

Listing 6-18. Cascading a Persist Event to Address

```
Customer customer = new Customer("Antony", "Balla", "tballa@mail.com");
Address address = new Address("Ritherdon Rd", "London", "8QE", "UK");
customer.setAddress(address);
```

```
tx.begin();
em.persist(customer);
tx.commit();
```

Without cascading, the customer would get persisted but not the address. Cascading an event is possible if the mapping of the relationship is changed. The annotations @OneToOne, @OneToMany, @ManyToOne, and @ManyToMany have a cascade attribute that takes an array of events to be cascaded, and a PERSIST event that can be cascaded as well as a REMOVE event (commonly used to perform delete cascades). To allow this, you must change the mapping of the Customer entity (see Listing 6-19) and add a cascade attribute to the @OneToOne annotation on Address.

Listing 6-19. Customer Entity Cascading Persist and Remove Events

```
@Entity
public class Customer {

    @Id @GeneratedValue
    private Long id;
    private String firstName;
    private String lastName;
    private String email;
    @OneToOne (fetch = FetchType.LAZY, cascade = {CascadeType.PERSIST, CascadeType.REMOVE})
    @JoinColumn(name = "address_fk")
    private Address address;

    // Constructors, getters, setters
}
```

You can choose from several events to cascade to a target association (Table 6-3 lists these events) and you can even cascade them all using the CascadeType.ALL type.

Table 6-3. *Possible Events to Be Cascaded*

Cascade Type	Description
PERSIST	Cascades persist operations to the target of the association
REMOVE	Cascades remove operations to the target of the association
MERGE	Cascades merge operations to the target of the association
REFRESH	Cascades refresh operations to the target of the association
DETACH	Cascades detach operations to the target of the association
ALL	Declares that all the previous operations should be cascaded

JPQL

You just saw how to manipulate entities individually with the EntityManager API. You know how to find an entity by ID, remove it, update its attributes, and so on. But finding an entity by ID is quite limiting, as you only retrieve a single entity using its unique identifier. In practice, you may need to retrieve an entity by criteria other than the ID (by name, ISBN, etc.) or retrieve a set of entities based on different criteria (e.g., all customers living in the United States). This possibility is inherent to relational databases, and JPA has a language that allows this interaction: JPQL.

JPQL is used to define searches against persistent entities independent of the underlying database. JPQL is a query language that takes its roots in the syntax of SQL, which is the standard language for database interrogation. But the main difference is that in SQL the results obtained are in the form of rows and columns (tables), whereas JPQL uses an entity or a collection of entities. JPQL syntax is object oriented and therefore more easily understood by developers whose experience is limited to object-oriented languages. Developers manage their entity domain model, not a table structure, by using the dot notation (e.g., myClass.myAttribute).

Under the hood, JPQL uses the mechanism of mapping to transform a JPQL query into language comprehensible by an SQL database. The query is executed on the underlying database with SQL and JDBC calls, and then entity instances have their attributes set and are returned to the application—all in a very simple and powerful manner using a rich query syntax.

The simplest JPQL query selects all the instances of a single entity.

```
SELECT b
FROM Book b
```

If you know SQL, this should look familiar to you. Instead of selecting from a table, JPQL selects entities, here Book. The FROM clause is also used to give an alias to the entity: b is an alias for Book. The SELECT clause of the query indicates that the result type of the query is the b entity (the Book). Executing this statement will result in a list of zero or more Book instances.

To restrict the result, add search criteria; you can use the WHERE clause as follows:

```
SELECT b
FROM Book b
WHERE b.title = 'H2G2'
```

The alias is used to navigate across entity attributes through the dot operator. Since the Book entity has a persistent attribute named title of type String, b.title refers to the title attribute of the Book entity. Executing this statement will result in a list of zero or more Book instances that have a title equal to *H2G2*.

The simplest select query consists of two mandatory parts: the SELECT and the FROM clause. SELECT defines the format of the query results. The FROM clause defines the entity or entities from which the results will be obtained, and the optional WHERE, ORDER BY, GROUP BY, and HAVING clauses can be used to restrict or order the result of a query. Listing 6-20 defines a simplified syntax of a JPQL statement.

Listing 6-20. Simplified JPQL Statement Syntax

```
SELECT <select clause>
FROM <from clause>
[WHERE <where clause>]
[ORDER BY <order by clause>]
[GROUP BY <group by clause>]
[HAVING <having clause>]
```

Listing 6-20 defines a SELECT statement, but DELETE and UPDATE statements can also be used to perform delete and update operations across multiple instances of a specific entity class.

Select

The SELECT clause follows the path expressions syntax and results in one of the following forms: an entity, an entity attribute, a constructor expression, an aggregate function, or some sequence of these Path expressions are the building blocks of queries and are used to navigate on entity attributes or across entity relationships (or a collection of entities) via the dot (.) navigation using the following syntax:

```
SELECT [DISTINCT] <expression> [[AS] <identification variable>]
expression ::= { NEW | TREAT | AVG | MAX | MIN | SUM | COUNT }
```

A simple SELECT returns an entity. For example, if a Customer entity has an alias called c, SELECT c will return an entity or a list of entities.

```
SELECT c
FROM Customer c
```

But a SELECT clause can also return attributes. If the Customer entity has a first name, SELECT c.firstName will return a String or a collection of Strings with the first names.

```
SELECT c.firstName
FROM Customer c
```

To retrieve the first name and the last name of a customer, you create a list containing the following two attributes:

```
SELECT c.firstName, c.lastName
FROM Customer c
```

Since JPA 2.0, an attribute can be retrieved depending on a condition (using a CASE WHEN ... THEN ... ELSE ... END expression). For example, instead of retrieving the price of a book, a statement can return a computation of the price (e.g., 50% discount) depending on the publisher (e.g., 50% discount on the Apress books, 20% discount for all the other books).

```
SELECT CASE b.editor WHEN 'Apress'
                     THEN b.price * 0.5
                     ELSE b.price * 0.8
       END
FROM Book b
```

If a Customer entity has a one-to-one relationship with Address, c.address refers to the address of the customer, and the result of the following query will return not a list of customers but a list of addresses:

```
SELECT c.address
FROM Customer c
```

Navigation expressions can be chained together to traverse complex entity graphs. Using this technique, path expressions such as c.address.country.code can be constructed, referring to the country code of the customer's address.

```
SELECT c.address.country.code
FROM Customer c
```

A constructor may be used in the SELECT expression to return an instance of a Java class initialized with the result of the query. The class doesn't have to be an entity, but the constructor must be fully qualified and match the attributes.

```
SELECT NEW org.agoncal.javaee7.CustomerDTO(c.firstName, c.lastName, c.address.street1)
FROM Customer c
```

The result of this query is a list of CustomerDTO objects that have been instantiated with the new operator and initialized with the first name, last name, and street of the customers.

Executing these queries will return either a single value or a collection of zero or more entities (or attributes) including duplicates. To remove the duplicates, the DISTINCT operator must be used.

```
SELECT DISTINCT c
FROM Customer c
```

```
SELECT DISTINCT c.firstName
FROM Customer c
```

The result of a query may be the result of an aggregate function applied to a path expression. The following aggregate functions can be used in the SELECT clause: AVG, COUNT, MAX, MIN, SUM. The results may be grouped in the GROUP BY clause and filtered using the HAVING clause.

```
SELECT COUNT(c)
FROM Customer c
```

Scalar expressions also can be used in the SELECT clause of a query as well as in the WHERE and HAVING clauses. These expressions can be used on numeric (ABS, SQRT, MOD, SIZE, INDEX), String (CONCAT, SUBSTRING, TRIM, LOWER, UPPER, LENGTH, LOCATE), and date-time (CURRENT_DATE, CURRENT_TIME, CURRENT_TIMESTAMP) values.

From

The FROM clause of a query defines entities by declaring identification variables. An *identification variable*, or *alias*, is an identifier that can be used in the other clauses (SELECT, WHERE, etc.). The syntax of the FROM clause consists of an entity and an alias. In the following example, Customer is the entity and c the identification variable:

```
SELECT c
FROM Customer c
```

Where

The WHERE clause of a query consists of a conditional expression used to restrict the result of a SELECT, UPDATE, or DELETE statement. The WHERE clause can be a simple expression or a set of conditional expressions used to filter the query.

The simplest way to restrict the result of a query is to use the attribute of an entity. For example, the following query selects all customers named Vincent:

```
SELECT c
FROM Customer c
WHERE c.firstName = 'Vincent'
```

You can further restrict queries by using the logical operators AND and OR. The following example uses AND to select all customers named Vincent, living in France:

```
SELECT c
FROM Customer c
WHERE c.firstName = 'Vincent' AND c.address.country = 'France'
```

The WHERE clause also uses comparison operators: =, >, >=, <, <=, <>, [NOT] BETWEEN, [NOT] LIKE, [NOT] IN, IS [NOT] NULL, IS [NOT] EMPTY, [NOT] MEMBER [OF]. The following shows an example using two of these operators:

```
SELECT c
FROM Customer c
WHERE c.age > 18

SELECT c
FROM Customer c
WHERE c.age NOT BETWEEN 40 AND 50

SELECT c
FROM Customer c
WHERE c.address.country IN ('USA', 'Portugal')
```

The LIKE expression consists of a String and optional escape characters that define the match conditions: the underscore (_) for single-character wildcards and the percent sign (%) for multicharacter wildcards.

```
SELECT c
FROM Customer c
WHERE c.email LIKE '%mail.com'
```

Binding Parameters

Until now, the WHERE clauses shown herein have only used fixed values. In an application, queries frequently depend on parameters. JPQL supports two types of parameter-binding syntax, allowing dynamic changes to the restriction clause of a query: positional and named parameters.

Positional parameters are designated by the question mark (?) followed by an integer (e.g., ?1). When the query is executed, the parameter numbers that should be replaced need to be specified.

```
SELECT c
FROM Customer c
WHERE c.firstName = ?1 AND c.address.country = ?2
```

Named parameters can also be used and are designated by a String identifier that is prefixed by the colon (:) symbol. When the query is executed, the parameter names that should be replaced need to be specified.

```
SELECT c
FROM Customer c
WHERE c.firstName = :fname AND c.address.country = :country
```

In the "Queries" section later in this chapter, you will see how an application binds parameters.

Subqueries

A subquery is a SELECT query that is embedded within a conditional expression of a WHERE or HAVING clause. The results of the subquery are evaluated and interpreted in the conditional expression of the main query. To retrieve the youngest customers from the database, a subquery with a MIN(age) is first executed and its result evaluated in the main query.

```
SELECT c
FROM Customer c
WHERE c.age = (SELECT MIN(cust. age) FROM Customer cust))
```

Order By

The ORDER BY clause allows the entities or values that are returned by a SELECT query to be ordered. The ordering applies to the entity attribute specified in this clause followed by the ASC or DESC keyword. The keyword ASC specifies that ascending ordering be used; DESC, the inverse, specifies that descending ordering be used. Ascending is the default and can be omitted.

```
SELECT c
FROM Customer c
WHERE c.age > 18
ORDER BY c.age DESC
```

Multiple expressions may also be used to refine the sort order.

```
SELECT c
FROM Customer c
WHERE c.age > 18
ORDER BY c.age DESC, c.address.country ASC
```

Group By and Having

The GROUP BY construct enables the aggregation of result values according to a set of properties. The entities are divided into groups based on the values of the entity field specified in the GROUP BY clause. To group customers by country and count them, use the following query:

```
SELECT c.address.country, count(c)
FROM Customer c
GROUP BY c.address.country
```

The GROUP BY defines the grouping expressions (c.address.country) over which the results will be aggregated and counted (count(c)). Note that expressions that appear in the GROUP BY clause must also appear in the SELECT clause.

The HAVING clause defines an applicable filter after the query results have been grouped, similar to a secondary WHERE clause, filtering the result of the GROUP BY. Using the previous query, by adding a HAVING clause, a result of countries other than the UK can be returned.

```
SELECT c.address.country, count(c)
FROM Customer c
GROUP BY c.address.country
HAVING c.address.country <> 'UK'
```

GROUP BY and HAVING can only be used within a SELECT clause (not a DELETE or an UPDATE).

Bulk Delete

You know how to remove an entity with the EntityManager.remove() method and query a database to retrieve a list of entities that correspond to certain criteria. To remove a list of entities, you can execute a query, iterate through it, and remove each entity individually. Although this is a valid algorithm, it is terrible in terms of performance (too many database accesses). There is a better way to do it: bulk deletes.

JPQL performs bulk delete operations across multiple instances of a specific entity class. These are used to delete a large number of entities in a single operation. The DELETE statement looks like the SELECT statement, as it can have a restricting WHERE clause and use parameters. As a result, the number of entity instances affected by the operation is returned. The syntax of the DELETE statement is

```
DELETE FROM <entity name> [[AS] <identification variable>]
[WHERE <where clause>]
```

As an example, to delete all customers younger than 18, you can use a bulk removal via a DELETE statement.

```
DELETE FROM Customer c
WHERE c.age < 18
```

Bulk Update

Bulk updates of entities are accomplished with the UPDATE statement, setting one or more attributes of the entity subject to conditions in the WHERE clause. The UPDATE statement syntax is

```
UPDATE <entity name> [[AS] <identification variable>]
SET <update statement> {, <update statement>}*
[WHERE <where clause>]
```

Rather than deleting all the young customers, their first name can be changed to "too young" with the following statement:

```
UPDATE Customer c
SET c.firstName = 'TOO YOUNG'
WHERE c.age < 18
```

Queries

You've seen the JPQL syntax and how to describe statements using different clauses (SELECT, FROM, WHERE, etc.). But how do you integrate a JPQL statement to your application? The answer: through queries. JPA 2.1 has five different types of queries that can be used in code, each with a different purpose.

- *Dynamic queries*: This is the simplest form of query, consisting of nothing more than a JPQL query string dynamically specified at runtime.

- *Named queries*: Named queries are static and unchangeable.

- *Criteria API*: JPA 2.0 introduced the concept of object-oriented query API.

- *Native queries*: This type of query is useful to execute a native SQL statement instead of a JPQL statement.

- *Stored procedure queries*: JPA 2.1 brings a new API to call stored procedures.

The central point for choosing from these five types of queries is the EntityManager interface, which has several factory methods, listed in Table 6-4, returning either a Query, a TypedQuery, or a StoredProcedureQuery interface (both TypedQuery and StoredProcedureQuery extend Query). The Query interface is used in cases when the result type is Object, and TypedQuery is used when a typed result is preferred. StoredProcedureQuery is used to control stored procedure query execution.

Table 6-4. *EntityManager Methods for Creating Queries*

Method	Description
Query createQuery(String jpqlString)	Creates an instance of Query for executing a JPQL statement for dynamic queries
Query createNamedQuery(String name)	Creates an instance of Query for executing a named query (in JPQL or in native SQL)
Query createNativeQuery(String sqlString)	Creates an instance of Query for executing a native SQL statement
Query createNativeQuery(String sqlString, Class resultClass)	Native query passing the class of the expected results
Query createNativeQuery(String sqlString, String resultSetMapping)	Native query passing a result set mapping
<T> TypedQuery<T> createQuery(CriteriaQuery<T> criteriaQuery)	Creates an instance of TypedQuery for executing a criteria query
<T> TypedQuery<T> createQuery(String jpqlString, Class<T> resultClass)	Typed query passing the class of the expected results
<T> TypedQuery<T> createNamedQuery(String name, Class<T> resultClass)	Typed query passing the class of the expected results
StoredProcedureQuery createStoredProcedureQuery(String procedureName)	Creates a StoredProcedureQuery for executing a stored procedure in the database
1. StoredProcedureQuery createStoredProcedureQuery(String procedureName, Class... resultClasses)	Stored procedure query passing classes to which the result sets are to be mapped
2. StoredProcedureQuery createStoredProcedureQuery(String procedureName, String... resultSetMappings)	Stored procedure query passing the result sets mapping
StoredProcedureQuery createNamedStoredProcedureQuery(String name)	Creates a query for a named stored procedure

When you obtain an implementation of the Query, TypedQuery, or StoredProcedureQuery interface through one of the factory methods in the EntityManager interface, a rich API controls it. The Query API, shown in Listing 6-21, is used for static queries (i.e., named queries) and dynamic queries using JPQL, and native queries in SQL. The Query API also supports parameter binding and pagination control.

Listing 6-21. Query API

```java
public interface Query {

    // Executes a query and returns a result
    List getResultList();
    Object getSingleResult();
    int executeUpdate();

    // Sets parameters to the query
    Query setParameter(String name, Object value);
    Query setParameter(String name, Date value, TemporalType temporalType);
    Query setParameter(String name, Calendar value, TemporalType temporalType);
    Query setParameter(int position, Object value);
    Query setParameter(int position, Date value, TemporalType temporalType);
    Query setParameter(int position, Calendar value, TemporalType temporalType);
    <T> Query setParameter(Parameter<T> param, T value);
    Query setParameter(Parameter<Date> param, Date value, TemporalType temporalType);
    Query setParameter(Parameter<Calendar> param, Calendar value, TemporalType temporalType);

    // Gets parameters from the query
    Set<Parameter<?>> getParameters();
    Parameter<?> getParameter(String name);
    Parameter<?> getParameter(int position);
    <T> Parameter<T> getParameter(String name, Class<T> type);
    <T> Parameter<T> getParameter(int position, Class<T> type);
    boolean isBound(Parameter<?> param);
    <T> T getParameterValue(Parameter<T> param);
    Object getParameterValue(String name);
    Object getParameterValue(int position);

    // Constrains the number of results returned by a query
    Query setMaxResults(int maxResult);
    int getMaxResults();
    Query setFirstResult(int startPosition);
    int getFirstResult();

    // Sets and gets query hints
    Query setHint(String hintName, Object value);
    Map<String, Object> getHints();

    // Sets the flush mode type to be used for the query execution
    Query setFlushMode(FlushModeType flushMode);
    FlushModeType getFlushMode();

    // Sets the lock mode type to be used for the query execution
    Query setLockMode(LockModeType lockMode);
    LockModeType getLockMode();

    // Allows access to the provider-specific API
    <T> T unwrap(Class<T> cls);
}
```

The methods that are mostly used in this API are ones that execute the query itself. To execute a SELECT query, you have to choose between two methods depending on the required result.

- The getResultList() method executes the query and returns a list of results (entities, attributes, expressions, etc.).

- The getSingleResult() method executes the query and returns a single result (throws a NonUniqueResultException if more than one result is found).

To execute an update or a delete, the executeUpdate() method executes the bulk query and returns the number of entities affected by the execution of the query.

As you saw in the "JPQL" section earlier, a query can use parameters that are either named (e.g., :myParam) or positional (e.g., ?1). The Query API defines several setParameter methods to set parameters before executing a query.

When you execute a query, it can return a large number of results. Depending on the application, these can be processed together or in chunks (e.g., a web application only displays ten rows at one time). To control the pagination, the Query interface defines setFirstResult() and setMaxResults() methods to specify the first result to be received (numbered from zero) and the maximum number of results to return relative to that point.

The flush mode indicates to the persistence provider how to handle pending changes and queries. There are two possible flush mode settings: AUTO and COMMIT. AUTO (the default) means that the persistence provider is responsible for ensuring pending changes are visible to the processing of the query. COMMIT is when the effect of updates made to entities does not overlap with changed data in the persistence context.

Queries can be locked using the setLockMode(LockModeType) method. Locks are intended to provide a facility that enables the effect of repeatable read whether optimistically or pessimistically.

The following sections illustrate the five different types of queries using some of the methods just described.

Dynamic Queries

Dynamic queries are defined on the fly as needed by the application. To create a dynamic query, use the EntityManager.createQuery() method, which takes a String as a parameter that represents a JPQL query.

In the following code, the JPQL query selects all the customers from the database. The result of this query is a list, so when you invoke the getResultList() method, it returns a list of Customer entities (List<Customer>). However, if you know that your query only returns a single entity, use the getSingleResult() method. It returns a single entity and avoids the work of retrieving the data as a list.

```
Query query = em.createQuery("SELECT c FROM Customer c");
List<Customer> customers = query.getResultList();
```

This JPQL query returns a Query object. When you invoke the query.getResultList() method, it returns a list of untyped objects. If you want the same query to return a list of type Customer, you need to use the TypedQuery as follows:

```
TypedQuery<Customer> query = em.createQuery("SELECT c FROM Customer c", Customer.class);
List<Customer> customers = query.getResultList();
```

This query string can also be dynamically created by the application, which can then specify a complex query at runtime not known ahead of time. String concatenation is used to construct the query dynamically depending on the criteria.

```
String jpqlQuery = "SELECT c FROM Customer c";
if (someCriteria)
    jpqlQuery += " WHERE c.firstName = 'Betty'";
query = em.createQuery(jpqlQuery);
List<Customer> customers = query.getResultList();
```

The previous query retrieves customers named Betty, but you might want to introduce a parameter for the first name. There are two possible choices for passing a parameter: using names or positions. In the following example, I use a named parameter called :fname (note the : symbol) in the query and bound it with the setParameter method:

```
query = em.createQuery("SELECT c FROM Customer c where c.firstName = :fname");
query.setParameter("fname", "Betty");
List<Customer> customers = query.getResultList();
```

Note that the parameter name fname does not include the colon used in the query. The code using a position parameter would look like the following:

```
query = em.createQuery("SELECT c FROM Customer c where c.firstName = ?1");
query.setParameter(1, "Betty");
List<Customer> customers = query.getResultList();
```

If you need to use pagination to display the list of customers by chunks of ten, you can use the setMaxResults method as follows:

```
query = em.createQuery("SELECT c FROM Customer c", Customer.class);
query.setMaxResults(10);
List<Customer> customers = query.getResultList();
```

An issue to consider with dynamic queries is the cost of translating the JPQL string into an SQL statement at runtime. Because the query is dynamically created and cannot be predicted, the persistence provider has to parse the JPQL string, get the ORM metadata, and generate the equivalent SQL. The performance cost of processing each of these dynamic queries can be an issue. If you have static queries that are unchangeable and want to avoid this overhead, then you can use named queries instead.

Named Queries

Named queries are different from dynamic queries in that they are static and unchangeable. In addition to their static nature, which does not allow the flexibility of a dynamic query, named queries can be more efficient to execute because the persistence provider can translate the JPQL string to SQL once the application starts, rather than every time the query is executed.

Named queries are static queries expressed in metadata inside either a @NamedQuery annotation or the XML equivalent. To define these reusable queries, annotate an entity with the @NamedQuery annotation, which takes two elements: the name of the query and its content. So let's change the Customer entity and statically define three queries using annotations (see Listing 6-22).

Listing 6-22. The Customer Entity Defining Named Queries

```
@Entity
@NamedQueries({
  @NamedQuery(name = "findAll", query="select c from Customer c"),
  @NamedQuery(name = "findVincent", ↪
              query="select c from Customer c where c.firstName = 'Vincent'"),
  @NamedQuery(name = "findWithParam", ↪
              query="select c from Customer c where c.firstName = :fname")
})
```

```
public class Customer {

    @Id @GeneratedValue
    private Long id;
    private String firstName;
    private String lastName;
    private Integer age;
    private String email;
    @OneToOne
    @JoinColumn(name = "address_fk")
    private Address address;

    // Constructors, getters, setters
}
```

Because the Customer entity defines more than one named query, it uses the @NamedQueries annotation, which takes an array of @NamedQuery. The first query, called findAll, selects all customers from the database with no restriction (no WHERE clause). The findWithParam query uses the parameter :fname to restrict customers by their first name. Listing 6-22 shows an array of @NamedQuery, but, if the Customer only had one query, it would have been defined as follows:

```
@Entity
@NamedQuery(name = "findAll", query="select c from Customer c")
public class Customer {...}
```

The way to execute these named queries resembles the way dynamic queries are used. The EntityManager.createNamedQuery() method is invoked and passed to the query name defined by the annotations. This method returns a Query or a TypedQuery that can be used to set parameters, the max results, fetch modes, and so on. To execute the findAll query, write the following code:

```
Query query = em.createNamedQuery("findAll");
```

Again, if you need to type the query to return a list of Customer objects, you'll need to use the TypedQuery as follows:

```
TypedQuery<Customer> query = em.createNamedQuery("findAll", Customer.class);
```

The following is a fragment of code calling the findWithParam named query, passing the parameter :fname, and setting the maximum result to 3:

```
Query query = em.createNamedQuery("findWithParam");
query.setParameter("fname", "Vincent");
query.setMaxResults(3);
List<Customer> customers = query.getResultList();
```

Because most of the methods of the Query API return a Query object, you can use the following elegant shortcut to write queries. You call methods one after the other (setParameter().setMaxResults(), etc.).

```
Query query = em.createNamedQuery("findWithParam").setParameter("fname", "Vincent") ➡
                                       .setMaxResults(3);
```

Named queries are useful for organizing query definitions and powerful for improving application performance. The organization comes from the fact that the named queries are defined statically on entities and are typically placed on the entity class that directly corresponds to the query result (here the findAll query returns customers, so it should be defined in the Customer entity).

There is a restriction in that the name of the query is scoped to the persistence unit and must be unique within that scope, meaning that only one findAll method can exist. A findAll query for customers and a findAll query for addresses should be named differently. A common practice is to prefix the query name with the entity name. For example, the findAll query for the Customer entity would be named Customer.findAll.

Another problem is that the name of the query, which is a String, is manipulated, and, if you make a typo or refactor your code, you may get some exceptions indicating that the query doesn't exist. To limit the risks, you can replace the name of a query with a constant. Listing 6-23 shows how to refactor the Customer entity.

Listing 6-23. The Customer Entity Defining a Named Query with a Constant

```
@Entity
@NamedQuery(name = Customer.FIND_ALL, query="select c from Customer c"),
public class Customer {

  public static final String FIND_ALL = "Customer.findAll";

  // Attributes, constructors, getters, setters
}
```

The FIND_ALL constant identifies the findAll query nonambiguously by prefixing the name of the query with the name of the entity. The same constant is then used in the @NamedQuery annotation, and you can use this constant to execute the query as follows:

```
TypedQuery<Customer> query = em.createNamedQuery(Customer.FIND_ALL, Customer.class);
```

Criteria API (or Object-Oriented Queries)

Until now, I've been using Strings to write JPQL (dynamic or named queries) statements. This has the advantage of writing a database query concisely but the inconvenience of being error prone and difficult for an external framework to manipulate: it is a String, you end up concatenating Strings and so many typos can be made. For example, you could have typos on JPQL keywords (SLECT instead of SELECT), class names (Custmer instead of Customer), or attributes (firstname instead of firstName). You can also write a syntactically incorrect statement (SELECT c WHERE c.firstName = 'John' FROM Customer). Any of these mistakes will be discovered at runtime, and it may sometimes be difficult to find where the bug comes from.

JPA 2.0 created a new API, called *Criteria API* and defined in the package javax.persistence.criteria. It allows you to write any query in an object-oriented and syntactically correct way. Most of the mistakes that a developer could make writing a statement are found at compile time, not at runtime. The idea is that all the JPQL keywords (SELECT, UPDATE, DELETE, WHERE, LIKE, GROUP BY...) are defined in this API. In other words, the Criteria API supports everything JPQL can do but with an object-based syntax. Let's have a first look at a query that retrieves all the customers named "Vincent." In JPQL, it would look as follows:

```
SELECT c FROM Customer c WHERE c.firstName = 'Vincent'
```

This JPQL statement is rewritten in Listing 6-24 in an object-oriented way using the Criteria API.

Listing 6-24. *A Criteria Query Selecting All the Customers Named Vincent*

```
CriteriaBuilder builder = em.getCriteriaBuilder();
CriteriaQuery<Customer> criteriaQuery = builder.createQuery(Customer.class);
Root<Customer> c = criteriaQuery.from(Customer.class);
criteriaQuery.select(c).where(builder.equal(c.get("firstName"), "Vincent"));
Query query = em.createQuery(criteriaQuery).getResultList();
List<Customer> customers = query.getResultList();
```

Without going into too much detail, you can see that the SELECT, FROM, and WHERE keywords have an API representation through the methods select(), from(), and where(). And this rule applies for every JPQL keyword. Criteria queries are constructed through the CriteriaBuilder interface that is obtained by the EntityManager (the em attribute in Listings 6-24 and 6-25). It contains methods to construct the query definition (this interface defines keywords such as desc(), asc(), avg(), sum(), max(), min(), count(), and(), or(), greaterThan(), lowerThan()...). The other role of the CriteriaBuilder is to serve as the main factory of criteria queries (CriteriaQuery) and criteria query elements. This interface defines methods such as select(), from(), where(), orderBy(), groupBy(), and having(), which have the equivalent meaning in JPQL. In Listing 6-24, the way you get the alias **c** (as in SELECT **c** FROM Customer) is through the Root interface (Root<Customer> c). Then you just have to use the builder, the query, and the root to write any JPQL statement you want: from the simplest (select all the entities from the database) to the most complex (joins, subqueries, case expressions, functions...).

Listing 6-25. *A Criteria Query Selecting All the Customers Older Than 40*

```
CriteriaBuilder builder = em.getCriteriaBuilder();
CriteriaQuery<Customer> criteriaQuery = builder.createQuery(Customer.class);
Root<Customer> c = criteriaQuery.from(Customer.class);
criteriaQuery.select(c).where(builder.greaterThan(c.get("age").as(Integer.class), 40));
Query query = em.createQuery(criteriaQuery).getResultList();
List<Customer> customers = query.getResultList();
```

Let's take another example. Listing 6-25 shows a query that retrieves all the customers older than 40. The c.get("age") gets the attribute age from the Customer entity and checks if it's greater than 40.

I started this section saying that the Criteria API allows you to write error-free statements. But it's not completely true yet. When you look at Listings 6-24 and 6-25, you can still see some strings ("firstName" and "age") that represent the attributes of the Customer entity. So typos can still be made. In Listing 6-25, we even need to cast the age into an Integer (c.get("age").as(Integer.class)) because there is no other way to discover that the age attribute is of type Integer. To solve these problems, the Criteria API comes with a static metamodel class for each entity, bringing type safety to the API.

Type-Safe Criteria API

Listings 6-24 and 6-25 are almost typesafe: each JPQL keyword can be represented by a method of the CriteriaBuilder and CriteriaQuery interface. The only missing part is the attributes of the entity that are string based: the way to refer to the customer's firstName attribute is by calling c.get("firstName"). The get method takes a String as a parameter. Type-safe Criteria API solves this by overriding this method with a path expression from the metamodel API classes bringing type safety.

Listing 6-26 shows the Customer entity with several attributes of different type (Long, String, Integer, Address).

Listing 6-26. A Customer Entity with Several Attributes' Types

```
@Entity
public class Customer {

  @Id @GeneratedValue
  private Long id;
  private String firstName;
  private String lastName;
  private Integer age;
  private String email;
  private Address address;

  // Constructors, getters, setters
}
```

To bring type safety, JPA 2.1 can generate a static metamodel class for each entity. The convention is that each entity X will have a metadata class called X_ (with an underscore). So, the Customer entity will have its metamodel representation described in the Customer_ class shown in Listing 6-27.

Listing 6-27. The Customer_ Class Describing the Metamodel of Customer

```
@Generated("EclipseLink")
@StaticMetamodel(Customer.class)
public class Customer_ {

  public static volatile SingularAttribute<Customer, Long> id;
  public static volatile SingularAttribute<Customer, String> firstName;
  public static volatile SingularAttribute<Customer, String> lastName;
  public static volatile SingularAttribute<Customer, Integer> age;
  public static volatile SingularAttribute<Customer, String> email;
  public static volatile SingularAttribute<Customer, Address> address;
}
```

In the static metamodel class, each attribute of the Customer entity is defined by a subclass of javax.persistence.metamodel.Attribute (CollectionAttribute, ListAttribute, MapAttribute, SetAttribute, or SingularAttribute). Each of these attributes uses generics and is strongly typed (e.g., SingularAttribute<Customer, Integer>, age). Listing 6-28 shows the exact same code as Listing 6-25 but revisited with the static metamodel class (the c.get("age") is turned into c.get(Customer_.age)). Another advantage of type safety is that the metamodel defines the age attribute as being an Integer, so there is no need to cast the attribute into an Integer using as(Integer.class).

Listing 6-28. A Type-Safe Criteria Query Selecting All the Customers Older Than 40

```
CriteriaBuilder builder = em.getCriteriaBuilder();
CriteriaQuery<Customer> criteriaQuery = builder.createQuery(Customer.class);
Root<Customer> c = criteriaQuery.from(Customer.class);
criteriaQuery.select(c).where(builder.greaterThan(c.get(Customer_.age), 40));
Query query = em.createQuery(criteriaQuery).getResultList();
List<Customer> customers = query.getResultList();
```

Again, these are just examples of what you can do with the Criteria API. It is a very rich API that is completely defined in Chapter 5 (*Metamodel API*) and Chapter 6 (*Criteria API*) of the JPA 2.1 specification.

■ **Note** The classes used in the static metamodel, such as `Attribute` or `SingularAttribute`, are standard and defined in the package `javax.persistence.metamodel`. But the generation of the static metamodel classes is implementation specific. EclipseLink uses an internal class called `CanonicalModelProcessor`. This processor can be invoked by your integrated development environment (IDE) while you develop a Java command, an Ant task, or a Maven plug-in.

Native Queries

JPQL has a very rich syntax that allows you to handle entities in any form and ensures portability across databases. JPA enables you to use specific features of a database by using native queries. Native queries take a native SQL statement (`SELECT`, `UPDATE`, or `DELETE`) as the parameter and return a `Query` instance for executing that SQL statement. However, native queries are not expected to be portable across databases.

If the code is not portable, why not use JDBC calls? The main reason to use JPA native queries rather than JDBC calls is because the result of the query will be automatically converted back to entities. If you want to retrieve all the customer entities from the database using SQL, you need to use the `EntityManager.createNativeQuery()` method that has as parameters the SQL query and the entity class that the result should be mapped to.

```
Query query = em.createNativeQuery("SELECT * FROM t_customer", Customer.class);
List<Customer> customers = query.getResultList();
```

As you can see in the preceding code fragment, the SQL query is a String that can be dynamically created at runtime (just like JPQL dynamic queries). Again, the query could be complex, and, because the persistence provider doesn't know in advance, it will interpret it each time. Like named queries, native queries can use annotations to define static SQL queries. Named native queries are defined using the @NamedNativeQuery annotation, which must be placed on any entity (see code below). Like JPQL named queries, the name of the query must be unique within the persistence unit.

```
@Entity
@NamedNativeQuery(name = "findAll", query="select * from t_customer")
@Table(name = "t_customer")
public class Customer {...}
```

Stored Procedure Queries

So far all the different queries (JPQL or SQL) have the same purpose: send a query from your application to the database that will execute it and send back a result. Stored procedures are different in the sense that they are actually stored in the database itself and executed within this database.

A stored procedure is a subroutine available to applications that access a relational database. Typical usage could be extensive or complex processing that requires execution of several SQL statements or a data-intensive repetitive task. Stored procedures are usually written in a proprietary language close to SQL and therefore not easily portable across database vendors. But storing the code inside the database even in a nonportable way provides many advantages, like

- Better performance due to precompilation of the stored procedure as well as reutilizing its execution plan,

- Keeping statistics on the code to keep it optimized,

- Reducing the amount of data passed over a network by keeping the code on the server,

- Altering the code in a central location without replicating in several different programs,

- Stored procedures, which can be used by multiple programs written in different languages (not just Java),

- Hiding the raw data by allowing only stored procedures to gain access to the data, and

- Enhancing security controls by granting users permission to execute a stored procedure independently of underlying table permissions.

Let's take a look at a practical example: archiving old books and CDs. After a certain date books and CDs have to be archived in a certain warehouse, meaning they have to be physically transferred from a warehouse to a reseller. Archiving books and CDs can be a time-consuming process as several tables have to be updated (Inventory, Warehouse, Book, CD, Transportation tables, etc.). So we can write a stored procedure to regroup several SQL statements and improve performance. The stored procedure sp_archive_books defined in Listing 6-29 takes an archive date and a warehouse code as parameters and updates the T_Inventory and the T_Transport tables.

Listing 6-29. Abstract of a Stored Procedure Archiving Books

```
CREATE PROCEDURE sp_archive_books @archiveDate DATE, @warehouseCode VARCHAR AS
  UPDATE T_Inventory
  SET Number_Of_Books_Left - 1
  WHERE Archive_Date < @archiveDate AND Warehouse_Code = @warehouseCode;

  UPDATE T_Transport
  SET Warehouse_To_Take_Books_From = @warehouseCode;
END
```

The stored procedure in Listing 6-29 is compiled into the database and can then be invoked through its name (sp_archive_books). As you can see, a stored procedure accepts data in the form of input or output parameters. Input parameters (@archiveDate and @warehouseCode in our example) are utilized in the execution of the stored procedure which, in turn, can produce some output result. This result is returned to the application through the use of a result set.

In JPA 2.1 the StoredProcedureQuery interface (which extends Query) supports stored procedures. Unlike dynamic, named, or native queries, the API only allows you to invoke a stored procedure that already exists in the database, not define it. You can invoke a stored procedure with annotations (with @NamedStoredProcedureQuery) or dynamically.

Listing 6-30 shows the Book entity that declares the sp_archive_books stored procedure using named query annotations. The NamedStoredProcedureQuery annotation specifies name of the stored procedure to invoke the types of all parameters (Date.class and String.class), their corresponding parameter modes (IN, OUT, INOUT, REF_CURSOR), and how result sets, if any, are to be mapped. A StoredProcedureParameter annotation needs to be provided for each parameter.

Listing 6-30. Entity Declaring a Named Stored Procedure

```
@Entity
@NamedStoredProcedureQuery(name = "archiveOldBooks", procedureName = "sp_archive_books",
  parameters = {
    @StoredProcedureParameter(name = "archiveDate", mode = IN, type = Date.class),
    @StoredProcedureParameter(name = "warehouse", mode = IN, type = String.class)
  }
)
```

```java
public class Book {

    @Id @GeneratedValue
    private Long id;
    private String title;
    private Float price;
    private String description;
    private String isbn;
    private String editor;
    private Integer nbOfPage;
    private Boolean illustrations;

    // Constructors, getters, setters
}
```

To invoke the sp_archive_books stored procedure, you need to use the entity manager and create a named stored procedure query by passing its name (archiveOldBooks). This returns a StoredProcedureQuery on which you can set the parameters and execute it as shown in Listing 6-31.

Listing 6-31. Calling a StoredProcedureQuery

```java
StoredProcedureQuery query = em.createNamedStoredProcedureQuery("archiveOldBooks");
query.setParameter("archiveDate", new Date());
query.setParameter("maxBookArchived", 1000);
query.execute();
```

If the stored procedure is not defined using metadata (@NamedStoredProcedureQuery), you can use the API to dynamically specify a stored procedure query. This means that parameters and result set information must be provided programmatically. This can be done using the registerStoredProcedureParameter method of the StoredProcedureQuery interface as shown in Listing 6-32.

Listing 6-32. Registering and Calling a StoredProcedureQuery

```java
StoredProcedureQuery query = em.createStoredProcedureQuery("sp_archive_old_books");
query.registerStoredProcedureParameter("archiveDate", Date.class, ParameterMode.IN);
query.registerStoredProcedureParameter("maxBookArchived", Integer.class, ParameterMode.IN);

query.setParameter("archiveDate", new Date());
query.setParameter("maxBookArchived", 1000);
query.execute();
```

Cache API

Most specifications (not just Java EE) focus heavily on functional requirements, leaving nonfunctional ones like performance, scalability, or clustering as implementation details. Implementations have to strictly follow the specification but may also add specific features. A perfect example for JPA would be caching.

Until JPA 2.0, caching wasn't mentioned in the specification. The entity manager is a first-level cache used to process data comprehensively for the database and to cache short-lived entities. This first-level cache is used on a per-transaction basis to reduce the number of SQL queries within a given transaction. For example, if an object is modified several times within the same transaction, the entity manager will generate only one UPDATE statement at the end of the transaction. A first-level cache is not a performance cache.

Nevertheless, all JPA implementations use a performance cache (a.k.a. a second-level cache) to optimize database access, queries, joins, and so on. As seen in Figure 6-3, the second-level cache sits between the entity manager and the database to reduce database traffic by keeping objects loaded in memory and available to the whole application.

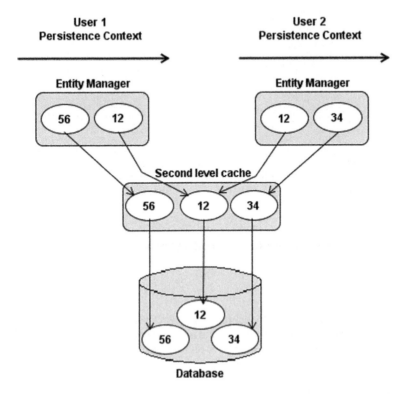

Figure 6-3. *Second-level cache*

Each implementation has its own way of caching objects, either by developing their own mechanism or by reusing existing ones (open source or commercial). Caching can be distributed across a cluster or not—anything is possible when the specification ignores a topic. JPA 2.0 acknowledged that second-level cache was needed and has added caching operations to the standard API. The API, shown in Listing 6-33, is very minimalist (because the goal of JPA is not to standardize a fully functional cache), but it allows code to query and remove some entities from the second-level cache in a standard manner. Like EntityManager, the javax.persistence.Cache is an interface implemented by the persistence provider caching system.

Listing 6-33. Cache API

```
public interface Cache {

    // Whether the cache contains the given entity
    public boolean contains(Class cls, Object id);

    // Removes the given entity from the cache
    public void evict(Class cls, Object id);
    // Removes entities of the specified class (and its subclasses) from the cache
    public void evict(Class cls);
```

```
  // Clears the cache.
  public void evictAll();

  // Returns the provider-specific cache implementation
  public <T> T unwrap(Class<T> cls);
}
```

You can use this API to check if a specific entity is in the second-level cache or not, remove it from the cache, or clear the entire cache. Combined with this API, you can explicitly inform the provider that an entity is cacheable or not by using the @Cacheable annotation as shown in Listing 6-34. If the entity has no @Cacheable annotation, it means that the entity and its state must not be cached by the provider.

Listing 6-34. The Customer Entity Is Cacheable

```
@Entity
@Cacheable(true)
public class Customer {

  @Id @GeneratedValue
  private Long id;
  private String firstName;
  private String lastName;
  private String email;

  // Constructors, getters, setters
}
```

The @Cacheable annotation takes a Boolean value. Once you've decided which entity should be cacheable or not, you need to inform the provider which caching mechanism to use. The way to do this with JPA is to set the shared-cache-mode attribute in the persistence.xml file. Following are the possible values:

- ALL: All entities and entity-related state and data are cached.

- DISABLE_SELECTIVE: Caching is enabled for all entities except those annotated with @Cacheable(false).

- ENABLE_SELECTIVE: Caching is enabled for all entities annotated with @Cacheable(true).

- NONE: Caching is disabled for the persistence unit.

- UNSPECIFIED: Caching behavior is undefined (the provider-specific defaults may apply).

Not setting one of these values leaves it up to the provider to decide which caching mechanism to use. The code in Listing 6-35 shows you how to use this caching mechanism. First, we create a Customer object and persist it. Because Customer is cacheable (see Listing 6-34), it should be in the second-level cache (by using the EntityManagerFactory.getCache().contains() method). Invoking the cache.evict(Customer.class) method removes the entity from the cache.

Listing 6-35. The Customer Entity Is Cacheable

```
Customer customer = new Customer("Patricia", "Jane", "plecomte@mail.com");

tx.begin();
em.persist(customer);
tx.commit();
```

```
// Uses the EntityManagerFactory to get the Cache
Cache cache = emf.getCache();

// Customer should be in the cache
assertTrue(cache.contains(Customer.class, customer.getId()));

// Removes the Customer entity from the cache
cache.evict(Customer.class);

// Customer should not be in the cache anymore
assertFalse(cache.contains(Customer.class, customer.getId()));
```

Concurrency

JPA can be used to change persistent data, and JPQL can be used to retrieve data following certain criteria. All this can happen within an application running in a cluster with multiple nodes, multiple threads, and one single database, so it is quite common for entities to be accessed concurrently. When this is the case, synchronization must be controlled by the application using a locking mechanism. Whether the application is simple or complex, chances are that you will make use of locking somewhere in your code.

To illustrate the problem of concurrent database access, let's see an example of an application with two concurrent threads, shown in Figure 6-4. One thread finds a book by its identifier and raises the price of the book by $2. The other does the same thing but raises the price by $5. If you execute these two threads concurrently in separate transactions and manipulate the same book, you can't predict the final price of the book. In this example, the initial price of the book is $10. Depending on which transaction finishes last, the price can be $12 or $15.

```
tx1.begin();                                      tx2.begin();

// The price of the book is 10$                   // The price of the book is 10$
Book book = em.find(Book.class, 12);              Book book = em.find(Book.class, 12);

book.raisePriceByTwoDollars();                    book.raisePriceByFiveDollars();

tx1.commit();                                     tx2.commit();
// The price is now 12$                           // The price is now 15$
```
time

Figure 6-4. *Transactions one (tx1) and two (tx2) updating the price of a book concurrently*

This problem of concurrency, where the "winner" is the last one to commit, is not specific to JPA. Databases have had to deal with this problem for a long time and have found different solutions to isolate one transaction from others. One common mechanism that databases use is to lock the row on which the SQL statement is being executed.

JPA 2.1 uses two different locking mechanisms (JPA 1.0 only had support for optimistic locking).

- *Optimistic locking* is based on the assumption that most database transactions don't conflict with other transactions, allowing concurrency to be as permissive as possible when allowing transactions to execute.

- *Pessimistic locking* is based on the opposite assumption, so a lock will be obtained on the resource before operating on it.

As an example from everyday life that reinforces these concepts, consider "optimistic and pessimistic street crossing." In an area with very light traffic, you might be able to cross the street without checking for approaching cars. But not in a busy city center!

JPA uses different locking mechanisms at different levels of the API. Both pessimistic and optimistic locks can be obtained via the `EntityManager.find` and `EntityManager.refresh` methods (in addition to the lock method), as well as through JPQL queries, meaning locking can be achieved at the `EntityManager` level and at the `Query` level with the methods listed in Tables 6-5 and 6-6.

Table 6-5. *EntityManager Methods to Lock Entities*

Method	Description
`<T> T find(Class<T> entityClass, Object primaryKey, LockModeType lockMode)`	Searches for an entity of the specified class and primary key and locks it with respect to the specified lock type
`void lock(Object entity, LockModeType lockMode)`	Locks an entity instance that is contained in the persistence context with the specified lock mode type
`void refresh(Object entity, LockModeType lockMode)`	Refreshes the state of the instance from the database, overwriting changes made to the entity, if any, and locks it with respect to the given lock mode type
`LockModeType getLockMode(Object entity)`	Gets the current lock mode for the entity instance

Table 6-6. *Query Method to Lock JPQL Queries*

Method	Description
`LockModeType getLockMode()`	Gets the current lock mode for the query
`Query setLockMode(LockModeType lockMode)`	Sets the lock mode type to be used for the query execution

Each of these methods takes a `LockModeType` as a parameter that can take different values.

- OPTIMISTIC: Uses optimistic locking.

- OPTIMISTIC_FORCE_INCREMENT: Uses optimistic locking and forces an increment to the entity's version column (see the upcoming "Versioning" section).

- PESSIMISTIC_READ: Uses pessimistic locking without the need to reread the data at the end of the transaction to obtain a lock.

- PESSIMISTIC_WRITE: Uses pessimistic locking and forces serialization among transactions attempting to update the entity.

- PESSIMISTIC_FORCE_INCREMENT: Uses pessimistic locking and forces an increment to the entity's version column (see the upcoming "Versioning" section).

- NONE: Specifies no locking mechanism should be used.

You can use these parameters in multiple places depending on how you need to specify locks. You can read *then* lock.

```
Book book = em.find(Book.class, 12);
// Lock to raise the price
em.lock(book, LockModeType.OPTIMISTIC_FORCE_INCREMENT);
book.raisePriceByTwoDollars();
```

Or you can read *and* lock.

```
Book book = em.find(Book.class, 12, LockModeType.OPTIMISTIC_FORCE_INCREMENT);
// The book is already locked, raise the price
book.raisePriceByTwoDollars();
```

Concurrency and locking are key motivators for versioning.

Versioning

Java specifications use versioning: Java SE 5.0, Java SE 6.0, EJB 3.1, JAX-RS 1.0, and so on. When a new version of JAX-RS is released, its version number is increased, and you upgrade to JAX-RS 1.1. JPA uses this exact mechanism when you need to version entities. So, when you persist an entity for the first time in the database, it will get the version number 1. Later, if you update an attribute and commit this change to the database, the entity version will get the number 2, and so on. This versioning will evolve each time a change is made to the entity.

In order for this to happen, the entity must have an attribute to store the version number, and it has to be annotated by @Version. This version number is then mapped to a column in the database. The attribute types supported for versioning can be int, Integer, short, Short, long, Long, or Timestamp. Listing 6-36 shows how to add a version attribute to the Book entity.

Listing 6-36. The Book Entity with a @Version Annotation on an Integer

```
@Entity
public class Book {

  @Id @GeneratedValue
  private Long id;
  @Version
  private Integer version;
  private String title;
  private Float price;
  private String description;
  private String isbn;
  private Integer nbOfPage;
  private Boolean illustrations;

  // Constructors, getters, setters
}
```

The entity can access the value of its version property but must not modify it. Only the persistence provider is permitted to set or update the value of the version attribute when the object is written or updated to the database. Let's look at an example to illustrate the behavior of this versioning. In Listing 6-37, a new Book entity is persisted to the database. Once the transaction is committed, the persistence provider sets the version to 1. Later, the price of the book is updated, and, once the data are flushed to the database, the version number is incremented to 2.

Listing 6-37. Transactions tx1 and tx2 Updating the Price of a Book Concurrently

```
Book book = new Book("H2G2", 21f, "Best IT book", "123-456", 321, false);

tx.begin();
em.persist(book);
tx.commit();
assertEquals(1, book.getVersion());

tx.begin();
book.raisePriceByTwoDollars();
tx.commit();
assertEquals(2, book.getVersion());
```

The version attribute is not required but is recommended when the entity can be concurrently modified by more than one process or thread. Versioning is the core of optimistic locking and provides protection for infrequent concurrent entity modification. In fact, an entity is automatically enabled for optimistic locking if it has a property mapped with a @Version annotation.

Optimistic Locking

As its name indicates, optimistic locking is based on the fact that database transactions don't conflict with each other. In other words, there is a good chance that the transaction updating an entity will be the only one that actually updates the entity during that interval. Therefore, the decision to acquire a lock on the entity is actually made at the end of the transaction. This ensures that updates to an entity are consistent with the current state of the database. Transactions that would cause this constraint to be violated result in an OptimisticLockException being thrown and the transaction marked for rollback.

How would you throw an OptimisticLockException? Either by explicitly locking the entity (with the lock or the find methods that you saw, passing a LockModeType) or by letting the persistence provider check the attribute annotated with @Version. The use of a dedicated @Version annotation on an entity allows the EntityManager to perform optimistic locking simply by comparing the value of the version attribute in the entity instance with the value of the column in the database. Without an attribute annotated with @Version, the entity manager will not be able to do optimistic locking automatically (implicitly).

Let's look again at the example of increasing the price of a book. Transactions tx1 and tx2 both get an instance of the same Book entity. At that moment, the version of the Book entity is 1. The first transaction raises the price of the book by $2 and commits this change. When the data are flushed to the database, the persistence provider increases the version number and sets it to 2. At that moment, the second transaction raises the price by $5 and commits the change. The entity manager for tx2 realizes that the version number in the database is different from that of the entity. This means the version has been changed by a different transaction, so an OptimisticLockException is thrown, as shown in Figure 6-5.

```
tx1.begin();                           tx2.begin();

// The price of the book is 10$         // The price of the book is 10$
Book book = em.find(Book.class, 12);    Book book = em.find(Book.class, 12);
// book.getVersion() == 1                // book.getVersion() == 1

book.raisePriceByTwoDollars();
                                        book.raisePriceByFiveDollars();
tx1.commit();
// The price is now 12$
// book.getVersion() == 2                tx2.commit();
                                        // version should be 1 but is 2
                                        // OptimisticLockException
                              time
```

Figure 6-5. OptimisticLockException thrown on transaction tx2

This is the default behavior when the @Version annotation is used: an OptimisticLockException is thrown when the data are flushed (at commit time or by explicitly calling the em.flush() method). You can also control where you want to add the optimistic lock using read then lock or read and lock. The code of read and lock, for example, would look like this:

```
Book book = em.find(Book.class, 12);
// Lock to raise the price
em.lock(book, LockModeType.OPTIMISTIC);
book.raisePriceByTwoDollars();
```

With optimistic locking, the LockModeType that you pass as a parameter can take two values: OPTIMISTIC and OPTIMISTIC_FORCE_INCREMENT (or READ and WRITE, respectively, but these values are deprecated). The only difference is that OPTIMISTIC_FORCE_INCREMENT will force an update (increment) to the entity's version column.

Applications are strongly encouraged to enable optimistic locking for all entities that may be concurrently accessed. Failure to use a locking mechanism may lead to inconsistent entity state, lost updates, and other state irregularities. Optimistic locking is a useful performance optimization that offloads work that would otherwise be required of the database and is an alternative to pessimistic locking, which requires low-level database locking.

Pessimistic Locking

Pessimistic locking is based on the opposite assumption to optimistic locking, because a lock is eagerly obtained on the entity before operating on it. This is very resource restrictive and results in significant performance degradation, as a database lock is held using a SELECT ... FOR UPDATE SQL statement to read data.

Databases typically offer a pessimistic locking service that allows the entity manager to lock a row in a table to prevent another thread from updating the same row. This is an effective mechanism to ensure that two clients do not modify the same row at the same time, but it requires expensive, low-level checks inside the database. Transactions that would cause this constraint to be violated result in a PessimisticLockException being thrown and the transaction marked for rollback.

Optimistic locking is appropriate in dealing with moderate contention among concurrent transactions. But in some applications with a higher risk of contentions, pessimistic locking may be more appropriate, as the database lock is immediately obtained as opposed to the often late failure of optimistic transactions. For example, in times of economic crises, stock markets receive huge numbers of selling orders. If 100 million Americans need to sell their stock options at the same time, the system needs to use pessimistic locks to ensure data consistency. Note that at the moment the market is rather pessimistic instead of optimistic, and that has nothing to do with JPA.

Pessimistic locking may be applied to entities that do not contain the annotated @Version attribute.

Entity Life Cycle

By now, you know most of the mysteries of entities, so let's look at their life cycle. When an entity is instantiated (with the new operator), it is just seen as a regular POJO by the JVM (i.e., detached) and can be used as a regular object by the application. Then, when the entity is persisted by the entity manager, it is said to be managed. When an entity is managed, the entity manager will automatically synchronize the value of its attributes with the underlying database (e.g., if you change the value of an attribute by using a set method while the entity is managed, this new value will be automatically synchronized with the database).

To have a better understanding of this process, take a look at Figure 6-6, a UML state diagram showing the transitions between each state of a Customer entity.

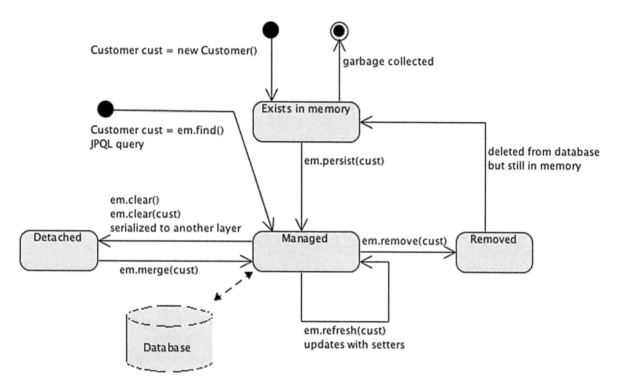

Figure 6-6. *Entity life cycle*

To create an instance of the Customer entity, you use the new operator. This object exists in memory, although JPA knows nothing about it. If you do nothing with this object, it will go out of scope and will end up being garbage collected, and that will be the end of its life cycle. What you can do next is persist an instance of Customer with the EntityManager.persist() method. At that moment, the entity becomes managed, and its state is synchronized with the database. During this managed state, you can update attributes using the setter methods (e.g., customer.setFirstName()) or refresh the content with anEntityManager.refresh() method. All these changes will be synchronized between the entity and the database. During this state, if you call the EntityManager.contains(customer) method, it will return true because customer is contained in the persistence context (i.e., managed).

Another way for an entity to be managed is when it is loaded from the database. When you use the EntityManager.find() method, or create a JPQL query to retrieve a list of entities, all are automatically managed, and you can start updating or removing their attributes.

217

In the managed state, you can call the `EntityManager.remove()` method, and the entity is deleted from the database and not managed anymore. But the Java object continues living in memory, and you can still use it until the garbage collector gets rid of it.

Now let's look at the detached state. You've seen in the previous chapter how explicitly calling the `EntityManager.clear()` or `EntityManager.detach(customer)` methods will clear the entity from the persistence context; it becomes detached. But there is also another, more subtle, way to detach an entity: when it's serialized. In many examples in this book, entities don't implement anything, but, if they need to cross a network to be invoked remotely or cross layers to be displayed in a presentation tier, they need to implement the `java.io.Serializable` interface. This is not a JPA restriction but a Java restriction. When a managed entity is serialized, crosses the network, and gets deserialized, it is seen as a detached object. To reattach an entity, you need to call the `EntityManager.merge()` method. A common-use case is when you use an entity in a JSF page. Let's say that a `Customer` entity is displayed in a form on a remote JSF page to be updated. Being remote, the entity needs to be serialized on the server side before being sent to the presentation layer. At that moment, the entity is automatically detached. Once displayed, if any data are changed and need to be updated, the form is submitted and the entity is sent back to the server, deserialized, and needs to be merged to be attached again.

Callback methods and listeners allow you to add your own business logic when certain life-cycle events occur on an entity, or broadly whenever a life-cycle event occurs on any entity.

Callbacks

The life cycle of an entity falls into four categories: persisting, updating, removing, and loading, which correspond to the database operations of inserting, updating, deleting, and selecting, respectively. Each life cycle has a "pre" and "post" event that can be intercepted by the entity manager to invoke a business method. These business methods have to be annotated by one of the annotations described in Table 6-7. These annotations may be applied to methods of an entity class, a mapped superclass, or a callback listener class.

Table 6-7. *Life-Cycle Callback Annotations*

Annotation	Description
@PrePersist	Marks a method to be invoked before `EntityManager.persist()` is executed.
@PostPersist	Marks a method to be invoked after the entity has been persisted. If the entity autogenerates its primary key (with `@GeneratedValue`), the value is available in the method.
@PreUpdate	Marks a method to be invoked before a database update operation is performed (calling the entity setters or the `EntityManager.merge()` method).
@PostUpdate	Marks a method to be invoked after a database update operation is performed.
@PreRemove	Marks a method to be invoked before `EntityManager.remove()` is executed.
@PostRemove	Marks a method to be invoked after the entity has been removed.
@PostLoad	Marks a method to be invoked after an entity is loaded (with a JPQL query or an `EntityManager.find()`) or refreshed from the underlying database. There is no `@PreLoad` annotation, as it doesn't make sense to preload data on an entity that is not built yet.

Adding the callback annotations to the UML state diagram shown previously in Figure 6-6 results in the diagram you see in Figure 6-7.

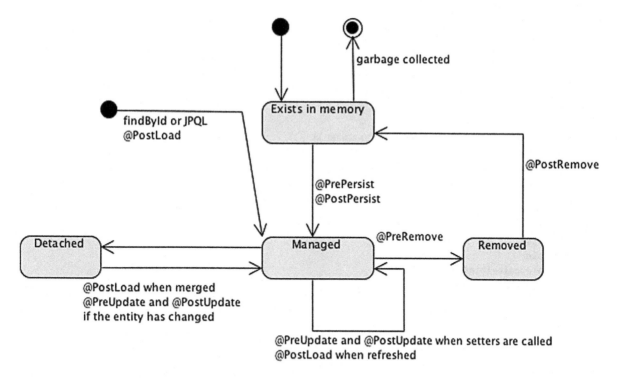

Figure 6-7. *Entity life cycle with callback annotations*

Before inserting an entity into the database, the entity manager calls the method annotated with `@PrePersist`. If the insert does not throw an exception, the entity is persisted, its identity is initialized, and the method annotated with `@PostPersist` is then invoked. This is the same behavior for updates (`@PreUpdate`, `@PostUpdate`) and deletes (`@PreRemove`, `@PostRemove`). A method annotated with `@PostLoad` is called when an entity is loaded from the database (via an `EntityManager.find()` or a JPQL query). When the entity is detached and needs to be merged, the entity manager first has to check whether there are any differences with the database (`@PostLoad`) and, if so, update the data (`@PreUpdate`, `@PostUpdate`).

How does it look in the code? Entities can have not only attributes, constructors, getters, and setters but also business logic used to validate their state or compute some of their attributes. These can consist of normal Java methods that are invoked by other classes or callback annotations (also referred to as callback methods), as shown in Listing 6-38. The entity manager invokes them automatically depending on the event triggered.

Listing 6-38. The Customer Entity with Callback Annotations

```
@Entity
public class Customer {

  @Id @GeneratedValue
  private Long id;
  private String firstName;
  private String lastName;
  private String email;
  private String phoneNumber;
  @Temporal(TemporalType.DATE)
  private Date dateOfBirth;
```

```
@Transient
private Integer age;
@Temporal(TemporalType.TIMESTAMP)
private Date creationDate;

@PrePersist
@PreUpdate
private void validate() {
  if (firstName == null || "".equals(firstName))
    throw new IllegalArgumentException("Invalid first name");
  if (lastName == null || "".equals(lastName))
    throw new IllegalArgumentException("Invalid last name");
}

@PostLoad
@PostPersist
@PostUpdate
public void calculateAge() {
  if (dateOfBirth == null) {
    age = null;
    return;
  }

  Calendar birth = new GregorianCalendar();
  birth.setTime(dateOfBirth);
  Calendar now = new GregorianCalendar();
  now.setTime(new Date());
  int adjust = 0;
  if (now.get(DAY_OF_YEAR) - birth.get(DAY_OF_YEAR) < 0) {
    adjust = -1;
  }
  age = now.get(YEAR) - birth.get(YEAR) + adjust;
}

// Constructors, getters, setters
}
```

In Listing 6-38, the Customer entity has a method to validate its data (checks the firstName and lastName attributes). This method is annotated with @PrePersist and @PreUpdate and will get called before inserting data into or updating data in the database. If the data are not valid, a runtime exception is launched, and the insert or update will roll back to ensure that the data inserted or updated in the database are valid.

The method calculateAge() calculates the age of the customer. The age attribute is transient and doesn't get mapped into the database. After the entity gets loaded, persisted, or updated, the calculateAge() method takes the date of birth of the customer, calculates the age, and sets the attribute.

The following rules apply to life-cycle callback methods:

- Methods can have public, private, protected, or package-level access but must not be static or final. Notice in Listing 6-38 that the validate() method is private.

- A method may be annotated with multiple life-cycle event annotations (the validateData() method is annotated with @PrePersist and @PreUpdate). However, only one life-cycle annotation of a given type may be present in an entity class (e.g., you can't have two @PrePersist annotations in the same entity).

- A method can throw unchecked (runtime) exceptions but not checked exceptions. Throwing a runtime exception will roll back the transaction if one exists.

- A method can invoke JNDI, JDBC, JMS, and EJBs but cannot invoke any `EntityManager` or `Query` operations.

- With inheritance, if a method is specified on the superclass, it will get invoked before the method on the child class. For example, if in Listing 6-38 `Customer` was inheriting from a `Person` entity, the `Person` `@PrePersist` method would be invoked before the `Customer` `@PrePersist` method.

- If event cascading is used in the relationships, the callback method will also be called in a cascaded way. For example, let's say a `Customer` has a collection of addresses, and a cascade remove is set on the relation. When you delete the customer, the `Address` `@PreRemove` method would be invoked as well as the `Customer` `@PreRemove` method.

Listeners

Callback methods in an entity work well when you have business logic that is only related to that entity. Entity listeners are used to extract the business logic to a separate class and share it between other entities. An entity listener is just a POJO on which you can define one or more life-cycle callback methods. To register a listener, the entity needs to use the `@EntityListeners` annotation.

Using the customer example, let's extract the `calculateAge()` and `validate()` methods to separate listener classes, `AgeCalculationListener` (see Listing 6-39) and `DataValidationListener` (see Listing 6-40), respectively.

Listing 6-39. A Listener Calculating the Customer's Age

```java
public class AgeCalculationListener {

  @PostLoad
  @PostPersist
  @PostUpdate
  public void calculateAge(Customer customer) {
    if (customer.getDateOfBirth() == null) {
      customer.setAge(null);
      return;
    }

    Calendar birth = new GregorianCalendar();
    birth.setTime(customer.getDateOfBirth());
    Calendar now = new GregorianCalendar();
    now.setTime(new Date());
    int adjust = 0;    if (now.get(DAY_OF_YEAR) - birth.get(DAY_OF_YEAR) < 0) {
      adjust = -1;
    }
    customer.setAge(now.get(YEAR) - birth.get(YEAR) + adjust);
  }
}
```

Listing 6-40. A Listener Validating the Customer's Attributes

```java
public class DataValidationListener {

    @PrePersist
    @PreUpdate
    private void validate(Customer customer) {
        if (customer.getFirstName() == null || "".equals(customer.getFirstName()))
            throw new IllegalArgumentException("Invalid first name");
        if (customer.getLastName() == null || "".equals(customer.getLastName()))
            throw new IllegalArgumentException("Invalid last name");
    }
}
```

Only simple rules apply to a listener class. The first is that the class must have a public no-arg constructor. Second, the signatures of the callback methods are slightly different from the ones in Listing 6-38. When you invoke the callback method on a listener, the method needs to have access to the entity state (e.g., the customer's first name and last name, which need to be validated). The methods must have a parameter of a type that is compatible with the entity type, as the entity related to the event is being passed into the callback. A callback method defined on an entity has the following signature with no parameter:

```java
void <METHOD>();
```

Callback methods defined on an entity listener can have two different types of signatures. If the method has to be used on several entities, it must have an Object argument.

```java
void <METHOD>(Object anyEntity)
```

If it is only for one entity or its subclasses (when there's inheritance), the parameter can be of the entity type.

```java
void <METHOD>(Customer customerOrSubclasses)
```

To designate that these two listeners are notified of life-cycle events on the Customer entity, you need to use the @EntityListeners annotation (see Listing 6-41). This annotation can take one entity listener as a parameter or an array of listeners. When several listeners are defined and the life-cycle event occurs, the persistence provider iterates through each listener in the order in which they are listed and will invoke the callback method, passing a reference of the entity to which the event applies. It will then invoke the callback methods on the entity itself (if there are any).

Listing 6-41. The Customer Entity Defining Two Listeners

```java
@EntityListeners({DataValidationListener.class, AgeCalculationListener.class})
@Entity
public class Customer {

    @Id @GeneratedValue
    private Long id;
    private String firstName;
    private String lastName;
    private String email;
    private String phoneNumber;
    @Temporal(TemporalType.DATE)
    private Date dateOfBirth;
```

```
@Transient
private Integer age;
@Temporal(TemporalType.TIMESTAMP)
private Date creationDate;

// Constructors, getters, setters
}
```

The result of this code is exactly the same as that of the previous example (shown earlier in Listing 6-38). The Customer entity validates its data before an insert or an update using the DataValidationListener.validate() method and calculates its age with the listener's AgeCalculationListener.calculateAge() method.

The rules that an entity listener's methods have to follow are similar to the entity callback methods except for a few details.

- Only unchecked exceptions can be thrown. This causes the remaining listeners and callback methods to not be invoked and the transaction to be roll backed if one exists.

- In an inheritance hierarchy, if multiple entities define listeners, the listeners defined on the superclass are invoked before the listeners defined on the subclasses. If an entity doesn't want to inherit the superclass listeners, it can explicitly exclude them by using the @ExcludeSuperclassListeners annotation (or its XML equivalent).

Listing 6-41 shows a Customer entity defining two listeners, but a listener can also be defined by more than one entity. This can be useful in cases where the listener provides more general logic that many entities can benefit from. For example, you could create a debug listener that displays the name of some triggered events, as shown in Listing 6-42.

Listing 6-42. A Debug Listener Usable by Any Entity

```
public class DebugListener {

  @PrePersist
  void prePersist(Object object) {
    System.out.println("prePersist");
  }

  @PreUpdate
  void preUpdate(Object object) {
    System.out.println("preUpdate");
  }

  @PreRemove
  void preRemove(Object object) {
    System.out.println("preRemove");
  }
}
```

Note that each method takes an Object as a parameter, meaning that any type of entity could use this listener by adding the DebugListener class to its @EntityListeners annotation. To have every single entity of your application use this listener, you would have to go through each one and add it manually to the annotation. For this case, JPA has a notion of default listeners that can cover all entities in a persistence unit. As there is no annotation targeted for the entire scope of the persistence unit, the default listeners can only be declared in an XML mapping file.

In the previous chapter you saw how to use XML mapping files instead of annotations. The same steps have to be followed to define the DebugListener as a default listener. A mapping file with the XML defined in Listing 6-43 needs to be created and deployed with the application.

Listing 6-43. A Debug Listener Defined as the Default Listener

```xml
<?xml version="1.0" encoding="UTF-8"?>
<entity-mappings xmlns="http://xmlns.jcp.org/xml/ns/persistence/orm"
                 xmlns:xsi="http://www.w3.org/2001/XMLSchema-instance" ↵
                 xsi:schemaLocation="http://xmlns.jcp.org/xml/ns/persistence/orm
                 http://xmlns.jcp.org/xml/ns/persistence/orm_2_1.xsd"
                 version="2.1">

  <persistence-unit-metadata>
     <persistence-unit-defaults>
        <entity-listeners>
           <entity-listener class="org.agoncal.book.javaee7.chapter06.DebugListener"/>
        </entity-listeners>
     </persistence-unit-defaults>
  </persistence-unit-metadata>

</entity-mappings>
```

In this file, the <persistence-unit-metadata> tag defines all the metadata that don't have any annotation equivalent. The <persistence-unit-defaults> tag defines all the defaults of the persistence unit, and the <entity-listener> tag defines the default listener. This file needs to be referred in the persistence.xml and deployed with the application. The DebugListener will then be automatically invoked for every single entity.

When you declare a list of default entity listeners, each listener gets called in the order in which it is listed in the XML mapping file. Default entity listeners always get invoked before any of the entity listeners listed in the @EntityListeners annotation. If an entity doesn't want to have the default entity listeners applied to it, it can use the @ExcludeDefaultListeners annotation, as shown in Listing 6-44.

Listing 6-44. The Customer Entity Excluding Default Listeners

```java
@ExcludeDefaultListeners
@Entity
public class Customer {

  @Id @GeneratedValue
  private Long id;
  private String firstName;
  private String lastName;
  private String email;
  private String phoneNumber;
  @Temporal(TemporalType.DATE)
  private Date dateOfBirth;
  @Transient
  private Integer age;
  @Temporal(TemporalType.TIMESTAMP)
  private Date creationDate;

  // Constructors, getters, setters
}
```

When an event is raised, the listeners are executed in the following order:

1. `@EntityListeners` for a given entity or superclass in the array order,

2. Entity listeners for the superclasses (highest first),

3. Entity listeners for the entity,

4. Callbacks of the superclasses (highest first), and

5. Callbacks of the entity.

Summary

In this chapter, you learned how to query entities. The entity manager is central to articulating entities with persistence. It can create, update, find by ID, remove, and synchronize entities with the database with the help of the persistence context, which acts as a level-one cache. JPA also comes with a very powerful query language, JPQL, which is database vendor independent. You can retrieve entities with a rich syntax using WHERE, ORDER BY, or GROUP BY clauses, and when concurrent access occurs to your entities, you know how to use versioning and when to use optimistic or pessimistic locking.

This chapter also described the entity life cycle and how the entity manager catches events to invoke callback methods. Callback methods can be defined on a single entity and annotated by several annotations (`@PrePersist`, `@PostPersist`, etc.). The method can also be extracted to listener classes and used by several or all entities (using default entity listeners). With callback methods, you see that entities are not just anemic objects (objects with no business logic, just attributes, getters, and setters); entities can have business logic that can be invoked by other objects in the application, or invoked automatically by the entity manager, depending on the life cycle of the entity.

CHAPTER 7

■ ■ ■

Enterprise JavaBeans

The previous chapter showed how to implement persistent objects using JPA and how to query them with JPQL. Entities can have methods to validate their attributes, but they are not made to represent complex tasks, which often require an interaction with other components (other persistent objects, external services, etc.). The persistence layer is not the appropriate layer for business processing. Similarly, the user interface should not perform business logic, especially when there are multiple interfaces (Web, Swing, portable devices, etc.). To separate the persistence layer from the presentation layer, to implement business logic, to add transaction management and security, applications need a business layer. In Java EE, we implement this layer using Enterprise JavaBeans (EJBs).

For most applications, layering is important. Following a bottom-up approach, the previous chapters on JPA modeled domain classes, usually defining nouns (Artist, CD, Book, Customer, etc.). On top of the domain layer, the business layer models the actions (or verbs) of the application (create a book, buy a book, print an order, deliver a book, etc.). Often, this business layer interacts with external web services (SOAP or RESTful web services), sends asynchronous messages to other systems (using JMS), or posts e-mails; it orchestrates several components from databases to external systems, and serves as the central place for transaction and security demarcation as well as the entry point to any kind of client such as web interfaces (Servlets or JSF backing beans), batch processing, or external systems. This logical separation between entities and session beans follows the "separation of concerns" paradigm wherein an application is split into separate components whose functions overlap as little as possible.

This chapter introduces you to EJBs and then explains the three different types of session beans: stateless, stateful, and singleton Stateless beans are the most scalable of the three, as they keep no state and complete business logic in a single method call. Stateful beans maintain a conversational state with one client. EJB 3.1 brought the singleton session bean (one instance per application) into the previous release. You will also see how to execute these EJBs in an embedded container and invoke them synchronously or asynchronously.

Understanding Enterprise JavaBeans

EJBs are server-side components that encapsulate business logic and take care of transactions and security. They also have an integrated stack for messaging, scheduling, remote access, web service endpoints (SOAP and REST), dependency injection, component life cycle, AOP (aspect-oriented programming) with interceptors, and so on. In addition, EJBs seamlessly integrate with other Java SE and Java EE technologies, such as JDBC, JavaMail, JPA, Java Transaction API (JTA), Java Messaging Service (JMS), Java Authentication and Authorization Service (JAAS), Java Naming and Directory Interface (JNDI), and Remote Method Invocation (RMI). This is why they are used to build the business logic layer (see Figure 7-1), sit on top of the database, and orchestrate the business model layer. EJBs act as an entry point for presentation-tier technologies like JavaServer Faces (JSF) but also for all external services (JMS or web services).

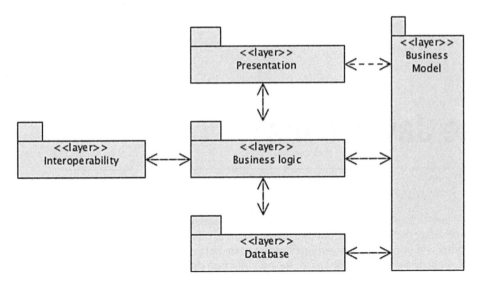

Figure 7-1. *Architecture layering*

EJBs use a very powerful programming model that combines ease of use and robustness. Today EJBs are a very simple Java server-side development model, reducing complexity while bringing reusability and scalability to mission-critical enterprise applications. All this comes from annotating a single POJO that will be deployed into a container. An EJB container is a runtime environment that provides services, such as transaction management, concurrency control, pooling, and security authorization. Historically, application servers have added other features such as clustering, load balancing, and failover. EJB developers can then concentrate on implementing business logic while the container deals with all the technical plumbing.

Today more than ever, with version 3.2, EJBs can be written once and deployed on any container that supports the specification. Standard APIs, portable JNDI names, lightweight components, CDI integration, and configuration by exception allow easy deployment of EJBs on open source as well as commercial implementations. The underlying technology was created more than 12 years ago, resulting in EJB applications that benefit from proven concepts.

Types of EJBs

Session beans are great for implementing business logic, processes, and workflow. And because enterprise applications can be complex, the Java EE platform defines several types of EJBs. A session bean may have the following traits:

- *Stateless*: The session bean contains no conversational state between methods, and any instance can be used for any client. It is used to handle tasks that can be concluded with a single method call.

- *Stateful*: The session bean contains conversational state, which must be retained across methods for a single user. It is useful for tasks that have to be done in several steps.

- *Singleton*: A single session bean is shared between clients and supports concurrent access. The container will make sure that only one instance exists for the entire application.

The three types of session beans all have their specific features, of course, but they also have a lot in common. First of all, they have the same programming model. As you'll see later on, a session bean can have a local and/or remote interface, or no interface at all. Session beans are container-managed components, so they need to be packaged in an archive (jar, war, or ear file) and deployed to a container.

Message-driven beans (MDBs) are used for integrating with external systems by receiving asynchronous messages using JMS. Even though MDBs are part of the EJB specification, I deal with them separately (in Chapter 13) because this component model is mainly used to integrate systems with message-oriented middleware (MOM). MDBs usually delegate the business logic to session beans.

EJBs can also be used as web service endpoints. Chapters 14 and 15 demonstrate SOAP and RESTful web services that can be either simple POJOs deployed in a web container or session beans deployed in an EJB container.

■ **Note** For compatibility reasons, the EJB 3.1 specification still included Entity CMP. This persistent component model has been pruned and is now optional in EJB 3.2. JPA is the preferred technology for mapping and querying relational databases. This book does not cover Entity CMP.

Process and Embedded Container

Right from the moment they were invented (EJB 1.0), EJBs had to be executed in a container that would run on top of a JVM. Think of GlassFish, JBoss, Weblogic, and so on, and you'll remember that the application server first needs to be started before deploying and using your EJB. This in-process container is appropriate for a production environment, where the server runs continuously. But it is time-consuming in a development environment where you frequently need to start, deploy, debug, and stop the container. Another issue with servers running in a different process is that testing capabilities are limited. Either you mock all the container services for unit testing or you need to deploy your EJB in a live server to perform integration tests. To solve these problems, some application server implementations came with embedded containers, but these were implementation specific. Since EJB 3.1 the expert group has standardized an embedded container that is portable across servers.

The idea of an embedded container is to be able to execute EJB applications within a Java SE environment allowing clients to run within the same JVM and class loader. This provides better support for integration testing, offline processing (e.g., batch processing), and the use of the EJB in desktop applications. The embeddable container API provides the same managed environment as the Java EE runtime container and includes the same services. You can now execute the embedded container on the same JVM as your IDE and debug your EJB without doing any deployment to a separate application server.

Services Given by the Container

No matter if the container is embedded or runs in a separate process, it provides core services common to many enterprise applications such as the following:

- *Remote client communication*: Without writing any complex code, an EJB client (another EJB, a user interface, a batch process, etc.) can invoke methods remotely via standard protocols.

- *Dependency injection*: The container can inject several resources into an EJB (JMS destinations and factories, datasources, other EJBs, environment variables, etc.) as well as any POJO thanks to CDI.

- *State management*: For stateful session beans, the container manages their state transparently. You can maintain state for a particular client, as if you were developing a desktop application.

- *Pooling*: For stateless beans and MDBs, the container creates a pool of instances that can be shared by multiple clients. Once invoked, an EJB returns to the pool to be reused instead of being destroyed.

- *Component life cycle*: The container is responsible for managing the life cycle of each component.

- *Messaging*: The container allows MDBs to listen to destinations and consume messages without too much JMS plumbing.

- *Transaction management*: With declarative transaction management, an EJB can use annotations to inform the container about the transaction policy it should use. The container takes care of the commit or the rollback.

- *Security*: Class or method-level access control can be specified on EJBs to enforce user and role authorization.

- *Concurrency support*: Except for singletons, where some concurrency declaration is needed, all the other types of EJB are thread-safe by nature. You can develop high-performance applications without worrying about thread issues.

- *Interceptors*: Cross-cutting concerns can be put into interceptors, which will be invoked automatically by the container.

- *Asynchronous method invocation*: Since EJB 3.1, it's now possible to have asynchronous calls without involving messaging.

Once the EJB is deployed, the container takes care of these features, leaving the developer to focus on business logic while benefiting from these services without adding any system-level code.

EJBs are managed objects. In fact they are considered to be Managed Beans. When a client invokes an EJB, it doesn't work directly with an instance of that EJB but rather with a proxy on an instance. Each time a client invokes a method on an EJB, the call is actually proxied and intercepted by the container, which provides services on behalf of the bean instance. Of course, this is completely transparent to the client; from its creation to its destruction, an enterprise bean lives in a container.

In a Java EE application, the EJB container will usually interact with other containers: the Servlet container (responsible for managing the execution of Servlets and JSF pages), the application client container (ACC) (for managing stand-alone applications), the message broker (for sending, queuing, and receiving messages), the persistence provider, and so on.

Containers give EJBs a set of service. On the other hand, EJBs cannot create or manage threads, access files using java.io, create a ServerSocket, load a native library, or use the AWT (Abstract Window Toolkit) or Swing APIs to interact with the user.

EJB Lite

Enterprise Java Beans are the predominant component model in Java EE 7, being the simplest method for transactional and secure business processing. However, EJB 3.2 still defines complex technologies that are less used today such as IIOP (Internet InterOrb Protocol) interoperability, meaning that any new vendor implementing the EJB 3.2 specification has to implement it. Developers getting started with EJBs would also be weighed down by many technologies that they would never use otherwise.

For these reasons, the specification defines a minimal subset of the full EJB API known as EJB Lite. It includes a small, powerful selection of EJB features suitable for writing portable transactional and secure business logic. Any EJB Lite application can be deployed on any Java EE product that implementsEJB 3.2. EJB Lite is composed of the subset of the EJB API listed in Table 7-1.

Table 7-1. *Comparison Between EJB Lite and Full EJB*

Feature	EJB Lite	Full EJB 3.2
Session beans (stateless, stateful, singleton)	Yes	Yes
No-interface view	Yes	Yes
Local interface	Yes	Yes
Interceptors	Yes	Yes
Transaction support	Yes	Yes
Security	Yes	Yes
Embeddable API	Yes	Yes
Asynchronous calls	No	Yes
MDBs	No	Yes
Remote interface	No	Yes
JAX-WS web services	No	Yes
JAX-RS web services	No	Yes
Timer service	No	Yes
RMI/IIOP interoperability	No	Yes

■ **Note**   Since the beginning the EJB specifications required the capability of using RMI/IIOP to export EJB components and to access EJB components over a network. This requirement allowed interoperability between Java EE products. This requirement has been pruned in EJB 3.2 and might become optional in future releases, because RMI/IIOP has been largely superseded by modern web technologies that provide interoperability support, such as SOAP and REST.

EJB Specification Overview

EJB 1.0 was created back in 1998, and EJB 3.2 was released in 2013 with Java EE 7. During these 15 years, the EJB specification went through many changes, but it still retains its mature foundations. From heavyweight components to annotated POJOs, from Entity Bean CMP to JPA, EJBs have reinvented themselves to meet the needs of developers and modern architectures.

More than ever, the EJB 3.2 specification helps to avoid vendor lock-in by providing features that were previously nonstandard (such as nonstandard JNDI names or embedded containers). Today, EJB 3.2 is much more portable than in the past.

A Brief History of the EJB Specification

Soon after the creation of the Java language, the industry felt the need for a technology that could address the requirements of large-scale applications, embracing RMI and JTA. The idea of creating a distributed and transactional business component framework arose, and as a result IBM first started creating what eventually became known as EJBs.

EJB 1.0 supported stateful and stateless session beans, with optional support for entity beans. The programming model used home and remote interfaces in addition to the session bean itself. EJBs were made accessible through an interface that offered remote access with arguments passed by value.

EJB 1.1 mandated support for entity beans and introduced the XML deployment descriptor to store metadata (which was then serialized as binary in a file). This version provided better support for application assembly and deployment by introducing roles.

In 2001, EJB 2.0 was the first version to be standardized by the Java Community Process (as JSR 19). It addressed the overhead of passing arguments by value by introducing local interfaces. Clients running inside the container would access EJBs through their local interface (using arguments passed by reference), and clients running in a different container would use the remote interface. This version introduced MDBs, and entity beans gained support for relationships and a query language (EJB QL).

Two years later, EJB 2.1 (JSR 153) added support for web services, allowing session beans to be invoked through SOAP/HTTP. A timer service was created to allow EJBs to be invoked at designated times or intervals.

Three years passed between EJB 2.1 and EJB 3.0, which allowed the expert group to remodel the entire design. In 2006, the EJB 3.0 specification (JSR 220) broke with previous versions as it focused on ease of use, with EJBs looking more like POJOs. The entity beans were replaced by a brand-new specification (JPA), and session beans no longer required home or EJB-specific component interfaces. Resource injection, interceptors, and life-cycle callbacks were introduced.

In 2009, the EJB 3.1 specification (JSR 318) shipped with Java EE 6, following the path of the previous version by simplifying the programming model even further. The 3.1 version brought an amazing number of new features such as the no-interface view, embedded container, singleton, a richer timer service, asynchrony, portable JNDI, and EJB Lite.

What's New in EJB 3.2?

The EJB 3.2 specification (JSR 345) is less ambitious than the previous release. To simplify future adoption of the specification, the Java EE 6 expert group had compiled a list of features for possible future removal (a.k.a. pruning). None of the following features were actually removed from EJB 3.1, but they all became optional in 3.2.

- Entity bean 2.*x*

- Client view of an entity bean 2.*x*

- EJB QL (query language for CMP)

- JAX-RPC–based web service endpoints

- Client view of a JAX-RPC web service

That's why the specification itself is organized into two different documents.

- *"EJB Core Contracts and Requirements:"* The main document that specifies EJBs.

- *"EJB Optional Features:"* The document that describes the previously listed features for which support has been made optional.

The EJB 3.2 specification includes the following minor updates and improvements:

- Transactions can now be used by Managed Beans (previously only EJBs could use transactions; more in Chapter 9).

- Stateful session bean life-cycle callback methods can opt-in to be transactional.

- Passivation for stateful session bean is now opted out.

- The rules to define all local/remote views of the bean have been simplified.

- Restriction to obtain the current class loader has been removed, and the use of the `java.io` package is now allowed.

- Allignment of JMS 2.0.

- Embeddable container implements `Autocloseable` to fit Java SE 7.

- RMI/IIOP has been pruned in this release. This means that it might be marked as optional in Java EE 8. Remote invocation would then be done with just RMI (without the IIOP interoperability).

Table 7-2 lists the main packages defined in EJB 3.2 today.

Table 7-2. *Main EJB Packages*

Package	Description
javax.ejb	Classes and interfaces that define the contracts between the EJB and its clients and between the EJB and the container
javax.ejb.embeddable	Classes for the embeddable API
javax.ejb.spi	Interfaces that are implemented by the EJB container

Reference Implementation

GlassFish is an open source application server project led by Oracle for the Java EE platform. Sun launched the project in 2005 and it became the reference implementation of Java EE 5 in 2006. Today, GlassFish v4 includes the reference implementation for EJB 3.2. Internally, the product is built around modularity (based on the Apache Felix OSGi runtime), allowing a very fast startup time and the use of various application containers (Java EE 7, of course, but also Ruby, PHP, etc.).

At the time of writing this book GlassFish is the only EJB 3.2 compliant implementation. But others will soon follow: OpenEJB, JBoss, Weblogic, Websphere . . .

Writing Enterprise Java Beans

Session beans encapsulate business logic, are transactional, and rely on a container that does pooling, multithreading, security, and so on. What artifacts do we need to create such a powerful component? One Java class and one annotation–that's all. Listing 7-1 shows how simple it is for a container to recognize that a class is a session bean and apply all the enterprise services.

Listing 7-1. A Simple Stateless EJB

```
@Stateless
public class BookEJB {

  @PersistenceContext(unitName = "chapter07PU")
  private EntityManager em;

  public Book findBookById(Long id) {
    return em.find(Book.class, id);
  }
```

```
public Book createBook(Book book) {
  em.persist(book);
  return book;
}
}
```

Previous versions of J2EE required developers to create several artifacts in order to create a session bean: a local or remote interface (or both), a local home or a remote home interface (or both), and a deployment descriptor. Java EE 5 and EJB 3.0 drastically simplified the model to the point where only one class and one or more business interfaces are sufficient and you don't need any XML configuration. As shown in Listing 7-1, since EJB 3.1 the class doesn't even have to implement any interface. We use only one annotation to turn a Java class into a transactional and secure component: @Stateless. Then, using the entity manager (as seen in the previous chapters), the BookEJB creates and retrieves books from the database in a simple yet powerful manner.

Anatomy of an EJB

Listing 7-1 shows the easiest programming model for session beans: an annotated POJO with no interface. But, depending on your needs, session beans can give you a much richer model, allowing you to perform remote calls, dependency injection, or asynchronous calls. An EJB is made of the following elements:

- *A bean class*: The bean class contains the business method implementation and can implement zero or several business interfaces. The session bean must be annotated with @Stateless, @Stateful, or @Singleton depending on its type.

- *Business interfaces*: These interfaces contain the declaration of business methods that are visible to the client and implemented by the bean class. A session bean can have local interfaces, remote interfaces, or no interface at all (a no-interface view with local access only).

As shown in Figure 7-2, a client application can access a session bean by one of its interfaces (local or remote) or directly by invoking the bean class itself.

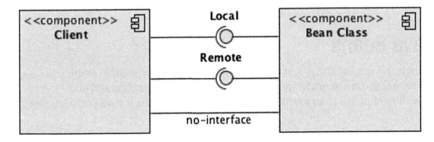

Figure 7-2. *Bean class has several types of business interfaces*

Bean Class

A session bean class is any standard Java class that implements business logic. The requirements to develop a session bean class are as follows:

- The class must be annotated with @Stateless, @Stateful, @Singleton, or the XML equivalent in a deployment descriptor.

- It must implement the methods of its interfaces, if any.

- The class must be defined as public, and must not be final or abstract.

- The class must have a public no-arg constructor that the container will use to create instances.

- The class must not define the finalize() method.

- Business method names must not start with ejb, and they cannot be final or static.

- The argument and return value of a remote method must be legal RMI types.

Remote, Local, and No-Interface Views

Depending from where a client invokes a session bean, the bean class will have to implement remote or local interfaces, or no interface at all. If your architecture has clients residing outside the EJB container's JVM instance, they must use a remote interface. As shown in Figure 7-3, this applies for clients running in a separate JVM (e.g., a rich client), in an application client container (ACC), or in an external web or EJB container. In this case, clients will have to invoke session bean methods through Remote Method Invocation (RMI). You can use local invocation when the bean and the client are running in the same JVM. That can be an EJB invoking another EJB or a web component (Servlet, JSF) running in a web container in the same JVM. It is also possible for your application to use both remote and local calls on the same session bean.

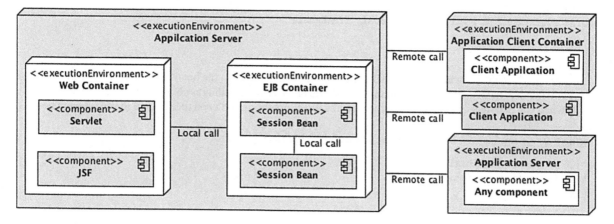

Figure 7-3. *Session beans invoked by several types of client*

A session bean can implement several interfaces or none. A business interface is a standard Java interface that does not extend any EJB-specific interfaces. Like any Java interface, business interfaces define a list of methods that will be available for the client application. They can use the following annotations:

- @Remote: Denotes a remote business interface. Method parameters are passed by value and need to be serializable as part of the RMI protocol.

- @Local: Denotes a local business interface. Method parameters are passed by reference from the client to the bean.

You cannot mark the same interface with more than one annotation. The session beans that you have seen so far in this chapter have no interface. The no-interface view is a variation of the local view that exposes all public business methods of the bean class locally without the use of a separate business interface.

Listing 7-2 shows a local interface (ItemLocal) and a remote interface (ItemRemote) implemented by the ItemEJB stateless session bean. With this code, clients will be able to invoke the findCDs() method locally or remotely as it is defined in both interfaces. The createCd() will only be accessible remotely through RMI.

Listing 7-2. Stateless Session Bean Implementing a Remote and Local Interface

```
@Local
public interface ItemLocal {
  List<Book> findBooks();
  List<CD> findCDs();
}


@Remote
public interface ItemRemote {
  List<Book> findBooks();
  List<CD> findCDs();
  Book createBook(Book book);
  CD createCD(CD cd);
}


@Stateless
public class ItemEJB implements ItemLocal, ItemRemote {
  // ...
}
```

Alternatively to the code in Listing 7-2, you might specify the interface in the bean's class. In this case, you would have to include the name of the interface in the @Local and @Remote annotations as shown in Listing 7-3. This is handy when you have legacy interfaces where you can't add annotations and need to use them in your session bean.

Listing 7-3. A Bean Class Defining a Remote, Local and No Interface

```
public interface ItemLocal {
  List<Book> findBooks();
  List<CD> findCDs();
}

public interface ItemRemote {
  List<Book> findBooks();
  List<CD> findCDs();
  Book createBook(Book book);
  CD createCD(CD cd);
}


@Stateless
@Remote(ItemRemote.class)
@Local(ItemLocal.class)
@LocalBean
public class ItemEJB implements ItemLocal, ItemRemote {
  // ...
}
```

If the bean exposes at least one interface (local or remote) it automatically loses the no-interface view. It then needs to explicitly specify that it exposes a no-interface view by using the @LocalBean annotation on the bean class. As you can see in Listing 7-3 the ItemEJB now has a local, remote, and no interface.

Web Services Interface

In addition to remote invocation through RMI, stateless beans can also be invoked remotely as SOAP web services or RESTful web services. Chapters 14 and 15 are dedicated to web services, so I won't describe them here. I just want to show you how a stateless session bean can be accessed in various forms just by implementing different annotated interfaces. Listing 7-4 shows a stateless bean with a local interface, a SOAP web services endpoint (@WebService), and a RESTful web service endpoint (@Path). Note that these annotations come, respectively, from JAX-WS (Chapter 14) and JAX-RS (Chapter 15) and are not part of EJB.

Listing 7-4. A Stateless Session Bean Implementing Several Interfaces

```
@Local
public interface ItemLocal {
  List<Book> findBooks();
  List<CD> findCDs();
}

@WebService
public interface ItemSOAP {
  List<Book> findBooks();
  List<CD> findCDs();
  Book createBook(Book book);
  CD createCD(CD cd);
}

@Path(/items)
public interface ItemRest {
    List<Book> findBooks();
}

@Stateless
public class ItemEJB implements ItemLocal, ItemSOAP, ItemRest {
  // ...
}
```

Portable JNDI Name

JNDI has been around for a long time. Its API is specified and is portable across application servers. But this wasn't the case with the JNDI name, which was implementation specific. When an EJB in GlassFish or JBoss was deployed, the name of the EJB in the directory service was different and thus not portable. A client would have to look up an EJB using one name for GlassFish, and another name for JBoss. Since EJB 3.1, JNDI names have been specified so the code could be portable. So now each time a session bean with its interfaces is deployed to the container, each bean/interface is automatically bound to a portable JNDI name. The Java EE specification defines portable JNDI names with the following syntax:

```
java:<scope>[/<app-name>]/<module-name>/<bean-name>[!<fully-qualified-interface-name>]
```

Each portion of the JNDI name has the following meaning:

- <scope> defines a series of standard namespaces that map to the various scopes of a Java EE application:

  - global: The java:global prefix allows a component executing outside a Java EE application to access a global namespace.

  - app: The java:app prefix allows a component executing within a Java EE application to access an application-specific namespace.

  - module: The java:module prefix allows a component executing within a Java EE application to access a module-specific namespace.

  - comp: The java:comp prefix is a private component-specific namespace and is not accessible by other components.

- <app-name> is only required if the session bean is packaged within an ear or war file. If this is the case, the <app-name> defaults to the name of the ear or war file (without the .ear or .war file extension).

- <module-name> is the name of the module in which the session bean is packaged. It can be an EJB module in a stand-alone jar file or a web module in a war file. The <module-name> defaults to the base name of the archive with no file extension.

- <bean-name> is the name of the session bean.

- <fully-qualified-interface-name> is the fully qualified name of each defined business interface. For the no-interface view, the name can be the fully qualified bean class name.

To illustrate this naming convention, let's take the example of an ItemEJB (defined in Listing 7-5), which has a remote interface, a local interface, and a no-interface view (using the @LocalBean annotation). All these classes and interfaces belong to the org.agoncal.book.javaee7 package. ItemEJB is the <bean-name> and is packaged in the cdbookstore.jar (the <module-name>).

Listing 7-5. A Stateless Session Bean Implementing Several Interfaces

```java
package org.agoncal.book.javaee7;
@Stateless
@Remote(ItemRemote.class)
@Local(ItemLocal.class)
@LocalBean
public class ItemEJB implements ItemLocal, ItemRemote {
  // ...
}
```

Once deployed, the container will create three JNDI names so an external component will be able to access the ItemEJB using the following global JNDI names:

```
java:global/cdbookstore/ItemEJB!org.agoncal.book.javaee7.ItemRemote
java:global/cdbookstore/ItemEJB!org.agoncal.book.javaee7.ItemLocal
java:global/cdbookstore/ItemEJB!org.agoncal.book.javaee7.ItemEJB
```

Note that, if the ItemEJB was deployed within an ear file (e.g., myapplication.ear), you would have to use the <app-name> as follow:

```
java:global/myapplication/cdbookstore/ItemEJB!org.agoncal.book.javaee7.ItemRemote
java:global/myapplication/cdbookstore/ItemEJB!org.agoncal.book.javaee7.ItemLocal
java:global/myapplication/cdbookstore/ItemEJB!org.agoncal.book.javaee7.ItemEJB
```

The container is also required to make JNDI names available through the java:app and java:module namespaces. So a component deployed in the same application as the ItemEJB will be able to look it up using the following JNDI names:

```
java:app/cdbookstore/ItemEJB!org.agoncal.book.javaee7.ItemRemote
java:app/cdbookstore/ItemEJB!org.agoncal.book.javaee7.ItemLocal
java:app/cdbookstore/ItemEJB!org.agoncal.book.javaee7.ItemEJB
java:module/ItemEJB!org.agoncal.book.javaee7.ItemRemote
java:module/ItemEJB!org.agoncal.book.javaee7.ItemLocal
java:module/ItemEJB!org.agoncal.book.javaee7.ItemEJB
```

This portable JNDI name can be applied to all session beans: stateless, stateful, and singleton.

Stateless Beans

In Java EE applications, stateless beans are the most popular session bean components. They are simple, powerful, and efficient and respond to the common task of doing stateless business processing. What does stateless mean? It means that a task has to be completed in a single method call.

As an example, we can go back to the roots of object-oriented programming where an object encapsulates its state and behavior. In object modeling, to persist a book to a database, you would do something like this: create an instance of a Book object (using the new keyword), set some values, and call a method so it could persist itself to a database (book.persistToDatabase()). In the following code, you can see that, from the very first line to the last one, the book object is called several times and keeps its state:

```
Book book = new Book();
book.setTitle("The Hitchhiker's Guide to the Galaxy");
book.setPrice(12.5F);
book.setDescription("Science fiction comedy series created by Douglas Adams.");
book.setIsbn("1-84023-742-2");
book.setNbOfPage(354);
book.persistToDatabase();
```

In a service architecture, you would delegate the business logic to an external service. Stateless services are ideal when you need to implement a task that can be concluded with a single method call (passing all the needed parameters). Stateless services are independent, are self-contained, and do not require information or state from one request to another. So, if you take the preceding code and introduce a stateless service, you need to create a Book object, set some values, and then use a stateless service to invoke a method that will persist the book on its behalf, in a single call. The state is maintained by Book but not by the stateless service:

```
Book book = new Book();
book.setTitle("The Hitchhiker's Guide to the Galaxy");
book.setPrice(12.5F);
book.setDescription("Science fiction comedy series created by Douglas Adams.");
```

```
book.setIsbn("1-84023-742-2");
book.setNbOfPage(354);
statelessService.persistToDatabase(book);
```

Stateless session beans follow the stateless service architecture and are the most efficient component model because they can be pooled and shared by several clients. This means that, for each stateless EJB, the container keeps a certain number of instances in memory (i.e., a pool) and shares them between clients. Because stateless beans have no client state, all instances are equivalent. When a client invokes a method on a stateless bean, the container picks up an instance from the pool and assigns it to the client. When the client request finishes, the instance returns to the pool to be reused. This means you need only a small number of beans to handle several clients, as shown in Figure 7-4. The container doesn't guarantee the same instance for the same client.

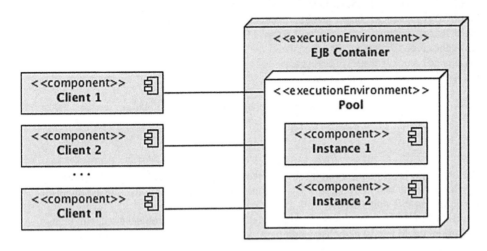

Figure 7-4. *Clients accessing stateless beans in a pool*

Listing 7-5 shows what a stateless EJB could look like: a standard Java class with just a single @Stateless annotation. Because it lives in a container, it can use any container-managed service, one of which is dependency injection. We use the @PersistenceContext annotation to inject a reference of an entity manager. For stateless session beans, the persistence context is transactional, which means that any method invoked in this EJB (createBook(), createCD(), etc.) is transactional. Chapter 9 explains this process in more detail. Notice that all methods have the needed parameters to process business logic in one single call. For example, the createBook() method takes a Book as a parameter and persists it without relying on any other state.

Listing 7-5. *Stateless Session Bean ItemEJB*

```
@Stateless
public class ItemEJB {

  @PersistenceContext(unitName = "chapter07PU")
  private EntityManager em;

  public List<Book> findBooks() {
    TypedQuery<Book> query = em.createNamedQuery(Book.FIND_ALL, Book.class);
    return query.getResultList();
  }
```

```java
  public List<CD> findCDs() {
    TypedQuery<CD> query = em.createNamedQuery(CD.FIND_ALL, CD.class);
    return query.getResultList();
  }

  public Book createBook(Book book) {
    em.persist(book);
    return book;
  }

  public CD createCD(CD cd) {
    em.persist(cd);
    return cd;
  }
}
```

Stateless session beans often contain several closely related business methods. For example, the ItemEJB bean in Listing 7-5 defines methods related to items sold by the CD-BookStore application. So you will find methods to create, update, or find books and CDs, as well as other related business logic.

The @Stateless annotation marks the ItemEJB POJO as a stateless session bean, thus turning a simple Java class into a container-aware component. Listing 7-6 describes the specification of the @javax.ejb.Stateless annotation.

Listing 7-6. @Stateless Annotation API

```java
@Target({TYPE}) @Retention(RUNTIME)
public @interface Stateless {
    String name() default "";
    String mappedName() default "";
    String description() default "";
}
```

The name parameter specifies the name of the bean and by default is the name of the class (ItemEJB in the example in Listing 7-5). This parameter can be used to look up an EJB with JNDI, for example. The description parameter is a String that can be used to describe the EJB. The mappedName attribute is the global JNDI name assigned by the container. Note that this JNDI name is vendor specific and is therefore not portable. mappedName has no relationship with the *portable* global JNDI name, which I described earlier.

Stateless session beans can support a large number of clients, minimizing any needed resources. Having stateless applications is one way to improve scalability (as the container doesn't have to store and manage state).

Stateful Beans

Stateless beans provide business methods to their clients but don't maintain a conversational state with them. Stateful session beans, on the other hand, preserve conversational state. They are useful for tasks that have to be done in several steps, each of which relies on the state maintained in a previous step. Let's take the example of a shopping cart in an e-commerce web site. A customer logs on (her session starts), chooses a first book, adds it to her shopping cart, chooses a second book, and adds it to her cart. At the end, the customer checks out the books, pays for them, and logs out (the session ends). The shopping cart keeps the state of how many books the customer has chosen throughout the interaction (which can take some time, specifically the time of the client's session). This interaction with a stateful component could be written as follows:

```
Book book = new Book();
book.setTitle("The Hitchhiker's Guide to the Galaxy");
book.setPrice(12.5F);
book.setDescription("Science fiction comedy series created by Douglas Adams.");
book.setIsbn("1-84023-742-2");
book.setNbOfPage(354);
statefulComponent.addBookToShoppingCart(book);
book.setTitle("The Robots of Dawn");
book.setPrice(18.25F);
book.setDescription("Isaac Asimov's Robot Series");
book.setIsbn("0-553-29949-2");
book.setNbOfPage(276);
statefulComponent.addBookToShoppingCart(book);
statefulComponent.checkOutShoppingCart();
```

The preceding code shows exactly how a stateful session bean works. Two books are created and added to a shopping cart of a stateful component. At the end, the checkOutShoppingCart() method relies on the maintained state and can check out the two books.

When a client invokes a stateful session bean in the server, the EJB container needs to provide the same instance for each subsequent method invocation. Stateful beans cannot be reused by other clients. Figure 7-5 shows the one-to-one correlation between a bean instance and a client. As far as the developer is concerned, no extra code is needed, as the EJB container automatically manages this one-to-one correlation.

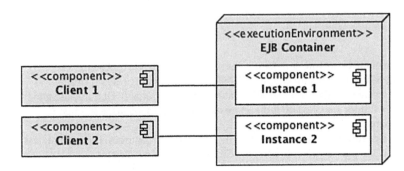

Figure 7-5. *Clients accessing stateful beans*

The one-to-one correlation comes at a price because, as you might have guessed, if you have one million clients, you will get one million stateful beans in memory. To avoid such a big memory footprint, the container temporarily clears stateful beans from memory before the next request from the client brings them back. This technique is called *passivation and activation*. Passivation is the process of removing an instance from memory and saving it to a persistent location (a file on a disk, a database, etc.). It helps you to free memory and release resources (a database or JMS connections, etc.). Activation is the inverse process of restoring the state and applying it to an instance. Passivation and activation are done automatically by the container; you shouldn't worry about doing it yourself, as it's a container service. What you should worry about is freeing any resource (e.g., database connection, JMS factories connection, etc.) before the bean is passivated. Since EJB 3.2, you can also disable passivation as you'll see in the next chapter with life-cycle and callback annotations.

Let's return to the shopping-cart example and apply it to a stateful bean (see Listing 7-7). A customer logs on to a web site, browses the catalog of items, and adds two books to the shopping cart (addItem() method). The cartItems attribute holds the content of the cart. Then the customer decides to get a coffee at a coffee machine. During this time, the container might passivate the instance to free some memory, which in turn saves the shopping content to permanent storage. A few minutes later, the customer comes back and wants to know the total price (getTotal() method) of his shopping cart before buying anything. The container activates the EJB and restores the data to the shopping cart. The customer can then check out (checkout() method) and buy the books. Once the customer logs off, the customer's session ends, and the container frees memory by permanently removing the instance of the stateful bean.

Listing 7-7. Stateful Session Bean ShoppingCartEJB

```
@Stateful
@StatefulTimeout(value = 20, unit = TimeUnit.SECONDS)
public class ShoppingCartEJB {

  private List<Item> cartItems = new ArrayList<>();

  public void addItem(Item item) {
    if (!cartItems.contains(item))
      cartItems.add(item);
  }

  public void removeItem(Item item) {
    if (cartItems.contains(item))
      cartItems.remove(item);
  }

  public Integer getNumberOfItems() {
    if (cartItems == null || cartItems.isEmpty())
      return 0;
    return cartItems.size();
  }

  public Float getTotal() {
    if (cartItems == null || cartItems.isEmpty())
      return 0f;

    Float total = 0f;
    for (Item cartItem : cartItems) {
      total += (cartItem.getPrice());
    }
    return total;
  }

  public void empty() {
    cartItems.clear();
  }

  @Remove
  public void checkout() {
    // Do some business logic
    cartItems.clear();
  }
}
```

The shopping-cart situation is a standard way of using stateful beans in which the container automatically takes care of maintaining the conversational state. The only needed annotation is @javax.ejb.Stateful, which has the same API as @Stateless, described in Listing 7-6.

Notice the optional @javax.ejb.StatefulTimeout and @javax.ejb.Remove annotations. @Remove decorates the checkout() method. This causes the bean instance to be permanently removed from memory after you invoke the checkout() method. @StatefulTimeout assigns a timeout value, which is the duration the bean is permitted to remain idle (not receiving any client invocations) before being removed by the container. The time unit of this annotation is a java.util.concurrent.TimeUnit, so it can go from DAYS, HOURS ... to NANOSECONDS (the default is MINUTES). Alternatively, you can avoid these annotations and rely on the container automatically removing an instance when the client's session ends or expires. However, making sure the stateful bean is removed at the appropriate moment might reduce memory consumption. This could be critical in highly concurrent applications.

Singletons

A singleton bean is a session bean that is instantiated once per application. It implements the widely used Singleton pattern from the famous book by the Gang of Four: *Design Patterns: Elements of Reusable Object-Oriented Software* by Erich Gamma, Richard Helm, Ralph Johnson, and John M. Vlissides (Addison-Wesley, 1995). A singleton ensures that only one instance of a class exists in the whole application and provides a global point to access to it. There are many situations that need singleton objects–that is, where your application only needs one instance of an object: a mouse, a window manager, a printer spooler, a file system, and so on.

Another common-use case is a caching system whereby the entire application shares a single cache (e.g., a Hashmap) to store objects. In an application-managed environment, you need to tweak your code a little bit to turn a class into a singleton, as shown in Listing 7-8. First, you need to prevent the creation of a new instance by having a private constructor. The public static method getInstance() returns the single instance of the CacheSingleton class. If a client class wants to add an object to the cache using the singleton, it needs to call

```
CacheSingleton.getInstance().addToCache(myObject);
```

If you want this code to be thread-safe, you will have to use the synchronized keyword to prevent thread interference and inconsistent data. Instead of a Map, you can also use a java.util.concurrent.ConcurrentMap which will result in much more concurrent and scalable behavior. This can be useful if those are critical considerations.

Listing 7-8. A Java Class Following the Singleton Design Pattern

```java
public class Cache {

    private static Cache instance = new Cache();
    private Map<Long, Object> cache = new HashMap<>();

    private Cache() {}

    public static synchronized Cache getInstance() {
        return instance;
    }

    public void addToCache(Long id, Object object) {
        if (!cache.containsKey(id))
            cache.put(id, object);
    }
```

```
  public void removeFromCache(Long id) {
    if (cache.containsKey(id))
      cache.remove(id);
  }

  public Object getFromCache(Long id) {
    if (cache.containsKey(id))
      return cache.get(id);
    else
      return null;
  }
}
```

EJB 3.1 introduced the singleton session bean, which follows the singleton design pattern. Once instantiated, the container makes sure there is only one instance of a singleton for the duration of the application. An instance is shared between several clients, as shown in Figure 7-6. Singletons maintain their state between client invocations.

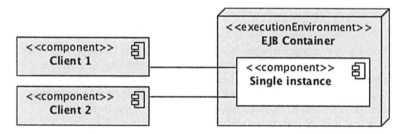

Figure 7-6. *Clients accessing a singleton bean*

■ **Note** Singletons are not cluster-aware. A cluster is a group of containers that work together closely (sharing the same resources, EJBs, etc.). So, in cases in which several distributed containers cluster together over several machines, each container will have its own instance of the singleton.

To turn the code in Listing 7-8 from a singleton Java class to a singleton session bean (see Listing 7-9), there is not much to do. In fact, you just need to annotate a class with @Singleton and not worry about the private constructor or the static getInstance() method. The container will make sure you create only one instance. The @javax.ejb.Singleton annotation has the same API as the @Stateless annotation described earlier in Listing 7-6.

Listing 7-9. Singleton Session Bean

```
@Singleton
public class CacheEJB {

  private Map<Long, Object> cache = new HashMap<>();

  public void addToCache(Long id, Object object) {
    if (!cache.containsKey(id))
      cache.put(id, object);
  }
```

```java
  public void removeFromCache(Long id) {
    if (cache.containsKey(id))
      cache.remove(id);
  }

  public Object getFromCache(Long id) {
    if (cache.containsKey(id))
      return cache.get(id);
    else
      return null;
  }
}
```

As you can see, stateless, stateful, and singleton session beans are very easy to develop: you just need one annotation. Singletons, though, have a bit more to them. They can be initialized at startup, be chained together, and have their concurrency access customized.

Startup Initialization

When a client class needs to access a method on a singleton session bean, the container makes sure to either instantiate it or use the one already living in the container. However, sometimes initializing a singleton can be time-consuming. Imagine if CacheEJB (shown previously in Listing 7-9) needs to access a database to load its cache with thousands of objects. The first call to the bean will be expensive, and the first client will have to wait for initialization to be completed.

To avoid such latency, you can ask the container to initialize a singleton bean at startup. If the @Startup annotation appears on the bean class, the container initializes it during the application startup, not when a client invokes it. The following code shows you how to use the annotation:

```java
@Singleton
@Startup
public class CacheEJB {...}
```

■ **Note** In Java EE 7 the expert group tried to extract the @Startup annotation from the EJB specification so it could be used by any Managed Bean or Servlet. This could not be done, but ideally it is something that will be possible in Java EE 8.

Chaining Singletons

In some cases, when you have several singleton beans, explicit initialization ordering can be important. Imagine if the CacheEJB needs to store data that come from another singleton bean (let's say a CountryCodeEJB that returns all the ISO country codes). The CountryCodeEJB then needs to be initialized before the CacheEJB. Dependencies can exist between multiple singletons, and the @javax.ejb.DependsOn annotation is there to express it. The following example illustrates the use of the annotation:

```java
@Singleton
public class CountryCodeEJB {...}

@DependsOn("CountryCodeEJB")
@Singleton
public class CacheEJB {...}
```

@DependsOn holds one or more Strings, where each specifies the name of the target singleton bean. The following code shows how CacheEJB depends on the initialization of CountryCodeEJB and ZipCodeEJB. @DependsOn("CountryCodeEJB", "ZipCodeEJB") tells the container to guarantee that singleton CountryCodeEJB and ZipCodeEJB are initialized before CacheEJB.

```
@Singleton
public class CountryCodeEJB {...}

@Singleton
public class ZipCodeEJB {...}
@DependsOn("CountryCodeEJB", "ZipCodeEJB")
@Startup
@Singleton
public class CacheEJB {...}
```

As you can see in this code, you can even combine dependencies with startup initialization. CacheEJB is eagerly initialized at startup (because it holds the @Startup annotation), and therefore CountryCodeEJB and ZipCodeEJB will also be initialized at startup before CacheEJB.

You can also use fully qualified names to refer to a singleton packaged within a different module in the same application. Let's say that both CacheEJB and CountryCodeEJB are packaged in the same application (same ear file) but in different jar files (respectively, technical.jar and business.jar). The following code shows how CacheEJB would depend on CountryCodeEJB:

```
@DependsOn("business.jar#CountryCodeEJB")
@Singleton
public class CacheEJB {...}
```

Note that this kind of reference introduces a code dependency on packaging details (in this case, the names of the module files).

Concurrency

As you understand by now, there is only one instance of a singleton session bean shared by multiple clients. So concurrent access by clients is allowed and can be controlled with the @ConcurrencyManagement annotation in two different ways.

- *Container-managed concurrency (CMC)*: The container controls concurrent access to the bean instance based on metadata (annotation or the XML equivalent).

- *Bean-managed concurrency (BMC)*: The container allows full concurrent access and defers the synchronization responsibility to the bean.

If no concurrency management is specified, the CMC demarcation is used by default. A singleton bean can be designed to use either CMC or BMC, but not both. As you'll see in the following sections, you can use the @AccessTimeout annotation to disallow concurrency (i.e., if a client invokes a business method that is being used by another client, the concurrent invocation will result in a ConcurrentAccessException).

Container-Managed Concurrency

With CMC, the default demarcation, the container is responsible for controlling concurrent access to the singleton bean instance. You can then use the @Lock annotation to specify how the container must manage concurrency when a client invokes a method. The annotation can take the value READ (shared) or WRITE (exclusive).

- @Lock(LockType.WRITE): A method associated with an exclusive lock will not allow concurrent invocations until the method's processing is completed. For example, if a client C1 invokes a method with an exclusive lock, client C2 will not be able to invoke the method until C1 has finished.

- @Lock(LockType.READ): A method associated with a shared lock will allow any number of other concurrent invocations to the bean's instance. For example, two clients, C1 and C2, can access simultaneously a method with a shared lock.

The @Lock annotation can be specified on the class, the methods, or both. Specifying on the class means that it applies to all methods. If you do not specify the concurrency locking attribute, it is assumed to be @Lock(WRITE) by default. The code in Listing 7-10 shows CacheEJB with a WRITE lock in the bean class. This implies that all methods will have WRITE concurrency except getFromCache(), which is overridden by READ.

Listing 7-10. A Singleton Session Bean with CMC

```java
@Singleton
@Lock(LockType.WRITE)
@AccessTimeout(value = 20, unit = TimeUnit.SECONDS)
public class CacheEJB {

  private Map<Long, Object> cache = new HashMap<>();

  public void addToCache(Long id, Object object) {
    if (!cache.containsKey(id))
      cache.put(id, object);
  }

  public void removeFromCache(Long id) {
    if (cache.containsKey(id))
      cache.remove(id);
  }

  @Lock(LockType.READ)
  public Object getFromCache(Long id) {
    if (cache.containsKey(id))
      return cache.get(id);
    else
      return null;
  }
}
```

In Listing 7-10, the class has an @AccessTimeout annotation. When a concurrent access is blocked, a timeout can be specified to reject a request if the lock is not acquired within a certain time. If a addToCache() invocation is locked for more than 20 seconds, the client will get a ConcurrentAccessTimeoutException.

Bean-Managed Concurrency

With BMC demarcation, the container allows full concurrent access to the singleton bean instance. You are then responsible for guarding its state against synchronization errors due to concurrent access. In this case, you are allowed to use Java synchronization primitives such as synchronized and volatile. The code in Listing 7-11 shows CacheEJB with BMC (@ConcurrencyManagement(BEAN)) using the synchronized keyword on the addToCache() and removeFromCache() methods.

Listing 7-11. A Singleton Session Bean with BMC

```
@Singleton
@ConcurrencyManagement(ConcurrencyManagementType.BEAN)
public class CacheEJB {

  private Map<Long, Object> cache = new HashMap<>();

  public synchronized void addToCache(Long id, Object object) {
    if (!cache.containsKey(id))
      cache.put(id, object);
  }

  public synchronized void removeFromCache(Long id) {
    if (cache.containsKey(id))
      cache.remove(id);
  }

  public Object getFromCache(Long id) {
    if (cache.containsKey(id))
      return cache.get(id);
    else
      return null;
  }
}
```

Concurrent Access Timeouts and Not Allowing Concurrency

A concurrent access attempt that cannot immediately acquire the appropriate lock is blocked until it can make forward progress. @AccessTimeout is used to specify the duration that the access attempt should be blocked before timing out. An @AccessTimeout value of -1 indicates that the client request will block indefinitely until forward progress can be made. An @AccessTimeout value of 0 indicates that concurrent access is not allowed. This will result in throwing a ConcurrentAccessException if a client invokes a method that is currently being used. This can have performance implications, as clients might have to handle the exception, try again to access the bean, potentially receive another exception, try again, and so on. In Listing 7-12, CacheEJB disallows concurrency on the addToCache() method. This means that if client A is adding an object to the cache and client B wants to do the same thing at the same time, client B will get an exception and will have to try again later (or manage the exception in another way).

Listing 7-12. A Singleton Session Bean Not Allowing Concurrency on a Method

```
@Singleton
public class CacheEJB {

  private Map<Long, Object> cache = new HashMap<>();

  @AccessTimeout(0)
  public void addToCache(Long id, Object object) {
    if (!cache.containsKey(id))
      cache.put(id, object);
  }

  public void removeFromCache(Long id) {
    if (cache.containsKey(id))
      cache.remove(id);
  }

  @Lock(LockType.READ)
  public Object getFromCache(Long id) {
    if (cache.containsKey(id))
      return cache.get(id);
    else
      return null;
  }
}
```

Dependency Injection

I've already talked about dependency injection in this book, and you will come across this mechanism several times in the next chapters. It is a simple yet powerful mechanism used by Java EE 7 to inject references of resources into attributes. Instead of the application looking up resources in JNDI, the container injects them. Injection is made at deployment time. If there is a chance that the data will not be used, the bean can avoid the cost of resource injection by performing a JNDI lookup. JNDI is an alternative to injection; through JNDI, the code pulls data only if they are needed, instead of accepting pushed data that may not be needed at all.

The containers can inject various types of resources into session beans using different annotations (or deployment descriptors).

- @EJB: Injects a reference of the local, remote, or no-interface view of an EJB into the annotated variable.

- @PersistenceContext and @PersistenceUnit: Expresses a dependency on an EntityManager and on an EntityManagerFactory, respectively (see the section "Obtaining an Entity Manager" in Chapter 6).

- @WebServiceRef: Injects a reference to a web service.

- @Resource: Injects several resources such as JDBC data sources, session context, user transactions, JMS connection factories and destinations, environment entries, the timer service, and so on.

- @Inject: Injects nearly everything with @Inject and @Produces, as explained in Chapter 2.

Listing 7-13 shows a snippet of a stateless session bean using various annotations to inject different resources into attributes. Note that these annotations can be set on instance variables as well as on setter methods.

Listing 7-13. A Stateless Bean Using Injection

```
@Stateless
public class ItemEJB {

  @PersistenceContext(unitName = "chapter07PU")
  private EntityManager em;

  @EJB
  private CustomerEJB customerEJB;

  @Inject
  private NumberGenerator generator;

  @WebServiceRef
  private ArtistWebService artistWebService;

  private SessionContext ctx;

  @Resource
  public void setCtx(SessionContext ctx) {
    this.ctx = ctx;
  }

  //...
}
```

Session Context

Session beans are business components that live in a container. Usually, they don't access the container or use the container services directly (transaction, security, dependency injection, etc.). These services are meant to be handled transparently by the container on the bean's behalf (this is called *inversion of control*). However, it is sometimes necessary for the bean to explicitly use container services in code (such as explicitly marking a transaction to be rolled back). And this can be done through the javax.ejb.SessionContext interface. The SessionContext allows programmatic access to the runtime context provided for a session bean instance. SessionContext extends the javax.ejb.EJBContext interface. Table 7-3 describes some methods of the SessionContext API.

Table 7-3. *Some Methods of the SessionContext Interface*

Method	Description
getCallerPrincipal	Returns the java.security.Principal associated with the invocation.
getRollbackOnly	Tests whether the current transaction has been marked for rollback.
getTimerService	Returns the javax.ejb.TimerService interface. Only stateless beans and singletons can use this method. Stateful session beans cannot be timed objects.
getUserTransaction	Returns the javax.transaction.UserTransaction interface to demarcate transactions. Only session beans with bean-managed transaction (BMT) can use this method.
isCallerInRole	Tests whether the caller has a given security role.
lookup	Enables the session bean to look up its environment entries in the JNDI naming context.
setRollbackOnly	Allows the bean to mark the current transaction for rollback.
wasCancelCalled	Checks whether a client invoked the cancel() method on the client Future object corresponding to the currently executing asynchronous business method.

As shown in Listing 7-14, a session bean can have access to its environment context by injecting a reference of SessionContext with an @Resource annotation. Here the createBook method checks that only admins can create a book. It also rolls back if the inventory level of books is too high.

Listing 7-14. A Stateless Bean Accessing the SessionContext API

```
@Stateless
public class ItemEJB {

  @PersistenceContext(unitName = "chapter07PU")
  private EntityManager em;

  @Resource
  private SessionContext context;

  public Book createBook(Book book) {

    if (!context.isCallerInRole("admin"))
      throw new SecurityException("Only admins can create books");

    em.persist(book);

    if (inventoryLevel(book) == TOO_MANY_BOOKS)
      context.setRollbackOnly();

    return book;
  }
}
```

Asynchronous Calls

By default, session bean invocations through remote, local, and no-interface views are synchronous: a client invokes a method, and it gets blocked for the duration of the invocation until the processing has completed, the result is returned, and the client can carry on its work. But asynchronous processing is a common requirement in many applications handling long-running tasks. For example, printing an order can be a very long task depending on whether the printer is online, there is enough paper, or dozens of documents are already waiting to be printed in the printer's spool. When a client calls a method to print a document, it wants to trigger a fire-and-forget process that will print the document so the client can carry on its processing.

Before EJB 3.1, asynchronous processing could only be handled by JMS and MDBs (see Chapter 13). You had to create administrated objects (JMS factories and destinations), deal with the low-level JMS API to send a message to a destination, and then develop an MDB that would consume and process the message. JMS comes with good reliability mechanisms (persistent message storage, delivery guarantees, integration with other systems, etc.) but it could be heavyweight for some use cases when you just want to call a method asynchronously.

Since EJB 3.1, you can call methods asynchronously simply by annotating a session bean method with `@javax.ejb.Asynchronous`. Listing 7-15 shows an `OrderEJB` that has one method for sending an e-mail to a customer and another for printing the order. Since these two methods are time-consuming, they are both annotated with `@Asynchronous`.

Listing 7-15. An OrderEJB That Declares Asynchronous Methods

```
@Stateless
public class OrderEJB {

  @Asynchronous
  public void sendEmailOrderComplete(Order order, Customer customer) {
    // Very Long task
  }

  @Asynchronous
  public void printOrder(Order order) {
    // Very Long task
  }
}
```

When a client invokes either the `printOrder()` or `sendEmailOrderComplete()` method, the container returns control to the client immediately and continues processing the invocation on a separate thread of execution. As you can see in Listing 7-15, the return type of the two asynchronous methods is void. This might be suitable in a vast majority of use cases, but sometimes you need a method to return a value. An asynchronous method can return void as well as a `java.util.concurrent.Future<V>` object, where V represents the result value. `Future` objects allow you to obtain a return value from a method executed in a separate thread. The client can then use the `Future` API to get the result or even cancel the call.

Listing 7-16 shows an example of a method that returns a `Future<Integer>`. The `sendOrderToWorkflow()` method uses a workflow to process an `Order` object. Let's imagine that it calls several enterprise components (messages, web services, etc.), and each step returns a status (an integer). When the client invokes the `sendOrderToWorkflow()` method asynchronously, it expects to receive the status of the workflow. The client can retrieve the result using the `Future.get()` method, or, if for any reason it wants to cancel the call, it can use `Future.cancel()`. If a client invokes `Future.cancel()`, the container will attempt to cancel the asynchronous call only if that call has not already started. Notice that the `sendOrderToWorkflow()` method uses the `SessionContext.wasCancelCalled()` method to check whether the client has requested to cancel the call or not. As a result, the method returns `javax.ejb.AsyncResult<V>`, which is a convenient implementation of `Future<V>`. Bear in mind that `AsyncResult` is used as a way to pass the result value to the container, not directly to the caller.

Listing 7-16. An Asynchronous Method Returning a Future

```
@Stateless
@Asynchronous
public class OrderEJB {

  @Resource
  SessionContext ctx;

  public Future<Integer> sendOrderToWorkflow(Order order) {
    Integer status = 0;

    // processing
    status = 1;

    if (ctx.wasCancelCalled()) {
      return new AsyncResult<>(2);
    }

    // processing

    return new AsyncResult<>(status);
  }
}
```

Notice in Listing 7-16 that you can also apply the @Asynchronous annotation at the class level. This defines all methods as being asynchronous. When the client invokes the sendOrderToWorkflow() method, it needs to call Future.get() in order to retrieve the result value.

```
Future<Integer> status = orderEJB.sendOrderToWorkflow (order);
Integer statusValue = status.get();
```

Deployment Descriptor

Java EE 7 components use configuration by exception, which means that the container, the persistence provider, or the message broker will apply a set of default services to that component. Configuring these default services is the exception. If you desire nondefault behavior, you need to explicitly specify an annotation, or its counterpart in XML. That's what you've already seen with JPA entities, where a set of annotations allows you to customize the default mapping. The same principle applies for session beans. A single annotation (@Stateless, @Stateful, etc.) is enough to inform the container to apply certain services (transaction, life cycle, security, interceptors, concurrency, asynchrony, etc.), but, if you need to change them, you use annotations or XML. Annotations attach additional information to a class, an interface, a method, or a variable, and so does an XML deployment descriptor.

An XML deployment descriptor is an alternative to annotations, which means that any annotation has an equivalent XML tag. If both annotations and deployment descriptors are used, the settings in the deployment descriptor will override the annotations during deployment process. I will not go into too much detail describing the structure of the XML deployment descriptor (called ejb-jar.xml), as it is optional and can end up being very verbose. As an example, Listing 7-17 shows what the ejb-jar.xml file of ItemEJB could look like (shown previously in Listing 7-2). It defines the bean class, the remote and local interface, its type (Stateless), and that it uses container-managed transaction (CMT) (Container).

Listing 7-17. The ejb-jar.xml File

```xml
<ejb-jar xmlns="http://xmlns.jcp.org/xml/ns/javaee"
         xmlns:xsi="http://www.w3.org/2001/XMLSchema-instance"
         xsi:schemaLocation="http://xmlns.jcp.org/xml/ns/javaee ↪
         http://xmlns.jcp.org/xml/ns/javaee/ejb-jar_3_2.xsd"
         version="3.2">

  <enterprise-beans>
    <session>
      <ejb-name>ItemEJB</ejb-name>
      <remote>org.agoncal.book.javaee7.chapter07.ItemRemote</remote>
      <local>org.agoncal.book.javaee7.chapter07.ItemLocal</local>
      <local-bean/>
      <ejb-class>org.agoncal.book.javaee7.chapter07.ItemEJB</ejb-class>
      <session-type>Stateless</session-type>
      <transaction-type>Container</transaction-type>
    </session>
  </enterprise-beans>
</ejb-jar>
```

If you deploy the session bean in a jar file, you need to store the deployment descriptor in the META-INF/ejb-jar.xml file. If you deploy it in a war file, you need to store it in the WEB-INF/ejb-jar.xml file. XML configuration is useful for details that are environment-specific and shouldn't be specified in the code through annotations (e.g., if an EJB needs to be run one way in development and another in test/production environments).

Environment Naming Context

When you work with enterprise applications, there are some situations where parameters of your application change from one deployment to another (depending on the country you are deploying in, the version of the application, etc.). For example, in the CD-BookStore application, ItemEJB (see Listing 7-18) converts the price of an item to the currency of the country where the application is deployed (applying a change rate based on the dollar). If you deploy this stateless bean somewhere in Europe, you need to multiply the price of the item by 0.80 and change the currency to euros.

Listing 7-18. A Stateless Session Bean Converting Prices to Euros

```java
@Stateless
public class ItemEJB {

  public Item convertPrice(Item item) {
    item.setPrice(item.getPrice() * 0.80F);
    item.setCurrency("Euros");
    return item;
  }
}
```

As you can understand, the problem of hard-coding these parameters is that you have to change your code, recompile it, and redeploy the component for each country in which the currency changes. The other option is to access a database each time you invoke the convertPrice() method. That's wasting resources. What you really want is to store these parameters somewhere you can change them at deployment time. The deployment descriptor is the perfect place to set these parameters.

The deployment descriptor (ejb-jar.xml) might be optional in EJB 3.2, but its use is legitimate with environment entries. Environment entries are specified in the deployment descriptor and are accessible via dependency injection (or via JNDI). They support the following Java types: String, Character, Byte, Short, Integer, Long, Boolean, Double, and Float. Listing 7-19 shows the ejb-jar.xml file of ItemEJB defining two entries: currencyEntry of type String with the value Euros and a changeRateEntry of type Float with the value 0.80.

Listing 7-19. ItemEJB Environment Entries in ejb-jar.xml

```
<ejb-jar xmlns="http://xmlns.jcp.org/xml/ns/javaee"
         xmlns:xsi="http://www.w3.org/2001/XMLSchema-instance"
         xsi:schemaLocation="http://xmlns.jcp.org/xml/ns/javaee ⮕
         http://xmlns.jcp.org/xml/ns/javaee/ejb-jar_3_2.xsd"
         version="3.2">

  <enterprise-beans>
    <session>
      <ejb-name>ItemEJB</ejb-name>
      <env-entry>
        <env-entry-name>currencyEntry</env-entry-name>
        <env-entry-type>java.lang.String</env-entry-type>
        <env-entry-value>Euros</env-entry-value>
      </env-entry>
      <env-entry>
        <env-entry-name>changeRateEntry</env-entry-name>
        <env-entry-type>java.lang.Float</env-entry-type>
        <env-entry-value>0.80</env-entry-value>
      </env-entry>
    </session>
  </enterprise-beans>
</ejb-jar>
```

Now that the parameters of the application are externalized in the deployment descriptor, ItemEJB can use dependency injection to get the value of each environment entry. In Listing 7-20, @Resource(name = "currencyEntry") injects the value of the currencyEntry into the currency attribute. Note that the datatypes of the environment entry and the injected variable must be compatible; otherwise, the container throws an exception.

Listing 7-20. An ItemEJB Using Environment Entries

```
@Stateless
public class ItemEJB {

  @Resource(name = "currencyEntry")
  private String currency;
  @Resource(name = "changeRateEntry")
  private Float changeRate;

  public Item convertPrice(Item item) {
    item.setPrice(item.getPrice() * changeRate);
    item.setCurrency(currency);
    return item;
  }
}
```

Packaging

Like most Java EE components (Servlets, JSF pages, web services, etc.); EJBs need to be packaged before they are deployed into a runtime container. In the same archive, you will usually find the enterprise bean class, its interfaces, any needed superclasses or superinterfaces, exceptions, helper classes, and an optional deployment descriptor (ejb-jar.xml). Once you package these artifacts in a jar (Java archive) file, you can deploy them directly into a container. Another option is also to embed the jar file into an ear (enterprise archive) file and deploy the ear file.

An ear file is used to package one or more modules (EJB jars or web applications) into a single archive so that deployment into an application server happens simultaneously and coherently. For example, as shown in Figure 7-7, if you need to deploy a web application, you might want to package your EJBs and entities into separate jar files, your Servlets into a war file, and the whole thing into an ear file. Deploy the ear file into an application server, and you will be able to manipulate entities from the Servlet using the EJB.

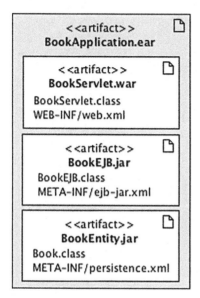
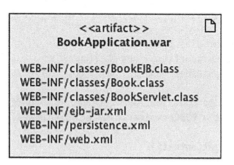

Figure 7-7. *Packaging EJBs*

Since EJB 3.1, EJB Lite can also be directly packaged within a web module (war file). On the right side of Figure 7-7, the Servlet, the EJB, and the entity are all packaged within the same war file with all the deployment descriptors. Note that in the EJB module the deployment descriptor is stored under META-INF/ejb-jar.xml and under WEB-INF/ejb-jar.xml for the web module. EJB Lite can be packaged directly in a war or in a jar file. If you need to use the full EJB specification (e.g., remote interface, JMS, asynchronous calls . . .), you have to package it into a jar, not in a war.

Deploying an EJB

Session beans are container-managed components, and that's their advantage. The container deals with all sorts of services (transaction, life cycle, asynchrony, interceptors, etc.), which leaves you to concentrate on business code. The downside is that you always need to execute your EJBs in a container. Historically these containers were running in a seperate process, so testing was a bit cumbersome. You had to start your container (a.k.a. server), package your EJBs, deploy them, test them, and eventually stop the server . . . to restart it later.

This problem has been solved since EJB 3.1 with the creation of an embeddable EJB container. EJB 3.1 brought a standard API to execute EJBs in a Java SE environment. The embeddable API (package javax.ejb.embeddable) allows a client to instantiate an EJB container that runs within its own JVM. The embeddable container provides a managed environment with support for the same basic services that exist within a Java EE container: injection, transactions, life cycle, and so forth. Embeddable EJB containers only work with the EJB Lite subset API (no MDBs, no remote calls, etc.), meaning it has the same capabilities as an EJB Lite container (but not a full EJB container).

Listing 7-21 shows a main class that uses the bootstrapping API to start the container (the javax.ejb. embeddable.EJBContainer abstract class), looks up an EJB, and invokes methods on it.

Listing 7-21. A Main Class Using the Embeddable Container

```
public class Main {

  public static void main(String[] args) throws NamingException {

    // Sets the container classpath
    Map<String, Object> properties = new HashMap<>();
    properties.put(EJBContainer.MODULES, new File("target/classes"));

    // Creates an Embedded Container and get the JNDI context
    try (EJBContainer ec = EJBContainer.createEJBContainer(properties)) {

      Context ctx = ec.getContext();

      // Creates an instance of book
      Book book = new Book();
      book.setTitle("The Hitchhiker's Guide to the Galaxy");
      book.setPrice(12.5F);
      book.setDescription("Science fiction comedy book");
      book.setIsbn("1-84173-742-2");
      book.setNbOfPage(354);
      book.setIllustrations(false);

      // Looks up the EJB with the no-interface view
      ItemEJB itemEJB = (ItemEJB) ctx.lookup("java:global/classes/ItemEJB ");

      // Persists the book to the database
      itemEJB.createBook(book);

      // Retrieves all the books from the database
      for (Book aBook : itemEJB.findBooks()) {
        System.out.println(aBook);
      }
    }
  }
}
```

As you can see in Listing 7-21, EJBContainer contains a factory method (createEJBContainer()) for creating a container instance. By default, the embeddable container searches the client's class path to find the set of EJBs for initialization (or you can set the class path using properties). Once you have initialized the container, the application gets the container JNDI context (EJBContainer.getContext(), which returns a javax.naming.Context) to look up the ItemEJB (using the portable global JNDI name syntax).

Note that ItemEJB (shown earlier in Listing 7-1) is a stateless session bean exposing business methods through a no-interface view. It uses injection, container-managed transactions, and a JPA Book entity. The embeddable container takes care of injecting an entity manager and committing or rolling back any transaction. EJBContainer implements java.lang.AutoCloseable so the try-with-resources block will automatically invoke the EJBContainer.close() method to shut down the embeddable container instance.

In Listing 7-21 I've used a main class to show you how to use an embeddable EJB container. But bear in mind that EJBs can now be used in any kind of Java SE environment: from test classes to Swing applications, or even batch processing.

Invoking Enterprise Java Beans

Now that you have seen examples of session beans and their different interfaces, you might want to take a look at how the client invokes these beans. The client of a session bean can be any kind of component: a POJO, a graphical interface (Swing), a CDI Managed Bean, a Servlet, a JSF-backing bean, a web service (SOAP or REST), or another EJB (deployed in the same or a different container).

Simplicity also is applied to the client side. To invoke a method on a session bean, a client does not directly instantiate the bean (using the new operator). It needs a reference to the bean (or to its interfaces). It can obtain it via dependency injection (with the @EJB or @Inject annotation) or via JNDI lookup. Dependency injection allows a container to automatically inject a reference on an EJB at deployment time. Unless specified, a client invokes a session bean synchronously.

Invoking with Injection

Java EE uses several annotations to inject references of resources (@Resource), entity managers (@PersistenceContext), web services (@WebServiceRef), and so on. But the @javax.ejb.EJB annotation is specifically intended for injecting session bean references into client code. Dependency injection is only possible within managed environments such as EJB containers, web containers, and application-client containers.

Let's take our initial examples in which session beans had no interface. For a client to invoke a session bean's no-interface view, it needs to obtain a reference to the bean class itself. For example, in the following code, the client gets a reference to the ItemEJB class using the @EJB annotation:

```
@Stateless
public class ItemEJB {...}

// Client code injecting a reference to the EJB
@EJB ItemEJB itemEJB;
```

If the session bean implements several interfaces, the client has to specify which one it wants a reference to. In the following code, the ItemEJB implements two interfaces and, thanks to the @LocalBean annotation, also exposes a no-interface view. The client can invoke the EJB through its local, remote, or no interface:

```
@Stateless
@Remote(ItemRemote.class)
@Local(ItemLocal.class)
@LocalBean
public class ItemEJB implements ItemLocal, ItemRemote {...}

// Client code injecting several references to the EJB or interfaces
@EJB ItemEJB itemEJB;
@EJB ItemLocal itemEJBLocal;
@EJB ItemRemote itemEJBRemote;
```

The @EJB API has several attributes; one of them is the JNDI name of the EJB you want to inject. This can be useful especially with remote EJBs living in a different server:

```
@EJB(lookup = "java:global/classes/ItemEJB") ItemRemote itemEJBRemote;
```

Invoking with CDI

As you just saw, invoking a method on an EJB requires only the annotation @EJB to get a reference injected to the client. It is pretty straightforward: it gives you a reference at deployment time. But @EJB doesn't give you something similar to CDI alternatives, for example. Instead you need to use the @Inject annotation.

Most of the time you can just replace @EJB by @Inject and your client code will work. By doing that you get all the CDI benefits you saw in Chapter 2. So if we take the previous examples, following is how a client would get EJB injection with CDI:

```
@Stateless
@Remote(ItemRemote.class)
@Local(ItemLocal.class)
@LocalBean
public class ItemEJB implements ItemLocal, ItemRemote {...}

// Client code injecting several references to the EJB or interfaces with @Inject
@Inject ItemEJB itemEJB;
@Inject ItemLocal itemEJBLocal;
@Inject ItemRemote itemEJBRemote;
```

For remote EJBs, as you just saw, you might need to use a JNDI string to look it up. The @Inject annotation cannot have a String parameter, so in this case, you need to produce the remote EJB to be able to inject it:

```
// Code producing a remote EJB
@Produces @EJB(lookup = "java:global/classes/ItemEJB") ItemRemote itemEJBRemote;

// Client code injecting the produced remote EJB
@Inject ItemRemote itemEJBRemote;
```

Depending on your client environment, you might not be able to use injection (if the component is not managed by a container). In this case, you can use JNDI to look up session beans through their portable JNDI name.

Invoking with JNDI

Session beans can also be looked up using JNDI. JNDI is mostly used for remote access when a client is not container managed and cannot use dependency injection. But JNDI can also be used by local clients, even if dependency injection results in simpler code. Injection is made at deployment time. If there is a chance that the data will not be used, the bean can avoid the cost of resource injection by performing a JNDI lookup. JNDI is an alternative to injection; through JNDI, the code pulls data only if they are needed, instead of accepting pushed data that may not be needed at all.

JNDI is an API for accessing different kinds of directory services, allowing clients to bind and look up objects via a name. JNDI is defined in Java SE and is independent of the underlying implementation, which means that you can look up objects in a Lightweight Directory Access Protocol (LDAP) directory or a Domain Name System (DNS) using a standard API.

The alternative to the preceding code is to use the `InitialContext` of JNDI and look up a deployed EJB using its portable JNDI name that I defined earlier in the section "Portable JNDI Name." The client code looks like the following:

```
Context ctx = new InitialContext();
ItemRemote itemEJB = (ItemRemote) ➥
        ctx.lookup("java:global/cdbookstore/ItemEJB!org.agoncal.book.javaee7.ItemRemote");
```

Summary

Starting with EJB 2.x, the EJB specification has evolved over the years since its creation from a heavyweight model where home and remote/local interfaces had to be packaged with tons of XML to a simple Java class with no interface and one annotation. The underlying functionality is always the same: transactional and secure business logic (more on that in the next chapters).

Session beans are container-managed components that are used to develop business layers. There are three different types of session beans: stateless, stateful, and singleton. Stateless beans are easily scalable because they keep no state, live in a pool, and process tasks that can be completed in a single method call. Stateful beans have a one-to-one correlation with a client and can be temporarily cleared from memory using passivation and activation. Singletons have a unique instance shared among several clients and can be initialized at startup time, chained together, and customized in their concurrency access.

Despite these differences, session beans share a common programming model. They can have a local, remote, or no-interface view, use annotations, or be deployed with a deployment descriptor. Session beans can use dependency injection to get references to several resources (JDBC datasources, persistence context, environment entries, etc.), as well as their runtime environment context (the SessionContext object). Since EJB 3.1, you can invoke methods asynchronously, look up EJBs with a portable JNDI name, or use the embeddable EJB container in the Java SE environment. EJB 3.2 follows the trajectory of its predecessor by bringing some minor enhancements.

The next chapter explains the life cycle of the different session beans and how you can interact with callback annotations. It also shows you how to use the enhanced timer service to schedule tasks and how to set security authorization.

CHAPTER 8

■ ■ ■

Callbacks, Timer Service, and Authorization

In the previous chapter, you learned that session beans are container-managed components. They live in an EJB container, which wraps business code behind the scenes with several services (dependency injection, transaction management, etc.). Three of these services are life-cycle management, scheduling, and authorization.

Life cycle means that a session bean goes through a predefined set of state transitions. Depending on the type of your bean (stateless, stateful, singleton), the life cycle will consist of different states. Each time the container changes the life-cycle state, it can invoke methods that are annotated with callback annotations.

The EJB timer service is the standard answer to scheduling tasks. Enterprise applications dependent on calendar-based notifications use this service to model workflow-type business processes.

Securing data is also important. You want your business tier to act like a firewall and authorize some actions to certain groups of users and deny access to others (e.g., only employees are allowed to persist data, but users and employees are authorized to read data).

In this chapter you will learn that stateless and singleton session beans share the same life cycle and that stateful beans have a slightly different one. You will also see how both stateless and singleton can use the timer service to schedule tasks declaratively or programmatically. This chapter finishes by showing how authorization works in the EJB container and how you can easily allow users with specific roles to access your code.

Session Beans Life Cycle

As you've seen in the previous chapter, a client doesn't create an instance of a session bean using the new operator. It gets a reference to a session bean either through dependency injection or through JNDI lookup. The container is the one creating the instance and destroying it. This means that neither the client nor the bean is responsible for determining when the bean instance is created, when dependencies are injected, or when the instance is destroyed. The container is responsible for managing the life cycle of the bean.

All session beans have two obvious phases in their life cycle: creation and destruction. In addition, stateful session beans go through the passivation and activation phases, which I mentioned in the previous chapter. Similar to the callback methods used in entities that you saw in previous chapters, EJBs allow the container, during certain phases of its life, to automatically invoke annotated methods (@PostConstruct, @PreDestroy, etc.). These methods may initialize state information on the bean, look up resources using JNDI, or release database connections.

Stateless and Singleton

Stateless and singleton beans have in common the fact that they don't maintain conversational state with a dedicated client. Both bean types allow access by any client—stateless does this on a per-instance basis, while singleton provides concurrent access to a single instance. Both share the same life cycle shown in Figure 8-1 and described as follows:

1. The life cycle of a stateless or singleton session bean starts when a client requests a reference to the bean (using either dependency injection or JNDI lookup). In the case of a singleton, it can also start when the container is bootstrapped (using the @Startup annotation). The container creates a new session bean instance.

2. If the newly created instance uses dependency injection through annotations (@Inject, @Resource, @EJB, @PersistenceContext, etc.) or deployment descriptors, the container injects all the needed resources.

3. If the instance has a method annotated with @PostContruct, the container invokes it.

4. The bean instance processes the call invoked by the client and stays in ready mode to process future calls. Stateless beans stay in ready mode until the container frees some space in the pool. Singletons stay in ready mode until the container is shut down.

5. The container does not need the instance any more. It invokes the method annotated with @PreDestroy, if any, and ends the life of the bean instance.

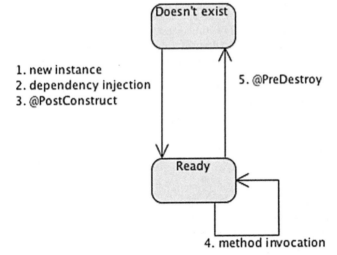

Figure 8-1. *Stateless and singleton bean life cycle*

Stateless and singleton beans share the same life cycle, but there are some differences in the way they are created and destroyed.

When you deploy a stateless session bean, the container creates several instances and adds them into a pool. When a client calls a method on a stateless session bean, the container selects one instance from the pool, delegates the method invocation to that instance, and returns it to the pool. When the container no longer needs the instance (usually when the container wants to reduce the number of instances in the pool), it destroys it.

■ **Note** EJB monitoring can be done through the GlassFish Administration Console. GlassFish then allows you to customize several EJB pool parameters. You can set a pool size (initial, minimum, and maximum number of beans in the pool), the number of beans to be removed when the pool idle timeout expires, and the number of milliseconds for the pool to time out. These options are implementation specific and may not be available on other EJB containers.

For singleton session beans, creation depends on whether they are instantiated eagerly (@Startup) or not, or whether they depend (@DependsOn) on another singleton that had been eagerly created. If the answer is yes, the container will create an instance at deployment time. If not, the container will create an instance when a client invokes a business method. Because singletons last for the duration of the application, the instance is destroyed when the container shuts down.

Stateful

Stateful session beans are programmatically not very different from stateless or singleton session beans: only the metadata change (@Stateful instead of @Stateless or @Singleton). But the real difference is that stateful beans maintain conversational state with their client, and therefore have a slightly different life cycle. The container generates an instance and assigns it only to one client. Then, each request from that client is passed to the same instance. Following this principle and depending on your application, you might end up with a one-to-one relationship between a client and a stateful bean (e.g., 1000 simultaneous users might produce 1000 stateful beans). If one client doesn't invoke its bean's instance for a long enough time, the container has to clear it before the JVM runs out of memory, preserve the instance state to a permanent storage, and then bring back the instance with its state when it's needed. The container employs the technique of passivation and activation.

Passivation is when the container serializes the bean instance to a permanent storage medium (file on a disk, database, etc.) instead of holding it in memory. Activation, which is the opposite, is done when the bean instance is needed again by the client. The container deserializes the bean from permanent storage and activates it back into memory. This means the bean's attributes have to be serializable (it must either be a Java primitive or implement the java.io.Serializable interface). Figure 8-2 shows the stateful bean life cycle and describes it as follows:

1. The life cycle of a stateful bean starts when a client requests a reference to the bean (either using dependency injection or JNDI lookup). The container creates a new session bean instance and stores it in memory.

2. If the newly created instance uses dependency injection through annotations (@Inject, @Resource, @EJB, @PersistenceContext, etc.) or deployment descriptors, the container injects all the needed resources.

3. If the instance has a method annotated with @PostContruct, the container invokes it.

4. The bean executes the requested call and stays in memory, waiting for subsequent client requests.

5. If the client remains idle for a period of time, the container invokes the method annotated with @PrePassivate, if any, and passivates the bean instance into a permanent storage.

6. If the client invokes a passivated bean, the container activates it back to memory and invokes the method annotated with @PostActivate, if any.

7. If the client does not invoke a passivated bean instance for the session timeout period, the container destroys it.

8. Alternatively to step 7, if the client calls a method annotated by @Remove, the container then invokes the method annotated with @PreDestroy, if any, and ends the life of the bean instance.

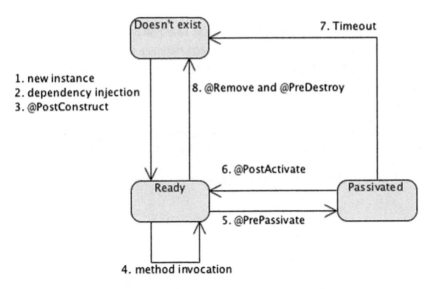

Figure 8-2. *Stateful bean life cycle*

In some cases, a stateful bean contains open resources such as network sockets or database connections. Because a container cannot keep these resources open for each bean, you will have to close and reopen the resources before and after passivation using callback methods. Another possibility is to deactivate the default activation/ passivation behavior or your stateful bean. You have to be very careful with that, but if it's what you really need you can annotate your stateful bean with @Stateful(passivationCapable=false).

Callbacks

As you just saw, each type of session bean has its own container-managed life cycle. The container lets you optionally provide your own business code when the state of the bean changes. The change from one state to another can be intercepted by the container to invoke methods annotated by one of the annotations listed in Table 8-1.

Table 8-1. *Life-Cycle Callback Annotations*

Annotation	Description
@PostConstruct	Marks a method to be invoked immediately after you create a bean instance and the container does dependency injection. This annotation is often used to perform any initialization.
@PreDestroy	Marks a method to be invoked immediately before the container destroys the bean instance. The method annotated with @PreDestroy is often used to release resources that had been previously initialized. With stateful beans, this happens after timeout or when a method annotated with @Remove has been completed.
@PrePassivate	Stateful beans only. Marks a method to be invoked before the container passivates the instance. It usually gives the bean the time to prepare for serialization and to release resources that cannot be serialized (e.g., it closes connections to a database, a message broker, a network socket, etc.).
@PostActivate	Stateful beans only. Marks a method to be invoked immediately after the container reactivates the instance. Gives the bean a chance to reinitialize resources that had been closed during passivation.

■ **Note** The javax.ejb package of the EJB 3.2 specification (JSR 345) defines the @PrePassivate and @PostActivate annotations. They are related to the stateful EJB life cycle and can happen many times during the EJB lifetime. @PostConstruct and @PreDestroy are part of the Common Annotations 1.2 specification (JSR 250) and come from the javax.annotation package (like @Resource or other security annotations that you'll see next). They are related to Managed Beans' life cycle and happen only once during the class lifetime (at creation and at destruction).

The following rules apply to a callback method:

- The method must not have any parameters and must return void.

- The method must not throw a checked exception but can throw runtime exceptions. Throwing a runtime exception will roll back the transaction if one exists (as explained in the next chapter).

- The method can have public, private, protected, or package-level access but must not be static or final.

- A method may be annotated with multiple annotations (the init() method shown later in Listing 8-2 is annotated with @PostConstruct and @PostActivate). However, only one annotation of a given type may be present on a bean (you can't have two @PostConstruct annotations in the same session bean, for example).

- A callback method can access the beans' environment entries (see the "Environment Naming Context" section in Chapter 7).

These callbacks are typically used to allocate and/or release the bean's resources. As an example, Listing 8-1 shows the singleton bean CacheEJB using a @PostConstruct annotation to initialize its cache. Straight after creating the single instance of the CacheEJB, the container invokes the initCache() method.

Listing 8-1. A Singleton Initializing Its Cache with the @PostConstruct Annotation

```
@Singleton
public class CacheEJB {

  private Map<Long, Object> cache = new HashMap<>();

  @PostConstruct
  private void initCache() {
    cache.put(1L, "First item in the cache");
    cache.put(2L, "Second item in the cache");
  }

  public Object getFromCache(Long id) {
    if (cache.containsKey(id))
      return cache.get(id);
    else
      return null;
  }
}
```

Listing 8-2 shows a snippet of code for a stateful bean. The container maintains conversational state, which can include heavy-duty resources such as a database connection. Because it is expensive to open a database connection, it should be shared across calls but released when the bean is idle (or passivated).

Listing 8-2. A Stateful Bean Initializing and Releasing Resources

```
@Stateful
public class ShoppingCartEJB {

  @Resource(lookup = "java:comp/defaultDataSource")
  private DataSource ds;
  private Connection connection;

  private List<Item> cartItems = new ArrayList<>();

  @PostConstruct
  @PostActivate
  private void init() {
    connection = ds.getConnection();
  }

  @PreDestroy
  @PrePassivate
  private void close() {
    connection.close();
  }

  // ...

  @Remove
  public void checkout() {
    cartItems.clear();
  }
}
```

After creating an instance of a stateful bean, the container injects the reference of a default data source (more on data sources later and in the next chapter) to the ds attribute. Once the injection is done, the container will call the designated @PostConstruct method (init()), which creates a database connection. If the container happens to passivate the instance, the close() method will be invoked (@PrePassivate). The purpose of this is to close the JDBC connection, which holds native resources and is no longer needed during passivation. When the client invokes a business method on the bean, the container activates it and calls the init() method again (@PostActivate). When the client invokes the checkout() method (annotated with the @Remove annotation), the container removes the instance but first will call the close() method again (@PreDestroy). Note that for better readability, I've omitted the SQL exception handling in the callback methods.

Timer Service

Some Java EE applications need to schedule tasks in order to provide notifications at certain times. For example, the CD-BookStore application needs to send a birthday e-mail to its customers every year, print monthly statistics about the items sold, generate nightly reports about inventory levels, and refresh a technical cache every 30 seconds.

As a result, EJB 2.1 introduced a scheduling facility called the timer service because clients couldn't use the Thread API directly. Compared with other proprietary tools or frameworks (the Unix cron utility, Quartz, etc.), the timer service was less feature rich. The EJB specification had to wait until the 3.1 version to see a drastic improvement of the timer service. It took its inspiration from Unix cron and other successful tools, and today competes with the other products as it responds to most scheduling use cases.

The EJB timer service is a container service that allows EJBs to be registered for callback invocation. EJB notifications may be scheduled to occur according to a calendar-based schedule, at a specific time, after a specific elapsed duration, or at specific recurring intervals. The container keeps a record of all the timers, and invokes the appropriate bean instance method when a timer has expired. Figure 8-3 shows the two steps involving the timer service. First, the EJB needs to create a timer (automatically or programmatically) and get registered for callback invocation, and then the timer service triggers the registered method on the EJB instance.

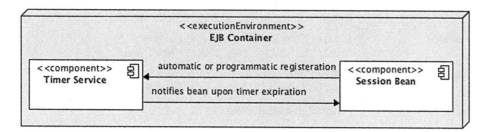

Figure 8-3. *Interaction between the timer service and the session bean*

Timers are intended for long-lived business processes and are by default persistent. This means they survive server shutdowns, and once the server starts again, the timers are executed as if no shutdown had happened. Optionally, you can specify timers to be nonpersistent.

■ **Note**   Stateless beans, singletons, and MDBs can be registered by the timer service, but stateful beans can't and shouldn't use the scheduling API.

Timers can be created automatically by the container at deployment time if the bean has methods annotated with the @Schedule annotation. But timers can also be created programmatically and must provide one callback method annotated with the @Timeout annotation.

Calendar-Based Expression

The timer service uses a calendar-based syntax that takes its roots from the Unix cron utility. This syntax is used for programmatic timer creation (using the ScheduleExpression class) and for automatic timer creation (via the @Schedule annotation or the deployment descriptor). A scheduling expression looks as follows:

```
year = "2008,2012,2016" dayOfWeek = "Sat,Sun" minute = "0-10,30,40"
```

Table 8-2 and Table 8-3 define the attributes creating calendar-based expressions.

Table 8-2. *Attributes of a Calendar-Based Expression*

Attribute	Description	Possible Values	Default Value
second	One or more seconds within a minute	[0,59]	0
minute	One or more minutes within an hour	[0,59]	0
hour	One or more hours within a day	[0,23]	0
dayOfMonth	One or more days within a month	[1,31] or {"1st", "2nd", "3rd",...,0th", "31st"} or {"Sun", "Mon", "Tue", "Wed", "Thu", "Fri", "Sat"} or "Last" (the last day of the month) or -x (means x day(s) before the last day of the month)	*
month	One or more months within a year	[1,12] or {"Jan", "Feb", "Mar", "Apr", "May", "Jun", "Jul", "Aug", "Sep", "Oct", "Nov", "Dec"}	
dayOfWeek	One or more days within a week	[0,7] or {"Sun", "Mon", "Tue", "Wed", Thu", "Fri", "Sat"}—"0" and "7" both refer to Sunday	*
year	A particular calendar year	A four-digit calendar year	*
timezone	A specific time zone	List of time zones as provided by the zoneinfo (or tz) database	

Each attribute of a calendar-based expression (second, minute, hour, etc.) supports values expressed in different forms. For example, you can have a list of days or a range of years. Table 8-3 defines the different forms that an attribute can take.

Table 8-3. *Forms of Expression*

Form	Description	Example
Single value	The attribute has only one possible value.	year = "2010" month= "May"
Wildcard	This form represents all possible values for a given attribute.	second = "*" dayOfWeek = "*"
List	The attribute has two or more values separated by a comma.	year = "2008,2012,2016" dayOfWeek = "Sat,Sun" minute = "0-10,30,40"
Range	The attribute has a range of values separated by a dash.	second = "1-10" dayOfWeek = "Mon-Fri"
Increments	The attribute has a starting point and an interval separated by a forward slash.	minute = "*/15" second = "30/10"

If you have used Unix cron syntax before, this might sound familiar and much simpler. With this rich syntax, you can express nearly any kind of calendar expression, as shown in Table 8-4.

Table 8-4. *Examples of Expressions*

Example	Expression
Every Wednesday at midnight	dayOfWeek="Wed"
Every Wednesday at midnight	second="0",minute="0",hour="0",dayOfMonth="*", month="*",dayOfWeek="Wed",year="*"
Every weekday at 6:55	minute="55",hour="6",dayOfWeek="Mon-Fri"
Every weekday at 6:55 Paris time	minute="55",hour="6",dayOfWeek="Mon-Fri", timezone="Europe/Paris"
Every minute of every hour of every day	minute="*",hour="*"
Every second of every minute of every hour of every day	second="*",minute="*",hour="*"
Every Monday and Friday at 30 seconds past noon	second="30", hour="12",dayOfWeek="Mon,Fri"
Every five minutes within the hour	minute="*/5",hour="*"
Every five minutes within the hour	minute="0,5,10,15,20,25,30,35, 40,45,50,55",hour="*"
The last Monday of December at 3 p.m.	hour="15",dayOfMonth="Last Mon",month="Dec"
Three days before the last day of each month at 1 p.m.	hour="13",dayOfMonth="-3"
Every other hour within the day starting at noon on the second Tuesday of every month	hour="12/2",dayOfMonth="2nd Tue"
Every 14 minutes within the hour, for the hours of 1 and 2 a.m.	minute = "*/14",hour="1,2"
Every 14 minutes within the hour, for the hours of 1 and 2 a.m.	minute = "0,14,28,42,56",our = "1,2"
Every 10 seconds within the minute, starting at second 30	second = "30/10"
Every 10 seconds within the minute, starting at second 30	second = "30,40,50"

Declarative Timer Creation

Timers can be created automatically by the container at deployment time based on metadata. The container creates a timer for each method annotated with @javax.ejb.Schedule or @Schedules (or the XML equivalent in the ejb-jar.xml deployment descriptor). By default, each @Schedule annotation corresponds to a single persistent timer, but you can also define nonpersistent timers.

Listing 8-3 shows the StatisticsEJB bean that defines several methods. statisticsItemsSold() creates a timer that will call the method every first day of the month at 5:30 a.m. The generateReport() method creates two timers (using @Schedules): one every day at 2 a.m. and another one every Wednesday at 2 p.m. refreshCache() creates a nonpersistent timer that will refresh the cache every ten minutes.

Listing 8-3. *A StatisticsEJB Registering Four Timers*

```
@Stateless
public class StatisticsEJB {

  @Schedule(dayOfMonth = "1", hour = "5", minute = "30")
  public void statisticsItemsSold() {
    // ...
  }

  @Schedules({
          @Schedule(hour = "2"),
          @Schedule(hour = "14", dayOfWeek = "Wed")
  })
  public void generateReport() {
    // ...
  }

  @Schedule(minute = "*/10", hour = "*", persistent = false)
  public void refreshCache() {
    // ...
  }
}
```

Programmatic Timer Creation

To create a timer programmatically, the EJB needs to access the javax.ejb.TimerService interface using either dependency injection or the SessionContext (SessionContext.getTimerService(), see section "Session Context" in Chapter 7), or through JNDI lookup. As listed in Table 8-5, the TimerService API has several methods that allow you to create different kinds of timers and get information about timers.

Table 8-5. *TimerService API*

Annotation	Description
createTimer	Creates a timer based on dates, intervals, or durations. These methods do not use calendar-based expressions.
createSingleActionTimer	Creates a single-action timer that expires at a given point in time or after a specified duration. The container removes the timer after the timeout callback method has been successfully invoked.
createIntervalTimer	Creates an interval timer whose first expiration occurs at a given point in time and whose subsequent expirations occur after specified intervals.
createCalendarTimer	Creates a timer using a calendar-based expression with the ScheduleExpression helper class.
getAllTimers	Returns the list of available timers (interface javax.ejb.Timer).

The ScheduleExpression helper class allows you to create calendar-based expressions programmatically. You will find methods related to the attributes defined in Table 8-2, and you will be able to program all the examples that you saw in Table 8-4. Following are some examples to give you an idea:

```
new ScheduleExpression().dayOfMonth("Mon").month("Jan");
new ScheduleExpression().second("10,30,50").minute("*/5").hour("10-14");
new ScheduleExpression().dayOfWeek("1,5").timezone("Europe/Lisbon");
new ScheduleExpression().dayOfMonth(customer.getBirthDay())
```

All the methods of TimerService (createSingleActionTimer, createCalendarTimer, etc.) return a javax.ejb.Timer object that contains information about the created timer (what time was it created, whether it is persistent, etc.). Timer also allows the EJB to cancel the timer prior to its expiration. When the timer expires, the container calls the associated @javax.ejb.Timeout method of the bean, passing the Timer object. A bean can have at most one @Timeout method.

When CustomerEJB (see Listing 8-4) creates a new customer in the system (createCustomer() method), it creates a calendar timer based on the date of birth of the customer. Thus, every year the container will trigger a bean to create and send a birthday e-mail to the customer. To do that, the stateless bean first needs to inject a reference of the timer service (using @Resource). The createCustomer() persists the customer in the database and uses the day and the month of her birth to create a ScheduleExpression. A calendar timer is created and given this ScheduleExpression and the customer object using a TimerConfig. new TimerConfig(customer, true) configures a persistent timer (as indicated by the true parameter) that passes the customer object.

Listing 8-4. A CustomerEJB Creating a Timer Programmatically

```java
@Stateless
public class CustomerEJB {

  @Resource
  TimerService timerService;

  @PersistenceContext(unitName = "chapter08PU")
  private EntityManager em;

  public void createCustomer(Customer customer) {
    em.persist(customer);

    ScheduleExpression birthDay = new ScheduleExpression().↪
            dayOfMonth(customer.getBirthDay()).month(customer.getBirthMonth());

    timerService.createCalendarTimer(birthDay, new TimerConfig(customer, true));
  }

  @Timeout
  public void sendBirthdayEmail(Timer timer) {
    Customer customer = (Customer) timer.getInfo();
    // ...
  }
}
```

Once you create the timer, the container will invoke the @Timeout method (sendBirthdayEmail()) every year, which passes the Timer object. Because the timer had been serialized with the customer object, the method can access it by calling the getInfo() method. Note that a bean can have at most one @Timeout method for handling programmatic timers.

Authorization

The primary purpose of the EJB security model is to control access to business code. In Java EE authentication is handled by the web tier (or a client application); the principal and its roles are then passed to the EJB tier, and the EJB checks whether the authenticated user is allowed to access a method based on its role. Authorization can be done either in a declarative or a programmatic manner.

With declarative authorization, access control is made by the EJB container. With programmatic authorization, access control is made in the code using the JAAS API.

Declarative Authorization

The declarative authorization can be defined in the bean using annotations or in the XML deployment descriptor. Declarative authorization involves declaring roles, assigning permission to methods (or to the entire bean), or changing temporarily a security identity. These controls are made by the annotations described in Table 8-6. Each annotation can be used on the bean and/or on the method.

Table 8-6. *Security Annotations*

Annotation	Bean	Method	Description
@PermitAll	X	X	Indicates that the given method (or the entire bean) is accessible by everyone (all roles are permitted).
@DenyAll	X	X	Indicates that no role is permitted to execute the specified method or all methods of the bean (all roles are denied). This can be useful if you want to deny access to a method in a certain environment (e.g., the method launchNuclearWar() should only be allowed in production but not in a test environment).
@RolesAllowed	X	X	Indicates that a list of roles is allowed to execute the given method (or the entire bean).
@DeclareRoles	X		Defines roles for security checking.
@RunAs	X		Temporarily assigns a new role to a principal.

The @RolesAllowed annotation is used to authorize a list of roles to access a method. It can be applied to a particular method or to the entire bean (then all business methods will inherit the bean's role access). This annotation can take either a single String (only one role can access the method) or an array of String (any of the roles can access the method). The @DeclareRoles annotation that you'll see later in this section can be used to declare other roles.

■ **Note**   Security annotations (@RolesAllowed, @DenyAll, etc.) are part of the Common Annotations 1.2 specification (JSR 250) and come from the javax.annotation.security package.

Listing 8-5 shows the ItemEJB using the @RolesAllowed annotation at the bean and method levels. This code indicates that any method is accessible by a principal associated with one of the following roles: user, employee, or admin. The deleteBook() method overrides the class-level settings and is only allowing access to the admin role.

Listing 8-5. A Stateless Bean Allowing Certain Roles

```
@Stateless
@RolesAllowed({"user", "employee", "admin"})
public class ItemEJB {

  @PersistenceContext(unitName = "chapter08PU")
  private EntityManager em;

  public Book findBookById(Long id) {
    return em.find(Book.class, id);
  }

  public Book createBook(Book book) {
    em.persist(book);
    return book;
  }

  @RolesAllowed("admin")
  public void deleteBook(Book book) {
    em.remove(em.merge(book));
  }
}
```

@RolesAllowed defines a list of roles that are allowed to access a method. The @PermitAll and @DenyAll annotations are applied for any role. So, you can use the @PermitAll annotation to mark an EJB, or a method, to be invoked by any role. Conversely, the @DenyAll forbids any role to have access to a method.

As you can see in Listing 8-6, because the findBookById() method is annotated with @PermitAll, it can now be accessible to any role, not just user, employee, and admin. On the other hand, the findConfidentialBook() method is not accessible at all (@DenyAll).

Listing 8-6. A Stateless Bean Using @PermitAll and @DenyAll

```
@Stateless
@RolesAllowed({"user", "employee", "admin"})
public class ItemEJB {

  @PersistenceContext(unitName = "chapter08PU")
  private EntityManager em;

  @PermitAll
  public Book findBookById(Long id) {
    return em.find(Book.class, id);
  }

  public Book createBook(Book book) {
    em.persist(book);
    return book;
  }
```

```
@RolesAllowed("admin")
public void deleteBook(Book book) {
  em.remove(em.merge(book));
}

@DenyAll
public Book findConfidentialBook(Long secureId) {
  return em.find(Book.class, secureId);
}
}
```

The @DeclareRoles annotation is slightly different as it doesn't permit or deny any access. It declares roles for the entire application. When you deploy the EJB in Listing 8-6, the container will automatically declare the user, employee, and admin roles by inspecting the @RolesAllowed annotation. But you might want to declare other roles in the security domain for the entire application (not just for a single EJB) through the @DeclareRoles annotation. This annotation, which only applies at the class level, takes an array of roles and declares them in the security domain. In fact, you declare security roles using either one of these two annotations or a combination of both. If both annotations are used, the aggregation of the roles in @DeclareRoles and @RolesAllowed are declared. We usually declare roles for the entire enterprise application, so in this case it makes more sense to declare roles in the deployment descriptor than with the @DeclareRoles annotation.

When you deploy the ItemEJB in Listing 8-7, the five roles HR, salesDpt, user, employee, and admin are declared. Then, with the @RolesAllowed annotation, certain of these roles are given access to certain methods (as previously explained).

Listing 8-7. A Stateless Bean Declaring Roles

```
@Stateless
@DeclareRoles({"HR", "salesDpt"})
@RolesAllowed({"user", "employee", "admin"})
public class ItemEJB {

  @PersistenceContext(unitName = "chapter08PU")
  private EntityManager em;

  public Book findBookById(Long id) {
    return em.find(Book.class, id);
  }

  public Book createBook(Book book) {
    em.persist(book);
    return book;
  }

  @RolesAllowed("admin")
  public void deleteBook(Book book) {
    em.remove(em.merge(book));
  }
}
```

The last annotation, @RunAs, is handy if you need to temporarily assign a new role to the existing principal. You might need to do this, for example, if you're invoking another EJB within your method, but the other EJB requires a different role.

For example, the ItemEJB in Listing 8-8 authorizes access to the user, employee, and admin role. When one of these roles accesses a method, the method is run with the temporary inventoryDpt role (@RunAs("inventoryDpt")). This means that when you invoke the createBook() method, the InventoryEJB.addItem() method will be invoked with an inventoryDpt role.

Listing 8-8. A Stateless Bean Running as a Different Role

```
@Stateless
@RolesAllowed({"user", "employee", "admin"})
@RunAs("inventoryDpt")
public class ItemEJB {

  @PersistenceContext(unitName = "chapter08PU")
  private EntityManager em;

  @EJB
  private InventoryEJB inventory;

  public List<Book> findBooks() {
    TypedQuery<Book> query = em.createNamedQuery("findAllBooks", Book.class);
    return query.getResultList();
  }

  public Book createBook(Book book) {
    em.persist(book);
    inventory.addItem(book);
    return book;
  }
}
```

As you can see, declarative authorization gives you easy access to a powerful authentication policy. But what if you need to provide security settings to an individual, or apply some business logic based on the current principal's role? This is where programmatic authorization comes into play.

Programmatic Authorization

Declarative authorization covers most security cases needed by an application. But sometimes you need a finer grain of authorizing access (allowing a block of code instead of the entire method, permitting or denying access to an individual instead of a role, etc.). You can use programmatic authorization to selectively permit or block access to a role or a principal. That's because you have direct access to the JAAS java.security.Principal interface, as well as the EJB context to check the principal's role in the code.

The SessionContext interface defines the following methods related to security:

- isCallerInRole(): This method returns a boolean and tests whether the caller has a given security role.

- getCallerPrincipal(): This method returns the java.security.Principal that identifies the caller.

To show how to use these methods, let's take a look at an example. The ItemEJB in Listing 8-9 doesn't use any declarative security but still needs to do some kind of checking programmatically. First of all, the bean needs to get a reference to its context (using the @Resource annotation). With this context, the deleteBook() method can check whether or not the caller has an admin role. If it doesn't, it throws a java.lang.SecurityException to notify the user about the authorization violation. The createBook() method does some business logic using the roles and the principal. Notice that the getCallerPrincipal() method returns a Principal object, which has a name. The method checks whether the principal's name is paul, and then sets the "special user" value to the book entity.

Listing 8-9. A Bean Using Programmatic Security

```java
@Stateless
public class ItemEJB {

  @PersistenceContext(unitName = "chapter08PU")
  private EntityManager em;

  @Resource
  private SessionContext ctx;

  public void deleteBook(Book book) {
    if (!ctx.isCallerInRole("admin"))
      throw new SecurityException("Only admins are allowed");

    em.remove(em.merge(book));
  }

  public Book createBook(Book book) {
    if (ctx.isCallerInRole("employee") && !ctx.isCallerInRole("admin")) {
      book.setCreatedBy("employee only");
    } else if (ctx.getCallerPrincipal().getName().equals("paul")) {
      book.setCreatedBy("special user");
    }
    em.persist(book);
    return book;
  }
}
```

Putting It All Together

In the "Putting It All Together" section in Chapter 4, I demonstrated the development of a Book entity (shown in Listing 4-3) that is mapped to a Derby database. Then I showed you a Main class (shown in Listing 4-4) that uses the entity manager to persist a book and retrieve all the books from the database (using explicit transactional demarcation: tx.begin() and tx.commit()).

The following example employs the same use case but replaces the Main class used in Chapter 4 with a stateless session bean (BookEJB). EJBs are transactional by nature (as you'll see in the next chapter), so our stateless session bean will handle CRUD operations on the Book entity with container-managed transactions (CMT). I will also add a singleton (DatabasePopulator) that will populate the database at startup so there are some data in the database, as well as a CDI producer to be able to inject the persistence unit (with @Inject). The BookEJB, the Book entity, the DatabasePopulator Singleton, the CDI producer, and all the needed XML configuration files will then be packaged and deployed into GlassFish. The BookEJB will be invoked remotely by a Main class (see Figure 8-4) and integration-tested with an embedded container (BookEJBIT).

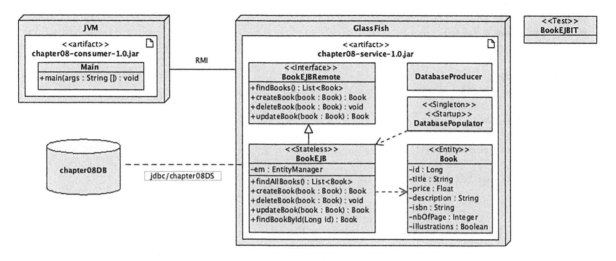

Figure 8-4. *Putting it all together*

To use transactions, the stateless session bean needs to access the database through a data source (jdbc/chapter08DS) that will have to be deployed in GlassFish and linked to the chapter08DB database (thanks to @DataSourceDefinition as you'll later see).

The directory structure for the project follows the Maven conventions, so you have to place classes and files in the following directories:

- src/main/java: For the Book entity, the BookEJB, the BookEJBRemote interface, the DatabasePopulator and the DatabaseProducer class.

- src/main/resources: The persistence.xml file containing the persistence unit used for the Derby database and the beans.xml that triggers CDI.

- src/test/java: The BookEJBIT class for integration-testing.

- pom.xml: The Maven Project Object Model (POM) describing the project, its dependencies on other external modules, and components.

Writing the Book Entity

Listing 8-10 refers to the same Book entity described in Chapter 4 (Listing 4-3), so I will not explain it in much detail (it uses JPA and Bean Validation annotations). One difference though is that the Book entity in Listing 8-10 implements Serializable because it needs to be accessed remotely by the Main class.

Listing 8-10. A Book Entity with a Named Query and Bean Validation Constraints

```
@Entity
@NamedQuery(name = FIND_ALL, query = "SELECT b FROM Book b")
public class Book implements Serializable {

  public static final String FIND_ALL = "Book.findAllBooks";

  @Id @GeneratedValue
  private Long id;
```

```
@NotNull
@Column(nullable = false)
private String title;
private Float price;
@Size(max = 2000)
@Column(length = 2000)
private String description;
private String isbn;
private Integer nbOfPage;
private Boolean illustrations;

// Constructors, getters, setters
}
```

Writing the BookEJB Stateless Session Bean

The BookEJB is a stateless session bean that acts like a façade and handles CRUD operations on the Book entity. Listing 8-11 shows the Java class that needs to be annotated with @javax.ejb.Stateless, exposes a no-interface view thanks to @LocalBean, and implements the BookEJBRemote interface (see Listing 8-12). The EJB obtains a reference of an entity manager using @Inject because the EntityManager is produced by the DatabaseProducer (Listing 8-13). Some explanations on each business method follow:

- findBooks: This method uses the findAllBooks named query defined in the Book entity to retrieve all the book instances from the database.

- createBook: This method takes a Book (that cannot be null) as a parameter, persists it to the database, and returns it.

- updateBook: This method takes a detached Book (that cannot be null) as a parameter and merges it. By using the merge() method, the object is attached to the entity manager and synchronized with the database.

- deleteBook: Before removing a Book entity from the database, this method has to reattach the object to the entity manager (using merge()) and then remove it.

Listing 8-11. A Stateless Session Bean Acting Like a Façade for CRUD Operations

```
@Stateless
@LocalBean
public class BookEJB implements BookEJBRemote {

    @Inject
    private EntityManager em;

    public List<Book> findBooks() {
        TypedQuery<Book> query = em.createNamedQuery(FIND_ALL, Book.class);
        return query.getResultList();
    }

    public @NotNull Book createBook(@NotNull Book book) {
        em.persist(book);
        return book;
    }
```

```
  public @NotNull Book updateBook(@NotNull Book book) {
    return em.merge(book);
  }

  public void deleteBook(@NotNull Book book) {
    em.remove(em.merge(book));
  }
}
```

The main differences between the Main class defined in Chapter 4 (Listing 4-4) and the class in Listing 8-11 is that an instance of EntityManager is directly injected into the session bean instead of using the EntityManagerFactory to create it. The EJB container deals with the EntityManager life cycle, so it injects an instance of it and then closes it when the EJB is destroyed. Also, JPA calls are not wrapped between tx.begin() and tx.commit() anymore, as session bean methods are implicitly transactional. This default behavior is known as a CMT and I discuss it in the next chapter.

Because the BookEJB is invoked remotely by the Main class, the BookEJB needs to implement a remote interface. The only difference between a normal Java interface and a remote interface is the presence of the @Remote annotation as shown in Listing 8-12.

Listing 8-12. A Remote Interface

```
@Remote
public interface BookEJBRemote {

  List<Book> findBooks();
  Book createBook(Book book);
  void deleteBook(Book book);
  Book updateBook(Book book);
}
```

Writing the CDI DatabaseProducer

In Listing 8-11 the BookEJB has an EntityManager injected using @Inject. As you now know, JPA allows an application to have several persistence units, each differentiated by a name (here "chapter08PU"). Because @Inject doesn't have String parameter (you can't write @Inject("chapter08PU")) the only way to inject an EntityManager is with @PersistenceContext(unitName = "chapter08PU"). Thanks to CDI producers (presented in Chapter 2) the bean in Listing 8-13 produces an EntityManager which is now injectable with the @Inject annotation.

Listing 8-13. CDI Bean Producing an EntityManager

```
public class DatabaseProducer {

  @Produces
  @PersistenceContext(unitName = "chapter08PU")
  private EntityManager em;
}
```

Persistence Unit for the BookEJB

In Chapter 4, the persistence unit (Listing 4-5) had to define the JDBC driver, the JDBC URL, the user, and the password to connect to the Derby database because the application managed the transactions (transaction-type ="RESOURCE_LOCAL"). In a container-managed environment, the container manages EJBs and transactions, not the application. So transaction-type of the persistent unit (see Listing 8-14) is set to "JTA". Another difference is that in Listing 4-5 we had to manually specify which JPA provider to use (EclipseLink) and list all the entities the provider had to manage. In a container-managed environment we rely on the default JPA provider (the one bundled with the EJB container). At deployment the container introspects the archive and finds all the entities it needs to manage (no need to explicitly use the <class> element in the persistence.xml).

Listing 8-14. A Persistence Unit Using the chapter08DS Datasource

```xml
<?xml version="1.0" encoding="UTF-8"?>
<persistence xmlns="http://xmlns.jcp.org/xml/ns/persistence"
             xmlns:xsi="http://www.w3.org/2001/XMLSchema-instance"
             xsi:schemaLocation="http://xmlns.jcp.org/xml/ns/persistence ➥
             http://xmlns.jcp.org/xml/ns/persistence/persistence_2_1.xsd"
             version="2.1">

  <persistence-unit name="chapter08PU" transaction-type="JTA">
    <jta-data-source>java:global/jdbc/chapter08DS</jta-data-source>
    <properties>
      <property name="eclipselink.target-database" value="DERBY"/>
      <property name="eclipselink.ddl-generation" value="drop-and-create-tables"/>
      <property name="eclipselink.logging.level" value="INFO"/>
    </properties>
  </persistence-unit>
</persistence>
```

In Listing 8-11, the BookEJB gets injected with a reference of an EntityManager associated with the chapter08PU persistence unit. This persistence unit (defined in Listing 8-14) needs to define the name of the data source to connect to (jdbc/chapter08DS) without specifying any access properties (URL, JDBC driver, etc.).

Writing the DatabasePopulator and Defining the Data Source

The jdbc/chapter08DS data source required by the persistence unit must be created within the EJB container. And there are several ways to do so. The simplest one is to have a @DataSourceDefinition annotation on any Managed Bean (see Listing 8-15). The container will deploy the bean and create the data source. Another way is to use the GlassFish interface, as you'll see next.

Listing 8-15. A Singleton Deploying a Datasource and Initializing the Database at Startup

```java
@Singleton
@Startup
@DataSourceDefinition(
        className = "org.apache.derby.jdbc.EmbeddedDataSource",
        name = "java:global/jdbc/chapter08DS",
        user = "app",
        password = "app",
        databaseName = "chapter08DB",
        properties = {"connectionAttributes=;create=true"}
)
public class DatabasePopulator {
```

```java
@Inject
private BookEJB bookEJB;

private Book h2g2;
private Book lord;

@PostConstruct
private void populateDB() {
   h2g2 = new Book("Beginning Java EE 7", 35F, "Great book", "1-8763-9125-7", 605, true);
   lord = new Book("The Lord of the Rings", 50.4f, "SciFi ", "1-84023-742-2", 1216, true);

   bookEJB.createBook(h2g2);
   bookEJB.createBook(lord);
}

@PreDestroy
private void clearDB() {
   bookEJB.deleteBook(h2g2);
   bookEJB.deleteBook(lord);
}
}
```

The DatabasePopulator singleton (Listing 8-15) is used to initialize some data at startup (@Startup). At deployment the container will initialize the singleton and will execute the populateDB() method because it is annotated with @PostConstruct. This method uses the BookEJB to create a few books in the database. At shutdown the container will invoke the clearDB() method (annotated with @PostConstruct) to remove the books from the database.

Instead of using the @DataSourceDefinition annotation to create a data source at deployment, you can also create it using the GlassFish administration console or the command line. The command-line method is quick and easy to reproduce. Make sure Derby and GlassFish are up and running before entering the following commands.

■ **Note**   @DataSourceDefinition defines a data source and, as you will see in Chapter 13 (Listing 13-18), JMS 2.0 also uses the same mechanism to define resources (ConnextionFactory and Destination) thanks to the @JMSConnectionFactoryDefinition and @JMSDestinationDefinition annotations.

Before creating a data source, you need a connection pool. GlassFish comes with a set of already-defined pools you can use, or you can create your own with the following command:

```
$ asadmin create-jdbc-connection-pool ↪
   --datasourceclassname=org.apache.derby.jdbc.ClientDataSource ↪
   --restype=javax.sql.DataSource ↪
   --property portNumber=1527:password=APP:user=APP:serverName=localhost:↪
   databaseName=chapter08DB:connectionAttributes=;create\=true Chapter08Pool
```

This command creates the Chapter08Pool using a Derby data source and a set of properties to connect to the database: its name (chapter08DB), the server (localhost) and the port (1527) it listens to, a user (APP), and a password (APP) to connect to. If you now ping this data source, Derby will create the database automatically (because you set connectionAttributes=;create\=true). To ping the data source, use the following command:

```
$ asadmin ping-connection-pool Chapter08Pool
```

After you successfully execute this command, you should see the directory chapter08DB on your hard drive where Derby stores the data. The database and the connection pool are created, and now you need to declare the jdbc/chapter08DS data source and link it to the newly created pool as follows:

```
$ asadmin create-jdbc-resource --connectionpoolid Chapter08Pool jdbc/chapter08DS
```

To list all the datasources hosted by GlassFish, enter the following command:

```
$ asadmin list-jdbc-resources
```

Writing the BookEJBIT Integration Test

In version 1.x and 2.x of EJBs, integration testing our BookEJB wasn't easy; you had to use specific features of certain application servers or make some twists to the code. With the new embedded container, an EJB becomes a testable class like any other, as it can run in a normal Java SE environment. The only thing necessary is to add a specific jar file to your class path, as done in the pom.xml file (shown later in Listing 8-17) with the glassfish-embedded-all dependency.

In Chapter 4, I explained how to integration-test an entity with an embedded database, so I will not go into too much detail here on the subject. To integration-test an EJB you use the in-memory Derby database, a different persistence unit, and the in-memory EJB embedded container. Everything is embedded and runs in the same process, necessitating only a JUnit test class (see Listing 8-16). This test initializes the EJBContainer (EJBContainer.createEJBContainer()), gets the JNDI context, looks up the EJB, and uses it to retrieve, create, and delete a book into/from the in-memory database. Thanks to try-with-resources, the embedded container gets closed automatically at the end of the try block.

Listing 8-16. Integration Test of the BookEJB Using the Embeddable Container

```
public class BookEJBIT {

  @Test
  public void shouldCreateABook() throws Exception {

    Map<String, Object> properties = new HashMap<>();
    properties.put(EJBContainer.MODULES, new File("target/classes"));

    try (EJBContainer ec = EJBContainer.createEJBContainer(properties)) {
      Context ctx = ec.getContext();

      // Check JNDI dependencies (Datasource and EJBs)
      assertNotNull(ctx.lookup("java:global/jdbc/chapter08DS"));
      assertNotNull( ↪
  ctx.lookup("java:global/classes/BookEJB!org.agoncal.book.javaee7.chapter08.BookEJBRemote"));
      assertNotNull( ↪
      ctx.lookup("java:global/classes/BookEJB!org.agoncal.book.javaee7.chapter08.BookEJB"));

      // Looks up the EJB
      BookEJB bookEJB = (BookEJB) ↪
        ctx.lookup("java:global/classes/BookEJB!org.agoncal.book.javaee7.chapter08.BookEJB");

      // Finds all the books and makes sure there are two (inserted by the DBPopulator)
      assertEquals(2, bookEJB.findBooks().size());
```

```java
    // Creates an instance of book
    Book book = new Book("H2G2", 12.5F, "Scifi book", "1-24561-799-0", 354, false);

    // Persists the book to the database
    book = bookEJB.createBook(book);
    assertNotNull("ID should not be null", book.getId());

    // Finds all the books and makes sure there is an extra one
    assertEquals(3, bookEJB.findBooks().size());

    // Removes the created book
    bookEJB.deleteBook(book);

    // Finds all the books and makes sure there is one less
    assertEquals(2, bookEJB.findBooks().size());
    }
  }
}
```

The shouldCreateABook() method is an integration test that checks the total number of books (there should be two because the DatabasePopulator has initialized the database with two books), creates a new one, checks that the total number of books has increased by one, removes it, and checks that the total number of books is back to two. For that, the test case creates an EJB container, gets the JNDI context, and uses that context to look up the BookEJB (to then retrieve and create books).

Compiling, Testing, and Packaging with Maven

Now you can use Maven to compile the Book entity, the BookEJB, the BookEJBRemote interface, the DatabasePopulator singleton, and the CDI DatabaseProducer class. Then Maven packages the whole lot in a jar file with the persistence unit (persistence.xml) as well as a CDI beans.xml file. Maven uses the pom.xml file in Listing 8-17 to describe the project and the external dependencies. This example needs the glassfish-embedded-all dependency that comes with all the Java EE 7 APIs, as well as JUnit for integration tests. The classes will be compiled and packaged in a jar file named chapter08- service-1.0.jar, and Maven needs to be informed that you are using Java SE 7 by configuring the maven-compiler-plugin as shown in Listing 8-17.

Listing 8-17. The pom.xml File to Compile, Test and Package the EJBs

```xml
<?xml version="1.0" encoding="UTF-8"?>
<project xmlns="http://maven.apache.org/POM/4.0.0" ➥
         xmlns:xsi="http://www.w3.org/2001/XMLSchema-instance" ➥
         xsi:schemaLocation="http://maven.apache.org/POM/4.0.0 ➥
         http://maven.apache.org/xsd/maven-4.0.0.xsd">
  <modelVersion>4.0.0</modelVersion>

  <parent>
    <artifactId>chapter08</artifactId>
    <groupId>org.agoncal.book.javaee7</groupId>
    <version>1.0</version>
  </parent>
```

```xml
<groupId>org.agoncal.book.javaee7.chapter08</groupId>
<artifactId>chapter08-service</artifactId>
<version>1.0</version>

<dependencies>
  <dependency>
    <groupId>org.glassfish.main.extras</groupId>
    <artifactId>glassfish-embedded-all</artifactId>
    <version>4.0</version>
    <scope>provided</scope>
  </dependency>
  <dependency>
    <groupId>junit</groupId>
    <artifactId>junit</artifactId>
    <version>4.11</version>
    <scope>test</scope>
  </dependency>
</dependencies>

<build>
  <plugins>
    <plugin>
      <groupId>org.apache.maven.plugins</groupId>
      <artifactId>maven-compiler-plugin</artifactId>
      <version>2.5.1</version>
      <configuration>
        <source>1.7</source>
        <target>1.7</target>
      </configuration>
    </plugin>
    <plugin>
      <artifactId>maven-failsafe-plugin</artifactId>
      <version>2.12.4</version>
      <executions>
        <execution>
          <id>integration-test</id>
          <goals>
            <goal>integration-test</goal>
            <goal>verify</goal>
          </goals>
        </execution>
      </executions>
    </plugin>
  </plugins>
</build>
</project>
```

Notice this code includes the glassfish-embedded-all dependency (<scope>provided</scope>), used by the test class (<scope>test</scope>), to invoke the embedded container and run the EJB.

To compile and package the classes, open a command-line interpreter and enter the following Maven command:

```
$ mvn package
```

The BUILD SUCCESSFUL message should appear, letting you know that compilation and packaging were successful. Further, if you check under the target subdirectory, you'll see that Maven has created the chapter08-service-1.0.jar file.

You can execute the integration test (Listing 8-16) with the Maven Failsafe plug-in by entering the following Maven command:

```
$ mvn integration-test
```

Deploying on GlassFish

Now that all the classes have been packaged into a jar archive, it can be deployed to the GlassFish application server. Before doing so, make sure GlassFish and Derby are up and running.

Use the asadmin utility to deploy the application into GlassFish. After you execute this command, it delivers a message informing you of the result of the deployment operation.

```
$ asadmin deploy --force=true target\chapter08-service-1.0.jar
```

Now that the EJB is deployed with the entity, helper classes, and the persistent unit in GlassFish; Derby is running; and the data source is created, it's time to write and run the Main class.

Writing the Main Class

Frequently, Java EE applications consist of web applications acting as clients for EJBs, as described in Chapter 10, where JSF backing beans would invoke EJBs. For now, let's use a plain Java class.

The Main class (see Listing 8-18) uses JNDI to get the InitialContext so it can look up the BookEJBRemote interface (using the portable JNDI name). Remember that this Main class is executed outside the EJB container, so injection is not possible. The main() method starts by looking up the remote interface of the EJB, displaying all the books from the database, creating a new instance of the Book object, and using the EJB createBook() method to persist the entity. It then changes the value of the book's title, updates the book, and removes it. Because the code of this Main class has no persistence context, the Book entity is seen as a detached object manipulated as a normal Java class by another Java class, with no JPA involved. The EJB is the one holding the persistence context and using the entity manager to access the database.

Listing 8-18. A Main Class Invoking the BookEJBRemote

```
public class Main {

  public static void main(String[] args) throws NamingException {

    // Looks up the EJB
    Context ctx = new InitialContext();
    BookEJBRemote bookEJB = (BookEJBRemote) ctx.lookup("java:global/ ↪
        chapter08-service-1.0/BookEJB!org.agoncal.book.javaee7.chapter08.BookEJBRemote");
```

```
    // Gets and displays all the books from the database
    List<Book> books = bookEJB.findBooks();
    for (Book aBook : books) {
      System.out.println(aBook);
    }

    // Creates an instance of book
    Book book = new Book("H2G2", 12.5F, "Scifi book", "1-24561-799-0", 354, false);

    book = bookEJB.createBook(book);
    System.out.println("Book created : " + book);

    book.setTitle("H2G2");
    book = bookEJB.updateBook(book);
    System.out.println("Book updated : " + book);

    bookEJB.deleteBook(book);
    System.out.println("Book deleted");
  }
}
```

Thanks to the Maven Exec plug-in, just enter the following command and Maven will execute the Main class (Listing 8-18). You should then see all the logs displayed in the prompt.

```
$ mvn exec:java
```

Summary

In this chapter, you learned that stateless and singleton session beans share the same life cycle and that stateful beans have a slightly different one. That's because stateful beans keep a conversational state with the client and need to temporarily serialize their state to a permanent storage (passivation). Callback annotations allow you to add business logic to your bean before or after an event occurs (@PostConstruct, @PreDestroy, etc.).

Since EJB 3.1 the timer service has been enhanced and can now effectively compete with other scheduling tools. It takes its roots from cron but adds more expressiveness so you can write complex but readable schedule expressions either declaratively or programmatically.

For security, you have to bear in mind that the business tier doesn't authenticate users; it authorizes roles to access methods. Declarative security is done through a relatively small number of annotations and allows you to cover most cases an enterprise application is likely to need. Again, you can switch to programmatic security and manipulate the JAAS API.

Transactions

Transaction management is an important matter for enterprises. It allows applications to have consistent data and process that data in a reliable manner. Transaction management is a low-level concern that a business developer shouldn't have to code himself. EJBs provide these services in a very simple way: either programmatically with a high level of abstraction or declaratively using metadata. Since Java EE 7, Managed Beans can also have declarative transactions in the same way.

Most of an enterprise application's work is about managing data: storing them (typically in a database), retrieving them, processing them, and so on. Often this is done simultaneously by several applications attempting to access the same data. A database has low-level mechanisms to preserve concurrent access, such as pessimistic locking, and uses transactions to ensure that data stay in a consistent state. EJBs make use of these mechanisms.

I devote the first part of this chapter to understanding transaction management as a whole. Then I discuss the different types of transaction demarcation supported by EJBs: CMT and BMT. I finish with the new transaction interceptor that can be used by Managed Beans.

Understanding Transactions

Data are crucial for business, and they must be accurate regardless of the operations you perform and the number of applications concurrently accessing the data. A *transaction* is used to ensure that the data are kept in a consistent state. It represents a logical group of operations that must be performed as a single unit, also known as a *unit of work*. These operations can involve persisting data in one or several databases, sending messages to a MOM (*message-oriented middleware*), or invoking web services. Companies rely on transactions every day for their banking and e-commerce applications or business-to-business interactions with partners

These indivisible business operations are performed either sequentially or in parallel over a relatively short period of time. Every operation must succeed in order for the transaction to succeed (we say that the transaction is committed). If one of the operations fails, the transaction fails as well (the transaction is rolled back). Transactions must guarantee a degree of reliability and robustness and follow the ACID properties.

ACID

ACID refers to the four properties that define a reliable transaction: Atomicity, Consistency, Isolation, and Durability (described in Table 9-1). To explain these properties, I'll take the classical example of a banking transfer: you need to debit your savings account to credit your current account.

Table 9-1. *ACID Properties*

Property	Description
Atomicity	A transaction is composed of one or more operations grouped in a unit of work. At the conclusion of the transaction, either these operations are all performed successfully (commit) or none of them is performed at all (rollback) if something unexpected or irrecoverable happens.
Consistency	At the conclusion of the transaction, the data are left in a consistent state.
Isolation	The intermediate state of a transaction is not visible to external applications.
Durability	Once the transaction is committed, the changes made to the data are visible to other applications.

When you transfer money from one account to the other, you can imagine a sequence of database accesses: the savings account is debited using a SQL update statement, the current account is credited using a different update statement, and a log is created in a different table to keep track of the transfer. These operations have to be done in the same unit of work (*Atomicity*) because you don't want the debit to occur but not the credit. From the perspective of an external application querying the accounts, only when both operations have been successfully performed are they visible (*Isolation*). With isolation, the external application cannot see the interim state when one account has been debited and the other is still not credited (if it could, it would think the user has less money than she really does). *Consistency* is when transaction operations (either with a commit or a rollback) are performed within the constraints of the database (such as primary keys, relationships, or fields). Once the transfer is completed, the data can be accessed from other applications (*Durability*).

Read Conditions

Transaction isolation can be defined using different read conditions (dirty reads, repeatable reads, and phantom reads). They describe what can happen when two or more transactions operate on the same data at the same time. Depending on the level of isolation you put in place you can totally avoid or allow concurrent access.

- *Dirty reads*: Occur when a transaction reads uncommitted changes made by the previous transaction.

- *Repeatable reads*: Occur when the data read are guaranteed to look the same if read again during the same transaction.

- *Phantom reads*: Occur when new records added to the database are detectable by transactions that started prior to the insert. Queries will include records added by other transactions after their transaction has started.

Transaction Isolation Levels

Databases use several different locking techniques to control how transactions access data concurrently. Locking mechanisms impact the read condition described previously. Isolation levels are commonly used in databases to describe how locking is applied to data within a transaction. The four types of isolation levels are

- *Read uncommitted* (less restrictive isolation level): The transaction can read uncommitted data. Dirty, nonrepeatable, and phantom reads can occur.

- *Read committed*: The transaction cannot read uncommitted data. Dirty reads are prevented but not nonrepeatable or phantom reads.

- *Repeatable read*: The transaction cannot change data that are being read by a different transaction. Dirty and nonrepeatable reads are prevented but phantom reads can occur

- *Serializable* (most restrictive isolation level): The transaction has exclusive read. The other transactions can neither read nor write the same data.

Generally speaking, as the isolation level becomes more restrictive the performance of the system decreases because transactions are prevented from accessing the same data. However, the isolation level enforces data consistency. Note that not all RDBMS (Relational Database Management Systems) implement these four isolation levels.

JTA Local Transactions

Several components have to be in place for transactions to work and follow the ACID properties. Let's first take the simplest example of an application performing several changes to a single resource (e.g., a database). When there is only one transactional resource, all that is needed is a local JTA transaction. A resource local transaction is a transaction that you have with a specific single resource using its own specific API. Figure 9-1 shows the application interacting with a resource through a transaction manager and a resource manager.

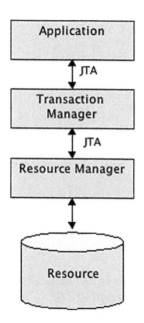

Figure 9-1. A transaction involving one resource

The components shown in Figure 9-1 abstract most of the transaction-specific processing from the application.

- The *transaction manager* is the core component responsible for managing the transactional operations. It creates the transactions on behalf of the application, informs the resource manager that it is participating in a transaction (an operation known as *enlistment*), and conducts the commit or rollback on the resource manager.

- The *resource manager* is responsible for managing resources and registering them with the transaction manager. An example of a resource manager is a driver for a relational database, a JMS resource, or a Java connector.

- The *resource* is the persistent storage from which you read or write (a database, a message destination, etc.).

It is not the application's responsibility to preserve ACID properties. The application just decides to either commit or roll back the transaction, and the transaction manager prepares all the resources to successfully make it happen.

Distributed Transactions and XA

As you've just seen, a transaction using a single resource (shown previously in Figure 9-1) is called a JTA local transaction. However, many enterprise applications use more than one resource. Returning to the example of the fund transfer, the savings account and the current account could be in separate databases. You would then need transaction management across several resources, or resources that are distributed across the network. Such enterprise-wide transactions require special coordination involving XA and the Java Transaction Service (JTS).

Figure 9-2 shows an application that uses transaction demarcation across several resources. This means that, in the same unit of work, the application can persist data in a database and send a JMS message, for example.

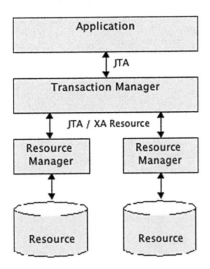

Figure 9-2. *An XA transaction involving two resources*

To have a reliable transaction across several resources, the transaction manager needs to use an XA (eXtended Architecture) resource manager interface. XA is a standard specified by the Open Group (www.opengroup.org) for distributed transaction processing (DTP) that preserves the ACID properties. It is supported by JTA and allows heterogeneous resource managers from different vendors to interoperate through a common interface. XA uses a two-phase commit (2pc) to ensure that all resources either commit or roll back any particular transaction simultaneously.

In our fund transfer example, suppose that the savings account is debited on a first database, and the transaction commits successfully. Then the current account is credited on a second database, but the transaction fails. We would have to go back to the first database and undo the committed changes. To avoid this data inconsistency problem, the two-phase commit performs an additional preparatory step before the final commit as shown in Figure 9-3. During phase 1, each resource manager is notified through a "prepare" command that a commit is about to be issued. This allows the resource managers to declare whether they can apply their changes or not. If they all indicate that they are prepared, the transaction is allowed to proceed, and all resource managers are asked to commit in the second phase.

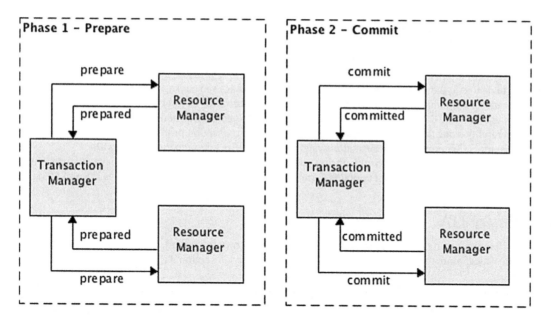

Figure 9-3. *Two-phase commit*

Most of the time, the resources are distributed across the network (see Figure 9-4). Such a system relies on JTS. JTS implements the Object Management Group (OMG) Object Transaction Service (OTS) specification, allowing transaction managers to participate in distributed transactions through Internet Inter-ORB Protocol (IIOP). Compared to Figure 9-2, where there is only one transaction manager, Figure 9-4 allows the propagation of distributed transactions using IIOP. This allows transactions to be distributed across different computers and different databases from different vendors. JTS is intended for vendors who provide the transaction system infrastructure. As an EJB developer, you don't have to worry about it; just use JTA, which interfaces with JTS at a higher level.

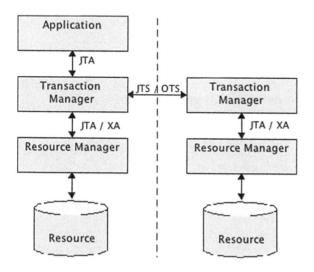

Figure 9-4. *A distributed XA transaction*

Transaction Specifications Overview

In Java EE 7, EJBs and Managed Beans handle transactions through the Java Transaction API (JTA) specified by JSR 907. JTA defines a set of interfaces for the application or the container to demarcate transactions' boundaries, and it also defines APIs to deal with the transaction manager. The `javax.transaction` package defines these interfaces.

JTS is a specification for building a transaction manager which supports the JTA interfaces at the high level and the standard Java mapping of the CORBA Object Transaction Service 1.1 specification at the low level. JTS provides transaction interoperability using the CORBA standard IIOP protocol for transaction propagation between servers. JTS is intended for vendors that provide the transaction system infrastructure for enterprise middleware.

Regarding transaction management, it is unlikely that you want to use the raw JTS/JTA APIs in Java. Instead you delegate transactions to the EJB container that contains a transaction manager (which internally uses JTS and JTA).

A Brief History of JTA

JTA is the general API for managing transactions in Java EE. It allows you to start, commit, and roll back transactions in a resource neutral way. If more than one resource participates in such a transaction, JTA also allows you to do XA transactions.

JTA 1.0 was introduced in 1999 and had some maintenance releases to reach a 1.1 version in 2002. It remained unchanged for a decade and was finally updated to JTA 1.2 with Java EE 7.

What's New in JTA 1.2?

Historically in Java EE, transactions were delegated to EJBs so developers didn't have to use the JTA APIs directly in their code. Both JTA (JSR 907) and EJBs (JSR 345) had been around since 1999. The EJB specification kept on evolving but not JTA, which was already a pretty mature and solid specification. With Managed Bean alignment happening in Java EE 7, one of the biggest challenges was to bring transactions to Managed Beans and not only EJBs. To accomplish that, the JTA specification needed to be updated. JTA 1.2 brings support for container-managed transactions independent of EJB and a `@TransactionScope` annotation for CDI bean scope.

The JTA API consists of classes and interfaces grouped in two packages described in Table 9-2.

Table 9-2. *Main JTA Packages*

Package	Description
javax.transaction	Contains the core JTA APIs
javax.transaction.xa	Interfaces and classes to accomplish distributed XA transactions

Reference Implementation

The reference implementation for JTA is the GlassFish Transaction Manager. It is a module of GlassFish but is not usable outside the server itself. Other open source or commercial stand-alone JTA implementations are available such as JBoss Transaction Manager, Atomikos, and Bitronix JTA.

Transaction Support in EJBs

When you develop business logic with EJBs, you don't have to worry about the internal structure of transaction managers or resource managers because JTA abstracts most of the underlying complexity. With EJBs, you can develop a transactional application very easily, leaving the container to implement the low-level transaction protocols, such as the two-phase commit or the transaction context propagation. An EJB container is a transaction manager that supports JTA as well as JTS to participate in distributed transactions involving other EJB containers and/or other transactional resources. In a typical Java EE application, session beans establish the boundaries of a transaction, call entities to interact with the database, or send JMS messages in a transaction context.

From its creation, the EJB model was designed to manage transactions. In fact, transactions are natural to EJBs, and by default each method is automatically wrapped in a transaction. This default behavior is known as a container-managed transaction (CMT), because transactions are managed by the EJB container (a.k.a. declarative transaction demarcation). You can also choose to manage transactions yourself using bean-managed transactions (BMTs), also called *programmatic transaction demarcation*. Transaction demarcation determines where transactions begin and end.

Container-Managed Transactions

When managing transactions declaratively, you delegate the demarcation policy to the container. You don't have to explicitly use JTA in your code (even if JTA is used underneath); you can leave the container to demarcate transaction boundaries by automatically beginning and committing transactions based on metadata. The EJB container provides transaction management services to session beans and MDBs (see Chapter 13 for more on MDBs). In an enterprise bean with a container-managed transaction, the EJB container sets the boundaries of the transactions.

In Chapter 7, you saw several examples of session beans, annotations, and interfaces, but never anything specific to transactions. Listing 9-1 shows the code of a stateless session bean using CMT. As you can see, there is no extra annotation added or any special interface to implement. EJBs are by nature transactional. With configuration by exception, all the transaction management defaults are applied (REQUIRED is the default transaction attribute as explained later in this section).

Listing 9-1. A Stateless Bean with CMT

```
@Stateless
public class ItemEJB {

  @PersistenceContext(unitName = "chapter09PU")
  private EntityManager em;
  @Inject
  private InventoryEJB inventory;

  public List<Book> findBooks() {
    TypedQuery<Book> query = em.createNamedQuery(FIND_ALL, Book.class);
    return query.getResultList();
  }

  public Book createBook(Book book) {
    em.persist(book);
    inventory.addItem(book);
    return book;
  }
}
```

You might ask what makes the code in Listing 9-1 transactional. The answer is the container. Figure 9-5 shows what happens when a client invokes the createBook() method. The client call is intercepted by the container, which checks immediately before invoking the method whether a transaction context is associated with the call. By default, if no transaction context is available, the container begins a new transaction before entering the method and then invokes the createBook() method. Once the method exits, the container automatically commits the transaction or rolls it back (if a particular type of exception is thrown, as you'll see later in the "Exceptions and Transactions" section).

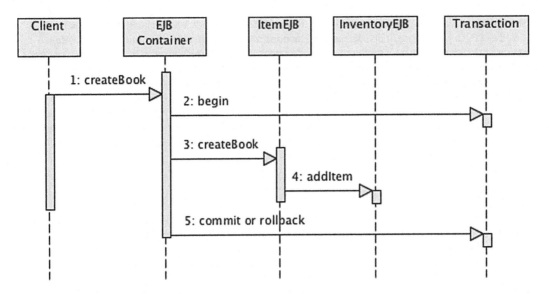

Figure 9-5. *The container handles the transaction*

The default behavior is that whatever transaction context is used for `3:createBook()` (from the client or created by the container) is applied to `4:addItem()`. The final commit happens if both methods have returned successfully. This behavior can be changed using metadata (annotation or XML deployment descriptor). Depending on the transaction attribute you choose (REQUIRED, REQUIRES_NEW, SUPPORTS, MANDATORY, NOT_SUPPORTED, or NEVER), you can affect the way the container demarcates transactions: on a client invocation of a transactional method, the container uses the client's transaction, runs the method in a new transaction, runs the method with no transaction, or throws an exception. Table 9-3 defines the transaction attributes.

Table 9-3. *CMT Attributes*

Attribute	Description
REQUIRED	This attribute (default value) means that a method must always be invoked within a transaction. The container creates a new transaction if the method is invoked from a nontransactional client. If the client has a transaction context, the business method runs within the client's transaction. You should use REQUIRED if you are making calls that should be managed in a transaction, but you can't assume that the client is calling the method from a transaction context.
REQUIRES_NEW	The container always creates a new transaction before executing a method, regardless of whether the client is executed within a transaction. If the client is running within a transaction, the container suspends that transaction temporarily, creates a second one, commits or rolls it back, and then resumes the first transaction. This means that the success or failure of the second transaction has no effect on the existing client transaction. You should use REQUIRES_NEW when you don't want a rollback to affect the client.
SUPPORTS	The EJB method inherits the client's transaction context. If a transaction context is available, it is used by the method; if not, the container invokes the method with no transaction context. You should use SUPPORTS when you have read-only access to the database table.

(continued)

Table 9-3. (*continued*)

Attribute	Description
MANDATORY	The container requires a transaction before invoking the business method but should not create a new one. If the client has a transaction context, it is propagated; if not, a `javax.ejb.EJBTransactionRequiredException` is thrown.
NOT_SUPPORTED	The EJB method cannot be invoked in a transaction context. If the client has no transaction context, nothing happens; if it does, the container suspends the client's transaction, invokes the method, and then resumes the transaction when the method returns.
NEVER	The EJB method must not be invoked from a transactional client. If the client is running within a transaction context, the container throws a `javax.ejb.EJBException`.

Figure 9-6 illustrates all the possible behaviors that an EJB can have depending on the presence or not of a client's transaction context. For example, if the createBook() method doesn't have a transaction context (top part of the figure) and invokes addItem() with a MANDATORY attribute, an exception is thrown. The bottom part of Figure 9-6 shows the same combinations but with a client that has a transaction context.

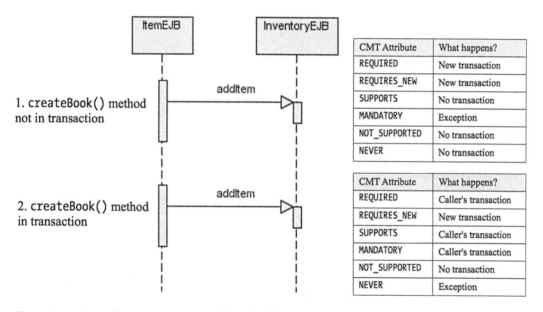

Figure 9-6. *Two calls made to InventoryEJB with different transaction policies*

To apply one of these six demarcation attributes to your session bean, you have to use the `@javax.ejb.TransactionAttribute` annotation or the deployment descriptor (setting the `<trans-attribute>` element in the `ejb-jar.xml`). These metadata can be applied either to individual methods or to the entire bean. If applied at the bean level, all business methods will inherit the bean's transaction attribute value. Listing 9-2 shows how the ItemEJB uses a SUPPORT transaction demarcation policy and overrides the createBook() method with REQUIRED.

Listing 9-2. A Stateless Bean with CMT

```
@Stateless
@TransactionAttribute(TransactionAttributeType.SUPPORTS)
public class ItemEJB {

  @PersistenceContext(unitName = "chapter09PU")
  private EntityManager em;
  @Inject
  private InventoryEJB inventory;

  public List<Book> findBooks() {
    TypedQuery<Book> query = em.createNamedQuery(FIND_ALL, Book.class);
    return query.getResultList();
  }

  @TransactionAttribute(TransactionAttributeType.REQUIRED)
  public Book createBook(Book book) {
    em.persist(book);
    inventory.addItem(book);
    return book;
  }
}
```

▪ **Note**   Client transaction context does not propagate with asynchronous method invocation (@Asynchronous).
MDBs support only the REQUIRED and NOT_SUPPORTED attributes as explained in Chapter 13.

Marking a CMT for Rollback

You've seen that the EJB container demarcates transactions automatically and invokes begin, commit, and rollback operations on your behalf. But, as a developer, you might want to prevent the transaction from being committed if some error or business condition is encountered. It is important to stress that a CMT bean is not allowed to roll back the transaction explicitly. Instead, you need to use the EJB context (see the "Session Context" section in Chapter 7) to inform the container to roll back.

As you can see in Listing 9-3, the InventoryEJB has a oneItemSold() method that accesses the database through the persistence manager and sends a JMS message to inform the shipping company that an item has been sold and should be delivered. If the inventory level is equal to zero (which means no more items are available), the method needs to explicitly roll back the transaction. To do so, the stateless bean first needs to obtain the SessionContext through dependency injection and then call its setRollbackOnly() method. Calling this method doesn't roll back the transaction immediately; instead, a flag is set for the container to do the actual rollback when it is time to end the transaction. Only session beans with CMT demarcation can use this method (BMT session beans roll back transactions directly, as shown in the "Bean-Managed Transactions" section).

Listing 9-3. A Stateless Bean CMT Marks the Transaction for Rollback

```
@Stateless
public class InventoryEJB {

  @PersistenceContext(unitName = "chapter09PU")
  private EntityManager em;
```

```
@Resource
private SessionContext ctx;

public void oneItemSold(Item item) {
  item.decreaseAvailableStock();
  sendShippingMessage();

  if (inventoryLevel(item) == 0)
    ctx.setRollbackOnly();
  }
}
```

Similarly, a bean can call the SessionContext.getRollbackOnly() method, which returns a boolean, to determine whether the current transaction has been marked for rollback.

Another way to programmatically inform the container to roll back is by throwing specific types of exceptions.

Exceptions and Transactions

Exception handling in Java has been confusing since the creation of the language (as it involves both checked exceptions and unchecked exceptions). Associating transactions and exceptions in EJBs is also quite intricate. Before going any further, I just want to say that throwing an exception in a business method will not always mark the transaction for rollback. It depends on the type of exception or the metadata defining the exception. In fact, the EJB 3.2 specification outlines two types of exceptions.

- *Application exceptions*: Exceptions related to business logic handled by the EJB. For example, an application exception might be raised if invalid arguments are passed to a method, the inventory level is too low, or the credit card number is invalid. Throwing an application exception does not automatically result in marking the transaction for rollback. As detailed later in this section in Table 9-4, the container doesn't roll back when checked exceptions (which extend java.lang.Exception) are thrown, but it does for unchecked exceptions (which extend RuntimeException).

- *System exceptions*: Exceptions caused by system-level faults, such as JNDI errors, JVM errors, failure to acquire a database connection, and so on. A system exception must be a subclass of a RuntimeException or java.rmi.RemoteException (and therefore a subclass of javax.ejb.EJBException). Throwing a system exception results in marking the transaction for rollback.

With this definition, we know now that if the container detects a system exception, such as an ArithmeticException, ClassCastException, IllegalArgumentException, or NullPointerException, it will roll back the transaction. Application exceptions depend on various factors. As an example, let's change the code from Listing 9-3 and use an application exception as shown in Listing 9-4.

Listing 9-4. A Stateless Bean Throwing an Application Exception

```
@Stateless
public class InventoryEJB {

  @PersistenceContext(unitName = "chapter09PU")
  private EntityManager em;

  public void oneItemSold(Item item) throws InventoryLevelTooLowException{
    item.decreaseAvailableStock();
    sendShippingMessage();
```

```
    if (inventoryLevel(item) == 0)
      throw new InventoryLevelTooLowException();
  }
}
```

InventoryLevelTooLowException is an application exception because it's related to the business logic of the oneItemSold() method. It is then a business concern to know whether you want to roll back the transaction or not. An application exception is one that extends from a checked or unchecked exception and is annotated with @javax.ejb.ApplicationException (or the XML equivalent in the deployment descriptor). This annotation has a rollback element that can be set to true to explicitly roll back the transaction. Listing 9-5 shows the InventoryLevelTooLowException as an annotated checked exception.

Listing 9-5. An Application Exception with rollback = true

```
@ApplicationException(rollback = true)
public class InventoryLevelTooLowException extends Exception {

  public InventoryLevelTooLowException() { }

  public InventoryLevelTooLowException(String message) {
    super(message);
  }
}
```

If the InventoryEJB in Listing 9-4 throws the exception defined in Listing 9-5, it will mark the transaction for rollback, and the container will do the actual rollback when it is time to end the transaction. That's because the InventoryLevelTooLowException is annotated with @ApplicationException(rollback = true). Table 9-4 shows all the possible combinations with application exceptions. The first line of the table could be interpreted as "If the application exception extends from Exception and has no @ApplicationException annotation, throwing it will not mark the transaction for rollback."

Table 9-4. *Combination of Application Exceptions*

Extends from	@ApplicationException	The transaction is marked for rollback
Exception	No annotation	No
Exception	rollback = true	Yes
Exception	rollback = false	No
RuntimeException	No annotation	Yes
RuntimeException	rollback = true	Yes
RuntimeException	rollback = false	No

Bean-Managed Transactions

With CMT, you leave the container to do the transaction demarcation just by specifying a transaction attribute and using the session context or exceptions to mark a transaction for rollback. In some cases, the declarative CMT may not provide the demarcation granularity that you require (e.g., a method cannot generate more than one transaction). To address this issue, EJBs offer a programmatic way to manage transaction demarcations with BMT. BMT allows you to explicitly manage transaction boundaries (begin, commit, rollback) using JTA.

To turn off the default CMT demarcation and switch to BMT mode, a bean simply has to use the `@javax.ejb.TransactionManagement` annotation (or the XML equivalent in the `ejb-jar.xml` file) as follows:

```
@Stateless
@TransactionManagement(TransactionManagementType.BEAN)
public class ItemEJB {...}
```

With BMT demarcation, the application requests the transaction, and the EJB container creates the physical transaction and takes care of a few low-level details. Also, it does not propagate transactions from one BMT to another.

The main interface used to carry out BMT is `javax.transaction.UserTransaction`. It allows the bean to demarcate a transaction, get its status, set a timeout, and so on. The `UserTransaction` is instantiated by the EJB container and made available through dependency injection, JNDI lookup, or the `SessionContext` (with the `SessionContext.getUserTransaction()` method). Table 9-5 describes the API.

Table 9-5. *Methods of the javax.transaction.UserTransaction Interface*

Method	Description
begin	Begins a new transaction and associates it with the current thread
commit	Commits the transaction attached to the current thread
rollback	Rolls back the transaction attached to the current thread
setRollbackOnly	Marks the current transaction for rollback
getStatus	Obtains the status of the current transaction
setTransactionTimeout	Modifies the timeout for the current transactions

Listing 9-6 shows how to develop a BMT bean. First of all, we get a reference of the `UserTransaction` using injection through the `@Resource` annotation. The `oneItemSold()` method begins the transaction, does some business processing, and then, depending on some business logic, commits or rolls back the transaction. Notice also that the transaction is marked for rollback in the `catch` block (I've simplified exception handling for better readability).

Listing 9-6. A Stateless Bean with BMT

```
@Stateless
@TransactionManagement(TransactionManagementType.BEAN)
public class InventoryEJB {

  @PersistenceContext(unitName = "chapter09PU")
  private EntityManager em;
  @Resource
  private UserTransaction ut;

  public void oneItemSold(Item item) {
    try {
      ut.begin();

      item.decreaseAvailableStock();
      sendShippingMessage();
```

```
      if (inventoryLevel(item) == 0)
        ut.rollback();
      else
        ut.commit();

    } catch (Exception e) {
      ut.rollback();
    }
    sendInventoryAlert();
  }
}
```

The difference with the CMT code shown in Listing 9-3 is that with CMT the container starts the transaction before the method execution and commits it immediately after. With the BMT code shown in Listing 9-6, you manually define transaction boundaries inside the method itself.

Transaction Support in Managed Beans

As you've just seen, CMT are one of the original ease-of-use facilities of EJB. With declarative transaction on enterprise bean classes or methods, the container can create new transactions (REQUIRED, REQUIRES_NEW), inherit from existing ones (SUPPORTS), or throw an exception if the transaction has not been already created (MANDATORY). That's because the container intercepts the corresponding method calls and interposes the necessary operations to initiate, suspend, or complete JTA transactions.

As part of better aligning Managed Beans across the platform, one of the improvements of Java EE 7 is the extension of CMT beyond EJBs. This was made possible thanks to interceptors and interceptor binding (see Chapter 2). Transaction management on Managed Beans has been implemented using a CDI interceptor binding as defined in Listing 9-7.

Listing 9-7. The @javax.transaction.Transactional Interceptor Binding

```
@Inherited
@InterceptorBinding
@Target({TYPE, METHOD})
@Retention(RUNTIME)
public @interface Transactional {

  TxType value() default TxType.REQUIRED;
  Class[] rollbackOn() default {};
  Class[] dontRollbackOn() default {};

  public enum TxType {
    REQUIRED,
    REQUIRES_NEW,
    MANDATORY,
    SUPPORTS,
    NOT_SUPPORTED,
    NEVER
  }
}
```

The javax.transaction.Transactional annotation (Listing 9-7) provides the application with the ability to control transaction boundaries on CDI Managed Beans, as well as Servlets, JAX-RS, and JAX-WS endpoints declaratively. This provides the semantics of EJB transaction attributes in CDI without dependencies on other EJB services such as RMI or timer service.

For example, Listing 9-8 shows a JAX-RS web service (more on that in Chapter 15) using the @Transactional annotation so it can use the EntityManager to persist books to the database. This code wasn't possible until Java EE 7. You had to either annotate the RESTful web service with @Stateless or delegate the persistence to a session bean layer.

Listing 9-8. A Book RESTful Web Service Creating Books with Transactions

```java
@Path("book")
@Transactional
public class BookRestService {

  @Context
  private UriInfo uriInfo;
  @PersistenceContext(unitName = "chapter09PU")
  private EntityManager em;

  @POST
  @Consumes(MediaType.APPLICATION_XML)
  public Response createBook(Book book) {
    em.persist(book);
    URI bookUri = uriInfo.getAbsolutePathBuilder().path(book.getId().toString()).build();
    return Response.created(bookUri).build();
  }

  @GET
  @Produces(MediaType.APPLICATION_XML)
  @Transactional(Transactional.TxType.SUPPORTS)
  public Books getAllBooks() {
    TypedQuery<Book> query = em.createNamedQuery(Book.FIND_ALL, Book.class);
    Books books = new Books(query.getResultList());
    return books;
  }
}
```

Like EJBs you can also change the default transactional policy (e.g., SUPPORTS) to a different one just by using the annotation attributes. As shown in Listing 9-8 the @Transactional annotation can be put on a class and/or on a method.

Exceptions and Transactions

Exceptions and transactions are slightly different in Managed Beans than in EJBs. As in EJBs, they use the same default exception handling: application exceptions (i.e., checked exceptions) do not result in the transactional interceptor marking the transaction for rollback, and system exceptions (i.e., unchecked exceptions) do. But this default behavior can be overridden in the @Transactional annotation using the rollbackOn and dontRollbackOn attributes. When you specify a class for either of these attributes, the designated behavior applies to subclasses of that class as well. If you specify both attributes, dontRollbackOn takes precedence.

To override the default behavior and cause transactions to be marked for rollback for all application exceptions you need to write the following:

```
@Transactional(rollbackOn={Exception.class})
```

On the other hand, if you want to prevent transactions from being marked for rollback by the interceptor when an IllegalStateException (unchecked exception) or any of its subclasses is caught, you can use the dontRollbackOn as follows:

```
@Transactional(dontRollbackOn={IllegalStateException.class})
```

You can use both attributes to refine the transactional behavior. Each attribute takes an array of classes and can be used as follows:

```
@Transactional(rollbackOn={SQLException.class},
        dontRollbackOn={SQLWarning.class, ArrayIndexOutOfBoundsException.class})
```

■ **Note**   There is no special, built-in knowledge about EJB application exceptions (i.e., exceptions annotated with @ApplicationException). As far as the interceptor is concerned, these would be treated just as any other exceptions unless otherwise specified with the rollbackOn and dontRollbackOn attributes.

Summary

In this chapter, I have shown you how to handle transactions within EJBs and Managed Beans. You can define transaction management either declaratively or programmatically.

Transactions allow the business tier to keep the data in an accurate state even when accessed concurrently by several applications. They follow the ACID properties and can be distributed across several resources (databases, JMS destinations, web services, etc.). CMT allows you to easily customize the EJB container behavior in terms of transaction demarcation. You can influence this behavior by marking a transaction for rollback through the EJB context or exceptions. You can always use BMT if you need finer control of the transaction demarcation directly using JTA. A novelty in Java EE 7 is to bring these concepts to other components such as Servlets or Web Services thanks to CDI interceptor binding.

CHAPTER 10

■ ■ ■

JavaServer Faces

If you want to graphically display information coming from the back end, you have to create a user interface. It can be of various types: desktop applications, web applications running in a browser, or mobile applications running in a portable device that displays a graphical interface and interacts with the end user.

Today we live in an Internet-dependent world. With our transactional back end processing thousands of requests, and communicating with heterogeneous systems through web services, we need a presentation layer to interact with end users, preferably one that runs in a browser. Browsers are everywhere, user interfaces are richer, more dynamic, and easier to use than before. Rich Internet applications are gaining in popularity as users expect more from their browsing experience. They need to consult catalogs of books and CDs online, but they also want to access e-mail and documents, receive e-mail notification, or have parts of their browser page selectively refreshed when a server event occurs. Add to that the Web 2.0 philosophy whereby people can share any kind of information with groups of friends and interact with each other, and the result is web interfaces that are becoming more and more complex to develop. JavaServer Faces (JSF, or simply Faces) was created to ease the creation of graphical interfaces.

Inspired by the Swing component model and other GUI (graphical user interface) frameworks, JSF allows developers to think in terms of components, events, backing beans, and their interactions, instead of requests, responses, and markup language. Its goal is to make web development faster and easier by supporting user interface components (such as text boxes, list boxes, tabbed panes, and data grids) in a rapid application development (RAD) approach.

This chapter introduces web pages with some basic concepts such as HTML, CSS, and JavaScript. Then it focuses on how to create web interfaces using JSF components or how to build your own custom components.

Understanding Web Pages

When we create a web application, we are interested in displaying dynamic content that can be read in a browser: a list of items from a catalog (CDs and books, for instance), the customer details for a given identifier, a shopping cart containing the items the customer wants to buy, and so on. Conversely, static content, such as the address of a book company and FAQs (frequently asked questions) with information on how to buy or ship items, rarely or never changes. Static content can also be the images, videos, or artwork that make up a page.

The final goal of creating a page is to display it in a browser. The page has to use languages that the browser can understand, of which there are several: HTML, XHTML, CSS, and JavaScript.

HTML

HyperText Markup Language (HTML) is the predominant language for web pages. It is based on Standard Generalized Markup Language (SGML), which is a standard metalanguage to define markup languages. HTML uses *markups*, or *tags*, to structure text into paragraphs, lists, links, buttons, text areas, and so on.

An HTML page is a text document used by browsers to present text and graphics. These documents are text files that often have an `.html` or `.htm` extension. A web page is made of content, tags to change some aspects of the content, and external objects such as images, videos, JavaScript, or CSS files. Listing 10-1 shows how to display a form to create a new book in HTML.

Listing 10-1. The newBook.html Page with Invalid HTML Structure

```
<H1>Create a new book</h1>
<hr>
<TABLE border=0>
  <TR>
    <TD>ISBN :</TD>
    <TD><input type=text/></td>
  </tr>
  <tr>
    <td>Title :</td>
    <TD><input type=text/></td>
  </tr>
  <tr>
    <td>Price :
    <TD><input type=text/>
  </tr>
  <tr>
    <td>Description :
    <td><textarea name=textarea cols=20 rows=5></textarea>
  </tr>
  <TR>
    <TD>Number of pages :
    <td><input type=text/>
  </tr>
  <tr>
    <td>Illustrations :
    <td><input type="checkbox"/>
  </tr>
</table>
<input type=submit value=Create>
<hr>
<em>APress - Beginning Java EE 7</em>
```

Normally, a valid HTML page starts with an `<html>` tag that acts like a container for the document. It is followed by a `<head>` and `<body>` tag. `<body>` contains the visible content such as the HTML code displaying a table, labels, input fields, and a button. As you can see in Listing 10-1, the `newBook.html` markup doesn't follow these rules, but browsers will display nonvalid HTML pages to a certain extent. So the visible result would look like Figure 10-1.

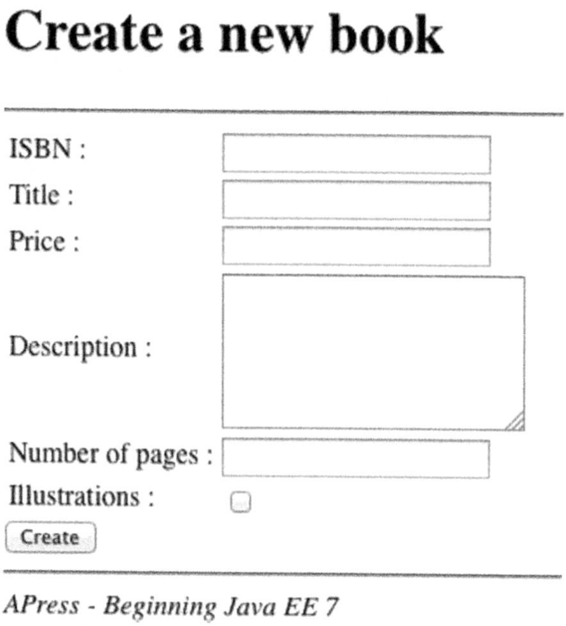

Create a new book

ISBN :

Title :

Price :

Description :

Number of pages :

Illustrations :

Create

APress - Beginning Java EE 7

Figure 10-1. *Graphical representation of the newBook.html page*

The graphical representation shown in Figure 10-1 is the one expected despite the fact that Listing 10-1 is not well formatted in terms of XML.

- The page does not have any `<html>`, `<head>`, or `<body>` tags.

- The `<input type=submit value=Create>` or `<hr>` tags are not closed.

- Attribute values are not between quotes (`border=0` instead of `border="0"`)

- Uppercase and lowercase are mixed in tags (e.g., `<TR>`and `</tr>` both appear in the listing).

Most browsers will permit such mistakes and display this form. However, if you want to process this document with XML parsers, for example, it would fail. To understand why this is, let's look at a web page that uses a strict XML structure with eXtensible HyperText Markup Language (XHTML).

■ **Note**   At the time of writing this book the HTML 5 specification has not been finalized. HTML5 will add many new features such as the `<video>`, `<audio>`, and `<canvas>` elements, as well as the integration of scalable vector graphics (SVG) content. These features are designed to make it easy to include and handle multimedia and graphical content on the Web without having to resort to proprietary plug-ins and APIs. HTML5 is also a potential candidate for cross-platform mobile applications as many features have been built with the consideration of being able to run on smartphones or tablets.

XHTML

XHTML was created shortly after HTML 4.01. It has its roots in HTML but is reformulated in strict XML. This means an XHTML document is an XML document that follows a certain schema and has a graphical representation on browsers. An XHTML file (which has the extension `.xhtml`) can be used as XML right away or displayed in a browser.

In contrast to HTML, this has the advantage of providing document validation using standard XML tools (XSL, or Extensible Stylesheet Language; XSLT, XSL Transformations; etc.). Hence, XHTML is much more flexible and powerful than HTML, because it allows you to define any set of tags you wish. Listing 10-2 shows how the XHTML version of the web page displaying a form to create a book would look.

Listing 10-2. The newBook.xhtml Page with a Valid XML Structure

```
<?xml version="1.0" encoding="UTF-8"?>
<!DOCTYPE html
        PUBLIC "-//W3C//DTD XHTML 1.0 Transitional//EN"
        "http://www.w3.org/TR/xhtml1/DTD/xhtml1-transitional.dtd">
<html xmlns="http://www.w3.org/1999/xhtml" xml:lang="en" lang="en">
<head>
  <title>Create a new book</title>
</head>
<body>
<h1>Create a new book</h1>
<hr/>
<table border="0">
  <tr>
    <td>ISBN :</td>
    <td><input type="text"/></td>
  </tr>
  <tr>
    <td>Title :</td>
    <td><input type="text"/></td>
  </tr>
  <tr>
    <td>Price :</td>
    <td><input type="text"/></td>
  </tr>
  <tr>
    <td>Description :</td>
    <td><textarea cols="20" rows="5"></textarea></td>
  </tr>
  <tr>
    <td>Number of pages :</td>
    <td><input type="text"/></td>
  </tr>
  <tr>
    <td>Illustrations :</td>
    <td><input type="checkbox"/></td>
  </tr>
</table>
<input type="submit" value="Create"/>
<hr/>
<em>APress - Beginning Java EE 7</em>
</body>
</html>
```

Some differences exist between Listing 10-1 and Listing 10-2: the document in Listing 10-2 follows a strict structure and has `<html>`, `<head>`, and `<body>` tags; all the tags are closed, even the ones with empty elements (each `<td>` is closed, and `<hr/>` is used instead of `<hr>`); attributes appear between single or double quotes (`<table border="0">` or `<table border='0'>`, but not `<table border=0>`); and tags are all lowercase (`<tr>` instead of `<TR>`). Compare this to Listing 10-1, which as mentioned previously shows invalid HTML that browsers will be able to display anyway.

The strict validation of XML syntax rules and schema constraints makes XHTML easier to maintain and to parse than HTML, and as a result it is now the preferred language for web pages. A conforming XHTML document is an XML document that follows the HTML 4.01 specification. A document can use three different validation formats.

- *XHTML 1.0 Transitional*: The most conciliatory variant of XHTML that lets you use presentational elements (such as center, font, and strike) that are excluded from the strict version.

- *XHTML 1.0 Frameset*: A transitional variant that also allows the definition of frameset documents (a common Web feature in the late 1990s).

- *XHTML 1.0 Strict*: The most restrictive variant of XHTML that strictly follows the HTML 4.01 specification.

CSS

Browsers live in a world of client-side languages such as HTML, XHTML, CSS, and JavaScript. Cascading Style Sheets (CSS) is a styling language used to describe the presentation of a document written in HTML or XHTML. CSS is used to define colors, fonts, layouts, and other aspects of document presentation. It allows separation of a document's content (written in XHTML) from its presentation (written in CSS). Like HTTP, HTML, and XHTML, the CSS specifications are maintained by the World Wide Web Consortium (W3C).

For example, say you want to alter the labels on the newBook.xhtml page by making them italic (`font-style: italic;`), changing the color to blue (`color: #000099;`), and increasing the font size (`font-size: 22px;`); you do not have to repeat these changes for each tag. You can define a CSS style (in a `<style type="text/css">` tag) and give it an alias (e.g., `.row`) or redefine existing tags styles (e.g., body, table or h1). The page (see Listing 10-3) will use these styles on elements that need to change their presentation (`<td class="row">`).

Listing 10-3. The newBook.xhtml Page with Some CSS Styles

```
<!DOCTYPE html PUBLIC "-//W3C//DTD XHTML 1.0 Transitional//EN"
        "http://www.w3.org/TR/xhtml1/DTD/xhtml1-transitional.dtd">
<html xmlns="http://www.w3.org/1999/xhtml" xml:lang="en" lang="en">
<head>
  <title>Create a new book</title>
  <style type="text/css">

    body {
      font-family: Arial, Helvetica, sans-serif;
    }

    table {
      border: 0;
    }

    h1 {
      font-size: 22px;
      color: blue;
      font-style: italic;
    }
```

```
    .row {
       font-style: italic;
    }
  </style>
</head>
<body>
<h1>Create a new book</h1>
<hr/>
<table>
  <tr>
    <td class="row">ISBN :</td>
    <td><input type="text"/></td>
  </tr>
  <tr>
    <td class="row">Title :</td>
    <td><input type="text"/></td>
  </tr>
  <tr>
    <td class="row">Price :</td>
    <td><input type="text"/></td>
  </tr>
  <tr>
    <td class="row">Description :</td>
    <td><textarea cols="20" rows="5"></textarea></td>
  </tr>
  <tr>
    <td class="row">Number of pages :</td>
    <td><input type="text"/></td>
  </tr>
  <tr>
    <td class="row">Illustrations :</td>
    <td><input type="checkbox"/></td>
  </tr>
</table>
<input type="submit" value="Create"/>
<hr/>
<em>APress - Beginning Java EE 7</em>
</body>
</html>
```

In Listing 10-3 the CSS code is embedded in the XHTML page. In a real application, all the styles would be written in a separate file and this file imported into the web page. The web designer can draw up one or more sets of CSS for various groups of pages, and then content contributors can write or change pages without needing to be concerned about the look and feel.

Compared with Figure 10-1, the end result is that all the labels are in italic and the title is blue (see Figure 10-2).

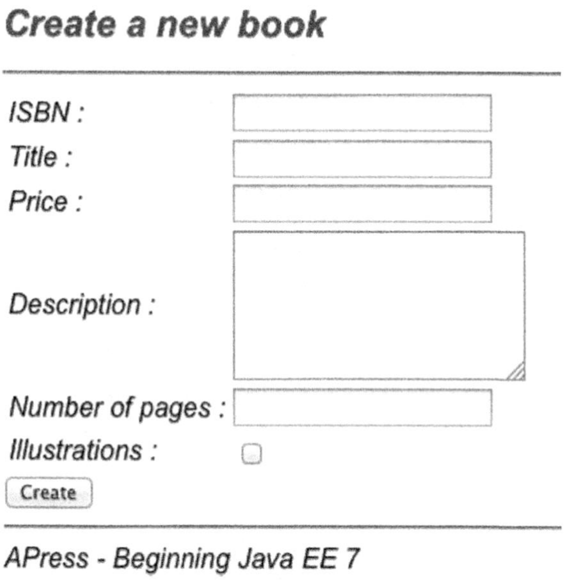

Create a new book

ISBN :

Title :

Price :

Description :

Number of pages :

Illustrations :

Create

APress - Beginning Java EE 7

Figure 10-2. Graphical representation of the newBook.xhtml page with CSS

DOM

An XHTML page is an XML document and thus has a Document Object Model (DOM) representation. DOM is a W3C specification for accessing and modifying the content and structure of XML documents as well as an abstract API for querying, traversing, and manipulating such documents. DOM can be thought of as a tree representation of the structure of a document. Figure 10-3 shows how the newBook.xhtml page might look as a DOM representation; at the root there's the html tag, one level below head and body, and under body a table with a list of tr tags.

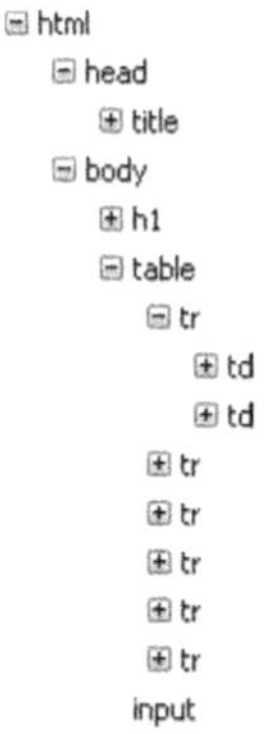

```
⊟ html
    ⊟ head
        ⊞ title
    ⊟ body
        ⊞ h1
        ⊟ table
            ⊟ tr
                ⊞ td
                ⊞ td
            ⊞ tr
            ⊞ tr
            ⊞ tr
            ⊞ tr
            ⊞ tr
            input
```

Figure 10-3. Tree representation of the newBook.xhtml page

DOM provides a standard way to interact with XML documents. You can traverse the tree and edit the content of a node (a leaf of the tree). With some JavaScript, you can introduce dynamism into your web pages. As you will see in Chapter 11, Ajax is based on JavaScript interacting with the DOM representation of a web page.

JavaScript

Until now, you've seen different languages used to represent static content and graphical aspects of a web page. But, often, a web page needs to interact with the end user by showing dynamic content. As you'll see, dynamic content can be handled with server-side technologies such as JSF, but browsers can also do so by executing JavaScript.

JavaScript is a scripting language used for client-side web development. Despite its name, it is unrelated to the Java programming language, as it is an interpreted, weakly typed language. JavaScript is a powerful way to create dynamic web applications by writing functions that interact with the DOM of a page. W3C standardized DOM, whereas the European Computer Manufacturers Association (ECMA) standardized JavaScript as the ECMAScript specification. Any page written with these standards (XHTML, CSS, and JavaScript) should look and behave more or less identically in any browser that adheres to these guidelines.

An example of JavaScript interacting with DOM is the newBook.xhtml page in Listing 10-4. This page displays a form where you can enter information about a book. The price of the book needs to be completed by the user on the client side before hitting the server. To make price a required entry, you can create a JavaScript function (priceRequired()) that checks whether the price text field is empty or not.

Listing 10-4. The newBook.xhtml Page with Some JavaScript

```
<?xml version="1.0" encoding="UTF-8"?>
<!DOCTYPE html PUBLIC "-//W3C//DTD XHTML 1.0 Transitional//EN"
        "http://www.w3.org/TR/xhtml1/DTD/xhtml1-transitional.dtd">
<html xmlns="http://www.w3.org/1999/xhtml" xml:lang="en" lang="en">
<head>
  <title>Create a new book</title>

  <script type="text/javascript">
    function priceRequired() {
      if (document.getElementById("price").value == "") {
          document.getElementById("priceError").innerHTML = "Please, enter a price !";
      }
    }
  </script>

</head>
<body>
<h1>Create a new book</h1>
<hr/>
<table border="0">
  <tr>
    <td>ISBN :</td>
    <td><input type="text"/></td>
  </tr>
  <tr>
    <td>Title :</td>
    <td><input type="text"/></td>
  </tr>
  <tr>
    <td>Price :</td>
    <td><input id="price" type="text" onblur="javascript:priceRequired()"/>
      <span id="priceError"/>
    </td>
  </tr>
```

```
    <tr>
      <td>Description :</td>
      <td><textarea cols="20" rows="5"></textarea></td>
    </tr>
    <tr>
      <td>Number of pages :</td>
      <td><input type="text"/></td>
    </tr>
    <tr>
      <td>Illustrations :</td>
      <td><input type="checkbox"/></td>
    </tr>
  </table>
  <input name="" type="submit" value="Create"/>
  <hr/>
  <em>APress - Beginning Java EE 7</em>
  </body>
  </html>
```

In Listing 10-4, the priceRequired() JavaScript function is embedded in the page within a <script> tag (but could have been externalized in a separate file). This function is called when the price text field loses the focus (that's what the onblur event does). The priceRequired() function uses the implicit document object that represents the DOM of the XHTML document. The getElementById("price") method looks for an element that has an identifier called price (<input id="price">) and checks whether it's empty. If so, the function looks for another element called priceError (getElementById("priceError")) and sets the value to Please, enter a price!. If the price is not completed, the client validation will display the message shown in Figure 10-4.

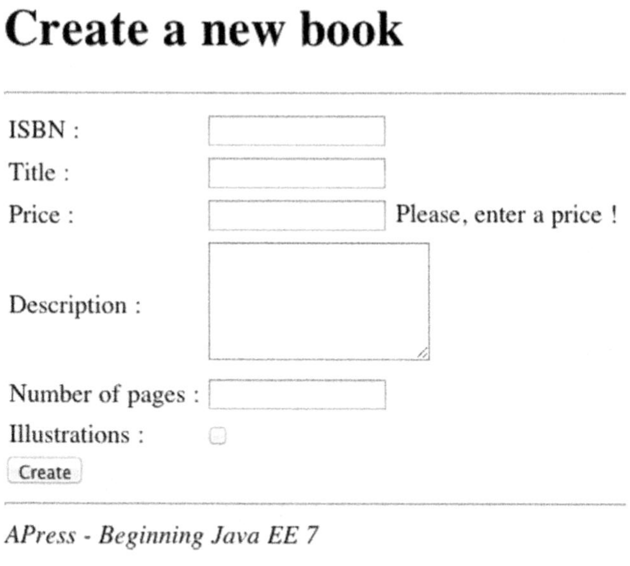

Create a new book

ISBN :

Title :

Price :   Please, enter a price !

Description :

Number of pages :

Illustrations :

Create

APress - Beginning Java EE 7

Figure 10-4. *The newBook.html page with an error message*

JavaScript is a rich language. The preceding section covers only a small part that demonstrates the interaction between JavaScript and DOM. It is important to understand that a JavaScript function can get to a node in the page (either by name or by ID such as the getElementById() method) and change its content dynamically on the client side. For details, see the "Ajax" section in Chapter 11.

Understanding JSF

You've just seen client-side technologies and languages, such as XHTML or CSS, which represent the content and the visual aspect of a static web page. To add some interaction and to dynamically change parts of the web page, you can use JavaScript functions that run on the browser. But, most of the time, you need to invoke a business layer of EJBs to display data from the database. This dynamic content can be obtained using JSF on the server side.

JSF's architecture is easy to understand (see Figure 10-5), if you are familiar with web frameworks. JSF applications are standard web applications that intercept HTTP requests via the Faces Servlet and produce HTML. Under the hood, the architecture allows you to plug in any page declaration language (PDL, or view declaration language, VDL), render it for different devices (web browser, mobile devices, tablets, etc.), and create pages using events, listeners, and components, à la Swing. Swing is a Java widget toolkit that has been part of Java SE since release 1.2. It is a GUI framework to create desktop applications (not web applications) using graphical components and the event-listener model to process user inputs. JSF also brings a standard set of user interface (UI) widgets (buttons, hyperlinks, check boxes, text fields, etc.) and allows the easy plug-in of third-party components. Figure 10-5 represents the JSF architecture at a very high level.

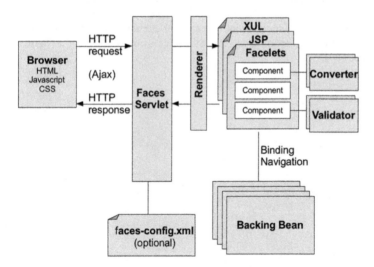

Figure 10-5. *JSF architecture*

Figure 10-5 represents several important pieces of JSF that make its architecture rich and flexible:

- FacesServlet *and* faces-config.xml: FacesServlet is the main Servlet for the application and can optionally be configured by a faces-config.xml descriptor file.

- *Pages and components*: JSF allows multiple PDLs but Facelets is the recommended one since JSF 2.0.

- *Renderers*: These are responsible for displaying a component and translating a user's input into the component property values.

- *Converters*: These convert a component's value (Date, Boolean, etc.) to and from markup values (String).

- *Validators*: These are responsible for ensuring that the value entered by a user is valid (most of the validation can be delegated to Bean Validation).

- *Backing beans and navigation*: The business logic is made in backing beans, which also control the navigation between pages.

- *Ajax support*: JSF 2.2 comes with built-in support for Ajax as explained in Chapter 11.

- *Expression language*: EL is used in JSF pages to bind variables and actions between a component and a backing bean.

FacesServlet

Most of the web frameworks use the Model-View-Controller (MVC) design pattern, as does JSF. The MVC pattern is used to decouple the view (the page) and the model (the data to be displayed in the view). The controller handles user actions that might result in changes in the model and updates to the views. In JSF, this controller is a Servlet called FacesServlet. The FacesServlet is a Servlet that manages the request processing life cycle for web applications. All user requests go through the FacesServlet, which examines the request and calls various actions on the model using backing beans.

This Servlet is internal and part of JSF. The only way it can be configured is by using external metadata. Up to JSF 1.2, the only source of configuration was the faces-config.xml file. Today, with JSF 2.2, this file is optional, and most metadata can be defined through annotations (on backing beans, converters, components, renderers, and validators).

Pages and Components

The JSF framework has to send a page to the client's output device (a browser, for example) and requires some sort of display technology. This display technology is the PDL. A JSF application is free to use several technologies for its PDL but Facelets is preferred for JSF 2.2 (more in the section "Facelets").

Facelets pages are made up of a tree of components (also called widgets or controls) that provide specific functionality for interacting with an end user (text field, button, list box, etc.). JSF has a standard set of components and allows you to easily create your own. The page goes through a rich life cycle to manage this tree of components (initialization, events, rendering, etc.).

The code in Listing 10-5 is a Facelets XHTML page that uses JSF tags (xmlns:h="http://xmlns.jcp.org/jsf/html") to display a form with two input fields (the ISBN and the title of a book) and a button. This page is composed of several JSF components. Some of them have no visual appearance, like the ones used to declare the header (<h:head>), the body (<h:body>), or the form (<h:form>). Others are visual and represent a label (<h:outputLabel>), a text field (<h:inputText>), or a button (<h:commandButton>). Notice that pure HTML tags can also be mixed in the page (<table>, <tr>, <hr/>, etc.).

Listing 10-5. Snippet of a JSF Page with a Mix of JSF Components and HTML

```
<!DOCTYPE html PUBLIC "-//W3C//DTD XHTML 1.0 Transitional//EN"
        "http://www.w3.org/TR/xhtml1/DTD/xhtml1-transitional.dtd">
<html xmlns="http://www.w3.org/1999/xhtml" xmlns:h="http://xmlns.jcp.org/jsf/html">
<h:head>
  <title>Create a new book</title>
</h:head>
<h:body>
  <h1>Create a new book</h1>
```

```
<hr/>
<h:form>
  <table border="0">

    <tr>
      <td><h:outputLabel value="ISBN : "/></td>
      <td><h:inputText value="#{bookController.book.isbn}"/></td>
    </tr>

    <tr>
      <td><h:outputLabel value="Title :"/></td>
      <td><h:inputText value="#{bookController.book.title}"/></td>
    </tr>

  </table>
  <h:commandButton value="Create a book"
                   action="#{bookController.doCreateBook}" styleClass="submit"/>

</h:form>
<hr/>
<em>APress - Beginning Java EE 7</em>
</h:body>
</html>
```

Facelets

When JSF was created, the intention was to reuse JSP (JavaServer Page) as the main PDL, as it was already part of Java EE. JSP was using EL and JSTL (JSP Standard Tag Library), so the idea was to make use of all these technologies within JSF. JSP is a page language, and JSF is a component layer on top of it. However, JSP and JSF life cycles don't fit together well. Tags in JSPs are processed once from top to bottom in order to produce a response. JSF has a more complex life cycle where the component tree generation and the rendering occur at different phases. This is where Facelets comes into play: to fit the JSF life cycle.

Facelets began life as an open source alternative to JSP. Unlike JSP, EL, and JSTL, it didn't have a JSR and was not part of Java EE. Facelets was a replacement for JSP and provided an XML-based alternative (XHTML) for pages in a JSF-based application. Facelets was designed with JSF in mind, and this is why it provided a simpler programming model than JSP's. Because of that, Facelets got specified in JSF 2.0 and comes today in Java EE 7 as the preferred PDL for JSF.

Renderers

JSF supports two programming models for displaying components: the direct implementation and the delegated implementation. When you use the direct model, components must decode themselves from, and encode themselves to, a graphical representation. When you use the delegated model, these operations are delegated to a renderer. which allows a component to be independent of a rendering technology (browser, portable device, etc.) and to have several graphical representations.

A renderer is responsible for displaying a component and translating user input into the component's value. Think of it as a translator between the client and the server: it decodes the user request to set values to the component, and encodes the response to create a representation of a component that the client understands and can display.

Renderers are organized into render kits, which focus on a specific type of output. To ensure application portability, JSF includes support for a standard render kit and associated renderers for HTML 4.01. JSF implementations can then create their own render kit to generate Wireless Markup Language (WML), scalable vector graphics (SVGs), and so on.

Converters and Validators

Once the page is rendered, the user can interact with it to enter data. As there are no type constraints, a renderer cannot know beforehand how to display the object. This is where converters come in: they translate an object (Integer, Date, Enum, Boolean, etc.) to a String for display, and from an input String back into an object. JSF comes with a set of converters for common types (in the javax.faces.convert package), but you can develop your own or incorporate third-party converters.

Sometimes these data also have to be validated before being processed in the back end. Validators are responsible for ensuring that the value entered by a user is acceptable. One or more validators can be associated with a single component. JSF comes with a few validators (LengthValidator, RegexValidator, etc.) and allows you to create your own using annotated classes. When there's a conversion or validation error, a message is sent back to the response to be displayed. Since JSF 2.0 part of the validation can be delegated to Bean Validation (presented in Chapter 3).

Backing Beans and Navigation

All the concepts so far have been related to a single page: what is a page, what is a component, how are they rendered, converted, and validated? Web applications are made up of multiple pages and need to perform business logic (e.g., by calling an EJB layer or RESTful web service). Backing beans handle going from one page to another, invoking EJBs, and synchronizing data with components.

A backing bean is a specialized Java class that synchronizes values with components, processes business logic, and handles navigation between pages (more on backing beans and navigation in Chapter 11). You associate a component with a specific backing bean property or action using EL. The following code binds the isbn attribute of the book bean and invokes the doCreateBook backing bean action:

```
<h:inputText value="#{bookController.book.isbn}"/>
<h:commandButton value="Create" action="#{bookController.doCreateBook}"/>
```

The first line of code hooks up the input text's value directly to the book.isbn property of a backing bean called bookController. The value of the input text is synchronized with the book.isbn property of the backing bean. A backing bean also handles events. The second line of code shows a submit button associated with an action. When the submit button is clicked, it triggers an event to the backing bean where an event listener method is executed (here the doCreateBook() method).

Listing 10-6 shows the BookController backing bean. This Java class is annotated with the CDI @Named annotation so it can be used within EL. It has a property book that is bound with the component's value of the page (value="#{bookController.book.isbn}"). The doCreateBook() method invokes a stateless EJB and then returns a string that allows navigation between pages (listBooks.xhtml).

Listing 10-6. BookController Backing Bean

```
@Named
@RequestScoped
public class BookController {

  @Inject
  private BookEJB bookEJB;

  private Book book = new Book();
```

```
public String doCreateBook() {
  book = bookEJB.createBook(book);
  return "listBooks.xhtml";
}

// Getters, setters
}
```

Expression Language

The binding between a JSF page and a Java backing bean is made through EL. You can use EL statements to print the value of variables, access objects' attributes in a page, or invoke a backing bean method. The basic syntax for an EL statement is

```
#{expr}
```

The #{expr} statements will be parsed and evaluated by the JSF runtime. EL expressions can use most of the usual Java operators.

- *Arithmetic*: +, -, *, / (div), % (mod),
- *Relational*: == (eq), != (ne), < (lt), > (gt), <= (le), >= (ge),
- *Logical*: && (and), || (or), ! (not), and
- *Other*: (), empty, [],.

Note that some operators have both symbolic and text variants (> can be gt, / can be div, etc.). These equivalents allow you to develop your JSF pages in an XML-compliant syntax. A "less than" could be coded #{2 lt 3} rather than #{2 < 3}.

The empty operator tests whether an object is null or whether it references an empty String, List, Map, or array. It returns true if empty; otherwise, it returns false. You could check whether the object or one of its attributes is null.

```
#{empty book}
#{empty book.isbn}
```

The dot operator is used to access the attribute isbn of the book object. Another syntax is possible by using the [ ] operator; the isbn attribute can be accessed using either notation, as follows:

```
#{book.isbn}
#{book[isbn]}
```

An enhancement in EL 3.0 is its ability to invoke methods. The following code fragment shows how to buy a book by calling the book.buy() method and how to pass a parameter (the currency used):

```
#{book.buy()}
#{book.buy('EURO')}
```

Ajax Support

A web application must provide a rich and responsive interface. This reactivity can be obtained by updating only small portions of the page in an asynchronous manner, which is what Ajax is all about. Previous 1.x versions of JSF didn't offer any out-of-the-box solution, so third-party libraries such as a4jsf filled this gap. Since JSF 2.0, Ajax support has been added in the form of a JavaScript library (jsf.js) defined in the specification and a <f:ajax> tag. For example, you can use the <f:ajax> tag to submit a form in an asynchronous way as shown in the following code:

```
<h:commandButton value="Create a book" action="#{bookController.doCreateBook}">
  <f:ajax execute="@form" render=":booklist"/>
</h:commandButton>
```

Don't worry if you don't understand this code; an entire section is dedicated to Ajax in Chapter 11.

JSF Specification Overview

Web development in Java started in 1996 with the Servlet API, a very rudimentary way to create dynamic web content. You had to manipulate a low-level HTTP API (HttpServletRequest, HttpServletResponse, HttpSession, etc.) to display HTML tags inside your Java code. JSPs arrived in 1999 and provided a higher level of abstraction than Servlets. In 2004, the first version of JSF arrived, with version 1.2 becoming part of Java EE 5 in 2006. JSF 2.2 is now bundled with Java EE 7.

A Brief History of Web Interfaces

At first, web pages were static. A user would request a resource (a web page, an image, a video, etc.), and the server would return it–simple, but very limited. With the growth of commercial activity on the Web, companies had to deliver dynamic content to their customers. The first solution for creating dynamic content was the Common Gateway Interface (CGI). By using HTML pages and CGI scripts written in any number of languages (from Perl to Visual Basic), an application could access databases and serve dynamic content, but it was clear that CGI was too low level (you had to handle HTTP headers, call HTTP commands, etc.) and needed to be improved.

In 1995, a new language called Java was released with a platform-independent user interface API called Abstract Window Toolkit (AWT). Later on, in Java SE 1.2, AWT, which relies on the operating system's user interface module, was superseded by the Swing API (which draws its own widgets by using Java 2D). During these early days of Java, Netscape's Navigator browser offered support for this new language, which opened the era of applets. *Applets* are applications that run on the client side, inside a browser. This allowed developers to write applications in AWT or Swing and embed them on a web page. However, applets never really took off. Netscape also created a scripting language called JavaScript, which executes directly in the browser. Despite some incompatibilities between browsers, JavaScript is now heavily used today and is a powerful way to create dynamic web applications.

After the failure of applets to become widely adopted, Sun introduced Servlets as a way to have thin, dynamic web clients. Servlets were an alternative to CGI scripts because they would offer a higher-level library for handling HTTP, had full access to the Java API (allowing database access, remote invocation, etc.), and could create HTML as a response to be displayed for the user.

Sun released JSP in 1999 as an enhancement of the Servlet model. But, because JSPs were mixing Java and HTML code, in 2001 an open source framework arrived and opened doors to a new approach: Struts. This extended the Servlet API and encouraged developers to adopt an MVC architecture. Recent history is full of other web frameworks, each trying to fill the gaps of the last (Tapestry, Wicket, WebWork, DWR, Spring MVC, etc.). Today, JSF 2.2 is the standard web framework in Java EE 7. It competes with Struts and Tapestry within the Java space. Rails and Grails compete with JSF overall, in the sense that Java competes with Ruby or Groovy. Google Web Toolkit (GWT), Flex, and JavaFX can be complementary to JSF.

■ **Note** JSP 1.2 and Servlet 2.3 were specified together in JSR 53. At the same time, the JSTL was specified in JSR 52. Since 2002, the JSP 2.0 specification has evolved separately from Servlets in JSR 152. In 2006, JSP 2.1 was part of Java EE 5 and facilitated the integration between JSF and JSP by introducing a unified EL. With Java EE 7, both JSP and EL specifications evolve separately (JSP 2.3 and Expression Language 3.0). This book does not cover JSP as it's becoming outdated, no major improvements have been made, and also JSF is the preferred web interface technology in Java EE.

A Brief History of JSF

JSF 1.0 was created in 2001 as JSR 127 and in 2004, a 1.1 maintenance version was released. Only in 2006 was JSF 1.2 introduced into Java EE as JSR 252 (with Java EE 5). The biggest challenge in this version was to preserve backward compatibility as well as to integrate JSP with a unified EL. Despite these efforts, JSF and JSP didn't fit well, so other frameworks such as Facelets were introduced as alternatives to JSPs.

JSF 2.0 was a major release evolving in JSR 314 and was part of Java EE 6. It brought easier navigation between pages, easier development with annotations (for backing beans, renderers, converters, validators), and easier graphical component development, and it brought GET requests as a first-class citizen as opposed to POST (allowing users to bookmark pages), new resource-handling mechanism (for images, CSS, JavaScript files . . .), and Ajax support. Today JSF 2.2 (JSR 344) follows up this ease of development and brings many new features.

What's New in JSF 2.2?

JSF 2.2 (JSR 344) is an evolution from 2.1 and a step forward as it brings the following new features:

- *HTML-friendly markup*: The ability to write the view in pure HTML but let JSF add all additional back-end features

- *Allowing id attribute on all elements for HTML5 content*: Contrary to previous HTML standards, HTML5 allows you to use an id attribute for every kind of element

- *Faces Flow*: A major JSF improvement, the concept of "flow" has been added to JSF 2.2. Flows take the user through a series of screens such as wizards, multiscreen subscriptions, bookings, etc.

- *Queue control for AJAX requests*: JSF adds support for controlling an Ajax request queue. If multiple requests arrive within this delay period, only the most recent one is sent to the server.

- *Injection in all JSF artifacts*: In JSF 2.1, relatively few JSF artifacts could use injection. In JSF 2.2 injection is possible everywhere (converters, validators, components, etc.).

- *Moving to CDI*: JSF 2.0 brought its own scoping mechanism and backing beans. Today CDI has become the drop-in replacement for the old JSF backing beans and JSF 2.2 supports the scopes directly for CDI (this means that the entire javax.faces.bean is deprecated and might get pruned in a future JSF release).

Table 10-1 lists the main packages defined in JavaServer Faces 2.2 today.

Table 10-1. *Main JavaServer Faces Packages*

Package	Description
javax.faces	The core JavaServer Faces APIs
javax.faces.application	APIs used to link an application's business logic objects to JavaServer Faces
javax.faces.component	Fundamental APIs for user interface components
javax.faces.context	Classes and interfaces defining per-request state information
javax.faces.convert	Classes and interfaces defining converters
javax.faces.event	Interfaces describing events and event listeners, and concrete event implementation classes
javax.faces.flow	Classes and runtime API for Faces Flow
javax.faces.lifecycle	Classes and interfaces defining life-cycle management for the JSF implementation
javax.faces.render	Classes and interfaces defining the rendering model
javax.faces.validator	Interface defining the validator model and concrete validator implementation classes
javax.faces.webapp	Classes required for integrating JSF into web applications, including the standard FacesServlet

Reference Implementation

Mojarra, named after a fish that is found on the South American and Caribbean coasts, is the Oracle open source reference implementation of JSF 2.2. Mojarra is available in GlassFish v4 and is used in the example presented next.

MyFaces is a project of the Apache Software Foundation which hosts several subprojects related to JavaServer Faces, including MyFaces Core which is a JSF runtime implementation.

Writing JSF Pages and Components

Writing a JSF page is different from writing an HTML page in the sense that JSF is a back-end technology. If you write a JSF page and run it straight in a browser, you will not see the graphical representation that you expect. A JSF page needs to be rendered in HTML on the server before being sent to the browser. A developer can combine JSF components with core HTML and CSS for styling if she wants, but all this will be rendered by the back end.

A JSF page can be seen as a component tree that uses several tag libraries (the ones defined by the JSF specification but also in-house or third-party libraries). The page body is compiled into a tree of graphical Java objects and their values are bound to a backing bean. Therefore, the page has a rich life cycle that handles many different phases.

Anatomy of a JSF Page

A JSF page is basically an XHTML file defining a list of tag libraries on the header and a body containing the graphical representation. As an example, let's reuse the page representing a form to create a new book (refer back to Figure 10-1). Listing 10-7 shows these two fragments. The xmlns:h="http://xmlns.jcp.org/jsf/html" is importing the tag library called http://xmlns.jcp.org/jsf/html and giving it the alias h. This is then used in the body of the page when we need to display a specific component that belongs to the tag library (e.g., <h:panelGrid> or <h:inputText>). In this example there is only one tag library that is being used but you can have as many as you need.

Listing 10-7. A JSF Page Using a Tag Library and Components

```
<!DOCTYPE html PUBLIC "-//W3C//DTD XHTML 1.0 Transitional//EN"
        "http://www.w3.org/TR/xhtml1/DTD/xhtml1-transitional.dtd">

<html xmlns="http://www.w3.org/1999/xhtml"
      xmlns:h="http://xmlns.jcp.org/jsf/html">

<h:head>
  <title>Create a new book</title>
</h:head>
<h:body>
  <h1>Create a new book</h1>
  <hr/>
  <h:form>
    <h:panelGrid columns="2">
      <h:outputLabel value="ISBN : "/>
      <h:inputText value="#{bookController.book.isbn}"/>

      <h:outputLabel value="Title :"/>
      <h:inputText value="#{bookController.book.title}"/>

      <h:outputLabel value="Price : "/>
      <h:inputText value="#{bookController.book.price}"/>

      <h:outputLabel value="Description  : "/>
      <h:inputTextarea value="#{bookController.book.description}" cols="20" rows="5"/>

      <h:outputLabel value="Number of pages : "/>
      <h:inputText value="#{bookController.book.nbOfPage}"/>

      <h:outputLabel value="Illustrations : "/>
      <h:selectBooleanCheckbox value="#{bookController.book.illustrations}"/>

    </h:panelGrid>
    <h:commandButton value="Create a book" action="#{bookController.doCreateBook}"/>

  </h:form>
  <hr/>
  <h:outputText value="APress - Beginning Java EE 7" style="font-style: italic"/>
</h:body>
</html>
```

Header

The header of a JSF page can be seen as the Java import mechanism: it is where you declare the set of component libraries that the page will be using. In the following code, an XML prologue is followed by the document type declaration (DTD) xhtml1-transitional.dtd. The root element of the page is html in the namespace http://www.w3.org/1999/xhtml. And then a set of XML namespaces declares the tag libraries used in the JSF page with a certain prefix (h and f).

```
<!DOCTYPE html PUBLIC "-//W3C//DTD XHTML 1.0 Transitional//EN"
        "http://www.w3.org/TR/xhtml1/DTD/xhtml1-transitional.dtd">
<html xmlns="http://www.w3.org/1999/xhtml"
      xmlns:h="http://xmlns.jcp.org/jsf/html"
      xmlns:f="http://xmlns.jcp.org/jsf/core">
```

Table 10-2 lists all the tag libraries that are defined in the JSF and JSTL specifications and that can be used in a Facelets page. There are the JSF's core and html graphical components as well as the templating and composite libraries (allowing you to create custom components). There are also the functions and core libraries that are part of JSTL.

Table 10-2. *Tag Libraries Allowed with Facelets PDL*

URI	Common Prefix	Description
http://xmlns.jcp.org/jsf/html	h	This tag library contains components and their HTML renderers (h:commandButton, h:commandLink, h:inputText, etc.).
http://xmlns.jcp.org/jsf/core	f	This library contains custom actions that are independent of any particular rendering (f:selectItem, f:validateLength, f:convertNumber, etc.).
http://xmlns.jcp.org/jsf/facelets	ui	Tags in this library add templating support.
http://xmlns.jcp.org/jsf/composite	composite	This tag library is used for declaring and defining composite components.
http://xmlns.jcp.org/jsp/jstl/core	c	Facelets pages can use some of the core JSP tag libraries (<c:if/>, <c:forEach/>, or <c:catch/>).
http://xmlns.jcp.org/jsp/jstl/functions	fn	Facelets pages can use all the function JSP tag libraries.

Body

As shown in Listing 10-7 the body of a JSF page describes a set of well-organized graphical (and nongraphical) components that ultimately, after being rendered on the server, will give you the HTML representation you want. A JSF page is a tree of components such as <h:outputText> that will be compiled into a tree of UI components. A UI component is a Java class that extends, directly or indirectly, the abstract javax.faces.component.UIComponent class. This class defines methods for navigating the component tree, interacting with backing beans, and validating and converting data as well as the rendering mechanism.

The JSF specification provides a number of built-in HTML and core components you need when building a web application. All these components extend UIComponent and are listed in Table 10-3. Notice that these classes are all defined in the javax.faces.component package. Later in the "JSF HTML Components Tags" section you'll see HTML components that are in javax.faces.component.html.

Table 10-3. *Standard JSF UI Components*

Component	Description
UIColumn	Represents a column in the parent UIData component
UICommand	Represents graphical components such as buttons, hyperlinks, or menus
UIComponent	Base class for all user interface components in JSF
UIComponentBase	Convenience class that implements the default concrete behavior of all methods defined by UIComponent
UIData	Supports data binding to a collection of objects; commonly used to render tables, lists, and trees
UIForm	Represents a user input form and is a container of other components
UIGraphic	Displays an image
UIInput	Represents components to input data such as input fields, text areas, and so on
UIMessage, UIMessages	Responsible for displaying one or several messages for a specific UIComponent
UIOutcomeTarget	Represents graphical buttons and hyperlinks that enable bookmarkability
UIOutput	Represents output components such as labels or any other textual data output
UIPanel	Represents UI components that server as containers for others without requiring form submission
UIParameter	Represents information that requires no rendering
UISelectBoolean	Represents check boxes
UISelectItem, UISelectItems	Represent a single or multiple items in a selection list
UISelectOne, UISelectMany	Represent components like combo boxes, list boxes, or groups of check boxes and allow the selection of one or many items
UIViewAction	Represents a method invocation that occurs during the request processing life cycle
UIViewParameter	Represents a bidirectional binding between a request parameter and a backing bean property
UIViewRoot	Represents the component tree root and has no graphical rendering

To have an HTML representation of the page described in Listing 10-7, the JSF runtime actually uses the HTML representation of each component defined in the page. These HTML components inherit from the ones listed in Table 10-3. For example, a <h:outputLabel> is defined by the javax.faces.component.html.HtmlOutputLabel class that extends UIOutput. A <h:panelGrid> is defined by the javax.faces.component.html.HtmlPanelGrid class that extends UIPanel, and so. The XML in Listing 10-8 is the tree representation of the page described in Listing 10-7.

Listing 10-8. Simplified View of the newBook XML Component Tree

```
<UIViewRoot>
  <html xmlns="http://www.w3.org/1999/xhtml">

    <UIOutput><title>Create a new book</title></UIOutput>

    <UIOutput>
```

```
<h1>Create a new book</h1>
<hr/>

<HtmlForm>
  <HtmlPanelGrid>

    <HtmlOutputLabel value="ISBN : "/>
    <HtmlInputText/>

    <HtmlOutputLabel value="Title :"/>
    <HtmlInputText/>

    <HtmlOutputLabel value="Price : "/>
    <HtmlInputText/>

    <HtmlOutputLabel value="Description : "/>
    <HtmlInputTextarea/>

    <HtmlOutputLabel value="Number of pages : "/>
    <HtmlInputText/>

    <HtmlOutputLabel value="Illustrations : "/>
    <HtmlSelectBooleanCheckbox/>
  </HtmlPanelGrid>

  <HtmlCommandButton value="Create a book"/>
</HtmlForm>

<hr/>
<HtmlOutputText value="APress - Beginning Java EE 7" style="font-style: italic"/>

    </UIOutput>
  </html>
</UIViewRoot>
```

■ **Tip**   You can easily get the component tree representation of a JSF page just by adding the `<ui:debug>` tag anywhere in the page and pressing CTRL+SHIFT+D.

Life Cycle

A JSF page is a component tree with a specific life cycle. You should understand this life cycle so you know when components are validated or the model is updated. Clicking a button causes a request to be sent from your web browser to the server. This request is translated into an event that can be processed by your application logic on the server. All data input by the user enters a phase of validation before the model is updated and any business logic invoked. JSF is then responsible for making sure that every graphical component (child and parent components) is properly rendered to the browser. Figure 10-6 shows the different phases of a JSF page life cycle.

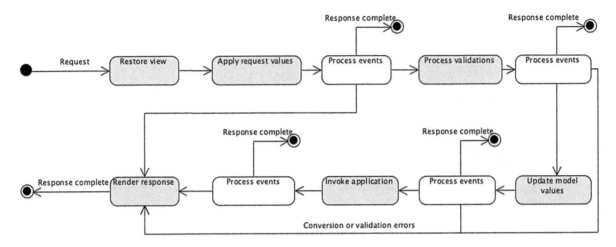

Figure 10-6. *The JSF life cyle*

The JSF life cycle is divided into six distinct phases.

1. *Restore view*: JSF finds the target view and applies the user's input to it. If this is the client's first visit to the page, JSF creates the view as a `UIViewRoot` component (root of the component tree that makes up a particular page as shown in Listing 10-8). If this is a subsequent request, the previously saved `UIViewRoot` is retrieved for processing the current HTTP request.

2. *Apply request values*: Values that have come from the request (from input fields in a web form, from cookies, or from request headers) are applied to the various components of the page. Note that only UI components update their state—not the backing bean that composes the model.

3. *Process validations*: After the preceding steps, the UI components have a value set. In the validation processing, JSF traverses the component tree and asks each component to ensure its submitted value is acceptable. If both conversion and validation are successful for all components, the life cycle continues to its next phase. Otherwise, the life cycle goes to the *Render response* phase with the appropriate validation and conversion error messages.

4. *Update model values*: All the validated component values are bound to the associated backing beans.

5. *Invoke application*: Now you can perform some business logic. Whatever action has been triggered will be executed on the backing bean, and this is where the navigation comes into effect, as its return will determine the render response.

6. *Render response*: Causes the response to be rendered to the client. The secondary goal of the phase is to save the state of the view so that it can be restored in the restore view phase if the user requests it again.

The thread of execution for a request/response cycle can flow through each phase or not, depending on the request and what happens during the processing; if an error occurs, the flow of execution transfers immediately to the render response phase. Note that four of these phases can generate messages: apply request values, process validations, update model values, and invoke application. With or without messages, it is the render response phase that sends output back to the user.

Anatomy of JSF Components

A JSF page is a tree of components. Some of these components have an HTML representation, others don't and allow you to validate, convert data, or enable Ajax invocation. You can use several components to design your Web pages.

- JSF built-in HTML, Core, and Templating components,
- JSTL tags,
- Your own homemade components, and
- Third-party components (open source or commercial).

Sometimes these components need external resources such as images, CSS, or JavaScript. JSF manages these resources in a very clever way, whereby you can bundle your resources depending on a locale, a library, or a version number (more on that in the "Resource Management" section). As you will see, JSF pages can also have access to implicit objects allowing components to use HTTP request parameters, cookie information, or HTTP headers.

JSF HTML Components Tags

JSF's architecture is designed to be independent of any particular protocol or markup language, and it is also made to write applications for HTML clients that communicate via HTTP. A user interface for a particular web page is created by assembling components. Components provide specific functionalities for interacting with an end user (labels, tables, check boxes, etc.). JSF provides a number of built-in HTML components that cover most of the common requirements.

A page is a tree of components; each component is represented by a class that extends `javax.faces.component. UIComponent` and has properties, methods, and events. The components in the tree have parent-child relationships with other components, starting at the root element of the tree, which is an instance of `UIViewRoot` (see Listing 10-8). Let's focus on using these components on web pages. The `javax.faces.component.html` package describes HTML components.

Commands

Commands (`UICommand`) are controls that a user can click to trigger an action. Such components are typically rendered as a button or a hyperlink. Table 10-4 lists the two command tags that can be used.

Table 10-4. *Command Tags*

Tag	Class	Description
`<h:commandButton>`	`HtmlCommandButton`	Represents an HTML input element for a button of type submit or reset
`<h:commandLink>`	`HtmlCommandLink`	Represents an HTML element for a hyperlink that acts like a submit button. This component must be placed inside a form

If on your page you need to add submit buttons, reset buttons, images that can be clicked, or hyperlinks that trigger an event, do so as follows:

```
<h:commandButton value="A submit button"/>
<h:commandButton type="reset" value="A reset button"/>
<h:commandButton image="book.gif" title="A button with an image"/>
<h:commandLink>A hyperlink</h:commandLink>
```

By default, a commandButton is of type submit, but it can be changed to type reset (type="reset"). If you want to turn a button into an image, don't use the value attribute (that's the name of the button), instead use the image attribute to specify the path of the image you want to display. The following is the graphical result of the previous code:

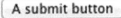

A hyperlink

Both buttons and links have an action attribute to invoke a method on a backing bean. For example, to call the doNew() method of the bookController, use the following EL statement to specify it in the action attribute:

```
<h:commandLink action="#{bookController.doNew}">
  Create a new book
</h:commandLink>
```

Targets

The previous command components invoke an action on a backing bean by generating an HTTP POST. If you need a button or a link to go directly to another page by generating an HTTP GET, then you need to use the target components (UIOutcomeTarget) defined in Table 10-5. Note that these components enable bookmarkability in JSF applications.

Table 10-5. *Target Tags*

Tag	Class	Description
<h:button>	HtmlOutcomeTargetButton	Renders an HTML input element for a button (produces a HTTP GET when clicked)
<h:link>	HtmlOutcomeTargetLink	Renders an HTML <a> anchor element (produces a HTTP GET when clicked)

If your need to navigate from one page to another one without calling a backing bean you can use outcome components as follows:

```
<h:button outcome="newBook.xhtml" value="A bookmarkable button link"/>
<h:link outcome="newBook.xhtml" value="A bookmarkable link"/>
```

The graphical representation is as expected.

```
A bookmarkable button link
```

A bookmarkable link

Inputs

Inputs (UIInput) are components that display their current value to the user and allow the user to enter different kinds of textual information. These can be text fields, text areas, or components to enter a password or hidden data. Table 10-6 lists the input tags.

Table 10-6. *Input Tags*

Tag	Class	Description
`<h:inputHidden>`	`HtmlInputHidden`	Represents an HTML input element of type hidden (which is useful to propagate values outside the session from page to page)
`<h:inputSecret>`	`HtmlInputSecret`	Represents an HTML input element of type password. On a redisplay, any previously entered value will not be rendered (for security reasons) unless the redisplay property is set to `true`
`<h:inputText>`	`HtmlInputText`	Represents an HTML input element of type text
`<h:inputTextarea>`	`HtmlInputTextarea`	Represents an HTML text area element
`<h:inputFile>`	`HtmlInputFile`	Allows you to browse a directory and pick up and upload a file

Many web pages contain forms in which a user has to enter some data or log on using a password. Input components have several attributes that allow you to change their length, content, or look and feel, as follows:

```
<h:inputHidden value="Hidden data"/>
<h:inputSecret maxlength="8"/>
<h:inputText value="An input text"/>
<h:inputText size="40" value="A longer input text"/>
<h:inputTextarea rows="4" cols="20" value="A text area"/>
<h:inputFile/>
```

All the components have a value attribute to set their default value. You can use the maxLength attribute to check that text entered doesn't go over a certain length or the size attribute to change the default size of the component. The previous code will have the following graphical representation:

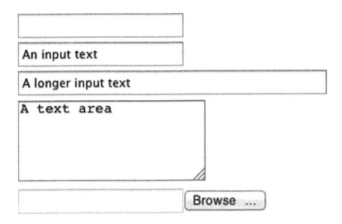

Outputs

Output components (classes that extend UIOutput) display a value, optionally retrieved from a backing bean, a value expression, or fixed text. The user cannot directly modify the value because it is for display purposes only. Table 10-7 lists the output tags available.

Table 10-7. *Output Tags*

Tag	Class	Description
<h:outputLabel>	HtmlOutputLabel	Renders an HTML <label> element
<h:outputLink>	HtmlOutputLink	Renders an HTML <a> anchor element
<h:outputText>	HtmlOutputText	Outputs text
<h:outputFormat>	HtmlOutputFormat	Renders parameterized text

Most of the web pages have to display some text. You can do this with normal HTML elements, but JSF output tags allow you to display the content of a variable bound to a backing bean using EL. You can display text with <h:outputText> and hypertext links with <h:outputLink>. Notice that the difference between <h:commandLink> and <h:outputLink> is that the latter displays the link but doesn't invoke any backing bean method when clicked. It just creates an external link or anchor.

```
<h:outputLabel value="#{bookController.book.title}"/>
<h:outputText value="A text"/>
<h:outputLink value="http://www.apress.com/">A link</h:outputLink>
<h:outputFormat value="Welcome {0}. You have bought {1} items">
  <f:param value="#{user.firstName}" />
  <f:param value="#{user.itemsBought}" />
</h:outputFormat>
```

The preceding code doesn't have any special graphical representation, just text. Following is the HTML rendering:

```
<label>The title of the book</label>
A text
<a href="http://www.apress.com/">A link</a>
Welcome Paul. You have bought 5 items
```

Selections

Check boxes, radio buttons, lists, or combo boxes represent selection components (see Table 10-8), which are used to select one or more values out of a list. Selection components allow the user to choose between a definite set of available options.

Table 10-8. *Select Tags*

Tag	Class	Description
<h:selectBooleanCheckbox>	HtmlSelectBooleanCheckbox	Renders one check box representing a single Boolean value. The check box will be rendered as checked or not based on the value of the property
<h:selectManyCheckbox>	HtmlSelectManyCheckbox	Renders a list of check boxes
<h:selectManyListbox>	HtmlSelectManyListbox	Renders a multiple-selection component where one or more options can be selected
<h:selectManyMenu>	HtmlSelectManyMenu	Renders an HTML <select> element
<h:selectOneListbox>	HtmlSelectOneListbox	Renders a single-selection component where only one available option can be selected
<h:selectOneMenu>	HtmlSelectOneMenu	Renders a single-selection component where only one available option can be selected. It only shows a single available option at a time
<h:selectOneRadio>	HtmlSelectOneRadio	Renders a list of radio buttons

The tags listed in this table have a graphical representation but require different tags to hold available options: <f:selectItem> or <f:selectItems>. These tags are nested inside the graphical components and create additional available options. To represent a combo box with a list of book genres, you should nest a set of <f:selectItem> tags in an <h:selectOneMenu> tag.

```
<h:selectOneMenu>
  <f:selectItem itemLabel="History"/>
  <f:selectItem itemLabel="Biography"/>
  <f:selectItem itemLabel="Literature"/>
  <f:selectItem itemLabel="Comics"/>
  <f:selectItem itemLabel="Child"/>
  <f:selectItem itemLabel="Scifi"/>
</h:selectOneMenu>
```

The graphic that follows shows all the possible representations. Some lists have multiple choices, others single choices, and, like all the other components, you can bind the value of a backing bean (List, Set, etc.) directly to one of the lists.

Tag	Rendering
h:selectBooleanCheckbox	☐
h:selectManyCheckbox	☑ History ☐ Biography ☐ Literature ☐ Comics ☐ Child ☐ Scifi
h:selectManyListbox	History Biography Literature Comics Child Scifi
h:selectManyMenu	History
h:selectOneListbox	History Biography Literature Comics Child Scifi
h:selectOneMenu	History ↕
h:selectOneRadio	○ History ⦿ Biography ○ Literature ○ Comics ○ Child ○ Scifi

Graphics

There is only one component for displaying images: `<h:graphicImage>` (class HtmlGraphicImage). It displays a graphical image to users that they cannot click on. This tag is rendered as an HTML `<img>` element. It has several attributes that allow you to resize the image, use a graphic as an image map, and so on. You can display an image that is bound to a property in a backing bean and comes from a file system or a database. The following code displays an image and resizes it:

```
<h:graphicImage value="book.gif" height="200" width="320"/>
```

Grid and Tables

Very often data need to be displayed in a table format (see Table 10-9). JSF has the very powerful `<h:dataTable>` tag that iterates through a list of elements and creates a table. Tables can also be used to create a layout for a grid-based UI. In this case, you can employ the `<h:panelGrid>` and `<h:panelGroup>` tags to lay out your components. `<h:dataTable>` is mostly used for displaying a table containing data from some of the models in your application while the `<h:panelGrid>` is for layout and placing of elements purpose.

Table 10-9. *Grid and Table Tags*

Tag	Class	Description
<h:dataTable>	HtmlDataTable	Represents a set of repeating data that will be rendered in an HTML <table> element
<h:column>	HtmlColumn	Renders a single column of data within an <h:dataTable> component
<h:panelGrid>	HtmlPanelGrid	Renders an HTML <table> element
<h:panelGroup>	HtmlPanelGroup	Is a container of components that can be embedded in an <h:panelGrid>

Unlike <h:dataTable>, the <h:panelGrid> tag does not use an underlying data model to render rows of data. Rather, this component is a layout container that renders other JSF components in a grid of rows and columns. You can specify how many columns are used to display the components, and the <h:panelGrid> will determine how many rows are needed. The columns attribute is the number of columns to render before starting a new row. For example, in the following code, the rendering will be three columns and two rows (displaying rows first and then columns):

```
<h:panelGrid columns="3" border="1">
  <h:outputLabel value="One"/>
  <h:outputLabel value="Two"/>
  <h:outputLabel value="Three"/>
  <h:outputLabel value="Four"/>
  <h:outputLabel value="Five"/>
  <h:outputLabel value="Six"/>
</h:panelGrid>
```

If you want to combine several components into a single column, you can use an <h:panelGroup> that will render its children as only one component. You can also define a header and a footer using the special <f:facet> tag:

```
<h:panelGrid columns="3" border="1">

  <f:facet name="header">
    <h:outputText value="Header"/>
  </f:facet>
  <h:outputLabel value="One"/>
  <h:outputLabel value="Two"/>
  <h:outputLabel value="Three"/>
  <h:outputLabel value="Four"/>
  <h:outputLabel value="Five"/>
  <h:outputLabel value="Six"/>
  <f:facet name="footer">
    <h:outputText value="Footer"/>
  </f:facet>
</h:panelGrid>
```

The two tables previously described will have the following graphical representation, one with a header and a footer and the other with neither.

One	Two	Three
Four	Five	Six

Header		
One	Two	Three
Four	Five	Six
Footer		

Error Messages

Applications can sometimes throw exceptions due to incorrectly formatted data or for technical reasons. But, as far as users are concerned, enough information should be displayed on the interface to draw their attention to correct the problem (not the entire exception stack trace). The mechanism for managing error messages is to include <h:message> and <h:messages> tags in a page (see Table 10-10). <h:message> is tied to a particular component, while <h:messages> can provide global messaging for all components on the page.

Table 10-10. *Message Tags*

Tag	Class	Description
<h:message>	HtmlMessage	Renders one error message
<h:messages>	HtmlMessages	Renders all the enqueued error messages

Messages can have different severities (INFO, WARN, ERROR, and FATAL), each of which corresponds to a CSS style (infoStyle, warnStyle, errorStyle, and fatalStyle). In this way, each type of message can have a different rendering style. For example, the following code will display all messages in red:

```
<h:messages style="color:red"/>
<h:form>
  Enter a title:
  <h:inputText value="#{bookController.title}" required="true"/>
  <h:commandButton action="#{bookController.save}" value="Save"/>
</h:form>
```

This will display an input field bound to a backing bean property. This property is required, so, if the user clicks the save button without filling it, an error message will be displayed:

- Validation Error: Value is required.

Enter a title: [   ] [Save]

Miscellaneous

There are other tags that don't have any graphical representation but do have an HTML equivalent. The native HTML tag can be used and will work. With JSF tags, extra attributes are available to make development easier. For example, you can add a JavaScript library to a page using the standard HTML `<script type="text/javascript">` tag. But, with the JSF `<h:outputScript>` tag, you can use new resource management, as you'll see in the "Resource Management" section. Table 10-11 shows these miscellaneous tags.

Table 10-11. *Miscellaneous Tags*

Tag	Class	Description
`<h:body>`	HtmlBody	Renders an HTML `<body>` element
`<h:head>`	HtmlHead	Renders an HTML `<head>` element
`<h:form>`	HtmlForm	Renders an HTML `<form>` element
`<h:doctype>`	HtmlDoctype	Renders an HTML `<doctype>` element
`<h:outputScript>`	Output	Renders the markup for a `<script>`
`<h:outputStylesheet>`	Output	Renders the markup for a `<link>` element

Basic Attributes

Each of the HTML component tags that you have been presented with vary in both complexity and the number of attributes you can utilize. For example, a `<h:message>` has a few attributes, including a CSS style (e.g. `<h:messages style="color:red"/>`), but the `<h:inputFile>`, being a more complex component, has more attributes (location of the file to upload, directory to browse, etc.). But all the HTML components share a few common attributes described in Table 10-12.

Table 10-12. *Some Basic Attributes*

Attribute	Description
id	Identifier for a component
rendered	Boolean to suppress rendering or not
value	A component's value (text or EL statement)
converter	Converter class name
validator	Validator class name
required	If true, requires a value to be entered in the associated field

JSF Core Tags

The JSF HTML component tags can only be used for HTML rendering (remember that JSF is indifferent to the final display device and can use several renderers). But some core JavaServer Faces actions are independent of any particular renderer. They don't have any visual representation and are mostly used for passing attributes or parameters to other components, as well as for conversion or validation. Table 10-13 presents these tags.

Table 10-13. *Some JSF Core Tags*

Tag	Description
`<f:facet>`	Adds a facet to a component
`<f:attribute>`	Adds an attribute to a component
`<f:param>`	Constructs a parameter child component
`<f:actionListener>` `<f:valueChangeListener>` `<f:propertyActionListener>`	Adds an action listener, value change listener, or property action listener to a component
`<f:phaseListener>`	Adds a phase listener to a page
`<f:converter>` `<f:convertDateTime>` `<f:convertNumber>`	Adds an arbitrary converter to a component or uses the specific date/time and number converter
`<f:validator>` `<f:validateDoubleRange>` `<f:validateLongRange>` `<f:validateLength>` `<f:validateRegex>`	Adds an arbitrary validator to a component or uses the specific double, long, length, and regular expression validator
`<f:validateBean>`	Specifies the validation groups for Bean Validation (see Chapter 3)
`<f:loadBundle>`	Loads a resource bundle
`<f:selectItem>` `<f:selectItems>`	Specifies one or several items for a select one, select many component
`<f:ajax>`	Enables Ajax behavior

JSF Templating Tags

A typical web application contains several pages that share a same look and feel, a header, a footer, a menu, and so forth. Facelets allows you to define a layout in a template file that can be used for all the pages in the Web application. A template defines areas (with the `<ui:insert>` tag) where the content can be replaced. The client page then uses the tags `<ui:component>`, `<ui:composition>`, `<ui:fragment>`, or `<ui:decorate>` to embed fragments into the template. Table 10-14 lists the various templating tags.

Table 10-14. *Templating Tags*

Tag	Description
`<ui:composition>`	Defines a composition that optionally uses a template. Multiple compositions can use the same template.
`<ui:component>`	Creates a component.
`<ui:debug>`	Captures debugging information.
`<ui:define>`	Defines content that is inserted into a page by a template.
`<ui:decorate>`	Allows you to decorate some content in a page.
`<ui:fragment>`	Adds a fragment of a page.
`<ui:include>`	Encapsulates and reuses content among multiple XHTML pages.
`<ui:insert>`	Inserts content into a template.
`<ui:param>`	Passes parameters to an included file (using `<ui:include>`) or a template.
`<ui:repeat>`	Iterates through a list of objects.
`<ui:remove>`	Removes content from a page.

As an example, let's reuse the page representing a form to create a new book (refer back to Figure 10-1). You could say that the title is the header of the page (*Create a new book*), and the footer would be the underlying text *Apress - Beginning Java EE 7*. So, the template called layout.xhtml would look like the code in Listing 10-9.

Listing 10-9. The layout.xhtml File Acting as a Template

```
<html xmlns="http://www.w3.org/1999/xhtml"
      xmlns:h="http://xmlns.jcp.org/jsf/html"
      xmlns:ui="http://xmlns.jcp.org/jsf/facelets">

<h:head>
  <title><ui:insert name="title">Default title</ui:insert></title>
</h:head>
<h:body>
  <h1><ui:insert name="title">Default title</ui:insert></h1>
  <hr/>

  <ui:insert name="content">Default content</ui:insert>

  <hr/>
  <h:outputText value="APress - Beginning Java EE 7" style="font-style: italic"/>

</h:body>
</html>
```

The template in Listing 10-9 must first define the needed tag library (xmlns:ui="http://xmlns.jcp.org/jsf/facelets"). Then, it uses the `<ui:insert>` tag to insert a title attribute into the `<title>` and `<h1>` tags. The body of the page will be inserted into the attribute called content.

To use this template, the newBook.xhtml page, shown in Listing 10-10, needs to declare which template it needs (`<ui:composition template="layout.xhtml">`). Then, the idea is to bind the attributes defined in the `<ui:define>` tag with the <ui:insert> tag in the template. For example, the title of the page is "Create a new book." This text is stored in the title variable (with <ui:define name="title">), which is bound to the matching tag <ui:insert name="title">. It is the same for the rest of the page, which is inserted into the content variable (<ui:define name="content">).

Listing 10-10. The newBook. xhtml Page Using the layout.xhtml Template

```
<html xmlns="http://www.w3.org/1999/xhtml"
      xmlns:h="http://xmlns.jcp.org/jsf/html"
      xmlns:ui="http://xmlns.jcp.org/jsf/facelets">


<ui:composition template="layout.xhtml">

  <ui:define name="title">Create a new book</ui:define>

  <ui:define name="content">

    <h:form>
      <h:panelGrid columns="2">
        <h:outputLabel value="ISBN : "/>
        <h:inputText value="#{bookController.book.isbn}"/>

        <h:outputLabel value="Title :"/>
        <h:inputText value="#{bookController.book.title}"/>

        <h:outputLabel value="Price : "/>
        <h:inputText value="#{bookController.book.price}"/>

        <h:outputLabel value="Description   : "/>
        <h:inputTextarea value="#{bookController.book.description}" cols="20" rows="5"/>

        <h:outputLabel value="Number of pages : "/>
        <h:inputText value="#{bookController.book.nbOfPage}"/>

        <h:outputLabel value="Illustrations : "/>
        <h:selectBooleanCheckbox value="#{bookController.book.illustrations}"/>

      </h:panelGrid>
      <h:commandButton value="Create a book" action="#{bookController.doCreateBook}"/>
    </h:form>

  </ui:define>

</ui:composition>
</html>
```

JSTL Tags

The JSP Standard Tag Library standardizes a number of common actions using tags. These actions range from setting the value of an object to catching exceptions, controlling the flow structure with conditions and iterators, XML parsing, and accessing databases. Table 10-15 lists these tags along with the URIs (uniform resource identifiers) used to reference the libraries and common associated prefixes.

Table 10-15. *JSTL Tag Libraries*

Functional Area	URI	Common Prefix
Core	`http://xmlns.jcp.org/jsp/jstl/core`	c
XML processing	`http://xmlns.jcp.org/jsp/jstl/xml`	x
I18N and formatting	`http://xmlns.jcp.org/jsp/jstl/fmt`	fmt
Database access	`http://xmlns.jcp.org/jsp/jstl/sql`	sql
Functions	`http://xmlns.jcp.org/jsp/jstl/functions`	fn

But Facelets only exposes a subset of the JSTL libraries. In fact, it only exposes a subset of the Core tag library and the entirety of the i18n and Formatting tag library (not the XML processing, functions, or database access).

Core Actions

The core actions provide tags for manipulating variables, dealing with errors, performing tests, and executing loops and iterations. Table 10-16 shows the actions supported by Facelets.

Table 10-16. *Subset of JSTL Core Actions Supported by Facelets*

Action	Description
`<c:set>`	Sets a value for a variable within a scope.
`<c:catch>`	Catches a `java.lang.Throwable` thrown by any of its nested actions.
`<c:if>`	Evaluates whether the expression is true.
`<c:choose>`	Provides mutually exclusive conditions.
`<c:when>`	Represents an alternative within a `<c:choose>` action.
`<c:otherwise>`	Represents the last alternative within a `<c:choose>` action.
`<c:forEach>`	Repeats the nested body over a collection of objects, or repeats it a fixed number of times.

To see some of these tags in action, let's write a JSF page that loops from number 3 to number 15, tests whether the number is odd or even, and displays this information in front of each number (see Listing 10-11).

Listing 10-11. A JSF Page Displaying a List of Odd and Even Numbers

```
<html xmlns="http://www.w3.org/1999/xhtml"
      xmlns:h="http://xmlns.jcp.org/jsf/html"
      xmlns:c="http://xmlns.jcp.org/jsp/jstl/core">
<h:head>
  <title>Checking numbers</title>
</h:head>
<h:body>
  <h1>Checking numbers</h1>
  <hr/>

  <c:set var="upperLimit" value="20"/>
  <c:forEach var="i" begin="3" end="#{upperLimit - 5}">
```

```
<c:choose>
  <c:when test="#{i%2 == 0}">
    <h:outputText value="#{i} is even"/><br/>
  </c:when>
  <c:otherwise>
    <h:outputText value="#{i} is odd"/><br/>
  </c:otherwise>
</c:choose>

</c:forEach>

<hr/>
<h:outputText value="APress - Beginning Java EE 7" style="font-style: italic"/>
</h:body>
</html>
```

To use the core tag library, the page needs to import its URI with a prefix (i.e., XML namespace). The code in Listing 10-11 assigns the value 20 to the upperLimit variable with the <c:set> tag and then iterates from the number 3 to number 15 (20 minus 5). You can see the usage of EL with the arithmetic expression #{upperLimit - 5}. Inside the loop, the value of the index (variable i) is tested to see whether its value is odd or even (<c:when test="#{i%2 == 0}">). The <h:outputText> tag displays the value of the index with the text ("#{i} is even").

The logic is only done via tags, and this page is totally XML compliant, using a markup language easy for non-Java programmers to read and understand.

Formatting Actions

Formatting actions provide support for formatting dates, numbers, currencies, and percentages, and they also support internationalization (i18n). You can get or set locales and time zones, or get the encoding of the web page. Table 10-17 shows the actions contained in the format library.

Table 10-17. *Formatting Actions*

Action	Description
<fmt:message>	Internationalizes a message by pulling it from a resource bundle.
<fmt:param>	Supplies a parameter for <fmt:message>.
<fmt:bundle>	Determines the resource bundle.
<fmt:setLocale>	Sets the locale.
<fmt:requestEncoding>	Sets the request's character encoding.
<fmt:timeZone>	Specifies the time zone in which time information is to be formatted.
<fmt:setTimeZone>	Stores the specified time zone on a variable.
<fmt:formatNumber>	Formats a numeric value (number, currency, percentage) in a locale-sensitive manner.
<fmt:parseNumber>	Parses the string representation of numbers, currencies, and percentages.
<fmt:formatDate>	Formats dates and times in a locale-sensitive manner.
<fmt:parseDate>	Parses the string representation of dates and times.

For an understanding of these tags, take a look at the JSF page shown in Listing 10-12, which uses some of these actions to format dates and numbers and internationalize currencies.

Listing 10-12. A JSF Page Formatting Dates and Numbers

```
<html xmlns="http://www.w3.org/1999/xhtml"
      xmlns:h="http://xmlns.jcp.org/jsf/html"
      xmlns:c="http://xmlns.jcp.org/jsp/jstl/core"
      xmlns:fmt="http://xmlns.jcp.org/jsp/jstl/fmt">

<h:head><title>Formatting data</title></h:head>
<h:body>

    Dates<br/>
    <c:set var="now" value="#{bookController.currentDate}"/>
    <fmt:formatDate type="time" value="#{now}"/><br/>
    <fmt:formatDate type="date" value="#{now}"/><br/>
    <fmt:formatDate type="both" dateStyle="short" timeStyle="short" value="#{now}"/><br/>
    <fmt:formatDate type="both" dateStyle="long" timeStyle="long" value="#{now}"/><br/>

    Currency<br/>
    <fmt:setLocale value="en_us"/>
    <fmt:formatNumber value="20.50" type="currency"/><br/>
    <fmt:setLocale value="en_gb"/>
    <fmt:formatNumber value="20.50" type="currency"/><br/>

</h:body>
</html>
```

The page imports the core and format tag libraries and uses the c and fmt prefixes. The `<c:set var="now" value="#{bookController.currentDate}"/>` line sets the current date to a variable named now. The `<fmt:formatDate>` tag formats this date using different patterns: shows only the time, only the date, both time and date. The `<fmt:setLocale value="en_us"/>` line sets the locale to the United States and formats currency so the result is $20.50. Then, the locale is changed to the UK and the result is changed to pounds sterling. This JSF page produces the following result:

```
Dates
11:31:12
14 may 2013
14/05/13 11:31
14 may 2013 11:31:12 CET

Currency
$20.50
£20.50
```

Resource Management

Most of the components may need external resources in order to be rendered properly. `<h:graphicImage>` needs an external image to display, `<h:commandButton>` can also display an image as a button, `<h:outputScript>` references an external JavaScript file, and components can apply CSS styles (with `<h:outputStylesheet>`). In JSF, a resource is a static element that can be transmitted to components so they can be displayed (images) or processed (JavaScript, CSS) by the browser.

Previous versions of JSF had no facility for serving resources. When you wanted to provide a resource, you had to put it in the web directory so that the client's browser could access it. The problem was that if you wanted to update it, you had to replace the file in the directory and have different directories to render localized resources (e.g., an image with English or Portuguese text). JSF 2.0 brought support for this functionality, so you can now put your resources directly under the resources directory or package them into a separate jar (with an optional version and/or locale). The resource can be placed in the web application root under the following path:

resources/<resourceIdentifier>

or under a jar file in the WEB-INF/lib directory.

WEB-INF/lib/{*.jar}/META-INF/**resources**/<resourceIdentifier>

<resourceIdentifier> consists of several subfolders, specified as follows:

[localePrefix/][libraryName/][libVersion/]resourceName[/resourceVersion]

Items in this resource identifier in [ ] are optional. The local prefix consists of the language code followed by an optional country code (en, en_US, pt, pt_BR). As this line indicates, you can add versioning to the library or the resource itself. Following are resource structures you might end up with:

```
book.gif
en/book.gif
en_us/book.gif
en/myLibrary/book.gif
myLibrary/book.gif
myLibrary/1_0/book.gif
myLibrary/1_0/book.gif/2_3.gif
```

You can then use a resource, such as the book.gif image, directly in the <h:graphicImage> component (value="book.gif") or by specifying the library name (library="myLibrary"). The resource with the right locale for your client will get pulled automatically. Notice that resource is an implicit object (more on that later) and that you can also use the syntax resource['book.gif'] or resource['myLibrary:book.gif'] to access a resource.

```
<h:graphicImage value="book.gif" />
<h:graphicImage value="book.gif" library="myLibrary" />
<h:graphicImage value="#{resource['book.gif']}" />
<h:graphicImage value="#{resource['myLibrary:book.gif']}" />
```

■ **Note** By default, resources are stored in the resources directory. Since JSF 2.2 you can change this default by setting the javax.faces.WEBAPP_RESOURCES_DIRECTORY variable in the web.xml deployment descriptor. If this parameter is set, the JSF runtime interprets its value as a path, relative to the web application root, where resources are to be located.

Implicit Objects

To access a resource you can use the implicit object called resources (e.g., #{resource['book.gif']}). This object doesn't have to be declared anywhere; it is simply available in JSF pages. These kinds of objects are called *implicit objects* (or *implicit variables*). Implicit objects are special identifiers that map to specific commonly used objects. They are implicit because a page has access to them and can use them without needing to explicitly declare or initialize them. Implicit objects are used within EL expressions. Table 10-18 lists all the implicit objects to which a page can have access.

Table 10-18. *Implicit Objects*

Implicit Object	Description	Returns
application	Represents the web application environment. Used to get application-level configuration parameters.	Object
applicationScope	Maps application-scoped attribute names to their values.	Map
component	Indicates the current component.	UIComponent
cc	Indicates the current composite component.	UIComponent
cookie	Specifies a Map containing cookie names (the key) and Cookie objects.	Map
facesContext	Indicates the FacesContext instance of this request.	FacesContext
flash	Represents the flash object (more on scopes in Chapter 11).	Object
header	Maps HTTP header names to a single String header value.	Map
headerValues	Maps HTTP header names to a String[] of all values for that header.	Map
initParam	Maps context initialization parameter names to their String parameter values.	Map
param	Maps request parameter names to a single String parameter value.	Map
paramValues	Maps request parameter names to a String[] of all values for that parameter.	Map
request	Represents the HTTP request object.	Object
requestScope	Maps request-scoped attribute names to their values.	Map
resource	Specifies the resource object.	Object
session	Represents the HTTP session object.	Object
sessionScope	Maps session-scoped attribute names to their values.	Map
view	Represents the current view.	UIViewRoot
viewScope	Maps view-scoped attribute names to their values.	Map

All these implicit objects are actual objects with interfaces, and once you know their API (refer to the specification or the javadoc), you can access their attributes with EL. For example, #{view.locale} will get the locale of the current view (en_US, pt_PT, etc.). If you store a book object in the session scope, you could access it like this: #{sessionScope.book}. You can even use a richer algorithm to display all the HTTP headers and their values such as in Listing 10-13.

Listing 10-13. *A Page Displaying the Locale and HTTP Headers Using Implicit Objects*

```
<html xmlns="http://www.w3.org/1999/xhtml"
      xmlns:h="http://xmlns.jcp.org/jsf/html"
      xmlns:c="http://xmlns.jcp.org/jsp/jstl/core">
<h:body>
  <h1>Implicit objects</h1>
  <hr/>

  <h3>Locale</h3>
  <h:outputText value="#{view.locale}"/>

  <h3>headerValues</h3>
  <c:forEach var="parameter" items="#{headerValues}">
    <h:outputText value="#{parameter.key}"/>   =
    <c:forEach var="value" items="#{parameter.value}">
      <h:outputText value="#{value}" escape="false"/><br/>
    </c:forEach>
  </c:forEach>

  <hr/>
  <h:outputText value="APress - Beginning Java EE 7" style="font-style: italic"/>
</h:body>
</html>
```

If you execute the code in Listing 10-13 you will get the page shown in Figure 10-7.

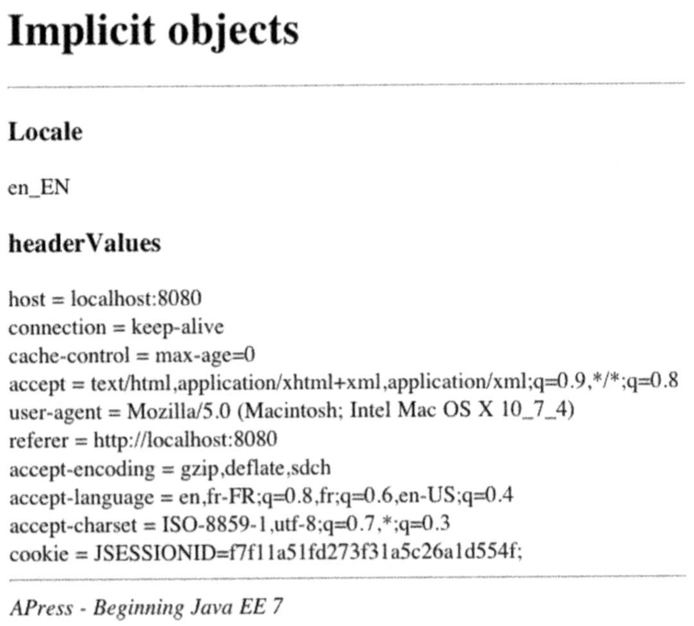

Implicit objects

***

Locale

en_EN

headerValues

host = localhost:8080
connection = keep-alive
cache-control = max-age=0
accept = text/html,application/xhtml+xml,application/xml;q=0.9,*/*;q=0.8
user-agent = Mozilla/5.0 (Macintosh; Intel Mac OS X 10_7_4)
referer = http://localhost:8080
accept-encoding = gzip,deflate,sdch
accept-language = en,fr-FR;q=0.8,fr;q=0.6,en-US;q=0.4
accept-charset = ISO-8859-1,utf-8;q=0.7,*;q=0.3
cookie = JSESSIONID=f7f11a51fd273f31a5c26a1d554f;

***

APress - Beginning Java EE 7

Figure 10-7. *A JSF page displaying implicit objects values*

Composite Components

All the previously discussed components and tag libraries are part of JSF and come with any implementation that follows the specification. Because JSF is based on reusable components, it provides a design that allows you to easily create and integrate your own components or third-party components into your applications.

Earlier, I mentioned that all components you've seen extend, directly or indirectly, the javax.faces.component. UIComponent class. Before JSF 2.0, if you wanted to create your own component, you had to extend the component class that most closely represented your component (UICommand, UIGraphic, UIOutput, etc.), declare it in the faces-config.xml file, and provide a tag handler and a renderer. These steps were complex, and other web frameworks such as Facelets showed that it was possible to create powerful components with less complexity. This is the point of composite components: to enable developers to write real, reusable JSF UI components without any Java code or configuration XML.

This new approach involves creating an XHTML page that contains components, and then using this page as a component in other pages. This XHTML page is then seen as a real component that can support validators, converters, and listeners. Any valid markup can be used inside a composite component, including the templating features. Composite components are handled as resources and therefore must reside within the standard resources directories. Table 10-19 lists all the tags involved in the creation and definition of a composite component.

Table 10-19. *Tags Used for Declaring and Defining Composite Components*

Tag	Description
<composite:interface>	Declares the contract for a component.
<composite:implementation>	Defines the implementation of a component.
<composite:attribute>	Declares an attribute that may be given to an instance of the component. There may be zero or many of these inside the <composite:interface> section.
<composite:facet>	Declares that this component supports a facet.
<composite:insertFacet>	Is used in the <composite:implementation> section. The inserted facet will be rendered in the component.
<composite:insertChildren>	Is used in the <composite:implementation> section. Any child components or template within the component will be inserted into the rendered output.
<composite:valueHolder>	Declares that the component whose contract is declared by the <composite:interface> in which this element is nested exposes an implementation of ValueHolder.
<composite:renderFacet>	Is used in the <composite:implementation> section to render a facet.
<composite:extension>	Is used within a <composite:interface> section to include XML content not defined by the JSF specification.
<composite:editableValueHolder>	Declares that the component whose contract is declared by the <composite:interface> in which this element is nested exposes an implementation of EditableValueHolder.
<composite:clientBehavior>	Defines a contract for behaviors that can enhance a component's rendered content.
<composite:actionSource>	Declares that the component whose contract is declared by the <composite:interface> in which this element is nested exposes an implementation of ActionSource.

Let's explore an example that shows how easy it is to create a graphical component and use it in other pages. You might remember from previous chapters that the CD-BookStore application sells two different items: books and CDs. In Chapter 4, I represented them as three different objects: Book and CD extending Item. Item contains the common attributes (a title, a price, and a description), and then the Book and the CD have specialized ones (isbn, publisher, nbOfPage, and illustrations for Book; musicCompany, numberOfCDs, totalDuration, and genre for CD). If you want your web application to be able to create new books and CDs, you need two different forms. But the common attributes of Item could be in a separate page that would act as a component. Figure 10-8 shows these two pages.

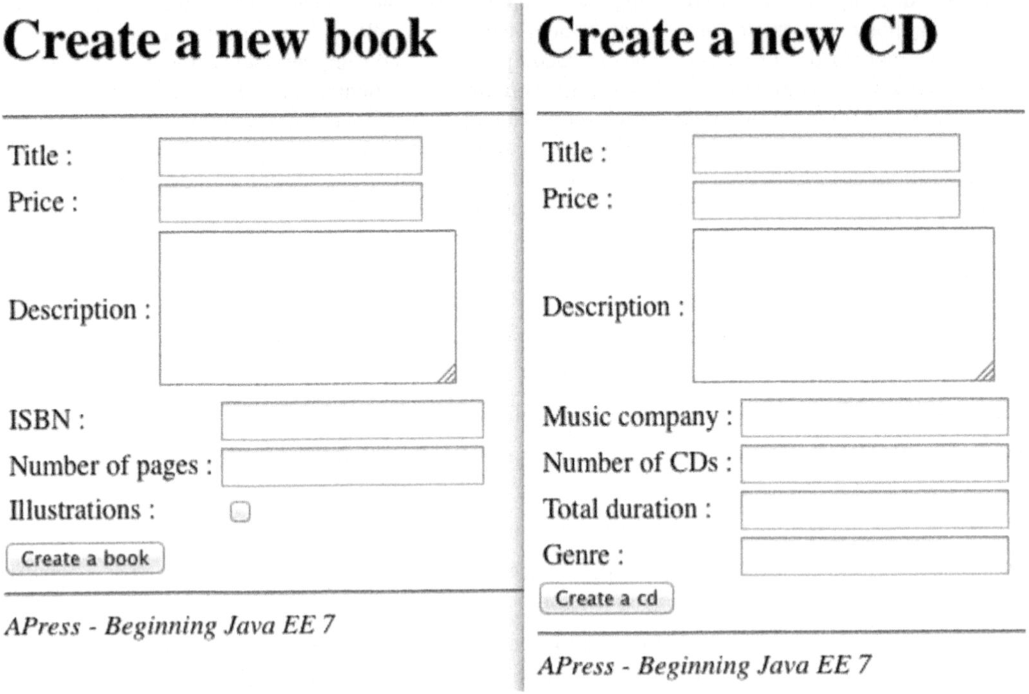

Figure 10-8. *Two forms, one to create a CD, another one to create a book*

So let's create a composite component with two input texts (for the title and the price) and one text area (for the description). The approach to writing a component with JSF 2.2 is relatively close to what you are used to in Java. You must first write an interface, <composite:interface> (see Listing 10-14), that acts as an entry point for the component. It describes the names and the parameters used by the component (here the item bean and a CSS style). Then comes the implementation, <composite:implementation>. This is the body, the graphical representation of the component written in XHTML and using any JSF tags you've seen so far. Interface and implementation are in the same XHTML page.

Listing 10-14. The newItem.xhtml Composite Component

```
<html xmlns="http://www.w3.org/1999/xhtml"
      xmlns:h="http://xmlns.jcp.org/jsf/html"
      xmlns:composite="http://xmlns.jcp.org/jsf/composite">

<composite:interface>
  <composite:attribute name="item" required="true"/>
  <composite:attribute name="style" required="false"/>
</composite:interface>
```

```
<composite:implementation>
  <h:panelGrid columns="2" style="#{cc.attrs.style}">

    <h:outputLabel value="Title : "/>
    <h:inputText value="#{cc.attrs.item.title}"/>

    <h:outputLabel value="Price : "/>
    <h:inputText value="#{cc.attrs.item.price}"/>

    <h:outputLabel value="Description : "/>
    <h:inputTextarea value="#{cc.attrs.item.description}" cols="20" rows="5"/>

  </h:panelGrid>
</composite:implementation>
</html>
```

The component in Listing 10-14 declares an interface with two attributes: item represents the Item bean (and the subclasses Book and CD), and style is a CSS style used for rendering. These attributes are then employed in the implementation of the composite component using the following syntax:

```
#{cc.attrs.[attributeName]}
```

This code indicates that the getAttributes() method will be called in the current composite component (as listed in Table 10-18, cc is an implicit object that indicates the current component); within the returned Map, the code will look for the value under the key attributeName. This is how a component uses attributes that are defined in the interface.

Before I explain how to use this component, recall the discussion on resource management earlier in this chapter and the notion of configuration by exception. The component has to be saved in a file that resides inside a resource library. For example, the file for this example is called newItem.xhtml and is saved under /resources/apress. If you leave all the defaults, to use this component you need to declare a library called apress and give it an XML namespace (ago in the following code):

```
<html xmlns:ago="http://xmlns.jcp.org/jsf/composite/apress">
```

Then, call the component newItem (the name of the page), passing any required parameters: item is the parameter that refers to the Item entity, and style is the optional parameter that refers to a CSS style.

```
<ago:newItem item="#{itemController.book}" style="myCssStyle"/>
<ago:newItem item="#{itemController.cd}"/>
```

To give you an overall picture of how to incorporate a component, Listing 10-15 shows the newBook.xhtml page representing the form to enter the book data. It includes the newItem composite component and adds input fields for the ISBN, the number of pages, and a check box to indicate whether the book has illustrations or not.

Listing 10-15. The newBook. xhtml Page Uses the newItem Component

```
<html xmlns="http://www.w3.org/1999/xhtml"
      xmlns:h="http://xmlns.jcp.org/jsf/html"
      xmlns:ago="http://xmlns.jcp.org/jsf/composite/apress">
<h:head>
  <title>Create a new book</title>
</h:head>
<h:body>
```

```
<h1>Create a new book</h1>
<hr/>
<h:form>

    <ago:newItem item="#{itemController.book}"/>

    <h:panelGrid columns="2">
      <h:outputLabel value="ISBN : "/>
      <h:inputText value="#{itemController.book.isbn}"/>

      <h:outputLabel value="Number of pages : "/>
      <h:inputText value="#{itemController.book.nbOfPage}"/>

      <h:outputLabel value="Illustrations : "/>
      <h:selectBooleanCheckbox value="#{itemController.book.illustrations}"/>

    </h:panelGrid>

    <h:commandButton value="Create a book" action="#{itemController.doCreateBook}"/>

</h:form>
<hr/>
<h:outputText value="APress - Beginning Java EE 7" style="font-style: italic"/>

</h:body>
</html>
```

■ **Note**   Writing a component is an easy task so developers should be encouraged to write their own business components so they can reuse them between pages. But some components are so common (a calendar, a color picker, a scroll panel, a breadcrumb . . .) that you don't have to develop them anymore; you just need to pick them up in third-party component libraries. Today there are three major open source projects that gather hundreds of already made graphical components: PrimeFaces, RichFaces, and IceFaces. Check their component libraries and you might get what you are looking for without developing anything, just using their libraries.

Summary

This chapter explained different ways of creating web pages using client languages such as HTML, XHTML, or CSS as well as creating dynamic content with server-side JSF pages. Today, the race between user interfaces continues, with the proliferation of rich desktop applications (RDAs), rich Internet applications (RIAs), mobile device applications (smartphones or tablets), and so forth. A few years ago, JSF entered this race, and today, with the 2.2 release, is holding its own.

JSF has an architecture based on components and a rich API for developing renderers, converters, validators, and more. It can render and convert several languages even if the preferred PDL for Web pages is Facelets. JSF provides a set of standard widgets (buttons, hyperlinks, check boxes, etc.) and a flexible model for creating your own widgets (composite components), and the community has developed a few open source third-party libraries.

But JSF can interact with backing beans to process data and navigate through pages. In Chapter 11 you will learn how navigation works, how components are bound to backing beans, and also how to write your own converter and validator.

CHAPTER 11

■ ■ ■

Processing and Navigation

In Chapter 10, I showed you how to create web pages using JSF components. However, drawing pages with graphical components is not enough; these pages need to interact with a back-end system, navigate through other pages, and also validate and convert data. JSF is a rich specification: backing beans allow you to invoke the business tier and to navigate in your application. A set of classes allows you to convert component values to and from a corresponding type or validate them to conform to business rules. Integration with Bean Validation also facilitates validation in JSF 2.2. With the use of annotations, it is now easy to develop backing beans, custom converters, and customer validators.

JSF 2.2 brings simplicity and richness in terms of dynamic user interfaces. It natively supports Ajax calls in a simple manner. The specification comes with a JavaScript library, allowing asynchronous calls to the server and refreshing small portions of the page.

Creating user interfaces, controlling navigation in the entire application, and calling business logic synchronously or asynchronously are possible because JSF is built on the Model-View-Controller (MVC) design pattern. Each part is separate from the other, allowing the user interface to change without impacting the business logic and vice versa. This chapter presents all these concepts, complementing Chapter 10.

The MVC Pattern

JSF, and most web frameworks, encourages separation of concerns by using variations of the MVC design pattern. MVC is an architectural pattern used to isolate business logic from the user interface. Business logic doesn't mix well with UI code. When the two are mixed, applications are much harder to maintain and less scalable. When MVC is applied, it results in a loosely coupled application; with this type of application, it is easier to modify either the visual appearance of the application or the underlying business rules without one affecting the other.

In MVC, the model represents the data of the application, the view corresponds to the UI, and the controller manages the communication between both (see Figure 11-1).

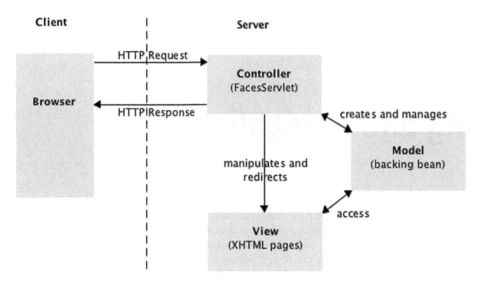

Figure 11-1. *The MVC design pattern*

The model is represented by the content, which is often stored in a database and displayed in the view. The model is built without concern for its look and feel when presented to the user. In JSF, it can consist of backing beans, EJB calls, JPA entities, and so forth.

The view in JSF is the actual XHTML page when we deal with web interfaces. As explained in Chapter 10, a view provides a graphical representation for a model. A model can also have several views, showing a book as a form or as a list, for example.

When a user manipulates a view, the view informs a controller of the desired changes. The controller then gathers, converts, and validates the data, invokes business logic, and generates the content in XHTML. In JSF, the controller is the FacesServlet.

FacesServlet

The FacesServlet is an implementation of javax.servlet.Servlet and acts as the central controller element, through which all user requests pass. As shown in Figure 11-2, when an event occurs (e.g., when the user clicks a button), the event notification is sent via HTTP to the server and is intercepted by the javax.faces.webapp. FacesServlet. It examines the request and calls various actions on the model using backing beans.

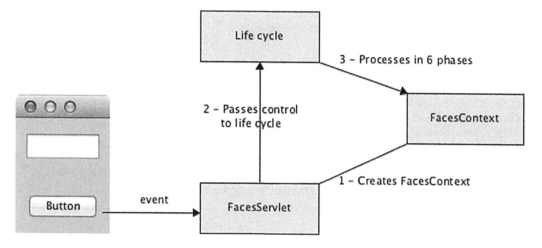

Figure 11-2. The FacesServlet interactions

Behind the scenes, the FacesServlet accepts incoming requests and hands control over to the javax.faces.lifecycle.Lifecycle object. Using a factory, it creates an object of type javax.faces.context.FacesContext, which contains and processes all the per-request state information. The Lifecycle object uses the FacesContext object during the six different phases of the page life cycle (previously described in Chapter 10) before rendering the response.

Out of the box, user requests are processed by the JSF runtime that declares a FacesServlet using common behavior, thanks to configuration by exception. If the defaults do not suit you, you can configure the FacesServlet in a web.xml file. Listing 11-1 shows the web.xml as an example.

Listing 11-1. web.xml Defining the FacesServlet

```xml
<?xml version='1.0' encoding='UTF-8'?>
<web-app xmlns="http://xmlns.jcp.org/xml/ns/javaee"
         xmlns:xsi="http://www.w3.org/2001/XMLSchema-instance"
         xsi:schemaLocation="http://xmlns.jcp.org/xml/ns/javaee ➥
         http://xmlns.jcp.org/xml/ns/javaee/web-app_3_1.xsd"
         version="3.1">

  <servlet>
    <servlet-name>Faces Servlet</servlet-name>
    <servlet-class>javax.faces.webapp.FacesServlet</servlet-class>
    <load-on-startup>1</load-on-startup>
  </servlet>
  <servlet-mapping>
    <servlet-name>Faces Servlet</servlet-name>
    <url-pattern>*.jsf</url-pattern>
  </servlet-mapping>

  <context-param>
    <param-name>javax.faces.PROJECT_STAGE</param-name>
    <param-value>Development</param-value>
  </context-param>
```

```
<context-param>
  <param-name>javax.faces.FACELETS_SKIP_COMMENTS</param-name>
  <param-value>true</param-value>
</context-param>
</web-app>
```

This web.xml file defines the javax.faces.webapp.FacesServlet by giving it a name (e.g., Faces Servlet) and a mapping. In this example, all requests that have the .jsf extension are mapped to be managed by the Servlet, and any request such as http://localhost:8080/chapter11-1.0/newBook.jsf will be handled by JSF.

■ **Note** The default Servlet mappings for JSF pages are *.faces or /faces/*. In Listing 11-1, this default value has been changed to .jsf but, if .faces suits you, you can omit the Servlet mapping configuration.

You can also configure a few JSF-specific parameters in the <context-param> element. Table 11-1 lists some of these parameters.

Table 11-1. *Some JSF-Specific Configuration Parameters*

Parameter	Description
javax.faces.CONFIG_FILES	Defines a comma-delimited list of context-relative resource paths under which the JSF implementation will look for resources.
javax.faces.DEFAULT_SUFFIX	Allows the web application to define a list of alternative suffixes for pages containing JSF content (e.g., .jsf).
javax.faces.FACELETS_BUFFER_SIZE	The buffer size to set on the response. By default, the value is –1, which will not assign a buffer size on the response.
javax.faces.FACELETS_REFRESH_PERIOD	When a page is requested, the interval in seconds that the compiler should check for changes. A value of –1 disables the compiler check.
javax.faces.FACELETS_SKIP_COMMENTS	If set to true, the runtime ensures that XML comments in the Facelets page are not delivered to the client.
javax.faces.LIFECYCLE_ID	Identifies the Lifecycle instance to be used when processing JSF requests.
javax.faces.STATE_SAVING_METHOD	Defines the location where state is saved. Valid values are server, which is the default (typically saved in HttpSession) and client (saved as a hidden field in the subsequent form submit).
javax.faces.PROJECT_STAGE	Describes where this particular JSF application is in the software development life cycle (Development, UnitTest, SystemTest, or Production). This could be used by a JSF implementation to cache resources in order to improve performance in production, for example.
javax.faces.DISABLE_FACELET_JSF_VIEWHANDLER	Disables Facelets as the default page declaration language (PDL) if set to true.
javax.faces.WEBAPP_RESOURCES_DIRECTORY	If this parameter is set, the JSF runtime interprets its value as a path, relative to the web application root, where resources are to be located.
javax.faces.LIBRARIES	Interprets each file found in the semicolon-separated list of paths as a Facelets tag library.

FacesContext

JSF defines the `javax.faces.context.FacesContext` abstract class for representing the contextual information associated with processing an incoming request and creating the corresponding response. This is the class that allows interaction with the UI and the rest of the JSF environment.

To gain access, you can either use the implicit `facesContext` object in your pages (see Chapter 10 for discussion on implicit objects) or obtain a reference in your backing beans using the static method `getCurrentInstance()`. This will return the `FacesContext` instance for the current thread, and then you can invoke the methods listed in Table 11-2.

Table 11-2. *Some Methods of the FacesContext*

Method	Description
addMessage	Appends a message (information, warning, error, or fatal).
getApplication	Returns the `Application` instance associated with this web application.
getAttributes	Returns a `Map` representing the attributes associated with the `FacesContext` instance.
getCurrentInstance	Returns the `FacesContext` instance for the request that is being processed by the current thread.
getELContext	Returns the `ELContext` instance for the current `FacesContext` instance.
getMaximumSeverity	Returns the maximum severity level recorded on any `FacesMessage` that has been queued.
getMessages	Returns a collection of `FacesMessage`.
getPartialViewContext	Returns the `PartialViewContext` object for this request. It is used to inject logic into the processing/rendering loop control (such as Ajax processing).
getViewRoot	Returns the root component that is associated with the request.
release	Releases any resources associated with this `FacesContext` instance.
renderResponse	Signals the JSF implementation that, as soon as the current phase of the request-processing life cycle has been completed, control should be passed to the *Render response* phase, bypassing any phases that have not been executed yet.
responseComplete	Signals the JSF implementation that the HTTP response for this request has already been generated (such as an HTTP redirect), and that the request-processing life cycle should be terminated as soon as the current phase is completed.

Faces Config

The `FacesServlet` is internal to JSF implementations, and, though you don't have access to its code; you do require metadata to configure it or some properties in the `web.xml` as seen in Listing 11.1. By now, you may be accustomed to the two possible choices of metadata in Java EE 7: annotations and XML deployment descriptors (`/WEB-INF/faces-config.xml`).

Before JSF 2.0, the only choice was to use XML; today, backing beans, converters, event listeners, renderers, and validators can have annotations, and so using XML configuration files has become optional. Even most of the navigation between pages can be orchestrated with either XML or Java code. Listing 11-2 shows an extract of what a `faces-config.xml` file looks like. In this example it defines a default locale (`fr`), a message bundle for internationalization, and some navigation rules. Soon you will see how to navigate with and without `faces-config.xml`.

Listing 11-2. Snippet of a faces-config.xml File

```xml
<?xml version='1.0' encoding='UTF-8'?>
<faces-config xmlns="http://xmlns.jcp.org/xml/ns/javaee"
              xmlns:xsi="http://www.w3.org/2001/XMLSchema-instance"
              xsi:schemaLocation="http://xmlns.jcp.org/xml/ns/javaee ⇥
              http://xmlns.jcp.org/xml/ns/javaee/web-facesconfig_2_2.xsd"
              version="2.2">

  <application>
    <locale-config>
      <default-locale>fr</default-locale>
    </locale-config>
    <resource-bundle>
      <base-name>messages</base-name>
      <var>msg</var>
    </resource-bundle>
  </application>

  <navigation-rule>
    <from-view-id>*</from-view-id>
    <navigation-case>
      <from-outcome>doCreateBook-success</from-outcome>
      <to-view-id>/listBooks.htm</to-view-id>
    </navigation-case>
  </navigation-rule>

</faces-config>
```

Writing Backing Beans

As noted earlier in this chapter, the MVC pattern encourages separation between the model, the view, and the controller: JSF pages form the view and the FacesServlet the controller. Backing beans are the gateway to the model.

Backing beans are annotated Java classes and are central to web applications. They can perform business logic (or delegate to EJBs, for example), handle navigation between pages, and hold data. A typical JSF application includes one or more backing beans that can be shared by several pages. The data are held within attributes of the backing bean and actions in a page trigger a method of the bean. To bind components to a backing bean, you need to use expression language (e.g., #{bookController.book.title}).

■ **Note**   I prefer to use the term "Backing Bean" rather than "Managed Bean" but they both historically mean the same thing in JSF. "Managed Bean" refers to the more general Java EE component model I introduced in Chapter 2 with CDI. In Java EE any POJO that is managed by a container or provider is called a Managed Bean. So a backing bean is actually a Managed Bean, but for JSF.

Writing a backing bean is as easy as writing an EJB or a JPA entity; it's simply a Java class annotated with the CDI @Named annotation (see Listing 11-3) and a CDI scope (in this case it's a @RequestScoped). There are no faces-config.xml entries, no helper classes, and no inheritance. JSF 2.2 also uses the configuration-by-exception mechanism, whereby, with only two annotations, you can use all defaults and deploy your web application with such a backing bean.

Listing 11-3. A Simple BookController Backing Bean

```
@Named
@RequestScoped
public class BookController {

  private Book book = new Book();

  public String doCreateBook() {
    createBook(book);
    return "newBook.xhtml";
  }

  // Constructors, getters, setters
}
```

Listing 11-3 shows the programming model of a backing bean: it holds state (the book attribute) for a certain duration (a scope), defines action methods (doCreateBook()), and handles navigation (return "newBook.xhtml"). With expression language a component can then bind its value to a property (e.g., <h:outputText value= "#{bookController.book.isbn}"/>) or invoke a method (<h:commandLink action="#{bookController.doCreateBook}">).

Anatomy of a Backing Bean

Backing beans are Java classes that are managed by the FacesServlet. The UI components are bound to the backing bean's properties and can invoke action methods. A backing bean needs to follow these requirements:

- The class must be annotated with @javax.inject.Named or the XML equivalent in the faces-config.xml deployment descriptor.

- It must have a scope (e.g., @RequestScoped).

- The class must be defined as public; it must not be final or abstract.

- The class must have a public no-arg constructor that the container will use to create instances.

- The class must not define the finalize() method.

- Attributes must have public getters and setters to be bound to a component.

Following the ease-of-use model of Java EE 7, a backing bean can simply be an annotated POJO, eliminating most of the configuration. Remember that in Chapter 2 I introduced CDI stereotypes. The @javax.enterprise.inject.Model is the perfect stereotype to use on backing beans as it is @Named and @RequestScoped (as shown in Listing 11-4). So you can rewrite the BookController showed in Listing 11-3, replace the annotations with @Model (Listing 11-5), and get the same behavior.

Listing 11-4. The Built-in CDI @Model Stereotype

```
@Named
@RequestScoped
@Documented
@Stereotype
@Target({ TYPE, METHOD, FIELD })
@Retention(RUNTIME)
public @interface Model {
}
```

Listing 11-5. The BookController Using the @Model Stereotype

```
@Model
public class BookController {

  private Book book = new Book();

  public String doCreateBook() {
    createBook(book);
    return "listBooks.xhtml";
  }

  // Constructors, getters, setters
}
```

The presence of the @javax.inject.Named annotation on a class allows expression language to use it in a page. @Named can also specify a different name for the backing bean (which by default is the name of the class starting with a lowercase letter). UI components are bound to backing bean properties; changing the default name has an impact on how you invoke a property or a method. The code in Listing 11-6 renames the backing bean to myBean.

Listing 11-6. A Renamed Backing Bean

```
@Named("myBean")
@RequestScoped
public class BookController06 {

  private Book book = new Book();

  public String doCreateBook() {
    createBook(book);
    return "listBooks.xhtml";
  }

  // Constructors, getters, setters
}
```

To invoke attributes or methods of this backing bean in your pages, you must use the overridden name as follows:

```
<h:outputText value="#{myBean.book.isbn}"/>
<h:form>
  <h:commandLink action="#{myBean.doCreateBook}">Create a new book</h:commandLink>
</h:form>
```

■ **Note** Before JSF 2.2 you had to annotate a backing bean with @javax.faces.bean.ManagedBean. First of all this was confusing because it was using the name "Managed Bean," which defines a more general Java EE component model which is part of the JSR-250 Common Annotations (@javax.annotation.ManagedBean). But more important, in JSF 2.2 the integration with CDI got stronger and it is now recommended to use CDI @Named as well as CDI scopes. The javax.faces.bean package will get deprecated in the next version of JSF.

Scopes

Objects that are created as part of a backing bean have a certain lifetime and may or may not be accessible to UI components or objects in the web application. The lifetime and accessibility of an object are known as *scope*. In a web application (backing beans and pages), you can specify the scope of an object using different durations:

- *Application*: This is the least restrictive duration (use the @ApplicationScoped annotation in your backing bean), with the longest life span. Objects that are created are available in all request/response cycles for all clients using the web application, for as long as the application is active. These objects can be called concurrently and need to be thread-safe (using the synchronized keyword). Objects with this scope can use other objects with no scope or application scope.

- *Session*: Objects are available for any request/response cycles that belong to the client's session (@SessionScoped). These objects have their state persisted between requests and last until the session is invalidated. Objects with this scope can use other objects with no scope, session scope, or application scope.

- *View*: Objects are available within a given view until the view is changed and have their state persisted until the user navigates to a new view, at which point they will be cleared out. Objects with this scope can use other objects with no scope, view scope, session scope, or application scope. Backing beans can be annotated with @ViewScoped.

- *Request*: State is available from the beginning of a request until the response has been sent to the client (@RequestScoped annotation). A client can execute several requests but stay on the same view. That's why the @ViewScoped duration lasts longer than that of @RequestScoped. Objects with this scope can use other objects with no scope, request scope, view scope, session scope, or application scope.

- *Flash*: Introduced in JSF 2.0, the new flash scope provides a short-lived conversation. It is a way to pass temporary objects that are propagated across a single-view transition and cleaned up before moving on to another view. The flash scope can only be used programmatically as there is no annotation.

- *Flow*: Objects in this scope are created when the user enters into the specified flow and deallocated when the user exits the flow (using the @FlowScoped annotation).

■ **Note** All the scoped annotations used in JSF 2.2 are now CDI scopes (i.e., they are all annotated with @javax. enterprise.context.NormalScope). But they come from different specifications: @ApplicationScoped, @RequestScoped, and @SessionScoped are part of CDI and @ViewScoped and @FlowScoped are defined in the JSF specification.

You need to be careful when you choose a scope for your backing beans. You should give them only as much scope as needed. Excessively scoped beans (e.g., @ApplicationScoped) will increase memory usage, and the potential need to persist them could cause increased disk and network usage. It makes no sense to give application scope to an object that is used only within a single component. Likewise, an object with too much restriction will be unavailable to different parts of your application. You should also be concerned with concurrent access. Multiple sessions accessing the same application scoped bean might create thread-safety issues.

The code in Listing 11-7 defines a backing bean with application scope. It initializes the defaultBook attribute as soon as it's constructed (@PostConstruct).

Listing 11-7. A Backing Bean with an Application Scope

```
@Named
@ApplicationScoped
public class InitController {

  private Book defaultBook;

  @PostConstruct
  private void init() {
    defaultBook = new Book("default title", OF, "default description");
  }

  // Constructors, getters, setters
}
```

Life Cycle and Callback Annotations

Chapter 10 explained the life cycle of a page (with six phases from receiving the request to rendering the response). Backing beans also have a life cycle (see Figure 11-3), which is completely different from that of the page. In fact, backing beans have a similar life cycle to Managed Beans, except that if they do exist, it is for the lifetime of the defined scope.

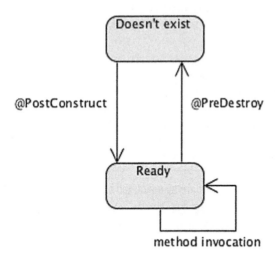

Figure 11-3. The backing bean life cycle

Backing beans running in a Servlet container can use the @PostConstruct and @PreDestroy annotations. After the container creates an instance of a backing bean, it calls the @PostConstruct callback method, if any. After this stage, the backing bean is bound to a scope and responds to any user's request. Before removing the backing bean, the container calls the @PreDestroy method. These methods can be used to initialize attributes or to create and release any external resource (see Listing 11-7).

Handling Exceptions and Messages

Backing beans process business logic, call EJBs, persist and retrieve data from databases, and so on, and sometimes things can go wrong. In this case, the user has to be informed through a message to take action. Messages can be split into two categories: application errors (involving business logic, database, or network connection) and user input errors (invalid ISBN or empty fields). Application errors can generate a completely different page asking the user to retry in a few moments, for example, or call a hotline service. Input errors can be displayed on the same page, with text describing the error, and messages can be informational, such as one indicating that a book was successfully added to the database.

In Chapter 10, you saw tags that are used to display messages on pages (<h:message> and <h:messages>). To produce these messages, JSF allows you to queue messages by calling the facesContext.addMessage() method in your backing beans. The signature of the method is as follows:

```
void addMessage(String clientId, FacesMessage message)
```

This method appends a FacesMessage to the set of messages to be displayed. The first parameter of this method specifies a client identifier. This parameter refers to the Document Object Model (DOM) location of the UI component that the message is registered to (e.g., bookForm:isbn refers to the UI component that has the isbn identifier within the bookForm form). If clientId is null, the message doesn't refer to any special component and is said to be global to the whole page. A message consists of a summary text, a detailed text, and a severity level (fatal, error, warning, and info). Messages can also be internationalized using message bundles.

```
FacesMessage(Severity severity, String summary, String detail)
```

The code in Listing 11-8 is a snippet of a backing bean that creates a book. If the creation succeeds, a global informational message is queued (the FacesMessage with a SEVERITY_INFO). If an exception is caught, an error message is added to the messages queue to be displayed. Note that both messages are global because the clientId is null. On the other hand, when we validate the ISBN and book title entered by the user, we want to display the warning messages (SEVERITY_WARN) related to the UI component (e.g., bookForm:title is the DOM identifier of the text field title located under the bookForm form).

Listing 11-8. Adding Different Severity Messages

```
@Named
@RequestScoped
public class BookController {

  @Inject
  private BookEJB bookEJB;
  private Book book = new Book();

  public String doCreateBook() {
    FacesContext ctx = FacesContext.getCurrentInstance();

    if (book.getIsbn() == null || "".equals(book.getIsbn())) {
      ctx.addMessage("bookForm:isbn", new FacesMessage(FacesMessage.SEVERITY_WARN, ↵
            "Wrong isbn", "You should enter an ISBN number"));
    }
    if (book.getTitle() == null || "".equals(book.getTitle())) {
      ctx.addMessage("bookForm:title", new FacesMessage(FacesMessage.SEVERITY_WARN, ↵
            "Wrong title", "You should enter a title for the book"));
    }
```

```
  if (ctx.getMessageList().size() != 0)
    return null;

  try {
    book = bookEJB.createBook(book);
    ctx.addMessage(null, new FacesMessage(FacesMessage.SEVERITY_INFO, "Book created", ↵
          "The book" + book.getTitle() + " has been created with id=" + book.getId()));

  } catch (Exception e) {
    ctx.addMessage(null, new FacesMessage(FacesMessage.SEVERITY_ERROR, ↵
          "Book hasn't been created", e.getMessage()));
  }
  return null;
}

// Constructors, getters, setters
}
```

The FacesContext is available in the page and so is the FacesMessage. The page can then display the global messages (with clientId equals to null) using a single <h:messages> tag. When we want to display a message at a specific place on the page for a specific component (as is usually the case with validation or conversion errors), we use <h:message>. Figure 11-4 shows a page with messages specifically aimed at the ISBN and title input fields.

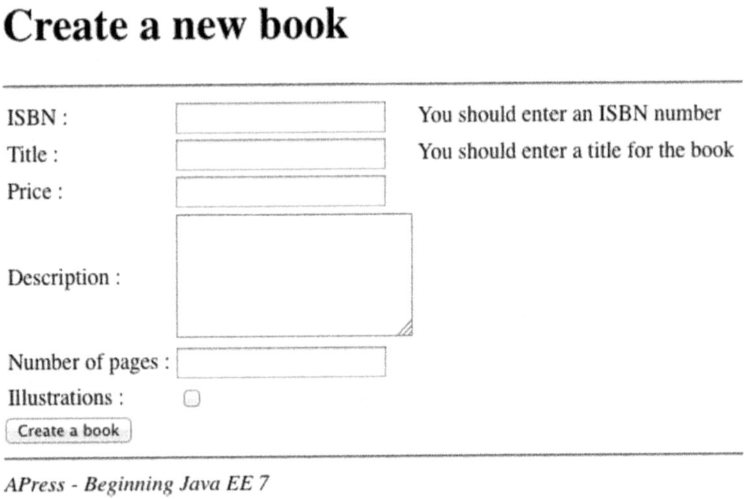

Create a new book

ISBN :   [   ]   You should enter an ISBN number

Title :   [   ]   You should enter a title for the book

Price :   [   ]

Description :   [   ]

Number of pages : [   ]

Illustrations :   ◻

[Create a book]

APress - Beginning Java EE 7

Figure 11-4. A page displaying a message per UI component

The page will have an input text field with an identifier (id="isbn"), and the <h:message> tag will refer to that component (for="isbn"). The result will be that this specific message will only be displayed for this component.

```
<h:messages infoStyle="color:blue" warnStyle="color:orange" errorStyle="color:red"/>
<h:form id="bookForm">
  <h:inputText id="isbn" value="#{bookController.book.isbn}"/>
  <h:message for="isbn"/>
</h:form>
```

If the ISBN field has not been filled, a warning message appears next to the ISBN input text field. JSF uses this messaging mechanism for converters, validators, and Bean Validation. Note that the <h:messages> tag can have different styles per severity (here errors are red and warnings orange).

Bringing JSF and EJBs Together

Until now all the binding and business invocation has been made through backing beans. As you'll soon see, backing beans also deal with navigation. So when you want to do some processing and then take the user to a different page, having a backing bean makes sense. But sometimes you just need to access an EJB to get a list of books to fill a datatable, for example. You could still go through a backing bean, but it would mostly delegate the call to the EJB. So why not directly call the EJB from the page?

One goal of CDI is to bring JSF and EJBs together. What do you need to do? Not much, just add a @Named annotation to your EJB and you can invoke it using expression language. Listing 11-9 shows a stateless EJB that uses JPA to get the list of all of the books from the database. It has a CDI @Named annotation and therefore can be invoked in a JSF page.

Listing 11-9. A Stateless EJB with a CDI @Named Annotation

```java
@Named
@Stateless
public class BookEJB {

  @Inject
  private EntityManager em;

  public List<Book> findAllBooks() {
    return em.createNamedQuery("findAllBooks", Book.class).getResultList();
  }
}
```

The findAllBooks() method in Listing 11-9 returns a list of books. To fill a datatable with this list, there is no need to use a backing bean. The page can directly invoke the bookEJB.findAllBooks() in the <h:dataTable> component using EL.

```html
<h:dataTable value="#{bookEJB.findAllBooks()}" var="book">
  <h:column>
    <h:outputText value="#{book.title}"/>
  </h:column>
</h:dataTable>
```

Navigation

Web applications are made of multiple pages that you need to navigate through. Depending on the application, you can have various levels of navigation with page flows that are more or less sophisticated. You can think of wizards, where you can go back to the previous or initial page, business cases where you go to a particular page depending on a certain rule, and so on. JSF has multiple options for navigation and allows you to control the flow, based on single pages or globally for the entire application.

Explicit Navigation

In JSF you can easily navigate to a page if you know its name. You just need to explicitly set the page's name either in a backing bean returned parameter method or in a JSF page. The FacesServlet, acting as a controller, will do the rest: intercept the call, get the page by its name, bind the values to the components, and render the page to the user. With explicit navigation you can choose between navigating straight to a page and doing some processing before navigating.

When you just want to go from page to page by clicking a link or a button without doing any processing, you can use the UI components <h:button>, <h:link> and <h:outputLink>.

```
<h:link value="Back to creating a new book" outcome="newBook.xhtml"/>
```

But sometimes this is not enough because you need to access a business tier or a database to retrieve or process data. In this case, you would use <h:commandButton> and <h:commandLink> with their action attribute that allows you to target backing bean methods, as opposed to targeting a page with <h:link> or <h:button>.

```
<h:commandButton value="Create a book" action="#{bookController.doCreateBook}">
```

Imagine there is a first page (newBook.xhtml) displaying a form to create a book. Once you click the *Create a book* button, a method on the backing bean is invoked, the book is created, and the user navigates to the listBooks.xhtml page, which lists all the books. Once the page is loaded into the browser, the *Back to creating a new book* link at the bottom of the page allows you to go straight to the previous page without doing any processing (as shown in Figure 11-5).

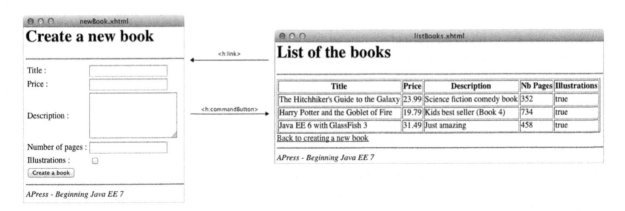

Figure 11-5. *Navigating between newBook.xhtml and listBooks.xhtml*

The page flow is simple but it still needs a backing bean (BookController) to do some business logic and navigation. Both pages use buttons and link components for navigating and interacting with the backing bean. The newBook.xhtml page uses a button to call the doCreateBook() method of the backing bean (<h:commandButton action="#{bookController.doCreateBook}"/>). The doCreateBook() method will then invoke an EJB to persist a Book entity in the database and return a String: the name of the following page. Then, the listBooks.xhtml page uses a normal link just to go back to the newBook.xhtml page without doing any processing (<h:link outcome="newBook.xhtml"/>).

The <h:commandButton> does not directly call the page it needs to go to. It invokes a method on the backing bean that is responsible for navigation and decides which page to load next. The navigation operates on a set of rules that define all the application's possible navigation paths. The code of the backing bean in Listing 11-10 uses the simplest form of navigation rules: it just returns the page it needs to go to.

Listing 11-10. *A Backing Bean Explicitly Defining Navigation*

```java
@Named
@RequestScoped
public class BookController {

  @Inject
  private BookEJB bookEJB;
  private Book book = new Book();
  private List<Book> bookList = new ArrayList<>();

  public String doCreateBook() {
    book = bookEJB.createBook(book);
    bookList = bookEJB.findBooks();
    return "listBooks.xhtml";
  }

  // Constructors, getters, setters
}
```

Navigation Rules

When a backing bean method returns a String, this String can take several forms. In Listing 11-10 you can see the simplest: it returns the page name. By default, the page file extension is .xhtml but you can change it if you configure the FacesServlet in the web.xml as seen previously.

With JSF, the page flow navigation can be defined externally via faces-config.xml. In faces-config.xml, navigation is specified in <navigation-rule> elements. A <navigation-rule> element identifies the start page, a condition, and the target page to navigate to when the condition occurs. The condition is based on a logical name rather than the name of the page. The code of the backing bean in Listing 11-10 could have used the logical name success as shown in Listing 11-11.

Listing 11-11. *Snippet of the Backing Bean Using Logical Names*

```java
@Named
@RequestScoped
public class BookController {
  // ...

  public String doCreateBook() {
    book = bookEJB.createBook(book);
    bookList = bookEJB.findBooks();
    return "success";
  }

  // Constructors, getters, setters
}
```

Listing 11-12 shows the structure of the faces-config.xml file. The <from-view-id> tag defines the page where you initially make the action request. In this case, you start on newBook.xhtml before making the call to the backing bean. If the returned logical name is success (<from-outcome>), the FacesServlet will forward the call to the listBooks.xhtml page (<to-view-id>).

Listing 11-12. A faces-config.xml File Defining Navigation

```
<?xml version='1.0' encoding='UTF-8'?>
<faces-config xmlns="http://xmlns.jcp.org/xml/ns/javaee"
              xmlns:xsi="http://www.w3.org/2001/XMLSchema-instance"
              xsi:schemaLocation="http://xmlns.jcp.org/xml/ns/javaee ↪
              http://xmlns.jcp.org/xml/ns/javaee/web-facesconfig_2_2.xsd"
              version="2.2">

  <navigation-rule>
    <from-view-id>newBook.xhtml</from-view-id>
    <navigation-case>
      <from-outcome>success</from-outcome>
      <to-view-id>listBooks.xhtml</to-view-id>
    </navigation-case>
  </navigation-rule>

</faces-config>
```

Navigation can be done directly in the backing beans or by faces-config.xml, but when should you use one over the other? The first reason to directly return the page name in backing beans is simplicity; the Java code is explicit, and there is no external XML file to work with. If the web application has an extensive page flow, you might want to keep it in a single place, so that any changes can be made in a central location instead of across several pages; and again, using a mix of both can result in having part of your navigation in your beans and another in the faces-config.xml file.

There is one case where using XML configuration is very useful; when there are global links on several pages (e.g., login or logout that can be done in an entire application), as you do not want to define them for every single page. Global navigation rules can be used in XML (but the same feature is not possible within backing beans).

```
<navigation-rule>
  <from-view-id>*</from-view-id>
  <navigation-case>
    <from-outcome>logout</from-outcome>
    <to-view-id>logout.xhtml</to-view-id>
  </navigation-case>
</navigation-rule>
```

If you have an action that applies to every page in the application, you can use a navigation-rule element without a <from-view-id> or you can use a wildcard (*). The preceding code indicates that, for any page the user is on, if the method of the backing bean returns the logical name logout, forward the user to the logout.xhtml page.

The previous examples showed simple navigation where one page has only one navigation rule and only one page to go to. This is not often the case, and, depending on certain rules or exceptions, users can be redirected to different pages. This is possible to achieve with either backing beans or the faces-config.xml file. The following code shows a switch case that redirects to different pages. Note that when the null value is returned, the user goes back to the page he is already on.

```
public String doCreateBook() {
  book = bookEJB.createBook(book);
  bookList = bookEJB.findBooks();
  switch (value) {
    case 1: return "page1.xhtml"; break;
    case 2: return "page2.xhtml"; break;
    default: return null; break;
  }
}
```

An enhancement made since JSF 2.0 is the addition of conditional navigation cases. It allows navigation cases to specify a precondition that must be met in order for the navigation case to be accepted. This precondition is specified as an EL expression using the new <if> configuration element. In the example that follows, if the user is in the admin role, the logout is specific and redirects the user to the logout_admin.xhtml page:

```
<navigation-rule>
    <from-view-id>*</from-view-id>
    <navigation-case>
        <from-outcome>logout</from-outcome>
        <to-view-id>logout_admin.xhtml</to-view-id>
        <if>#{userController.isAdmin}</if>
    </navigation-case>
</navigation-rule>
```

Bookmarkability

Prior to JSF 2.0, every client server interaction was an HTTP POST (<h:commandButton> and <h:commandLink>). While this was fine in many situations, it did not work well when it came to bookmarking pages in a web application. JSF 2.0 introduced bookmarking capability mainly with the use of two new tags–<h:button>, <h:link>–and also a ViewParam tag. This provided support for HTTP GET requests. But still the model wasn't polished enough and so we had to use the preRenderView phase in order to do the job. JSF 2.2 introduced the ViewAction to enable smoother bookmarkability.

ViewParam and ViewAction provide a mechanism to process GET requests and bind the parameters passed in the HTTP request to properties in the model using EL. A page including a <f:viewParam> tag can pull the parameters from the GET request into bound properties. The following code allows access to the viewBook.xhtml page with an id parameter in the request (such as viewBook.xhtml?id=123) and binds it to the bookController.book.id attribute:

```
<f:metadata>
  <f:viewParam name="id" value="#{bookController.book.id}"/>
</f:metadata>
```

Once the id of the book is extracted from the HTTP request and bound to a property, you need to invoke an action on a backing bean. JSF 2.2 defines the new tag <f:viewAction> that specifies an application-specific action. To retrieve the book from the database based on the id you need to invoke the doFindBookById method as follows:

```
<f:metadata>
  <f:viewParam name="id" value="#{bookController.book.id}"/>
  <f:viewAction action="#{bookController.doFindBookById}"/>
</f:metadata>
```

This technique allows you to directly change the URL (uniform resource locator) in your browser to point at the desired book (e.g., viewBook.xhtml?id=123 or viewBook.xhtml?id=456) and bookmark the page.

Conversion and Validation

You've seen how to handle messages to inform the end user about actions to be taken. One possible action is to correct an invalid input value (e.g., invalid ISBN). JSF provides a standard conversion and validation mechanism that can process user inputs to ensure data integrity. In this way, when you invoke business methods to process, you can safely rely on valid data. Conversion and validation allow the developer to focus on business logic rather than checking whether the input data are not null, fit a range of values, and so on.

Conversion takes place when data input by the end user has to be converted from a String to an object and vice versa. It ensures that data are of the right type—for example, in converting a String to a java.util.Date, a String to an Integer, or a price in dollars to euros. As for validation, it ensures data contain the expected content (a date following the dd/MM/yyyy format, a float between 3.14 and 3.15, etc.).

Conversion and validation occur during different phases of the page life cycle (which you saw in the previous chapter) as shown in Figure 11-6.

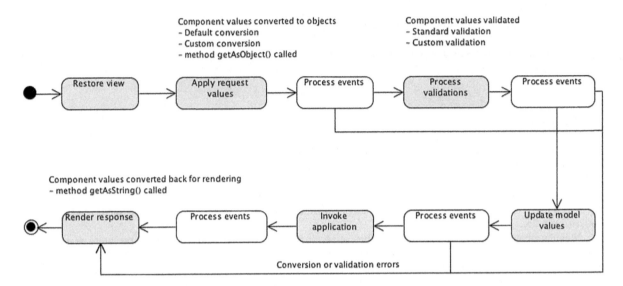

Figure 11-6. *Conversion and validation during page life cycle*

During the *Apply request values* phase in Figure 11-6, the UI component value is converted to the targeted object (e.g., from a String to a date) and then validated during the *Process validation* phase. It makes sense that conversion and validation occur before component data are bound to the backing bean (which happens during the *Update model values* phase). If any error is found, it will result in adding error messages and shortening the life cycle, so it goes straight to *Render response* (and messages will be displayed on the user interface with <h:messages/>). During this phase, the backing bean properties are converted back to a String to be displayed.

JSF has a set of standard converters and validators and allows you to easily create your own.

Converters

When a form is displayed on a browser, the end user fills the input fields and hits a button, resulting in transporting the data to the server in an HTTP request using String formats. Before updating the model on the backing bean, these data have to be converted from Strings to the target objects (Float, Integer, BigDecimal, etc.). The reverse action will take place when the data have to be sent back to the client in the response and be rendered in the browser.

JSF ships with converters for common types like dates and numbers. In cases where the backing bean property is a primitive type (Integer, int, Float, float, etc.), JSF will automatically convert the UI component value to the correct type and back. When the property is some other datatype, you need to provide your own converter. Table 11-3 lists all the standard converters that are in the javax.faces.convert package.

Table 11-3. *Standard Converters*

Converter	Description
BigDecimalConverter	Converts a String to a java.math.BigDecimal and vice versa.
BigIntegerConverter	Converts a String to a java.math.BigInteger and vice versa.
BooleanConverter	Converts a String to a Boolean (and boolean primitive) and vice versa.
ByteConverter	Converts a String to a Byte (and byte primitive) and vice versa.
CharacterConverter	Converts a String to a Character (and char primitive) and vice versa.
DateTimeConverter	Converts a String to a java.util.Date and vice versa.
DoubleConverter	Converts a String to a Double (and double primitive) and vice versa.
EnumConverter	Converts a String to an Enum (and enum primitive) and vice versa.
FloatConverter	Converts a String to a Float (and float primitive) and vice versa.
IntegerConverter	Converts a String to an Integer (and int primitive) and vice versa.
LongConverter	Converts a String to a Long (and long primitive) and vice versa.
NumberConverter	Converts a String to an abstract java.lang.Number class and vice versa.
ShortConverter	Converts a String to a Short (and short primitive) and vice versa.

JSF will automatically convert input values to numbers when the backing bean property is some primitive numeric type and to date or time when the property is some date type. If automatic conversion doesn't suit you, you can explicitly control it through the standard convertNumber and convertDateTime tags. To use these tags, you need to nest the converter inside any of the input or output tags. The converter will be called by JSF during the life cycle.

The convertNumber tag has attributes that allow conversion of the input value to a number (default), a currency, or a percentage. You can specify a currency symbol or a number of decimal digits, as well as a formatting pattern, determining how the number should be formatted and parsed.

```
<h:inputText value="#{bookController.book.price}">
  <f:convertNumber currencySymbol="$" type="currency"/>
</h:inputText>
```

The convertDateTime tag can convert dates in various formats (date, time, or both). It has several attributes that control the date conversion and time zones. A pattern attribute allows identification of the pattern of the date String that will be converted.

```
<h:inputText value="#{bookController.book.publishedDate}">
    <f:convertDateTime pattern="MM/dd/yy"/>
</h:inputText>
```

Custom Converters

Sometimes converting numbers, dates, enums, and so on is insufficient, and you may require custom conversion. It is easy to develop your own converters and use them in pages with JSF. You simply have to write a class that implements the javax.faces.convert.Converter interface and register it with metadata. This interface has two methods.

```
Object getAsObject(FacesContext ctx, UIComponent component, String value)
String getAsString(FacesContext ctx, UIComponent component, Object value)
```

The getAsObject() method converts the String value of a UI component into the corresponding supported type and returns the new instance. This method throws a ConverterException if the conversion fails. Conversely, the getAsString() method converts the provided type to a String, to be rendered in markup language (such as XHTML).

Once you develop the custom converter, it must be registered to allow it to be used in the web application. One method is by declaring the converter in the faces-config.xml file; the other is to use the @FacesConverter annotation.

Listing 11-13 shows how to write a custom converter that converts a price from dollars to euros. It starts by associating this converter with the name euroConverter using the @FacesConverter("euroConverter") annotation, and implements the Converter interface. This example only overrides the getAsString() method, which returns a String representation of a given price in euros.

Listing 11-13. A Euro Converter

```
@FacesConverter("euroConverter")
public class EuroConverter implements Converter {

  @Override
  public Object getAsObject(FacesContext context, UIComponent component, String value) {
    return value;
  }

  @Override
  public String getAsString(FacesContext ctx, UIComponent component, Object value) {
    float amountInDollars = Float.parseFloat(value.toString());
    double ammountInEuros = amountInDollars * 0.8;
    DecimalFormat df = new DecimalFormat("###,##0.##");
    return df.format(ammountInEuros);
  }
}
```

To use this converter, use either the converter attribute of the <h:outputText> tag or the <f:converter> tag. In both cases, you must pass the name of the custom converter defined in the @FacesConverter annotation (euroConverter). The following code displays two output texts, one representing the price in dollars and the other converting this price to euros:

```
<h:outputText value="#{book.price}"/> // in dollar
<h:outputText value="#{book.price}">  // converted in euro
  <f:converter converterId="euroConverter"/>
</h:outputText>
```

Or you can use the converter attribute of the outputText tag.

```
<h:outputText value="#{book.price}" converter="euroConverter"/>
```

Validators

When working with web applications, the accuracy of user-entered data must be ensured. Accurate data entry can be enforced on the client side using JavaScript or on the server side using validators and Bean Validation. JSF simplifies data validation through the use of standard and custom server-side validators. Validators act as a first level of control by validating the value of UI components before being processed by the backing bean.

UI components generally handle simple validation, such as whether or not a value is required. For example, the following tag would require that a value in the text field be entered:

```
<h:inputText value="#{bookController.book.title}" required="true"/>
```

If you do not enter a value, JSF returns the page with a message indicating that a value should be entered (the page must have a <h:messages> tag). This uses the same message mechanism that I described before. But JSF comes with a set of richer validators that can be used (described in Table 11-4), which are defined in the javax.faces.validator package.

Table 11-4. *Standard Validators*

Converter	Description
DoubleRangeValidator	Checks the value of the corresponding component against specified minimum and maximum double values.
LengthValidator	Checks the number of characters in the String value of the associated component.
LongRangeValidator	Checks the value of the corresponding component against specified minimum and maximum long values.
MethodExpressionValidator	Performs validation by executing a method on an object.
RequiredValidator	Equivalent to setting the required attribute on the input component to true.
RegexValidator	Checks the value of the corresponding component against a regular expression.

These validators are useful for generic cases like the length of a field or a number range and can be easily associated within a component, in the same way as converters are (both can be used on the same component). The following code ensures the book's title is between 2 and 20 characters in length and its price is from $1 to $500:

```
<h:inputText value="#{bookController.book.title}" required="true">
  <f:validateLength minimum="2" maximum="20"/>
</h:inputText>
<h:inputText value="#{bookController.book.price}">
  <f:validateLongRange minimum="1" maximum="500"/>
</h:inputText>
```

Custom Validators

Perhaps the standard JSF validators might not suit your needs; you may have data that have to follow certain business formats such as a ZIP code, a state, or an e-mail address. You must create your own custom validator to address these cases. Like converters, a validator is a class that needs to implement an interface and override some method. In the case of a validator, the interface is javax.faces.validator.Validator, which has a single validate() method:

```
void validate(FacesContext context, UIComponent component, Object value)
```

In this method, the value argument is the one that has to be checked, based on some business logic. If it passes the validation check, you can simply return from the method, and the life cycle of the page will continue. If not, you can throw a ValidatorException and include a FacesMessage with a summary and a detail message describing the validation error. You must register the validator either in the faces-config.xml or by using the @FacesValidator annotation.

As an example, create an ISBN validator that ensures the ISBN entered by the user for the book follows a certain format (using a regular expression). Listing 11-14 shows the code for the IsbnValidator.

Listing 11-14. An ISBN Validator

```
@FacesValidator("isbnValidator")
public class IsbnValidator implements Validator {

    private Pattern pattern;
    private Matcher matcher;

    @Override
    public void validate(FacesContext context, UIComponent component, ➥
                         Object value) throws ValidatorException {

      String componentValue = value.toString();

      pattern = Pattern.compile("(?=[-0-9xX]{13}$)");
      matcher = pattern.matcher(componentValue);

      if (!matcher.find()) {
        String message = MessageFormat.format("{0} not a valid isbn format", componentValue);
        FacesMessage facesMessage = new FacesMessage(FacesMessage.SEVERITY_ERROR, msg, msg);
        throw new ValidatorException(facesMessage);
      }
    }
}
```

The code in Listing 11-14 starts by associating the validator with the name isbnValidator, to allow it to be used in a page. It implements the Validator interface and adds the validation logic in the validate() method. It checks, with a regular expression, that the ISBN has the right format. If not, it adds a message to the context and throws an exception. JSF will automatically resume the life cycle of the page, recall the page, and display the error message. You can employ this custom validator in your pages using the validator attribute or embedding a <f:validator> tag.

```
<h:inputText value="#{bookController.book.isbn}" validator="isbnValidator"/>
// or
<h:inputText value="#{bookController.book.isbn}">
  <f:validator validatorId="isbnValidator" />
</h:inputText>
```

Integration with Bean Validation

Since JSF 2.0, the support for Bean Validation has been made mandatory (i.e., a JSF implementation must support it). The way it works is pretty simple. If a JSF page has several text fields and each text field is bound to a backing bean property that has at least one Bean Validation constraint annotation, the javax.validation.Validator.validate() method is called during the validation phase. Bean Validation is therefore invoked automatically without the developer doing anything on the JSF page or calling any Bean Validation method in the backing bean. The JSF runtime also ensures that every ConstraintViolation that resulted in attempting to validate the model data is wrapped in a FacesMessage and added to the FacesContext as is normal with every other kind of validator. So a simple <h:messages> in a page will display the list of messages of the violated ConstraintViolation.

In Chapter 3, I presented validation groups. If in your page you need to validate certain components for a certain group, you can use the <f:validateBean> tag. The code that follows validates the title and the price of a book for the Delivery group only:

```
<f:validateBean validationGroups="org.agoncal.book.javaee7.Delivery">
  <h:inputText value="#{bookController.book.title}"/>
  <h:inputText value="#{bookController.book.price}"/>
</f:validateBean>
```

Ajax

The HTTP protocol is based on a request/response mechanism: a client needs something, sends a request, and receives a response from the server, usually an entire web page. The communication follows this direction: a client requests something from the server, and not the other way around. However, web applications must provide rich and responsive interfaces and must react to server events, update parts of the page, aggregate widgets, and so on. In a normal request/response situation, the server would have to send the entire web page back even if only a small portion had to change. If the page has a significant size, you'll overload the bandwidth and have poor responsiveness as the browser would need to load the entire page. If you want to increase the browser's responsiveness and improve the user's browsing experience, you need to update only small portions of the page. And this can be done with Ajax.

Ajax (Asynchronous JavaScript and XML) is a set of web development techniques used to create interactive web applications. Ajax allows web applications to retrieve portions of data from the server asynchronously without interfering with the display and behavior of the existing page. Once the browser receives the data, it only needs the portions requiring updating using the DOM of the page and JavaScript.

General Concepts

The term "Ajax" was coined in 2005 as a set of alternative techniques for loading asynchronous data into web pages. Back in 1999, Microsoft created the XMLHttpRequest object as an ActiveX control in Internet Explorer 5. In 2006, the World Wide Web Consortium (W3C) released the first specification draft for the XMLHttpRequest object, which is now supported by most browsers. At the same time, several companies brainstormed about how to ensure that Ajax could be the industry standard for a rich application platform based on open technologies. The result of this work was the creation of the OpenAjax Alliance, which consists of vendors, open source projects, and companies using Ajax-based technologies.

As shown in Figure 11-7, in traditional web applications, the browser has to ask for the full HTML documents from the server. The user clicks a button to send or get the information, waits for the server to respond, and then receives the entire page that the browser loads. Ajax, on the other hand, uses asynchronous data transfer (HTTP requests) between the browser and the server, allowing web pages to request small bits of information (JSON or XML data) from the server instead of whole pages. The user stays on the same page while a piece of JavaScript requests or sends data to a server asynchronously, and only portions of the page are actually updated, making web application faster and more user friendly.

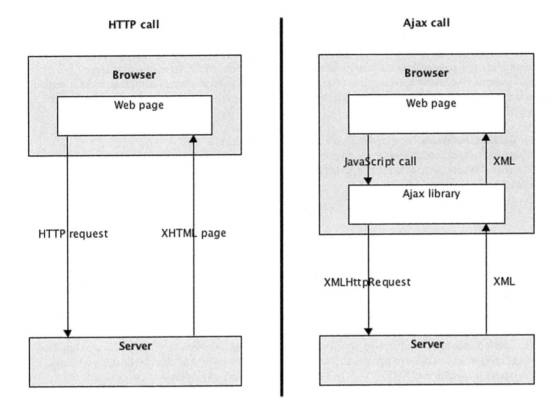

Figure 11-7. *Plain HTTP calls vs. Ajax HTTP calls*

In principle, Ajax is based on the following:

- XHTML and CSS for presentation.

- DOM for dynamic display and interaction with data.

- XML and XSLT for the interchange, manipulation, and display of XML data.

- The XMLHttpRequest object for asynchronous communication.

- JavaScript to bring these technologies together on the browser.

XMLHttpRequest is an important part of Ajax, as it's a DOM API used by JavaScript to transfer XML from the browser to the server. The data returned have to be fetched on the client side to update portions of the page dynamically with JavaScript. The data can have several formats such as XHTML, JSON, or even plain text.

Since JSF 2.0, Ajax is supported natively, so you don't have to develop JavaScript to handle the XMLHttpRequest, but you do need to use a JavaScript library that has been specified and shipped with JSF implementations.

Support in JSF

Previous versions of JSF offered no native Ajax solution, so third-party libraries had to be used to fill the gap. Sometimes this increased the complexity of the code at the expense of performance. Since JSF 2.0, things are much easier, as Ajax support has been specified and is built into any JSF implementation.

First of all, there is a specified JavaScript library (jsf.js) for performing Ajax interaction, which means you don't have to develop your own scripts or manipulate the XMLHttpRequest objects directly. Without developing any JavaScript, you can use a set of standardized functions to send asynchronous requests and receive data. In order to use this library in your pages, you need to add the jsf.js resource with the following line of code:

```
<h:outputScript name="jsf.js" library="javax.faces" target="head"/>
```

The <h:outputScript> tag renders a <script> markup element referring to the jsf.js JavaScript file in the javax.faces library (which follows the new resource management of JSF, meaning that the jsf.js file is under the META-INF/resources/javax/faces directory). Note that the top-level javax namespace is registered within the OpenAjax Alliance. This JavaScript API is used to initiate client-side interactions with JSF including partial tree traversal and partial page update. The function that we will be directly using in our pages is the request function, as it is responsible for sending an Ajax request to the server. Its signature is as follows:

```
jsf.ajax.request(ELEMENT, |event|, { |OPTIONS| });
```

ELEMENT is any JSF component or XHTML element from which you trigger the event. Typically, for submitting a form, the element would be a button. EVENT is any JavaScript event supported by that element, such as onmousedown, onclick, onblur, and so forth. The OPTIONS argument is an array that may contain the following name/value pairs:

- execute:'<space-separated list of UI component IDs>': Sends the list of component IDs to the server in order to be processed during the execute phase of the request.

- render:'<space-separated list of UI component IDs>': Renders the list of component IDs that have been processed during the render phase of the request.

As an example, the following code shows a button that calls asynchronously the doCreateBook method passing all the parameters of a book form. The button calls the jsf.ajax.request function when the user clicks it (onclick event). The this argument refers to the element itself (the button), and the options refer to components IDs (isbn, title, price . . .):

```
<h:commandButton value="Create a book" onclick="jsf.ajax.request(this, event,
        {execute:'isbn title price description nbOfPage illustrations',
         render:'booklist'}); return false;"
        actionListener="#{bookController.doCreateBook}" />
```

When the client makes an Ajax request, the page life cycle on the server side stays the same (it goes through the same six phases). The key benefit is that the response is simply the return of a small chunk of data rather than a large HTML page to the browser. The *Apply request* phase determines whether the current request is a "partial request" or not, and the PartialViewContext object is used throughout the page's life cycle. It contains methods and properties that pertain to partial request processing and partial response rendering. At the end of the life cycle, the Ajax response (or, strictly speaking, the partial response) is sent to the client during the *Render response* phase. It usually consists of XHTML, XML, or JSON that the client-side JavaScript will parse.

JSF 2 also includes a declarative approach that is intended to be more convenient and easier to use. This approach leverages the new <f:ajax> tag. Instead of manually coding the JavaScript for the Ajax request call, you can declaratively specify the same behavior without requiring any JavaScript code.

```
<h:commandButton value="Create a book" action="#{bookController.doCreateBook}">
    <f:ajax execute="@form" render=":booklist"/>
</h:commandButton>
```

In this example, render points to the component id we want to render back (the booklist component). The execute attribute refers to all the components that belong to the form. Table 11-5 shows all the possible values that the render and execute attribute can take.

Table 11-5. *Possible Values of the Render and Execute Attribute*

Value	Description
@all	Renders or executes all components in view.
@none	Renders or executes no components in view (this is the default value if render or execute is not specified).
@this	Renders or executes only this component (the component that triggered the Ajax request).
@form	Renders or executes all components within this form (from which Ajax request was fired).
Space separated list of IDs	One or more IDs of components to be rendered or executed.
Expression language	Expression which resolves to Collection of Strings.

Putting It All Together

Now let's put all these concepts together and write a web application allowing the user to create a new book, list all the books from the database, and visualize the details of a book. This web application consists of two web pages:

- newBook.xhtml displays a form at the top, letting you create a book, and lists all the books at the bottom. When you create a book and press the *Create a book* button, only the list at the bottom is updated using Ajax. When you click a book's title link at the bottom, the user navigates to a different page and visualizes the book's details.

- viewBook.xhtml displays the book's details (title, price, description, etc.). Thanks to bookmarkability you can display the content of any book by simply changing the URL (e.g., viewBook.xhtml?id=123 or viewBook.xhtml?id=456).

These two pages share the same template displaying a link at the top (to go back to the newBook.xhtml page) and a label at the bottom. Figure 11-8 shows these two pages and the different navigations (either with <h:link> or <h:commandButton>).

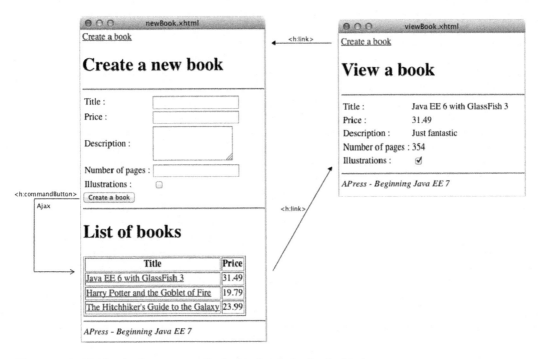

Figure 11-8. *Navigating between newBook.xhtml and viewBook.xhtml*

These two pages use the BookController backing bean to store the necessary properties and for navigation. Using persistence with JPA and business logic with EJB, everything can be plugged together (JSF, EJB, JPA, Bean Validation, and CDI). The backing bean delegates all the business logic to the BookEJB, which contains three methods: one to persist a book into a database (createBook()), one to retrieve all the books (findAllBooks()), and another one to get a book by its identifier (findBookById()). This stateless session bean uses the EntityManager API to manipulate a Book entity (which uses some Bean Validation annotations).

Figure 11-9 shows the interacting components in this web application. They are packaged in a war file and deployed in a running instance of GlassFish and an in-memory Derby database.

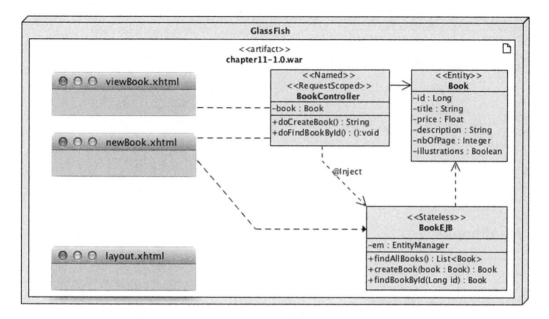

Figure 11-9. *Pages and classes involved in the web application*

This web application follows the Maven directory structure, so classes, files, and web pages have to be placed in the following directories:

- src/main/java: Contains the Book entity, the BookEJB, and the BookController backing bean.

- src/main/resources: Contains the META-INF/persistence.xml file used to map the entity in the database.

- src/main/webapp: Contains the two web pages newBook.xhtml and viewBook.xhtml.

- src/main/webapp/WEB-INF: Contains the faces-config.xml and beans.xml files used to trigger JSF and CDI.

- pom.xml: Represents the Maven Project Object Model (POM) describing the project, its dependencies, and plug-ins.

Writing the Book Entity

I will not go into too much detail about Listing 11-15, as you should by now understand the code of the Book entity. Despite the JPA mapping and Bean Validation annotations, notice the named query, findAllBooks, that retrieves books from the database ordered by title.

Listing 11-15. A Book Entity with a Named Query and Bean Validation Annotations

```java
@Entity
@NamedQuery(name = "findAllBooks", query = "SELECT b FROM Book b ORDER BY b.title DESC")
public class Book {

    @Id @GeneratedValue
    private Long id;
    @NotNull @Size(min = 4, max = 50)
    @Column(nullable = false)
    private String title;
    private Float price;
    @Column(length = 2000)
    private String description;
    private Integer nbOfPage;
    private Boolean illustrations;

    // Constructors, getters, setters
}
```

As you know, this entity also has to be packaged with a persistence.xml file, but in the interests of simplicity I won't show it here (refer to Chapter 4).

Writing the BookEJB

Listing 11-16 represents a stateless session bean that exposes a no-interface view. This means that the client (i.e., the backing bean) doesn't need an interface (local or remote) and can directly invoke the EJB. This EJB gets injected with a reference to an entity manager using @Inject. For that it needs a CDI DatabaseProducer similar to Listing 8-13 (not shown here, refer to Chapter 8). With this EntityManager it persists a Book entity (createBook() method), retrieves all the books from the database (using the findAllBooks named query), and finds a book by its identifier. Notice that the EJB is @Named, so it can be invoked from a JSF page (more on that later) and it defines a Datasource with the @DataSourceDefinition annotation. This EJB doesn't need any deployment descriptor.

Listing 11-16. A Stateless EJB That Creates and Retrieves Books

```java
@Named
@Stateless
@DataSourceDefinition(name = "java:global/jdbc/lab11DS",
        className = "org.apache.derby.jdbc.EmbeddedDriver",
        url = "jdbc:derby:memory:lab11DB;create=true;user=app;password=app"
)
public class BookEJB {

    @Inject
    private EntityManager em;

    public Book createBook(Book book) {
        em.persist(book);
        return book;
    }
```

```
  public List<Book> findAllBooks() {
    return em.createNamedQuery("findAllBooks", Book.class).getResultList();
  }

  public Book findBookById(Long id) {
    return em.find(Book.class, id);
  }
}
```

Writing the BookController Backing Bean

One of the roles of a backing bean is to interact with other layers of the application (e.g., the EJB layer) or perform validation. The BookController in Listing 11-17 is annotated with @Named; therefore it can be used in the JSF pages. The second annotation, @RequestScoped, defines the life duration of the bean; it lasts for the duration of the request. This backing bean contains one attribute book that will be used by the pages. book is the object that will get mapped to the form (newBook.xhtml page), displayed in viewBook.xhtml and persisted to the database.

Listing 11-17. The BookController Backing Bean Invoking the EJB

```
@Named
@RequestScoped
public class BookController {

  @Inject
  private BookEJB bookEJB;
  private Book book = new Book();

  public String doCreateBook() {
    bookEJB.createBook(book);

    FacesContext.getCurrentInstance().addMessage(null,
            new FacesMessage(FacesMessage.SEVERITY_INFO, "Book created",
            "The book" + book.getTitle() + " has been created with id=" + book.getId()));

    return "newBook.xhtml";
  }

  public void doFindBookById() {
    book = bookEJB.findBookById(book.getId());
  }

  // Getters, setters
}
```

All the business processing (creating and retrieving books) is done through the BookEJB. The backing bean is injected with a reference to the EJB using the @Inject annotation and has two methods that will be invoked by the pages.

- doCreateBook(): This method allows book creation by invoking the stateless EJB and passing the book attribute. If the persist succeeds, an INFO message is displayed on the page. Then the method returns the name of the page it needs to navigate to.

- doFindBookById(): This method is used by the viewBook.xhtml page to retrieve a book by its identifier using the stateless EJB.

Listing 11-17 shows the BookController backing bean. All the getters and setters in this snippet of code have been omitted for better readability but are required for the attribute book.

Writing the layout.xhtml Template

Both pages newBook.xhtml and viewBook.xhtml use the same template (layout.xhtml defined in Listing 11-18). As you can see in Figure 11-8 the template has a title, a header with a <h:link> *Create a book* to navigate to the newBook.xhtml, and a <h:messages> tag to display error and informational messages, as well as a footer.

Listing 11-18. The layout.xhtml Template Used by Both Pages

```
<!DOCTYPE html PUBLIC "-//W3C//DTD XHTML 1.0 Transitional//EN"
        "http://www.w3.org/TR/xhtml1/DTD/xhtml1-transitional.dtd">
<html xmlns="http://www.w3.org/1999/xhtml"
      xmlns:ui="http://xmlns.jcp.org/jsf/facelets"
      xmlns:h="http://xmlns.jcp.org/jsf/html">

<h:head>
  <title><ui:insert name="title">Default title</ui:insert></title>
</h:head>
<h:body>
  <h:link value="Create a book" outcome="newBook.xhtml"/>

  <h1><ui:insert name="title">Default title</ui:insert></h1>
  <hr/>

  <h:messages id="errors" infoStyle="color:blue" warnStyle="color:orange" ↵
                                                 errorStyle="color:red"/>

  <ui:insert name="content">Default content</ui:insert>

  <hr/>
  <h:outputText value="APress - Beginning Java EE 7" style="font-style: italic"/>
</h:body>
</html>
```

Writing the newBook.xhtml Page

The newBook.xhtml page is a single page that has a form at the top to enter the book data (title, price, description, number of pages, and illustrations), and a list of books at the bottom (see Figure 11-8). Each time a new book is created by clicking the button, the list is refreshed, showing the newly created book. Once the form is submitted, only the list portion of the page needs to be refreshed. For that we use Ajax.

The code in Listing 11-19 shows the top part of the page that represents the form. The bookController variable refers to the BookController backing bean responsible for all the business logic (see Listing 11-17). Book is the entity, and its attributes are accessed using expression language (#{bookController.book.title} binds to the title).

Listing 11-19. The Top Part of the newBook.xhtml Page

```
<!DOCTYPE html PUBLIC "-//W3C//DTD XHTML 1.0 Transitional//EN"
        "http://www.w3.org/TR/xhtml1/DTD/xhtml1-transitional.dtd">
<html xmlns="http://www.w3.org/1999/xhtml"
      xmlns:h="http://xmlns.jcp.org/jsf/html"
      xmlns:ui="http://xmlns.jcp.org/jsf/facelets"
      xmlns:f="http://xmlns.jcp.org/jsf/core">
```

```
<ui:composition template="layout.xhtml">

  <ui:define name="title">Create a new book</ui:define>

  <ui:define name="content">

    <h:form id="bookForm">

      <h:panelGrid columns="2">
        <h:outputLabel value="Title : "/>
        <h:inputText value="#{bookController.book.title}"/>

        <h:outputLabel value="Price : "/>
        <h:inputText value="#{bookController.book.price}"/>

        <h:outputLabel value="Description : "/>
        <h:inputTextarea value="#{bookController.book.description}" cols="16" rows="3"/>

        <h:outputLabel value="Number of pages : "/>
        <h:inputText value="#{bookController.book.nbOfPage}"/>

        <h:outputLabel value="Illustrations : "/>
        <h:selectBooleanCheckbox value="#{bookController.book.illustrations}"/>
      </h:panelGrid>

      <h:commandButton value="Create a book" action="#{bookController.doCreateBook}">
        <f:ajax execute="@form" render=":booklist :errors"/>
      </h:commandButton>

    </h:form>
    ...
```

The `<h:commandButton>` tag represents the button where the Ajax call is made. When the user clicks, the `<f:ajax>` tag passes all the form parameters using the @form shortcut (instead, it could have passed a list of all the components identifiers). The values of all the UI components that make up the form are then posted to the server. The doCreateBook() method of the backing bean is invoked, the new book is persisted, and the list of books is retrieved. If no exception is thrown, the name of the page to navigate to is returned: newBook.xhtml so the user stays on the same page. The rendering of this list on the client side is made asynchronously thanks to Ajax. The render element refers to the booklist ID as the identifier of the data table displaying all the books (see Listing 11-20) but also the errors ID which is defined in the layout.xhtml page (see Listing 11-18) in case a message needs to be displayed.

Listing 11-20. The Bottom Part of the newBook.xhtml Page

```
...
<hr/>
<h1>List of books</h1>

<h:dataTable id="booklist" value="#{bookEJB.findAllBooks()}" var="bk" border="1">
```

```
  <h:column>
    <f:facet name="header">
      <h:outputText value="Title"/>
    </f:facet>
    <h:link outcome="viewBook.xhtml?id=#{bk.id}" value="#{bk.title}"/>
  </h:column>

  <h:column>
    <f:facet name="header">
      <h:outputText value="Price"/>
    </f:facet>
    <h:outputText value="#{bk.price}"/>
  </h:column>

  </h:dataTable>
 </ui:define>

</ui:composition>
</html>
```

Listing 11-20 shows the bottom part of the page. To display the list of all books, the page uses a <h:dataTable> whose values come straight from the BookEJB (instead of the BookController) thanks to the @Named annotation (see Listing11-16). The <h:dataTable> tag binds to the bookEJB.findAllBooks() method that returns a List<Book> and declares the variable bk to iterate through the list. Then, inside the <h:dataTable> tag, you can use expressions such as #{bk.price} to get the price attribute of a book and display. The <h:link> tag creates an HTML link that, when clicked, navigates to the viewBook.xhtml passing the identifier of the book (viewBook.xhtml?id=#{bk.id}).

Writing the viewBook.xhtml Page

The viewBook.xhtml page allows you to view the details of a book (title, price, description, number of pages, and illustrations). It uses the bookmarkability functionality of JSF 2, meaning that you can access any book detail just by changing the URL with an HTTP GET, thanks to ViewAction.

You can see in Listing 11-21 that the page binds the id parameter (e.g., viewBook.xhtml?id=123) to the #{bookController.book.id} attribute. Once the identifier is bound, the action #{bookController.doFindBookById} is invoked. The BookController.doFindBookById method (Listing 11-17) calls the EJB and gets the book from the database, and then the page can bind the book attributes (e.g., #{bookController.book.title}) to output text components.

Listing 11-21. The viewBook.xhtml Page

```
<!DOCTYPE html PUBLIC "-//W3C//DTD XHTML 1.0 Transitional//EN"
        "http://www.w3.org/TR/xhtml1/DTD/xhtml1-transitional.dtd">
<html xmlns="http://www.w3.org/1999/xhtml"
      xmlns:h="http://xmlns.jcp.org/jsf/html"
      xmlns:ui="http://xmlns.jcp.org/jsf/facelets"
      xmlns:f="http://xmlns.jcp.org/jsf/core">

<ui:composition template="layout.xhtml">
```

```
<f:metadata>
  <f:viewParam name="id" value="#{bookController.book.id}"/>
  <f:viewAction action="#{bookController.doFindBookById}"/>
</f:metadata>

<ui:define name="title">View a book</ui:define>

<ui:define name="content">

  <h:panelGrid columns="2">
    <h:outputLabel value="Title : "/>
    <h:outputText value="#{bookController.book.title}"/>

    <h:outputLabel value="Price : "/>
    <h:outputText value="#{bookController.book.price}"/>

    <h:outputLabel value="Description : "/>
    <h:outputText value="#{bookController.book.description}" cols="16" rows="3"/>

    <h:outputLabel value="Number of pages : "/>
    <h:outputText value="#{bookController.book.nbOfPage}"/>

    <h:outputLabel value="Illustrations : "/>
    <h:selectBooleanCheckbox value="#{bookController.book.illustrations}"/>
  </h:panelGrid>

</ui:define>

</ui:composition>
</html>
```

Compiling and Packaging with Maven

The web application needs to be compiled and packaged in a war file (`<packaging>war</packaging>`). The pom.xml shown in Listing 11-22 declares all the dependencies necessary for compiling code (`glassfish-embedded-all`) and uses version 1.7 of the JDK.

Listing 11-22. Maven pom.xml File for Compiling and Packaging the Web Application

```
<?xml version="1.0" encoding="UTF-8"?>
<project xmlns="http://maven.apache.org/POM/4.0.0" ⮕
         xmlns:xsi="http://www.w3.org/2001/XMLSchema-instance" ⮕
         xsi:schemaLocation="http://maven.apache.org/POM/4.0.0 ⮕
         http://maven.apache.org/xsd/maven-4.0.0.xsd">
  <modelVersion>4.0.0</modelVersion>

  <parent>
    <artifactId>chapter11</artifactId>
    <groupId>org.agoncal.book.javaee7</groupId>
    <version>1.0</version>
  </parent>
```

```xml
<groupId>org.agoncal.book.javaee7.chapter11</groupId>
<artifactId>chapter11</artifactId>
<version>1.0</version>
<packaging>war</packaging>

<dependencies>
  <dependency>
    <groupId>org.glassfish.main.extras</groupId>
    <artifactId>glassfish-embedded-all</artifactId>
    <version>4.0</version>
    <scope>provided</scope>
  </dependency>
</dependencies>

<build>
  <plugins>
    <plugin>
      <artifactId>maven-compiler-plugin</artifactId>
      <version>2.5.1</version>
      <configuration>
        <source>1.7</source>
        <target>1.7</target>
      </configuration>
    </plugin>
    <plugin>
      <artifactId>maven-war-plugin</artifactId>
      <version>2.2</version>
      <configuration>
        <failOnMissingWebXml>false</failOnMissingWebXml>
      </configuration>
    </plugin>
  </plugins>
</build>
</project>
```

To compile and package the classes, open a command-line interpreter in the directory that contains the pom.xml file and enter the following Maven command:

```
$ mvn package
```

Go to the target directory to find the chapter11-1.0.war file. Open it, and you will see that it contains the Book entity, the BookEJB, the BookController backing bean, the three deployment descriptors (persistence.xml, faces-config.xml, and beans.xml), and the two web pages (newBook.xhtml and viewBook.xhtml).

Deploying on GlassFish

Once you have packaged the web application, it needs to be deployed into GlassFish. Ensure GlassFish is up and running. Open a command line, go to the target directory where the chapter11-1.0.war file is located, and enter the following:

```
$ asadmin deploy chapter11-1.0.war
```

If the deployment is successful, the following command should return the name of the deployed application and its type. There are two types: web, because it's a web application, and ejb, because the application contains an EJB.

```
$ asadmin list-components
chapter11-1.0 <ejb, web>
```

Running the Example

Now that the application is deployed, open your browser and go to the following URL:

```
http://localhost:8080/chapter11-1.0/newBook.faces
```

The browser is pointing to newBook.faces, not newBook.xhtml, because of the default mapping of the FacesServlet. With the .faces extension, JSF knows it has to process the page before rendering it. Once the newBook page shows up, enter some data, and click the submit button. The book is persisted in the database and appears in the list at the bottom of the page.

If you take a web developer tool to check what happens on the network between the browser and GlassFish, you'll see Ajax in action. The rendering is a partial XML response instead of the entire HTML page. The partial response from the server contains the XHTML portion of the page to be updated. The JavaScript looks for the errors and booklist elements of the page and applies the changes needed (updating the DOM). The partial response on Listing 11-23 is self-explanatory; it specifies that an update has to be made to the components identified by errors and booklist (<update id="booklist">). The body of the <update> element is the fragment of XHTML that has to override the actual data table. Of course, this XML is handled automatically by the JSF Ajax handlers—the developer doesn't need to do anything with it manually.

Listing 11-23. The Partial Response Received by the Browser

```xml
<?xml version='1.0' encoding='UTF-8'?>
<partial-response>
  <changes>
    <update id="errors">
      <![CDATA[
      <ul id="errors"><li style="color:blue">Book created</li></ul>
      ]]>
    </update>
    <update id="booklist">
      <![CDATA[
      <table id="booklist" border="1">
        <thead>
          <tr>
            <th scope="col">Title</th>
            <th scope="col">Price</th>
          </tr>
        </thead>
        <tbody>
          <tr>
            <td><a href="/chapter11-1.0/viewBook.faces?id=54">Java EE 6</a></td>
            <td>31.49</td>
          </tr>
```

```
      <tr>
        <td><a href="/chapter11-1.0/viewBook.faces?id=1">Harry Potter </a></td>
        <td>19.79</td>
      </tr>
      <tr>
        <td><a href="/chapter11-1.0/viewBook.faces?id=51">H2G2</a></td>
        <td>23.99</td>
      </tr>
    </tbody>
  </table>
  ]]>
  </update>
 </changes>
</partial-response>
```

Summary

Chapter 10 examined the graphical aspect of JSF, and this chapter focused on its dynamic side. JSF follows the MVC design pattern, and its specification ranges from creating user interfaces with components to processing data with backing beans.

Backing beans are at the heart of JSF as they are used to process business logic, call EJBs, databases, and so on, as well as navigating between pages. They have a scope and a life cycle (resembling stateless session beans), and they declare methods and properties that are bound to UI components using expression language. Annotations and configuration by exception have greatly simplified JSF 2.2, as most of the XML configuration is now optional.

This chapter then showed how conversion and validation are handled on any input component. JSF defines a set of converters and validators for most common cases, but it also allows you to easily create and register custom ones. Integration with Bean Validation is natural and you don't need any plumbing code to integrate it with JSF.

While the Ajax technique has been around for some years, JSF brings standard support, allowing web pages to invoke backing beans asynchronously. It defines a standard JavaScript library, and the developer doesn't need to write scripts but instead uses functions to refresh portions of pages.

The next four chapters will focus on how to interoperate with systems through messaging, SOAP web services, and RESTful web services using XML or JSon.

CHAPTER 12

■ ■ ■

XML and JSon Processing

XML (eXtensible Markup Language) has been used in the Java EE platform since the beginning of deployment descriptors and metadata information. We deal with XML in `persistence.xml`, `beans.xml` or `ejb-jar.xml` files. That's often how Java developers first entered the rich world of XML. But we quickly discovered that there was more to XML than just deploying a web application or an EJB.

XML is an industry standard defined by the World Wide Web Consortium (W3C). Although it is not tied to any programming language or software vendor, it has solved the problem of data independence and interoperability. Because XML is extensible, platform-independent, and supports internationalization, it became the preferred language to interchange data among software components, systems, and enterprises (e.g., by leveraging SOAP Web Services that will be described in Chapter 14).

On the other hand, JSON (JavaScript Object Notation) originated with JavaScript for representing simple data structures in a less verbose manner than XML. To be precise, the JSON format is often used for serializing and transmitting structured data over a network connection. It rapidly became so popular that today recent web browsers have native JSON encoding/decoding support. But, in addition to its relationship with browsers and JavaScript, JSON works nicely as a data interchange format (e.g., extensively used in RESTful Web Services; described in Chapter 15).

In this chapter, I will describe both XML and JSON formats focusing on the document structure and the APIs to manipulate these structures. The XML world is richer, so you will notice that several specifications help you in parsing, validating or binding XML to Java objects. It is so ingrained in our ecosystem that most of these XML specifications belong to Java SE. JSON is a relative newcomer in the Java platform and therefore has less standard support in Java SE/EE.

Understanding XML

The eXtensible Markup Language (XML), derived from the Standard Generalized Markup Language (SGML), was originally envisioned as a language for defining new document formats for the World Wide Web. XML can actually be considered to be a meta-language as it is used to construct other languages. Today it provides the basis for a wide variety of industry specific languages such as Mathematical Markup Language (MathML), Voice Markup Language (VXML), or OpenOffice and LibreOffice (OpenDocument).

XML is used to create human-readable structured data and self-describing documents that conform to a set of rules. XML parsers can then validate the structure of any XML document, given the rules of its language. XML documents are text-based structures described using markup tags (words surrounded by '<' and '>').

XML Document

Listing 12-1 shows an XML document representing a customer's purchase order for the CD-BookStore application (see Chapter 1). Note that this document is easily readable as well as being structured and therefore can be understood by an external system. In this case it describes information about the purchase order, the customer who made the order, the items bought by the customer as well as the credit card information used to pay the order.

Listing 12-1. An XML Document Representing a Purchase Order

```xml
<?xml version="1.0" encoding="UTF-8" ?>
<order id="1234" date="05/06/2013">
  <customer first_name="James" last_name="Rorrison">
    <email>j.rorri@me.com</email>
    <phoneNumber>+44 1234 1234</phoneNumber>
</customer>
<content>
    <order_line item="H2G2" quantity="1">
      <unit_price>23.5</unit_price>
    </order_line>
    <order_line item="Harry Potter" quantity="2">
      <unit_price>34.99</unit_price>
    </order_line>
  </content>
  <credit_card number="1357" expiry_date="10/13" control_number="234" type="Visa"/>
</order>
```

The document begins with an optional XML declaration (specifying which version of XML and character encoding is being used by the document) and then is composed of both markups and content. Markups, also referred to as tags, describe the structure of the document, allowing you to easily send and receive data, or transform data from one format to another.

As you can see in Table 12-1, the XML terminology is quite simple. Despite this simplicity and readability, XML can be used to describe any kind of document, data structure, or deployment descriptor when it comes to Java EE.

Table 12-1. *XML Terminology*

Terminology	Definition
Unicode character	An XML document is a string of characters represented by almost every legal Unicode character
Markup and content	The Unicode characters are divided into markup and content. Markups begin with the character < and end with a > (<email>) and what is not markup is considered to be content (such as j.rorri@me.com)
Tag	Tags come in three flavors of markups: start-tags (<email>), end-tags (</email>) and empty-element tags (<email/>)
Element	An element begins with a start-tag and ends with a matching end-tag (or consists only of an empty-element tag). It can also include other elements, which are called child elements. An example of an element is <email>j.rorri@me.com</email>
Attribute	An attribute consists of a name/value pair that exists within a start-tag or empty-element tag. In the following example item is the attribute of the order_line tag: <order_line item="H2G2">
XML Declaration	XML documents may begin by declaring some information about themselves, as in the following example: <?xml version="1.0" encoding="UTF-8" ?>

Validating with XML Schema

The XML terminology is so broad that it allows you to write anything you want with XML and declare your own language. In fact, you can write so many things that your XML structure can become meaningless if you don't define a grammar. This grammar can be set using an XML Schema Definition (XSD). By having a grammar attached to your XML document, you can have any validating XML parser enforce the rules of a particular XML dialect. This removes a tremendous burden from your application's code as the parser will automatically validate your XML document.

■ **Note** The first and earliest language definition mechanism is the document type definition (DTD). Still being used in several legacy frameworks, the DTD mechanism has been replaced by XSD due to DTD's numerous limitations. One basic and major limitation is that a DTD is not itself a valid XML document. Therefore, it cannot be handled by XML parsing tools, just like XML itself. More problematic, DTDs are quite limited in their ability to constrain the structure and content of XML documents.

An XML Schema Definition (XSD) is an XML-based grammar declaration used to describe the structure and content of an XML document. For instance, the schema in Listing 12-2 can be used to specify the XML document described in Listing 12-1, giving it an extra meaning: "This is not just a text file, it's a structured document representing an order with items and customer details." During document interchange, the XSD describes the contract between the producer and consumer because it describes what constitutes a valid XML message between the two parties.

Listing 12-2. XSD Describing the Purchase Order XML Document

```xml
<?xml version="1.0" encoding="UTF-8" ?>
<xs:schema version="1.0" xmlns:xs="http://www.w3.org/2001/XMLSchema">

  <xs:element name="order" type="order"/>

  <xs:complexType name="creditCard">
    <xs:sequence/>
    <xs:attribute name="number" type="xs:string"/>
    <xs:attribute name="expiry_date" type="xs:string"/>
    <xs:attribute name="control_number" type="xs:int"/>
    <xs:attribute name="type" type="xs:string"/>
  </xs:complexType>

  <xs:complexType name="customer">
    <xs:sequence>
      <xs:element name="email" type="xs:string" minOccurs="0"/>
      <xs:element name="phoneNumber" type="xs:string" minOccurs="0"/>
    </xs:sequence>
    <xs:attribute name="first_name" type="xs:string"/>
    <xs:attribute name="last_name" type="xs:string"/>
  </xs:complexType>
```

```xml
<xs:complexType name="order">
  <xs:sequence>
    <xs:element name="customer" type="customer" minOccurs="0"/>
    <xs:element name="content" minOccurs="0">
      <xs:complexType>
        <xs:sequence>
          <xs:element name="order_line" type="orderLine" minOccurs="0" ↪
                      maxOccurs="unbounded"/>
        </xs:sequence>
      </xs:complexType>
    </xs:element>
    <xs:element name="credit_card" type="creditCard" minOccurs="0"/>
  </xs:sequence>
  <xs:attribute name="id" type="xs:long"/>
  <xs:attribute name="date" type="xs:dateTime"/>
</xs:complexType>

<xs:complexType name="orderLine">
  <xs:sequence>
    <xs:element name="unit_price" type="xs:double" minOccurs="0"/>
  </xs:sequence>
  <xs:attribute name="item" type="xs:string"/>
  <xs:attribute name="quantity" type="xs:int"/>
</xs:complexType>
</xs:schema>
```

As you can see in Listing 12-2, the XSD allows a very precise definition of both simple (`<xs:attribute name="expiry_date" type="xs:string"/>`) and complex data types (`<xs:complexType name="creditCard">`), and even allows types to inherit properties from other types. The purchase order schema consists of a variety of subelements, most notably elements, complex types, and attributes that determine the appearance of the content. Thanks to XSD, elements and attributes become strongly typed and have datatype information associated with them. Such strongly typed XML can now be mapped to objects using technologies such as JAXB, which you'll see later in this chapter.

Table 12-2 only lists a subset of the XSD elements and attributes. XSD is a much richer language, but it's not the goal of this book to be an exhaustive XSD resource. If you want to know more about XSD, its structure, and its datatypes, you should check the related W3C website.

Table 12-2. XSD Elements and Attributes

Element	Description
schema	Is the root element of every XML Schema. It may contain some attributes such as the schema version
xmlns	Each element in the schema has a default prefix xs: (or sometimes xsd: although any prefix can be used) which is associated with the XML Schema namespace (xmlsn) through the declaration, xmlns:xsd="http://www.w3.org/2001/XMLSchema"
element	Elements are declared using the element element. For example, order is defined as an element and appears as <order id="1234" date="11/08/2013" total_amount="93.48"> in the XML document
type	An element can be of a simple type such as string, decimal, long, double and so on (type="xs:long") or a complex type (type="customer")
minOccurs, maxOccurs	Define the minimum and maximum occurrence of a type. This value may be a positive integer or the term unbounded to indicate there is no maximum number of occurrences
complexType	It describes a complex type with elements, sub-elements, and attributes. A complexType element can contain another complexType. For example, the complex type order contains a complexType
sequence	An element may include other elements, which are called child elements. The sequence element specifies that the child elements must appear in a sequence. Each child element can occur from 0 to any number of times
attribute	A complex type may have one or more attributes that are defined by attribute elements. The orderLine type has two attributes; item and quantity
choice	Used to indicate only one set of elements can be present in the containing element
complexContent	A complex type can extend or restrict another complex type using complexContent element
extension	The extension element extends an existing simpleType or complexType element

Once you have an XML document and its associated XML Schema Definition you can use a parser to do the validation for you. Parsers come in two major flavors: DOM and SAX.

Parsing with SAX and DOM

Before a document can be used, it must be parsed and validated by an XML parser. The parser, a.k.a. processor, analyzes the markup and makes the data contained in the XML available to the application that needs to use it. Most XML parsers can be used in two distinct modes. One mode is the Document Object Model (DOM) that reads in an entire XML data source and constructs a treelike representation of it in memory. The other mode is an event-based model called the Simple API for XML (SAX) that reads in the XML data source and makes callbacks to the application whenever it encounters a distinct section (the end of an element).

DOM

The Document Object Model (DOM) API is generally an easy API to use. It provides a familiar tree structure of objects enabling the application to rearrange nodes, add or delete contents as needed.

DOM is generally easy to implement, but constructing the DOM requires reading the entire XML structure and holding the object tree in memory. Therefore, it is better to use DOM with small XML data structures in situations in which speed is not of paramount importance to the application and random access to the entire content of the document is essential. There are also other technologies such as JDOM and DOM4J that provide a simple object-oriented XML-programming API for applications with less complexity.

SAX

The streaming model in parsers is used for local processing of resources where random access to the other parts of the data in the resource is not required. The Simple API for XML (SAX) is based on a push parsing streaming model in which data is pushed to the client reader application.

SAX is an event-driven, serial-access mechanism that does element-by-element processing. Using a SAX parser, a SAX event is fired whenever the end of an XML element has been encountered. The event includes the name of the element that has just ended. The SAX handler is a state machine that can only operate on the portion of the XML document that has already been parsed.

SAX is the fastest parsing method for XML, and it is appropriate for handling large documents that could not be read into memory all at once. It tends to be preferred for server-side, high-performance applications and data filters that do not require an in-memory representation of the data. Though, it places greater demands on the software developer's skills.

Querying with XPath

XPath is a query language designed to query XML structures that is used by a variety of other XML standards, including XSLT, XPointer, and XQuery. It defines the syntax for creating expressions, which are evaluated against an XML document.

XPath expressions can represent a node, a boolean, a number, or a string. The most common type of XPath expression is a location path, which represents a node. For example, the XPath expression / is an expression that represents all nodes in the XML document from the root. Below is an XPath expression representing all the unit_price nodes whose value is greater than 20 (see the purchase order XML in Listing 12-1):

```
//content/order_line[unit_price>=20]/unit_price
```

Also, XPath has a set of built-in functions that enable you to develop very complex expressions. The following expression returns the children text node of unit_price elements:

```
//content/order_line[unit_price>=20]/unit_price/text()
```

XQuery is another query language that is designed to query collections of XML data using XPath expressions. XQuery is syntactically similar to SQL, with a set of keywords including FOR, LET, WHERE, ORDER BY or RETURN. The following is a simple XQuery expression that is using the doc() function (that reads the order.xml document) to return all order_line children nodes which have a quantity greater than 1 and unit_price less than 50;

```
for $orderLine in doc("order.xml")//content/order_line[@quantity>1]
where $orderLine/unit_price < 50
return $orderLine/unit_price/text()
```

There are more complex queries you can do with XQuery like joining XML documents, making complex conditions or ordering the result on an element.

In some cases, extracting information from an XML document using an API may be too cumbersome mostly because the criteria for finding the data are complex and a bunch of code is needed to iterate through the nodes. XML query languages such as XPath 1.0 and XQuery provide rich mechanisms for extracting information from XML documents.

Transforming with XSLT

A key advantage of XML over other data formats is the ability to transform an XML document from one vocabulary to another, in a generic manner. For example you can render an XML document into a print-friendly format or into a web page. The technology that enables this translation is the eXtensible Stylesheet Language Transformations (XSLT).

Simply stated, XSLT provides a framework for transforming the structure of an XML document by combining it with an XSL stylesheet to produce an output document. All you have to do is to create an XSL stylesheet that contains a set of transformation instructions for transforming a source tree into a result tree. Then an XSLT processor will transform the source document by associating patterns within the source XML tree with XSL stylesheet templates that are to be applied to them.

A pattern is an XPath expression that is matched against elements in the source tree. On a successful match, a template is instantiated to create part of the result tree. In constructing the result tree, elements from the source can be filtered and reordered, and arbitrary structure can be added.

The XSLT stylesheet in Listing 12-3 converts the order.xml document shown in Listing 12-1 into an XHTML Web page showing a table of sold items whose price is greater than 30.

Listing 12-3. XSLT Stylesheet for Purchase Order XML Document

```xml
<?xml version="1.0" encoding="UTF-8"?>
<xsl:stylesheet version="2.0" xmlns:xsl="http://www.w3.org/1999/XSL/Transform">
  <xsl:template match="/">
    <html>
      <body>
        <h2>Sold Items</h2>
        <table border="1">
          <tr>
            <th>Title</th>
            <th>Quantity</th>
            <th>Unit Price</th>
          </tr>

          <xsl:for-each select="order/content/order_line">
            <tr>
              <td>
                <xsl:value-of select="@item"/>
              </td>
              <td>
                <xsl:value-of select="@quantity"/>
              </td>

              <xsl:choose>
                <xsl:when test="unit_price > 30">
                  <td bgcolor="#FF0000">
                    <xsl:value-of select="unit_price"/>
                  </td>
                </xsl:when>
                <xsl:otherwise>
                  <td>
                    <xsl:value-of select="unit_price"/>
                  </td>
                </xsl:otherwise>
              </xsl:choose>
```

```
      </tr>
    </xsl:for-each>

    </table>
   </body>
  </html>
 </xsl:template>
</xsl:stylesheet>
```

The generic XSLT APIs in the `javax.xml.transform` package are used for compiling stylesheet instructions, and performing a transformation from XML source to a XML result. XSLT can also be used with the SAX APIs to convert data to XML.

XML Specifications Overview

XML specification became a W3C (World Wide Web Consortium) recommendation in 1998, after which, several XML specifications like XSLT, XPath, XML Schema, and XQuery were introduced and became standard in W3C. Java platform-independent code and XML platform-independent data were two complementary points that led to standardization and simplification of various Java APIs for XML. This has made developing XML-aware applications in Java much simpler.

A Brief History of XML Specifications

The W3C is a consortium that is known for developing and maintaining web technologies like HTML, XHTML, RDF, or CSS. But, W3C is also the central organ for XML and all the related XML technologies like XML Schema, XSLT, XPATH, and DOM.

Development of XML (Extensible Markup Language) started in 1996 by the XML Working Group of the W3C and led to a W3C recommendation in February 1998. However, the technology was not entirely new. It was based on SGML (Standard Generalized Markup Language), which had been developed in the early 1980s and became an ISO standard in 1986.

XSD (XML Schema) offers the facilities to describe the structure of XML documents in an `.xsd` file. This structure constrains the contents of XML documents and therefore, can be used to validate XML documents. XSD is one of several XML schema languages and it was the first separate schema language for XML, published as a W3C recommendation in 2001.

XSLT (EXtensible Stylesheet) is one of the first XML specifications, influenced by functional languages and by text-based pattern matching languages, to transform XML documents. Its most direct predecessor is DSSSL (Document Style Semantics and Specification Language), which did for SGML what XSLT does for XML. XSLT 1.0 became part of W3C in 1999 and the project led to the creation of XPath. Xalan, Saxon, and AltovaXML are some of several XSLT processors available for XML transformation.

XPath 1.0 is a query language for addressing nodes in an XML document. It was introduced and accepted as a W3C Recommendation in 1999. It was originally motivated by a desire to provide a common syntax between XPointer and XSLT. It can be directly used inside Java or it can be embedded in languages such as XSLT, XQuery or XML Schema.

The mission of the XML Query project is to provide flexible query facilities to extract data from documents. The development of XQuery 1.0 by the XML Query Working Group was closely coordinated with the development of XSLT 2.0 by the XSL Working Group; the two groups shared responsibility for XPath 2.0, which is a subset of XQuery 1.0. XQuery 1.0 became a W3C Recommendation on January 23, 2007.

The Document Object Model (DOM) is a tree-based interface for representing and interacting with contents, structures and styles in HTML, XHTML, and XML documents. At the beginning, DOM was an effort to develop a standard for scripting languages used in browsers. The current release of the DOM specification, DOM Level 3, supports XPath as well as an interface for serializing documents into XML.

The Simple API for XML (SAX) is the first widely adopted API for XML in Java. It is a streaming, event-based interface to parse XML data. SAX was originally implemented in Java, but is now supported by nearly all major programming languages.

From the start, the development of XML specifications has been intertwined with a focus to improve the usability of XML.

Table 12-3 contains some of the specifications for XML technologies.

Table 12-3. *W3C XML Specifications*

Specification	Version	URL
Extensible Markup Language (XML)	1.1	http://www.w3.org/TR/xml11/
XML Schema	1.0	http://www.w3.org/TR/xmlschema-1
EXtensible Stylesheet (XSLT)	1.0	http://www.w3.org/TR/xslt
XML Path (XPath)	1.0	http://www.w3.org/TR/xpath
Document Object Model (DOM)	level 3	http://www.w3.org/TR/DOM-Level-3-Core/
Simple API for XML (SAX)	2.0.2	http://sax.sourceforge.net/

XML Specifications in Java

The XML ecosystem was created by the W3C. But because it works hand in hand with Java, there are several XML-related specifications that were created within the JCP. Examples include from processing XML to binding documents into Java objects.

JAXP (Java Architecture for XML Processing) is a low-level specification (JSR 206) that gives you the possibility to process XML in a very flexible manner; allowing you to use SAX, DOM, or XSLT. It is the API used under the hood for JAXB or StAX.

The JAXB (Java Architecture for XML Binding) specification provides a set of APIs and annotations for representing XML documents as Java artifacts, allowing developers to work with Java objects representing XML documents. JAXB (JSR 222) facilitates unmarshalling XML documents into objects and marshalling objects back into XML documents. Even if JAXB can be used for any XML purpose, it is tightly integrated with JAX-WS (see Chapter 14).

StAX (Streaming API for XML) version 1.0 (JSR 173) is an API to read and write XML documents. Its main focus is to gather the benefits of tree-based APIs (DOM parsers) and event-based APIs (SAX parsers). DOM parsers allow random, unlimited access to the document, while SAX parsers provide a smaller memory footprint and have reduced processor requirements.

Table 12-4 lists all the Java specifications related to XML.

Table 12-4. *XML-related Specifications*

Specification	Version	JSR	URL
JAXP	1.3	206	http://jcp.org/en/jsr/detail?id=206
JAXB	2.2	222	http://jcp.org/en/jsr/detail?id=222
StAX	1.0	173	http://jcp.org/en/jsr/detail?id=173

Reference Implementations

The primary goal of a Reference Implementation (RI) is to support the development of the specification and to validate it. StAX RI is the reference implementation for the JSR-173 specification which is based on a standard pull parser streaming model. StAX has been included in JDK since version 1.6 and can be downloaded separately for JDK 1.4 and 1.5. The RI for the JAXP specification is also integrated into Java SE as well as Metro, which is the reference implementation for JAXB. Metro is a production-quality implementation of JAXB that is used directly in a number of Oracle products.

Java Architecture for XML Processing

Java Architecture for XML Processing (JAXP) is an API that provides a common, implementation-independent interface for creating and using the SAX, DOM, and XSLT APIs in Java.

Prior to JAXP, there were different incompatible versions of XML parsers and transformers from different vendors. JAXP has provided an abstraction layer on top of these vendor-specific XML API implementations to parse and transform XML resources.

Note that JAXP doesn't use a different mechanism to parse and transform XML documents. Instead, applications can use it to access the underlying XML APIs indirectly in a common manner. Applications can then replace a vendor's implementation with another.

Using JAXP, you can parse XML documents with SAX or DOM as the underlying strategy, or transform them to a new format using XSLT. The JAXP API architecture is depicted in Figure 12-1.

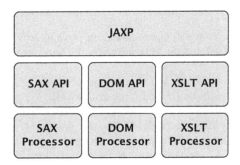

Figure 12-1. *JAXP Architecture*

JAXP consists of four packages summarized in Table 12-5. In these packages you'll find interfaces and classes to parse and transform XML data in a generic way.

Table 12-5. *The JAXP Packages*

Package	Description
`javax.xml.parsers`	A common interface to DOM and SAX parsers
`org.w3c.dom`	The generic DOM API for Java
`org.xml.sax`	Defines the interfaces used for the SAX parser
`javax.xml.transform`	The XSLT APIs to transform XML into other forms

Configuring JAXP

As JAXP is flexible, you can configure it to use any processing implementation you need. But you can always use the defaults as the JAXP reference implementation uses Xerces as the default XML parser and Xalan as the default XSLT processor to transform XML documents.

Imagine a scenario in which there are more than one JAXP-compliant implementations in your classpath. In this case, you have to tell JAXP which API to use. Depending if your application either runs in a standalone client mode or an application server mode, you can provide your application with an XML parser or transformer through a property file. For example, putting a `jaxp.properties` file (a standard file following the `java.util.Properties` format) in lib subdirectory of the JRE directory causes the JAXP implementation to use the specified factories. The following is the content of a `jaxp.properties` file that defines which DOM builder, SAX parser, and XSLT transformer is to be used:

```
javax.xml.parsers.DocumentBuilderFactory=org.apache.xerces.jaxp.DocumentBuilderFactoryImpl
javax.xml.parsers.SAXParserFactory=org.apache.xerces.jaxp.SAXParserFactoryImpl
javax.xml.transform.TransformerFactory=org.apache.xalan.processor.TransformerFactoryImpl
```

The other way is to configure Java system properties before running the application. For example, the following system property informs the JVM to use Xerces as XML parser:

```
-Djavax.xml.parsers.DocumentBuilderFactory=org.apache.xerces.jaxp.DocumentBuilderFactoryImpl
```

The main system properties that can be modified to introduce new parsers or transformers are listed in Table 12-6.

Table 12-6. *System Properties for XML Parser/Transformer Configuration*

System Property	Description
javax.xml.parsers.DocumentBuilderFactory	Sets the DOM builder
javax.xml.parsers.SAXParserFactory	Configures the SAX parser
javax.xml.transform.TransformerFactory	Determines which XSLT implementation to use

JAXP with SAX

SAX is known for its low memory requirements and fast processing functionality. SAX is an event-driven, serial access mechanism to parse XML documents. You have to provide the parser with callback methods that are invoked by the parser as it reads the XML document. For example, the SAX parser calls a method in your application each time an element is reached and calls a different method when a text node is encountered.

The way in which you process the current element in an XML document without maintaining any state from previously parsed elements is called state-independent processing. This is the most suited model for processing XML resources with SAX parsers. The other model is state-dependent parsing, which is handled with pull parsers like StAX parsers.

Listing 12-4 shows a class that parses the `order.xml` document using the SAX event-model. The `SaxParsing` class extends `DefaultHandler` which is required for different parsing needs and implements four different handlers (`ContentHandler`, `ErrorHandler`, `DTDHandler`, and `EntityResolver`). The `SAXParserFactory` configures and creates a SAX parser instance. As mentioned earlier, it is possible to manually configure the system property `javax.xml.parsers.SAXParserFactory` to use a third-party SAX parser. The `SAXParser` wraps a `SAXReader` object which can be referenced by `getXMLReader()`. Therefore, when the SAX parser's `parse()` method is invoked, the reader invokes one of several handler methods implemented by the application (e.g. the `startElement` method).

Listing 12-4. SAX Parser Parsing the Purchase Order Document

```java
public class SaxParsing extends DefaultHandler {

  private List<OrderLine> orderLines = new ArrayList<>();
  private OrderLine orderLine;
  private Boolean dealingWithUnitPrice = false;
  private StringBuffer unitPriceBuffer;

  public List<OrderLine> parseOrderLines() {

    try {
      File xmlDocument = Paths.get("src/main/resources/order.xml").toFile();

      // SAX Factory
      SAXParserFactory factory = SAXParserFactory.newInstance();
      SAXParser saxParser = factory.newSAXParser();

      // Parsing the document
      saxParser.parse(xmlDocument, this);
    } catch (SAXException | IOException | ParserConfigurationException e) {
      e.printStackTrace();
    }
    return orderLines;
  }

  @Override
  public void startElement(String namespaceURI, String localName, String qualifiedName, ↪
                                      Attributes attrs) throws SAXException {

    switch (qualifiedName) {
      // Getting the order_line node
      case "order_line":
        orderLine = new OrderLine();
        for (int i = 0; i < attrs.getLength(); i++) {
          switch (attrs.getLocalName(i)) {
            case "item":
              orderLine.setItem(attrs.getValue(i));
              break;
            case "quantity":
              orderLine.setQuantity(Integer.valueOf(attrs.getValue(i)));
              break;
          }
        }
        break;
      case "unit_price":
        dealingWithUnitPrice = true;
        unitPriceBuffer = new StringBuffer();
        break;
    }
  }
}
```

```java
    @Override
    public void characters(char[] ch, int start, int length) throws SAXException {
        if (dealingWithUnitPrice)
            unitPriceBuffer.append(ch, start, length);
    }

    @Override
    public void endElement(String namespaceURI, String localName, String qualifiedName) ➥
                                                            throws SAXException {

        switch (qualifiedName) {
          case "order_line":
            orderLines.add(orderLine);
            break;
          case "unit_price":
            orderLine.setUnitPrice(Double.valueOf(unitPriceBuffer.toString()));
            dealingWithUnitPrice = false;
            break;
        }
    }
}
```

The ContentHandler interface handles the basic document-related events like the start and end of elements with startDocument, endDocument, startElement, and endElement methods. These methods are called when the starting or ending of XML document or tags occur. In Listing 12-4 the startElement method checks that the element is either order_line or unit_price to either create an OrderLine object or get the unit price value. The ContentHandler interface also defines the method characters(), which is invoked when the parser encounters a chunk of characters in an XML element (in Listing 12-4 the characters() method buffers the unit price of each item).

To ensure error handling while parsing an XML document, an ErrorHandler can be registered to the SAXReader. The ErrorHandler interface methods (warning, error, and fatalError) are invoked in response to various types of parsing errors.

The DTDHandler interface defines methods to handle DTD-related events. The parser uses the DTDHandler to report notation and unparsed entity declarations to the application. This is useful when processing a DTD to recognize and act on declarations for an unparsed entity.

JAXP with DOM

JAXP provides interfaces to parse and modify the XML data using DOM APIs. The entry point is the javax.xml.parsers. DocumentBuilderFactory class. It is used to produce a DocumentBuilder instance as shown in Listing 12-5. Using one of the parse methods in DocumentBuilder, you can create a tree structure of the XML data in an org.w3c.dom.Document instance. This tree contains tree nodes (such as elements and text nodes), which are implementations of the org.w3c. dom.Node interface. Alternatively, to create an empty Document object, you can use the newDocument() method on the DocumentBuilder instance.

Listing 12-5. DOM Parser Parsing the Purchase Order Document

```java
public class DomParsing {

  public List<OrderLine> parseOrderLines() {

    List<OrderLine> orderLines = new ArrayList<>();
```

```
    try {
      File xmlDocument = Paths.get("src/main/resources/order.xml").toFile();

      // DOM Factory
      DocumentBuilderFactory factory = DocumentBuilderFactory.newInstance();

      // Parsing the document
      DocumentBuilder documentBuilder = factory.newDocumentBuilder();
      Document document = documentBuilder.parse(xmlDocument);

      // Getting the order_line node
      NodeList orderLinesNode = document.getElementsByTagName("order_line");
      for (int i = 0; i < orderLinesNode.getLength(); i++) {
        Element orderLineNode = (Element) orderLinesNode.item(i);
        OrderLine orderLine = new OrderLine();
        orderLine.setItem(orderLineNode.getAttribute("item"));
        orderLine.setQuantity(Integer.valueOf(orderLineNode.getAttribute("quantity")));

        Node unitPriceNode = orderLineNode.getChildNodes().item(1);
        orderLine.setUnitPrice(Double.valueOf(unitPriceNode.getFirstChild().getNodeValue()));

          orderLines.add(orderLine);
      }

    } catch (SAXException | IOException | ParserConfigurationException e) {
      e.printStackTrace();
    }
    return orderLines;
  }
}
```

Listing 12-5 parses the order.xml document, which results in a tree representation in memory. Thanks to the numerous Document methods, you can then get the list of order_line nodes or the quantity attribute (e.g., getAttribute("quantity")) to create an OrderLine object.

As previously mentioned, it is possible to override the platform's default DOM parser by setting the system property javax.xml.parsers.DocumentBuilderFactory for a different DOM API to be used.

JAXP with XSLT

JAXP is also used to transform XML documents using the XSLT API. XSLT interacts with XML resources to transform an XML source to an XML result using a transformation stylesheet (see Listing 12-3).

Listing 12-6 takes the order.xml document (Listing 12-1) and transforms it into an HTML page using the XSLT defined in Listing 12-3. The code first uses the newInstance() method of the javax.xml.transform.TransformerFactory class, to instantiate a transformer factory. Then, it calls the newTransformer() method to create a new XSLT Transformer. Then it transforms the order.xml document to a stream resulting in an HTML page.

Listing 12-6. Transforming an XML Document with XSLT

```java
public class XsltTransforming {

  public String transformOrder() {

    StringWriter writer = new StringWriter();

    try {
      File xmlDocument = Paths.get("src/main/resources/order.xml").toFile();
      File stylesheet = Paths.get("src/main/resources/order.xsl").toFile();

      TransformerFactory factory = ↩
        TransformerFactory.newInstance("net.sf.saxon.TransformerFactoryImpl", null);

      // Transforming the document
      Transformer transformer = factory.newTransformer(new StreamSource(stylesheet));
      transformer.transform(new StreamSource(xmlDocument), new StreamResult(writer));

    } catch (TransformerException e) {
      e.printStackTrace();
    }

    return writer.toString();
  }
}
```

Java Architecture for XML Binding

Java offers various ways to manipulate XML, from common APIs that are bundled in the JDK such as javax.xml.stream. XmlStreamWriter and java.beans.XMLEncoder to more complex and low-level models such as SAX, DOM, or JAXP.

The Java Architecture for XML Binding (JAXB) specification (JSR 222) provides a higher level of abstraction than SAX or DOM and is based on annotations. JAXB defines a standard to bind Java representations to XML and vice versa. This allows developers to work with Java objects that represent XML documents.

Listing 12-7 shows a simple CreditCard class annotated with the JAXB annotation @javax.xml.bind. annotation.XmlRootElement. JAXB will then bind the CreditCard object back and forth from XML to Java.

Listing 12-7. A CreditCard Class with a JAXB Annotation

```java
@XmlRootElement
public class CreditCard {

  private String number;
  private String expiryDate;
  private Integer controlNumber;
  private String type;

  // Constructors, getters, setters
}
```

Except for the @XmlRootElement annotation, Listing 12-7 shows the code of a simple Java class. With this annotation and a marshalling mechanism, JAXB is able to create an XML representation of a CreditCard instance that could look like the XML document shown in Listing 12-8.

Listing 12-8. An XML Document Representing Credit Card Data

```xml
<?xml version="1.0" encoding="UTF-8" standalone="yes"?>
<creditCard>
    <controlNumber>566</controlNumber>
    <expiryDate>10/14</expiryDate>
    <number>12345678</number>
    <type>Visa</type>
</creditCard>
```

Marshalling is the action of transforming an object into XML (see Figure 12-2). The inverse is also possible with JAXB. Unmarshalling would take the XML document in Listing 12-8 as an input and instantiate a CreditCard object with the values defined in the document.

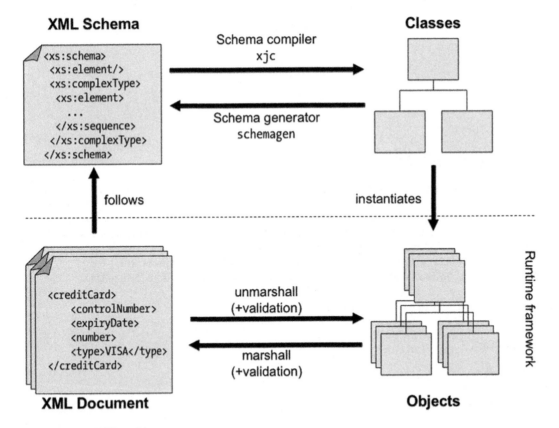

Figure 12-2. *JAXB architecture*

JAXB manages XML documents and XML Schema Definitions (XSD) in a transparent, object-oriented way that hides the complexity of the XSD language. JAXB can automatically generate the schema that would validate the credit card XML structure to ensure that it would have the correct structure and data types (thanks to the schemagen utility in the JDK). Listing 12-9 shows the XML Schema Definition (XSD) of the CreditCard class.

Listing 12-9. XML Schema Validating the Previous XML Document

```
<?xml version="1.0" encoding="UTF-8" standalone="yes"?>
<xs:schema version="1.0" xmlns:xs="http://www.w3.org/2001/XMLSchema">
  <xs:element name="creditCard" type="creditCard"/>
  <xs:complexType name="creditCard">
    <xs:sequence>
      <xs:element name="controlNumber" type="xs:int" minOccurs="0"/>
      <xs:element name="expiryDate" type="xs:string" minOccurs="0"/>
      <xs:element name="number" type="xs:string" minOccurs="0"/>
      <xs:element name="type" type="xs:string" minOccurs="0"/>
    </xs:sequence>
  </xs:complexType>
</xs:schema>
```

The schema in Listing 12-9 is made of simple elements (controlNumber, expiryDate, etc.) and a complex type (creditCard). Notice that all of the tags use the xs prefix (xs:element, xs:string, etc.). This prefix is called a *namespace* and is defined in the xmlns (XML namespace) header tag of the document:

```
<xs:schema version="1.0" xmlns:xs="http://www.w3.org/2001/XMLSchema">
```

Namespaces create unique prefixes for elements in separate documents or applications that are used together. They are used primarily to avoid conflict problems that may be caused if the same element name appears in several documents (for example, the <element> tag could appear in several documents and have different meanings).

JAXB provides a lightweight, two-way mapping between Java objects and XML structures. It enables the conversion of Java objects to XML data without the need to create complex code that is hard to maintain and debug. For example, JAXB allows you to easily transfer the state of an object to XML data and serialize it to network stream for example. On the other hand, JAXB enables you to work with XML documents as if they are Java objects without the need to explicitly perform SAX or DOM parsing in your application code.

Binding

The JAXB API, defined in the javax.xml.bind package, provides a set of interfaces and classes to produce XML documents and to generate Java classes. In other words, it binds the two models. The JAXB runtime framework implements the marshall and unmarshall operations. Table 12-7 contains the main JAXB packages for marshalling and unmarshalling operations.

Table 12-7. *The JAXB Packages*

Package	Description
javax.xml.bind	A runtime binding framework including marshalling, unmarshalling, and validation capabilities
javax.xml.bind.annotation	Annotations for customizing the mapping between the Java program and XML data
javax.xml.bind.annotation.adapters	Adapter classes to be used with JAXB
javax.xml.bind.attachment	Enables marshalling to optimize storage of binary data and unmarshalling a root document containing binary data formats
javax.xml.bind.helpers	Contains partial default implementations for some of the javax.xml.bind interfaces
javax.xml.bind.util	Provides useful utility classes

As shown in Figure 12-2, marshalling is the process of converting instances of JAXB-annotated classes to XML representations. Likewise, unmarshalling is the process of converting an XML representation to a tree of objects. During the process of marshalling/unmarshalling, JAXB can also validate the XML against an XSD (Listing 12-9). JAXB can also work at the class level and is able to automatically generate a schema from a set of classes and vice versa.

The center of the JAXB API is the javax.xml.bind.JAXBContext class. This abstract class manages the binding between XML documents and Java objects as it provides:

- An Unmarshaller class that transforms an XML document into an object graph and optionally validates the XML

- A Marshaller class that takes an object graph and transforms it into an XML document

For example, to transform our CreditCard object into an XML document (see Listing 12-10), the Marshaller. marshal() method must be used. This method takes an object as a parameter and marshalls it into several supports (StringWriter to have a string representation of the XML document or FileOutputStream to store it in a file).

Listing 12-10. A Main Class Marshalling a CreditCard Object

```
public class Main {

  public static void main(String[] args) throws JAXBException {

    CreditCard creditCard = new CreditCard("1234", "12/09", 6398, "Visa");
    StringWriter writer = new StringWriter();

    JAXBContext context = JAXBContext.newInstance(CreditCard.class);
    Marshaller m = context.createMarshaller();
    m.marshal(creditCard, writer);

    System.out.println(writer.toString());
  }
}
```

The code in Listing 12-10 creates an instance of JAXBContext by using the static method newInstance(), to which it passes the root class that needs to be marshalled (CreditCard.class). From the created Marshaller object, it then calls the marshal() method that generates the XML representation (shown previously in Listing 12-8) of the credit card object into a StringWriter and displays it. The same approach could be used to unmarshall an XML document into objects using the Unmarshaller.unmarshal() method.

Metro the JAXB reference implementation, has other tools, specifically the schema compiler (xjc) and the schema generator (schemaGen). While marshalling/unmarshalling deals with objects and XML documents, the schema compiler and the schema generator deal with classes and XML Schemas. These tools can be used in the command line (they are bundled with Java SE 7) or as Maven goals.

Annotations

JAXB is similar to JPA in many ways. However, instead of mapping objects to a database, JAXB does the mapping to an XML document. Also, like JPA, JAXB defines a set of annotations (in the javax.xml.bind.annotation package) to customize this mapping, and relies on configuration by exception to minimize the work of the developer. If persistent objects have to be annotated with @Entity, the correspondent in JAXB is @XmlRootElement (see Listing 12-11).

Listing 12-11. A Customized CreditCard Class

```
@XmlRootElement
@XmlAccessorType(XmlAccessType.FIELD)
public class CreditCard {

    @XmlAttribute(required = true)
    private String number;
    @XmlElement(name = "expiry-date", defaultValue = "01/10")
    private String expiryDate;
    private String type;
    @XmlElement(name = "control-number")
    private Integer controlNumber;

    // Constructors, getters, setters
}
```

In Listing 12-11 the @XmlRootElement annotation notifies JAXB that the CreditCard class is the root element of the XML document. If this annotation is missing, JAXB will throw an exception when trying to marshall it. This class is then mapped to the schema shown in Listing 12-12 using all the JAXB default mapping rules (each attribute is mapped to an element and has the same name).

Listing 12-12. The Credit Card Schema with Attributes and Default Values

```
<?xml version="1.0" encoding="UTF-8" standalone="yes"?>
<xs:schema version="1.0" xmlns:xs="http://www.w3.org/2001/XMLSchema">

    <xs:element name="creditCard" type="creditCard"/>

    <xs:complexType name="creditCard">
        <xs:sequence>
            <xs:element name="expiry-date" type="xs:string" default="01/10" minOccurs="0"/>
            <xs:element name="type" type="xs:string" minOccurs="0"/>
            <xs:element name="control-number" type="xs:int" minOccurs="0"/>
        </xs:sequence>
        <xs:attribute name="number" type="xs:string" use="required"/>
    </xs:complexType>
</xs:schema>
```

With a Marshaller object, you can easily get an XML representation of a CreditCard object (shown earlier in Listing 12-10). The root element <creditCard> represents the CreditCard object, and it includes the value of each attribute.

JAXB provides a way to customize and control this XML structure. An XML document is made of elements (<element>value</element>) and attributes (<element attribute="value"/>). JAXB uses two annotations to differentiate them: @XmlAttribute and @XmlElement. Each annotation has a set of parameters that allows you to rename an attribute, allow null values or not, give default values, and so forth. The class properties are mapped to XML elements by default if they are not annotated with @XmlAttribute annotation.

Listing 12-11 uses these annotations to turn the credit card number into an attribute (instead of an element) and to rename the expiry date and control number. This class will get mapped to a different schema in which the credit card number is represented as a required <xs:attribute>, and the expiry date is renamed and has a default value set to 01/10, as shown in Listing 12-12.

The XML representation of the CreditCard will also change as you can see Listing 12-13 (compared with the one in Listing 12-8).

Listing 12-13. An XML Document Representing a Customized CreditCard Object

```xml
<?xml version="1.0" encoding="UTF-8" standalone="yes"?>
<creditCard number="1234">
  <expiry-date>12/09</expiry-date>
  <type>Visa</type>
  <control-number>6398</control-number>
</creditCard>
```

Table 12-8 lists the main JAXB annotations. Some can annotate attributes (or getters), others classes, and some can be used on an entire package (such as @XmlSchema).

Table 12-8. *JAXB Annotations*

Annotation	Description
@XmlAccessorType	Controls whether attributes or getters should be mapped (FIELD, NONE, PROPERTY, PUBLIC_MEMBER)
@XmlAttribute	Maps an attribute or a getter to an XML attribute of simple type (String, Boolean, Integer, and so on)
@XmlElement	Maps a nonstatic and nontransient attribute or getter to an XML element
@XmlElements	Acts as a container for multiple @XmlElement annotations
@XmlEnum	Maps an enum to an XML representation
@XmlEnumValue	Identifies an enumerated constant
@XmlID	Identifies the key field of an XML element (of type String), which can be used when referring back to an element using the @XmlIDREF annotation (XML Schema ID and IDREF concepts)
@XmlIDREF	Maps a property to an XML IDREF in the schema
@XmlList	Maps a property to a list
@XmlMimeType	Identifies a textual representation of the MIME type for a property
@XmlNs	Identifies an XML namespace
@XmlRootElement	Represents an annotation required by any class that is to be bound as the root XML element
@XmlSchema	Maps a package name to an XML namespace
@XmlTransient	Informs JAXB not to bind an attribute (analogous to the Java transient keyword or @Transient annotation in JPA)
@XmlType	Annotates a class as being a complex type in XML Schema
@XmlValue	Allows the mapping of a class to a simple schema content or type

When using these annotations, you can map objects to a specific XML Schema. And sometimes you need this flexibility with legacy web services, as you will see in the coming chapters. Referring to JPA, when you need to map entities to a legacy database, there is a set of annotations that allows the customization of every part of the mapping (columns, table, foreign keys, etc.). With web services, it's similar: web services are described in a WSDL file written in XML. If it's a legacy web service, its WSDL cannot change. Instead, a mechanism to map it to objects must be used, which is why JAXB is used with web services.

■ **Note**　In this section, I've mentioned JPA several times because both JPA and JAXB technologies heavily rely on annotations and are used to map objects to a different media (database or XML). In terms of architecture, entities should only be used to map data to a database, and JAXB classes to map data to XML. But sometimes you may want the same object to have a database representation as well as an XML one. As you'll see in Chapter 14, it is possible to annotate the same class with @Entity and @XmlRootElement.

Understanding JSON

JavaScript Object Notation (JSON) is a lightweight data-interchange format that is less verbose and more readable than XML. It is often used for serializing and transmitting structured data over a network connection between a server and web application.

As an alternative to XML, JSON is directly consumable by JavaScript code in web pages. This is the major reason for using JSON over other representations. Listing 12-14 is the JSON representation of the purchase order XML document show in Listing 12-1.

Listing 12-14.　The JSON Representation of Purchase Order

```
{
   "order": {
     "id": "1234",
     "date": "05/06/2013",
     "customer": {
       "first_name": "James",
       "last_name": "Rorrison",
       "email": "j.rorri@me.com",
       "phoneNumber": "+44 1234 1234"
     },
     "content": {
       "order_line": [
         {
           "item": "H2G2",
           "quantity": "1",
           "unit_price": "23.5"
         },
         {
           "item": "Harry Potter",
           "quantity": "2",
           "unit_price": "34.99"
         }
       ]
     },
     "credit_card": {
       "number": "1357",
       "expiry_date": "10/13",
       "control_number": "234",
       "type": "Visa"
     }
   }
}
```

JSON objects can be serialized in JSON, which will end up in a less complex structure than XML. By enclosing the variable's value in curly braces, it indicates that the value is an object. Inside the object, we can declare any number of properties using a `"name":"value"` pair, separated by commas. To access the information stored in JSON, we can simply refer to the object and name of the property.

JSON Document

JSON is a text-based language-independent format that uses a set of conventions to represent simple data structures. Many languages have implemented APIs to parse JSON documents. Data structures in JSON are human-readable and are much like data structures in Java. JSON can represent four primitive types (number, string, booleans, and null) and two structured types (objects and arrays). Table 12-9 lists the JSON conventions to represent data.

Table 12-9. *JSON Terminology*

Terminology	Definition
Number	Number in JSON is much like number in Java except that the octal and hexadecimal formats are not used
String	A string is a sequence of zero or more Unicode characters, wrapped in double quotes, using backslash escapes
Value	A value in JSON can be in one of these formats; a string in double quotes, a number, true, false, null, an object, or an array
Array	An array is an ordered set of values. Brackets ([,]) mark the beginning and end of an array. Values in an array are separated by commas (,) and can be of object type
Object	JSON and Java have the same definition for objects. In JSON, an object is an unordered set of name/value pairs. Braces ({,}) mark the beginning and the end of an object. The name/value pairs in JSON are separated by comma (,) and represent attributes for a POJO in Java

Colon (:) is used as the name-separator and comma as the value-separator in JSON. Valid JSON data is a serialized object or array of data structures that can be nested. For example, a JSON object can contain a JSON array. In Listing 12-14, content is an object that contains an array of order_line.

JSON Specifications Overview

JSON is derived from the object literals of JavaScript. JSON was submitted as RFC 4627 in the Internet Engineering Task Force (IETF) in 2006. The IETF is an open international community of network designers, researchers, operators, and vendors concerned with the evolution of the Internet architecture.

The official Internet media type for JSON is `application/json` (see Chapter 15 with RESTful Web services) and the JSON filename extension is `.json`. Though JSON is not currently submitted as a W3C recommendation, there are many W3C specifications and APIs that are based directly or indirectly on JSON or that use JSON such as JSON-LD, JSONPath, JSONT, and JSONiq. Also, a large variety of programming languages have implemented APIs to parse and generate data in JSON format.

Java has several implementations to process, transform, serialize/deserialize, or generate JSON data such as Json-lib, fastjson, Flexjson, Jettison, Jackson, and so on (check `http://json.org`, which lists several Java APIs for JSON); each could be useful for different scenarios.

To provide a standard Java API for processing JSON, the JSR 353 (Java API for JSON Processing) was submitted to the JCP in 2011 and was released with Java EE 7.

JSON-P

Java API for JSON Processing (JSR 353) known as JSON-P, is a specification that allows JSON processing in Java. The processing includes mechanisms to parse, generate, transform, and query JSON data. JSON-P provides a standard to build a Java object in JSON using an API similar to DOM for XML. At the same time, it provides a mechanism to produce and consume JSON by streaming in a manner similar to StAX for XML.

Although it is not a strict requirement in the original JSR, some JSON-P implementations may also provide binding of JSON data to Java objects and vice versa (but this will be specified in a future JSR, which could be called JSON-B, 'B' for Binding). Table 12-10 lists the important JSON-P packages.

Table 12-10. *The JSON-P Packages*

Package	Description
javax.json	Provides an API to describe JSON data structure (e.g. JsonArray class for JSON array and JsonObject class for JSON object), provides the entry point to parse, build, read, and write JSON objects and arrays by streaming
javax.json.spi	Service Provider Interface (SPI) to plug JsonParser and JsonGenerator implementations
javax.json.stream	Provides a streaming API to parse and generate JSON

Reference Implementation

There are several JSON processors implemented in Java, but the open source reference implementation for JSON-P (JSR 353) is JSON RI.

JSON Processing

JSON-P provides two different programming models to process JSON documents: the Object Model API, and the Streaming API. Similar to the DOM API for XML, the Object Model API provides classes to model JSON objects and arrays in a treelike structure that represent JSON data in memory. As with the DOM API, the Object Model API provides flexible navigation and queries to the whole content of the tree.

The streaming API is a low-level API designed to process large amounts of JSON data efficiently. The Streaming API is much like the StAX API for XML. It provides a way to stream JSON without maintaining the whole document in memory. The streaming API provides an event-based parser based on a pull parsing streaming model, enabling the user to process or discard the parser event, and ask for the next event (pull the event). JSON Generator also helps you to generate and write JSON in by streaming.

The JSR 353 has a main javax.json.Json API, which is a class for creating JSON processing objects. This central API has methods to create a JsonParser, JsonGenerator, JsonWriter, JsonReader, JsonArrayBuilder and JsonObjectBuilder.

Building JSON

The object and array structures in JSON are represented by the javax.json.JsonObject and javax.json.JsonArray classes. The API lets you navigate and query the tree structure of data.

JsonObject provides a Map view to access the unordered collection of zero or more name/value pairs. Similarly, JsonArray provides a List view to access the ordered sequence of zero or more values. The API uses the builder patterns to create the tree representation of JsonObject and JsonArray through the javax.json.JsonObjectBuilder and javax.json.JsonArrayBuilder interfaces.

Listing 12-15 shows how to build the purchase order in JSON described in Listing 12-14. As you can see, the Json class is used to create JsonObjectBuilder and JsonArrayBuilder objects that will end up building a JsonObject (using the final build() method). JsonObject provides a map view to the JSON object name/value mappings.

Listing 12-15. The OrderJsonBuilder Class Building a Purchase Order in JSON

```java
public class OrderJsonBuilder {

  public JsonObject buildPurchaseOrder() {

    return Json.createObjectBuilder().add("order", Json.createObjectBuilder()
            .add("id", "1234")
            .add("date", "05/06/2013")
            .add("customer", Json.createObjectBuilder()
                .add("first_name", "James")
                .add("last_name", "Rorrison")
                .add("email", "j.rorri@me.com")
                .add("phoneNumber", "+44 1234 1234"))
            .add("content", Json.createObjectBuilder()
                .add("order_line", Json.createArrayBuilder()
                        .add(Json.createObjectBuilder()
                                .add("item", "H2G2")
                                .add("quantity", "1")
                                .add("unit_price", "23.5"))
                        .add(Json.createObjectBuilder()
                                .add("item", "Harry Potter")
                                .add("quantity", "2")
                                .add("unit_price", "34.99"))))
            .add("credit_card", Json.createObjectBuilder()
                    .add("number", "1357")
                    .add("expiry_date", "10/13")
                    .add("control_number", "234")
                    .add("type", "Visa"))).build();
  }
}
```

The JsonObject can also be created from an input source (such as InputStream or Reader) using the interface javax.json.JsonReader. The following example shows how to read and create the JsonObject using the interface JsonReader. A JsonReader is created from an order.json file (Listing 12-14). Then, to access the order object, the getJsonObject() method is called and returns a JsonObject. If no object is found, null is returned:

```java
JsonReader reader = Json.createReader(new FileReader("order.json"));
JsonObject jsonObject = reader.readObject();
jsonObject  = jsonObject.getJsonObject("order");
```

JsonReader also provides the general read() method to read any javax.json.JsonStructure subtype (JsonObject and JsonArray). Using the JsonStructure.getValueType() method returns the ValueType (ARRAY, OBJECT, STRING, NUMBER, TRUE, FALSE, NULL) and then you can read the value. The toString() method on JsonStructure returns the JSON representation of the object model.

Similarly, JsonObject and JsonArray can be written to an output source (such as OutputStream or Writer) using the class javax.json.JsonWriter. The builder method Json.createWriter()can create a JsonWriter for different outputs.

Parsing JSON

The Streaming API (package javax.json.stream) facilitates parsing JSON via streaming with forward and read-only access. It provides the javax.json.stream.JsonParser interface to parse a JSON document. The entry point is the javax.json.Json factory class, which provides a createParser() method that returns a javax.json.stream.JsonParser from a specified input source (such as a Reader or an InputStream). As an example, a JSON parser for parsing an empty JSON object could be created as follows:

```
StringReader reader = new StringReader("{}");
JsonParser parser = Json.createParser(reader);
```

You can configure the parser by passing a Map property to the createParserFactory() method. This factory creates a JsonParser specifically configured to parse your JSON data:

```
StringReader reader = new StringReader("{}");
JsonParserFactory factory = Json.createParserFactory(properties);
JsonParser parser = factory.createParser(reader);
```

The JsonParser is based on a pull parsing streaming model. Meaning that the parser generates events when a JSON name/value is reached or the beginning/end of an object/array is read. Table 12-11 lists all of the events triggered by the parser.

Table 12-11. *JSon Parsing Events*

Package	Description
START_OBJECT	Event for start of a JSON object (fired when { is reached)
END_OBJECT	Event for end of an object (fired when } is reached)
START_ARRAY	Event for start of a JSON array (fired when [is reached)
END_ARRAY	Event for end of an array (fired when] is reached)
KEY_NAME	Event for a name in name(key)/value pair of a JSON object
VALUE_STRING	Event for a string value
VALUE_NUMBER	Event for a number value
VALUE_TRUE	Event for a true value
VALUE_FALSE	Event for a false value
VALUE_NULL	Event for a null value

The class in Listing 12-16 parses the JSON in Listing 12-14 (saved in an order.json file) to extract the customer's e-mail. The parser moves forward until it encounters an email property name. The next() method causes the parser to advance to the next parsing state. It returns the next javax.json.stream.JsonParser.Event enum (Table 12-11) of for the next parsing state. When the parser reaches the email property value, it returns it.

Listing 12-16. The OrderJsonParser Class Parsing the JSON Representation of the Purchase Order

```
public class OrderJsonParser {

  public String parsePurchaseOrderAndReturnEmail() throws FileNotFoundException {
    String email = null;

    JsonParser parser = Json.createParser(new FileReader("src/main/resources/order.json"));
    while (parser.hasNext()) {
      JsonParser.Event event = parser.next();
      while (parser.hasNext() && !(event.equals(JsonParser.Event.KEY_NAME) && ↪
                                   parser.getString().matches("email"))) {
        event = parser.next();
      }

      if (event.equals(JsonParser.Event.KEY_NAME) && parser.getString().matches("email")) {
        parser.next();
        email = parser.getString();
      }
    }
    return email;
  }
}
```

By using the Event.equals() method, you can determine the type of the event and process the JSON based on the event. While the JsonParser streams the JSON, you can use the getString() method to get a String representation for each name (key) and value depending on the state of the parser. The name is returned if the event is KEY_NAME, the String value is returned when the event is VALUE_STRING, and the number value when the event is VALUE_NUMBER. In addition to getString(), which returns a String value, you can use other methods such as getIntValue(), getLongValue(), and getBigDecimalValue(), depending on the type.

If an incorrect data format is encountered while parsing, the parser will throw runtime exceptions such as javax.json.stream.JsonParsingException and java.lang.IllegalStateException, depending on the source of the problem.

Generating JSON

The JSON builder APIs allow you to build a JSON tree structure in memory. The JsonParser parses a JSON object via streaming, whereas the javax.json.stream.JsonGenerator allows the writing of JSON to a stream by writing one event at a time.

The class in Listing 12-17 uses the createGenerator() method from the main javax.json.Json factory to get a JsonGenerator and generates the JSON document defined in Listing 12-14. The generator writes name/value pairs in JSON objects and JSON arrays.

Listing 12-17. Generating a Purchase Order Object In JSON

```
public class OrderJsonGenerator {

    public StringWriter generatePurchaseOrder() throws IOException {
        StringWriter writer = new StringWriter();
        JsonGenerator generator = Json.createGenerator(writer);
        generator.writeStartObject()
                    .write("id", "1234")
                    .write("date", "05/06/2013")
                    .writeStartObject("customer")
                        .write("first_name", "James")
                        .write("last_name", "Rorrison")
                        .write("email", "j.rorri@me.com")
                        .write("phoneNumber", "+44 1234 1234")
                    .writeEnd()
                    .writeStartArray("content")
                        .writeStartObject()
                            .write("item", "H2G2")
                            .write("unit_price", "23.5")
                            .write("quantity", "1")
                        .writeEnd()
                        .writeStartObject()
                            .write("item", "Harry Potter")
                            .write("unit_price", "34.99")
                            .write("quantity", "2")
                        .writeEnd()
                    .writeEnd()
                    .writeStartObject("credit_card")
                        .write("number", "123412341234")
                        .write("expiry_date", "10/13")
                        .write("control_number", "234")
                        .write("type", "Visa")
                    .writeEnd()
                .writeEnd()
                .close();
        return writer;
    }
}
```

Familiarity with object and array contexts is needed when generating JSON. JSON name/value pairs can be written to an object, whereas JSON values can be written to an array. While the writeStartObject() method writes a JSON start object character ({), the writeStartArray() method is used to write a JSON start array character ([). Each opened context must be terminated using the writeEnd() method. After writing the end of the current context, the parent context becomes the new current context.

The writeStartObject() method is used to start a new child object context and the writeStartArray() method starts a new child array context. Both methods can be used only in an array context or when a context is not yet started and both can only be called when no context is started. A context is started when one of these methods are used.

The JsonGenerator class provides other methods, such as write(), to write a JSON name/value pair in the current object context or to write a value in current array context.

Although the flush() method can be used to write any buffered output to the underlying stream, the close() method closes the generator and frees any associated resources.

Putting It All Together

By putting the concepts of this chapter all together, let's write a CreditCard POJO and use JAXB and JSON-P to get an XML and JSON representation of the credit card. To test both formats we will write unit tests. The CreditCardXMLTest class marshalls and unmarshalls the CreditCard to check that the XML representation is correct. The CreditCardJSonTest class checks that the generated JSON is also well formatted.

Writing the CreditCard Class

The CreditCard class in Listing 12-18 is annotated with the JAXB @XmlRootElement annotation to be marshalled into XML. The other JAXB annotation @XmlAccessorType, with parameter XmlAccessType.FIELD, tells JAXB to bind the attributes rather than the getters.

Listing 12-18. The CreditCard Class with a JAXB Annotation

```
@XmlRootElement
@XmlAccessorType(XmlAccessType.FIELD)
public class CreditCard {

    @XmlAttribute
    private String number;
    @XmlElement(name = "expiry_date")
    private String expiryDate;
    @XmlElement(name = "control_number")
    private Integer controlNumber;
    private String type;

    // Constructors, getters, setters
}
```

The CreditCard object has some basic fields such as the credit card number, the expiry date (formatted as MM/YY), a credit card type (Visa, Master Card, American Express, etc.), and a control number. Some of these attributes are annotated with @XmlAttribute to be mapped to an XML attribute. The @XmlElement is used to override the XML element name.

Writing the CreditCardXMLTest Unit Test

The CreditCardXMLTest class shown in Listing 12-19 marshalls and unmarshalls a CreditCard object back and forth from XML to Java using the JAXB marshalling mechanism. The shouldMarshallACreditCard method creates an instance of the CreditCard class and checks it has the correct XML representation. The method shouldUnmarshallACreditCard does the opposite as it unmarshalls the XML document into a CreditCard instance and checks that the object is correctly set.

Listing 12-19. The CreditCardXMLTest Unit Test Marshalls and Unmarshalls XML

```
public class CreditCardXMLTest {

    public static final String creditCardXML =
            "<?xml version=\"1.0\" encoding=\"UTF-8\" standalone=\"yes\"?>\n" +
            "<creditCard number=\"12345678\">\n" +
            "    <expiry_date>10/14</expiry_date>\n" +
            "    <control_number>566</control_number>\n" +
            "    <type>Visa</type>\n" +
            "</creditCard>";
```

```java
@Test
public void shouldMarshallACreditCard() throws JAXBException {

  CreditCard creditCard = new CreditCard("12345678", "10/14", 566, "Visa");

  StringWriter writer = new StringWriter();
  JAXBContext context = JAXBContext.newInstance(CreditCard.class);
  Marshaller m = context.createMarshaller();
  m.setProperty(Marshaller.JAXB_FORMATTED_OUTPUT, Boolean.TRUE);
  m.marshal(creditCard, writer);

  System.out.println(writer);

  assertEquals(creditCardXML, writer.toString().trim());

}

@Test
public void shouldUnmarshallACreditCard() throws JAXBException {
  StringReader reader = new StringReader(creditCardXML);
  JAXBContext context = JAXBContext.newInstance(CreditCard.class);
  Unmarshaller u = context.createUnmarshaller();
  CreditCard creditCard = (CreditCard) u.unmarshal(reader);

  assertEquals("12345678", creditCard.getNumber());
  assertEquals("10/14", creditCard.getExpiryDate());
  assertEquals((Object) 566, creditCard.getControlNumber());
  assertEquals("Visa", creditCard.getType());
  }
}
```

Writing the CreditCardJSonTest Unit Test

The CreditCardJSonTest class shown in Listing 12-20 uses the JsonGenerator API to write a JSON object representation of a CreditCard. It then checks that the JSonObject has a valid syntax by comparing it to the creditCardJSon constant.

Listing 12-20. The CreditCardJSonTest Unit Test Generates JSon

```java
public class CreditCardJSonTest {

  public static final String creditCardJSon =
        "{\"creditCard\":" +
              "{\"number\":\"12345678\"," +
              "\"expiryDate\":\"10/14\"," +
              "\"controlNumber\":566," +
              "\"type\":\"Visa\"}" +
        "}";
```

```java
@Test
public void shouldGenerateACreditCard(){

    CreditCard creditCard = new CreditCard("12345678", "10/14", 566, "Visa");

    StringWriter writer = new StringWriter();
    JsonGenerator generator = Json.createGenerator(writer);
    generator.writeStartObject()
            .writeStartObject("creditCard")
              .write("number", creditCard.getNumber())
              .write("expiryDate", creditCard.getExpiryDate())
              .write("controlNumber", creditCard.getControlNumber())
              .write("type", creditCard.getType())
            .writeEnd()
          .writeEnd()
          .close();

    assertEquals(creditCardJSon, writer.toString().trim());

    }
}
```

Summary

XML is more than just a text format for describing documents. It is a mechanism for describing platform-independent complex structured data. Java provides a set of powerful, lightweight APIs to parse, validate, and generate XML data. Different parsing models such as DOM, SAX, and StAX are supported in Java. Although you can use low-level Java APIs to work with XML based on DOM or SAX models, the JAXP API provides the wrapper classes to parse your XML resources based on the DOM or SAX model and transfers the XML document using XSLT and XPath.

Java Architecture for XML Binding (JAXB) defines a standard to bind Java representations to XML and vice versa. It provides a high level of abstraction, as it is based on annotations. Even if JAXB can be used in any kind of Java application, it fits well in the web service space because any information exchanged is written in XML, as you will see in Chapter 14.

JSON is a lightweight data-interchange format. It is an alternative to XML, and its suggested use is for simpler data structures. JSON-P facilitates parsing and generating data in JSON format via streaming. Even if the JAXB equivalent in JSON doesn't exist yet, specifications such as JAX-RS use JSON-P to return JSON objects from RESTful web services (see Chapter 15).

Messaging

Most of the communications between components that you have seen so far are synchronous: one class calls another, a managed bean invokes an EJB, which calls an entity, and so on. In such cases, the invoker and the target have to be up and running for the communication to succeed, and the invoker must wait for the target to complete before proceeding. With the exception of asynchronous calls in EJB (thanks to the @Asynchronous annotation), most Java EE components use synchronous calls (local or remote). When we talk about messaging, we mean loosely coupled, asynchronous communication between components.

Message-oriented middleware) (MOM) is software (a provider) that enables the exchange of messages asynchronously between heterogeneous systems. It can be seen as a buffer between systems that produce and consume messages at their own pace (e.g., one system is 24/7, the other runs only at night). It is inherently loosely coupled, as producers don't know who is at the other end of the communication channel to consume the message and perform actions. The producer and the consumer do not have to be available at the same time in order to communicate. In fact, they do not even know about each other, as they use an intermediate buffer. In this respect, MOM differs completely from technologies, such as remote method invocation (RMI), which require an application to know the signature of a remote application's methods.

Today, a typical organization has many applications, often written in different languages, that perform well-defined tasks. MOM is based on an asynchronous interaction model so it allows these applications to work independently and, at the same time, form part of an information workflow process. Messaging is a good solution for integrating existing and new applications in a loosely coupled, asynchronous way, as long as the producer and consumer agree on the message format and the intermediate destination. This communication can be local within an organization or distributed among several external services.

Understanding Messaging

MOM (Message-oriented middleware), which has been around for a while, uses a special vocabulary. When a message is sent, the software that stores the message and dispatches it is called a *provider* (or sometimes a *broker*). The message sender is called a *producer*, and the location where the message is stored is called a *destination*. The component receiving the message is called a *consumer*. Any component interested in a message at that particular destination can consume it. Figure 13-1 illustrates these concepts.

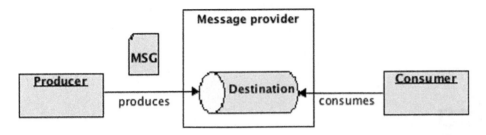

Figure 13-1. *MOM architecture*

In Java EE, the API that deals with these concepts is called Java Message Service (JMS). It has a set of interfaces and classes that allow you to connect to a provider, create a message, send it, and receive it. JMS doesn't physically carry messages, it's just an API; it requires a provider that is in charge of handling messages. When running in an EJB container, Message-Driven Beans (MDBs) can be used to receive messages in a container-managed way.

At a high level, a messaging architecture consists of the following components (see Figure 13-2):

- *A provider:* JMS is only an API, so it needs an underlying implementation to route messages, that is, the provider (a.k.a. a message broker). The provider handles the buffering and delivery of messages.

- *Clients:* A client is any Java application or component that produces or consumes a message to/from the provider. "Client" is the generic term for producer, sender, publisher, consumer, receiver, or subscriber.

- *Messages:* These are the objects that clients send to or receive from the provider.

- *Administered objects:* A message broker must provide administered objects to the client (connection factories and destinations) either through JNDI lookups or injection (as you'll see later).

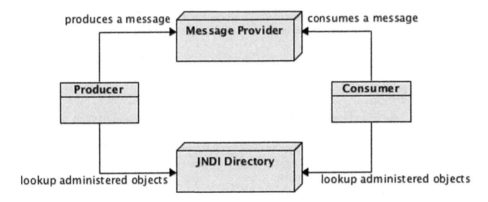

Figure 13-2. *Messaging architecture*

The messaging provider enables asynchronous communication by providing a destination where messages can be held until they can be delivered to a client (see Figure 13-1). There are two different types of destination, each applying to a specific messaging model:

- *The point-to-point (P2P) model:* In this model, the destination used to hold messages is called a *queue*. When using point-to-point messaging, one client puts a message on a queue, and another client receives the message. Once the message is acknowledged, the message provider removes the message from the queue.

- *The publish-subscribe (pub-sub) model:* The destination is called a *topic*. When using publish/subscribe messaging, a client publishes a message to a topic, and all subscribers to that topic receive the message.

Point-to-Point

In the P2P model, a message travels from a single producer to a single consumer. The model is built around the concept of message queues, senders, and receivers (see Figure 13-3). A queue retains the messages sent by the sender until they are consumed, and a sender and a receiver do not have timing dependencies. This means that the sender can produce messages and send them in the queue whenever he likes, and a receiver can consume them whenever he likes. Once the receiver is created, it will get all the messages that were sent to the queue, even those sent before its creation.

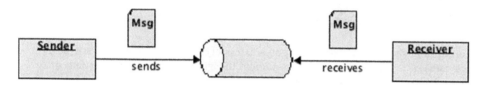

Figure 13-3. *P2P model*

Each message is sent to a specific queue, and the receiver extracts the messages from the queue. Queues retain all messages sent until they are consumed or until they expire.

The P2P model is used if there is only one receiver for each message. Note that a queue can have multiple consumers, but once a receiver consumes a message from the queue, it is taken out of the queue, and no other consumer can receive it. In Figure 13-4, you can see one sender producing three messages.

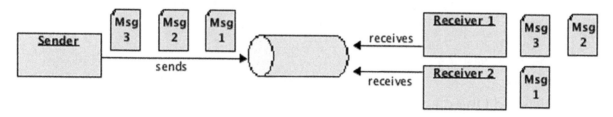

Figure 13-4. *Multiple receivers*

Note that P2P doesn't guarantee messages are delivered in any particular order (the order is not defined). A provider might pick them in arrival order, or randomly, or some other way.

Publish-Subscribe

In the pub-sub model, a single message is sent by a single producer to potentially several consumers. The model is built around the concept of topics, publishers, and subscribers (Figure 13-5). Consumers are called *subscribers* because they first need to subscribe to a topic. The provider manages the subscribing/unsubscribing mechanism as it occurs dynamically.

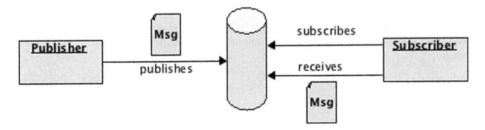

***Figure 13-5.** Pub-sub model*

The topic retains messages until they are distributed to all subscribers. Unlike the P2P model, there is a timing dependency between publishers and subscribers; subscribers do not receive messages sent prior to their subscription, and, if the subscriber is inactive for a specified period, it will not receive past messages when it becomes active again. Note that this can be avoided, because the JMS API supports the concept of a durable subscriber, as you'll later see.

Multiple subscribers can consume the same message. The pub-sub model can be used for broadcast-type applications, in which a single message is delivered to several consumers. In Figure 13-6, the publisher sends three messages that each subscriber will receive (in an undefined order).

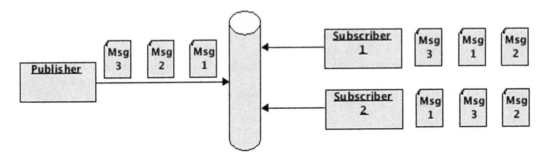

***Figure 13-6.** Multiple subscribers*

Administered Objects

Administered objects are objects that are configured administratively, as opposed to programmatically. The message provider allows these objects to be configured, and makes them available in the JNDI namespace. Like JDBC datasources, administered objects are created only once. The two types of administered objects:

- *Connection factories*: Used by clients to create a connection to a destination.

- *Destinations*: Message distribution points that receive, hold, and distribute messages. Destinations can be queues (P2P) or topics (pub-sub).

Clients access these objects through portable interfaces by looking them up in the JNDI namespace or through injection. In GlassFish, there are several ways to create these objects as you'll later see: by using the administration console, the asadmin command-line, or the REST interface. Since JMS 2.0 you can even use the @JMSConnectionFactoryDefinition and @JMSDestinationDefinition annotations to define programmatically these objects.

Message-Driven Beans

Message-Driven Beans (MDBs) are asynchronous message consumers that are executed inside an EJB container. As you've seen in Chapters 7 through 9, the EJB container takes care of several services (transactions, security, concurrency, message acknowledgment, etc.), while the MDB focuses on consuming messages. MDBs are stateless, meaning that the EJB container can have numerous instances, executing concurrently, to process messages coming in from various producers. Even if they look like stateless beans, client applications cannot access MDBs directly; the only way to communicate with an MDB is to send a message to the destination that the MDB is listening to.

In general, MDBs listen to a destination (queue or topic) and, when a message arrives, they consume and process it. They can also delegate business logic to other stateless session beans in a safe, transactional manner. Because they are stateless, MDBs do not maintain state across separate invocations from one message received to the next. MDBs respond to messages received from the container, whereas stateless session beans respond to client requests through an appropriate interface (local, remote, or no-interface).

Messaging Specifications Overview

Messaging in Java is mostly represented by JMS, which can be used in applications running in a standard (Java SE) or an enterprise (Java EE) environment. MDBs simply represent a way for stateless session EJBs to be message consumers and are bound to the EJB specification.

A Brief History of Messaging

Up until the late 1980s, companies did not have any easy way to link different applications. Developers had to write separate software adapters for systems to translate data from source applications into a format that the destination system could understand (and vice versa). Because of the disparity of servers' processing capabilities and availabilities, buffers were created to de-couple the processing so that the overall time wouldn't be prolonged. A lack of homogeneous transport protocols created low-level protocol adapters. Toward the end of the 1980s, middleware began to emerge, which solved these integration issues. The first MOMs were created as separate pieces of software that could sit in the middle of applications and manage the "plumbing" between systems. They were able to manage different platforms, different programming languages, various network protocols, and diverse hardware.

The JMS specification was first published in August 1998. It was created by the major middleware vendors to bring messaging capabilities to Java. JSR 914 went through minor changes (JMS 1.0.1, 1.0.2, and 1.0.2b) to finally reach the 1.1 version in April 2002. JMS 1.1 was integrated into J2EE 1.2 and has been a part of Java EE since. However, JMS and MDBs are not part of the Web Profile specification. This means they are only available on application servers implementing the full Java EE 7 platform.

What's New in JMS 2.0?

JMS 1.1 didn't change for more than a decade. Since Java EE 5 the APIs have slowly been modernized to fit the language changes (annotations, generics…) except for JMS. It was time for JMS to follow the same path, make use of annotations and simplify its API. In fact, several changes have been made to the JMS API to make it simpler and easier to use:

- Connection, Session and other objects with a close() method now implement the java.jang.AutoCloseable interface to allow them to be used in a Java SE 7 try-with-resources statement

- A new "simplified API" has been added which offers a simpler alternative to the standard and legacy APIs

- A new method getBody has been added to allow an application to extract the body directly from a Message without the need to cast it first to an appropriate subtype

- A set of new unchecked exceptions have been created, all extending from JMSRuntimeException

- New send methods have been added to allow an application to send messages asynchronously

What's New in EJB 3.2?

MDBs were introduced in EJB 2.0 and were improved with EJB 3.0 and the general Java EE 5 paradigm of "ease of use." They were not internally modified as they continued to be message consumers, but the introduction of annotations and configuration by exception made them much easier to write. The new EJB 3.2 specification (JSR 345) brought some changes to MDBs by adding more portable configuration (more on that later).

As you've seen in Chapter 7, asynchronous calls are now possible within stateless session beans (using the @Asynchronous annotation). In previous versions of Java EE, it was impossible to have asynchronous calls between EJBs. Therefore, the only possible solution was to use JMS and MDBs—expensive, as many resources had to be used (JMS destinations, connections, factories, etc.) just to call a method asynchronously. Today asynchronous calls are possible between session beans without the need for MDBs, allowing them to focus on integrating systems through messaging.

Reference Implementation

Open Message Queue (OpenMQ) is the reference implementation of JMS. It has been open source since 2006 and can be used in stand-alone JMS applications or embedded in an application server. OpenMQ is the default messaging provider for GlassFish and, as this book is being written, is reaching version 5.0. It also adds many nonstandard features such as the Universal Message Service (UMS), wildcard topic destinations, XML message validation, clustering, and more.

Java Messaging Service API

JMS is a standard Java API that allows applications to create, send, receive, and read messages asynchronously. It defines a common set of interfaces and classes that allow programs to communicate with other message providers. JMS is analogous to JDBC: the latter connects to several databases (Derby, MySQL, Oracle, DB2, etc.), and JMS connects to several providers (OpenMQ, MQSeries, SonicMQ, etc.).

The JMS API has evolved ever since its creation. For historical reasons JMS offers three alternative sets of interfaces for producing and consuming messages. These very different interfaces evolved in JMS 1.0, 1.1 and 2.0 and are referred to as legacy API, classic API and simplified API.

JMS 1.0 made a clear difference between the point-to-point and publish-subscribe model. It defined two domain-specific APIs, one for point-to-point (queues) and one for pub-sub (topics). That's why you can find QueueConnectionFactory and TopicConnectionFactory API instead of the generic ConnectionFactory for example. Note also the different vocabulary; a consumer is called a receiver in P2P and a subscriber in pub-sub.

The JMS 1.1 API (referred to as the classic API) provided a unified set of interfaces that can be used with both P2P and pub-sub messaging. Table 13-1 shows the generic name of an interface (e.g., Session) and the legacy names for each model (QueueSession, TopicSession).

Table 13-1. *Interfaces Depending on JMS Version*

Classic API	Simplified API	Legacy API (P2P)	Legacy API (Pub-Sub)
ConnectionFactory	ConnectionFactory	QueueConnectionFactory	TopicConnectionFactory
Connection	JMSContext	QueueConnection	TopicConnection
Session	JMSContext	QueueSession	TopicSession
Destination	Destination	Queue	Topic
Message	Message	Message	Message
MessageConsumer	JMSConsumer	QueueReceiver	TopicSubscriber
MessageProducer	JMSProducer	QueueSender	TopicPublisher
JMSException	JMSRuntimeException	JMSException	JMSException

But JMS 1.1 was still a verbose and low-level API compared to JPA or EJB. JMS 2.0 introduces a simplified API that offers all the features of the classic API but requires fewer interfaces and is simpler to use. Table 13-1 highlights the differences between these APIs (all located under the javax.jms package).

I will not discuss the legacy API but I need to introduce the classic API; first of all because you will still find millions of lines of code using the JMS 1.1 classic API and second, because technically the simplified API relies on the classical one.

Classic API

The JMS classic API provides classes and interfaces for applications that require a messaging system (see Figure 13-7). This API enables asynchronous communication between clients by providing a connection to the provider, and a session where messages can be created and sent or received. These messages can contain text or other different kinds of objects.

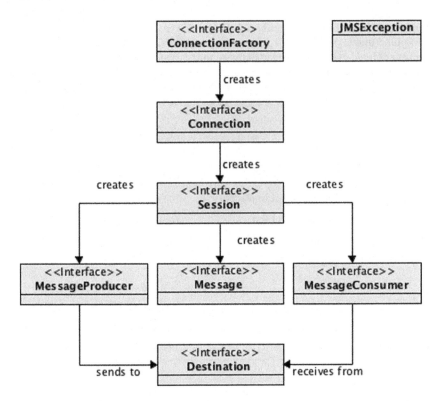

Figure 13-7. *JMS Classic API*

ConnectionFactory

Connection factories are administered objects that allow an application to connect to a provider by creating a Connection object programmatically. A javax.jms.ConnectionFactory is an interface that encapsulates the configuration parameters that have been defined by an administrator.

To use an administered object such as a ConnectionFactory, the client needs to perform a JNDI lookup (or use injection). For example, the following code fragment obtains the JNDI InitialContext object and uses it to look up a ConnectionFactory by its JNDI name:

```
Context ctx = new InitialContext();
ConnectionFactory ConnectionFactory = ➥
            (ConnectionFactory) ctx.lookup("jms/javaee7/ConnectionFactory");
```

The methods available in this interface (see Listing 13-1) are createConnection methods that return a Connection object and new JMS 2.0 createContext methods that return a JMSContext. You can create a Connection or a JMSContext either with the default user identity or by specifying a username and password.

Listing 13-1. ConnectionFactory Interface

```
public interface ConnectionFactory {

  Connection createConnection() throws JMSException;
  Connection createConnection(String userName, String password) throws JMSException;
  JMSContext createContext();
  JMSContext createContext(String userName, String password);
  JMSContext createContext(String userName, String password, int sessionMode);
  JMSContext createContext(int sessionMode);
}
```

Destination

A destination is an administered object that contains provider-specific configuration information such as the destination address. But this configuration is hidden from the JMS client by using the standard javax.jms.Destination interface. Like the connection factory, a JNDI lookup is needed to return such objects:

```
Context ctx = new InitialContext();
Destination queue = (Destination) ctx.lookup("jms/javaee7/Queue");
```

Connection

The javax.jms.Connection object, which you create using the createConnection() method of the connection factory, encapsulates a connection to the JMS provider. Connections are thread-safe and designed to be shareable, as opening a new connection is resource intensive. However, a session (javax.jms.Session) provides a single-threaded context for sending and receiving messages, using a connection to create one or more sessions. Once you have a connection factory, you can use it to create a connection as follows:

```
Connection connection = connectionFactory.createConnection();
```

Before a receiver can consume messages, it must call the start() method. If you need to stop receiving messages temporarily without closing the connection, you can call the stop() method:

```
connection.start();
connection.stop();
```

When the application completes, you need to close any connections created. Closing a connection also closes its sessions and its producers or consumers:

```
connection.close();
```

Session

You create a session from the connection using the createSession() method. A session provides a transactional context in which a set of messages to be sent or received are grouped in an atomic unit of work, meaning that, if you send several messages during the same session, JMS will ensure that either they all are sent or none. This behavior is set at the creation of the session:

```
Session session = connection.createSession(true, Session.AUTO_ACKNOWLEDGE);
```

The first parameter of the method specifies whether or not the session is transactional. In the code, the parameter is set to true, meaning that the request for sending messages won't be realized until either the session's commit() method is called or the session is closed. If the parameter was set to false, the session would not be transactional, and messages would be sent as soon as the send() method is invoked. The second parameter means that the session automatically acknowledges messages when they have been received successfully. A session is single-threaded and is used to create messages, producers, and consumers.

Messages

To communicate, clients exchange messages; one producer will send a message to a destination, and a consumer will receive it. Messages are objects that encapsulate information and are divided in three parts (see Figure 13-8):

- A *header:* contains standard information for identifying and routing the message.

- *Properties:* are name-value pairs that the application can set or read. Properties also allow destinations to filter messages based on property values.

- A *body:* contains the actual message and can take several formats (text, bytes, object, etc.).

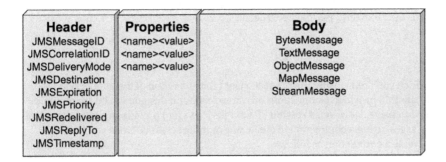

Figure 13-8. *Structure of a JMS message*

Header

The header has predefined name-value pairs, common to all messages that both clients and providers use to identify and route messages. They can be seen as message metadata as they give information about the message. Each field has associated getter and setter methods defined in the javax.jms.Message interface. Some header fields are intended to be set by a client, but many are set automatically by the send() or the publish() method. Table 13-2 describes each JMS message header field.

Table 13-2. *Fields Contained in the Header*

Field	Description	Set By
JMSDestination	This indicates the destination to which the message is being sent.	send() or publish() method
JMSDeliveryMode	JMS supports two modes of message delivery. PERSISTENT mode instructs the provider to ensure the message is not lost in transit due to a failure. NON_PERSISTENT mode is the lowest-overhead delivery mode because it does not require the message to be logged to a persistent storage.	send() or publish() method
JMSMessageID	This provides a value that uniquely identifies each message sent by a provider.	send() or publish() method
JMSTimestamp	This contains the time a message was handed off to a provider to be sent.	send() or publish() method
JMSCorrelationID	A client can use this field to link one message with another such as linking a response message with its request message.	Client
JMSReplyTo	This contains the destination where a reply to the message should be sent.	Client
JMSRedelivered	This Boolean value is set by the provider to indicate whether a message has been redelivered.	Provider
JMSType	This serves as a message type identifier.	Client
JMSExpiration	When a message is sent, its expiration time is calculated and set based on the time-to-live value specified on the send() method.	send() or publish() method
JMSPriority	JMS defines a 10-level priority value, with 0 as the lowest priority and 9 as the highest.	send() or publish() method

Properties

In addition to the header fields, the javax.jms.Message interface supports property values, which are just like headers, but explicitly created by the application, instead of being standard across messages. This provides a mechanism for adding optional header fields to a message that a client will choose to receive or not via selectors. Property values can be boolean, byte, short, int, long, float, double, and String. The code to set and get properties looks like this:

```
message.setFloatProperty("orderAmount", 1245.5f);
message.getFloatProperty("orderAmount");
```

Body

The body of a message is optional, and contains the data to send or receive. Depending on the interface that you use, it can contain different formats of data, as listed in Table 13-3.

Table 13-3. *Types of Messages*

Interface	Description
StreamMessage	A message whose body contains a stream of Java primitive values. It is filled and read sequentially.
MapMessage	A message whose body contains a set of name-value pairs where names are strings and values are Java primitive types.
TextMessage	A message whose body contains a string (for example, it can contain XML).
ObjectMessage	A message that contains a serializable object or a collection of serializable objects.
BytesMessage	A message that contains a stream of bytes.

It is possible to create your own message format, if you extend the javax.jms.Message interface. Note that, when a message is received, its body is read-only. Depending on the message type, you have different methods to access its content. A text message will have a getText() and setText() method, an object message will have a getObject() and setObject(), and so forth:

```
textMessage.setText("This is a text message");
textMessage.getText();
bytesMessage.readByte();
objectMessage.getObject();
```

Note that since JMS 2.0, the new method <T> T getBody(Class<T> c) returns the message body as an object of the specified type.

Sending and Receiving a Message with Classic API

Now let's take a look at a simple example to get an idea of how to use the classic JMS API to send and receive a message. JMS employs producers, consumers, and destinations. The producer sends a message to the destination, where the consumer is waiting for the message to arrive. Destinations can be of two kinds: queues (for point-to-point communication) and topics (for publish-subscribe communication). In Listing 13-2, a producer sends a text message to a queue to which the consumer is listening.

Listing 13-2. *The Producer Class Produces a Message into a Queue using the Classic API*

```
public class Producer {

  public static void main(String[] args) {

    try {
      // Gets the JNDI context
      Context jndiContext = new InitialContext();

      // Looks up the administered objects
      ConnectionFactory connectionFactory = (ConnectionFactory) ➥
                      jndiContext.lookup("jms/javaee7/ConnectionFactory");
      Destination queue = (Destination) jndiContext.lookup("jms/javaee7/Queue");

      // Creates the needed artifacts to connect to the queue
      Connection connection = connectionFactory.createConnection();
      Session session = connection.createSession(false, Session.AUTO_ACKNOWLEDGE);
      MessageProducer producer = session.createProducer(queue);
```

```
    // Sends a text message to the queue
    TextMessage message = session.createTextMessage("Text message sent at " + new Date());
    producer.send(message);

    connection.close();

  } catch (NamingException | JMSException e) {
    e.printStackTrace();
  }
 }
}
```

The code in Listing 13-2 represents a Producer class that has a main() method only. In this method, the first thing that occurs is that a JNDI context is instantiated and used to obtain a ConnectionFactory and a Destination. Connection factories and destinations (queues and topics) are called administered objects; they have to be created and declared in the message provider (in our case, OpenMQ in GlassFish). They both have a JNDI name (e.g., the queue is called jms/javaee7/Queue) and need to be looked up in the JNDI tree.

When the two administered objects are obtained, the Producer class uses the ConnectionFactory to create a Connection from which a Session is obtained. With this session, a MessageProducer and a message are created on the destination queue (session.createProducer(queue)). The producer then sends this message (of type text). Note that this main class catches the JNDI NamingException as well as the checked JMSException.

Fortunately, once you've written this code to send a message, the code to receive it looks almost the same. In fact, the first lines of the Consumer class in Listing 13-3 are exactly the same: create a JNDI context, lookup for the connection factory and the destination, and then connect. The only differences are that a MessageConsumer is used instead of a MessageProducer, and that the receiver enters an infinite loop to listen to the queue (you'll later see that this loop can be avoided by using the more standard message listener). When the message arrives, it is consumed and the content displayed.

Listing 13-3. The Consumer Class Consumes a Message from a Queue using the Classic API

```
public class Consumer {

  public static void main(String[] args) {

    try {
      // Gets the JNDI context
      Context jndiContext = new InitialContext();

      // Looks up the administered objects
      ConnectionFactory connectionFactory = (ConnectionFactory) ➥
                        jndiContext.lookup("jms/javaee7/ConnectionFactory");
      Destination queue = (Destination) jndiContext.lookup("jms/javaee7/Queue");

      // Creates the needed artifacts to connect to the queue
      Connection connection = connectionFactory.createConnection();
      Session session = connection.createSession(false, Session.AUTO_ACKNOWLEDGE);
      MessageConsumer consumer = session.createConsumer(queue);

      connection.start();

      // Loops to receive the messages
      while (true) {
        TextMessage message = (TextMessage) consumer.receive();
        System.out.println("Message received: " + message.getText());
      }
```

```
    } catch (NamingException | JMSException e) {
      e.printStackTrace();
    }
  }
}
```

Simplified API

As you can see, the code in Listing 13-2 and 13-3 is quite verbose and low level. You need several artifacts to be able to produce or consume a message (ConnectionFactory, Connection, Session...). On top of that you also need to deal with the JMSException which is a checked exception (JMSException has several sub classes). This API was created with JMS 1.1 in 2002 and was not changed until JMS 2.0.

JMS 2.0 introduces a new simplified API, which consists mainly of three new interfaces (JMSContext, JMSProducer and JMSConsumer). These interfaces rely internally on the ConnectionFactory and other classic APIs but leave the boilerplate code aside. Thanks to the new JMSRuntimeException, which is an unchecked exception, the code to send or receive a message is now much easier to write and read (code examples to follow).

Figure 13-9 shows a simplified class diagram of this new API. Note that the legacy, classic, and simplified APIs are all under the javax.jms package.

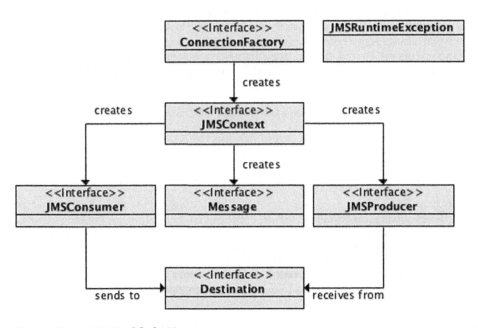

Figure 13-9. JMS Simplified API

The simplified API provides the same messaging functionality as the classic API but requires fewer interfaces and is simpler to use. These main interfaces are:

- JMSContext: active connection to a JMS provider and a single-threaded context for sending and receiving messages

- JMSProducer: object created by a JMSContext that is used for sending messages to a queue or topic

- JMSConsumer: object created by a JMSContext that is used for receiving messages sent to a queue or topic

JMSContext

The JMSContext is the main interface in the simplified JMS API introduced by JMS 2.0. It combines the functionality of two separate objects from the JMS 1.1 classic API: a Connection (the physical link to the JMS provider) and a Session (a single-threaded context for sending and receiving messages).

A JMSContext may be created by the application by calling one of several createContext methods on a ConnectionFactory (see Listing 13-1) and then closed (i.e., application-managed). Alternatively, if the application is running in a container (EJB or Web), the JMSContext can be injected using the @Inject annotation (i.e., container-managed).

When an application needs to send messages it uses the createProducer method to create a JMSProducer, which provides methods to configure and send messages. Messages may be sent either synchronously or asynchronously. To receive messages, an application can use one of several createConsumer methods to create a JMSConsumer. Table 13-4 shows you a subset of the JMSContext API.

Table 13-4. *Subset of the JMSContext API*

Property	Description
void start()	Starts (or restarts) delivery of incoming messages
void stop()	Temporarily stops the delivery of incoming messages
void close()	Closes the JMSContext
void commit()	Commits all messages done in this transaction and releases any locks currently held
void rollback()	Rolls back any messages done in this transaction and releases any locks currently held
BytesMessage createBytesMessage()	Creates a BytesMessage object
MapMessage createMapMessage()	Creates a MapMessage object
Message createMessage()	Creates a Message object
ObjectMessage createObjectMessage()	Creates an ObjectMessage object
StreamMessage createStreamMessage()	Creates a StreamMessage object
TextMessage createTextMessage()	Creates a TextMessage object
Topic createTopic(String topicName)	Creates a Topic object
Queue createQueue(String queueName)	Creates a Queue object
JMSConsumer createConsumer(Destination destination)	Creates a JMSConsumer for the specified destination
JMSConsumer createConsumer(Destination destination, String messageSelector)	Creates a JMSConsumer for the specified destination, using a message selector
JMSProducer createProducer()	Creates a new JMSProducer object which can be used to configure and send messages
JMSContext createContext(int sessionMode)	Creates a new JMSContext with the specified session mode

JMSProducer

A JMSProducer is used to send messages on behalf of a JMSContext. It provides various send methods to send a message to a specified destination. An instance of JMSProducer is created by calling the createProducer method on a JMSContext. It also provides methods to allow send options, message properties and message headers (see Figure 13-8) to be specified prior to sending the message. Table 13-5 shows a subset of the JMSProducer API.

Table 13-5. *Subset of the JMSProducer API*

Property	Description
get/set[Type]Property	Sets and returns a message property where [Type] is the type of the property and can be Boolean, Byte, Double, Float, Int, Long, Object, Short, String
JMSProducer clearProperties()	Clears any message properties set
Set<String> getPropertyNames()	Returns an unmodifiable Set view of the names of all the message properties that have been set
boolean propertyExists(String name)	Indicates whether a message property with the specified name has been set
get/set[Message Header]	Sets and returns a message header where [Message Header] can be DeliveryDelay, DeliveryMode, JMSCorrelationID, JMSReplyTo, JMSType, Priority, TimeToLive
JMSProducer send(Destination destination, Message message)	Sends a message to the specified destination, using any send options, message properties and message headers that have been defined
JMSProducer send(Destination destination, String body)	Sends a TextMessage with the specified body to the specified destination

JMSConsumer

A JMSConsumer is used to receive messages from a queue or topic. It is created with one of the createConsumer methods on a JMSContext by passing a Queue or a Topic. As you will later see, a JMSConsumer can be created with a message selector so it can restrict messages delivered.

A client may receive a message synchronously or asynchronously as they arrive. For asynchronous delivery, a client can register a MessageListener object with a JMSConsumer. As messages arrive, the provider delivers them by calling the MessageListener's onMessage method. Table 13-6 shows you a subset of the JMSConsumer API.

Table 13-6. *Subset of the JMSConsumer API*

Property	Description
void close()	Closes the JMSConsumer
Message receive()	Receives the next message produced
Message receive(long timeout)	Receives the next message that arrives within the specified timeout interval
<T> T receiveBody(Class<T> c)	Receives the next message produced and returns its body as an object of the specified type
Message receiveNoWait()	Receives the next message if one is immediately available
void setMessageListener(MessageListener listener)	Sets the MessageListener
MessageListener getMessageListener()	Gets the MessageListener
String getMessageSelector()	Gets the message selector expression

Writing Message Producers

The new JMS simplified API allows you to write producers and consumers in a less verbose manner than with the classic API. But it still needs both of the administered objects: ConnectionFactory and Destination. Depending if you are running outside or inside a container (EJB, Web or ACC) you will either use JNDI lookups or injection. As you've seen previously, the JMSContext API is the central API to produce and consume messages. If your application runs outside a container you will need to manage the lifecycle of the JMSContext (by creating and closing it programmatically). If you run inside a container you can just inject it and leave the container to manage its lifecycle.

Producing a Message outside a Container

A message producer (JMSProducer) is an object created by the JMSContext and is used to send messages to a destination. The following steps explain how to create a producer that sends a message to a queue (see Listing 13-4) outside any container (in a pure Java SE environment):

- Obtain a connection factory and a queue using JNDI lookups

- Create a JMSContext object using the connection factory (notice the try-with-resources statement that will automatically close the JMSContext object)

- Create a javax.jms.JMSProducer using the JSMContext object

- Send a text message to the queue using the JMSProducer.send() method

Listing 13-4. The Producer Class Produces a Message into a Queue

```
public class Producer {

  public static void main(String[] args) {

    try {
      // Gets the JNDI context
      Context jndiContext = new InitialContext();
```

```
// Looks up the administered objects
ConnectionFactory connectionFactory = (ConnectionFactory) ↪
                    jndiContext.lookup("jms/javaee7/ConnectionFactory");
Destination queue = (Destination) jndiContext.lookup("jms/javaee7/Queue");

// Sends a text message to the queue
try (JMSContext context = connectionFactory.createContext()) {
  context.createProducer().send(queue, "Text message sent at " + new Date());
}

} catch (NamingException e) {
  e.printStackTrace();
  }
 }
}
```

If you compare the code in Listing 13-4 with the one using the classic API in Listing 13-2, you will notice that the code is less verbose. Exception handling is also neater as the new JMSRuntimeException is used in the new API and is an unchecked exception.

Producing a Message inside a Container

Connection factories and destinations are administered objects that reside in a message provider and have to be declared in the JNDI namespace, which is why you use the JNDI API to look them up. When the client code runs inside a container, dependency injection can be used instead. Java EE 7 has several containers: EJB, servlet, and application client container (ACC). If the code runs in one of these containers, the @Resource annotation can be used to inject a reference to that resource by the container. With Java EE 7, using resources is much easier, as you don't have the complexity of JNDI or are not required to configure resource references in deployment descriptors. You just rely on the container injection capabilities.

Table 13-7 lists the attributes that belong to the @Resource annotation.

Table 13-7. *API of the @javax.annotation.Resource Annotation*

Element	Description
name	The JNDI name of the resource (the name is implementation specific and not portable)
type	The Java type of the resource (e.g., javax.sql.DataSource or javax.jms.Topic)
authenticationType	The authentication type to use for the resource (either the container or the application)
shareable	Whether the resource can be shared
mappedName	A product-specific name that the resource should map to
lookup	The JNDI name of a resource that the resource being defined will be bound to. It can link to any compatible resource using the portable JNDI names
description	Description of the resource

To use the @Resource annotation let's take the example of the producer in Listing 13-4, change it to a stateless session bean and use injection instead of JNDI lookups. In Listing 13-4, both the connection factory and the queue are looked up using JNDI. In Listing 13-5, the JNDI name is on the @Resource annotation. When the ProducerEJB runs in a container, references of ConnectionFactory and Queue are injected at initialization.

Listing 13-5. The ProducerEJB Running inside a Container and using @Resource

```
@Stateless
public class ProducerEJB {

  @Resource(lookup = "jms/javaee7/ConnectionFactory")
  private ConnectionFactory connectionFactory;
  @Resource(lookup = "jms/javaee7/Queue")
  private Queue queue;

  public void sendMessage() {

    try (JMSContext context = connectionFactory.createContext()) {
      context.createProducer().send(queue, "Text message sent at " + new Date());
    }
  }
}
```

The code in Listing 13-5 is simpler than the one in Listing 13-4 because it doesn't deal with JNDI lookups or the JNDI `NamingException`. The container injects the administered objects once the EJB is initialized.

Producing a Message inside a Container with CDI

When the producer is executed in a container (EJB or Servlet container) with CDI enabled, it can inject the JMSContext. The container will then manage its lifecycle (no need to create or close the JMSContext). This can be done thanks to the @Inject and @JMSConnectionFactory annotations.

The annotation `javax.jms.JMSConnectionFactory` may be used to specify the JNDI lookup name of the ConnectionFactory used to create the JMSContext (see Listing 13-6). If the JMSConnectionFactory annotation is omitted, then the platform default JMS connection factory will be used.

Listing 13-6. A Managed Bean Producing a Message using @Inject

```
public class Producer {

  @Inject
  @JMSConnectionFactory("jms/javaee7/ConnectionFactory")
  private JMSContext context;
  @Resource(lookup = "jms/javaee7/Queue")
  private Queue queue;

  public void sendMessage() {
    context.createProducer().send(queue, "Text message sent at " + new Date());
  }
}
```

The code in Listing 13-6 is quite minimalist. The container does all the work of injecting the needed components and managing their lifecycle. As a developer you just need one line of code to send a message.

The annotation `javax.jms.JMSPasswordCredential` can also be used to specify a user name and password for when the JMSContext is created:

```
@Inject
@JMSConnectionFactory("jms/connectionFactory")
@JMSPasswordCredential(userName="admin",password="mypassword")
private JMSContext context;
```

Writing Message Consumers

A client uses a JMSConsumer to receive messages from a destination. A JMSConsumer is created by passing a Queue or Topic to the JMSContext's createConsumer() method. Messaging is inherently asynchronous, in that there is no timing dependency between producers and consumers. However, the client itself can consume messages in two ways:

- *Synchronously*: A receiver explicitly fetches the message from the destination by calling the receive() method.

- *Asynchronously*: A receiver decides to register to an event that is triggered when the message arrives. It has to implement the MessageListener interface, and, whenever a message arrives, the provider delivers it by calling the onMessage() method.

Figure 13-10 illustrates these two types of consumer.

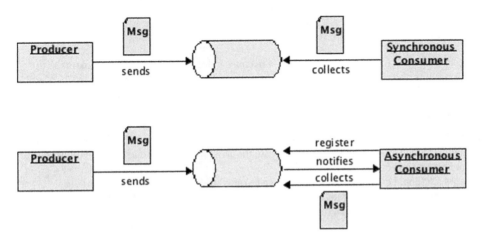

Figure 13-10. *Synchronous and asynchronous consumers*

Synchronous Delivery

A synchronous consumer needs to start a JMSContext, loop to wait until a new message arrives, and request the arrived message using one of its receive() methods (see Table 13-6). There are several variations of receive() that allow a client to pull or wait for the next message. The following steps explain how you can create a synchronous consumer that consumes a message from a queue (see Listing 13-7):

- Obtain a connection factory and a topic using JNDI lookups (or injection)
- Create a JMSContext object using the connection factory
- Create a javax.jms.JMSConsumer using the JSMContext object
- Loop and call the receive() method (or in this case receiveBody) on the consumer object. The receive() methods block if the queue is empty and wait for a message to arrive. Here, the infinite loop waits for other messages to arrive

Listing 13-7. The Consumer Class Consumes Messages in a Synchronous Manner

```java
public class Consumer {

  public static void main(String[] args) {

    try {
      // Gets the JNDI context
      Context jndiContext = new InitialContext();

      // Looks up the administered objects
      ConnectionFactory connectionFactory = (ConnectionFactory) ↪
                    jndiContext.lookup("jms/javaee7/ConnectionFactory");
      Destination queue = (Destination) jndiContext.lookup("jms/javaee7/Queue");

      // Loops to receive the messages
      try (JMSContext context = connectionFactory.createContext()) {
        while (true) {
          String message = context.createConsumer(queue).receiveBody(String.class);
        }
      }

    } catch (NamingException e) {
      e.printStackTrace();
    }
  }
}
```

Again, if you compare the code in Listing 13-7 with the one using the classic API in Listing 13-3, you will see how the new simplified API is easier to use and more expressive.

■ **Note**   Just like producers that can use injection with @Resource, @Inject or @JMSConnectionFactory when executed inside a container (see Listing 13-5 and 13-6), consumers can benefit from the same functionalities. Here I am just showing how a consumer can receive a message in a pure Java SE environment, but you can guess the simplifications made to the code if running inside a container and using injection.

Asynchronous Delivery

Asynchronous consumption is based on event handling. A client can register an object (including itself) that implements the MessageListener interface. A *message listener* is an object that acts as an asynchronous event handler for messages. As messages arrive, the provider delivers them by calling the listener's onMessage() method, which takes one argument of type Message. With this event model, the consumer doesn't need to loop indefinitely to receive a message. MDBs use this event model (more on that later).

The following steps describe the process used to create an asynchronous message listener (see Listing 13-8):

- The class implements the javax.jms.MessageListener interface, which defines a single method called onMessage()

- Obtain a connection factory and a topic using JNDI lookups (or injection)

- Create a javax.jms.JMSConsumer using the JSMContext object

- Call the setMessageListener() method, passing an instance of a MessageListener interface (in Listing 13-8, the Listener class itself implements the MessageListener interface)

- Implement the onMessage() method and process the received message. Each time a message arrives, the provider will invoke this method, passing the message

Listing 13-8. The Consumer Is a Message Listener

```java
public class Listener implements MessageListener {

  public static void main(String[] args) {

    try {
      // Gets the JNDI context
      Context jndiContext = new InitialContext();

      // Looks up the administered objects
      ConnectionFactory connectionFactory = (ConnectionFactory) ➥
                      jndiContext.lookup("jms/javaee7/ConnectionFactory");
      Destination queue = (Destination) jndiContext.lookup("jms/javaee7/Queue");

      try (JMSContext context = connectionFactory.createContext()) {
        context.createConsumer(queue).setMessageListener(new Listener());
      }

    } catch (NamingException e) {
      e.printStackTrace();
    }
  }

  public void onMessage(Message message) {
    System.out.println("Async Message received: " + message.getBody(String.class));
  }
}
```

Reliability Mechanisms

You've seen how to connect to a provider, create different types of messages, send them to queues or topics, and receive them. But what if you rely heavily on JMS and need to ensure reliability or other advanced features? JMS defines several levels of reliability to ensure your message is delivered, even if the provider crashes or is under load, or if destinations are filled with messages that should have expired. The mechanisms for achieving reliable message delivery are as follows:

- *Filtering messages*: Using selectors you can filter messages you want to receive

- *Setting message time-to-live*: Set an expiration time on messages so they are not delivered if they are obsolete

- *Specifying message persistence*: Specify that messages are persistent in the event of a provider failure

- *Controlling acknowledgment*: Specify various levels of message acknowledgment

- *Creating durable subscribers*: Ensure messages are delivered to an unavailable subscriber in a pub-sub model

- *Setting priorities*: Set the priority for delivering a message

Filtering messages

Some messaging applications need to filter the messages they receive. When a message is broadcast to many clients, it becomes useful to set criteria so that it is only consumed by certain receivers. This eliminates both the time and bandwidth the provider would waste transporting messages to clients that don't need them.

You've seen that messages are composed of three parts: header, properties, and body (see Figure 13-8). The header contains a fixed number of fields (the message metadata), and the properties are a set of custom name-value pairs that the application can use to set any values. Selection can be done on those two areas. Producers set one or several property values or header fields, and the consumer specifies message selection criteria using selector expressions. Only messages that match the selector are delivered. Message selectors assign the work of filtering messages to the JMS provider, rather than to the application.

A message selector is a string that contains an expression. The syntax of the expression is based on a subset of the SQL92 conditional expression syntax and looks like this:

```
context.createConsumer(queue, "JMSPriority < 6").receive();
context.createConsumer(queue, "JMSPriority < 6 AND orderAmount < 200").receive();
context.createConsumer(queue, "orderAmount BETWEEN 1000 AND 2000").receive();
```

In the preceding code, a consumer is created with the JMSContext.createConsumer() method, passing a selector string. This string can use header fields (JMSPriority < 6) or custom properties (orderAmount < 200). The producer sets these properties into the message as follows:

```
context.createTextMessage().setIntProperty("orderAmount", 1530);
context.createTextMessage().setJMSPriority(5);
```

Selector expression can use logical operators (NOT, AND, OR), comparison operators (=, >, >=, <, <=, <>), arithmetic operators (+, -, *, /), expressions ([NOT] BETWEEN, [NOT] IN, [NOT] LIKE, IS [NOT] NULL), and so on.

Setting Message Time-to-Live

Under heavy load, a time-to-live can be set on messages to ensure that the provider will remove them from the destination when they become obsolete, by either using the JMSProducer API or setting the JMSExpiration header field. The JMSProducer has a setTimeToLive() method that takes a number of milliseconds:

```
context.createProducer().setTimeToLive(1000).send(queue, message);
```

Specifying Message Persistence

JMS supports two modes of message delivery: persistent and nonpersistent. *Persistent delivery* ensures that a message is delivered only once to a consumer, whereas *nonpersistent delivery* requires a message be delivered once at most. Persistent delivery (which is the default) is more reliable, but at a performance cost, as it prevents losing a message if a provider failure occurs. The delivery mode can be specified by using the setDeliveryMode() method of the JMSProducer interface:

```
context.createProducer().setDeliveryMode(DeliveryMode.NON_PERSISTENT).send(queue, message);
```

Controlling Acknowledgment

So far, the scenarios we've explored have assumed that a message is sent and received without any acknowledgment. But sometimes, you will want a receiver to acknowledge the message has been received (see Figure 13-11). An acknowledgment phase can be initiated either by the JMS provider or by the client, depending on the acknowledgment mode.

Figure 13-11. *A consumer acknowledging a message*

In transactional sessions, acknowledgment happens automatically when a transaction is committed. If a transaction is rolled back, all consumed messages are redelivered. But in nontransactional sessions, an acknowledgment mode must be specified:

- `AUTO_ACKNOWLEDGE`: The session automatically acknowledges the receipt of a message

- `CLIENT_ACKNOWLEDGE`: A client acknowledges a message by explicitly calling the `Message.acknowledge()` method

- `DUPS_OK_ACKNOWLEDGE`: This option instructs the session to lazily acknowledge the delivery of messages. This is likely to result in the delivery of some duplicate messages if the JMS provider fails, so it should be used only by consumers that can tolerate duplicate messages. If the message is redelivered, the provider sets the value of the `JMSRedelivered` header field to `true`

The following code uses the `@JMSSessionMode` annotation to set the acknowledgment mode to the `JMSContext` on the producer. The consumer explicitly acknowledges the message by calling the `acknowledge()` method:

```
// Producer
@Inject
@JMSConnectionFactory("jms/connectionFactory")
@JMSSessionMode(JMSContext.AUTO_ACKNOWLEDGE)
private JMSContext context;
...
context.createProducer().send(queue, message);

// Consumer
message.acknowledge();
```

Creating Durable Consumers

The disadvantage of using the pub-sub model is that a message consumer must be running when the messages are sent to the topic; otherwise, it will not receive them. By using durable consumers, the JMS API provides a way to keep messages in the topic until all subscribed consumers receive them. With durable subscription, the consumer can be offline for some time, but, when it reconnects, it receives the messages that arrived during its disconnection. To achieve this, the client creates a durable consumer using the JMSContext:

```
context.createDurableConsumer(topic, "javaee7DurableSubscription").receive();
```

At this point, the client program starts the connection and receives messages. The name javaee7DurableSubscription is used as an identifier of the durable subscription. Each durable consumer must have a unique ID, resulting in the declaration of a unique connection factory for each potential, durable consumer.

Setting Priorities

You can use message priority levels to instruct the JMS provider to deliver urgent messages first. JMS defines ten priority values, with 0 as the lowest and 9 as the highest. You can specify the priority value by using the setPriority() method of the JMSProducer:

```
context.createProducer().setPriority(2).send(queue, message);
```

Most of these methods return the JMSProducer to allow method calls to be chained together, allowing a fluid programming style. For example:

```
context.createProducer().setPriority(2)
                        .setTimeToLive(1000)
                        .setDeliveryMode(DeliveryMode.NON_PERSISTENT)
                        .send(queue, message);
```

Writing Message-Driven Beans

Until now, this chapter showed how asynchronous messaging provides loose coupling and increased flexibility between systems, using the JMS API. MDBs provide this standard asynchronous messaging model for enterprise applications running in an EJB container.

An MDB is an asynchronous consumer that is invoked by the container as a result of the arrival of a message. To a message producer, an MDB is simply a message consumer, hidden behind a destination to which it listens.

MDBs are part of the EJB specification, and their model is close to stateless session beans as they do not have any state and run inside an EJB container. The container listens to a destination and delegates the call to the MDB upon message arrival. Like any other EJB, MDBs can access resources managed by the container (other EJBs, JDBC connections, JMS resources, Entity Manager etc.).

Why use MDBs when you can use stand-alone JMS clients, as you've seen previously? Because of the container, which manages multithreading, security, and transactions, thereby greatly simplifying the code of your JMS consumer. It also manages incoming messages among multiple instances of MDBs (available in a pool) that have no special multithreading code themselves. As soon as a new message reaches the destination, an MDB instance is retrieved from the pool to handle the message. A simple consumer MDB is described in Listing 13-9.

Listing 13-9. A Simple MDB

```
@MessageDriven(mappedName = "jms/javaee7/Topic")
public class BillingMDB implements MessageListener {

  public void onMessage(Message message) {
    System.out.println("Message received: " + message.getBody(String.class));
  }
}
```

The code in Listing 13-9 (omitting exception handling for clarity) shows that MDBs relieve the programmer of all mechanical aspects of processing the types of messages explained so far. An MDB implements the MessageListener interface and the onMessage() method, but no other code is needed to connect to the provider or start message consumption. MDBs also rely on the configuration-by-exception mechanism, and only a few annotations are needed to make it work (see the @MessageDriven annotation).

Anatomy of an MDB

MDBs are different from session beans, as they do not implement a local or remote business interface but instead implement the javax.jms.MessageListener interface. Clients cannot invoke methods directly on MDBs; however, like session beans, MDBs have a rich programming model that includes a life cycle, callback annotations, interceptors, injection, and transactions. Taking advantage of this model provides applications with a high level of functionality.

It is important to be aware that MDBs are not part of the EJB Lite model, meaning that they cannot be deployed in a simple web profile application server, but still need the full Java EE stack.

The requirements to develop an MDB class are as follows:

- The class must be annotated with @javax.ejb.MessageDriven or its XML equivalent in a deployment descriptor

- The class must implement, directly or indirectly, the MessageListener interface

- The class must be defined as public, and must not be final or abstract

- The class must have a public no-arg constructor that the container will use to create instances of the MDB

- The class must not define the finalize() method.

The MDB class is allowed to implement other methods, invoke other resources, and so on. MDBs are deployed in a container and can be optionally packaged with an ejb-jar.xml file. Following the "ease of use" model of Java EE 7, an MDB can be simply an annotated POJO, eliminating most of the configuration. However, if you still need to customize the JMS configuration, you can use the elements of the @MessageDriven and @ActivationConfigProperty annotations (or XML equivalent).

@MessageDriven

MDBs are one of the simplest kinds of EJBs to develop, as they support the smallest number of annotations. The @MessageDriven annotation (or XML equivalent) is mandatory, as it is the piece of metadata the container requires to recognize that the Java class is actually an MDB.

The API of the @MessageDriven annotation, shown in Listing 13-10, is very simple, and all elements are optional.

Listing 13-10. @MessageDriven Annotation API

```
@Target(TYPE) @Retention(RUNTIME)
public @interface MessageDriven {
  String name() default "";
  Class messageListenerInterface default Object.class;
  ActivationConfigProperty[] activationConfig() default {};
  String mappedName();
  String description();
}
```

The name element specifies the name of the MDB (which by default is the name of the class). messageListenerInterface specifies which message listener the MDB implements (if the MDB implements multiple interfaces, it tells the EJB container which one is the MessageListener interface). The mappedName element is the JNDI name of the destination that the MDB should be listening to. description is just a string, used to give a description of the MDB once deployed. The activationConfig element is used to specify configuration properties and takes an array of @ActivationConfigProperty annotations.

@ActivationConfigProperty

JMS allows configuration of certain properties such as message selectors, acknowledgment mode, durable subscribers, and so on. In an MDB, these properties can be set using the @ActivationConfigProperty annotation. This optional annotation can be provided as one of the parameters for the @MessageDriven annotation, and, compared to the JMS equivalent, the @ActivationConfigProperty is very basic, consisting of a name-value pair (see Listing 13-11).

Listing 13-11. ActivationConfigProperty Annotation API

```
@Target({}) @Retention(RUNTIME)
public @interface ActivationConfigProperty {
  String propertyName();
  String propertyValue();
}
```

The activationConfig property allows you to provide standard and nonstandard (provider-specific) configuration. The code in Listing 13-12 sets the acknowledge mode and the message selector.

Listing 13-12. Setting Properties on MDBs

```
@MessageDriven(mappedName = "jms/javaee7/Topic", activationConfig = {
  @ActivationConfigProperty(propertyName = "acknowledgeMode", ⮑
                            propertyValue = "Auto-acknowledge"),
  @ActivationConfigProperty(propertyName = "messageSelector", ⮑
                            propertyValue = "orderAmount < 3000")
})
public class BillingMDB implements MessageListener {

  public void onMessage(Message message) {
    System.out.println("Message received: " + message.getBody(String.class));
  }
}
```

Each activation property is a name-value pair that the underlying messaging provider understands and uses to set up the MDB. Table 13-8 lists some standard properties you can use.

Table 13-8. *Activation Properties for OpenMQ*

Property	Description
acknowledgeMode	The acknowledgment mode (default is AUTO_ACKNOWLEDGE)
messageSelector	The message selector string used by the MDB
destinationType	The destination type, which can be TOPIC or QUEUE
destinationLookup	The lookup name of an administratively-defined Queue or Topic
connectionFactoryLookup	The lookup name of an administratively defined ConnectionFactory
destination	The name of the destination.
subscriptionDurability	The subscription durability (default is NON_DURABLE)
subscriptionName	The subscription name of the consumer
shareSubscriptions	Used if the message-driven bean is deployed into a clustered
clientId	Client identifier that will be used when connecting to the JMS provider

Dependencies Injection

Like all the other EJBs that you've seen in Chapter 7, MDBs can use dependency injection to acquire references to resources such as JDBC datasources, EJBs, or other objects. *Injection* is the means by which the container inserts dependencies automatically after creating the object. These resources have to be available in the container or environment context, so the following code is allowed in an MDB:

```
@PersistenceContext
private EntityManager em;
@Inject
private InvoiceBean invoice;
@Resource(lookup = "jms/javaee7/ConnectionFactory")
private ConnectionFactory connectionFactory;
```

The MDB context can also be injected using the @Resource annotation:

```
@Resource private MessageDrivenContext context;
```

MDB Context

The MessageDrivenContext interface provides access to the runtime context that the container provides for an MDB instance. The container passes the MessageDrivenContext interface to this instance, which remains associated for the lifetime of the MDB. This gives the MDB the possibility to explicitly roll back a transaction, get the user principal, and so on. The MessageDrivenContext interface extends the javax.ejb.EJBContext interface without adding any extra methods.

If the MDB injects a reference to its context, it will be able to invoke the methods listed in Table 13-9.

Table 13-9. Methods of the MessageDrivenContext Interface

Method	Description
getCallerPrincipal	Returns the java.security.Principal associated with the invocation
getRollbackOnly	Tests whether the current transaction has been marked for rollback
getTimerService	Returns the javax.ejb.TimerService interface
getUserTransaction	Returns the javax.transaction.UserTransaction interface to use to demarcate transactions. Only MDBs with bean-managed transaction (BMT) can use this method
isCallerInRole	Tests whether the caller has a given security role
Lookup	Enables the MDB to look up its environment entries in the JNDI naming context
setRollbackOnly	Allows the instance to mark the current transaction as rollback. Only MDBs with BMT can use this method

Life Cycle and Callback Annotations

The MDB life cycle (see Figure 13-12) is identical to that of the stateless session bean: either the MDB exists and is ready to consume messages or it doesn't exist. Before exiting, the container first creates an instance of the MDB and, if applicable, injects the necessary resources as specified by metadata annotations (@Resource, @Inject, @EJB, etc.) or deployment descriptor. The container then calls the bean's @PostConstruct callback method, if any. After this, the MDB is in the ready state and waits to consume any incoming message. The @PreDestroy callback occurs when the MDB is removed from the pool or destroyed.

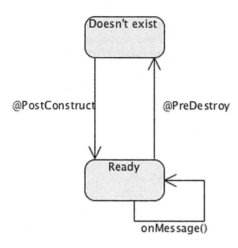

Figure 13-12. *MDB life cycle*

This behavior is identical to that of stateless session beans (see Chapter 8 for more details about callback methods), and, like other EJBs, you can add interceptors with the @javax.ejb.AroundInvoke annotation.

MDB as a Consumer

As explained in the "Writing Message Consumers" section earlier in this chapter, consumers can receive a message either synchronously, by looping and waiting for a message to arrive, or asynchronously, by implementing the MessageListener interface. By nature, MDBs are designed to function as asynchronous message consumers. MDBs implement a message listener interface, which is triggered by the container when a message arrives.

Can an MDB be a synchronous consumer? Yes, but this is not recommended. Synchronous message consumers block and tie up server resources (the EJBs will be stuck looping without performing any work, and the container will not be able to free them). MDBs, like stateless session beans, live in a pool of a certain size. When the container needs an instance, it takes one out of the pool and uses it. If each instance goes into an infinite loop, the pool will eventually empty, and all the available instances will be busy looping. The EJB container can also start generating more MDB instances, growing the pool and eating up more and more memory. For this reason, session beans and MDBs should not be used as synchronous message consumers. Table 13-10 shows you the different receiving modes for MDBs and session beans.

Table 13-10. *MDB Compared with Session Beans*

Enterprise Beans	Producer	Synchronous Consumer	Asynchronous Consumer
Session beans	Yes	Not recommended	Not possible
MDB	Yes	Not recommended	Yes

MDB as a Producer

MDBs are capable of becoming message producers, something that often occurs when they are involved in a workflow, as they receive a message from one destination, process it, and send it to another destination. To add this capability, the JMS API must be used.

A destination and a connection factory can be injected by using the @Resource and @JMSConnectionFactory annotations or via JNDI lookup, and then methods on the javax.jms.JMSContext object can be invoked to create and send a message. The code of the BillingMDB (see Listing 13-13) listens to a topic (jms/javaee7/Topic), receives messages (onMessage() method), and sends a new message to a queue (jms/javaee7/Queue).

Listing 13-13. A MDB Consuming and Producing Messages

```
@MessageDriven(mappedName = "jms/javaee7/Topic", activationConfig = { ↪
            @ActivationConfigProperty(propertyName  = "acknowledgeMode", ↪
                                      propertyValue = "Auto-acknowledge"), ↪
            @ActivationConfigProperty(propertyName  = "messageSelector", ↪
                                      propertyValue = "orderAmount BETWEEN 3 AND 7")
})
public class BillingMDB implements MessageListener {

  @Inject
  @JMSConnectionFactory("jms/javaee7/ConnectionFactory")
  @JMSSessionMode(JMSContext.AUTO_ACKNOWLEDGE)
  private JMSContext context;
  @Resource(lookup = "jms/javaee7/Queue")
  private Destination printingQueue;

  public void onMessage(Message message) {
    System.out.println("Message received: " + message.getBody(String.class));
    sendPrintingMessage();
  }

  private void sendPrintingMessage() throws JMSException {
    context.createProducer().send(printingQueue, "Message has been received and resent");
  }
}
```

This MDB uses most of the concepts introduced thus far. First, it uses the @MessageDriven annotation to define the JNDI name of the topic it is listening to (mappedName = "jms/javaee7/Topic"). In this same annotation, it defines a set of properties, such as the acknowledge mode and a message selector using an array of @ActivationConfigProperty annotations, and it implements MessageListener and its onMessage() method.

This MDB also needs to produce a message. Therefore, it is injected with the two administered objects required: a connection factory (using JMSContext) and a destination (the queue named jms/javaee7/Queue). Finally, the business method that sends messages (the sendPrintingMessage() method) looks like what you've seen earlier: a JMSProducer is created and used to create and send a text message. For better readability, exception handling has been omitted in the entire class.

Transactions

MDBs are EJBs (see Chapter 7 and 8 for more information). MDBs can use BMTs or container-managed transactions (CMTs); they can explicitly roll back a transaction by using the MessageDrivenContext.setRollbackOnly() method, and so on. However, there are some specifics regarding MDBs that are worth explaining.

When we talk about transactions, we always think of relational databases. However, other resources are also transactional, such as messaging systems. If two or more operations have to succeed or fail together, they form a transaction (see Chapter 9). With messaging, if two or more messages are sent, they have to succeed (commit) or fail (roll back) together. How does this work in practice? The answer is that messages are not released to consumers until the transaction commits. The container will start a transaction before the onMessage() method is invoked and will commit the transaction when the method returns (unless the transaction was marked for rollback with setRollbackOnly()).

Even though MDBs are transactional, they cannot execute in the client's transaction context, as they don't have a client. Nobody explicitly invokes methods on MDBs, they just listen to a destination and consume messages. There is no context passed from a client to an MDB, and similarly the client transaction context cannot be passed to the onMessage() method. Table 13-11 compares CMTs with session beans and MDBs.

Table 13-11. *MDB Transactions Compared with Session Beans*

Transaction Attribute	Session Beans	MDB
NOT_SUPPORTED	Yes	Yes
REQUIRED	Yes	Yes
MANDATORY	Yes	No
REQUIRES_NEW	Yes	No
SUPPORTS	Yes	No
NEVER	Yes	No

In CMTs, MDBs can use the @javax.ejb.TransactionAttribute annotation on business methods with the two following attributes:

- REQUIRED *(the default)*: If the MDB invokes other enterprise beans, the container passes the transaction context with the invocation. The container attempts to commit the transaction when the message listener method has completed

- NOT_SUPPORTED: If the MDB invokes other enterprise beans, the container passes no transaction context with the invocation

Handling Exceptions

In the snippets of code in this chapter, exception handling has been omitted, as the JMS API can be verbose in dealing with exceptions. The classic API defines 12 different exceptions, all inheriting from javax.jms.JMSException. The simplified API defines 10 runtime exceptions all inheriting from javax.jms.JMSRuntimeException.

It is important to note that JMSException is a checked exception (see the discussion on application exception in the "Exception Handling" section in Chapter 9) and JMSRuntimeException is unchecked. The EJB specification outlines two types of exceptions:

- *Application exceptions*: Checked exceptions that extend Exception and do not cause the container to roll back

- *System exceptions*: Unchecked exceptions that extend RuntimeException and cause the container to roll back

Throwing a JMSRuntimeException will cause the container to roll back, but throwing a JMSException will not. If a rollback is needed, the setRollBackOnly() must be explicitly called or a system exception (such as EJBException) rethrown:

```
public void onMessage(Message message) {
  try {
    System.out.println("Message received: " + message.getBody(String.class));
```

```
  } catch (JMSException e) {
    context.setRollBackOnly();
  }
}
```

Putting It All Together

In this chapter we have covered the basic concepts of messaging (P2P and pub-sub models), administered objects (connection factories and destinations), learned how to connect to a provider, to produce and consume messages, to use some reliability mechanisms, and to use container-managed components (MDBs) to listen to destinations. So now let's see how these concepts work together through an example; we'll compile and package it with Maven, and deploy it to GlassFish.

This example uses a stand-alone class (OrderProducer) that sends messages to a topic (called jms/javaee7/Topic). These messages are objects representing a customer purchase order of books and CDs. The purchase order (OrderDTO) has several attributes, including the total amount of the order. The consumers that listen to the topic are OrderConsumer and ExpensiveOrderMDB (see Figure 13-13). The OrderConsumer receives any order, but the MDB only consumes orders that have a total amount greater than $1,000 (using a selector).

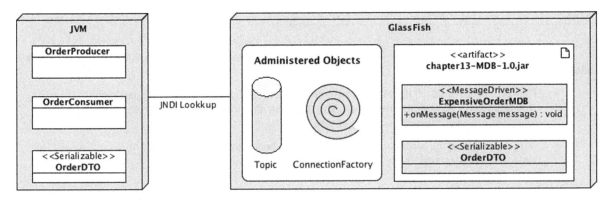

Figure 13-13. *Putting It All Together*

Because Maven needs to structure the code based on the final packaging artifacts, the ExpensiveOrderMDB and the OrderDTO will get packaged in one jar file (chapter13-MDB-1.0.jar file) and then deployed to GlassFish. The OrderProducer, OrderConsumer and, again, the OrderDTO will run in a Java SE environment.

Writing the OrderDTO

The object that will be sent in the JMS message is a POJO that needs to implement the Serializable interface. The OrderDTO class, shown in Listing 13-14, gives some information about the order, including its total amount; it is the object that will be set into a JMS ObjectMessage and sent from the OrderProducer to the topic and then consumed by the OrderConsumer and ExpensiveOrderMDB.

Listing 13-14. *The OrderDTO Is Passed in a JMS ObjectMessage*

```
public class OrderDTO implements Serializable {

  private Long orderId;
  private Date creationDate;
```

```
    private String customerName;
    private Float totalAmount;

// Constructors, getters, setters
}
```

Writing the OrderProducer

The OrderProducer, shown in Listing 13-15, is a stand-alone client that uses the JMS simplified API to send an ObjectMessage to the jms/javaee7/Topic topic. It looks up for the necessary connection factory and destination, and in the main() method creates an instance of an OrderDTO class. Note that the totalAmount of the order is an argument passed to the class (args[0]). The JSMProducer sets the orderAmount property in the message for selection later, and the order is then sent to the topic.

Listing 13-15. The OrderProducer Sends an OrderDTO

```
public class OrderProducer {

  public static void main(String[] args) throws NamingException {

    // Creates an orderDto with a total amount parameter
    Float totalAmount = Float.valueOf(args[0]);
    OrderDTO order = new OrderDTO(12341, new Date(), "Betty Moreau", totalAmount);

    // Gets the JNDI context
    Context jndiContext = new InitialContext();

    // Looks up the administered objects
    ConnectionFactory connectionFactory = (ConnectionFactory) ↪
                    jndiContext.lookup("jms/javaee7/ConnectionFactory");
    Destination topic = (Destination) jndiContext.lookup("jms/javaee7/Topic");

    try (JMSContext jmsContext = connectionFactory.createContext()) {
      // Sends an object message to the topic
      jmsContext.createProducer().setProperty("orderAmount", totalAmount).send(topic, order);
    }
  }
}
```

Writing the OrderConsumer

The OrderConsumer, shown in Listing 13-16, is also a stand-alone JMS client listening to the jms/javaee7/Topic topic and using the JMSConsumer API to receive all the OrderDTO (there are no selectors).

Listing 13-16. The OrderConsumer Consumes all the OrderDTO Messages

```
public class OrderConsumer {

  public static void main(String[] args) throws NamingException {

    // Gets the JNDI context
    Context jndiContext = new InitialContext();
```

```
    // Looks up the administered objects
    ConnectionFactory connectionFactory = (ConnectionFactory) ↪
                      jndiContext.lookup("jms/javaee7/ConnectionFactory");
    Destination topic = (Destination) jndiContext.lookup("jms/javaee7/Topic");

    // Loops to receive the messages
    try (JMSContext jmsContext = connectionFactory.createContext()) {
      while (true) {
        OrderDTO order = jmsContext.createConsumer(topic).receiveBody(OrderDTO.class);
        System.out.println("Order received: " + order);
      }
    }
  }
 }
}
```

Writing the ExpensiveOrderMDB

The ExpensiveOrderMDB class (see Listing 13-17) is an MDB annotated with @MessageDriven that listens to the jms/javaee7/Topic destination. This MDB is only interested in orders greater than $1,000, using a message selector (orderAmount > 1000). At message arrival, the onMessage() method consumes it, casts it to an OderDTO (getBody(OrderDTO.class)), and gets the body of the message. For this example, only the message is displayed (System. out.println), but other processing could have also been done (by delegating to a stateless session bean for example).

Listing 13-17. The ExpensiveOrderMDB only Consumes Orders with an Amount Greater than $1000

```
@MessageDriven(mappedName = "jms/javaee7/Topic", activationConfig = { ↪
        @ActivationConfigProperty(propertyName  = "acknowledgeMode", ↪
                                  propertyValue = "Auto-acknowledge"), ↪
        @ActivationConfigProperty(propertyName  = "messageSelector", ↪
                                  propertyValue = "orderAmount > 1000")
})
public class ExpensiveOrderMDB implements MessageListener {

  public void onMessage(Message message) {
    try {
      OrderDTO order = message.getBody(OrderDTO.class);
      System.out.println("Expensive order received: " + order.toString());
    } catch (JMSException e) {
      e.printStackTrace();
    }
  }
}
```

Compiling and Packaging with Maven

The ExpensiveOrderMDB and the OrderDTO should be packaged together in a jar file so they can be deployed to GlassFish. Because MDBs use annotations from the EJB package (@MessageDriven) and the JMS API (ConnectionFactory, Destination, etc.) the pom.xml shown in Listing 13-18 uses the glassfish-embedded-all dependency (which contains all the Java EE 7 APIs). This dependency has the scope provided because GlassFish, as an EJB container and a JMS provider, provides these APIs at runtime. Maven should be informed that you are using Java SE 7 by configuring the maven-compiler-plugin.

Listing 13-18. The pom.xml to Build and Package the MDB

```xml
<?xml version="1.0" encoding="UTF-8"?>
<project xmlns="http://maven.apache.org/POM/4.0.0" ↪
        xmlns:xsi="http://www.w3.org/2001/XMLSchema-instance" ↪
        xsi:schemaLocation="http://maven.apache.org/POM/4.0.0 ↪
        http://maven.apache.org/xsd/maven-4.0.0.xsd">
  <modelVersion>4.0.0</modelVersion>

  <parent>
    <artifactId>chapter13</artifactId>
    <groupId>org.agoncal.book.javaee7</groupId>
    <version>1.0</version>
  </parent>

  <groupId>org.agoncal.book.javaee7.chapter13</groupId>
  <artifactId>chapter13-mdb</artifactId>
  <version>1.0</version>

  <dependencies>
    <dependency>
      <groupId>org.glassfish.main.extras</groupId>
      <artifactId>glassfish-embedded-all</artifactId>
      <version>4.0</version>
      <scope>provided</scope>
    </dependency>
  </dependencies>

  <build>
    <plugins>
      <plugin>
        <groupId>org.apache.maven.plugins</groupId>
        <artifactId>maven-compiler-plugin</artifactId>
        <version>2.5.1</version>
        <configuration>
          <source>1.7</source>
          <target>1.7</target>
        </configuration>
      </plugin>
    </plugins>
  </build>
</project>
```

To compile and package the classes, open a command-line interpreter in the directory that contains the pom.xml file, and enter the following Maven command:

```
$ mvn package
```

Go to the target directory, where you should see the file chapter13-MDB-1.0.jar. If you open it, you will see that it contains the class file for the ExpensiveOrderMDB and OrderDTO.

Creating the Administered Objects

The administered objects required to send and receive messages need to be created in the JMS provider. Each one has a JNDI name, allowing clients to obtain a reference of the object through a JNDI lookup:

- The connection factory is called jms/javaee7/ConnectionFactory

- The topic is called jms/javaee7/Topic

As these objects are created administratively, GlassFish needs to be up and running. Once you've made sure that the asadmin command-line is in your path, execute the following command in the console:

```
$ asadmin create-jms-resource --restype javax.jms.ConnectionFactory ⟶
                                 jms/javaee7/ConnectionFactory
$ asadmin create-jms-resource --restype javax.jms.Topic jms/javaee7/Topic
```

GlassFish's web console can be used to set up the connection factory and the queue. Note, however, that in my experience the easiest and quickest way to administer GlassFish is through the asadmin script. Use another command to list all the JMS resources and ensure that the administered objects are created successfully:

```
$ asadmin list-jms-resources
jms/javaee7/Topic
jms/javaee7/ConnectionFactory
```

Since JMS 2.0, there is a programmatic way to declare administered objects. The idea is to annotate any managed bean (managed bean, EJB, MDB...) with @JMSConnectionFactoryDefinition and @JMSDestinationDefinition, deploy the bean, and the container will make sure to create the factory and the destination. This mechanism is similar to the one you saw in Chapter 8 Listing 8-15 with the @DataSourceDefinition annotation. Listing 13-19 shows the ExpensiveOrderMDB with two definition annotations.

Listing 13-19. The ExpensiveOrderMDB Defining Administered Objects Programmatically

```
@JMSConnectionFactoryDefinition(name = "jms/javaee7/ConnectionFactory",
                         className = "javax.jms.ConnectionFactory")
@JMSDestinationDefinition(name = "jms/javaee7/Topic",
                    className = "javax.jms.Topic")
public class ExpensiveOrderMDB implements MessageListener {...}
```

Deploying the MDB on GlassFish

Once the MDB is packaged in the jar, it needs to be deployed into GlassFish. This can be done in several ways, including via the web administration console. However, the asadmin command-line does the job simply: open a command-line, go to the target directory where the chapter13-MDB-1.0.jar file is, make sure GlassFish is still running, and enter the following command:

```
$ asadmin deploy chapter13-MDB-1.0.jar
```

If the deployment is successful, the following command should return the name of the deployed jar and its type (ejb in the example):

```
$ asadmin list-components
chapter13-MDB-1.0 <ejb>
```

Running the Example

The MDB is deployed on GlassFish and is listening to the `jms/javaee7/Topic` destination, waiting for a message to arrive. It's time to run the `OrderConsumer` and `OrderProducer` clients. These classes are stand-alone applications with a `main` method that has to be executed outside of GlassFish, in a pure Java SE environment. Enter the following command to run the `OrderConsumer`:

```
$ java -cp target/classes OrderConsumer
```

The consumer loops indefinitely and waits for an order to arrive. Now enter the following command to send a message with an order of $2,000:

```
$ java -cp target/classes OrderProducer 2000
```

Because the amount is greater than $1,000 (the amount defined in the selector message), the `OrderExpensiveMDB` and `OrderConsumer` should both receive the message. Check the GlassFish logs to confirm this. If you pass a parameter lower than $1,000, the MDB will not receive the message, just the `OrderConsumer`:

```
$ java -cp target/classes OrderProducer 500
```

Summary

This chapter showed that integration with messaging is a loosely coupled, asynchronous form of communication between components. MOM can be seen as a buffer between systems that need to produce and consume messages at their own pace. This is different from the RPC architecture (such as RMI) in which clients need to know the methods of an available service.

The first section of this chapter concentrated on the JMS API (classical and simplified) and its vocabulary. The asynchronous model is a very powerful API that can be used in a Java SE or a Java EE environment, and is based on P2P and pub-sub, connection factories, destinations, connections, sessions, messages (header, properties, body) of different types (text, object, map, stream, bytes), selectors, and other reliability mechanisms such as acknowledgment or durability.

Java EE has a special enterprise component to consume messages: MDBs. The second section of this chapter showed how MDBs could be used as asynchronous consumers and how they rely on their container to take care of several services (life cycle, interceptors, transactions, security, concurrency, message acknowledgment, etc.).

This chapter also showed how to put these pieces together with Maven, GlassFish, and OpenMQ, and gave an example with a stand-alone sender and an MDB receiver.

The following chapters will demonstrate other technologies used to interoperate with external systems: SOAP web services and RESTful web services.

SOAP Web Services

The term *web service* implies "something" accessible on the "web" that gives you a "service." The first example that comes to our mind is an HTML page: it's accessible online and, once read, it gives you the information you were looking for. Another kind of web service is the Servlets. They are bound to a URL, therefore accessible on the web, and they perform any kind of processing. But the term "web services" quickly became a buzzword, got assimilated to Service Oriented Architecture (SOA) and today web services are part of our day-to-day architectural life. Web services applications can be implemented with different technologies such as SOAP, described in this chapter, or REST (see next chapter).

SOAP (Simple Object Access Protocol) web services are said to be "loosely coupled" because the client, a.k.a. the consumer, of a web service doesn't have to know its implementation details (such as the language used to develop it, the method signature or the platform it runs on). The consumer is able to invoke a SOAP web service using a self-explanatory interface describing the available business methods (parameters and return value). The underlying implementation can be done in any language (Visual Basic, C#, C, C++, Java, etc.). A consumer and a service provider will still be able to exchange data in a loosely coupled way: using XML documents. A consumer sends a request to a SOAP web service in the form of an XML document, and, optionally, receives a reply, also in XML.

SOAP web services are also about distribution. Distributed software has been around for a long time, but, unlike existing distributed systems, SOAP web services are adapted to the Web. The default network protocol is HTTP, a well-known and robust stateless protocol.

SOAP web services are everywhere. They can be invoked from a simple desktop or used for business-to-business (B2B) integration so that operations that previously required manual intervention are performed automatically. SOAP web services integrate applications run by various organizations through the Internet or within the same company (which is known as Enterprise Application Integration, or EAI). In all cases, they provide a standard way to connect diverse pieces of software.

This chapter will first introduce some important notions to understand SOAP Web Services such as WSDL or SOAP. Then it will show how to write a SOAP Web Service before explaining how to consume it.

Understanding SOAP Web Services

Simply put, SOAP web services constitute a kind of business logic exposed via a service (i.e., the service provider) to a client (i.e., the service consumer). However, unlike objects or EJBs, SOAP web services provide a loosely coupled interface using XML. SOAP web service standards specify that the interface to which a message is sent should define the format of the message request and response, and mechanisms to publish and to discover web service interfaces (the service registry).

In Figure 14-1, you can see a high-level picture of a SOAP web service interaction. The SOAP web service can optionally register its interface into a registry (Universal Description Discovery and Integration, or UDDI) so a consumer can discover it. Once the consumer knows the interface of the service and the message format, it can send a request to the service provider and receive a response.

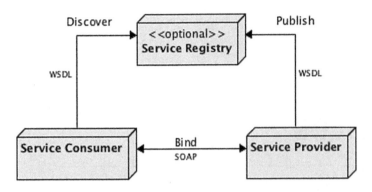

Figure 14-1. *The consumer discovers the service through a registry*

SOAP web services depend on several technologies and protocols to transport and to transform data from a consumer to a service provider in a standard way. The ones that you will come across more often are the following:

- Extensible Markup Language (XML) is the basic foundation on which SOAP web services are built and defined (SOAP, WSDL, and UDDI).

- Web Services Description Language (WSDL) defines the protocol, interface, message types, and interactions between the consumer and the provider.

- Simple Object Access Protocol (SOAP) is a message-encoding protocol based on XML technologies, defining an envelope for web services communication.

- Messages are exchanged using a transport protocol. Although Hypertext Transfer Protocol (HTTP) is the most widely adopted transport protocol, others such as SMTP or JMS can also be used.

- Universal Description Discovery, and Integration (UDDI) is an optional service registry and discovery mechanism, similar to the Yellow Pages; it can be used for storing and categorizing SOAP web services interfaces (WSDL).

With these standard technologies, SOAP web services provide almost unlimited potential. Clients can call a service, which can be mapped to any program and accommodate any data type and structure to exchange messages through XML.

XML

I've already described XML in Chapter 12 and you now know how to manipulate, parse, and bind XML documents. Because XML is the perfect integration technology that solves the problem of data independence and interoperability, it is the DNA of SOAP web services. It is used not only as the message format but also as the way the services are defined (WSDL) or exchanged (SOAP). Associated with these XML documents, schemas (XSD) are used to validate the data exchanged between the consumer and the provider. Historically, SOAP web services evolved from the basic idea of "RPC (Remote Procedure Call) using XML."

WSDL

WSDL is the interface definition language (IDL) that defines the interactions between consumers and SOAP web services (see Figure 14-2). It is central to a SOAP web service as it describes the message type, port, communication protocol, supported operations, location, and what the consumer should expect in return. It defines the contract to which the service guarantees it will conform. You can think of WSDL as a Java interface but written in XML.

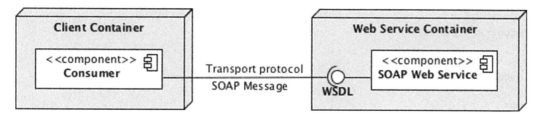

Figure 14-2. *WSDL interface between the consumer and the web service*

To ensure interoperability, a standard web service interfaceis needed for a consumer and a producer to share and understand a message. That's the role of WSDL. Listing 14-1 shows you an example of a WSDL that represents a credit card validation SOAP web service (this service takes a credit card as an input and validates it). This WSDL is pure XML and, if you read carefully, you will see all the information needed for a consumer to locate a web service (soap:address location), invoke a method (operation name="validate"), and use an appropriate transport protocol (soap:binding transport).

Listing 14-1. A WSDL File Representing a Credit Card Validation Service

```xml
<?xml version="1.0" encoding="UTF-8" ?>
<definitions
        xmlns:wsam="http://www.w3.org/2007/05/addressing/metadata"
        xmlns:soap="http://schemas.xmlsoap.org/wsdl/soap/"
        xmlns:tns="http://chapter14.javaee7.book.agoncal.org/"
        xmlns:xsd="http://www.w3.org/2001/XMLSchema"
        xmlns="http://schemas.xmlsoap.org/wsdl/"
        targetNamespace="http://chapter14.javaee7.book.agoncal.org/"
        name="CardValidatorService">
  <types>
    <xsd:schema>
      <xsd:import namespace="http://chapter14.javaee7.book.agoncal.org/"
          schemaLocation="http://localhost:8080/chapter14/CardValidatorService?xsd=1"/>
    </xsd:schema>
  </types>
  <message name="validate">
    <part name="parameters" element="tns:validate"/>
  </message>
  <message name="validateResponse">
    <part name="parameters" element="tns:validateResponse"/>
  </message>
  <portType name="CardValidator">
    <operation name="validate">
      <input message="tns:validate"/>
      <output message="tns:validateResponse"/>
    </operation>
  </portType>
  <binding name="CardValidatorPortBinding" type="tns:CardValidator">
    <soap:binding transport="http://schemas.xmlsoap.org/soap/http" style="document"/>
    <operation name="validate">
      <soap:operation soapAction=""/>
```

```
    <input>
      <soap:body use="literal"/>
    </input>
    <output>
      <soap:body use="literal"/>
    </output>
  </operation>
</binding>
<service name="CardValidatorService">
  <port name="CardValidatorPort" binding="tns:CardValidatorPortBinding">
    <soap:address location="http://localhost:8080/chapter14/CardValidatorService"/>
  </port>
</service>
</definitions>
```

WSDL uses XML to describe what a service does, how to invoke its operations, and where to find it. It follows a fixed structure containing several parts (types, message, portType, binding, service). Table 14-1 lists a subset of the WSDL elements and attributes. WSDL is a much richer language than what's listed in Table 14-1 and is defined by the W3C. If you want to know more about WSDL, its structure, and its datatypes, you should check the related W3C website.

Table 14-1. *WSDL Elements and Attributes*

Element	Description
definitions	Is the root element of the WSDL, and it specifies the global declarations of namespaces that are visible throughout the document
types	Defines the data types to be used in the messages. In this example, it is the XML Schema Definition (CardValidatorService?xsd=1) that describes the parameters passed to the web service request and the response
message	Defines the format of data being transmitted between a web service consumer and the web service itself. Here you have the request (the validate method) and the response (validateResponse)
portType	Specifies the operations of the web service (the validate method). Each operation refers to an input and output message
binding	Describes the concrete protocol (here SOAP) and data formats for the operations and messages defined for a particular port type
service	Contains a collection of <port> elements, where each port is associated with an endpoint (a network address location or URL)
port	Specifies an address for a binding, thus defining a single communication endpoint

The <xsd:import namespace> element refers to an XML Schema that has to be available on the network to the consumers of the WSDL. Listing 14-2 shows this schema defining the data types used in the web service: the structure of the CreditCard object (with number, expiry date, and so on) sent in the request (validate), and a boolean (the credit card is valid or not) received in the response (validateResponse).

Listing 14-2. The Schema Imported by the WSDL File

```xml
<xs:schema xmlns:tns="http://chapter14.javaee7.book.agoncal.org/" ↵
           xmlns:xs="http://www.w3.org/2001/XMLSchema" ↵
           targetNamespace="http://chapter14.javaee7.book.agoncal.org/" version="1.0">
  <xs:element name="validate" type="tns:validate"/>
  <xs:element name="validateResponse" type="tns:validateResponse"/>
  <xs:complexType name="validate">
    <xs:sequence>
      <xs:element name="arg0" type="tns:creditCard" minOccurs="0"/>
    </xs:sequence>
  </xs:complexType>
  <xs:complexType name="creditCard">
    <xs:sequence/>
    <xs:attribute name="number" type="xs:string" use="required"/>
    <xs:attribute name="expiry_date" type="xs:string" use="required"/>
    <xs:attribute name="control_number" type="xs:int" use="required"/>
    <xs:attribute name="type" type="xs:string" use="required"/>
  </xs:complexType>
  <xs:complexType name="validateResponse">
    <xs:sequence>
      <xs:element name="return" type="xs:boolean"/>
    </xs:sequence>
  </xs:complexType>
</xs:schema>
```

If you remember JAXB described in Chapter 12, you will realize that the XSD in Listing 14-2 has all the information needed to be bound to Java classes. With a WSDL and a schema any consumer can then generate the needed artifacts to invoke the web service (as you'll see later, JAX-WS comes with utilities that automatically generate these artifacts).

SOAP

WSDL describes an abstract interface of the web service while SOAP provides a concrete implementation, defining the XML messages exchanged between the consumer and the provider (see Figure 14-3). SOAP is the standard web services application protocol. It provides the communication mechanism to connect web services, exchanging formatted XML data across a network protocol, commonly HTTP. Like WSDL, SOAP relies heavily on XML because a SOAP message is an XML document containing several elements (an envelope, a header, a body, etc.). Instead of using HTTP to request a web page from a browser, SOAP sends an XML message via a HTTP request and receives a reply via a HTTP response.

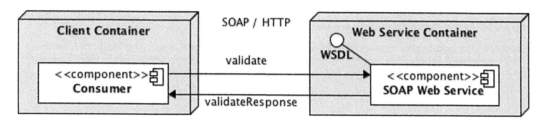

Figure 14-3. *A consumer invoking a SOAP web service*

SOAP is designed to provide an independent, abstract communication protocol capable of connecting distributed services. The connected services can be built using any combination of hardware and software that supports a given transport protocol.

Let's use the credit card validation example shown in Figure 14-3. The consumer calls the SOAP web service to validate a credit card passing all the needed parameters (credit card number, expiry date, type and control number) and receives a Boolean that informs the consumer if the card is valid or not. Listings 14-3 and 14-4, respectively, show the structure of these two SOAP messages.

Listing 14-3. The SOAP Envelope Sent for the Request

```
<soap:Envelope xmlns:soap="http://schemas.xmlsoap.org/soap/envelope/" ↩
               xmlns:cc="http://chapter14.javaee7.book.agoncal.org/">
  <soap:Header/>
  <soap:Body>
    <cc:validate>
      <arg0 number="123456789011" expiry_date="10/12" control_number="544" type="Visa"/>
    </cc:validate>
  </soap:Body>
</soap:Envelope>
```

Listing 14-4. The SOAP Envelope Received for the Response

```
<soap:Envelope xmlns:soap="http://schemas.xmlsoap.org/soap/envelope/" ↩
               xmlns:cc="http://chapter14.javaee7.book.agoncal.org/">
  <soap:Body>
    <cc:validateResponse>
      <return>true</return>
    </cc:validateResponse>
  </soap:Body>
</soap:Envelope>
```

The consumer sends all the credit card information within a SOAP envelope (Listing 14-3) to the validate method of the credit card validator web service. The service returns another SOAP envelope (Listing 14-4) with the result of the validation (true or false).

Table 14-2 lists a subset of the SOAP elements and attributes. Like WSDL, SOAP is defined by the W3C standard body.

Table 14-2. *SOAP Elements and Attributes*

Element	Description
Envelope	Defines the message and the namespace used in the document. This is a required root element
Header	Contains any optional attributes of the message or application-specific infrastructure such as security information or network routing
Body	Contains the message being exchanged between applications
Fault	Provides information about errors that occur while the message is processed. This element is optional

UDDI

Consumers and providers that interact with one another over the Web need to be able to find information that allows them to interconnect. Either the consumer knows the exact location of the service it wants to invoke or it has to find it. UDDI provides a standard approach to locating information about a web service and how to invoke it. The service provider publishes a WSDL into a UDDI registry available on the Internet. Then it can be discovered and downloaded by potential consumers. It is optional as you can invoke a web service without UDDI if you already know the web service's location.

UDDI is an XML-based registry of web services, similar to a Yellow Pages directory, where businesses can register their services. This registration includes the business type, geographical location, web site, phone number, and so on. Other businesses can then search the registry and discover information about specific web services. This information provides additional metadata about the service, describing its behavior and the actual location of the WSDL document.

■ **Note**   UDDI has not been as widely adopted as its designers (IBM, Microsoft, and SAP) had hoped. In January 2006 the three companies announced they were closing their public UDDI registries. In late 2007, the group defining UDDI at OASIS announced the closure of the Technical Committee.

Transport Protocol

For a consumer to communicate with a web service it needs a way to send messages. SOAP messages can be transported over a network using a protocol that both parties can support. Given that web services are used mostly on the Web, they usually use HTTP, but they can also use other network protocols such as HTTPS (HTTP Secure), TCP/IP, SMTP (Simple Mail Transport Protocol), FTP (File Transfer Protocol), and so on.

SOAP Web Services Specifications Overview

As seen in Chapter 4, persistence is mostly covered by one specification: JPA. For web services, the situation is more complex, as you have to deal with many specifications coming from different standard bodies. Moreover, because other programming languages use web services, these specifications are not all directly related to the Java Community Process (JCP).

A Brief History of SOAP Web Services Specifications

SOAP web services are a standard way for businesses to communicate over a network. There have been precursors:Common Object Request Broker Architecture (CORBA), initially used by Unix systems, and Distributed Component Object Model (DCOM), its Microsoft competitor. On a lower level, there is Remote Procedure Call (RPC) and, closer to our Java world, Remote Method Invocation (RMI).

Before the Web, it was difficult to get all major software vendors to agree on a transport protocol. When the HTTP protocol became a mature standard, it gradually became a universal business medium of communication. At about the same time, XML officially became a standard when the World Wide Web Consortium (W3C) announced that XML 1.0 was suitable for deployment in applications. By 1998, both ingredients, HTTP and XML, were ready to work together.

SOAP 1.0, started in 1998 by Microsoft, was finally shipped at the end of 1999, and modeled typed references and arrays in XML Schema. By 2000, IBM started working on SOAP 1.1, and WSDL was submitted to the W3C in 2001. UDDI was written in 2000 by the Organization for the Advancement of Structured Information Standards (OASIS) to allow businesses to publish and discover web services. With SOAP, WSDL, and UDDI in place, the de facto standards to create web services had arrived with the support of major IT companies.

Java introduced web services capabilities with the Java API for XML-based RPC 1.0 (JAX-RPC 1.0) in June 2002 and added JAX-RPC 1.1 to J2EE 1.4 in 2003. This specification was quite verbose and not easy to use. With the arrival of Java EE 5 and annotations in Java, the brand new Java API for XML-based Web Services 2.0 (JAX-WS 2.0) specification was introduced as the preferred SOAP web service model. Today Java EE 7 is shipped with JAX-WS 2.2a.

SOAP Web Services Related Specifications

To master all web services standards, you would have to spend some time reading all the specifications listed in Table 14-3 coming from the W3C, the JCP, and OASIS.

Table 14-3. *SOAP Web Services Related Specifications and Standard Bodies*

Specification	Version	Stand. body	JSR	URL
JAX-WS	2.2a	JCP	224	http://jcp.org/en/jsr/detail?id=224
Web Services	1.3	JCP	109	http://jcp.org/en/jsr/detail?id=109
Web Services Metadata	2.1	JCP	181	http://jcp.org/en/jsr/detail?id=181
JAXB	2.2	JCP	222	http://jcp.org/en/jsr/detail?id=222
SAAJ	1.3	JCP	67	http://jcp.org/en/jsr/detail?id=67
JAX-RPC	*1.1*	*JCP*	*101*	*http://jcp.org/en/jsr/detail?id=101*
JAXR	*1.1*	*JCP*	*93*	*http://jcp.org/en/jsr/detail?id=93*
SOAP	1.2	W3C		http://www.w3.org/TR/soap/
XML	1.1	W3C		http://www.w3.org/TR/xml
WSDL	1.1	W3C		http://www.w3.org/TR/wsdl
UDDI	1.0	OASIS		http://uddi.org/pubs/uddi_v3.htm

The W3C is a consortium that develops and maintains web technologies such as HTML, XHTML, RDF, CSS, and so forth and, more interestingly for web services, XML, XML Schemas, SOAP, and WSDL.

OASIS hosts several web service-related standards such as UDDI, WS-Addressing, WS-Security, WS-Reliability, and many others (known as WS-*).

Returning to Java, the JCP has a set of specifications that are part of Java EE 7 and Java SE 7. They include JAX-WS 2.2a (JSR 224), Web Services 1.3 (JSR 109), Web Services Metadata 2.3 (JSR 181) and JAXB 2.2 (JSR 222). Taken together, these specifications are usually referred to by the informal term Java Web Services (JWS). SAAJ (SOAP with Attachments API for Java), defined in JSR 67, is part of Java SE and enables developers to produce and consume SOAP messages with attachments.

Other related specifications have been part of previous Java EE versions and have been pruned or evolve now separately from Java EE. JAX-WS is the successor of JAX-RPC (JSR 101) which was too verbose and complex. JAX-RPC has been pruned in Java EE 6, meaning that it has been removed from Java EE 7. The Java API for XML Registries (JAXR) specification defines a standard set of APIs that allow Java clients to access UDDI. Because UDDI has not had the momentum initially expected, this JSR 93 has been pruned and is not included in Java EE 7.

Looking at this huge list of specifications may make you think that writing a SOAP web service in Java is difficult, especially when it comes to getting your head around the APIs. However, the beauty of it is that you don't need to worry about the underlying technologies (XML, WSDL, SOAP, HTTP, etc.), as just a few JWS standards will do the work for you as you'll see in a few paragraphs.

JAX-WS 2.2a

JAX-WS 2.2a defines a set of APIs (main packages listed in Table 14-4) and annotations that allow you to build and consume web services with Java. It provides the consumer and service facilities to send and receive web service requests via SOAP, masking the complexity of the protocol. Therefore, neither the consumer nor the service has to generate or parse SOAP messages, as JAX-WS deals with the low-level processing. The JAX-WS specification depends on other specifications such as Java Architecture for XML Binding (JAXB) that you saw in Chapter 12.

Table 14-4. *Main JAX-WS Packages*

Package	Description
javax.xml.ws	This package contains the core JAX-WS APIs
javax.xml.ws.http	Defines APIs specific to the XML/HTTP binding
javax.xml.ws.soap	Defines APIs specific to the SOAP 1.1/HTTP or SOAP 1.2/HTTP binding
javax.xml.ws.handler	This package defines APIs for message handlers

Web Services 1.3

JSR 109 ("Implementing Enterprise Web Services") defines the programming model and runtime behavior of web services in the Java EE container. It also defines packaging to ensure portability of web services across application server implementations.

WS-Metadata 2.3

Web Services Metadata (WS-Metadata, specification JSR 181) provides annotations to facilitate the definition and deployment of web services (main packages listed in Table 14-5). The primary goal of JSR 181 is to simplify the development of web services. It provides mapping facilities between WSDL and Java interfaces, and vice versa, through annotations. These annotations can be used within simple Java classes or EJBs.

Table 14-5. *Main WS-Metadata Packages*

Package	Description
javax.jws	This package contains the Java to WSDL mapping annotations
javax.jws.soap	APIs to specify the mapping of the web service onto the SOAP message protocol

What's New in SOAP Web Services Specifications?

Unfortunately there is nothing new in JAX-WS or WS-Metadata in Java EE 7. SOAP web services specifications have not been updated in this Java EE release. For instance, in Java EE 7, SOAP web services are not considered Managed Beans so you can't use interceptors, interceptor binding, injection of context, and so on. Bean Validation hasn't been integrated either, meaning you cannot use method level validation (see Chapter 3).

Reference Implementation

Metro is the open source reference implementation of the Java web services specifications. It consists of JAX-WS and JAXB, and also supports the legacy JAX-RPC APIs. It allows you to create and deploy secure, reliable, transactional, interoperable SOAP web services as well as SOAP web service consumers. The Metro stack is produced by the GlassFish community, but it can also be used outside GlassFish in a Java SE environment or other web containers (e.g. Tomcat, Jetty).

Apache CXF (formerly known as XFire) and Apache Axis2 also implement the JWS stack. In addition to not being the reference implementation, both frameworks are also heavily used in SOAP web services.

Writing SOAP Web Services

So far you've seen lots of low-level concepts such as HTTP protocol, WSDL documents, SOAP messages, or XML. But how do you write a SOAP web service with all the specifications that have been previously presented? You can either start from the WSDL or go straight to coding some Java.

Because the WSDL document is the contract between the consumer and the service, it can be used to generate the Java code for the consumer and the service. This is the *top-down approach*, also known as *contract first*. This approach starts with the contract (the WSDL) by defining operations, messages, and so forth. When both the consumer and provider agree on the contract, you can then implement the Java classes based on that contract. Metro provides some tools (wsimport) that generate classes from a WSDL.

With the other approach, called *bottom-up*, the implementation class already exists, and all that is needed is to create the WSDL. Again, Metro provides utilities (wsgen) to generate a WSDL from existing classes. In both cases, the code may need to be adjusted to fit the WSDL or vice versa. That is when JAX-WS comes to your aid. With a simple development model and a few annotations, Java-to-WSDL mapping can be adjusted. But be careful, the bottom-up approach can result in very inefficient applications, as the Java methods and classes have no bearing on the ideal granularity of messages crossing the network. If latency is high and/or bandwidth low, it pays to use the fewer, larger messages, and this can be done more efficiently by using the contract-first approach.

Despite all these specifications, concepts, standards, and organizations, writing and consuming a web service in the bottom-up approach is very easy. SOAP web services follow the "ease of development" paradigm of Java EE 7 and do not require you to write any WSDL or SOAP. The web service is just an annotated POJO that needs to be deployed in a web service container. Listing 14-5 shows you the code of a web service that validates a credit card.

Listing 14-5. The CardValidator Web Service

```
@WebService
public class CardValidator {

  public boolean validate(CreditCard creditCard) {
    Character lastDigit = creditCard.getNumber().charAt( ↪
                          creditCard.getNumber().length() - 1);

    if (Integer.parseInt(lastDigit.toString()) % 2 != 0) {
      return true;
    } else {
      return false;
    }
  }
}
```

Like entities or EJBs, a SOAP web service uses the annotated POJO model with the configuration-by-exception policy. This means that a web service can just be a Java class annotated with @javax.jws.WebService if all the defaults suit you. Then, the JAX-WS runtime will generate all the plumbing that will transform a Java method invocation into a XML over HTTP call. This CardValidator SOAP web service has one method to validate a credit card. It takes a credit card as a parameter and returns true or false according to whether the card is valid or not. In this instance, it assumes that credit cards with an even number are valid, and those with an odd number are not.

A CreditCard object (see Listing 14-6) is exchanged between the consumer and the SOAP web service. When describing the web service architecture, the data exchanged needs to be an XML document, so a method to transform a Java object into an XML document is needed. This is where JAXB comes into play with its simple annotations and powerful API. As seen in Chapter 12, the CreditCard object has to be annotated with @javax.xml.bind.annotation. XmlRootElement, and a few other mapping annotations (e.g. @XmlAttribute) if you need to customize the mapping, and JAXB will transform it back and forth from XML to Java.

Listing 14-6. The CreditCard Class with JAXB Annotations

```
@XmlRootElement
public class CreditCard {

  @XmlAttribute(required = true)
  private String number;
  @XmlAttribute(name = "expiry_date", required = true)
  private String expiryDate;
  @XmlAttribute(name = "control_number", required = true)
  private Integer controlNumber;
  @XmlAttribute(required = true)
  private String type;

  // Constructors, getters, setters
}
```

With JAXB annotations, you avoid developing all the low-level XML parsing, as it happens behind the scenes. The web service manipulates a Java object, and the same is true for the consumer.

Anatomy of a SOAP Web Service

Like most of the Java EE 7 components, SOAP web services rely on the configuration-by-exception paradigm, which specifies that configuring a component is the exception. Only one annotation is actually needed to turn a POJO into a SOAP web service @WebService. The requirements to write a web service are as follows:

- The class must be annotated with @javax.jws.WebService or the XML equivalent in a deployment descriptor (webservices.xml).

- The class (a.k.a service implementation bean) can implement zero or more interfaces (a.k.a service endpoint interface) that have to be annotated with @WebService.

- The class must be defined as public, and it must not be final or abstract.

- The class must have a default public constructor.

- The class must not define the finalize() method.

- To turn a SOAP web service into an EJB endpoint, the class has to be annotated with @javax.ejb.Stateless or @javax.ejb.Singleton (see Chapter 7).

- A service must be a stateless object and should not save client-specific state across method calls.

The WS-Metadata specification (JSR 181) says that, as long as it meets these requirements, a POJO can be used to implement a web service deployed to the servlet container. This is commonly referred to as a *servlet endpoint*. A stateless or singleton session bean can also be used to implement a web service that will be deployed in an EJB container (a.k.a. an EJB endpoint).

SOAP Web Service Endpoints

JAX-WS allows both regular Java classes and EJBs to be exposed as web services. We call it service endpoint interfaces (SEI). Referring to the code for a POJO (Listing 14-5) and for an EJB web service (Listing 14-7) reveals hardly any differences, with the exception that the EJB web service has the extra annotation @Stateless (or @Singleton). Although, the packaging can be different as you'll later see.

Listing 14-7. The CardValidator Web Service as an EJB Endpoint

```
@WebService
@Stateless
public class CardValidator {

  public boolean validate(CreditCard creditCard) {
    Character lastDigit = creditCard.getNumber().charAt(↪
                          creditCard.getNumber().length() - 1);

    if (Integer.parseInt(lastDigit.toString()) % 2 != 0) {
      return true;
    } else {
      return false;
    }
  }
}
```

Both endpoints have almost identical behavior, but a few extra benefits are gained from using EJB endpoints. As the web service is also an EJB, the benefits of transaction and security being managed by the container are automatic, and interceptors can be used, which is not possible with servlet endpoints. The business code can be exposed as a web service and as an EJB at the same time, meaning that the business logic can be exposed through SOAP and also through RMI by adding a remote interface.

WSDL Mapping

At the service level, systems are defined in terms of XML messages, WSDL operations, and SOAP messages. Meanwhile, at the Java level, applications are defined in terms of objects, interfaces, and methods. A translation from Java objects to WSDL operations is needed. The JAXB runtime uses annotations to determine how to marshal/unmarshal a class to/from XML. Similarly, JWS uses annotations to map Java classes into WSDL and to determine how to marshal a method invocation to a SOAP request and unmarshal a SOAP response into an instance of the method's return type.

The JAX-WS (JSR 224) and WS-Metadata specifications (JSR 181) define two different kinds of annotations:

- *WSDL mapping annotations*: These annotations belong to the javax.jws package and allow you to change the WSDL/Java mapping. The @WebMethod, @WebResult, @WebParam, and @OneWay annotations are used on the web service to customize the signature of the exposed methods.

- *SOAP binding annotations*: These annotations belong to the javax.jws.soap package and allow customizing of the SOAP binding (@SOAPBinding and @SOAPMessageHandler).

Like all the other Java EE 7 specifications, web services annotations can be overridden by an XML deployment descriptor (`webservices.xml`), which is optional. Let's take a closer look at the WSDL mapping annotations.

@WebService

The `@javax.jws.WebService` annotation marks a Java class or interface as being a web service. If used directly on the class (as in all the examples so far), the annotation processor of the container will generate the interface, so the following snippets of code are equivalent. Here is the annotation on the class:

```
@WebService
public class CardValidator {...}
```

And the following snippet shows the annotation on an interface implemented by a class. As you can see, the implementation needs to define the fully qualified name of the interface in the `endpointInterface` attribute:

```
@WebService
public interface Validator {...}

@WebService(endpointInterface = "org.agoncal.book.javaee7.chapter14.Validator")
public class CardValidator implements Validator {...}
```

The @WebService annotation has a set of attributes (see Listing 14-8) that allow you to customize the name of the web service in the WSDL file (the `<wsdl:portType>` or `<wsdl:service>` element) and in its namespace, as well as change the location of the WSDL itself (the `wsdlLocation` attribute).

Listing 14-8. The @WebService API

```
@Retention(RUNTIME) @Target(TYPE)
public @interface WebService {
  String name() default "";
  String targetNamespace() default "";
  String serviceName() default "";
  String portName() default "";
  String wsdlLocation() default "";
  String endpointInterface() default "";
}
```

So when the default WSDL mapping rules are not appropriate for your SOAP web service, just use the needed attributes. The code below changes the port and service name:

```
@WebService(portName = "CreditCardValidator", serviceName = "ValidatorService")
public class CardValidator {...}
```

If you compare with the default WSDL described in Listing 14-1 you'll see the following changes:

```
<service name="ValidatorService">
 <port name="CreditCardValidator" binding="tns:CreditCardValidatorBinding">
 <soap:address location="http://localhost:8080/chapter14/ValidatorService"/>
 </port>
</service>
```

When you use the @WebService annotation, all public methods of the web service are exposed except when using the @WebMethod annotation.

@WebMethod

By default, all the public methods of a SOAP web service are exposed in the WSDL and use all the default mapping rules. To customize some elements of this mapping, you can apply the @javax.jws.WebMethod annotation on methods. The API of this annotation is quite simple as it allows the renaming of a method or exclusion of it from the WSDL. Listing 14-9 shows how the CardValidator web service renames the two first methods and excludes the last one.

Listing 14-9. Two Methods Are Renamed, the Last One Excluded

```
@WebService
public class CardValidator {

  @WebMethod(operationName = "ValidateCreditCard")
  public boolean validate(CreditCard creditCard) {
    // Business logic
  }

  @WebMethod(operationName = "ValidateCreditCardNumber")
  public void validate(String creditCardNumber) {
    // Business logic
  }

  @WebMethod(exclude = true)
  public void validate(Long creditCardNumber) {
    // Business logic
  }
}
```

As you can see in the WSDL fragment described in Listing 14-10, only the two methods ValidateCreditCard and ValidateCreditCardNumber are defined. The last method got excluded from the WSDL.

Listing 14-10. Fragment of WSDL with Renamed Methods

```
<message name="ValidateCreditCard">
  <part name="parameters" element="tns:ValidateCreditCard"/>
</message>
<message name="ValidateCreditCardResponse">
  <part name="parameters" element="tns:ValidateCreditCardResponse"/>
</message>
<message name="ValidateCreditCardNumber">
  <part name="parameters" element="tns:ValidateCreditCardNumber"/>
</message>
<message name="ValidateCreditCardNumberResponse">
  <part name="parameters" element="tns:ValidateCreditCardNumberResponse"/>
</message>
<portType name="CardValidator">
  <operation name="ValidateCreditCard">
    <input message="tns:ValidateCreditCard"/>
    <output message="tns:ValidateCreditCardResponse"/>
  </operation>
```

```
    <operation name="ValidateCreditCardNumber">
      <input message="tns:ValidateCreditCardNumber"/>
      <output message="tns:ValidateCreditCardNumberResponse"/>
    </operation>
</portType>
```

@WebResult

The @javax.jws.WebResult annotation controls the generated name of the message returned value in the WSDL. In Listing 14-11, the returned result of the validate() method is renamed to IsValid.

Listing 14-11. The Return Result of the Method Is Renamed

```
@WebService
public class CardValidator {

  @WebResult(name = "IsValid")
  public boolean validate(CreditCard creditCard) {
    // Business logic
  }
}
```

By default the name of the returned value in the WSDL is set to return. But with the @WebResult annotation you can be more specific and have a more expressive contract:

```
<!-- Default -->
<xs:element name="return" type="xs:boolean"/>
<!-- Renamed to IsValid -->
<xs:element name="IsValid" type="xs:boolean"/>
```

This annotation also has other elements to customize the WSDL, such as the XML namespace for the returned value, and looks like the @WebParam annotation shown in Listing 14-12.

Listing 14-12. The @WebParam API

```
@Retention(RUNTIME) @Target(PARAMETER)
public @interface WebParam {
  String name() default "";
  public enum Mode {IN, OUT, INOUT};
  String targetNamespace() default "";
  boolean header() default false;
  String partName() default "";
};
```

@WebParam

The @javax.jws.WebParam annotation, shown in Listing 14-12, is similar to @WebResult as it customizes the parameters for the web service methods. Its API permits changing the name of the parameter in the WSDL (see Listing 14-13), the namespace, and the type. Valid types are IN, OUT, or INOUT (both), which determine how the parameter is flowing (default is IN).

Listing 14-13. The Method Parameter Is Renamed

```
@WebService
public class CardValidator {

  public boolean validate(@WebParam(name= "Credit-Card", mode = IN) CreditCard creditCard) {
    // Business logic
  }
}
```

Again, if you compare this with the default XSD defined in Listing 14-2 you'll notice that, by default, the name of the parameter is arg0. The @WebParam annotation overrides this default with the name Credit-Card:

```
<!-- Default -->
<xs:element name="arg0" type="tns:creditCard" minOccurs="0"/>
<!-- Renamed to Credit-Card -->
<xs:element name="Credit-Card" type="tns:creditCard" minOccurs="0"/>
```

@OneWay

The @OneWay annotation can be used on methods that do not have a return value such as methods returning void. This annotation has no elements and can be seen as a markup interface that informs the container that invocation can be optimized, as there is no return (using an asynchronous invocation, for example).

@SOAPBinding

A binding describes how the web service is bound to a messaging protocol, particularly the SOAP messaging protocol. There are two programming styles for SOAP binding defined in WSDL 1.1: RPC and document (a.k.a. messaging). This choice corresponds to how the SOAP body content is structured:

- Document: The SOAP message contains the document. It is sent as one document in the <soap:Body> element without additional formatting rules; it contains whatever the sender and the receiver agree upon. Document style is the default choice.

- RPC: The SOAP message contains the parameters and the return values. The <soap:Body> contains an element with the name of the method or remote procedure being invoked. This element in turn contains an element for each parameter of that procedure.

A SOAP binding (Document or RPC) has then to choose from two different serialization/deserialization formats:

- Literal: Data is serialized according to an XML schema.

- Encoded: SOAP encoding specifies how objects, structures, arrays, and object graphs should be serialized.

This gives you four style/use models:

- Document/Literal (default)

- Document/Encoded (not WS-* compliant)

- RPC/Literal

- RPC/Encoded

By default the generated WSDL that you've seen so far uses the document/literal style of binding. Specifying the @SOAPBinding annotation on the class as seen in Listing 14-14 can change this.

Listing 14-14. Web Service Using an RPC/Literal Binding

```
@WebService
@SOAPBinding(style = RPC, use = LITERAL)
public class CardValidator {

  public boolean validate(CreditCard creditCard) {
    // Business logic
  }
}
```

Listing 14-14 overrides the default binding by using the RPC style instead of Document. This has an effect on the WSDL as well as the XML schema generated for the SOAP web service provider and consumer. Listing 14-15 shows these differences.

Listing 14-15. WSDL Differences Between Document and RPC Style

```
<!-- Document style -->
<message name="validate">
  <part name="parameters" element="tns:validate"/>
</message>
<message name="validateResponse">
  <part name="parameters" element="tns:validateResponse"/>
</message>
...
<soap:binding transport="http://schemas.xmlsoap.org/soap/http" style="document"/>

<!-- RPC Style -->
<message name="validate">
  <part name="arg0" type="tns:creditCard"/>
</message>
<message name="validateResponse">
  <part name="return" type="xsd:boolean"/>
</message>
...
<soap:binding transport="http://schemas.xmlsoap.org/soap/http" style="rpc"/>
```

Putting the Mapping All Together

To have a better understanding of what influence these annotations have on the SOAP web service, let's put them all together and look at the different artifacts. I'll use the basic CardValidator web service defined in Listing 14-5 and add most of the mapping annotations we've seen so far (see Listing 14-16).

Listing 14-16. The CardValidator Web Service with Mapping Annotations

```
@WebService(portName = "CreditCardValidator", serviceName = "ValidatorService")
@SOAPBinding(style = RPC, use = LITERAL)
public class CardValidator {
```

```
@WebResult(name = "IsValid")
@WebMethod(operationName = "ValidateCreditCard")
public boolean validate(@WebParam(name = "Credit-Card") CreditCard creditCard) {
  // Business logic
}

@WebResult(name = "IsValid")
@WebMethod(operationName = "ValidateCreditCardNumber")
public void validate(@WebParam(name = "Credit-Card-Number") String creditCardNumber) {
  // Business logic
}

@WebMethod(exclude = true)
public void validate(Long creditCardNumber) {
  // Business logic
}
}
```

Listing 14-16 defines an RPC/Literal web services with only two methods exposed (note that the method validate(Long creditCardNumber) is not exposed because of @WebMethod(exclude = true)). Every method parameter and returned value is renamed to have a more expressive WSDL. Listing 14-17 shows the resulting WSDL document that you can compare with the original one in Listing 14-1 (the differences are highlighted in bold in the code).

Listing 14-17. The WSDL After Customization

```
<?xml version="1.0" encoding="UTF-8" ?>
<definitions ↪
        xmlns:soap="http://schemas.xmlsoap.org/wsdl/soap/" ↪
        xmlns:tns="http://chapter14.javaee7.book.agoncal.org/" ↪
        xmlns:xsd="http://www.w3.org/2001/XMLSchema" ↪
        xmlns="http://schemas.xmlsoap.org/wsdl/" ↪
        targetNamespace="http://chapter14.javaee7.book.agoncal.org/" ↪
        name="ValidatorService">
  <types>
    <xsd:schema>
      <xsd:import namespace="http://chapter14.javaee7.book.agoncal.org/" ↪
                  schemaLocation="http://localhost:8080/chapter14/ValidatorService?xsd=1"/>
    </xsd:schema>
  </types>
  <message name="ValidateCreditCard">
    <part name="Credit-Card" type="tns:creditCard"/>
  </message>
  <message name="ValidateCreditCardResponse">
    <part name="IsValid" type="xsd:boolean"/>
  </message>
  <message name="ValidateCreditCardNumber">
    <part name="Credit-Card-Number" type="xsd:string"/>
  </message>
  <message name="ValidateCreditCardNumberResponse"/>
  <portType name="CardValidator">
```

```
      <operation name="ValidateCreditCard">
        <input message="tns:ValidateCreditCard"/>
        <output message="tns:ValidateCreditCardResponse"/>
      </operation>
      <operation name="ValidateCreditCardNumber">
        <input message="tns:ValidateCreditCardNumber"/>
        <output message="tns:ValidateCreditCardNumberResponse"/>
      </operation>
    </portType>
    <binding name="CreditCardValidatorBinding" type="tns:CardValidator">
      <soap:binding transport="http://schemas.xmlsoap.org/soap/http" style="rpc"/>
      <operation name="ValidateCreditCard">
        <soap:operation soapAction=""/>
        <input>
          <soap:body use="literal"/>
        </input>
        <output>
          <soap:body use="literal"/>
        </output>
      </operation>
      <operation name="ValidateCreditCardNumber">
        <soap:operation soapAction=""/>
        <input>
          <soap:body use="literal"/>
        </input>
        <output>
          <soap:body use="literal"/>
        </output>
      </operation>
    </binding>
    <service name="ValidatorService">
      <port name="CreditCardValidator" binding="tns:CreditCardValidatorBinding">
        <soap:address location="http://localhost:8080/chapter14/ValidatorService"/>
      </port>
    </service>
</definitions>
```

The @WebService annotation renames the <portType name> and <port name> elements of the WSDL. @WebMethod renames the <operation name> element, @WebResult and @WebParam rename the <part name> which is part of the <message> element.

The XML schema also gets customized as both the request and the response, are defined in the <xs:complexType> element. Compared with the XSD defined in Listing 14-2 you can see that the one in Listing 14-18 is very different. That's because the SOAP web service uses an RPC style (no request/response documents are defined, but instead it uses the types creditCard and boolean).

Listing 14-18. The XML Schema After Customization

```
<xs:schema xmlns:xs="http://www.w3.org/2001/XMLSchema"
           targetNamespace="http://chapter14.javaee7.book.agoncal.org/" version="1.0">
  <xs:complexType name="creditCard">
    <xs:sequence/>
    <xs:attribute name="number" type="xs:string" use="required"/>
    <xs:attribute name="expiry_date" type="xs:string" use="required"/>
```

```
      <xs:attribute name="control_number" type="xs:int" use="required"/>
      <xs:attribute name="type" type="xs:string" use="required"/>
   </xs:complexType>
</xs:schema>
```

The WSDL (Listing 14-17) and the XSD (Listing 14-18) are used to define the contract between the service consumer and provider. But at runtime they are not used anymore and only SOAP envelopes are exchanged between the consumer and the provider. Listing 14-19 shows the SOAP request that is sent to the web service. It defines the method to be called (ValidateCreditCard) and the parameters to pass to this method (Credit-Card).

Listing 14-19. The SOAP Envelope for the ValidateCreditCard Request After Customization

```
<soap:Envelope xmlns:soap="http://schemas.xmlsoap.org/soap/envelope/" ↩
                xmlns:cc="http://chapter14.javaee7.book.agoncal.org/">
   <soap:Header/>
   <soap:Body>
     <cc:ValidateCreditCard>
       <Credit-Card number="123456789011" expiry_date="10/12" control_number="544" ↩
                                                               type="Visa"/>
     </cc:ValidateCreditCard>
   </soap:Body>
</soap:Envelope>
```

Listing 14-20 shows the SOAP response that is sent back to the consumer. It indicates that the credit card sent in the request is valid (<IsValid>true</IsValid>).

Listing 14-20. The SOAP Envelope for the ValidateCreditCard Response After Customization)

```
<soap:Envelope xmlns:soap="http://schemas.xmlsoap.org/soap/envelope/"
                xmlns:cc="http://chapter14.javaee7.book.agoncal.org/">
   <soap:Body>
     <cc:ValidateCreditCardResponse>
       <IsValid>true</IsValid>
     </cc:ValidateCreditCardResponse>
   </soap:Body>
</soap:Envelope>
```

Handling Exceptions

So far everything is working well: the data exchanged between the consumer and the provider is valid, the web service doesn't crash, and the network is reliable. But that's not always the case. In Java, when something goes wrong, an exception is thrown and some other class inside the JVM has to handle it. With SOAP web services this mechanism cannot work as the consumer and the service may not be written in the same language and are separated by a network. So the idea is to use a SOAP fault in the SOAP message. The JAX-WS runtime automatically converts Java exceptions into SOAP fault messages that are returned to the client. This feature saves you a lot of time and energy by eliminating the need to write code that maps your service exceptions to SOAP faults.

If you look at the validate method of the CardValidator web service defined in Listing 14-5, you'll notice that if the CreditCard parameter is null, the validation crashes with a NullPointerException. When this happens, the JAX-WS runtime catches the NullPointerException exception on the server, creates a SOAP Fault message (Listing 14-21) and sends it back to the consumer.

Listing 14-21. A SOAP Fault is Sent in the SOAP Response

```
<soap:Envelope xmlns:soap="http://schemas.xmlsoap.org/soap/envelope/">
  <soap:Body>
    <soap:Fault>
      <faultcode>soap:Server</faultcode>
      <faultstring>java.lang.NullPointerException</faultstring>
    </soap:Fault>
  </soap:Body>
</soap:Envelope>
```

As you can see in Listing 14-21, the JAX-WS runtime automatically sets the faultstring to the qualified name of the Java exception. The specification also provides a mechanism to differentiate between the types of fault using the faultcode element. In this case it is set to soap:Server indicating that the server is responsible for the fault (soap:Client is the other option).

One other option for returning a SOAP fault is to throw an application exception as shown in Listing 14-22. Here the web service throws a check exception (but same mechanism applies to uncheck exceptions) if the credit card number is odd. This application exception will automatically be translated into the appropriate soap:Fault message, wrapped in the SOAP body, and returned to the client.

Listing 14-22. Validation Throws an Exception

```
@WebService
public class CardValidator throws CardValidatorException {

public boolean validate(CreditCard creditCard) {
    Character lastDigit = creditCard.getNumber().charAt( ↪
                        creditCard.getNumber().length() - 1);

    if (Integer.parseInt(lastDigit.toString()) % 2 == 0) {
      return true;
    } else {
      throw new CardValidatorException("The credit card number is invalid");
    }
  }
}
```

The application exception can inherit from Exception, RuntimeException, or a SOAP web service exception such as javax.xml.ws.WebServiceException or one of its subclasses (e.g., javax.xml.ws.soap.SOAPFaultException). These exceptions can also be annotated with @WebFault to have a more explicit SOAP envelope as show in Listing 14-23.

Listing 14-23. Exception with a WebFault Annotation

```
@WebFault(name = "CardValidationFault")
public class CardValidatorException extends Exception {

  public CardValidatorRTException() {
    super();
  }

  public CardValidatorRTException(String message) {
    super(message);
  }
}
```

When the SOAP web service throws the exception defined in Listing 14-23, the JAX-WS runtime generates the SOAP fault message defined in Listing 14-24.

Listing 14-24. SOAP Fault in a SOAP Envelope

```
<soap:Envelope xmlns:soap="http://schemas.xmlsoap.org/soap/envelope/">
  <soap:Body>
    <soap:Fault>
      <faultcode>soap:Server</faultcode>
      <faultstring>org.agoncal.book.javaee7.chapter14.CardValidatorException</faultstring>
      <detail>
        <ns2:CardValidationFault xmlns:ns2="http://chapter14.javaee7.book.agoncal.org/">
          <message>The credit card number is invalid</message>
        </ns2:CardValidationFault>
      </detail>
    </soap:Fault>
  </soap:Body>
</soap:Envelope>
```

But if you want to produce a more accurate SOAP fault message with a different faultcode and so on, then you can use the javax.xml.soap.SOAPFactory API to create a javax.xml.soap.SOAPFault object (shown in Listing 14-25).

Listing 14-25. Validation Uses a SOAPFactory to Create a SOAPFault

```
@WebService
public class CardValidator {

public boolean validate(CreditCard creditCard) {
    Character lastDigit = creditCard.getNumber().charAt( ↩
                        creditCard.getNumber().length() - 1);

    if (Integer.parseInt(lastDigit.toString()) % 2 == 0) {
      return true;
    } else {
      SOAPFactory soapFactory = SOAPFactory.newInstance();
      SOAPFault fault = soapFactory.createFault("The credit card number is invalid", ↩
                                        new QName("ValidationFault"));

      throw new CardValidatorException(fault);
    }
  }
}
```

Listing 14-25 creates a SOAPFault with a reason text ("The credit card number is invalid") and a fault code (ValidationFault) that will produce the SOAP envelope shown in Listing 14-26.

Listing 14-26. SOAP Fault in a SOAP Envelope

```
<soap:Envelope xmlns:soap="http://schemas.xmlsoap.org/soap/envelope/">
  <soap:Body>
    <soap:Fault>
      <faultcode>ValidationFault</faultcode>
      <faultstring>The credit card number is invalid</faultstring>
```

```
    </soap:Fault
  </soap:Body>
</soap:Envelope>
```

Life Cycle and Callback

As you can see in Figure 14-4, SOAP web services also have a life cycle that resembles managed beans. It is the same life cycle found for components that do not hold any state: either they do not exist or they are ready to process a request. The container manages this life cycle.

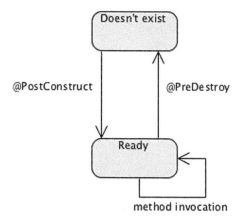

Figure 14-4. *SOAP web service life cycle*

Both the servlet and EJB endpoint support dependency injection (because they run in a container) and life-cycle methods such as @PostConstruct and @PreDestroy. The container calls the @PostConstruct callback method, if any, when it creates an instance of a web service, and calls the @PreDestroy callback when it destroys it. One difference between servlet and EJB endpoints is that EJBs can use interceptors (described in Chapter 2).

WebServiceContext

A SOAP web service has an environment context and can access it by injecting a reference of javax.xml.ws.WebServiceContext with a @Resource annotation. Within this context, the web service can obtain runtime information such as the endpoint implementation class, the message context, and security information relative to a request being served.

■ **Note** JAX-WS and WS-Metadata specifications haven't been updated in Java EE 7 so, even if your application uses CDI, you cannot use the @Inject annotation to inject the WebServiceContext, you still need to use @Resource.

The code in Listing 14-27 uses the WebServiceContext to check if the caller has the Admin role to validate a credit card. Table 14-6 lists the methods defined in the javax.xml.ws.WebServiceContext interface.

Listing 14-27. SOAP Web Service Using the WebServiceContext

```
@WebService
public class CardValidator {

    @Resource
    private WebServiceContext context;

    public boolean validate(CreditCard creditCard) {

        if (!context.isUserInRole("Admin"))
            throw new SecurityException("Only Admins can validate cards");

        // Business logic
        }
    }
}
```

Table 14-6. *Methods of the WebServiceContext Interface*

Method	Description
getMessageContext	Returns the MessageContext for the request being served at the time this method is called. It can be used to access the SOAP message headers, body, and so on.
getUserPrincipal	Returns the Principal that identifies the sender of the request currently being serviced.
isUserInRole	Returns a Boolean indicating whether the authenticated user is included in the specified logical role.
getEndpointReference	Returns the EndpointReference associated with this endpoint.

Deployment Descriptor

Like most Java EE 7 technologies, SOAP web services allow you to define metadata using annotations (what I've been doing so far in all the examples) as well as XML. Located under the WEB-INF directory, the webservices.xml file overrides or augments the annotations. Like most deployment descriptors in Java EE 7, webservices.xml is optional since the annotations can be used to specify most of the information specified in this deployment descriptor. For example, Listing 14-28 shows how you can override the WSDL port (OverriddenPort) for the CardValidator web service.

Listing 14-28. A webservices.xml Deployment Descriptor

```
<webservices xmlns="http://java.sun.com/xml/ns/javaee" ↪
             xmlns:xsi="http://www.w3.org/2001/XMLSchema-instance" ↪
             xsi:schemaLocation="http://java.sun.com/xml/ns/javaee ↪
             http://java.sun.com/xml/ns/javaee/javaee_web_services_1_3.xsd" ↪
             version="1.3">
```

```
<webservice-description>
  <webservice-description-name>CardValidatorWS</webservice-description-name>

  <port-component>
    <port-component-name>CardValidator</port-component-name>
    <wsdl-port>OverriddenPort</wsdl-port>
    <service-endpoint-interface>
      org.agoncal.book.javaee7.chapter14.Validator
    </service-endpoint-interface>
    <service-impl-bean>
      <servlet-link>CardValidatorServlet</servlet-link>
    </service-impl-bean>
  </port-component>
</webservice-description>
</webservices>
```

Packaging

SOAP web services may be packaged in a war or EJB jar file. Those packaged in a war file can use servlet or EJB Lite endpoints. SOAP web services packaged in an EJB jar file can only use Stateless/Singleton session beans. The developer is responsible for packaging:

- The service implementation bean and its dependent classes

- The service endpoint interfaces (optional)

- The WSDL file either by containment or reference (not required when annotations are used because the WSDL can be automatically generated by the JAX-WS runtime)

- Generated artifacts for the SOAP request and response (optional as they are automatically generated by the JAX-WS runtime)

- An optional deployment descriptor

Publishing a SOAP Web Service

Once packaged in a war/jar file, publishing a SOAP web service is just a matter of deploying the archive into a Java EE container such as GlassFish or JBoss. That's because JAX-WS is part of Java EE 7 and the runtime is bundled in the application server. But you can also publish a SOAP web service in a web container such as Tomcat or Jetty if you embed a JAX-WS implementation such as Metro, CXF, or Axis2.

But remember that JAX-WS also comes in Java SE and sometimes you do not require the full power of a servlet or EJB container (for example when testing your web service). In this case you can use the javax.xml.ws.Endpoint API to programmatically publish a SOAP web service. The method Endpoint.publish (see Listing 14-29) uses by default a lightweight HTTP server that is included in the Oracle's JVM (defined in the package com.sun.net.httpserver).

Listing 14-29. A SOAP Web Service Publishing Itself and Accepting Incoming Requests

```
@WebService
public class CardValidator {

  public boolean validate(CreditCard creditCard) {
    // Business logic
  }
```

```java
  public static void main(String[] args) {
    Endpoint.publish("http://localhost:8080/cardValidator", new CardValidator());
  }
}
```

In Listing 14-29 the `publish` method is used to publish the `CardValidator` SOAP web service, at which point it starts accepting incoming requests at the address `http://localhost:8080/cardValidator`. You can then invoke methods on your web service. There is also a `stop` method that can be used to stop accepting incoming requests and to take the endpoint down (as you'll later see when developing an integration test).

Invoking SOAP Web Services

So far you've seen how to write, package, and publish a SOAP web service. Now let's look at how to invoke such a service. With the WSDL and some tools to generate the Java client stubs (or proxies), you can easily invoke a web service without caring about all the plumbing around HTTP or SOAP. Invoking a web service is similar to invoking a distributed object with RMI. Like RMI, JAX-WS enables the programmer to use a local method call to invoke a distributed service. The difference is that, on the remote host, the web service can be written in another programming language (note that you can also invoke non-Java code using RMI-IIOP). The WSDL is the standard contract between the consumer and the service. Metro provides a WSDL-to-Java utility tool (`wsimport`) that generates Java interfaces and classes from a WSDL. Such proxies give you a Java representation of a web service endpoint (servlet or EJB). This proxy then routes the local Java call to the remote web service using HTTP.

When a method on this proxy is invoked (see Figure 14-5), it converts the parameters of the method into a SOAP message (the request) and sends it to the web service endpoint. To obtain the result, the SOAP response is converted back into an instance of the returned type. You don't need to understand the internal work of the proxy nor even look at the code. Before compiling your client consumer, you need to generate the SEI to get the proxy class to call it in your code.

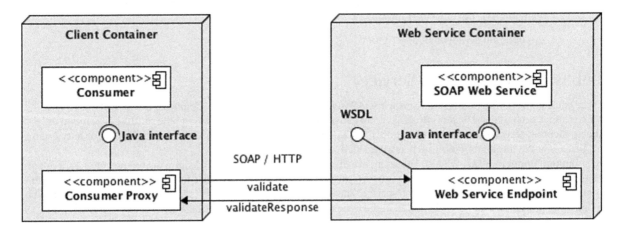

Figure 14-5. *A consumer invoking a web service through a proxy*

When developing SOAP consumers using a contract first, the client has to get the WSDL, generate the needed artifacts, invoke the CardValidator web service to validate a credit card (the validate SOAP message), and receive a response (the validateResponse SOAP message).

■ **Note** The `wsimport` and `wsgen` tools are shipped with JDK 1.7 as well as GlassFish or Metro. `wsimport` takes a WSDL as an input and generates JAX-WS artifacts, such as an SEI. `wsgen` reads a web service endpoint class and generates the WSDL. You can access these tools directly with a Java SE 7 installation, or through the GlassFish command-line interface (CLI), an Ant task, or a Maven plug-in.

Anatomy of a SOAP Consumer

Because JAX-WS is available in Java SE, a SOAP web service consumer can be any kind of Java code from a main class running on the JVM to any Java EE component running in a container (Web, EJB or application client container). If it runs in a container the consumer can get an instance of the proxy either through injection or by programmatically creating it. To inject a web service, you need to use the `@javax.xml.ws.WebServiceRef` annotation or a CDI producer.

Invoking Programmatically

If your consumer is running outside a container, you need to programmatically invoke your SOAP web service. As you can see in Listing 14-30, the `CardValidator` web service is not directly invoked. The consumer uses an instance of `CardValidatorService` (which has been generated from the WSDL thanks to `wsimport`) using the new keyword. It then has to get the proxy `CardValidator` class (`getCardValidatorPort()`) to invoke business methods locally. A local call is made on the `validate()` method of the proxy, which in turn will invoke the remote web service, create the SOAP request, marshal the credit card messages, and so on. The proxy finds the target service because the default endpoint URL is embedded in the WSDL file, and is subsequently integrated into the proxy implementation.

Listing 14-30. A Java SE Class Invoking a SOAP Web Service Programmatically

```
public class WebServiceConsumer {

  public static void main(String[] args) {

    CreditCard creditCard = new CreditCard();
    creditCard.setNumber("12341234");
    creditCard.setExpiryDate("10/12");
    creditCard.setType("VISA");
    creditCard.setControlNumber(1234);

    CardValidator cardValidator = new CardValidatorService().getCardValidatorPort();
    cardValidator.validate(creditCard);
  }
}
```

Although this code is straightforward, there's a lot of magic happening behind the scenes. Several artifacts have been generated from a WSDL file to make this work. They contain all the information required to connect to the URL where the web service is located, marshal the `CreditCard` object into XML, invoke the web service through a SOAP request, and obtain a result from the SOAP response.

Invoking with Injection

On the other hand, if your consumer runs in a container you can use injection to get a reference to the SOAP web service client proxy. Listing 14-31 shows a simple main Java class running in an application client container (ACC) and using the @WebServiceRef annotation. It follows the @Resource or @EJB annotation pattern shown in previous chapters, but for web services. When this annotation is applied on an attribute (or a getter method), the container will inject an instance of the web service client proxy when the application is initialized.

Listing 14-31. A Java SE Class Running in ACC and Using Injection

```
public class WebServiceConsumer {

    @WebServiceRef
    private static CardValidatorService cardValidatorService;

    public static void main(String[] args) {

        CreditCard creditCard = new CreditCard();
        creditCard.setNumber("12341234");
        creditCard.setExpiryDate("10/12");
        creditCard.setType("VISA");
        creditCard.setControlNumber(1234);

        CardValidator cardValidator = cardValidatorService.getCardValidatorPort();
        cardValidator.validate(creditCard);
    }
}
```

Note that the code in Listing 14-31 would be very similar if your consumer is an EJB, a Servlet or a JSF backing bean. To get injection you need to run your code in a container otherwise the @WebServiceRef annotation cannot be used.

Invoking with CDI

The JAX-WS specification hasn't been updated in Java EE 7 and therefore does not embrace all the CDI goodies. For example, you cannot directly inject a reference of the web service proxy using the @Inject annotation. But as seen in Chapter 2, you can use the CDI producers to produce such a reference (see Listing 14-32).

Listing 14-32. Utility Class Producing a Web Service Reference

```
public class WebServiceProducer {

    @Produces
    @WebServiceRef
    private CardValidatorService cardValidatorService;

}
```

Thanks to the WebServiceProducer utility class in Listing 14-32, any EJB or Servlet can now inject the produced CardValidatorService with @Inject and invoke a business method on it (Listing 14-33). With this mechanism you can even use the CDI alternatives to route your method invocation to an alternative SOAP web service as explained in Chapter 2.

Listing 14-33. An EJB Using a CDI Producer to Inject a Web Service Reference

```
@Stateless
public class EJBConsumerWithCDI {

  @Inject
  private CardValidatorService cardValidatorService;

  public boolean validate(CreditCard creditCard) {

    CardValidator cardValidator = cardValidatorService.getCardValidatorPort();
    return cardValidator.validate(creditCard);
  }
}
```

Putting It All Together

Now let's put all these concepts together and write a consumer, a SOAP web service, test it, deploy it in GlassFish and invoke it. We will use JAXB and JAX-WS annotations, as well as generate a service endpoint interface with the wsimport Maven goal. To write a web service, several steps are needed. I'll demonstrate these steps by revisiting the CardValidator web service.

The CardValidator SOAP web service checks that a credit card is valid. It has one method that takes a CreditCard object as a parameter, applies some algorithm, and returns true if the card is valid, false if not. This business logic will be unit tested but also tested in integration (with an embedded HTTP server). Once this web service is tested and deployed on GlassFish, wsimport is used to generate all the needed artifacts for the consumer. The consumer can then invoke the web service to validate credit cards.

As shown in Figure 14-6, you will use two Maven projects: one to package the web service into a war file (chapter14-service-1.0.war) and another to package the consumer into a jar file (chapter14-consumer-1.0.jar). These archives will have code developed by you but also generated code on both the consumer (generated by wsimport) and the service (generated by the JAX-WS runtime).

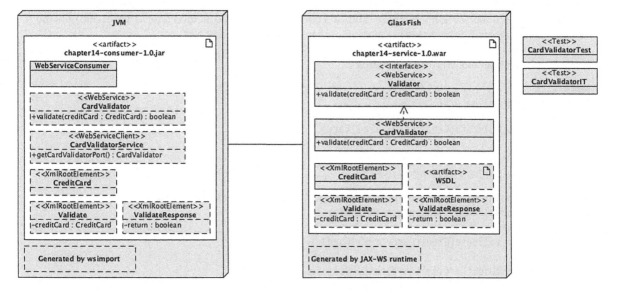

Figure 14-6. *Putting It All Together*

Writing the CreditCard Class

The CreditCard class, shown in Listing 14-34, is the POJO used as a parameter of the web service validate() method. SOAP web services exchange XML messages, not Java objects. The CreditCard class is annotated with several JAXB annotations (e.g., @XmlRootElement) allowing it to be marshaled into XML so that it can be sent in a SOAP request. The CreditCard object has some basic required attributes such as the credit card number, the expiry date (formatted as MM/YY), a credit card type (Visa, MasterCard, American Express, etc.), and a control number.

Listing 14-34. The CreditCard Class with JAXB Annotations

```java
@XmlRootElement
@XmlAccessorType(XmlAccessType.FIELD)
public class CreditCard {

  @XmlAttribute(required = true)
  private String number;
  @XmlAttribute(name = "expiry_date", required = true)
  private String expiryDate;
  @XmlAttribute(name = "control_number", required = true)
  private Integer controlNumber;
  @XmlAttribute(required = true)
  private String type;

  // Constructors, getters, setters
}
```

Writing the CardValidator SOAP Web Service

The CardValidator (see Listing 14-36) implements the Validator interface (see Listing 14-35) and both are annotated with the JAX-WS @WebService annotation. CardValidator is just a POJO so it is considered a Servlet endpoint and not an EJB endpoint (as it doesn't have the @Stateless or @Singleton annotation). It has a validate() method that takes a CreditCard object as a parameter. The algorithm to check whether the card is valid or not is based on the card number: even numbers are valid, odd numbers are not. The method returns a boolean. Both the class and the interface will be packaged in the war file (chapter14-service-1.0.war).

Listing 14-35. The Validator Web Service Interface

```java
@WebService
public interface Validator {

  public boolean validate(CreditCard creditCard);
}
```

Listing 14-36. The CardValidator Web Service Bean

```java
@WebService(endpointInterface = "org.agoncal.book.javaee7.chapter14.Validator")
public class CardValidator implements Validator {

  public boolean validate(CreditCard creditCard) {

    Character lastDigit = creditCard.getNumber().charAt( ➥
                          creditCard.getNumber().length() - 1);
```

```
      if (Integer.parseInt(lastDigit.toString()) % 2 == 0) {
        return true;
      } else {
        return false;
      }
    }
  }
}
```

For simplicity, no extra Java-to-WSDL mapping is used, so there are no @WebMethod, @WebResult, or @WebParam annotations, allowing you to see how easy it is to write a web service using all the default mapping rules.

Writing the CardValidatorTest Unit Test

Unit testing a SOAP web service can be pretty simple if you only test the business logic in isolation (i.e., with no container services such as injection, security, and so on). Unit testing the CardValidator POJO means testing the credit card validation algorithm. As shown in Listing 14-37, the test case creates an instance of the CardValidator POJO, a CreditCard with an even number, validates it, and checks that the card is valid. Then it changes the number to odd, validates the card again, and checks it is invalid.

Listing 14-37. The CardValidatorTest Unit Test

```
public class CardValidatorTest {

  @Test
  public void shouldCheckCreditCardValidity() {

    CardValidator cardValidator = new CardValidator();

    CreditCard creditCard = new CreditCard("12341234", "10/10", 1234, "VISA");
    assertTrue("Credit card should be valid", cardValidator.validate(creditCard));

    creditCard.setNumber("12341233");
    assertFalse("Credit card should not be valid", cardValidator.validate(creditCard));
  }
}
```

But what do you do if your SOAP web service needs injection, for example? If you review the code in Listing 14-27, you'll notice that the container injects the WebServiceContext so the bean can check if the user is in role Admin or not. Without the container the WebServiceContext will be null and the test will fail. To solve this problem you can either mock the container's services (e.g., mock the WebServiceContext injection) or test your SOAP web service in integration mode, that is, inside the container.

Writing the CardValidatorIT Integration Test

Integration testing a SOAP web service means deploying it to a web server, accessing its WSDL, having full container services, and so on. This used to be a tedious task, as you had to start a runtime container, package your application, and deploy and test it. But since Java SE 6, you can now use an embedded web server thanks to the javax.xml.ws.Endpoint API.

Listing 14-38 shows a JUnit test class that publishes our CardValidator SOAP web service at a given URL (http://localhost:8080/cardValidator). Once published (endpoint.isPublished()), it can access the generated WSDL at URL http://localhost:8080/cardValidator?wsdl and use it to create a Service (Service.create(wsdlDocumentLocation, serviceQN)). The service.getPort method returns the client proxy to the SOAP web service where you can then invoke a method (cardValidator.validate(creditCard)). Before finishing the test you need to undeploy the web service (endpoint.stop()).

Listing 14-38. The CardValidatorIT Integration Test

```java
public class CardValidatorIT {

    @Test
    public void shouldCheckCreditCardValidity() throws MalformedURLException {

        // Publishes the SOAP Web Service
        Endpoint endpoint = Endpoint.publish("http://localhost:8080/cardValidator", ↪
                                             new CardValidator());
        assertTrue(endpoint.isPublished());
        assertEquals("http://schemas.xmlsoap.org/wsdl/soap/http", ↪
                    endpoint.getBinding().getBindingID());

        // Needed properties to access the web service
        URL wsdlDocumentLocation = new URL("http://localhost:8080/cardValidator?wsdl");
        String namespaceURI = "http://chapter14.javaee7.book.agoncal.org/";
        String servicePart = "CardValidatorService";
        String portName = "CardValidatorPort";
        QName serviceQN = new QName(namespaceURI, servicePart);
        QName portQN = new QName(namespaceURI, portName);

        // Creates a service instance
        Service service = Service.create(wsdlDocumentLocation, serviceQN);
        Validator cardValidator = service.getPort(portQN, Validator.class);

        // Invokes the web service
        CreditCard creditCard = new CreditCard("12341234", "10/10", 1234, "VISA");
        assertTrue("Credit card should be valid", cardValidator.validate(creditCard));

        creditCard.setNumber("12341233");
        assertFalse("Credit card should not be valid", cardValidator.validate(creditCard));

        // Unpublishes the SOAP Web Service
        endpoint.stop();
        assertFalse(endpoint.isPublished());
    }
}
```

Now that the CardValidator SOAP web service is developed and tested, we can package it and deploy it to GlassFish.

Compiling, Testing and Packaging with Maven

The CardValidator web service (interface in Listing 14-35 and implementation in Listing 14-36) needs to be compiled, tested and packaged in a war file (`<packaging>` war `</packaging>`). The pom.xml file (see Listing 14-39) declares the glassfish-embedded-all dependency, which is a convenient way to have access to all the Java EE 7 specifications including JAX-WS and Web Services Metadata. In fact, glassfish-embedded-all contains the full GlassFish 4.0 implementation in a single JAR, useful for compilation and embedded use. Setting the version to 1.7 in the maven-compiler-plugin explicitly specifies that you want to use Java SE 7 (`<source>` 1.7 `</source>`).

Listing 14-39. The pom.xml File to Compile, Test and Package the Web Service

```
<?xml version="1.0" encoding="UTF-8"?>
<project xmlns="http://maven.apache.org/POM/4.0.0" ↪
         xmlns:xsi="http://www.w3.org/2001/XMLSchema-instance" ↪
         xsi:schemaLocation="http://maven.apache.org/POM/4.0.0 ↪
         http://maven.apache.org/xsd/maven-4.0.0.xsd">
  <modelVersion>4.0.0</modelVersion>

  <parent>
    <artifactId>chapter14</artifactId>
    <groupId>org.agoncal.book.javaee7</groupId>
    <version>1.0</version>
  </parent>

  <groupId>org.agoncal.book.javaee7.chapter14</groupId>
  <artifactId>chapter14-service</artifactId>
  <version>1.0</version>
  <packaging>war</packaging>

  <dependencies>
    <dependency>
      <groupId>org.glassfish.main.extras</groupId>
      <artifactId>glassfish-embedded-all</artifactId>
      <version>4.0</version>
      <scope>provided</scope>
    </dependency>

    <dependency>
      <groupId>junit</groupId>
      <artifactId>junit</artifactId>
      <version>4.11</version>
      <scope>test</scope>
    </dependency>
  </dependencies>

  <build>
    <plugins>
      <plugin>
        <groupId>org.apache.maven.plugins</groupId>
        <artifactId>maven-compiler-plugin</artifactId>
        <version>2.5.1</version>
        <configuration>
```

```
        <source>1.7</source>
        <target>1.7</target>
      </configuration>
    </plugin>
    <plugin>
      <groupId>org.apache.maven.plugins</groupId>
      <artifactId>maven-war-plugin</artifactId>
      <version>2.2</version>
      <configuration>
        <failOnMissingWebXml>false</failOnMissingWebXml>
      </configuration>
    </plugin>
    <plugin>
      <groupId>org.apache.maven.plugins</groupId>
      <artifactId>maven-failsafe-plugin</artifactId>
      <version>2.12.4</version>
      <executions>
        <execution>
          <id>integration-test</id>
          <goals>
            <goal>integration-test</goal>
            <goal>verify</goal>
          </goals>
        </execution>
      </executions>
    </plugin>
  </plugins>
  </build>
</project>
```

With Java EE 7, deployment descriptors are optional; therefore, you don't need a web.xml or webservices.xml file. However, as Maven still obliges you to add a web.xml file into a war by default, you need to change the failOnMissingWebXml attribute of the maven-war-plugin to false; otherwise, Maven will fail the build.

To compile and package the web service, open a command-line in the root directory containing the pom.xml file and enter the following Maven command:

```
$ mvn package
```

Go to the target directory, where you should see a file named chapter14-service-1.0.war. If you open it, you will see that Validator.class, CardValidator.class and CreditCard.class are under the WEB-INF\classes directory. The war file doesn't contain anything else, not even a WSDL file (which will be generated by the JAX-WS runtime).

You can execute the unit test (Listing 14-37) and integration test (Listing 14-38) with the Maven Surefire and Failsafe plugin by enter the following Maven command:

```
$ mvn integration-test
```

Now that the CardValidator SOAP web service is developed and tested we can deploy it to GlassFish.

Deploying on GlassFish

Once the web service is packaged in the war file, it needs to be deployed into GlassFish. This can be done using the asadmin command line. Open a console and go to the target directory of your project where the chapter14-service-1.0.war file is located, make sure GlassFish is running, and enter the following command:

```
$ asadmin deploy chapter14-service-1.0.war
Application deployed with name chapter14-service-1.0.
Command deploy executed successfully.
```

If the deployment is successful, the following command should return the name of the deployed components and their types:

```
$ asadmin list-components
chapter14-service-1.0 <webservices, web>
```

It's interesting to note that GlassFish recognizes the web module (the war file could have contained web pages, servlets, and so on) as being a web service. If you go to the GlassFish administration console shown in Figure 14-7 (http://localhost:4848/), you will see that chapter14-service-1.0 is deployed under the Applications menu.

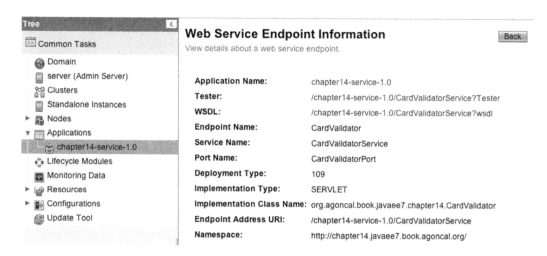

Figure 14-7. *Web services deployed in the GlassFish administration console*

On this page, if you click the WSDL link, it will open the browser at the following URL and show the generated WSDL of the CardValidator SOAP web service (see Figure 14-8):

```
http://localhost:8080/chapter14-service-1.0/CardValidatorService?wsdl
```

This XML file does not appear to have any style information associated with it. The document tree is shown below.

```
▼<!--
    Published by JAX-WS RI at http://jax-ws.dev.java.net. RI's version is Metro/2.3 (tags/2.3-7528; 2013-04-29T19:34:10+0000) JAXWS-RI/2.2.8 JAXWS/2.2 svn-revision#unknown.
  -->
▼<!--
    Generated by JAX-WS RI at http://jax-ws.dev.java.net. RI's version is Metro/2.3 (tags/2.3-7528; 2013-04-29T19:34:10+0000) JAXWS-RI/2.2.8 JAXWS/2.2 svn-revision#unknown.
  -->
▼<definitions xmlns:wsu="http://docs.oasis-open.org/wss/2004/01/oasis-200401-wss-wssecurity-utility-1.0.xsd" xmlns:wsp="http://www.w3.org/ns/ws-policy"
    xmlns:wsp1_2="http://schemas.xmlsoap.org/ws/2004/09/policy" xmlns:wsam="http://www.w3.org/2007/05/addressing/metadata" xmlns:soap="http://schemas.xmlsoap.org/wsdl/soap/"
    xmlns:tns="http://chapter14.javaee7.book.agoncal.org/" xmlns:xsd="http://www.w3.org/2001/XMLSchema" xmlns="http://schemas.xmlsoap.org/wsdl/"
    targetNamespace="http://chapter14.javaee7.book.agoncal.org/" name="CardValidatorService">
  ▼<types>
    ▼<xsd:schema>
        <xsd:import namespace="http://chapter14.javaee7.book.agoncal.org/" schemaLocation="http://localhost:8080/chapter14-service-1.0/CardValidatorService?xsd=1"/>
      </xsd:schema>
    </types>
  ▼<message name="validate">
      <part name="parameters" element="tns:validate"/>
    </message>
  ▼<message name="validateResponse">
      <part name="parameters" element="tns:validateResponse"/>
    </message>
  ▼<portType name="Validator">
    ▼<operation name="validate">
        <input wsam:Action="http://chapter14.javaee7.book.agoncal.org/Validator/validateRequest" message="tns:validate"/>
        <output wsam:Action="http://chapter14.javaee7.book.agoncal.org/Validator/validateResponse" message="tns:validateResponse"/>
      </operation>
    </portType>
  ▼<binding name="CardValidatorPortBinding" type="tns:Validator">
      <soap:binding transport="http://schemas.xmlsoap.org/soap/http" style="document"/>
    ▼<operation name="validate">
        <soap:operation soapAction=""/>
      ▼<input>
          <soap:body use="literal"/>
        </input>
      ▼<output>
          <soap:body use="literal"/>
        </output>
      </operation>
    </binding>
  ▼<service name="CardValidatorService">
    ▼<port name="CardValidatorPort" binding="tns:CardValidatorPortBinding">
        <soap:address location="http://localhost:8080/chapter14-service-1.0/CardValidatorService"/>
      </port>
    </service>
  </definitions>
```

Figure 14-8. *The WSDL has been generated by Metro*

It is interesting to note that you didn't create this WSDL or deploy it in the war file. The Metro stack automatically generates the WSDL based on the annotations contained in the web service (as well as the Validate SOAP request and ValidateResponse SOAP response shown in Figure 14-6). That's the WSDL we'll use to generate the client proxy so that the consumer can remotely access the web service.

Writing the WebServiceConsumer Class

The web service is now deployed, GlassFish is up and running, and you know which URL the WSDL has been generated to. Thanks to this WSDL, the consumer will be able to generate the necessary artifacts to invoke the web service with the wsimport tool. First, let's write the consumer code, as shown in Listing 14-40.

Listing 14-40. The WebServiceConsumer Class Invokes the Web Service Using Injection

```java
public class WebServiceConsumer {

    @WebServiceRef
    private static CardValidatorService cardValidatorService;

    public static void main(String[] args) {

        CreditCard creditCard = new CreditCard();
        creditCard.setNumber("12341234");
        creditCard.setExpiryDate("10/12");
        creditCard.setType("VISA");
        creditCard.setControlNumber(1234);
```

```
CardValidator cardValidator = cardValidatorService.getCardValidatorPort();

    System.out.println(cardValidator.validate(creditCard));
  }
}
```

This WebServiceConsumer class creates an instance of the CreditCard object, sets some data, injects a reference to the web service, invokes the validate() method, and displays the result (true or false depending on whether the credit card is valid). The interesting thing is that the consumer does not have any of these classes. The CardValidatorService, CardValidator, and CreditCard are totally unknown to the consumer. This code will not compile until all of these classes are generated.

Generating Consumer's Artifacts and Packaging with Maven

Before compiling the WebServiceConsumer class, you need to generate the artifacts with the wsimport tool. The good news is that Maven has a JAX-WS plugin with a wsimport goal, and this goal is executed automatically during the generate-sources life-cycle phase. As described in Appendix A, Maven uses a rich life cycle to build applications. The generate-sources phase is used to generate code and is executed before compilation. The only thing to do is tell this wsimport goal where to find the WSDL document. You have this information because you've deployed the web service into GlassFish, and you have displayed the content of the WSDL. Its location is:

```
http://localhost:8080/chapter14-service-1.0/CardValidatorService?wsdl
```

The pom.xml file in Listing 14-41 specifies the needed dependencies, the glassfish-embedded-all version 4.0, as well as the JDK version (1.7). The WebServiceConsumer class is packaged in the chapter14-consumer-1.0.jar file, and, like every jar file, it has a META-INF\MANIFEST.MF file. This file can be used to define some metadata about the jar, and that's what you do when you use the maven-jar-plugin. You add a Main-Class element to the MANIFEST pointing to the WebServiceConsumer class. This will allow execution of the jar file (with the java -jar command, for example).

Listing 14-41. The pom.xml File Generates and Packages the Consumer's Artifacts

```xml
<?xml version="1.0" encoding="UTF-8"?>
<project xmlns="http://maven.apache.org/POM/4.0.0" ⮑
         xmlns:xsi="http://www.w3.org/2001/XMLSchema-instance" ⮑
         xsi:schemaLocation="http://maven.apache.org/POM/4.0.0 ⮑
         http://maven.apache.org/xsd/maven-4.0.0.xsd">
  <modelVersion>4.0.0</modelVersion>

  <parent>
    <artifactId>chapter14</artifactId>
    <groupId>org.agoncal.book.javaee7</groupId>
    <version>1.0</version>
  </parent>

  <groupId>org.agoncal.book.javaee7.chapter14</groupId>
  <artifactId>chapter14-consumer</artifactId>
  <packaging>jar</packaging>
  <version>1.0</version>
```

```xml
<dependencies>
  <dependency>
    <groupId>org.glassfish.main.extras</groupId>
    <artifactId>glassfish-embedded-all</artifactId>
    <version>4.0</version>
    <scope>provided</scope>
  </dependency>
</dependencies>

<build>

  <plugins>
    <plugin>
      <groupId>org.apache.maven.plugins</groupId>
      <artifactId>maven-jar-plugin</artifactId>
      <version>2.4</version>
      <configuration>
        <archive>
          <manifest>
            <mainClass>org.agoncal.book.javaee7.chapter14.WebServiceConsumer</mainClass>
          </manifest>
        </archive>
      </configuration>
    </plugin>

    <plugin>
      <groupId>org.jvnet.jax-ws-commons</groupId>
      <artifactId>jaxws-maven-plugin</artifactId>
      <version>2.2</version>
      <executions>
        <execution>
          <goals>
            <goal>wsimport</goal>
          </goals>
          <configuration>
            <wsdlUrls>
              <wsdlUrl>
                http://localhost:8080/chapter14-service-1.0/CardValidatorService?wsdl
              </wsdlUrl>
            </wsdlUrls>
            <keep>true</keep>
          </configuration>
        </execution>
      </executions>
    </plugin>

    <plugin>
      <artifactId>maven-compiler-plugin</artifactId>
      <version>2.5.1</version>
      <configuration>
        <source>1.7</source>
```

```
        <target>1.7</target>
      </configuration>
    </plugin>

  </plugins>
</build>
</project>
```

To have a better understanding of what happens behind the scenes, first generate the artifacts by entering the following Maven command:

```
$ mvn generate-sources
```

This command executes the Maven generate-sources life-cycle phase, and thus the wsimport goal that is defined with it. wsimport connects to the web service WSDL URL, downloads it, and generates all the artifacts. Here is the output of the Maven command:

```
[INFO] --- jaxws-maven-plugin:2.2:wsimport (default) @ chapter14-consumer ---
[INFO] Processing: http://localhost:8080/chapter14-service-1.0/CardValidatorService?wsdl
[INFO] jaxws:wsimport args: [-keep, chapter14-consumer/target/generated-sources/wsimport, ↪
-encoding, UTF-8, -Xnocompile, ↪
 http://localhost:8080/chapter14-service-1.0/CardValidatorService?wsdl]

parsing WSDL...
Generating code...

[INFO] ------------------------------------------------------------------------
[INFO] BUILD SUCCESS
[INFO] ------------------------------------------------------------------------
```

If you are curious, you can go to the target/generated-sources/wsimport directory and check the classes that have been generated. You will find the CardValidator, CardValidatorService, and CreditCard classes, of course, but also one class for the SOAP request (Validate) and another one for the response (ValidateResponse). These classes are full of JAXB and JAX-WS annotations as they marshal the CreditCard object and connect to the remote web service. You don't have to worry about the generated code. The jar file can be compiled and packaged:

```
$ mvn package
```

This creates the chapter14-consumer-1.0.jar file, which contains the WebServiceConsumer class you wrote plus all the generated classes (see Figure 14-6 to have a better overview of all the generated classes). This jar is self-contained and can now be executed to invoke the web service.

Running the WebServiceConsumer Class

Remember that the WebServiceConsumer class uses the @WebServiceRef annotation to get injected a reference to the web service endpoint interface. This means that the code needs to be executed in the application client container (ACC). Also remember that the chapter14-consumer-1.0.jar file is executable, as you've added a Main-Class element to the MANIFEST.MF file. The only thing that you have to do is to invoke the appclient utility that comes with GlassFish and pass it the jar file as follows:

```
$ appclient -client chapter14-consumer-1.0.jar
```

This will invoke the web service through HTTP and get a response back telling you whether the credit card is valid or not.

Summary

Companies need to exchange data in a secure, reliable, transactional, and interoperable manner. That's why distribution history has seen technologies such as CORBA, DCOM, RPC, or RMI. With the wide adoption of HTTP, several standard bodies (W3C, OASIS) have developed SOAP web services as a loosely (XML) standard way for businesses to communicate over a network. Today, many organizations use SOAP web services heavily to integrate applications run by various external organizations (Internet) or internal departments (intranet).

This chapter has introduced some relevant SOAP web service standards (WSDL, SOAP, etc.) and has focused on the Java EE specifications that cover these standards (JAX-WS, JAXB, WS-Metadata, etc.). These specifications are vital if you want to hide network complexity and simplify development. Leaving these specifications behind, JAX-WS follows a simple development model and uses only a small set of annotations to adjust the Java-to-WSDL mapping. It is then easy to write a web service (servlet or EJB endpoint) or a consumer as simple annotated POJOs with optional deployment descriptors.

This chapter ended with an example of how to write a web service, compile, test (unit testing and integration testing), and package it with Maven. Thanks to the WSDL and some tooling, you can generate the consumer's artifacts to remotely invoke the SOAP web service.

Amazon, eBay, Google, Yahoo!, and many others have provided SOAP web services for the use of their customers. But in recent years they have all shifted to RESTful web service (described in the next chapter), mainly for performance reasons.

■ ■ ■

CHAPTER 15

RESTful Web Services

The SOAP web services stack (SOAP, WSDL, WS-*) described in the previous chapter, delivers interoperability in both message integration and RPC style. Still heavily used in the B2B industry, SOAP web services didn't have the momentum expected of them on the Internet. With the rise of Web 2.0, new web frameworks have emerged and brought more agile web development and more reactive user interfaces. Mobile devices, with their native and web applications aggregating data, started to be part of our day-to-day lives. HTML 5 and JavaScript revolutionized our surfing experience. With all that, a new kind of web services has gained in popularity: RESTful web services. With that in mind, many key web players such as Amazon, eBay, Google, and Yahoo! have decommissioned their SOAP web services in favor of RESTful resource-oriented services.

Representational State Transfer (REST) is an architectural style based on how the Web works. Applied to services, it tries to put the Web back into web services. To design a RESTful web service, you need to know Hypertext Transfer Protocol (HTTP) and Uniform Resource Identifiers (URIs), and to observe a few design principles. This basically means that each unique URL is a representation of some object. You can interact with that object using an HTTP GET (to get its content), DELETE, POST (to create it), or PUT (to update the content).

RESTful architectures quickly became popular because they rely on a very robust transport protocol: HTTP. RESTful web services reduce the client/server coupling, making it much easier to evolve a REST interface over time without breaking existing clients. Like the protocol they are based on, RESTful web services are stateless and can make use of HTTP cache and proxy servers to help you handle high load and scale much better. Furthermore, they are easy to build as no special toolkit or WSDL-like is required.

The beginning of this chapter will cover a series of concepts to understand what REST is. Then it will put all these concepts together to write RESTful web services and to consume them.

Understanding RESTful Web Services

SOAP web services are meant to be able to use several transport protocols, HTTP being one of them. As a result, they only use a very small subset of its capabilities. On the other hand, RESTful web services are HTTP-centric and make the most of this very rich protocol. In the REST architectural style, every piece of information is a resource, and these resources are addressed using Uniform Resource Identifiers (URIs), typically links on the Web. The resources are acted on by using a set of simple, well-defined operations. The REST client-server architectural style is designed to exchange representations of these resources using a defined interface and protocol. These principles encourage RESTful applications to be simple and lightweight, and to have high performance.

A Web-Browsing Experience

Because REST is derived from the Web, to better understand it, I'll start with a real-life web-browsing experience. How would you proceed to reach the list of Java technology books at Apress? You point your browser to the Apress web site: http://www.apress.com. Although it is likely that this page will not contain the exact information you're seeking, you're expecting it to give you access in one way or another to the Java book list. The home page offers a search engine on all Apress books, but there is also a book directory sorted by technologies. Click the Java node, and the hypermedia magic happens: here is the full list of Apress Java books at http://www.apress.com/java. You get a page showing you 20 books out of 191. If you want to have all of the books displayed on the page in a list format, click on http://www.apress.com/java?limit=all&mode=list.

Say you save the link in your favorite bookmark manager and, as you go through the book list, *The Definitive Guide to Grails 2* by Graeme Rocher and Jeff Brown captures your attention. The hyperlink on the book title takes you to the book page (http://www.apress.com/9781430243779) where you can read the abstract, author biography, and so on, and you notice one of the books listed in the Related Titles section might be as valuable for your current project. You would like to compare Graeme Rocher's book with *Practical JRuby on Rails Web 2.0 Projects: Bringing Ruby on Rails to Java* by Ola Bini (http://www.apress.com/9781590598818). Apress book pages give you access to a more concrete representation of its books in the form of online previews: open a preview, go through the table of contents, and make your choice.

Here is what we do on a day-to-day basis with our browsers. REST applies the same principles to your services where books, search results, table of contents, or book's covers can be defined as resources.

Resources and URIs

Resources are given a central role in RESTful architectures. In the Web-Browsing Experience above you've noticed that a resource is anything the client might want to reference or interact with, any piece of information that might be worthwhile referencing in a hyperlink (a book, a search result, a table of contents ...). A resource can be stored in a database, a file ... anywhere it can be addressed. Avoid as much as possible exposing abstract concepts as resources; instead opt for simple objects. Some resources used in the CD-BookStore application could be:

- A list of Java books

- The book *The Definitive Guide to Grails 2*

- Ola Bini's résumé

Resources on the Web are identified by a URI (Uniform Resource Identifier). A URI is a unique identifier for a resource, made of a name and a structured address indicating where to find this resource. Various types of URIs exist: WWW addresses, Universal Document Identifiers, Universal Resource Identifiers, and finally the combination of Uniform Resource Locators (URLs) and Uniform Resource Names (URNs). Examples of resources and URIs are listed in Table 15-1.

Table 15-1. *Examples of Resources and URIs*

Resource	URI
The catalog of Apress books	http://www.apress.com/book/catalog
The cover of the Java EE 6 book	http://www.apress.com/book/catalog/beginning-javaee6.jpg
Information about jobs at Apress	http://www.apress.com/info/jobs
The weather in Paris for 2013	http://www.weather.com/weather/2013?location=Paris,France
Interesting photos on Flickr for January 1, 2013	http://www.flickr.com/explore/interesting/2013/01/01
Interesting photos on Flickr for the last 24 hours	http://www.flickr.com/explore/interesting/24hours
The list of adventure movies	http://www.movies.com/categories/adventure

URIs should be as descriptive as possible and should target a unique resource. Note that different URIs identifying different resources may lead to the same data. Actually, at some point in time, the list of the interesting photos uploaded to Flickr on 01/01/2013 was the same as the list of the uploaded photos in the last 24 hours, but the information conveyed by the two corresponding URIs is not the same. The standard format of a URI is as follow:

```
http://host:port/path?queryString#fragment
```

HTTP is the protocol, `host` is a DNS name or IP address and the `port` is optional. The `path` is a set of text segment delimited by the "/" character. Following this there is an optional query string (list of parameters represented as a name/value pair, each pair delimited with the "&" character. The last part delimited by "#" is the fragment that is used to point to a certain place in the document. The following URI points to the weather in Lisbon (Portugal) on the morning of the 1st January 2013:

```
http://www.weather.com:8080/weather/2013/01/01?location=Lisbon,Portugal&time=morning
```

Representations

So far I've explained what a resource is and where you can find it. But what is the representation of the resource the URI is pointing to? Are there several representations for a single resource? Actually you might want to get the representation of a resource as text, JSON, XML, PDF document, JPG image, or another data format. When the client deals with a resource, it is always through its representation; the resource itself remains on the server. *Representation* is any useful information about the state of a resource. For example, the list of Java books mentioned previously has at least two representations:

- The HTML page rendered by your browser: `http://www.apress.com/java`

- The comma-separated value (CSV) file of books:
  `http://www.apress.com/resource/csv/bookcategory?cat=32`

How do you choose between the different representations of a given resource? Two solutions are possible. The service could expose one URI per representation as shown above. However, the two URIs are really different and do not seem directly related. Following is a neater set of URIs:

- `http://www.apress.com/java`

- `http://www.apress.com/java/csv`

- `http://www.apress.com/java/xml`

The first URI is the default representation of the resource, and additional representations append their format extension to it: `/csv` (for `text/csv`), `/xml`, `/pdf`, and so on.

Another solution is to expose one single URI for all representations (e.g., `http://www.apress.com/java`) and to rely on the mechanism called *content negotiation*, which I'll discuss in more detail a little later in this chapter. For instance, a URI could have a human-readable and a machine-processable representation.

Addressability

An important tenet to follow when designing RESTful web services is addressability. Your web service should make your application as addressable as possible, which means that every valuable piece of information in your application should be a resource and have a URI, making that resource easily accessible. The URI is the only piece of data you need to publish to make the resource accessible, so your business partner won't have guesswork to do in order to reach the resource.

For example, you're dealing with a bug in your application, and your investigations lead you to line 42 of the class `CreditCardValidator.java` as the place where the bug occurs. Because you're not responsible for this domain of the application, you want to file an issue so a qualified person will take care of it. How would you point her to the incriminating line? You could say, "Go to line 42 of the class `CreditCardValidator`," or, if your source code is addressable through a repository browser, you could save the URI of the line itself in the bug report. This raises the issue of defining the granularity of your RESTful resources in your application: it could be at the line, method, or class level, and so forth.

Unique URIs make your resources linkable, and, because they are exposed through a uniform interface, everyone knows exactly how to interact with them, allowing people to use your application in ways you would have never imagined.

Connectedness

In graph theory, a graph is called connected if every pair of distinct vertices in the graph can be connected through some path. It is said to be strongly connected if it contains a direct path from u to v and a direct path from v to u for every pair of vertices u,v. REST advocates that resources should be as connected as possible.

Once again, this daunting statement resulted from an examination of the success of the Web. Web pages embed links to navigate through pages in a logical and smooth manner and, as such, the Web is very well connected. If there is a strong relationship between two resources, they should be connected. REST states that web services should also take advantage of hypermedia to inform the client of what is available and where to go. It promotes the discoverability of services. From a single URI, a user agent accessing a well-connected web service could discover all available actions, resources, their various representations, and so forth.

For instance, when a user agent (e.g., a Web browser) looks up the representation of a CD (see Listing 15-1), this representation could have not only the names of the artist, but also a link, or a URI, to the biography. It's up to the user agent to actually retrieve it or not. The representation could also link to other representations of the resource or available actions.

Listing 15-1. A CD Representation Connected to Other Services

```
<cd>
   <title>Ella and Louis</title>
   <year ref="http://music.com/year/1956">1956</year>
   <artist ref="http://music.com/artists/123">Ella Fitzgerald</artist>
   <artist ref="http://music.com/artists/456">Louis Armstrong</artist>
   <link rel="self" type="text/json" href="http://music.com/album/789"/>
   <link rel="self" type="text/xml" href="http://music.com/album/789"/>
   <link rel="http://music.com/album/comments" type="text/xml" ↪
       href="http://music.com/album/789/comments"/>
</cd>
```

Another crucial aspect of the hypermedia principle is the state of the application, which must be led by the hypermedia. In short, the fact that the web service provides a set of links enables the client to move the application from one state to the next by simply following a link.

In the preceding XML snippet, the client could change the state of the application by commenting on the album. The list of comments on the album is a resource addressable with the URI `http://music.com/album/789/comments`. Because this web service uses a uniform interface, once the client knows the URI format, the available content types and the data format, it will know exactly how to interact with it: a GET will retrieve the list of existing comments, a PUT will update the comment, and so on. From this single initial request, the client can take many actions: the hypermedia drives the state of the application.

Uniform Interface

One of the main constraints that make an architecture RESTful is the use of a uniform interface to manage your resources. Pick whatever interface suits you, but use it in the same way across the board, from resource to resource, from service to service. Never stray from it or alter the original meaning. By using a uniform interface, "the overall system architecture is simplified and the visibility of interactions is improved" (Roy Thomas Fielding, *Architectural Styles and the Design of Network-based Software Architectures*). Your services become part of a community of services using the exact same semantic.

The de facto web protocol is HTTP, which is a document-based standardized request/response protocol between a client and a server. HTTP is the uniform interface of RESTful web services. Web services built on SOAP, WSDL, and other WS-* standards also use HTTP as the transport layer, but they leverage only a very few of its capabilities (as SOAP web services can also use other transport protocols such as JMS). You have to discover the semantic of the service by analyzing the WSDL and then invoke the right methods. RESTful web services have a uniform interface (HTTP methods and URIs), so, once you know where the resource is (URI), you can invoke the HTTP method (GET, POST, etc.).

In addition to familiarity, a uniform interface promotes interoperability between applications; HTTP is widely supported, and the number of HTTP client libraries guarantees that you won't have to deal with communication issues.

Statelessness

The last feature of REST is statelessness, which means that every HTTP request happens in complete isolation, as the server should never keep track of requests that were executed before. For the sake of clarity, resource state and application state are usually distinguished. The resource state must live on the server and is shared by everybody, while the application state must remain on the client and is its sole property. Going back to the example in Listing 15-1, the application state is that the client has fetched a representation of the album *Ella and Louis*, but the server should not hold onto this information. The resource state is the album information itself; the server should obviously maintain this information. The client may change the resource state. If the shopping cart is a resource with restricted access to just one client, the application needs to keep track of the shopping cart ID in the client session.

Statelessness comes with many advantages such as better scalability: no session information to handle, no need to route subsequent requests to the same server (load-balancing), failure handling (e.g., service interruptions), and so on. If you need to keep state, the client has to do extra work to store it.

HTTP

HTTP, a protocol for distributed, collaborative, hypermedia information systems, led to the establishment of the World Wide Web together with URIs, HTML, and the first browsers. Coordinated by the World Wide Web Consortium (W3C) and the Internet Engineering Task Force (IETF), HTTP is the result of several Requests For Comment (RFC), notably RFC 216, which defines HTTP 1.1.

Request and Response

HTTP is based on requests and responses exchanged between a client and a server. A client sends a request to a server and expects an answer (see Figure 15-1). The messages exchanged are made of an envelope and a body, also called a payload or entity.

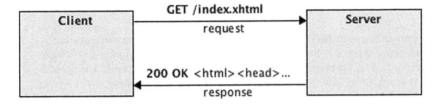

Figure 15-1. *HTTP request and response*

When you navigate on the APress web site you only see the web pages, not the technical details of the HTTP request and response. To have an idea of what's happening behind the scenes, you can use another tool such as cURL. For instance, here is a request sent to the server when you go to http://www.apress.com/java?limit=all&mode=list:

```
$ curl -v -X GET http://www.apress.com/java?limit=all&mode=list
> GET /java?limit=all&mode=list HTTP/1.1
> User-Agent: curl/7.23.1 (x86_64-apple-darwin11.2.0) libcurl/7.23.1 zlib/1.2.5
> Host: www.apress.com
> Accept: */*
```

This request has several pieces of information sent from the client to the server:

- The HTTP method, here GET

- The path, here /java?limit=all&mode=list

- Several other request headers (User-Agent)

Notice that there is no body as part of the request. Actually, a GET never has a body. To this request, the server will send the following response:

```
< HTTP/1.1 200 OK
< Date: Sat, 17 Nov 2012 17:42:15 GMT
< Server: Apache/2.2.3 (Red Hat)
< X-Powered-By: PHP/5.2.17
< Vary: Accept-Encoding,User-Agent
< Transfer-Encoding: chunked
< Content-Type: text/html; charset=UTF-8
<!DOCTYPE HTML PUBLIC "-//W3C//DTD HTML 4.01 Transitional//EN">
<html>
  <head>
  <title>
  ...
```

This response is made up of the following:

- *A response code*: In this case, the response code is 200-OK.

- *Several response headers*: In the preceding code, the response headers are Date, Server, Content-Type. Here the content type is text/html, but it could be any other media such as XML (application/xml) or images (image/jpeg).

- *Entity body, or representation*: The content of the returned web page is the entity body in this example (here I just showed a fragment of an HTML page).

■ **Note**   cURL (`http://curl.haxx.se/`) is a command-line tool for transferring files with URL syntax via protocols such as HTTP, FTP, SFTP, SCP, and many more. You can send HTTP commands, change HTTP headers, and so on. It is a good tool for simulating a user's actions at a web browser.

Headers

HTTP header fields are components of the message header of requests and responses. Header fields are colon-separated name-value pairs in clear-text string format, terminated by a carriage return and line feed character sequence. A core set of fields is standardized by the Internet Engineering Task Force (IETF) and must be implemented by all HTTP-compliant protocol implementations. But additional field names may be defined by each application if needed. Table 15-2 lists a subset of common defined header values that you can find either in the request or response.

Table 15-2. *Subset of Common Defined Header Values*

Header Name	Description
Accept	Content-Types that are acceptable (e.g., text/plain)
Accept-Charset	Character sets that are acceptable (e.g., utf-8)
Accept-Encoding	Acceptable encodings (e.g., gzip, deflate)
Accept-Language	Acceptable languages for response (en-US)
Cookie	An HTTP cookie previously sent by the server
Content-Length	The length of the request body in bytes
Content-Type	The MIME type of the body of the request (e.g., text/xml)
Date	The date and time that the message was sent
ETag	An identifier for a specific version of a resource (e.g., 8af7ad3082f20958)
If-Match	Only performs the action if the client supplied entity matches the same entity on the server
If-Modified-Since	Allows a 304-Not Modified to be returned if content is unchanged since a date
User-Agent	The user agent string of the user agent (e.g., Mozilla/5.0)

HTTP Methods

The Web consists of well-identified resources linked together and accessed through simple HTTP requests. The main types of requests standardized in HTTP are GET, POST, PUT, DELETE. These are also called verbs, commands, or methods. HTTP defines four other methods that are less frequently used: HEAD, TRACE, OPTIONS, CONNECT.

GET

GET is a simple read that requests a representation of a resource. GET should be implemented in a safe way, meaning it shouldn't change the state of the resource. In addition, GET must be idempotent, which means it must leave the resource in the same state when called once, twice, or more. Safety and idempotence bring greater stability. When a client does not get a response (e.g., due to a network failure), it might renew its requests, and those new requests will expect the same answer it should have received originally, without corrupting the resource state on the server.

POST

Given a representation (text, XML, etc.), calling a POST method creates a new resource identified by the requested URI. Examples of POST could be appending a message to a log file, a comment to a blog, a book to a booklist, and so on. Consequently, POST is not safe (the resource state is updated) nor idempotent (sending the request twice will result in two new subordinates). If a resource has been created on the origin server, the response should be status 201-Created. Most modern browsers generate only GET and POST requests.

PUT

A PUT request is intended to update the state of the resource stored under a given URI. If the request URI refers to a nonexistent resource, the resource will be created under this same URI. Examples of PUT could be updating the price of a book or the address of a customer. PUT is not safe (because the state of the resource gets updated), but it is idempotent: you can send the same PUT request many times, and the final resource state will always be the same.

DELETE

A DELETE request deletes the resource. The response to a DELETE may be a status message as part of the body or no status at all. DELETE is also idempotent but not safe.

Others

As mentioned previously, other HTTP methods exist, even if they are less used:

- HEAD is identical to GET except that the server doesn't return a message body in the response. HEAD might be useful for checking the validity of a link or the size of an entity without transferring it.

- When a server receives a TRACE request from the client, it echoes back the received request. This can be useful to see what intermediate servers, proxies or firewalls are adding or changing in the request.

- OPTIONS represents a request for information about the communication options available on the request/response chain identified by the URI. This method allows the client to determine the options and/or requirements associated with a resource, or the capabilities of a server, without implying a resource action or initiating resource retrieval.

- CONNECT is used in conjunction with a proxy that can dynamically switch to being a tunnel (a technique by which the HTTP protocol acts as a wrapper for various network protocols).

Content Negotiation

Content negotiation, described in section 12 of the HTTP standard, is defined as "the process of selecting the best representation for a given response when there are multiple representations available." Clients' needs, desires, and capabilities vary; the best representation for a mobile-device user in Japan might not be the best for a feed-reader application in the United States.

Content negotiation is based on, but not limited to, the HTTP request headers Accept, Accept-Charset, Accept-Encoding, Accept-Language, and User-Agent. For example, to get the CSV representation of Apress Java books, the client application (the user agent) will request http://www.apress.com/java with a header Accept set to text/csv. You could also imagine that, based on the Accept-Language header, the server selects the proper CSV document to match the corresponding language (Japanese or English).

Content Types

HTTP uses Internet media types (originally called MIME types) in the Content-Type and Accept header fields in order to provide open and extensible data typing and type negotiation. Internet media types are divided into five discrete, top-level categories: text, image, audio, video, and application. These types are further divided into several subtypes (text/plain, text/xml, text/xhtml, etc.). Some of the most common public content types are as follows:

- text/plain: This is the default content type, as it's used for simple text messages.

- text/html: Very commonly used in our browsers, this content-type informs the user-agent that the content is an HTML page.

- image/gif, image/jpeg, image/png: This image top-level media type requires a display device (such as a graphical display, a graphics printer, etc.) to view the information.

- text/xml, application/xml: Format used for XML exchanges.

- application/json: JavaScript Object Notation (JSON) is a lightweight data-interchange text format independent of the programming language (see Chapter 12).

Status Codes

Each time a response is received, an HTTP code is associated with it. The specification defines around 60 status codes. The Status-Code element is a three-digit integer that describes the context of a response and is part of the response envelope. The first digit specifies one of five classes of response:

- *1xx*: Informational. The request was received, and the process is continuing.

- *2xx*: Success. The action was successfully received, understood, and accepted.

- *3xx*: Redirection. Further action must be taken in order to complete the request.

- *4xx*: Client Error. The request contains bad syntax or cannot be fulfilled.

- *5xx*: Server Error. The server failed to fulfill an apparently valid request.

Table 15-3 lists some status codes you might have already come across.

Table 15-3. *Subset of HTTP Status Code*

Status Code	Description
100-Continue	The server has received the request headers and the client should proceed to send the request body
101-Switching Protocols	The requester has asked the server to switch protocols and the server is acknowledging that it will do so
200-OK	The request has succeeded. The entity body, if any, contains the representation of the resource
201-Created	The request has been fulfilled and resulted in a new resource being created
204-No Content	The server successfully processed the request, but is not returning any content
206-Partial Content	The server is delivering only part of the resource due to a range header sent by the client
301-Moved Permanently	The requested resource has been assigned a new, permanent URI and any future reference to this resource should use one of the returned URIs
304-Not Modified	Indicates the resource has not been modified since last requested
307-Temporary Redirect	The request should be repeated with another URI; however, future requests should still use the original URI
308-Permanent Redirect	The request, and all future requests should be repeated using another URI
400-Bad Request	The request cannot be fulfilled due to bad syntax
401-Unauthorized	Similar to 403 but when authentication is required and has failed
403-Forbidden	The request was valid, but the server is refusing to respond to it
404-Not Found	The server has not found anything matching the request URI
405-Method Not Allowed	A request was made using a request method not supported by the resource
406-Not Acceptable	The requested resource is only capable of generating content not acceptable according to the Accept headers sent in the request
500-Internal Server Error	The server encountered an unexpected condition that prevented it from fulfilling the request
501-Not Implemented	The server either does not recognize the request method, or it lacks the ability to fulfill the request
503-Service Unavailable	The server is currently unavailable (because it is overloaded or down for maintenance); generally, this is a temporary state
505-HTTP Version Not Supported	The server does not support the HTTP protocol version used in the request

Caching and Conditional Requests

In most distributed systems, caching is crucial. Caching aims at improving performance by avoiding unnecessary requests or by reducing the amount of data in responses. HTTP provides mechanisms to allow caching and make sure cached data is correct. But, if the client decides not to use any caching mechanism, it will always need to request data even if it hasn't been modified since the last request.

When a response to a GET is sent, it could include a Last-Modified header indicating the time that the resource was last modified. The next time the user agent requests this resource, it can pass this date in the If-Modified-Since header. The web server (or a proxy) will compare this date with the latest modification date. If the date sent by the user agent is equal or newer, a 304-Not Modified status code with no response body is returned. Otherwise, the requested operation is performed or forwarded.

But dates can be difficult to manipulate and imply that all the interacting agents are, and stay, synchronized. The ETag response header solves this issue. The easiest way to think of an ETag is as an MD5 or SHA1 hash of all the bytes in a representation; if just one byte in the representation changes, the ETag will change.

Figure 15-2 gives an example of how to use ETags. To get a book resource, you use the GET action and give it the URI of the resource (GET /book/12345). The server will return a response with the XML representation of the book, a 200 OK status code, and a generated ETag. The second time you ask for the same resource, if you pass the ETag as a value in an If-None-Match header, the server will not send the representation of the resource assuming the resource has not actually changed since the earlier request. This will instead return a 304-Not Modified status code informing the client that the resource hasn't changed since last access.

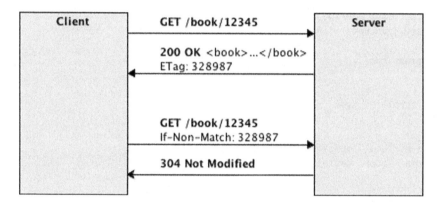

Figure 15-2. *Using caching and the 304 Not Modified status code*

Requests using the HTTP headers If-Modified-Since, If-Unmodified-Since, If-Match, If-None-Match, and If-Range are said to be conditional. Conditional requests can save bandwidth and CPU (on both the server and client side) by avoiding unnecessary round-trips or data transmissions. The If-* headers are most often used for GET and PUT requests.

From the Web to Web Services

We all use the Web and know how it works, so why should web services behave differently? After all, services also often exchange uniquely identified resources, linked with others like hyperlinks. Web architecture has proven its scalability for years; why reinvent the wheel? To create, update, and delete a book resource, why not use the common HTTP verbs? For example:

- Use POST to **create** a book resource (passing XML, JSON, or any other format) with the URI http://www.apress.com/book/. Once created, the response sends back the URI of the new resource: http://www.apress.com/book/123456.

- Use GET to **read** the resource (and possible links to other resources from the entity body) at http://www.apress.com/book/123456.

- Use PUT on data to **update** the book resource at http://www.apress.com/book/123456.

- Use DELETE to **delete** the resource at http://www.apress.com/book/123456.

By using HTTP verbs, we have access to all possible Create, Read, Update, Delete (CRUD) actions on a resource.

WADL

While SOAP-based services rely on WSDL to describe the format of possible requests for a given web service, Web Application Description Language (WADL) is used to expose the possible interactions with a given RESTful web service. It eases client development, which can load and interact directly with the resources. WADL was submitted to the W3C but the consortium has no current plans to standardize it because it is not widely supported. Listing 15-2 shows you what it can look like.

Listing 15-2. WADL Defining Several Operations That Can Be Invoked on a Resource

```
<application xmlns="http://wadl.dev.java.net/2009/02">
  <doc xmlns:jersey="http://jersey.java.net/" jersey:generatedBy="Jersey: 2.0"/>

  <resources base="http://www.apress.com/">

      <resource path="{id}">
        <param name="id" style="template" type="xs:long"/>
        <method name="GET">
          <response>
            <representation element="book" mediaType="application/xml"/>
            <representation element="book" mediaType="application/json"/>
          </response>
        </method>
        <method name="DELETE"/>
      </resource>

      <resource path="book">
        <method name="GET">
          <response>
            <representation element="book" mediaType="application/xml"/>
            <representation element="book" mediaType="application/json"/>
          </response>
        </method>
      </resource>

  </resources>
</application>
```

Listing 15-2 describes a resource root (http://www.apress.com/) to where you can pass an id ({id}) to GET or DELETE a book. Another resource allows you to GET all the books from APress in JSON or XML.

RESTful Web Services Specifications Overview

Contrary to SOAP and the WS-* stack, which rely on W3C standards, REST has no standard and is just a style of architecture with design principles. REST applications rely heavily on many other standards:

- HTTP

- URI, URL

- XML, JSON, HTML, GIF, JPEG, and so forth (resource representations)

The Java side has been specified through JAX-RS (Java API for RESTful Web Services), but REST is like a design pattern: a reusable solution to a common problem that can be implemented by several languages.

A Brief History of REST

The term REST was first introduced by Roy Thomas Fielding in Chapter 5 of his PhD thesis, *Architectural Styles and the Design of Network-based Software Architectures* (University of California, Irvine, 2000, http://www.ics.uci.edu/~fielding/pubs/dissertation/top.htm). The dissertation is a retrospective explanation of the architecture chosen to develop the Web. In his thesis, Fielding takes a look at the parts of the World Wide Web that work very well and extracts design principles that could make any other distributed hypermedia system—whether related to the Web or not—as efficient.

The original motivation for developing REST was to create an architectural model of the Web. Roy T. Fielding is also one of the authors of the HTTP specification, so it's not surprising that HTTP fits quite well the architectural design he described in his dissertation.

Java API for RESTful Web Services

To write RESTful web services in Java, you would only need a client and a server that support HTTP. Any browser and an HTTP servlet container will do the job at the cost of some XML configuration and glue-code pain to parse HTTP requests and responses. Once completed, this technical code would be barely readable and maintainable. This is where JAX-RS comes to the rescue. As you'll see, with just a few annotations you get the full power of invoking HTTP resources and parsing them.

The first version of the JAX-RS specification (JSR 311), finalized in October 2008, defined a set of APIs that promoted the REST architecture style. But it only covered the server-side aspect of REST. With Java EE 7, JAX-RS has been updated to a 2.0 version and now defines a client API among other novelties.

What's New in JAX-RS 2.0?

JAX-RS 2.0 (JSR 339) is a major release focusing on integration with Java EE 7 and its new features. The major new features of JAX-RS 2.0 are as follows:

- A client API was missing from JAX-RS 1.x so each implementation defined its own proprietary API. JAX-RS 2.0 fills this gap with a fluent, low-level, request building API.

- Like SOAP handlers or Managed Bean interceptors, JAX-RS 2.0 now has filters and interceptors so you can intercept request and response and do some processing.

- With the new asynchronous processing you can now implement long-polling interfaces or server-side push.

- Integration with Bean Validation has been achieved so you can constrain your RESTful web services.

Table 15-4 lists the main packages defined in JAX-RS.

Table 15-4. *Main JAX-RS Packages*

Package	Description
javax.ws.rs	High-level interfaces and annotations used to create RESTful web service
javax.ws.rs.client	Classes and interfaces of the new JAX-RS client API
javax.ws.rs.container	Container-specific JAX-RS API
javax.ws.rs.core	Low-level interfaces and annotations used to create RESTful web resources
javax.ws.rs.ext	APIs that provide extensions to the types supported by the JAX-RS API

Reference Implementation

Jersey is the reference implementation of JAX-RS. It is an open source project under dual CDDL and GPL licenses. Jersey also provides a specific API so that you can extend Jersey itself.

Other implementations of JAX-RS are also available such as CXF (Apache), RESTEasy (JBoss), and Restlet (a senior project that existed even before JAX-RS was finalized).

Writing RESTful Web Services

Some of the low-level concepts (such as the HTTP protocol) might have you wondering how the code would look when developing a RESTful web service. The good news is that you don't have to write plumbing code to digest HTTP requests, nor create HTTP responses by hand. JAX-RS is a very elegant API allowing you to describe a RESTful web service with only a few annotations. RESTful web services are POJOs that have at least one method annotated with @ javax.ws.rs.Path. Listing 15-3 shows a typical resource.

Listing 15-3. A Simple Book RESTful Web Service

```
@Path("/book")
public class BookRestService {

    @GET
    @Produces("text/plain")
    public String getBookTitle() {
        return "H2G2";
    }
}
```

The BookRestService is a Java class annotated with @Path, indicating that the resource will be hosted at the URI path /book. The getBookTitle() method is marked to process HTTP GET requests (using @GET annotation) and produces text (the content is identified by the MIME Media text/plain; I could have also used the constant MediaType.TEXT_PLAIN). To access this resource, you need an HTTP client such as a browser to point to the URL http://www.myserver.com/**book**.

JAX-RS is HTTP-centric by nature and has a set of clearly defined classes and annotations to deal with HTTP and URIs. A resource can have several representations, so the API provides support for a variety of content types and uses JAXB to marshall and unmarshall XML representations from/into objects. JAX-RS is also independent of the container, so resources can be deployed in GlassFish, of course, but also in a variety of servlet containers.

Anatomy of a RESTful Web Service

From Listing 15-3, you can see that the REST service doesn't implement any interface nor extend any class; the only mandatory annotation to turn a POJO into a REST service is @Path. JAX-RS relies on configuration by exception, so it has a set of annotations to configure the default behavior. Following are the requirements to write a REST service:

- The class must be annotated with @javax.ws.rs.Path (in JAX-RS 2.0 there is no XML equivalent to meta-data as there is no deployment descriptor).

- The class must be defined as public, and it must not be final or abstract.

- Root resource classes (classes with a @Path annotation) must have a default public constructor. Non-root resource classes do not require such a constructor.

- The class must not define the finalize() method.

- To add EJB capabilities to a REST service, the class has to be annotated with @javax.ejb.Stateless or @javax.ejb.Singleton (see Chapter 7).

- A service must be a stateless object and should not save client-specific state across method calls.

CRUD Operations on a RESTful Web Service

Listing 15-3 shows how to write a very simple REST service that returns a String. But most of the time you need to access a database, retrieve or store data in a transactional manner. For this you can have a REST service and add stateless session beans functionalities by adding the @Stateless annotation. This will allow transactional access to a persistent layer (JPA entities), as shown in Listing 15-4.

Listing 15-4. A Book RESTful Web Service Creating, Deleting, and Retrieving Books from the Database

```
@Path("book")
@Stateless
public class BookRestService {

  @Context
  private UriInfo uriInfo;
  @PersistenceContext(unitName = "chapter15PU")
  private EntityManager em;

  @GET
  @Produces(MediaType.APPLICATION_XML)
  public Books getBooks() {
    TypedQuery<Book> query = em.createNamedQuery(Book.FIND_ALL, Book.class);
    Books books = new Books(query.getResultList());
    return books;
  }

  @POST
  @Consumes(MediaType.APPLICATION_XML)
  public Response createBook(Book book) {
    em.persist(book);
    URI bookUri = uriInfo.getAbsolutePathBuilder().path(book.getId().toString()).build();
    return Response.created(bookUri).build();
  }
```

```
@DELETE
@Path("{id}")
public Response deleteBook(@PathParam("id") Long bookId) {
  em.remove(em.find(Book.class, bookId));
  return Response.noContent().build();
}
}
```

The code in Listing 15-4 represents a REST service that can consume and produce an XML representation of a book. The getBooks() method retrieves the list of books from the database and returns an XML representation (using content negotiation) of this list, accessible through a GET method. The createBook() method takes an XML representation of a book and persists it to the database. This method is invoked with an HTTP POST and returns a Response with the URI (bookUri) of the new book as well as the created status. The deleteBook method takes a book id as a parameter and deletes it from the database.

The code in Listing 15-4 follows a very simple JAX-RS model and uses a set of powerful annotations. Let's now take a deeper look at all the concepts shown in the code.

URI Definition and Binding URIs

The @Path annotation represents a relative URI that can annotate a class or a method. When used on classes, it is referred to as the *root resource*, providing the root of the resource tree and giving access to subresources. Listing 15-5 shows a REST service that can be access at http://www.myserver.com/**items**. All the methods of this service will have /items as root.

Listing 15-5. Root Path to an Item Resource

```
@Path("/items")
public class ItemRestService {

  @GET
  public Items getItems() {
    // ...
  }
}
```

You can then add subpaths to your methods, which can be useful to group together common functionalities for several resources as shown in Listing 15-6 (you may ignore for the moment the @GET, @POST, and @DELETE annotations in the listing, as they will be described later in the "HTTP Method Matching" section).

Listing 15-6. Several Subpaths in the ItemRestService

```
@Path("/items")
public class ItemRestService {

  @GET
  public Items getItems() {
    // URI : /items
  }
```

```
@GET
@Path("/cds")
public CDs getCDs() {
  // URI : /items/cds
}

@GET
@Path("/books")
public Books getBooks() {
  // URI : /items/books
}

@POST
@Path("/book")
public Response createBook(Book book) {
  // URI : /items/book
  }
}
```

Listing 15-6 represents a RESTful web service that will give you methods to get all the items (CDs and books) from the CD-BookStore Application. When requesting the root resource /items, the only method without sub @Path will be selected (getItems()). Then, when @Path exists on both the class and method, the relative path to the method is a concatenation of both. For example, to get all the CDs, the path will be /items/cds. When requesting /items/books, the getBooks() method will be invoked. To create a new book you need to point at /items/book.

If @Path("/items") only existed on the class, and not on any methods, the path to access each method would be the same. The only way to differentiate them would be the HTTP verb (GET, PUT, etc.) and the content negotiation (text, XML, etc.), as you'll later see.

Extracting Parameters

Having nice URIs by concatenating paths to access your resource is very important in REST. But paths and subpaths are not enough: you also need to pass parameters to your RESTful web services, extract and process them at runtime. Listing 15-4 showed how to get a parameter out of the path with @javax.ws.rs.PathParam. JAX-RS provides a rich set of annotations to extract the different parameters that a request could send (@PathParam, @QueryParam, @MatrixParam, @CookieParam, @HeaderParam, and @FormParam).

Listing 15-7 shows how the @PathParam annotation is used to extract the value of a URI template parameter. A parameter has a name and is represented by a variable between curly braces or by a variable that follows a regular expression. The searchCustomers method takes any String parameter while getCustomerByLogin only allows lowercase/uppercase alphabetical letters ([a-zA-Z]*) and getCustomerById only digits (\\d+).

Listing 15-7. Extracting Path Parameters and Regular Expressions

```
@Path("/customer")
@Produces(MediaType.APPLICATION_JSON)
public class CustomerRestService {

  @Path("search/{text}")
  public Customers searchCustomers(@PathParam("text") String textToSearch) {
    // URI : /customer/search/smith
  }
```

```java
@GET
@Path("{login: [a-zA-Z]*}")
public Customer getCustomerByLogin(@PathParam("login") String login) {
  // URI : /customer/foobarsmith
}

@GET
@Path("{customerId : \\d+}")
public Customer getCustomerById(@PathParam("customerId") Long id) {
  // URI : /customer/12345
}
}
```

The @QueryParam annotation extracts the value of a URI query parameter. Query parameters are key/value pairs separated by an & symbol such as http://www.myserver.com/customer?zip=75012&city=Paris. The @MatrixParam annotation acts like @QueryParam, except it extracts the value of a URI matrix parameter (; is used as a delimiter instead of ?). Listing 15-8 shows how to extract both query and matrix parameters from URIs.

Listing 15-8. Extracting Query and Matrix Parameters

```java
@Path("/customer")
@Produces(MediaType.APPLICATION_JSON)
public class CustomerRestService {

  @GET
  public Customers getCustomersByZipCode(@QueryParam("zip") Long zip, ↩
                                          @QueryParam("city") String city) {
    // URI : /customer?zip=75012&city=Paris
  }

  @GET
  @Path("search")
  public Customers getCustomersByName(@MatrixParam("firstname") String firstname, ↩
                                      @MatrixParam("surname") String surname) {
    // URI : /customer/search;firstname=Antonio;surname=Goncalves
  }
}
```

Two other annotations are related to the innards of HTTP, things you don't see directly in URIs: cookies and HTTP headers @CookieParam extracts the value of a cookie, while @HeaderParam extracts the value of a header field. Listing 15-9 extracts the session ID from the cookie and the User Agent from the HTTP header.

Listing 15-9. Extracting Values From the Cookie and HTTP Header

```java
@Path("/customer")
@Produces(MediaType.TEXT_PLAIN)
public class CustomerRestService {

  @GET
  public String extractSessionID(@CookieParam("sessionID") String sessionID) {
    // ...
  }
```

```
@GET
public String extractUserAgent(@HeaderParam("User-Agent") String userAgent) {
  // ...
}
}
```

The @FormParam annotation specifies that the value of a parameter is to be extracted from a form in a request entity body. @FormParam is not required to be supported on fields or properties.

With all these annotations, you can add a @DefaultValue annotation to define the default value for a parameter you're expecting. The default value is used if the corresponding parameter is not present in the request. Listing 15-10 sets default values to query and matrix parameters. For example, in the method getCustomersByAge, if the query parameter age is not in the request, the default value is set to 50.

Listing 15-10. Defining Default Values

```
@Path("/customer")
public class CustomerRestService {

  @GET
  public Customers getCustomersByAge(@DefaultValue("50") @QueryParam("age") int age) {
    // ...
  }

  @GET
  public Customers getCustomersByCity(@DefaultValue("Paris") @MatrixParam("city") ↪
                                                             String city) {
    // ...
  }
}
```

Consuming and Producing Content Types

With REST, the same resource can have several representations; a book can be represented as a web page, a PDF, or an image showing the book cover. JAX-RS specifies a number of Java types that can represent a resource such as String, InputStream and JAXB beans. The @javax.ws.rs.Consumes and @javax.ws.rs.Produces annotations may be applied to a resource where several representations are possible. It defines the media types of the representation exchanged between the client and the server. JAX-RS has a javax.ws.rs.core.MediaType class that acts like an abstraction for a MIME type. It has several methods and defines the constants listed in Table 15-5.

Table 15-5. *MIME Types Defined in* `MediaType`

Constant name	MIME type
`APPLICATION_ATOM_XML`	"application/atom+xml"
`APPLICATION_FORM_URLENCODED`	"application/x-www-form-urlencoded"
`APPLICATION_JSON`	"application/json"
`APPLICATION_OCTET_STREAM`	"application/octet-stream"
`APPLICATION_SVG_XML`	"application/svg+xml"
`APPLICATION_XHTML_XML`	"application/xhtml+xml"
`APPLICATION_XML`	"application/xml"
`MULTIPART_FORM_DATA`	"multipart/form-data"
`TEXT_HTML`	"text/html"
`TEXT_PLAIN`	"text/plain"
`TEXT_XML`	"text/xml"
`WILDCARD`	"*/*"

Using the @Consumes and @Produces annotations on a method overrides any annotations on the resource class for a method argument or return type. In the absence of either of these annotations, support for any media type (*/*) is assumed. By default, `CustomerRestService` produces plain text representations that are overridden in some methods (see Listing 15-11). Note that the `getAsJsonAndXML` produces an array of representations (XML or JSON).

Listing 15-11. A Customer Resource with Several Representations

```
@Path("/customer")
@Produces(MediaType.TEXT_PLAIN)
public class CustomerRestService {

  @GET
  public Response getAsPlainText() {
    // ...
  }

  @GET
  @Produces(MediaType.TEXT_HTML)
  public Response getAsHtml() {
    // ...
  }

  @GET
  @Produces({MediaType.APPLICATION_JSON, MediaType.APPLICATION_XML})
  public Response getAsJsonAndXML() {
    // ...
  }
```

```
@PUT
@Consumes(MediaType.TEXT_PLAIN)
public void putName(String customer) {
  // ...
  }
}
```

If a RESTful web service is capable of producing more than one media type, the targeted method will correspond to the most acceptable media type, as declared by the client in the Accept header of the HTTP request. For example, if the Accept header is:

```
Accept: text/plain
```

and the URI is /customer, the getAsPlainText() method will be invoked. But the client could have used the following HTTP header:

```
Accept: text/plain; q=0.8, text/html
```

This header declares that the client can accept media types of text/plain and text/html but prefers the latter using the quality factor (or preference weight) of 0.8 ("I prefer text/html, but send me text/plain if it is the best available after an 80% markdown in quality"). By including such header and pointing at the /customer URI, the getAsHtml() method will be invoked.

Returned Types

So far you've seen mostly how to invoke a method (using parameters, media type, HTTP methods ...) without caring about the returned type. What can a RESTful web service return? Like any Java class, a method can return any standard Java type, a JAXB bean or any other object as long as it has a textual representation that can be transported over HTTP. In this case, the runtime determines the MIME type of the object being returned and invokes the appropriate Entity Provider (see later) to get its representation. The runtime also determines the appropriate HTTP return code to send to the consumer (204-No Content if the resource method's return type is void or null; 200-OK if the returned value is not null). But sometimes you want finer control of what you are returning: the response body (a.k.a. an entity) of course, but also the response code and/or response headers or cookies. That's when you return a Reponse object. It is a good practice to return a javax.ws.rs.core.Response with an entity since it would guarantee a return content type. Listing 15-12 shows you different return types.

Listing 15-12. A Customer Service Returning Data Types, a JAXB Bean, and a Response

```
@Path("/customer")
public class CustomerRestService {

  @GET
  public String getAsPlainText() {
    return new Customer("John", "Smith", "jsmith@gmail.com", "1234565").toString();
  }

  @GET
  @Path("maxbonus")
  public Long getMaximumBonusAllowed() {
    return 1234L;
  }
```

```
@GET
@Produces(MediaType.APPLICATION_XML)
public Customer getAsXML() {
    return new Customer("John", "Smith", "jsmith@gmail.com", "1234565");
}

@GET
@Produces(MediaType.APPLICATION_JSON)
public Response getAsJson() {
    return Response.ok(new Customer("John", "Smith", "jsmith@gmail.com", "1234565"),↪
                                            MediaType.APPLICATION_JSON).build();

}
}
```

The getAsPlainText method returns a String representation of a customer and the getMaximumBonusAllowed returns a numerical constant. The defaults will apply so the return HTTP status on both methods will be 200-OK (if no exception occurs). The getAsXML returns a Customer JAXB POJO meaning that the runtime will marshall the object into an XML representation.

The getAsJson method doesn't return an entity but instead a javax.ws.rs.core.Response object. A Response wraps the entity that is returned to the consumer and it's instantiated using the ResponseBuilder class as a factory. In this example, we still want to return a JAXB object (the Customer) with a 200-OK status code (the ok() method), but we also want to specify the MIME type to be JSON. Calling the ResponseBuilder.build() method creates the final Response instance.

It is recommended to return a custom Response for all requests rather than the entity itself (you can then set a specific status code if needed). Table 15-6 shows a subset of the Response API.

Table 15-6. *The Response API*

Method	Description
accepted()	Creates a new ResponseBuilder with an accepted status
created()	Creates a new ResponseBuilder for a created resource (with its URI)
noContent()	Creates a new ResponseBuilder for an empty response
notModified()	Creates a new ResponseBuilder with a not-modified status
ok()	Creates a new ResponseBuilder with an ok status
serverError()	Creates a new ResponseBuilder with an server error status
status()	Creates a new ResponseBuilder with the supplied status
temporaryRedirect()	Creates a new ResponseBuilder for a temporary redirection
getCookies()	Gets the cookies from the response message
getHeaders()	Gets the headers from the response message
getLinks()	Get the links attached to the message as header
getStatus()	Get the status code associated with the response
readEntity()	Read the message entity as an instance of specified Java type using a MessageBodyReader that supports mapping the message onto the requested type

The Response and ResponseBuilder follow the fluent API design pattern. Meaning you can easily write a response by concatenating methods. This also makes the code more readable. Here are some examples of what you can write with this API:

```
Response.ok().build();
Response.ok().cookie(new NewCookie("SessionID", "5G79GDIFYO9")).build();
Response.ok("Plain Text").expires(new Date()).build();
Response.ok(new Customer ("John", "Smith"), MediaType.APPLICATION_JSON).build();
Response.noContent().build();
Response.accepted(new Customer("John", "Smith", "jsmith@gmail.com", "1234565")).build();
Response.notModified().header("User-Agent", "Mozilla").build();
```

HTTP Method Matching

You've seen how the HTTP protocol works with its requests, responses, and action methods (GET, POST, PUT, etc.). JAX-RS defines these common HTTP methods using annotations: @GET, @POST, @PUT, @DELETE, @HEAD, and @OPTIONS. Only public methods may be exposed as resource methods. Listing 15-13 shows a customer RESTful web service exposing CRUD methods: @GET methods to retrieve resources, @POST methods to create a new resource, @PUT methods to update an existing resource, and @DELETE methods to delete a resource.

Listing 15-13. A Customer Resource Exposing CRUD Operations and Retuning Responses

```
@Path("/customer")
@Produces(MediaType.APPLICATION_XML)
@Consumes(MediaType.APPLICATION_XML)
public class CustomerRestService {

  @GET
  public Response getCustomers() {
    // ..
    return Response.ok(customers).build();
  }

  @GET
  @Path("{customerId}")
  public Response getCustomer(@PathParam("customerId") String customerId) {
    // ..
    return Response.ok(customer).build();
  }

  @POST
  public Response createCustomer(Customer customer) {
    // ..
    return Response.created(createdCustomerURI).build();
  }

  @PUT
  public Response updateCustomer(Customer customer) {
    // ..
    return Response.ok(customer).build();
  }
```

```
@DELETE
@Path("{customerId}")
public Response deleteCustomer(@PathParam("customerId") String customerId) {
    // ..
    return Response.noContent().build();
  }
}
```

The HTTP specification defines what HTTP response codes should be on a successful request. You can expect JAX-RS to return the same default response codes:

- GET methods retrieve whatever information (in the form of an entity) is identified by the requested URI. GET should return 200-OK.

- The PUT method refers to an already existing resource that needs to be updated. If an existing resource is modified, either the 200-OK or 204-No Content response should be sent to indicate successful completion of the request.

- The POST method is used to create a new resource identified by the request URI. The response should return 201-CREATED with the URI of this new resource or 204-No Content if it does not result in a resource that can be identified by a URI.

- The DELETE method requests that the server deletes the resource identified by the requested URI. A successful response should be 200-OK if the response includes an entity, 202-Accepted if the action has not yet been enacted, or 204-No Content if the action has been enacted but the response does not include an entity.

Building URIs

Hyperlinks are a central aspect of REST applications. In order to evolve through the application states, RESTful web services need to be agile at managing transition and building URIs. JAX-RS provides a javax.ws.rs.core.UriBuilder that aims at replacing java.net.URI for making it easier to build URIs in a safe manner. UriBuilder has a set of methods that can be used to build new URIs or build from existing URIs. Listing 15-14 gives you some examples of how you can use the UriBuilder to create any kind of URI with path, query, or matrix parameters.

Listing 15-14. Using UriBuilder

```
public class URIBuilderTest {

  @Test
  public void shouldBuildURIs() {
    URI uri = ↵
        UriBuilder.fromUri("http://www.myserver.com").path("book").path("1234").build();
    assertEquals("http://www.myserver.com/book/1234", uri.toString());

    uri = UriBuilder.fromUri("http://www.myserver.com").path("book") ↵
                              .queryParam("author", "Goncalves").build();
    assertEquals("http://www.myserver.com/book?author=Goncalves", uri.toString());

    uri = UriBuilder.fromUri("http://www.myserver.com").path("book") ↵
                              .matrixParam("author", "Goncalves").build();
    assertEquals("http://www.myserver.com/book;author=Goncalves", uri.toString());
```

```
uri = UriBuilder.fromUri("http://www.myserver.com").path("{path}")  ↪
        .queryParam("author", "{value}").build("book", "Goncalves");
assertEquals("http://www.myserver.com/book?author=Goncalves", uri.toString());


uri = UriBuilder.fromResource(BookRestService.class).path("1234").build();
assertEquals("/book/1234", uri.toString());

uri = UriBuilder.fromUri("http://www.myserver.com").fragment("book").build();
assertEquals("http://www.myserver.com/#book", uri.toString());

  }
}
```

Contextual Information

When a request is being processed, the resource provider needs contextual information to perform the request properly. The @javax.ws.rs.core.Context annotation is intended to inject into an attribute or a method parameter the following classes: HttpHeaders, UriInfo, Request, SecurityContext, and Providers. For example, Listing 15-15 shows the code that injects UriInfo so it can build URIs and HttpHeaders to return some headers information.

Listing 15-15. A Customer Resource Getting HttpHeaders and UriInfo

```
@Path("/customer")
public class CustomerRestService {

  @Context
  UriInfo uriInfo;

  @Inject
  private CustomerEJB customerEJB;

  @GET
  @Path("media")
  public String getDefaultMediaType(@Context HttpHeaders headers) {
    List<MediaType> mediaTypes = headers.getAcceptableMediaTypes();
    return mediaTypes.get(0).toString();
  }

  @GET
  @Path("language")
  public String getDefaultLanguage(@Context HttpHeaders headers) {
    List<String> mediaTypes = headers.getRequestHeader(HttpHeaders.ACCEPT_LANGUAGE);
    return mediaTypes.get(0);
  }

  @POST
  @Consumes(MediaType.APPLICATION_XML)
  public Response createCustomer(Customer cust) {
    Customer customer = customerEJB.persist(cust);
```

```
    URI bookUri = uriInfo.getAbsolutePathBuilder().path(customer.getId()).build();
    return Response.created(bookUri).build();
  }
}
```

As you saw earlier with HTTP, information is transported between the client and the server not only in the entity body, but also in the headers (Date, Server, Content-Type, etc.). HTTP headers take part in the uniform interface, and RESTful web services use them in their original meanings. As a resource developer, you may need to access HTTP headers; that's what the javax.ws.rs.core.HttpHeaders interface serves. An instance of HttpHeaders can be injected into an attribute or a method parameter using the @Context annotation, as the HttpHeaders class is a map with helper methods to access the header values in a case-insensitive manner. In Listing 15-15 the service returns the default Accept-Language and MediaType.

■ **Note**   JAX-RS 2.0 uses @Context to inject contextual information. Unfortunately @Inject doesn't work because the CDI alignment couldn't be completely archived in this release. Hopefully in the future releases of JAX-RS we will be able to use CDI extensively and just focus on a single annotation: @Inject.

Entity Provider

When entities are received in requests or sent in responses, the JAX-RS implementation needs a way to convert the representations to a Java type and vice versa. This is the role of entity providers that supply mapping services between representations and their associated java types. An example is JAXB, which maps an object to an XML representation and vice versa. If the default XML and JSON providers are not sufficient, then you can develop your own custom entity providers. You can even define your own format. What you need then is to give the JAX-RS runtime a way to read/write your custom format into/from an entity by implementing your own entity provider. Entity providers come in two flavors: MessageBodyReader and MessageBodyWriter.

Let's say you want to exchange your Customer bean into a custom/format that would look like this: 1234/John/Smith. As you can see, the delimiter is the '/' symbol, the first token is the customer id, the second the first name and the last one the surname. You first need a class (a writer) that takes a Customer bean and maps it to a response body. Listing 15-16 shows the CustomCustomerWriter class that must implement the javax.ws.rs.ext.MessageBodyWriter interface and be annotated with @Provider. The annotation @Produces specifies our custom media type (**"custom/format"**). As you can see, the writeTo method converts a Customer bean into a stream following the custom format.

Listing 15-16. A Provider Producing a Custom Representation of a Customer

```
@Provider
@Produces("custom/format")
public class CustomCustomerWriter implements MessageBodyWriter<Customer> {

  @Override
  public boolean isWriteable(Class<?> type, Type genericType, Annotation[] annotations, ⮑
                                                         MediaType mediaType) {

    return Customer.class.isAssignableFrom(type);
  }
```

```java
@Override
public void writeTo(Customer customer, Class<?> type, Type gType, Annotation[] ➥
            annotations, MediaType mediaType, MultivaluedMap<String, Object> httpHeaders, ➥
                OutputStream outputStream) throws IOException, WebApplicationException {

    outputStream.write(customer.getId().getBytes());
    outputStream.write('/');
    outputStream.write(customer.getFirstName().getBytes());
    outputStream.write('/');
    outputStream.write(customer.getLastName().getBytes());
}

@Override
public long getSize(Customer customer, Class<?> type, Type genericType, Annotation[] ➥
                                            annotations, MediaType mediaType) {
    return customer.getId().length() + 1 + customer.getFirstName().length() + 1 + ➥
                                customer.getLastName().length();
}
}
```

On the other hand, to map a request body to a Java type, a class must implement the javax.ws.rs.ext. MessageBodyReader interface and be annotated with @Provider. By default, the implementation is assumed to consume all media types (*/*). The annotation @Consumes in Listing 15-17 is used to specify our custom media type. The method readFrom takes the input stream, tokenizes it using the '/' delimiter and converts it into a Customer object. MessageBodyReader and MessageBodyWriter implementations may throw a WebApplicationException if they can't produce any representation.

Listing 15-17. A Provider Consuming a Custom Stream and Creating a Customer

```java
@Provider
@Consumes("custom/format")
public class CustomCustomerReader implements MessageBodyReader<Customer> {

    @Override
    public boolean isReadable(Class<?> type, Type genericType, Annotation[] annotations, ➥
                                                MediaType mediaType) {
        return Customer.class.isAssignableFrom(type);
    }

    @Override
    public Customer readFrom(Class<Customer> type, Type gType, Annotation[] annotations, ➥
                        MediaType mediaType, MultivaluedMap<String, String> httpHeaders, ➥
                        InputStream inputStream) throws IOException, WebApplicationException {

        String str = convertStreamToString(inputStream);
        StringTokenizer s = new StringTokenizer(str, "/");

        Customer customer = new Customer();
        customer.setId(s.nextToken());
        customer.setFirstName(s.nextToken());
        customer.setLastName(s.nextToken());

        return customer;
    }
}
```

Thanks to our `CustomCustomerWriter` and `CustomCustomerReader` we can now exchange data represented by our custom format, back and forth from the service to the consumer. The RESTful web service just has to declare the correct media type and the JAX-RS runtime will do the rest:

```
@GET
@Produces("custom/format")
public Customer getCustomCustomer () {
  return new Customer("1234", "John", "Smith");
}
```

Our custom format is a specific case, but for common media types, the JAX-RS implementation comes with a set of default entity providers (see Table 15-7). So for most common cases you don't have to worry about implementing your own reader and writer.

Table 15-7. *Default Providers of the JAX-RS Implementation*

Type	Description
byte[]	All media types (*/*)
java.lang.String	All media types (*/*)
java.io.InputStream	All media types (*/*)
java.io.Reader	All media types (*/*)
java.io.File	All media types (*/*)
javax.activation.DataSource	All media types (*/*)
javax.xml.transform.Source	XML types (text/xml, application/xml)
javax.xml.bind.JAXBElement	JAXB class XML media types (text/xml, application/xml)
MultivaluedMap<String,String>	Form content (application/x-www-form-urlencoded)
javax.ws.rs.core StreamingOutput	All media types (*/*), MessageBodyWriter only

Handling Exceptions

The code so far was executed in a happy world where everything works and no exception handling has been necessary. Unfortunately, life is not that perfect, and sooner or later you'll have to face a resource being blown up either because the data you received is not valid or because pieces of the network are not reliable.

A resource method may throw any checked or unchecked exception. Unchecked exceptions can be rethrown and allowed to propagate to the underlying container. Conversely, checked exceptions cannot be thrown directly and must be wrapped in a container-specific exception (`ServletException`, `WebServiceException` or `WebApplicationException`). But you can also throw a `javax.ws.rs.WebApplicationException` or subclasses of it (`BadRequestException`, `ForbiddenException`, `NotAcceptableException`, `NotAllowedException`, `NotAuthorizedException`, `NotFoundException`, `NotSupportedException`). The exception will be caught by the JAX-RS implementation and converted into an HTTP response. The default error is a 500 with a blank message, but the class `javax.ws.rs.WebApplicationException` offers various constructors so you can pick a specific status code (defined in the enumeration `javax.ws.rs.core.Response.Status`) or an entity. In Listing 15-18 the method `getCustomer` throws an unchecked exception (`IllegalArgumentException`) if the customer id is lower than 1000, and a 404-Not Found if the customer is not found in the database (instead it could have thrown a `NotFoundException`).

Listing 15-18. A Method Throwing Exceptions

```
@Path("/customer")
public class CustomerRestService {

  @Inject
  private CustomerEJB customerEJB;

  @Path("{customerId}")
  public Customer getCustomer(@PathParam("customerId") Long customerId) {
    if (customerId < 1000)
      throw new IllegalArgumentException("Id must be greater than 1000!");

    Customer customer = customerEJB.find(customerId);
    if (customer == null)
      throw new WebApplicationException(Response.Status.NOT_FOUND);
    return customer;
  }
}
```

To keep your code DRY (which stands for Don't Repeat Yourself), you can supply exception mapping providers. An exception mapping provider maps a general exception to a Response. If this exception is thrown, the JAX-RS implementation will catch it and invoke the corresponding exception mapping provider. An exception mapping provider is an implementation of ExceptionMapper<E extends java.lang.Throwable>, annotated with @Provider. Listing 15-19 maps a javax.persistence.EntityNotFoundException to a 404-Not Found status code.

Listing 15-19. An JPA Exception Mapped to a 404-Not Found Status Code

```
@Provider
public class EntityNotFoundMapper implements ExceptionMapper<EntityNotFoundException> {

  public Response toResponse(javax.persistence.EntityNotFoundException ex) {
    return Response.status(404).entity(ex.getMessage()).type(MediaType.TEXT_PLAIN).build();
  }
}
```

Life Cycle and Callback

When a request comes in, the targeted RESTful web service is resolved, and a new instance of the matching class is created. Thus, the life cycle of a RESTful web service is per request so the service does not have to worry about concurrency and can use instance variables safely.

If deployed in a Java EE container (servlet or EJB), JAX-RS resource classes and providers may also make use of the JSR 250 life-cycle management and security annotations: @PostConstruct, @PreDestroy, @RunAs, @RolesAllowed, @PermitAll, @DenyAll, and @DeclareRoles. The life cycle of a resource can use @PostConstruct and @PreDestroy to add business logic after the resource is created or before it is destroyed. Figure 15-3 shows the life cycle that is equivalent to most components in Java EE.

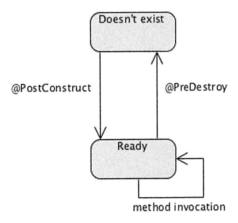

Figure 15-3. *Resource life cycle*

Packaging

RESTful web services may be packaged in a war or an EJB jar file depending if you are targeting the Web Profile or Full Java EE 7 services. Remember that a RESTful web service can also be annotated with @Stateless or @Singleton to benefit from the services of session beans. SOAP web services had several generated artifacts to package but that's not the case for REST. The developer is responsible for just packaging the classes annotated with @Path (and other helper classes). Note that there is no deployment descriptor in JAX-RS 2.0.

Invoking RESTful Web Services

So now you know how to develop RESTful web services that can process data, make CRUD operations on a database, bring information from the server and so on. How do you access them? Well, if you look back at Figure 15-1 it is just a matter of being able to make an HTTP request on a URI. Take any tool that is able to do so and you can invoke all the RESTful web services seen so far.

The first tool that comes to our mind is the Web browser. Open your browser, point it to a URI and you will get the visual representation. Unfortunately Web browsers only know how to do GET and POST HTTP methods. If you want more from your Web browser, you can always add a few plugins to allow more flexibility and use PUT and DELETE, too (e.g., Postman on Chrome, but there are more). Another very rich tool you can use is cUrl. With this command-line tool you can have access to all the details of the HTTP protocol and so invoke your RESTful web services.

Before JAX-RS 2.0 there was no standard Java way to easily invoke your RESTful web services. You would either rely on the low-level java.net.HttpURLConnection API or use a proprietary framework API (such as Jersey, Resteasy or Restlet). JAX-RS 2.0 fills this gap with a fluent, easy to use, request building API.

The Client API

JAX-RS 2.0 introduces a new client API so that you can make HTTP requests to your remote RESTful web services easily (despite all the low-level details of the HTTP protocol). It is a fluent request building API (i.e., using the Builder design pattern) that uses a small number of classes and interfaces (see Table 15-8 to have an overview of the javax.ws.rs.client package as well as Table 15-6 for the Response API). Very often, you will come across three main classes: Client, WebTarget, and Response. The Client interface (obtained with the ClientBuilder) is a builder of WebTarget instances. A WebTarget represents a distinct URI from which you can invoke requests on to obtain a Response. From this Response you can check HTTP status, length or cookies but more importantly you can get its content (a.k.a. entity, message body or payload) through the Entity class.

Table 15-8. *Main Classes and Interfaces of the* `javax.ws.rs.client` *Package*

Class/Interface	Description
`Client`	Is the main entry point to the fluent API used to build and execute client requests in order to consume responses returned
`ClientBuilder`	Entry point to the client API used to bootstrap `Client` instances
`Configurable`	Client-side configuration form `Client`, `WebTarget`, and `Invocation`
`Entity`	Encapsulates message entity including the associated variant information
`Invocation`	Is a request that has been prepared and is ready for execution
`Invocation.Builder`	A client request invocation builder
`WebTarget`	A resource target identified by the resource URI

Let's take it step by step to discover how to use this new API and then put it all together to test a RESTful web service.

Bootstrapping the Client

The main entry point for the API is the `Client` interface. The `Client` interface manages and configures HTTP connections. It is also a factory for `WebTargets` and has a set of methods for creating resource links and invocations. The `Client` instances are created using one of the static methods of the `ClientBuilder` class:

```
Client client = ClientBuilder.newClient();
```

This example demonstrates the way to create a `Client` instance using the default implementation. It is also possible to request a particular custom `Client` implementation using a specific configuration. For example, this code registers the `CustomCustomerReader` provider (see Listing 15-17) and sets some properties:

```
Client client = ClientBuilder.newClient();
client.configuration().register(CustomCustomerReader.class).setProperty("MyProperty", 1234);
```

Targets and Invocations

Once you have a `Client` you can now target a RESTful web service URI and invoke some HTTP methods on it. That's what the `WebTarget` and `Invocation` interfaces allow you to do. The `Client.target()` methods are factories for web targets that represent a specific URI. You build and execute requests from a `WebTarget` instance. You can create a `WebTarget` with the String representation of a URI:

```
WebTarget target = client.target("http://www.myserver.com/book");
```

You can also obtain a `WebTarget` from a java.net.URI, javax.ws.rs.core.UriBuilder or javax.ws.rs.core.Link:

```
URI uri = new URI("http://www.myserver.com/book ");
WebTarget target = client.target(uri);
```

Now that you have a URI to target, you need to build your HTTP resquest. The `WebTarget` allows you to do that by using the `Invocation.Builder`. To build a simple HTTP GET on a URI just write:

```
Invocation invocation  = target.request().buildGet()
```

Invocation.Builder allows you to build a GET method as well as POST, PUT and DELETE methods. You can also build a request for different MIME types and even add path, query and matrix parameters. For PUT and POST methods you need to pass an Entity, which represents the payload to send to your RESTful web service:

```
target.request().buildDelete();
target.queryParam("author", "Eloise").request().buildGet();
target.path(bookId).request().buildGet();
target.request(MediaType.APPLICATION_XML).buildGet();
target.request(MediaType.APPLICATION_XML).acceptLanguage("pt").buildGet();
target.request().buildPost(Entity.entity(new Book()));
```

This code just builds an Invocation. You then need to call the invoke()method to actually invoke your remote RESTful web service and get a Response object back. The Response is what defines the contract with the returned instance and is what you will consume:

```
Response response = invocation.invoke();
```

So if you put everything together, these are the lines of code to invoke a GET method on a remote RESTful web service located at http://www.myserver.com/book and return a text/plain value:

```
Client client = ClientBuilder.newClient();
WebTarget target = client.target("http://www.myserver.com/book");
Invocation invocation  = target.request(MediaType.TEXT_PLAIN).buildGet();
Response response = invocation.invoke();
```

Thanks to the builder API and some shortcuts, you can write the same behavior in a single line of code:

```
Response response = ClientBuilder.newClient().target("http://www.myserver.com/book") ➥
                                  .request(MediaType.TEXT_PLAIN).get();
```

Now let's see how to manipulate the Response and how to consume entities.

Consuming Responses

The Response class allows the consumer to have some control over the HTTP response returned from the RESTful web service. With its API you can check HTTP status, headers, cookies and, of course, the message body (a.k.a. entity). The code below uses the built-in methods to get access to some low-level HTTP information such as the status code, body length, message date or any HTTP header:

```
assertTrue(response.getStatusInfo() == Response.Status.OK);
assertTrue(response.getLength() == 4);
assertTrue(response.getDate() != null);
assertTrue(response.getHeaderString("Content-type").equals("text/plain"));
```

But most of the time what we really want from a Response is the entity sent from the RESTful web service. The readEntity method reads the message input stream, as an instance of specified Java, using a MessageBodyReader that supports the mapping of the message entity stream to the requested type. This means that if you specify that you want a String, the JAX-RS runtime will use the default String reader:

```
String body = response.readEntity(String.class);
```

When the `readEntity()` method is invoked with POJO, the JAX-RS runtime needs a `MessageBodyReader` that matches the response's content-type. So, for example, if Book is a JAXB bean and if your content type is XML, then JAX-RS will delegate the JAXB runtime to unmarshall the XML stream into your Book POJO:

```
Book book = response.readEntity(Book.class);
```

Putting everything together, the code below invokes a remote RESTful web service and gets the returned String entity:

```
Response response = ClientBuilder.newClient().target("http://www.myserver.com/book") ↩
                                          .request().get();
String body = response.readEntity(String.class);
```

But there is actually a shortcut on the Get method that allows you to specify the desired type and get an entity in a single line of code (without using an intermediate Response object):

```
String body = ClientBuilder.newClient().target("http://www.myserver.com/book") ↩
                                    .request().get(String.class);
```

Anatomy of a REST Consumer

Contrary to JAX-WS, which is embedded in Java SE and allows you to invoke SOAP web services out of the box with a JDK, with JAX-RS you need the client API in your classpath. But that's the only constraint. Unlike SOAP you don't have to generate any artifacts. So RESTful web service consumers can be from any Java class running on the JVM (main class, integration test, batch processing), to any Java EE component running in a container (Servlet, EJB, Managed Bean).

Of course, one of the strength of RESTful web services is interoperability. So if you expose a set of resources on the Internet you will be able to have mobile devices (smartphones, tablets) and other web technologies (e.g., JavaScript) accessing them.

Putting It All Together

Let's put all these concepts together and write a book RESTful web service, package and deploy it into GlassFish, and test it with cURL and with an integration test using the new client API. The idea is to have a Books JAXB bean that has a list of Book JPA entities that are mapped to a database. The BookRestService gives CRUD operations on the book. Despite being a RESTful web service it is also a stateless session bean allowing transactional demarcation (using an EntityManager). Once deployed, you will be able to create, retrieve, or delete books using HTTP methods with cURL and the JAX-RS client API. Thanks to JAXB and an extension of Jersey, you will be able to have both XML and JSON representations of these books.

The example follows the Maven directory structure and packages all the classes into a war file (`chapter15-service-1.0.war`). The classes described in Figure 15-4 have to be placed in the following directories:

- `src/main/java`: The directory for the Books, Book entity and BookRestService as well as a technical classes used to configure the runtime (more on ApplicationConfig later)

- `src/main/resources`: The persistence.xml file used by the resource that maps the Book entity to the Derby database

- `src/test/java`: The directory for the integration test BookRestServiceIT

- `pom.xml`: The Maven Project Object Model (POM) describing the project and its dependencies

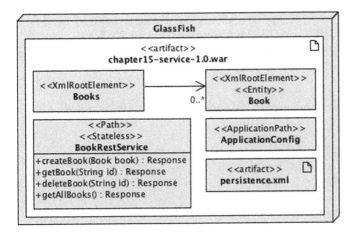

Figure 15-4. *Putting It All Together*

Writing the Book Entity

By now you understand the code of the Book entity, but there is one very important element to notice: this entity is also annotated with the JAXB @XmlRootElement annotation (see Listing 15-20), which allows it to have an XML representation of a book (and JSON with a Jersey extension that you will see later).

Listing 15-20. A Book Entity with a JAXB Annotation

```
@Entity
@XmlRootElement
@NamedQuery(name = Book.FIND_ALL, query = "SELECT b FROM Book b")
public class Book {

    public static final String FIND_ALL = "Book.findAll";

    @Id
    @GeneratedValue
    private String id;
    @Column(nullable = false)
    private String title;
    private Float price;
    @Column(length = 2000)
    private String description;
    private String isbn;
    private Integer nbOfPage;
    private Boolean illustrations;

    // Constructors, getters, setters
}
```

This entity also has to be packaged with a persistence.xml file (not shown here for simplicity).

Writing the Books JAXB Bean

One of the methods of the RESTful web service retrieves all the books from the database. This method could have returned a List<Book> but that would not allow JAXB marshalling. To have an XML representation of a list of books we need to have a JAXB annotated POJO. As you can see in Listing 15-21, the Books class inherits from ArrayList<Book> and has an @XmlRootElement annotation.

Listing 15-21. A Books JAXB Bean Containing a List of Book

```
@XmlRootElement
@XmlSeeAlso(Book.class)
public class Books extends ArrayList<Book> {

  public Books() {
    super();
  }

  public Books(Collection<? extends Book> c) {
    super(c);
  }

  @XmlElement(name = "book")
  public List<Book> getBooks() {
    return this;
  }

  public void setBooks(List<Book> books) {
    this.addAll(books);
  }
}
```

Writing the BookRestService

The BookRestService is a RESTful web service, implemented as a stateless session bean, using an entity manager to create, delete, and retrieve books. Let's split the class in several parts and explain them all.

Header Class

The header of the BookRestService (see Listing 15-22) is important as it uses several metadata annotations. In JAX-RS, users access services by invoking a URI. The @Path("/book") annotation indicates the root path of the resource (the URL used to access it)—in this case, it's something like http://localhost:8080/book.

Listing 15-22. Header of the BookRestService Class

```
@Path("/book")
@Produces({MediaType.APPLICATION_XML, MediaType.APPLICATION_JSON})
@Consumes({MediaType.APPLICATION_XML, MediaType.APPLICATION_JSON})
@Stateless
public class BookRestService {
```

```
@PersistenceContext(unitName = "chapter15PU")
private EntityManager em;
@Context
private UriInfo uriInfo;
// ...
```

The @Produces and @Consumes annotations define the default content type that this resource produces or consumes: XML and JSON. Finally, we find the @Stateless annotation that you've seen in Chapter 7, which informs the container that this RESTful web service should also be treated as an EJB and allow transaction demarcation when accessing the database. This service has a reference to an entity manager and a UriInfo injected into it.

Creating a New Book

Following the REST semantic, we use an HTTP POST method to create a new resource in XML or JSON (as specified in the header with the @Consumes annotation). By default, every method consumes XML or JSON, and this is true for the createBook() method. As seen in Listing 15-23 this method takes a Book as a parameter; remember that the Book entity is also a JAXB object and, once the XML has been unmarshalled to a Book object, the entity manager can persist it. If the book parameter is null, a BadRequestException is thrown (400-Bad Request).

Listing 15-23. The createBook Method of the BookRestService

```
// ...
@POST
public Response createBook(Book book) {
  if (book == null)
    throw new BadRequestException();

  em.persist(book);
  URI bookUri = uriInfo.getAbsolutePathBuilder().path(book.getId()).build();
  return Response.created(bookUri).build();
}
// ...
```

This method returns a Response, which is the URI of the newly created book. We could have returned a status code 200-OK (Response.ok()), indicating that the creation of the book was successful, but, following the REST principles, the method should return a 201 (or 204), specifying the request has been fulfilled and resulting in the creation (Response.created()) of a new resource. The newly created resource can be referenced by the URI returned in the response (bookUri).

To create a resource with the code in Listing 15-23, we have the choice of sending either XML or JSON. JSON is less verbose. The cURL command line uses a POST method and passes data in a JSON format that must follow the JSON/XML mapping used in Jersey (remember that the XML in turn is mapped from the Book object using JAXB rules):

```
$ curl -X POST --data-binary "{\"description\":\"Science fiction comedy book\", ↪
  \"illustrations\":false,\"isbn\":\"1-84023-742-2\",\"nbOfPage\":354,\"price\":12.5, ↪
  \"title\":\"The Hitchhiker's Guide to the Galaxy\"}" ↪
  -H "Content-Type: application/json" http://localhost:8080/chapter15-service-1.0/rs/book -v
```

The verbose mode of cURL (the -v argument) displays the HTTP request and response (as shown in the following output). You can see in the response the URI of the created book resource with an ID set to 601:

```
> POST /chapter15-service-1.0/rs/book HTTP/1.1
> User-Agent: curl/7.23.1 (x86_64-apple-darwin11.2.0) libcurl/7.23.1
> Host: localhost:8080
> Accept: */*
> Content-Type: application/json
> Content-Length: 165
>
< HTTP/1.1 201 Created
< Server: GlassFish Server Open Source Edition  4.0
< Location: http://localhost:8080/chapter15-service-1.0/rs/book/601
< Date: Thu, 29 Nov 2012 21:49:44 GMT
< Content-Length: 0
```

Getting a Book by ID

To retrieve a book by its identifier, the request must have a URL of the form /book/{id of the book}. The id is used as a parameter to find the book in the database. In Listing 15-24 if the book is not found a NotFoundException (404) is thrown. Depending on the MIME type, the getBook() method will return an XML or a JSON representation of the book.

Listing 15-24. The getBook Method of the BookRestService

```
// ...
@GET
@Path("{id}")
public Response getBook(@PathParam("id") String id) {
  Book book = em.find(Book.class, id);

  if (book == null)
    throw new NotFoundException();

  return Response.ok(book).build();
}
// ...
```

The @Path annotation indicates the subpath within the already specified path at the class level. The use of the {id} syntax binds the URL element to the method parameter. Let's use cURL to access the book with id 601 and get a JSON representation:

```
$ curl -X GET -H "Accept: application/json" ↩
                http://localhost:8080/chapter15-service-1.0/rs/book/601
{"description":"Science fiction comedy book","id":"1","illustrations":false, ↩
                "isbn":"1-84023-742-2","nbOfPage":354,"price":12.5,"title":"H2G2"}
```

By just changing the Accept header property, the same code will return the XML representation of book 601:

```
$ curl -X GET -H "Accept: application/xml" ↩
                http://localhost:8080/chapter15-service-1.0/rs/book/601
```

```
<?xml version="1.0" encoding="UTF-8" standalone="yes"?><book><description>Science fiction ↩
 comedy book</description><id>601</id><illustrations>false</illustrations>978-1-4302-4188-1 ↩
 1-84023-742-2</isbn><nbOfPage>354</nbOfPage><price>12.5</price><title>H2G2</title></book>
```

Getting all the Books

To get all the books from the database the code in Listing 15-25 uses a TypedQuery the result of which is set into the Books class. Remember that this class extends ArrayList<Book> and gives an XML representation of the list thanks to its JAXB annotations. The response returns a 200-OK status with the books representation in the message body.

Listing 15-25. The getBooks Method of the BookRestService

```
// ...
@GET
public Response getBooks() {
  TypedQuery<Book> query = em.createNamedQuery(Book.FIND_ALL, Book.class);
  Books books = new Books(query.getResultList());
  return Response.ok(books).build();
}
// ...
```

Again, if you want to quickly test this code with a cUrl, fire a command line and type the following commands to get either an XML or JSON representation of the list of books:

```
$ curl -X GET -H "Accept: application/json" ↩
                      http://localhost:8080/chapter15-service-1.0/rs/book
$ curl -X GET -H "Accept: application/xml" ↩
                      http://localhost:8080/chapter15-service-1.0/rs/book
```

Deleting a Book

The deleteBook()method in Listing 15-26 follows the format of the getBook() method because it uses a subpath and an ID as a parameter, with the only difference being the HTTP request used (DELETE instead of GET). If the book is not found in the database a NotFoundException is thrown, otherwise the book is deleted and a 204-No Content is sent back.

Listing 15-26. The deleteBook Method of the BookRestService

```
// ...
@DELETE
@Path("{id}")
public Response deleteBook(@PathParam("id") String id) {
  Book book = em.find(Book.class, id);

  if (book == null)
    throw new NotFoundException();

  em.remove(book);

  return Response.noContent().build();
}
// ...
```

If we use the verbose mode of cURL (-v argument), we'll see the DELETE request is sent, and the 204-No Content status code appears in the response to indicate that the resource doesn't exist anymore.

```
$ curl -X DELETE http://localhost:8080/chapter15-service-1.0/rs/book/601 -v
> DELETE /chapter15-service-1.0/rs/book/601 HTTP/1.1
> User-Agent: curl/7.23.1 (x86_64-apple-darwin11.2.0) libcurl/7.23.1
> Host: localhost:8080
> Accept: */*
>
< HTTP/1.1 204 No Content
< Server: GlassFish Server Open Source Edition  4.0
```

Configuring JAX-RS

Before deploying the BookRestService and Book entity, we need to register a url pattern in Jersey to intercept HTTP calls to the services. This way the requests sent to the /rs path will get intercepted by Jersey. You can either set this url pattern by configuring the Jersey servlet in the web.xml file, or use the @ApplicationPath annotation (see Listing 15-27). The ApplicationConfig class needs to extend javax.ws.rs.core.Application and define all the RESTful web services of the application (here c.add(BookRestService.class)) as well as any other needed extension (c.add(MOXyJsonProvider.class)).

Listing 15-27. The ApplicationConfig Class Declaring the /rs URL Pattern

```
@ApplicationPath("rs")
public class ApplicationConfig extends Application {

  private final Set<Class<?>> classes;

  public ApplicationConfig() {
    HashSet<Class<?>> c = new HashSet<>();
    c.add(BookRestService.class);

    c.add(MOXyJsonProvider.class);

    classes = Collections.unmodifiableSet(c);
  }

  @Override
  public Set<Class<?>> getClasses() {
    return classes;
  }
}
```

This class has to be somewhere in your project (no particular package) and, thanks to the @ApplicationPath annotation, it will map the requests to the /rs/* URL pattern. This means, each time a URL starts with /rs/, it will be handled by Jersey. And, indeed, in the examples that I have used with cURL, all the resource URLs start with /rs:

```
$ curl -X GET -H "Accept: application/json" ↪
                   http://localhost:8080/chapter15-service-1.0/rs/book
```

■ **Note** In Chapter 12 you've seen several specifications around XML and JSON. Two groups of specifications exist: processing (JAXP and JSON-P) and binding (JAXB). Thanks to binding, JAX-RS will convert the list of beans into XML using the built-in `MessageBodyReader` and `MessageBodyWriter` which are based on JAXB. Unfortunately the binding technology for JSON does not exist yet (it is supposed to arrive in the coming years and will probably be called JSON-B). So, for now, marshalling a bean to JSON automatically is impossible. That's why in the `ApplicationConfig` class we need to add a Jersey specific provider (`MOXyJsonProvider`) to have a JSON `MessageBodyReader` and `MessageBodyWriter`. But that's not portable across JAX-RS implementations.

Compiling and Packaging with Maven

All the classes need now to be compiled and packaged in a war file (`<packaging>war</packaging>`). The pom.xml in Listing 15-28 declares all necessary dependencies to compile the code (which are all in `glassfish-embedded-all`). Remember that JAXB is part of Java SE, so we don't need to add this dependency. Notice that the pom.xml declares the Failsafe plugin that is designed to run integration tests (used later to run the `BookRestServiceIT` integration test class).

Listing 15-28. The pom.xml File to Compile, Test, and Package the RESTful Web Service

```xml
<?xml version="1.0" encoding="UTF-8"?>
<project xmlns="http://maven.apache.org/POM/4.0.0" ➥
         xmlns:xsi="http://www.w3.org/2001/XMLSchema-instance" ➥
         xsi:schemaLocation="http://maven.apache.org/POM/4.0.0 ➥
         http://maven.apache.org/xsd/maven-4.0.0.xsd">
  <modelVersion>4.0.0</modelVersion>

  <parent>
    <artifactId>chapter15</artifactId>
    <groupId>org.agoncal.book.javaee7</groupId>
    <version>1.0</version>
  </parent>

  <groupId>org.agoncal.book.javaee7.chapter15</groupId>
  <artifactId>chapter15-service</artifactId>
  <version>1.0</version>
  <packaging>war</packaging>

  <dependencies>
    <dependency>
      <groupId>org.glassfish.main.extras</groupId>
      <artifactId>glassfish-embedded-all</artifactId>
      <version>4.0</version>
      <scope>provided</scope>
    </dependency>

    <dependency>
      <groupId>junit</groupId>
      <artifactId>junit</artifactId>
      <version>4.11</version>
```

```xml
        <scope>test</scope>
      </dependency>
    </dependencies>

  <build>
    <plugins>
      <plugin>
        <groupId>org.apache.maven.plugins</groupId>
        <artifactId>maven-compiler-plugin</artifactId>
        <version>2.5.1</version>
        <configuration>
          <source>1.7</source>
          <target>1.7</target>
        </configuration>
      </plugin>
      <plugin>
        <groupId>org.apache.maven.plugins</groupId>
        <artifactId>maven-war-plugin</artifactId>
        <version>2.2</version>
        <configuration>
          <failOnMissingWebXml>false</failOnMissingWebXml>
        </configuration>
      </plugin>
      <plugin>
        <groupId>org.apache.maven.plugins</groupId>
        <artifactId>maven-failsafe-plugin</artifactId>
        <version>2.12.4</version>
        <executions>
          <execution>
            <id>integration-test</id>
            <goals>
              <goal>integration-test</goal>
              <goal>verify</goal>
            </goals>
          </execution>
        </executions>
      </plugin>
    </plugins>
  </build>
</project>
```

To compile and package the classes, open a command line in the root directory containing the pom.xml file and enter the following Maven command:

```
$ mvn package
```

Go to the target directory, look for a file named chapter15-service-1.0.war, and open it. Notice that Book.class, Books.class, ApplicationConfig.class, and BookRestService.class are all under the WEB-INF\classes directory. The persistence.xml file is also packaged in the war file.

Deploying on GlassFish

Once the code is packaged, make sure GlassFish and Derby are up and running and deploy the war file by issuing the asadmin command-line interface. Open a console, go to the `target` directory where the `chapter15-service-1.0.war` file is located, and enter:

```
$ asadmin deploy chapter15-service-1.0.war
```

If the deployment is successful, the following command should return the name of the deployed component and its type:

```
$ asadmin list-components
chapter15-service-1.0 <ejb, web>
```

Now that the application is deployed, you can use cURL in a command line to create book resources by sending POST requests and get all or a specific resource with GET requests. DELETE will remove book resources.

WADL

I introduced the WADL (Web Application Description Language) at the beginning of the chapter saying that it wasn't standardized and not very much used in RESTful architecture. But if you want to have a look at what it could look like for our BookRestService RESTful web service, check the following URL: `http://localhost/8080/chapter15-service-1.0/rs/application.wadl`. Listing 15-29 shows an abstract of this WADL.

Listing 15-29. Extract of the WADL Generated by GlassFish for the BookRestService RESTful web service

```
<application xmlns="http://wadl.dev.java.net/2009/02">
  <resources base="http://localhost:8080/chapter15-service-1.0/rs/">
    <resource path="/book">
      <method id="POST" name="POST">
        <request>
          <representation element="book" mediaType="application/xml"/>
          <representation element="book" mediaType="application/json"/>
        </request>
      </method>
      <resource path="{id}">
        <param name="id" style="template" type="xs:string"/>
        <method id="GET{id}" name="GET">
          <response>
            <representation mediaType="application/xml"/>
            <representation mediaType="application/json"/>
          </response>
        </method>
        <method id="DELETE{id}" name="DELETE"/>
      </resource>
    </resource>
    ...
  </resources>
</application>
```

The WADL in Listing 15-29 describes the root path (http://localhost:8080/chapter15-service-1.0/rs/) and all the subpaths available in the RESTful service (/book and {id}). It also gives you the HTTP method you can invoke (POST, GET, DELETE ...).

Writing the BookRestServiceIT Integration Test

Now that the code is packaged and deployed into GlassFish we can write an integration test that will make HTTP requests to the RESTful web service using the new JAX-RS 2.0 Client API. Integration tests are different from unit tests because they don't test your code in isolation, they need all the containers services. Typically, if GlassFish and Derby are not up and running, the code in Listing 15-30 will not work.

The two first methods test failures. shouldNotCreateANullBook makes sure you cannot create a book with a null Book object. So it posts a null entity and expects a 400-Bad Request. The shouldNotFindTheBookID test case passes an unknown book id and expects a 404-Not Found.

The shouldCreateAndDeleteABook test case is a bit more complex as it invokes several operations. First, it posts an XML representation of a Book object and makes sure the status code is 201-Created. The bookURI variable is the URI of the newly created book. The test case uses this URI to request the new book, then reads the message body, casts it to a Book class (book = response.readEntity(Book.class)) and asserts that the values are correct. Then a DELETE invocation deletes the book from the database and checks the response status code is 204-No Content. A last GET on the resource makes sure it has been deleted by checking the 404-Not Found status code.

Listing 15-30. The ApplicationConfig Class Declaring the /rs URL Pattern

```java
public class BookRestServiceIT {

  private static URI uri = UriBuilder.
                fromUri("http://localhost/chapter15-service-1.0/rs/book").port(8080).build();
  private static Client client = ClientBuilder.newClient();

  @Test
  public void shouldNotCreateANullBook() throws JAXBException {

    // POSTs a Null Book
    Response response = client.target(uri).request().post(Entity.entity(null, ↵
                                            MediaType.APPLICATION_XML));
    assertEquals(Response.Status.BAD_REQUEST, response.getStatusInfo());
  }

  @Test
  public void shouldNotFindTheBookID() throws JAXBException {

    // GETs a Book with an unknown ID
    Response response = client.target(uri).path("unknownID").request().get();
    assertEquals(Response.Status.NOT_FOUND, response.getStatusInfo());
  }

  @Test
  public void shouldCreateAndDeleteABook() throws JAXBException {

    Book book = new Book("H2G2", 12.5F, "Science book", "1-84023-742-2", 354, false);
```

```
    // POSTs a Book
    Response response = client.target(uri).request().post(Entity.entity(book, ↪
                                                        MediaType.APPLICATION_XML));
    assertEquals(Response.Status.CREATED, response.getStatusInfo());
    URI bookURI = response.getLocation();

    // With the location, GETs the Book
    response = client.target(bookURI).request().get();
    book = response.readEntity(Book.class);
    assertEquals(Response.Status.OK, response.getStatusInfo());
    assertEquals("H2G2", book.getTitle());

    // Gets the book id and DELETEs it
    String bookId = bookURI.toString().split("/")[6];
    response = client.target(uri).path(bookId).request().delete();
    assertEquals(Response.Status.NO_CONTENT, response.getStatusInfo());

    // GETs the Book and checks it has been deleted
    response = client.target(bookURI).request().get();
    assertEquals(Response.Status.NOT_FOUND, response.getStatusInfo());

  }
}
```

Make sure GlassFish and Derby are up and running, that the application is deployed, and execute this integration test with the Maven Failsafe plugin by entering the following Maven command:

```
$ mvn failsafe:integration-test
```

Summary

The previous chapter explained SOAP web services and by now you should know the difference between JAX-WS and JAX-RS web services. REST embraces HTTP so this chapter commenced with a general introduction to resources, representation, addressability, connectedness, and uniform interfaces. With simple verbs (GET, POST, PUT, etc.), you learned how you can access any resource deployed on the Web.

The chapter then zoomed into HTTP, a protocol based on a request/response mechanism, exchanging messages made of headers, cookies, and a body. Using HTTP headers and content negotiation, RESTful web services can choose an appropriate content type from the same URI. Caching can be employed to optimize network traffic with conditional requests using dates and ETags. This optimization can also be used with REST as it is based on HTTP. Thanks to the new JAX-RS 2.0 client API, we've managed to programmatically invoke a few RESTful web services.

JAX-RS is a Java API, shipped with Java EE 7 that simplifies RESTful web service development. With a set of annotations, you can define the path and subpaths of your resource, extract different kinds of parameters, or map to HTTP methods (@GET, @POST, etc.). When developing RESTful web services, you must think about resources, how they are linked together, and how to manage their state using HTTP. Now you are ready to expose a few services on the Web and see how many different devices will be able to consume them.

Setting Up the Development Environment

This appendix focuses on setting up your development environment so you can do some hands-on work by following the code snippets listed in the previous chapters. This book has lots of code, and most of the chapters have a "Putting It All Together" section. This section provides a step-by-step example showing how to develop, compile, deploy, execute, unit-test, and integration-test a component. To run these examples, you need to install the required software:

- JDK 1.7
- Maven 3
- JUnit 4
- Derby 10.8 database (a.k.a. Java DB)
- GlassFish 4 application server

JDK 1.7

Essential for the development and the execution of the examples in the book is the Java Development Kit (JDK). It includes several tools such as a compiler (javac), a virtual machine, a documentation generator (javadoc), monitoring tools (Visual VM), and so on. To install the JDK 1.7, go to the official Oracle web site (http://www.oracle.com/technetwork/java/javase/downloads/index.html), select the appropriate platform and language, and download the distribution.

If you are running on Mac OS X (Linux and Windows environments are not tested in this book but the code should be portable), double-click the jdk-7u15-macosx-x64.dmg file and the screen shown in Figure A-1 will ask you to double-click the JDK package. A wizard will then invite you to accept the license of the software and will install the JDK.

Figure A-1. *Setting up the JDK installation*

Once the installation is complete, it is necessary to set the JAVA_HOME variable and the $JAVA_HOME/bin directory to the PATH variable. Check that your system recognizes Java by entering java -version (see Figure A-2).

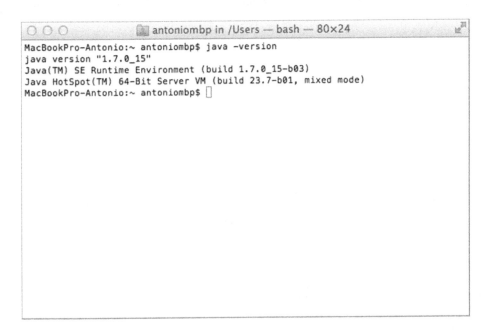

Figure A-2. *Displaying the JDK version*

Maven 3

To reflect what you'll find in the real development world, I've decided to use Apache Maven (http://maven.apache.org) to build the examples of this book. The purpose of this book is not to explain Maven. You will find plenty of resources for Maven on the Internet or in bookstores. But I will introduce some elements so that you can easily understand and use the examples.

Building a Java EE application requires different operations.

- Generating code and resources,

- Compiling Java classes and test classes,

- Running unit and integration tests, and

- Packaging the code in an archive (jar, ear, war, etc.) with potentially external jar libraries.

Doing these tasks manually can be time-consuming and can generate errors. Thus, development teams have looked for ways of automating these tasks. That's how Maven was created–to fulfill these gaps.

A Brief History of Maven

In 2000, Java developers started to use Apache Ant (`http://ant.apache.org`), allowing them to create scripts for building applications. Ant itself is written in Java and offers a range of commands that, unlike a Unix Make tool, are portable across platforms. Development teams started to create their own scripts to fulfill their needs. Yet Ant was quickly pushed to its limits when projects had to start encompassing complex heterogeneous systems. Companies faced difficulties to industrialize their build system. There was no real tool to easily reuse a build script between different projects (copy/paste was the only way).

In 2002, Apache Maven was born, and this project not only addressed these issues but also went beyond being a simple building tool. Maven offers projects a building solution, shared libraries, and a plug-in platform, allowing you to do quality control, documentation, teamwork, and so forth. Based on the "convention over configuration" principle, Maven brings a standard project description and a number of conventions such as a standard directory structure (as shown in Figure A-3). With an extensible architecture based on plug-ins (a.k.a. mojos), Maven can offer many different services.

Figure A-3. *Standard Maven directory structure*

Project Descriptor

Maven is based on the fact that a majority of Java and Java EE projects face similar needs when building applications. A Maven project needs to follow standards as well as define specific features in a project descriptor, or Project Object Model (POM). The POM is an XML file (pom.xml) placed at the root of the project that contains all the metadata of the project. As shown in Listing A-1, the minimum required information to describe the identity of the project is the groupId, the artifactId, the version, and the packaging type.

Listing A-1. Minimal pom.xml

```xml
<?xml version="1.0" encoding="UTF-8"?>
<project xmlns="http://maven.apache.org/POM/4.0.0" ↪
         xmlns:xsi="http://www.w3.org/2001/XMLSchema-instance"↪
         xsi:schemaLocation="http://maven.apache.org/POM/4.0.0 ↪
         http://maven.apache.org/xsd/maven-4.0.0.xsd">

  <modelVersion>4.0.0</modelVersion>
  <groupId>org.agoncal.book.javaee7</groupId>
  <artifactId>chapter01</artifactId>
  <version>1.0-SNAPSHOT</version>
  <packaging>jar</packaging>
</project>
```

A project is often divided into different artifacts. These artifacts are then grouped under the same groupId (similar to packages in Java) and uniquely identified by the artifactId. Packaging allows Maven to produce the artifact following a standard format (jar, war, ear, etc.). Finally, the version allows identifying an artifact during its lifetime (version 1.1, 1.2, 1.2.1, etc.). Maven imposes versioning so a team can manage the life of its project development. Maven also introduces the concept of SNAPSHOT versions (the version number ends with the string -SNAPSHOT) to identify an artifact when it's being developed.

The POM defines much more information about your project. Some is purely descriptive (name, description, etc.); other information concerns the application execution such as the list of external libraries used, and so on. Finally, the pom.xml defines environmental information to build the project (versioning tool, continuous integration server, artifacts repositories), and any other specific process to build your project.

Managing Artifacts

Maven goes beyond building artifacts; it also offers a genuine approach to archive and share these artifacts. Maven uses a local repository on your hard drive (by default in ~/.m2/repository) where it stores all the artifacts that the project's descriptor manipulates. The local repository (see Figure A-4) is filled either by the local developer's artifacts (e.g., myProject-1.1.jar) or by external ones (e.g., javax.ejb-3.2.jar) that Maven downloads from remote repositories. By default, Maven uses a main repository at http://search.maven.org to download the missing artifacts.

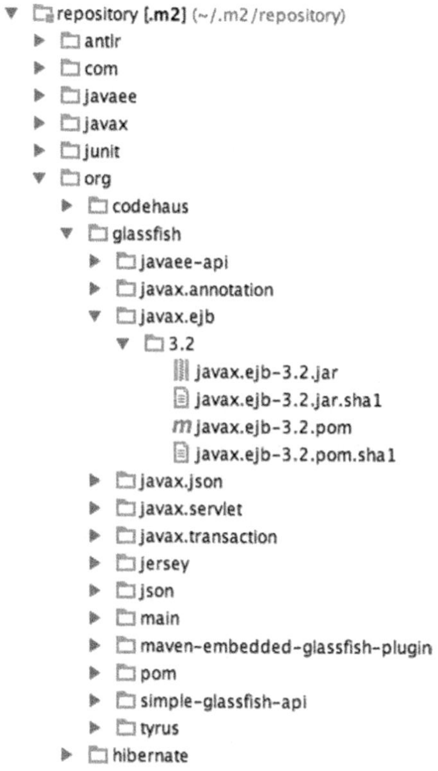

```
▼ 🗁 repository [.m2] (~/.m2/repository)
    ▶ 🗀 antlr
    ▶ 🗀 com
    ▶ 🗀 javaee
    ▶ 🗀 javax
    ▶ 🗀 junit
    ▼ 🗀 org
        ▶ 🗀 codehaus
        ▼ 🗀 glassfish
            ▶ 🗀 javaee-api
            ▶ 🗀 javax.annotation
            ▼ 🗀 javax.ejb
                ▼ 🗀 3.2
                        ▦ javax.ejb-3.2.jar
                        🗎 javax.ejb-3.2.jar.sha1
                        𝑚 javax.ejb-3.2.pom
                        🗎 javax.ejb-3.2.pom.sha1
            ▶ 🗀 javax.json
            ▶ 🗀 javax.servlet
            ▶ 🗀 javax.transaction
            ▶ 🗀 jersey
            ▶ 🗀 json
            ▶ 🗀 main
            ▶ 🗀 maven-embedded-glassfish-plugin
            ▶ 🗀 pom
            ▶ 🗀 simple-glassfish-api
            ▶ 🗀 tyrus
        ▶ 🗀 hibernate
```

Figure A-4. *Example of a local repository*

A Maven project defines a single artifact in a declarative way with its dependencies in the POM (groupId, artifactId, version, type) as shown in Listing A-2. If necessary, Maven will download them to the local repository from remote repositories. Moreover, using the POM descriptors of these external artifacts, Maven will also download the artifacts they need, and so on. Therefore, the development team doesn't have to manually deal with project dependencies. Maven automatically adds the necessary libraries.

Listing A-2. Dependencies in the pom.xml

```xml
<dependencies>
  <dependency>
    <groupId>org.eclipse.persistence</groupId>
    <artifactId>javax.persistence</artifactId>
    <version>2.1</version>
    <scope>provided</scope>
  </dependency>
  <dependency>
    <groupId>org.glassfish</groupId>
    <artifactId>javax.ejb</artifactId>
    <version>3.2</version>
    <scope>provided</scope>
  </dependency>
</dependencies>
```

Dependencies may have limited visibility (called scope).

- test: The library is used to compile and run test classes but is not packaged in the produced artifact.

- provided: The library is provided by the environment (persistence provider, application server, etc.) and is only used to compile the code.

- compile: The library is necessary for compilation and execution.

- runtime: The library is only required for execution but is excluded from the compilation (e.g., JSF components and JSTL tag libraries).

Project Modularity

To address project modularity, Maven provides a mechanism based on modules. Each module is a Maven project in its own right. Maven is able to build a project with different modules by calculating the dependencies they have between them (see Figure A-5). To facilitate reusing common parameters, POM descriptors can inherit from parent POM projects.

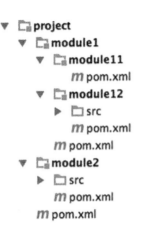

Figure A-5. *A project and its modules*

Plug-ins and Life Cycle

Maven uses a life cycle made of several phases (see Figure A-6): it cleans the resources, validates the project, generates any needed sources, compiles Java classes, runs test classes, packages the project, and installs it to the local repository. This life cycle is the vertebral column on which Maven plug-ins hang. Depending on the type of project you build, the associated mojos can be different (a mojo to compile, another to test, another to build, etc.). In the project description, you can link new plug-ins to a life-cycle phase, change the configuration of a plug-in, and so on. For example, when you build a web service client, you might add a mojo that generates web service artifacts during the generate-sources phase.

▼ ⌂ Lifecycle
    ⚙ clean
    ⚙ validate
    ⚙ generate-sources
    ⚙ process-sources
    ⚙ generate-resources
    ⚙ process-resources
    ⚙ compile
    ⚙ process-classes
    ⚙ generate-test-sources
    ⚙ process-test-sources
    ⚙ generate-test-resources
    ⚙ process-test-resources
    ⚙ test-compile
    ⚙ test
    ⚙ prepare-package
    ⚙ package
    ⚙ pre-integration-test
    ⚙ integration-test
    ⚙ post-integration-test
    ⚙ verify
    ⚙ install
    ⚙ site
    ⚙ deploy

Figure A-6. *Project life cycle*

Installation

The examples of this book have been developed with Apache Maven 3.0.5. Once you have installed JDK 1.7, make sure the JAVA_HOME environment variable is set. Then download Maven from http://maven.apache.org/, unzip the file on your hard drive, and add the apache-maven/bin directory to your PATH variable.

Once you've done this, open a command line and enter mvn -version to validate your installation. Maven should print its version and the JDK version as shown in Figure A-7.

```
○ ○ ○                     🖾 antoniombp in /Users — bash — 95×24
MacBookPro-Antonio:~ antoniombp$ mvn -version
Apache Maven 3.0.5 (r01de14724cdef164cd33c7c8c2fe155faf9602da; 2013-02-19 14:51:28+0100)
Maven home: /usr/share/java/maven-3.0.5
Java version: 1.7.0_15, vendor: Oracle Corporation
Java home: /Library/Java/JavaVirtualMachines/jdk1.7.0_15.jdk/Contents/Home/jre
Default locale: fr_FR, platform encoding: UTF-8
OS name: "mac os x", version: "10.7.4", arch: "x86_64", family: "mac"
MacBookPro-Antonio:~ antoniombp$ 
```

Figure A-7. *Maven displaying its version*

Be aware that Maven needs Internet access so it can download plug-ins and project dependencies from the main repository. If you are behind a proxy, see the documentation to configure your settings.

Usage

Here are some commands that you will be using to run the examples in the book. They all invoke a different phase of the project life cycle (clean, compile, install, etc.) and use the pom.xml to dd libraries, customize the compilation, or extend some behaviors with plug-ins:

- mvn clean: Deletes all generated files (compiled classes, generated code, artifacts, etc.).
- mvn compile: Compiles the main Java classes.
- mvn test-compile: Compiles the test classes.
- mvn test: Compiles the main Java classes as well as the test classes and executes the tests.
- mvn package: Compiles, executes the tests and packages the code into an archive.
- mvn install: Builds and installs the artifacts in your local repository.
- mvn clean install: Cleans and installs. (Note that you can add several commands separated by a space.)

■ **Note** Maven allows you to compile, run, and package the examples of this book. It decouples the fact that you need to write your code (within an IDE) and build it. To develop you need an integrated development environment (IDE). I use IntelliJ IDEA from JetBrains, and you will see some screenshots of it throughout these pages. But you can use any IDE you want because this book only relies on Maven, not on specific IntelliJ IDEA features.

JUnit 4

JUnit is an open source framework to write and run repeatable tests. JUnit features include

- Assertions for testing expected results,

- Fixtures for sharing common test data, and

- Runners for running tests.

JUnit is the de facto standard testing library for the Java language, and it stands in a single jar file that you can download from http://www.junit.org/ (or use Maven dependency management to do it). The library contains a complete API to help you write your unit tests and a tool to execute them. Unit and integration tests help your code to be more robust, bug free, and reliable.

A Brief History of JUnit

JUnit was originally written by Erich Gamma and Kent Beck in 1998. It was inspired by Smalltalk's SUnit test framework, also written by Kent Beck. It quickly became one of the most popular frameworks in the Java world.

Bringing the benefits of unit testing to a wide range of languages, JUnit has inspired a family of *x*Unit tools like nUnit (.NET), pyUnit (Python), CppUnit (C++), dUnit (Delphi), and others. JUnit took an important place in achieving test-driven development (TDD).

How Does It Work?

Since JUnit 4, writing unit and integration tests is simplified by using annotations, static import, and other Java features. Compared to the previous versions of JUnit, it provides a simpler, richer, and easier testing model, as well as introducing more flexible initialization, cleanup, timeouts, and parameterized test cases.

Let's see some of the JUnit features through a simple example. Listing A-3 represents a Customer POJO. It has some attributes, including a date of birth, constructors, getters, and setters. It also provides a utility method to calculate the age of the customer (calculateAge()).

Listing A-3. A Customer Class

```java
public class Customer {

  private Long id;
  private String firstName;
  private String lastName;
  private String email;
  private String phoneNumber;
  private Date dateOfBirth;
  private Integer age;

  // Constructors, getters, setters

  public void calculateAge() {
    if (dateOfBirth == null) {
      age = null;
      return;
    }
```

```
      Calendar birth = new GregorianCalendar();
      birth.setTime(dateOfBirth);
      Calendar now = new GregorianCalendar();
      now.setTime(new Date());
      int adjust = 0;
      if (now.get(Calendar.DAY_OF_YEAR) - birth.get(Calendar.DAY_OF_YEAR) < 0) {
        adjust = -1;
      }
      age = now.get(Calendar.YEAR) - birth.get(Calendar.YEAR) + adjust;
  }
}
```

The calculateAge() method uses the dateOfBirth attribute to set the customer's age. To test the calculateAge() method, we could use the JUnit class CustomerTest described in Listing A-4.

Listing A-4. A Unit Test Class for Customer

```
public class CustomerTest {

  private Customer customer;

  @Before
  public void clearCustomer () {
    customer.clear();
  }

  @Test
  public void ageShouldBeGretaterThanZero() {
    customer = new Customer("Rita", "Navalhas", "rnavalhas@gmail.com");
    customer.setDateOfBirth(new GregorianCalendar(1975, 5, 27).getTime());

    customer.calculateAge();

    int calculatedAge = customer.getAge();

    assertTrue(calculatedAge >= 0);
  }

  @Test
  public void ageShouldBe42() {
    int expectedAge = 42;

    Calendar birth = new GregorianCalendar();
    birth.roll(Calendar.YEAR, expectedAge * (-1));
    birth.roll(Calendar.DAY_OF_YEAR, -1);

    customer = new Customer("Rita", "Navalhas", "rnavalhas@gmail.com");
    customer.setDateOfBirth(birth.getTime());

    customer.calculateAge();

    assertEquals(new Long(expectedAge), new Long(customer.getAge()));
  }
```

```
@Test(expected = NullPointerException.class)
public void shouldThrowAnExceptionCauseDateOfBirtheIsNull() {
  customer = new Customer();

  customer.calculateAge();
}

@Test @Ignore("Test is not ready yet")
public void shouldCalculateOldAge() {
  // some work to do
  }
}
```

The test class in Listing A-4 contains four test methods all annotated with @Test. The JUnit framework will execute the four methods and will return the execution result (i.e., how many have succeeded and how many have failed).

Test Methods

In JUnit 4, test classes do not have to extend anything. To be executed as a test case, a JUnit class needs at least one method annotated with @Test. If you write a class without at least one @Test method, you will get an error when trying to execute it (java.lang.Exception: No runnable methods).

A test method must use the @Test annotation, return void, and take no parameters. This is controlled at runtime and throws an exception if not respected. The @Test annotation supports the optional expected parameter, which declares that a test method should throw an exception. If it doesn't or if it throws a different exception than the one declared, the test fails. In Listing A-4, trying to calculate the age of a null customer object should throw a NullPointerException (method shouldThrowAnExceptionCauseDateOfBirtheIsNull).

Listing A-4 does not implement the shouldCalculateOldAge method. However, you don't want the test to fail; you just want to ignore it. You can add the @Ignore annotation in front or after @Test. Test runners will report the number of ignored tests, along with the number of tests that succeeded and failed. Note that @Ignore takes an optional parameter (a String) in case you want to record why a test is being ignored.

Assert Methods

Test cases must assert that objects conform to an expected result. For that, JUnit has an Assert class that contains several methods. In order to use it, you can either use the prefixed syntax (e.g., Assert.assertEquals()) or import statically the Assert class.

Fixtures

Fixtures are methods to initialize and release any common object during tests. JUnit uses @Before and @After annotations to execute code before or after each test. These methods can be given any name (clearCustomer() in Listing A-4), and you can have multiple methods in one test class. JUnit uses @BeforeClass and @AfterClass annotations to execute specific code only once per class. These methods must be unique and static. @BeforeClass and @AfterClass can be very useful if you need to allocate and release expensive resources.

Launching JUnit

To run the JUnit launcher, you must add the JUnit jar file to your CLASSPATH variable (or add a Maven dependency). After that, you can run your tests through the Java launcher as shown in the following code:

```
java org.junit.runner.JUnitCore org.agoncal.book.javaee7.CustomerTest
```

The preceding command will provide the following result:

```
JUnit version 4.11
..E.I
Time: 0.016
There was 1 failure:
1) ageShouldBe33(org.agoncal.book.javaee7.CustomerTest)
java.lang.AssertionError: at CustomerTest. ageShouldBe33(CustomerTest.java:52)

FAILURES!!!
Tests run: 3, Failures: 1
```

The first displayed information is the JUnit version number (4.11 in this case). Then JUnit gives the number of executed tests (here, three) and the number of failures (one in this example). The letter I indicates that a test has been ignored. Remember that you can run your tests with the following Maven command:

```
mvn test
```

JUnit Integration

JUnit is currently very well integrated with most IDEs (IntelliJ IDEA, Eclipse, NetBeans, etc.). When working with these IDEs, in most cases, JUnit highlights in green to indicate successful tests and in red to indicate failures. Most IDEs also provide facilities to create test classes.

JUnit is also integrated to Maven through the Surefire plug-in used during the test phase of the build life cycle. It executes the JUnit test classes of an application and generates reports in XML and text file formats. The following Maven command runs the JUnit tests through the plug-in:

```
mvn test
```

Derby 10.8

Initially called Cloudscape, the Derby database developed in Java was given to the Apache foundation by IBM and became open source. Sun Microsystems and then Oracle have released their own distribution called JavaDB. Of small footprint (2MB), Derby is a fully functional and transactional relational database that can easily be embedded in any Java-based solution.

Derby provides two different modes: embedded and network server. The embedded mode refers to Derby being started by a simple single-user Java application. With this option, Derby runs in the same JVM as the application. In this book, I use this mode during integration testing. The network server mode refers to Derby being started as a separate process and providing multiuser connectivity. I use this mode throughout the book when running applications.

Installation

Installing Derby is very easy; in fact, you may find it is already installed because it is bundled with the JDK 1.7. During the installation of JDK 1.7, the wizard proposed you install Java DB. And by default it does. If you don't have it installed, you can download the binaries from http://db.apache.org.

Once installed, set the DERBY_HOME variable to the path where you've installed it, and add $DERBY_HOME/bin to your PATH variable. Start the Derby network server by launching the $DERBY_HOME/bin/startNetworkServer script. Derby displays some information to the console such as the port number it listens to (1527 by default).

Derby comes with several utilities, one of them being sysinfo. Open a command interpreter, enter the sysinfo command line, and you should see information about your Java and Derby environment, as shown in Figure A-8.

```
○ ○ ○              📁 bin in ~/Tools/Software/Derby/db-derby-10.8.2.2-bin — bash — 110×22
------------------ Java Information ------------------
Java Version:      1.7.0_15
Java Vendor:       Oracle Corporation
Java home:         /Library/Java/JavaVirtualMachines/jdk1.7.0_15.jdk/Contents/Home/jre
Java classpath:    /Users/antoniombp/Tools/Software/Derby/db-derby-10.8.2.2-bin/lib/derby.jar:/Users/antoniombp/
Tools/Software/Derby/db-derby-10.8.2.2-bin/lib/derbynet.jar:/Users/antoniombp/Tools/Software/Derby/db-derby-10
.8.2.2-bin/lib/derbytools.jar:/Users/antoniombp/Tools/Software/Derby/db-derby-10.8.2.2-bin/lib/derbyclient.jar
OS name:           Mac OS X
OS architecture:   x86_64
OS version:        10.7.4
Java user name:    antoniombp
Java user home:    /Users/antoniombp
Java user dir:     /Users/antoniombp/Tools/Software/Derby/db-derby-10.8.2.2-bin/bin
java.specification.name: Java Platform API Specification
java.specification.version: 1.7
java.runtime.version: 1.7.0_15-b03
--------- Derby Information ---------
JRE - JDBC: Java SE 7 - JDBC 4.0
[/Users/antoniombp/Tools/Software/Derby/db-derby-10.8.2.2-bin/lib/derby.jar] 10.8.2.2 - (1181258)
[/Users/antoniombp/Tools/Software/Derby/db-derby-10.8.2.2-bin/lib/derbytools.jar] 10.8.2.2 - (1181258)
[/Users/antoniombp/Tools/Software/Derby/db-derby-10.8.2.2-bin/lib/derbynet.jar] 10.8.2.2 - (1181258)
[/Users/antoniombp/Tools/Software/Derby/db-derby-10.8.2.2-bin/lib/derbyclient.jar] 10.8.2.2 - (1181258)
```

Figure A-8. sysinfo output after installing Derby

Usage

Derby provides several tools (located under the bin subdirectory) to interact with the database. The simplest are probably ij, which allows you to enter SQL commands at a command prompt, and dblook, which lets you view all or part of a database's data definition language (DDL).

Make sure you've started the Derby network server, and type the command ij to enter the command prompt and run interactive queries against a Derby database. Then, enter the following commands to create a database and a table, insert data into the table, and query the data:

```
ij> connect 'jdbc:derby://localhost:1527/Chapter01DB;create=true';
```

This connects to the Chapter01DB database. Because it doesn't exist already, the create=true parameter forces the database creation. Now let's create the customer table by entering the following command line:

```
ij> create table customer (custId int primary key, firstname varchar(20), lastname varchar(20));
```

This creates a customer table with a primary key column and two `varchar(20)` columns for the first name and last name. You can display the description of the table by entering the following command: `ij> describe customer;`

```
COLUMN_NAME |TYPE_NAME   |DEC&    |NUM&    |COLUM&  |COLUMN_DEF  |CHAR_OCTE&  |IS_NULL&
------------------------------------------------------------------------------------
CUSTID      |INTEGER     |0       |10      |10      |NULL        |NULL        |NO
FIRSTNAME   |VARCHAR     |NULL    |NULL    |20      |NULL        |40          |YES
LASTNAME    |VARCHAR     |NULL    |NULL    |20      |NULL        |40          |YES
```

Now that you have created the table, you can add data using the `insert` SQL statement as follows:

```
ij> insert into customer values (1, 'Fred', 'Chene');
ij> insert into customer values (2, 'Sylvain', 'Verin');
ij> insert into customer values (3, 'Robin', 'Riou');
```

You can then use all the power of the SQL `select` statement to retrieve, order, or aggregate data.

```
ij> select count(*) from customer;
1
-----------
3

ij> select * from customer where custid=3;
CUSTID |FIRSTNAME |LASTNAME
-----------------------------------------------------
3      |Robin     |Riou

ij> exit;
```

To get the DDL of the created table, you can exit `ij` and run `dblook` against the `Chapter01DB` database. Figure A-9 shows the output of the `dblook` command.

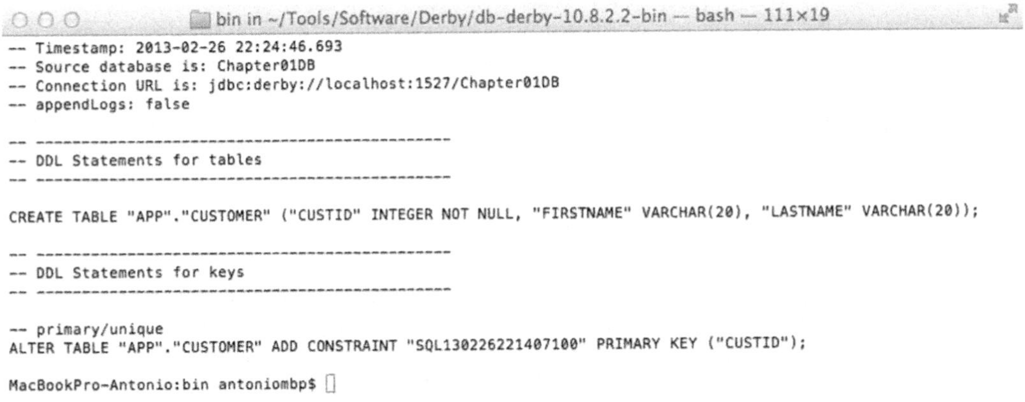
bin in ~/Tools/Software/Derby/db-derby-10.8.2.2-bin — bash — 111×19
-- Timestamp: 2013-02-26 22:24:46.693
-- Source database is: Chapter01DB
-- Connection URL is: jdbc:derby://localhost:1527/Chapter01DB
-- appendLogs: false
-- --
-- DDL Statements for tables
-- --
CREATE TABLE "APP"."CUSTOMER" ("CUSTID" INTEGER NOT NULL, "FIRSTNAME" VARCHAR(20), "LASTNAME" VARCHAR(20));
-- --
-- DDL Statements for keys
-- --
-- primary/unique
ALTER TABLE "APP"."CUSTOMER" ADD CONSTRAINT "SQL130226221407100" PRIMARY KEY ("CUSTID");
MacBookPro-Antonio:bin antoniombp$

Figure A-9. *`dblook` output of the Chapter01DB database*

GlassFish v4

While a fairly new application server, GlassFish is already used by a large number of developers and corporations. Not only is it the Reference Implementation (RI) for the Java EE technology, it is also what you get when downloading the Java EE SDK. You can also deploy critical production applications on the GlassFish application server. Besides being a product, GlassFish is also a community that has gathered around the open source code and lives on `http://glassfish.java.net`. The community is quite responsive on mailing lists and forums. Today GlassFish has support for a diverse ecosystem: Java EE, of course, but also for Ruby on Rails or PHP applications.

A Brief History of GlassFish

The origins of GlassFish take us back to the early Tomcat days when Sun and the JServ group donated this technology to Apache. In 2005, Sun created the GlassFish project. The initial main goal was to produce a fully certified Java EE application server. GlassFish version 1.0 shipped in May 2006. At its core, the web container part of GlassFish had a lot of Tomcat heritage (in fact, at that time, an application running on Tomcat would run unmodified on GlassFish).

GlassFish v2 was released by Sun in September 2007 and had several updates. GlassFish tended to be pretty good at maintaining the same user experience across major releases, not breaking code or changing developers' habits. Also, there is no quality difference between the "community" and "supported" versions of GlassFish. While paying customers have access to patches and additional monitoring tools (GlassFish Enterprise Manager), the open source version available from `http://glassfish.java.net` and the supported version available from `http://www.oracle.com/goto/glassfish` have undergone the same amount of testing, making it easy to switch to a supported version at any time in the project cycle.

In March 2010, soon after the acquisition of Sun Microsystems by Oracle, a roadmap for the community was published, with version 3.0.1, and 3.1, 3.2, and 4.0, planned for the next few years, and clustering being brought back into the 3.1 version (it was not initially in the 3.0 release, which had full Java EE 6 support and modularity as higher priorities).

For the purpose of this book, I have used GlassFish Open Source Edition 4.0 which shipped in May 2013. The main goal of GlassFish 4 is modularization of the core features, with an OSGi-based kernel and full support for Java EE 7. A number of developer-friendly features such as fast startup time and session preservation across redeployments are also part of this release.

■ **Note** The GlassFish team has put a tremendous effort toward having rich and up-to-date documentation, making available many different guides: Quick Start Guide, Installation Guide, Administration Guide, Administration Reference, Application Deployment Guide, Developer's Guide, and more. Check them out at `http://glassfish.java.net/docs`. Also check the FAQs, how-to's, and the GlassFish forum for more information.

GlassFish v4 Architecture

As an application programmer (and not one of the GlassFish developers), you do not need to understand the internal architecture of GlassFish v4, but you might be interested in the main architectural choices and guiding principles. Being built on a modular kernel powered by OSGi, GlassFish ships and runs straight on top of the Apache Felix implementation. It also runs with Equinox or Knopflerfish OSGi runtimes. HK2 (the Hundred-Kilobyte Kernel) abstracts the OSGi module system to provide components, which can also be viewed as services. Such services can be discovered and injected at runtime. OSGi is not exposed to Java EE developers for the time being but it is quite possible to inject OSGi Declarative Services into Java EE components using the standard @Resource annotation.

> ■ **Note** OSGi is a standard for dynamic component management and discovery. Applications or components can be remotely installed, started, stopped, updated, and uninstalled without requiring a reboot. Components can also detect the addition or removal of new services dynamically and adapt accordingly. Apache Felix, Equinox, and Knopflerfish are OSGi implementations.

This modularity and extensibility are how GlassFish v4 can grow from a simple web server listening to administrative commands to a more capable runtime by simply deploying artifacts such as war files (a web container is loaded and started, and the application deployed) or EJB jar files (which will dynamically load and start the EJB container). Additionally, the bare-bones server starts in just a few seconds (less than five seconds on reasonably modern hardware), and you only pay for what you use in terms of startup time and memory consumption. Starting the web container on the fly takes about three more seconds, and deployments are often less than one second. This all makes GlassFish v4 a very developer-friendly environment.

No matter how many modules GlassFish v4 dynamically loads, the administration console, the command-line interface, and the centralized configuration file are all extensible, and each remains unique. Also worth mentioning is the Grizzly framework, which started out as a nonblocking, I/O-based HTTP server to become one of the key elements in GlassFish as shown in Figure A-10.

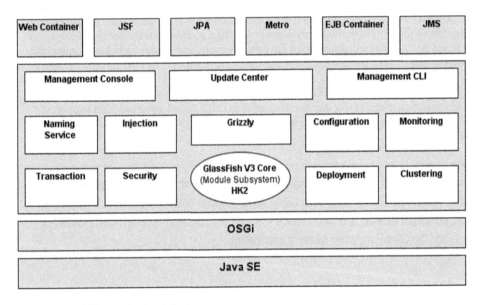

Figure A-10. *GlassFish v4 architecture*

Update Center

Once you're given a modular application server, you can start to mix and match various modules to build your own environment just like you would with IDEs and Linux distributions, or similar to the way Firefox or Chrome let you manage your extensions. The GlassFish Update Center is a set of graphical and command-line tools to manage your runtime. The technology behind this is the Image Packaging System (IPS, also known as pkg), which is what the OpenSolaris project uses for package management. GlassFish v4 is available in two distributions: Web Profile (defined by the Java EE 7 Web Profile) and Full Profile. These distributions each ship with a specific set of modules, the web profile being a strict subset of the full profile. Beyond this default combination, a user can connect to one or more repositories to update the existing features (such as move from the Web Profile to the Full Java EE 7 Profile), add new features (Grails support, a JDBC driver, a portlet container, etc.) or even add new third-party applications. In a corporate environment, you can set up your own repository and use the update center pkg command-line tool to provision and bootstrap the installation of GlassFish-based software.

In practice, with GlassFish v4, the update center can be accessed via theadmin console, the graphical client available at $GLASSFISH_HOME/bin/updatetool, or the pkg command line. All three allow you to list, add, and remove components available from a set of multiple repositories (although, in the case of the admin console, a number of operations are not available since the application server should not be running at the time of install). In the case of pkg (also located in $GLASSFISH_HOME/bin), the most common commands are pkg list, pkg install, pkg uninstall, and pkg image-update.

GlassFish Subprojects

There are many different parts to the GlassFish application server, so the project was broken up into subprojects. This helps you to further understand not only the different pieces but also the adoption of individual features outside the GlassFish environment, in stand-alone mode or within another container. Figure A-11 shows a high-level architecture of the functional parts of the application server.

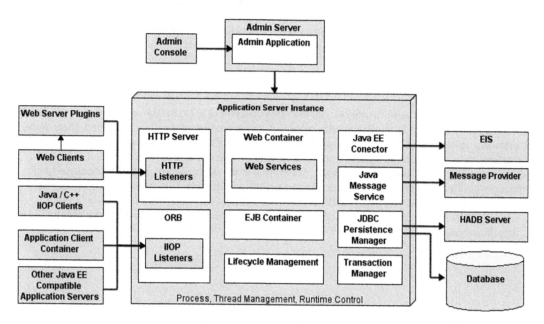

Figure A-11. *Functional parts of GlassFish*

OpenMQ, for instance, is a production-quality open source implementation of JMS. Although it is often used stand-alone for message-oriented architectures, OpenMQ can also be integrated in various ways with GlassFish (in-process, out-of-process, or remote). The administration of OpenMQ can be done via the GlassFish admin console or the asadmin command-line interface (see the "The asadmin CLI" section). The community web site is at http://mq.dev.java.net.

Metro is the one-stop shop for web services. This complete stack builds on the JAX-WS development paradigm and augments it with advanced features such as trusted, end-to-end security; optimized transport (MTOM, FastInfoset); reliable messaging; and transactional behavior for SOAP web services. Such quality of service (QoS) for web services is based on standards (OASIS, W3C), is expressed in the form of policies, and does not require the use of a new API in addition to JAX-WS. Metro is also regularly tested with Microsoft against .NET implementations to ensure interoperability between the two technologies. The community web site is at `http://metro.java.net`.

Mojarra is the name of the JSF 2.2 implementation in GlassFish and is available at `http://mojarra.java.net`. It is certainly one of the most often reused projects by other application servers.

Jersey is the production-quality RI for the new JAX-RS 2.0 specification. Both the specification and the implementation were the early comers to Java EE 7 and GlassFish. Jersey is also used internally by GlassFish v4 to offer a RESTful administration API which complements the existing tools described in the next section. The Jersey community web site is at `http://jersey.java.net`.

Administration

Obviously, being a compliant application server means that GlassFish implements 100% of the Java EE 7 specifications, but it also has additional features that make it a polished product, such as its administrative capabilities, be it through the admin console or via a powerful `asadmin` command-line interface. Almost all the configuration is stored in a file called `domain.xml` (located in `domains/domain1/config`), which can be useful for troubleshooting, but this file should not be edited by hand; instead, one of these two administration tools should be used. Both of them rely on the extensive JMX instrumentation provided by GlassFish.

Admin Console

The admin console is a browser-based administration user interface (see Figure A-12) for the application server. This tool is for both administrators and developers. It provides graphical representation of the objects under management, enhanced log file viewing, system status, and monitoring data. At a minimum, the console manages the creation and modification of configurations (JVM tuning, log level, pool and cache tuning, etc.), JDBC, JNDI, JavaMail, JMS, and connector resources, as well as applications (deployment). At any time in the navigation of the tool, contextual help is available via the top-right Help button. With a default installation, the admin console is available upon GlassFish startup at `http://localhost:4848`. Starting with GlassFish v4, an anonymous user can be set up at install time, removing the need to log in. Note that the admin console is loaded in the application server on the first hit to the preceding URL, thus illustrating the load-on-demand feature of GlassFish v4.

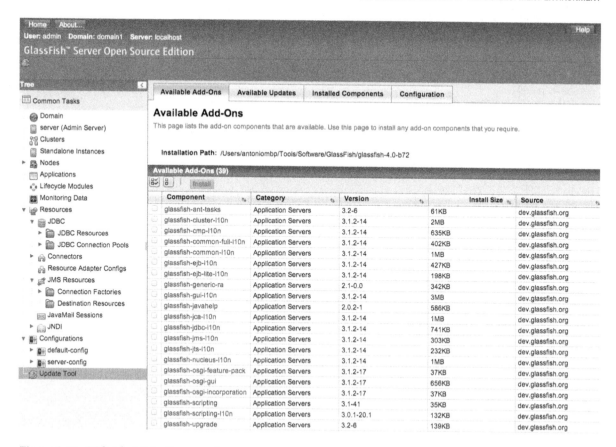

Figure A-12. *Web administration console*

The asadmin CLI

The asadmin command-line interface (CLI) is quite powerful and often what people use in production, as it can be scripted to create instances and resources, deploy applications, and provide monitoring data on a running system. The command is located under the bin subdirectory of GlassFish and can manage multiple local or remote application server domains. asadmin offers several hundred commands, but you should get away with using only a small subset of these. If you are curious about the commands, try asadmin help. Useful commands in a simple developer profile include asadmin start-domain, asadmin stop-domain, asadmin deploy, asadmin deploydir, and asadmin undeploy. In case of a typo, asadmin will give you a choice of the closest matching command. Try asadmin resource, for instance, and asadmin will give you the related commands as shown in Figure A-13.

```
⊙ ○ ○      bin in ~/Tools/Software/GlassFish/glassfish-4.0-b72/glassfish — java — 99×32
asadmin> resource
Command resource not found.
Check the entry of command name. This command may be provided by a package that is not installed.
Closest matching local and remote command(s):
    add-resources
    create-connector-resource
    create-custom-resource
    create-javamail-resource
    create-jdbc-resource
    create-jms-resource
    create-jndi-resource
    create-resource-adapter-config
    create-resource-ref
    delete-connector-resource
    delete-custom-resource
    delete-javamail-resource
    delete-jdbc-resource
    delete-jms-resource
    delete-jndi-resource
    delete-resource-adapter-config
    delete-resource-ref
    list-connector-resources
    list-custom-resources
    list-javamail-resources
    list-jdbc-resources
    list-jms-resources
    list-jndi-resources
    list-resource-adapter-configs
    list-resource-refs

Command resource executed successfully.
asadmin> ▯
```

Figure A-13. *asadmin CLI*

Installing GlassFish

GlassFish can be downloaded via multiple distribution mechanisms. The most obvious choices are to get it from
http://glassfish.java.net/, or with the Java EE SDK (it also ships with the NetBeans IDE 7.3 and above).
I'll document here how to download and install GlassFish from the community web site.

Go to the main download page, http://glassfish.java.net/public/downloadsindex.html, and select the
download link for "GlassFish Open Source Edition 4." You are then offered the choice of both a graphical installer
download and a simple Zip download. Each option further offers the choice between the Java EE 7 Full Profile and
Web Profile. I will document here the installer version of the Full Profile. Note that GlassFish is available for Windows,
Linux, Solaris, and Mac OS X. Executing the shell will start the graphical installer, which will

- Ask you to agree to the license.

- Request an install location.

- Let you configure an admin username and password (or default to an anonymous user).

- Let you configure HTTP and admin ports (while checking that they're not already in use).

- Install and enable the update tool (pkg and updatetool clients). With the Zip installer, the
  updatetool is not installed by default and will be installed from the network on the first run.

It will then decompress a simple preconfigured GlassFish install with default settings: admin port is 4848, HTTP port is 8080, and no explicit admin user configured. Once properly installed, GlassFish can be started with the asadmin command line (see Figure A-14).

```
asadmin start-domain -v
```

```
○ ○ ○                    📁 bin in ~/Tools/Software/GlassFish/glassfish-4.0-b72/glassfish — java — 145×47

[#|2013-02-27T06:14:05.905+0100|INFO|glassfish 4.0||_ThreadID=42;_ThreadName=Thread-8;_TimeMillis=1361942045905;_LevelValue=800;|this.makeModuleF
or(org.glassfish.main.admingui.console-common, 4.0.0.b72) returned OSGiModuleImpl:: Bundle = [org.glassfish.main.admingui.console-common [50]], S
tate = [READY]|#]

[#|2013-02-27T06:14:05.906+0100|INFO|glassfish 4.0||_ThreadID=42;_ThreadName=Thread-8;_TimeMillis=1361942045906;_LevelValue=800;|this.makeModuleF
or(org.glassfish.main.admingui.console-jts-plugin, 4.0.0.b72) returned OSGiModuleImpl:: Bundle = [org.glassfish.main.admingui.console-jts-plugin
[65]], State = [READY]|#]

[#|2013-02-27T06:14:05.906+0100|INFO|glassfish 4.0||_ThreadID=42;_ThreadName=Thread-8;_TimeMillis=1361942045906;_LevelValue=800;|this.makeModuleF
or(org.glassfish.main.admingui.console-cluster-plugin, 4.0.0.b72) returned OSGiModuleImpl:: Bundle = [org.glassfish.main.admingui.console-cluster
-plugin [46]], State = [READY]|#]

[#|2013-02-27T06:14:05.906+0100|INFO|glassfish 4.0||_ThreadID=42;_ThreadName=Thread-8;_TimeMillis=1361942045906;_LevelValue=800;|this.makeModuleF
or(org.glassfish.main.admingui.console-jca-plugin, 4.0.0.b72) returned OSGiModuleImpl:: Bundle = [org.glassfish.main.admingui.console-jca-plugin
[59]], State = [READY]|#]

[#|2013-02-27T06:14:05.907+0100|INFO|glassfish 4.0||_ThreadID=42;_ThreadName=Thread-8;_TimeMillis=1361942045907;_LevelValue=800;|this.makeModuleF
or(org.glassfish.main.admingui.console-jdbc-plugin, 4.0.0.b72) returned OSGiModuleImpl:: Bundle = [org.glassfish.main.admingui.console-jdbc-plugi
n [61]], State = [READY]|#]

[#|2013-02-27T06:14:05.907+0100|INFO|glassfish 4.0||_ThreadID=42;_ThreadName=Thread-8;_TimeMillis=1361942045907;_LevelValue=800;|this.makeModuleF
or(org.glassfish.main.admingui.console-updatecenter-plugin, 4.0.0.b72) returned OSGiModuleImpl:: Bundle = [org.glassfish.main.admingui.console-up
datecenter-plugin [67]], State = [READY]|#]

[#|2013-02-27T06:14:05.907+0100|INFO|glassfish 4.0||_ThreadID=42;_ThreadName=Thread-8;_TimeMillis=1361942045907;_LevelValue=800;|this.makeModuleF
or(org.glassfish.main.admingui.console-jms-plugin, 4.0.0.b72) returned OSGiModuleImpl:: Bundle = [org.glassfish.main.admingui.console-jms-plugin
[63]], State = [READY]|#]

[#|2013-02-27T06:14:05.907+0100|INFO|glassfish 4.0||_ThreadID=42;_ThreadName=Thread-8;_TimeMillis=1361942045907;_LevelValue=800;|this.makeModuleF
or(org.glassfish.main.admingui.console-web-plugin, 4.0.0.b72) returned OSGiModuleImpl:: Bundle = [org.glassfish.main.admingui.console-web-plugin
[69]], State = [READY]|#]

[#|2013-02-27T06:14:06.741+0100|INFO|glassfish 4.0|javax.enterprise.resource.webcontainer.jsf.config|_ThreadID=42;_ThreadName=Thread-8;_TimeMilli
s=1361942046741;_LevelValue=800;_MessageID=jsf.config.listener.version;|Initialisation de Mojarra 2.2.0-m08 (-SNAPSHOT 20130107-2105 https://svn.
java.net/svn/mojarra~svn/tags/2.2.0-m08@11337) pour le contexte «»|#]

[#|2013-02-27T06:14:07.756+0100|INFO|glassfish 4.0|org.hibernate.validator.internal.util.Version|_ThreadID=42;_ThreadName=Thread-8;_TimeMillis=13
61942047756;_LevelValue=800;|HV000001: Hibernate Validator 5.0.0.Alpha1|#]

[#|2013-02-27T06:14:08.596+0100|INFO|glassfish 4.0|javax.enterprise.web|_ThreadID=42;_ThreadName=Thread-8;_TimeMillis=1361942048596;_LevelValue=8
00;_MessageID=AS-WEB-00324;|Loading application [__admingui] at [/]|#]

[#|2013-02-27T06:14:08.597+0100|INFO|glassfish 4.0|javax.enterprise.system.core|_ThreadID=42;_ThreadName=Thread-8;_TimeMillis=1361942048597;_Leve
lValue=800;_MessageID=NCLS-CORE-0022;|Loading application __admingui done in 6 366 ms|#]
```

Figure A-14. *Starting GlassFish*

You can then go to the admin console (shown earlier in Figure A-12) at http://localhost:4848 or to the default welcome page at http://localhost:8080.

■ **Tip** If you only have one domain, you can omit the default domain name and start GlassFish with only asadmin start-domain. If you'd like to have the log file appear inline rather than checking the content of the dedicated log file (domains/domain1/logs/server.log), you can use asadmin start-domain --verbose or -v.

There are many more things that GlassFish has to offer; I show you some of them in this book, but I'll leave it to you to explore its support for session preservation across redeployments, incremental deployment in NetBeans, Eclipse and IntelliJ IDEA, advanced OSGi hybrid application support, diagnostic services, RESTful management, monitoring, and the various security configurations.

Index

■ L

layout.xhtml Template, 379
logMethod(), 45

■ M

CPSIA information can be obtained
at www.ICGtesting.com
Printed in the USA
LVOW02s2203130916

504490LV00023B/287/P